AF600100

POETS, PLAYERS, AND PREACHERS

Remembering the Gunpowder Plot in Seventeenth-Century England

ANNE JAMES

Poets, Players, and Preachers

Remembering the Gunpowder Plot in Seventeenth-Century England

UNIVERSITY OF TORONTO PRESS
Toronto Buffalo London

Toronto Buffalo London
www.utppublishing.com

ISBN 978-1-4426-4937-8

Library and Archives Canada Cataloguing in Publication

James, Anne, 1958–, author
Poets, players, and preachers : remembering the Gunpowder Plot in seventeenth-century England / Anne James.

Includes bibliographical references and index.
ISBN 978-1-4426-4937-8 (hardback)

1. Gunpowder Plot, 1605 – Early works to 1800. 2. English literature – Early modern, 1500–1700 – History and criticism. 3. English literature – Political aspects. 4. Literature and history. 5. Conspiracy in literature. I. Title.

PR438.P65J36 2016 820.9′358 C2016-901906-3

This book has been published with the help of a grant from the Federation for the Humanities and Social Sciences, through the Awards to Scholarly Publications Program, using funds provided by the Social Sciences and Humanities Research Council of Canada.

University of Toronto Press acknowledges the financial assistance to its publishing program of the Canada Council for the Arts and the Ontario Arts Council, an agency of the Government of Ontario.

Canada Council for the Arts | Conseil des Arts du Canada

Funded by the Government of Canada | Financé par le gouvernement du Canada

Contents

Acknowledgments

I am grateful to those who read this manuscript and offered both helpful suggestions and encouragement at various stages of its development: David Gay, Rick Bowers, Beverley Lemire, Paul Harland, Richard Dutton, and Jeanne Shami, as well as the anonymous readers for the Press. Thanks to Greg Kneidel for his assistance with the Latin in chapters 4 and 5. I would also like to thank the librarians and staff at the following repositories for access to their collections: The Bodleian Library, The British Library, Cambridge University Library, Dr Williams's Library (Dr David Wykes), McGill University Library, St Paul's Cathedral Library (Mr Joseph Wisdom), The National Archives, Worcester College (Oxford) Library (Dr Joanna Parker), University of Alberta libraries, and the University of Regina Library. My research was supported generously by the Social Sciences and Humanities Research Council of Canada and by the University of Alberta.

Parts of several chapters have been presented at conferences over the past few years, and I am appreciative of those who asked questions and offered comments on those occasions. An opportunity to attend the "Making Publics" Summer Seminar in 2009 allowed me to work out parts of chapter 4. I would also like to thank the members of the John Donne Society for their collegiality over the past decade.

Thank you to the people at University of Toronto Press, particularly Suzanne Rancourt, whose patience and encouragement are much appreciated.

Finally, I am grateful to the family members who have supported me in every way over the years. My parents started me on a journey of learning that took longer than they could have imagined, and my husband, Warren, has taken every new direction easily in stride.

Illustrations

POETS, PLAYERS, AND PREACHERS

Remembering the Gunpowder Plot in Seventeenth-Century England

1 Introduction: Writing the Gunpowder Plot

1.1 Preface

Over four hundred years after its discovery, the Gunpowder Plot still sparks the imaginations of writers and readers, regardless of the event's meagre results. No explosion on 5 November 1605 destroyed the English Houses of Parliament, and only thirteen alleged conspirators, a few supporters of the Midlands revolt, and two Jesuit priests lost their lives, most either killed resisting capture or executed by the crown.[1] Objectively, the plot was a failure, a non-event, but it has seldom been discussed objectively. Annual commemoration, both voluntary and enforced, ensured it a deep and lasting place in the collective memory and historical consciousness of the English people. Nevertheless, its meaning has never been stable, shifting with the winds of political, religious, and social change. This book explores how the literature that celebrated, chronicled, and critiqued the plot and its discovery from 1605 to 1688 both participated in and reflected these changes. In doing so, it queries both the role of literature in public events and the role of public events in literary history, negotiating the boundaries between imagination and memory, literature and history, fiction and reality.

From the beginning, both polemical imperatives and the desire to create a coherent narrative out of fragmentary, and frequently conflicting, evidence shaped Gunpowder narratives. The one provided by official contemporary sources, and still current in many popular histories, tells of a conspiracy by a small group of Catholic gentlemen, impoverished by the Elizabethan penal laws, further embittered by their new king's failure to rescind them, and seduced by Jesuit doctrine and the personal magnetism of their leader, Robert Catesby.[2] Rejecting the idea of a simple attempt on the king's life, Catesby and his followers determined on the bold scheme of blowing up the House of Lords on the opening day of James I's second parliament with most of the royal family, as well as the lords spiritual and temporal, in attendance.[3] A solid wall impeded their efforts to tunnel beneath the building, but Thomas Percy, another of the plotters, obtained access to an adjacent cellar they could rent. Here they piled barrels of gunpowder, covering them with kindling, iron bars, and coal, both to conceal their stores and to maximize the damage of the projected explosion. When the original opening date of 7 February 1605 was postponed first to 30 October and then to 5 November, they seized the opportunity to consider how they would govern the country after destroying the ruling elite.[4] Uncertainty about which of the royal children would attend the opening hampered their planning, but they apparently agreed upon kidnapping the young princess Elizabeth and crowning her as figurehead under a Catholic regent. This part of the plan required developing a second base of operations in the Midlands, where several wealthier Catholics were recruited to supply funds and horses to seize the princess and put down any local resistance. At least one conspirator, however, allegedly spent some of his time fretting about the ethics of killing the Catholic lords who would be in Parliament.

On the night of 26 October 1605, an unidentified messenger delivered a cryptic letter in the street to a servant of the Catholic noble William Parker, Lord Monteagle,[5] warning him not to attend the opening, where a "terrible blowe" was to be struck. Wary of being compromised by the activities of his hotter headed co-religionists, Monteagle took the letter immediately to Whitehall, where several members of the Privy Council happened to be meeting. Robert Cecil, first Earl of Salisbury and Secretary of State, claiming to be mystified by the enigmatic construction of its contents, chose to wait until the king returned from hunting on 30 October to initiate any investigation. Reading the letter several days after his return, James immediately suspected gunpowder and ordered the cellars searched. A first search revealed nothing suspicious; a second, on the night of 4 November, uncovered the gunpowder along with a man who gave his name as John Johnson but is known to history as Guy Fawkes. Imprisonment, and possibly torture, shook Fawkes's initial bravado, and within a few days he began naming his fellow conspirators. By this time, however, the authorities had captured or killed most of the others, who had unwisely attempted to proceed with rebellion in the Midlands. Hunting down the last conspirators, rebels, and priests dragged into the beginning of 1606, but by early May all of the alleged conspirators were dead.[6]

Virtually every detail of this narrative, however, has been repeatedly challenged over the past four hundred years. An enduring subject of speculation is the authorship of the mysterious warning sent to Lord Monteagle. Given his suspicious death in the Tower before he could be tried, Francis Tresham remains the favourite suspect, but none of the conspirators ever confessed to penning the letter. Moreover, did the letter really alert the authorities, or had they been following the plotters' movements and awaiting the most dramatic moment to capture them? Equally contentious is the role of the priests, particularly Henry Garnett. The Jesuit superior eventually admitted to knowledge of the plot, but claimed he had obtained it only under the inviolable seal of confession. The third, and perhaps greatest, puzzle is why Salisbury, with the Monteagle letter in hand, waited until the last minute to act against the plotters. Critics accuse Salisbury of complicity ranging from inventing the plot for political purposes to simply allowing it to mature so he could claim the credit for thwarting it. Daring contemporaries observed that he benefitted from the plot in two ways – it solidified his position with his new monarch and it allowed him to neutralize his closest political rival, Henry Percy, ninth Earl of Northumberland, compromised by his cousin Thomas Percy's role in the conspiracy. Those who credited Salisbury with the second Earl of Essex's fall in 1601 were quick to see a repetition of a successful strategy for disposing of a competitor.[7] Almost from the beginning, Cecil's detractors contested his actions, from his handling of the letter to his hand in shaping the official narratives. Sceptics continue to ask questions: Was there any evidence of a tunnel? What happened to the gunpowder? How much powder was there, was it "decayed" as some have claimed, and how much damage could it have done? Finally, was the real plot a government conspiracy to entrap a few malcontented Catholics?

1.2 Contesting Conspiracy: Studying the Plot

While such speculations have frequently engaged popular writers, political and religious historians, unconvinced by allegations of government conspiracy, have for the most part lost interest in the plot. Joel Hurstfield concluded in 1970 that "the question of the authenticity of Gunpowder Plot is no longer a rewarding subject of historical research … Trying to prove that it was a fabrication has become a game, like dating Shakespeare's sonnets: a pleasant way to pass a wet afternoon but hardly a challenging occupation for adult men and women."[8] Satisfied that a plot existed, historians seem disinclined to probe its workings, leaving Jenny Wormald to lament more than a decade later that

> after almost 400 years, we still lack a coherent historical explanation of how it was that thirteen Catholic conspirators sought to destroy the political structure of society within two years of the admittedly tortured birth of Great Britain. We still need answers to the two most basic questions, Why was there a Gunpowder Plot, and what did the Plotters really want?[9]

Compelling answers to such fundamental questions remain elusive largely because conflicting narratives quickly became weapons in confessional warfare. Early published accounts were exclusively Protestant, not only because texts required pre-publication scrutiny, but also, as Alison Shell points out, because most Catholics preferred to forget the incident.[10] The primary sources of contemporary information, both published by royal authority, consisted of two pamphlets, one containing the king's speech to Parliament on 9 November 1605 and a "Discourse of the maner of this late intended treason," possibly written by the king, while a second offered the official account of the plotters' trials. Even as modern historical methodologies developed, however, they frequently served to construct or affirm Protestant narratives.

The first history based upon primary sources was David Jardine's *Narrative of the Gunpowder Plot* published in 1857. Jardine claimed to offer a balanced and accurate account by comparing newly rediscovered documents in the Public Record Office with the official contemporary pamphlets. He discounted the official "Discourse," which he believed to have been written by Francis Bacon, on the grounds of its narrative coherence, as an attempt "to surround fictions by undoubted truths with such apparent simplicity and carelessness, but in fact with such consummate art and depth of design, that the reader is beguiled into an unsuspecting belief in the whole narration." Jardine conceded that laws against Catholics were severe and accused James of increasing fines in order to reward his Scottish retainers, but he did not exonerate the plotters.[11] Nevertheless, he showed a grudging respect for Fawkes, whose "language and conduct after the discovery of the Plot are characteristic of a resolute fanatic, acting upon perverted notions of right and wrong, but by no means destitute of piety or humanity."[12]

Despite admitting that a Catholic might be pious, however, Jardine still saw the conspirators in thrall to superstition. Convinced of Garnett's legal guilt, he was less certain of the priest's moral guilt. Garnett was probably more involved in the plot than he admitted, but he was unfairly charged with all the crimes committed by the Jesuits during the previous twelve years. Sir Everard Digby, whom his judges had treated with respect based on his superior social status, Jardine dismissed as a "weak and bigoted young man," completely under the Jesuits' spell.[13] He argued that Tresham had written the Monteagle warning, but saw the letter as a ruse to conceal the government's real source of information. Nevertheless, he emphatically denied that Cecil had fabricated the plot and concluded that the plotters had been justly executed, regardless of any mitigating factors. Dismissing the familiar parallel of the Catilinarian conspiracy, he insisted that this one was *not* enacted by desperate men, but by men of wealth and position who deliberately rebelled against the state. Jardine's use of documents initiated archival research into the plot and made his study the most authoritative plot history until Samuel Gardiner published the first volume of his *History of England* in 1883.

Although Gardiner also relied upon documentary evidence, he found the coherence of the traditional narrative convincing, concluding that "The whole story of the plot, as far as it relates to the lay conspirators, rests upon indisputable evidence," while he declared the evidence against Garnett mainly circumstantial.[14] Gardiner's history ignited a heated exchange with Father John Gerard that smouldered for the remainder of the century. Gerard's resentment of Gardiner's status as a professional historian exacerbated their confessional differences, but some of their disagreement centred on the problem of narrative. Emulating Gardiner's use of documentary evidence, in his *What Was the Gunpowder Plot?* (1897) Gerard shrewdly compared Cecil's narrative for the foreign ambassadors, the 7 November "minute" for the Privy Council, and the "Discourse," concluding that discrepancies among their stories pointed to manipulation of the official version .[15] Gerard offered the first serious challenge, based upon documentary evidence, to Protestant accounts, but Gardiner prevailed, not only through superior research but also by assailing Gerard's personal and narrative credibility.

Responding with *What Gunpowder Plot Was* (1897), the historian focused on confessional differences: as a Catholic and a Jesuit, Gerard had reason to discredit the traditional story. Presuming that the original account is substantially true, Gardiner refutes the priest's arguments step by step in the manner of seventeenth-century religious disputation. He also complains, however, that his opponent has no believable narrative to substitute for the traditional Protestant one he is intent upon demolishing. Joseph Levine observes that notwithstanding Gardiner's reliance on documentary evidence, his project also required him to "imagine the conspirators at every step of their failed plot."[16] Gardiner's conclusions, mostly endorsed by a leading twentieth-century plot historian, Mark Nicholls, are thus based upon both documentary evidence and narrative coherence.

Along with Wormald, the only historian sensitive to the role of anti-Scots feelings among the plotters, Nicholls has done much to revive historical interest in the plot. In his most extensive study, *Investigating Gunpowder Plot*, Nicholls rejects the temptation to which most earlier historians succumbed, that of a chronological narrative, beginning instead with the government's response to the discovery of the gunpowder. He supports his hypothesis "that the plot came as a genuine surprise to the authorities" by demonstrating that they reacted as most governments would to the sudden revelation of a conspiracy.[17] Although hampered by the destruction of the Privy Council records for the relevant period in a 1619 Whitehall fire, he finds no evidence of prior knowledge or fabrication by the government. In a subsequent article on the composition and dissemination of the popularly titled "King's Book" containing the anonymous "Discourse," he once again insists that in the days following the discovery "ignorance, embarrassment, even panic ran through the highest counsels in the land."[18] Even if they do not materially advance our understanding of the plotters' motives or long-term plans, Nicholls's conclusions, like Gardiner's, rebut the government conspiracy theories to the satisfaction of professional historians, leaving them to writers of popular history and sensational fiction.[19]

Perhaps this situation should not surprise us, for the Gunpowder Plot has appealed to the popular imagination since James I claimed it as the founding event of his new Protestant Britain and initiated a deliberate memorialization campaign that produced poetry, prose pamphlets, and sermons. Studying this long-neglected literature allows us to explore topics at the forefront of seventeenth-century literary and interdisciplinary scholarship, including reciprocal relationships between literary and non-literary events, the beginnings of a "public sphere" in the early modern period, and the role played by narrative in public memory. In this sense, plot literature can function as a case study, providing a body of texts related to a single discrete event to be analysed with these questions in mind. At the same time, the plot deserves attention as a literary event in its own right because its treatment, not only by canonical authors including Shakespeare, Jonson, Milton, and Donne, but also by less notable writers, contributed to new generic configurations. Specialized studies of individual texts have gradually given way to broader thematic treatments: Rebecca Lemon analyses the impact of the plot on discourses of treason, particularly in the theatre, and Paul Wake examines the relationship between history and imagination in the use of the Troy story in Gunpowder narratives.[20] Until now, however, no study has extensively sampled this literature from the perspective of its uses and reinterpretations of genre. The purpose of this book, then, is to examine a broad range of texts in three distinct genres in order to offer some preliminary conclusions first about the development and use of the Gunpowder narrative in seventeenth-century literary works, and second about how these works helped to reshape literary discourse in the period.

1.3 Reading Conspiracy: The Plot in Literary History

If historians have relinquished the Gunpowder Plot largely to amateurs, literary critics during much of the twentieth century relegated its literature to specialized literary historians, who sought the sources of canonical works such as *Paradise Lost* in the writings of neglected authors such as Phineas Fletcher and Francis Herring as well as in Milton's own youthful *In Quintum Novembris*. These studies produced some important work, including Stella Revard's insight that the Gunpowder sermons to which he would have been exposed annually might have been as important a source for Milton's narrative of the war in heaven as classical epic.[21] More provocatively, Barbara De Luna proposed in 1967 that Ben Jonson wrote *Catiline, his Conspiracy* as a "parallelograph" of the Gunpowder Plot.[22] De Luna broke new ground in taking seriously the relationship between a literary text and the Gunpowder Plot, but she restricted Jonson's purpose to justifying his own role in the aftermath of the conspiracy, and, while recognizing the play as a source for works by later writers, she failed to trace the contexts of its periodic revivals. Since early modern sermons, except those by well-known preachers such as John Donne and Lancelot Andrewes, remained unknown territory to most literary scholars, however, this large collection of texts continued to be neglected. In the final quarter of the twentieth century, however, two developments in literary theory provided a basis for new ways of looking at the Gunpowder texts. First, reception studies began replacing source studies as critics increasingly recognized relationships between texts as dialogic and accorded new importance to the reader's role. Second, New Historicism offered serious attention to non-canonical works, grappling, like reception studies, with the question of how literary and non-literary histories might inform each other. Increased attention to the historical contexts of literary works has encouraged interdisciplinary studies in aspects of early modern culture such as the growth of a public sphere and the relationship between public memory and narrative. The texts arising from the Gunpowder Plot, both those traditionally considered literary and those not, present an excellent case study in which we can observe the unfolding of a narrative in an ever-changing religious and political context as well as develop methodologies for interdisciplinary work in these areas.

New Historicist methodologies of contextualizing literary texts by juxtaposing them with texts previously read as historical documents inform this study first by turning our attention to works that have been traditionally slighted, recognizing them as texts in their own right rather than simply as contexts or sources. While early New Historicists sought in such texts evidence for the repressive exercise of power and authority, literary scholars of the seventeenth-century have more recently begun wrestling with more complex understandings of relationships between writers and rulers.[23] I argue that the Gunpowder texts are not simply propaganda forced upon subjects by an authoritarian government, but that by reading, writing, and even listening, subjects actively participated in developing and revising plot narratives. Consequently, as readers we must be sensitive to changes over time, a problem New Historicists have been reluctant to address for fear of recreating the teleological narratives that characterized older historicisms. Reception studies, a cluster of related methodologies based on initial theorizations by Hans Robert Jauss in the 1970s, offers a solution to this problem by tracing the histories of texts as readers shape them into new texts.[24]

Jauss's seven theses reoriented the relationship between text and context by giving literary texts a role beyond mere commentary. His seventh thesis proposes that "The social function of literature takes place when the reader's literary experience informs his understanding of the world and affects his social behaviour."[25] Jauss sees literary history as a series of ongoing dialogues between works and their audiences involving refutation, emulation, and imitation. Although he invited criticism by failing to define the "horizon of expectations" against which a text is initially read, this methodology both accounts for literary change and traces the relationship between literary and non-literary history.[26] Complementing or even replacing source studies, reception studies presents a new way of understanding the texts written in the wake of the Gunpowder Plot, which encouraged various responses that in turn created new texts and fostered incremental generic changes.

In critiquing both reception studies and New Historicism, Robert Hume argues that simply placing examples in chronological order tells us nothing about progression. To write credible literary history, we must situate texts within a broader cultural history, considering and contextualizing both production and reception. Rejecting Jauss's more theoretical models, which imply homogeneous audiences with a uniform horizon of expectations, Hume advocates reconstructing audiences using data obtained about real readers when possible and carefully hypothesized readers when we lack evidence for actual reception. In such cases, dedications and other paratextual materials provide valuable clues about how authors expected their texts to be understood and what readers they sought. The importance of examining such materials can be seen in Richard Dutton's reading of the preliminaries of *Volpone* as evidence of Jonson's engagement with recent history in the play.[27] Genre also informs us about both the ways in which a writer expected a text to be understood and the reading strategies with which an audience likely approached it.

To Hume's suggestive remarks about genre, we may add Alastair Fowler's proposal that genre studies can help to resolve the problem of accounting for change in literary history. Central to Fowler's approach is a definition of genres less as systems of classification than as "fields of association" modified over time.[28] He argues that every literary work modifies a genre and that these incremental generic changes constitute literary history. Changes, however, result from both internal and external factors, in other words from both literary and extra-literary events, an insight that offers the possibility of situating literary within non-literary history. Similarly, Kevin Sharpe and Steven Zwicker affirm that "The history both of the creation of genres and of the awareness and manipulation of genres is a literary subject, but its exposition is part of social and cultural history." Perhaps more audaciously, they argue that "Literature ... not only divines the important changes in history but can mold, accelerate, and even enact them." Most frequently it does so by changing literary history.[29] Both readers and writers are vital to this process. Nigel Smith also argues that genre is the connection between text and society. Genres, "with their capacity for transformation as well as representation, define the parameters of public debate, the nature of change, and the means for comprehending that change." They "are always engaged in the social relations in which they originate"; however, "texts have a power in their circulation, interpretation and use, not necessarily connected with the circumstances of their production."[30] In the case of the Gunpowder Plot, texts and their responses formed and transformed genres as authors wrote and rewrote the story to inform, persuade, and entertain their audiences.

This is the first study to examine a wide range of Gunpowder texts as literary works both composed and read with attention to their genres. In contrast, cultural studies such as David Cressy's have used literary texts as evidence for various commemorative practices without accounting for generic differences. Similarly, Jason C. White, who cites numerous poems and prose pamphlets written in the plot's aftermath as evidence for the development of national identity, categorizes these texts simply as polemics.[31] To understand these texts historically, however, we need to recreate contexts that include occasions, real or anticipated audiences, and the associations evoked by genre. Foregrounding genre, I trace changes to individual texts, their receptions, and their genres over time, assuming that generic change happens gradually through the reception of texts and their assimilation, through positive and negative responses, into new texts. This method resolves one of the dilemmas posed by New Historicism – that, as David Quint observes, "attention to synchronous historical relationships can cause the text's participation in a diachronic *literary* history to be overlooked."[32] For example, we will see in chapter 6 that Henry Burton signalled his challenge to Laudianism in 1636 by preaching on a biblical text that Lancelot Andrewes had chosen for a conformist sermon in 1614. Thus, combining these methodologies nuances our understanding of the interactions between literary and non-literary history more than relying upon a single methodology.

1.4 Debating Conspiracy: The Plot and the Public Sphere

Responses to the plot provide a case study for examining the circulation of news and opinions in oral, print, and manuscript forms during the seventeenth century. Building upon and responding to Jürgen Habermas's *Structural Transformation of the Public Sphere*, historians and literary scholars over the past several decades have explored how a culture of discussion and debate in England, what Habermas calls a public sphere, originated in various venues and media predating the periodical press and the coffee house. In particular, Peter Lake, in collaborations with Steve Pincus and Michael Questier, has traced its earliest beginnings to the arrival of the Jesuit mission in England.[33] Their research has stimulated interest in the transmission of news and views within public spaces including both the theatre and the church, and also through such previously neglected printed materials as pamphlets and sermons. Rebecca Lemon suggests that "the reading and writing communities that emerged out of the Gunpowder Plot offer a story of origins in the creation of the early modern public sphere," and examines how rulers and subjects negotiated the idea of treason in post-plot England, analysing plays by Jonson, Hayward, and Shakespeare as well as Donne's *Pseudo-Martyr*.[34] The current study endorses and extends Lemon's conclusion by demonstrating that the plot encouraged discussion and debate of other topics and through other media, such as sermons.

One of the features that increasingly distinguished both popular and official responses to the attempted rebellions and assassinations of the late sixteenth and early seventeenth centuries was the use of print to disseminate multiple interpretations of these events. While there were doubtless competing, and even conflicting, understandings of earlier incidents, the increasing availability of print opened up new avenues for discussion. Censorship at times restricted the printing of more extreme views, but Annabel Patterson has pointed out that the authorities permitted a significant degree of critique, provided that authors avoided open sedition.[35] For more dangerous works, the options of oral or manuscript transmission remained, although a letter might fall into the wrong hands or a libel writer be identified.

Early in Elizabeth's reign, official proclamations, accounts of executions that the state had scripted, and popular ballads publicized acts of treason. Those with court connections or hopes of preferment might also extol Elizabeth and celebrate the preservation of the Protestant state in literary texts intended for select audiences, as Thomas Churchyard did after the Northern Rebellion.[36] Even in such texts, however, and particularly in official ones, chronicling conspiracies and rebellions served an admonitory function and consequently focused on occasions of punishment. Witnessing public executions and participating in occasional ceremonies of thanksgiving involving homilies and special liturgies warned subjects against treasonous behaviour. Such media discouraged, although they could not prevent, individual interpretation. The government's need to control interpretative acts may be seen in K.J. Kesselring's description of how the queen and William Cecil drafted a defence of Elizabeth's reign immediately after the Northern revolt. The document, however, "ended with a note that as the bulk of her good subjects were unable to read, the text was to be read aloud in all parish churches."[37] Whether or not the defence was disseminated in this way, Kesselring found no surviving print copies nor any evidence of publication. The setting of the parish church doubtless discouraged dissonant responses, contributing to the monologic nature of the discourse surrounding treason.

Nevertheless, the drafting of this document suggests a subtle change in official responses to threats against the state. Despite continuing to produce accounts of conspiracies and executions, the government apparently shifted its emphasis from displays of authority to attempts at persuasion. In 1583 William Cecil, Lord Burghley penned a defence of Edmund Campion's execution, and four years later a pamphlet, appearing anonymously but reputed to be the work of his son Robert, justified the beheading of Mary Stuart.[38] Produced explicitly in response to rumours and libels, such accounts acknowledged the possibility of alternative interpretations and expressed the government's commitment to convincing readers to trust official versions.[39] Between 1569 and 1583, then, the government seems to have acknowledged an increasing level of popular print literacy and to have developed a strategy for using printed texts both to pre-empt and to respond to discordant voices. However, the materiality of these texts and their ongoing availability to anyone who could read or hear them read offered possibilities for discussion and dialogue not only at the time but in succeeding years. Consequently, it became increasingly necessary for writers to establish the truth of their narratives against competing versions.

As sermons came to dominate Reformation culture, the pulpit offered an apparent solution to the problem of establishing truth claims. Delivering official accounts of events through clergymen could align political with divine authority, but this process too was fraught with uncertainties. Sermons reached both the literate and illiterate, but they required the cooperation of preachers, who quickly realized that political sermons allowed them to question, or even reject, official versions of events. As God's servants as well as the monarch's, these men also needed to believe the story they were telling. After Essex's execution the Elizabethan authorities struggled to find a preacher willing to endorse the crown's version of the rebellion at Paul's Cross, and William Barlow, who reluctantly accepted the assignment, was derided for his pains, while some of James VI's Scottish preachers stubbornly refused to publicize his narrative of the Gowrie Conspiracy.[40] The pulpit thus remained a necessary but not entirely reliable instrument of official communication, and sermons joined pamphlets in providing a range of interpretations of political events to an increasingly sophisticated audience of hearers and readers. Although they form an extensive and important body of texts, these sermons have generally been either neglected or relegated to specialized studies.[41]

Lake and Questier identify three characteristics necessary to the development of a "public sphere": messages sent through various media, an assumption of general public interest, and a belief that individuals are capable of considering public events critically. They suggest that the commencement of the English Jesuit mission helped to create these conditions, particularly the third. Examining the interactions between the Elizabethan government and the first missionaries,

Edmund Campion and Robert Persons, they conclude that "in Elizabethan England the creation of something like a rudimentary public sphere was not a product of Puritan opposition to the establishment or state but rather a product of the regime's own efforts to perpetuate and protect itself from a popish threat variously conceived."[42] In a more recent collaboration, Lake and Pincus develop the complementary idea that a public sphere emerged gradually from traditions of giving counsel, and that exceptional events such as threats of conspiracies and rebellions permitted occasional openings and closings of the public sphere that gradually normalized more widespread participation in public affairs.[43] Thus, increasingly frequently, the crown's attempts to warn people about the threat of militant Catholicism were countered by writers exhorting the king to maintain true religion.

As a significant threat from a religious group disadvantaged in England but powerful on the Continent, the Gunpowder Plot required an official narrative that would inform the English public of what had taken place, warn others against similar attempts, and justify the traitors' punishments to both national and international audiences. Like his predecessor, James used pamphlets, liturgies, and sermons to achieve these objectives. The sermon at Paul's Cross, again by the unlucky Barlow, the official narrative (possibly penned by James), and the account of the trials and executions compiled by the Earl of Northampton all offered a reasonably homogeneous narrative. As we shall see later, however, subsequent writers discovered and exploited gaps within and between them.[44] Although the new king acted more assertively than Elizabeth ever had by instituting annual commemorations to sustain a powerful collective memory of this event, pulpit, stage, and pamphlet helped to destabilize its meanings.

1.5 Remembering Conspiracy: Plot Narratives and National Memory

That public memory had political consequences in this period has been demonstrated by Jonathan Scott, who argues in *England's Troubles: Seventeenth-Century English Political Instability in European Context* that recollections of incidents such as the Gunpowder Plot fuelled the fear of Catholicism that helped to detonate the civil wars and the 1688 revolution.[45] Building upon Scott's work, Jason C. White shows how militant Protestants used the memory of the plot to appeal for a political union that could strengthen their defences against international Catholicism. In other words, these writers assert the political significance of perceptions, regardless of their truth content. James I seems to have shared the belief that perceptions influence political activity, hastening to counteract rumours that Catholic nations had supported the plotters in order to prevent his subjects from jeopardizing the new peace with Spain. I suggest that the king also sought to create a cultural memory that supported his bid for union, solidifying his position as the founder of a new dynasty and a new Britain as well as the preserver of Protestantism. The following chapters will show that he was successful in creating a powerful memory, but less successful in retaining control of that memory, perhaps because he underestimated the interpretative capabilities of his reading and writing subjects.

Although public memorials shaped national memory, literature perpetuated it, particularly as the immediacy of the event faded. According to Astrid Erll and Ann Rigney, once the witnesses to events die, cultural memories must be actively cultivated through texts, material objects, and rituals. Memories of the Gunpowder Plot survived not only in annual commemorative rituals, but also in texts accessible throughout the year in print or manuscript. Erll and Rigney propose that literature plays three roles in the production of cultural memory, acting as a medium of remembrance, an object of remembrance, and a medium for the production of cultural memory. Although these roles may overlap, literary texts first "help produce collective memories in the form of narratives."[46] Paul Ricoeur and Paul Connerton also insist upon the role of narrative in memory, Connerton arguing that remembering requires creating "meaningful narrative sequences," while Ricoeur proposes that narrative incorporates memories into our identities, individual and collective.[47]

If we accept Connerton's distinction between two types of remembrance – incorporation and inscription – we may see the early seventeenth century at a crossroads between the two. Incorporation involves ritual acts requiring physical participation, while inscription involves the creation of myths. Although Connerton admits that the two may overlap, he argues that the "transition from an oral culture to a literate culture is a transition from incorporating practices to inscribing practices."[48] In the seventeenth century, commemoration included both such incorporating rituals as attending church, participating in the liturgy, and ringing church bells and such inscribing practices as hearing sermons and watching plays, as well as reading and writing various print and manuscript texts. While the two types frequently reinforced each other, they could also open up differences of interpretation. As Connerton points out, ritual may be more conservative than myth, since the "*reservoir of meanings*" in a myth may be reshaped for different purposes, while "the structure of ritual has significantly less potential for *variance*."[49] Although Cressy's study of the "vocabulary" of celebration demonstrates that practices such as bell ringing expressed changing meanings over time, they could not accommodate the full range of interpretations that narratives could.[50]

Despite requiring his subjects' participation in both incorporating and inscribing practices, James encountered several obstacles to creating a new national identity through shared memory. As Ricoeur reminds us, the "duty of memory consists essentially in a duty not to forget," which meant subjects had to be exhorted continually to recall their own deliverance from this threat.[51] While remembrance needed to begin on this personal level, writers frequently threatened that individual forgetfulness could endanger the state: if England's people forgot God's blessings, then God would forget England.[52] One of the difficulties of memory, however, is its tendency to become confused with imagination. This problem became acute when individuals were required to remember an event that had been prevented from happening. To impress people with the magnitude of their deliverance, speakers and writers had to describe the extent of the proposed destruction, which could only be accomplished by appealing to their imaginations.[53] In his sermon at Paul's Cross on 10 November 1605, Barlow painted a vivid picture of London after an explosion. In this "*fierie massacre*," "(beside the place it selfe at the which hee aymed) the *Hall of Iudgement, the Courtes of Recordes, the Collegiate Church, the Citie of Westminster*, yea, *White-Hall* the Kinges house, had beene trushed and ouerthrowne." A "D*eluge of Bloode*," in which people would have been torn "parcell meale" as if by beasts would have followed the explosion.[54] So many sermons and pamphlets during the remainder of the century repeated this word picture that even the Royalist James Howell felt compelled to satirize it in his letter to the "knowing reader" at the beginning of his *Epistolae Ho-Elianae*.[55] Expanding on the capabilities of letters, he reminds his readers that "Had not the Eagle's *Letter* brought to Light / That subterranean horrid Work of Night":

> Witness that fiery *Pile*, which would have blown
> Up to the Clouds, Prince, People, Peers and Town,
> Tribunals, Church, and Chapel; and had dry'd
> The *Thames*, tho' swelling in her highest Pride,
> And parboil'd the poor Fish, which from her Sands
> Had been toss'd up to the adjoining Lands.
> Lawyers, as *Vultures*, had soar'd up and down;
> Prelates, like *Magpies*, in the Air had flown.[56]

Howell's poem demonstrates how imagination stimulates literature by providing the possibility of multiple, even competing, memories.[57]

Individuals recall public events differently, according to Maurice Halbwachs, because they have different social identities. Halbwachs and other memory theorists also suggest that individuals identify more fully with smaller, more tightly knit social groups than with the more abstract notion of the state.[58] In the years after the plot's discovery, preachers occasionally reminded elite congregations that they would have lost their lives had the plot been successful. Members of the lower social orders, however, likely recalled the threat of economic and political chaos rather than that of immediate death. Those outside London may have felt less personally affected by the plot, receiving the news after the danger was averted and having to rely on second-hand accounts of the trials and executions witnessed by Londoners. Walter Yonge, living in Devonshire, recorded the plot's discovery in his diary with interest but no apparent fear. His observation that the Midlands rising comprised only "sixty or eighty horse" suggests that he did not exaggerate the threat.[59] In these cases, social cohesion within a smaller group did not preclude identification with the Protestant nation.

For others, however, conflicted loyalties arose. This was particularly true for Catholics, expressly denied full participation in a Protestant state.[60] Recent research depicts the post-Reformation Catholic community in England as a close and supportive network,[61] yet many Catholics, including Ben Jonson, considered themselves both Catholics and loyal Englishmen. James acknowledged this dilemma, insisting from the beginning that Catholics could be loyal subjects without changing their religion, provided they repudiated the pope's power of deposition. Many writers nevertheless saw all Catholics as potential if not actual traitors, forcing them to choose between their religious and political allegiances. For many, a less explicit conflict centred on James's unpopular project of Anglo-Scottish union. Undercurrents of anti-Scots feelings, expressed in post-plot drama and perhaps more covertly in Anglo-Latin epic, indicate that many were unwilling to subsume their English identity within a British one.[62] James, however, apparently recognized the necessity of overcoming these challenges. Recent scholarship has described how the English Reformation disrupted medieval sites of memory, initiating a crisis of memory as the sermon replaced the Mass, prayers for the dead were abolished, and the old calendar of saints' days was radically pruned.[63] As Cressy suggests, the institution of political anniversaries helped to smooth this transition by replacing these traditions with new rituals and myths.[64]

While rituals could be legislated, mythmaking required the work of authors mostly outside direct state control. Some wrote to obtain patronage, others for more immediate monetary gain, and still others to persuade readers of their political or religious views. For all Renaissance authors, however, writing about the recent past posed a theoretical challenge that continues to trouble both historians and literary critics. Aristotle's *Poetics*, echoed by Sidney's *Defence of Poetry*, distinguished poetry from history, classifying poetry as general, plot-driven, and focused upon the possible, while history is particular, episodic, and deals with the actual.[65] Aristotle does not preclude poets from representing historical subjects; however, Sidney favours imagined events, claiming that the historian has fewer opportunities to encourage virtuous action because the actual events he must narrate may not supply appropriate morals.[66] Historical narratives, he fears, may actually promote vicious rather than virtuous action. According to Eric MacPhail, Aristotle developed the idea of plot or *mythos* "as a distinctly poetic form of rationality and coherence absent from history," but Renaissance theorists transferred this idea from poetry to history. In the reversal that he posits, "humanist historiography sought to portray the pattern and the logic of historical events while Renaissance literary criticism undertook to reevaluate the historicity of fiction."[67]

The relationship of narrative to literary form in historical representation remains contentious. Hayden White proposes that all narrative histories are "verbal fictions" shaped according to literary conventions.[68] Jauss similarly argues that narrative history perpetrates three "illusions": the illusion of a clear beginning and end, since these are actually selected from a range of possibilities; the illusion of completeness even when events are obviously incomplete; and the illusion of objectivity.[69] According to White, the literary form the author chooses to impose upon an event determines the selection of beginning and end. As Ricoeur points out, however, White's equation of historical and fictional narratives neglects a fundamental difference between the two. While fictional narratives require only a sign and a signifier, historical narratives also need a referent to legitimate their truth claims, although these may be compromised by the selectivity of both archive and researcher.

From the beginning, the crown needed to assert the truth of the plot in order to squelch powerful counter-narratives by religiously and politically disaffected individuals and communities. Recognizing testimony as the link between memory and history, the crown first polished and published the confessions of Guy Fawkes and Thomas Winter in the "Discourse" published with James's 9 November speech, then documented the plotters' trials.[70] By including his account of Catholic interference beginning with the bull against Elizabeth in the latter pamphlet, however, Northampton began situating the event within a lengthier history. Subsequent authors adopted this chronicle form to offer credible history while demonstrating England's providential preservation. The form promised objectivity, since most readers were unlikely to reflect upon the absence of incidents that had been silently elided.[71] Listing the Catholic plots from which Protestant England had been saved, frequently beginning with the Elizabethan Settlement, these texts made the Gunpowder Plot the finale in a series of increasingly daring Catholic attempts to subvert English Protestantism. As White points out, however, closure remains elusive in the chronicle form, making it singularly appropriate to a series of incidents that could only end with the papal Antichrist's final defeat at the apocalypse.[72]

One of the earliest prose chronicles to include the Gunpowder Plot, Thomas Mason's 1615 *Christs victorie ouer Sathans tyrannie*, a continuation of Foxe's *Acts and Monuments*, places the conspiracy within a lengthy list of domestic rebellions, assassination attempts, the thwarted Spanish invasion of 1588, and the Gowrie Conspiracy.[73] Contextualizing the plot within a chronology of Protestant martyrdoms both emphasizes its place in providential history and openly contests Catholic claims that Garnett and Oldcorne died as martyrs.[74] A new polemical imperative shaped the chronicles of the 1620s, as authors garnered support for their political positions on intervening in the continental war by mobilizing fears that the next generation might forget the plot. Bishop George Carleton's providential history, *A Thankfull Remembrance of God's Mercy* (1624), exhorted England to remember her deliverances, implicitly warning that forgetfulness could imperil the nation. Like Mason, Carleton situated the plot within a detailed list of attacks on English Protestantism, attributing the conspiracy to the Jesuits without entirely dismissing the possibility of diabolical agency.[75] Dedicating his pamphlet to Prince Charles, to whom he was chaplain, however, Carleton chose as his final evidence of divine favour God's preservation of England from the continental wars in which Charles was then attempting to embroil his country. Carleton's isolationism contrasts with the repeated injunctions of the puritan printer Michael Sparke to pray for German Protestants and particularly for the dispossessed Elector Palatine and his wife, Princess Elizabeth, in his immensely popular *Crumms of Comfort*, a collection of prayers and thanksgivings reprinted in numerous editions from the mid-1620s into the eighteenth century. Although these texts displayed the widening interpretative gap between conformists and radical Protestants, both authors consciously sought to instil memories of former deliverances in the next generation, providing foldout illustrations of the Armada and the Gunpowder Plot to be used when instructing children about these events.[76]

The new sense of solidarity engendered by the Thirty Years' War encouraged radical Protestants like Sparke to integrate their list of deliverances with those of their co-religionists on the continent, and by mid-century their chronicles were able even to represent the civil wars as part of the Counter-Reformation. The anonymous *Papa Patens or The Pope in his Colours* (1652) promised on its title page an "Exact account" of the Armada, the Gunpowder Plot, the Massacre at Paris, the murders of Henri III and IV, and the Irish Rebellion.[77] No longer was the plot simply an attack on an individual monarch, or even a nation; it had become part of an international conspiracy against Protestantism directed from Rome itself. The nation's enemies, in their efforts to restore Catholicism, begin "by striving to make our selves hate our own Religion, and leave that God which brought us out of the Land of *Ægypt*," but if this fails they resort to "poyson, murder, and force of Arms."[78] The pamphlet's underlying message is that people err in hating puritans more than papists when their behaviour is in fact much more moderate and less politically dangerous. Thus, Catholics can be blamed even for the dissensions among Protestants that have caused the civil wars. Rather curiously, a brief recital of William Watson's 1603 plot (also known as the Bye Plot), the truth of which the writer questions, follows the account of the Gunpowder Plot.[79] Possibly the author thought narrating the events chronologically would undermine the truth claims he makes for the Gunpowder Plot, condemning those who either consider it the work of "a few male-contents" or "an invention of him whom in reverence I forbeare to name."[80] For the first time in this text, however, narrative struggles against the chronicle form.

Nevertheless, J.H. could still use this form at the Restoration to span the divide of the civil wars, celebrating Charles II's accession by recalling his grandfather's deliverances in *A True and Perfect Relation of that Most Horrid & Hellish Conspiracy of the Gunpowder Treason* (1662) and claiming he had collected his information "out of the Best and most Authentique Writers." Indeed, the author seems to have drawn eclectically from various sources. He follows the author of the "Discourse" in giving Fawkes three matches and the author of *Papa Patens* in having the plotters encounter the wall about Candlemas.[81] From the "Discourse," also, comes the image of the rebels' support melting away like a snowball in spring that John Vicars borrowed when expanding a brief epic by Francis Herring. His main purpose is to celebrate the Stuart dynasty, beginning the story with James's accession and the Watson and Ralegh conspiracies and concluding with the executions of the Gunpowder traitors. Thomas Howard, the Lord Chamberlain, takes precedence over Salisbury in the plot's discovery, possibly because the Howard line had continued to support the Stuarts.[82] This royalist text warns readers that their ingratitude caused Charles I's execution, thus linking Catholicism and separatism at the same time that 30 January joined 5 November on the political calendar, one celebrating a Stuart monarch's deliverance from a Catholic plot and the other commemorating his son's betrayal by puritans. While the chronicle structure had proved remarkably flexible for both political and religious purposes, fidelity to history was becoming incompatible with fidelity to a polemical narrative. The result was a movement away from the chronicle format towards single-incident narratives representing themselves as trustworthy histories.

For early writers of histories the only available documentary evidence comprised the testimonies of Fawkes and Winter, the Monteagle letter, and the trial itself, all mediated through official accounts that Catholic writers actively contested.[83] In his 1658 *Englands warning peece or the history of the gun-powder treason*, Thomas Spencer cited John Speed and Bishop Carleton rather than more radical sources to prove his neutrality, and he supplemented the conspirators' testimonies with that of the Littletons' cook, who guessed the rebels were hiding at Holbeach House after the failed Midlands rebellion when his master ordered more food than he could possibly eat. Although unsubstantiated, this anecdote offers readers an immediate first-person narrative. By the 1670s, amid fears of a Catholic succession, authors turned to Catholic sources to assert an increasingly elusive impartiality. Edward Stephens' *Discourse Concerning the Original of the Powder-Plot* (1674) tackles both Catholicism and separatism, warning that the laxity of preferment-seeking clergy is driving more godly clerics from the Church of England, leaving the country more vulnerable to Catholicism. Although he implicates even the pope in the plotting of the conspiracy, his primary targets are the Jesuits, and he exploits Catholic anti-Jesuitism by citing Catholics like Jacques Auguste de Thou, who concede the Society's role in the conspiracy. An English edition of de Thou's narrative appeared the same year.[84]

As the urgency to validate the traditional narrative escalated in response to the Popish Plot, the original account of the discovery appeared in 1679 for the first time since 1606, with a new preface signed by T.L., probably Thomas Barlow, Bishop of Lincoln. Hoping to quell rumours that there was no plot or that Cecil invented one, Barlow insists in his introduction that the story is "no lying Legend, no vain Romance, no spurious or unlicenc'd-seditious Pamphlet, but an Authentique History." Rejecting various generic labels, Barlow claims objectivity, relying upon Catholic authors to show that even their co-religionists repudiate the Jesuits, although he blames the puritans as well, asserting that they "had set a foot a scandalous report of the King, *THAT HE MEANT TO GRANT A TOLERATION TO POPERY.*"[85] Barlow's main contribution to plot historiography, however, was publishing some letters by Everard Digby, found upon the death of his son, Sir Kenelm Digby. Although they provide little insight into the event, they augmented the documentary evidence for the first time since the confessions of Fawkes and Winter and the Monteagle letter had been printed with the original narrative.[86]

The earlier chronicles had relied upon the method of example, which, according to Jauss, "extracts a clearly formulated moral lesson from some earlier deed in order to guide future actions."[87] As long as human nature was regarded as constant, understanding the past could explain the present and anticipate the future. Thus, on the journey from Reformation to apocalypse, Catholics and Spaniards would always attack or undermine Protestant England, but they would do so in various ways. By the 1670s, this approach was abandoned in favour of the parallel, which, as Achsah Guibbory explains, represents a more cyclical view of history than the chronicle, for it suggests that certain patterns repeat themselves, although with varying degrees of exactness.[88] In 1678 John Williams, Bishop of Chichester, followed Stephens's formula in his *History of the Gunpowder-Treason* to insist that the plotters were highly placed Jesuits, that even some Catholics condemned the plot, and that the evidence of Garnett's complicity had conveniently perished with Catesby. Williams also makes an impassioned plea for the continuing celebration of the plot lest it, like the Armada, be forgotten and England continue to fall prey to Jesuit treachery. Responding to his critics, in 1681 he published a "vindication" of the earlier text, adding to it "A PARALLEL betwixt That and the Present Popish Plot," reiterating his previous assertions that the plot was formulated in the highest Jesuit councils, but using the strategy of the parallel to demonstrate that if the Gunpowder Plot was genuine, then the Popish Plot must also be. He elaborates on the similarities between the two – both were perpetrated by Jesuits, were intended to re-Catholicize England, and were planned and discovered in comparable ways.[89] The argument is logically weak, but in the highly charged atmosphere of the time its rhetoric may have been compelling. Williams's pamphlets were reprinted with Gilbert Burnet's 1684 Gunpowder sermon and various items related to the Popish Plot in *A Collection of Several Tracts and Dsicourses* [*sic*] in 1685. In his controversial sermon, published to vindicate himself of charges of popery, Burnet used a strategy similar to Williams's by choosing as his text Psalm 22.31, in which David requests God's assistance on the strength of a former deliverance.[90] The subsequent discovery that the Popish Plot had been fabricated, however, seems to have revived an element of scepticism regarding traditional plot narratives from which they have never fully recovered.

While these prose texts, despite their obvious polemical stances, represented themselves as histories, the commemorative texts with which this study is largely concerned were not required to establish truth claims by using testimony or printed sources. Commemoration, as Ricoeur points out, requires fidelity to the original narrative rather than to historical truth.[91] Most of these texts were self-consciously literary or rhetorical, taking the forms of occasional poetry, epigram, Virgilian epic, or sermon. The theatre from the beginning challenged both the historical and commemorative traditions by querying official accounts. The relationships among these texts demonstrate a developing intertextuality that blends fiction and reality, memory and imagination. While at times authors' engagements with previous texts seem eclectic or merely pragmatic, they frequently serve to turn their works into "object[s] of remembrance," making intertextuality part of collective memory. Erll and Rigney argue that "recollecting texts composed or written in earlier periods is an integral part of cultural remembrance."[92] Rewriting texts, as Jauss has made clear, also enables literary history.

Responses to the plot helped to create a radically Protestant epic tradition, influenced the development of the occasional political sermon, and fostered the late-seventeenth-century ghost poem genre inspired by Jonson's *Catiline, his Conspiracy*. Equally importantly, they helped to create audiences sensitive to religious and political nuances in the selection and manipulation of various generic codes. Consequently, the impact of these developments extends beyond literary history. While the relationship between public memory and history is complex, and it is difficult to trace a direct path from reading to political action, it is clear that memory creates narratives, narratives shape beliefs, and beliefs inform actions.

The present study examines texts in their relations not only to the original plot, but also to events taking place when they were composed, published, and received. Since the number of artefacts, even within the three genres I have selected, precludes analysis of every plot-related work, I have chosen a smaller number of texts representing the range of this material and its literary and historical influence in the seventeenth century, contextualizing them as broadly as possible.[93] The selected texts either take the plot as their main subject or theme, or were written as a direct result of the discovery or its annual celebration. I have deliberately omitted some specific groups of texts, particularly the polemical texts related to the Oath of Allegiance controversy. This vast body of materials merits its own study, and its relationship to the Gunpowder Plot is tangential although clearly significant. The best known of these texts, Donne's *Pseudo-Martyr*, has already been discussed in the context of post-plot representations of treason by Rebecca Lemon. With a few notable exceptions, the texts I discuss are by Protestant authors. Although it is not essential to my argument, I assume, with them and with most modern historians, that there was a plot and that its discovery unfolded roughly according to the official narratives. The majority of these texts, not surprisingly, were produced in the first half of the seventeenth century; however, their influence extends through the century and even into the next. Because generic development and mutation occurred at different paces among the selected genres, terminal dates for inclusion of texts vary between chapters; however, changing interpretations of the plot after 1688, when William III represented his own arrival on 5 November as England's second great deliverance from Catholicism, stimulated new forms of Gunpowder literature that cannot be discussed here but deserve their own study.

I begin in chapter 2 by reviewing the way in which, between 1569 and 1605, the English church and state developed and disseminated a providential account of the country's Protestant history through occasional liturgies, sermons, and prose narratives celebrating the monarch's deliverances from Catholic threats, both domestic and international. James VI followed a similar prescription in Scotland after his alleged kidnapping by the Gowrie brothers, with the important distinction that he made celebrating his deliverance an annual event. Bringing this celebration with him to England enabled him to claim a place in a developing narrative demonstrating God's care for English Protestantism by establishing an annual thanksgiving service and modelling the liturgy for the occasion on the one for Elizabeth's accession day. Early in his English reign, the discovery of the Gunpowder Plot allowed James to enhance this identification by the same means. Nevertheless, from the beginning rumours, libels, manuscript testimonies, and even printed sources offering alternative interpretations countered the sermons and authorized print accounts of these events. As time passed, James's insistence upon perpetual memorialization paradoxically both strengthened his self-representation as a British Protestant monarch and opened him and his heirs to critique. Although he could perpetuate the myth that all the plots against both himself and Elizabeth were, like Samson's foxes, joined at their tails, he had created regular occasions that his critics as well as his supporters could exploit.[94] This chapter, then, establishes how the development of the occasional thanksgiving liturgy, anniversary sermon, and narrative of deliverance helped to create a "rudimentary public sphere" during the late Elizabethan period by enabling members of various social and religious groups to interpret public events. Furthermore, these texts not only commented on events, but also created these events in the public memory using evolving generic conventions. By reading the texts created in the immediate aftermath of the Gunpowder Plot both in chronological order and against one another, we can see that a narrative develops through negotiation and dialogue rather than being simply imposed by the authorities.

Each of the remaining chapters concentrates upon a single genre, tracing its changing role in the narrative and its transformations over time. Chapter 3 explores the repercussions of the state's failure to create a univocal narrative, particularly in the very public trials and executions of the plotters, which opened the door to theatrical representations that engaged with unresolved questions about ambition, religion, and rhetoric. While no surviving play dramatizes the plot, contemporary dramas allude to it in various ways. Investigating the possibility of a dialogic relationship among three early plays – John Day's *Isle of Gulls*, Ben Jonson's *Volpone*, and Thomas Dekker's *Whore of Babylon* – I suggest that they challenge their audiences to re-examine the events that had recently taken place on the public stage of London, and particularly Robert Cecil's part in them. Jonson's later *Catiline, his Conspiracy* reprises these questions, offering a sweeping indictment of institutional rather than merely individual corruption and its lengthy afterlife. Memory plays a crucial role in this play, beginning with the appearance of Sylla's ghost in Catiline's study. This striking ghost, which functions differently than other stage spectres in the period, reappears in Restoration satire to raise once again the problem of the connection between religion and ambition that had not been safely buried with the plotters. The apparition highlights another absent presence in plot narratives – the women who cared for and protected the plotters, especially the priests, but were erased from the plot narratives until scholars in the late twentieth century began to reinstate them.[95] The female characters in *Catiline* have suffered from a similar neglect through most of the play's history, despite the significance of their actions and the liberties Jonson took with his classical sources in representing them. Why did the women, particularly Anne Vaux, who had sheltered Garnett, drop out of the narrative so quickly and completely? The play's conclusion raises further questions about the rhetorical self-representations of those who tried the plotters and about the futility of trying to eliminate English Catholicism. The ghost thus serves as a reminder of all that haunts Jacobean England and the hazards of applying simple solutions to complex problems. Briefly tracing the play's reception through the later seventeenth century we watch its central concerns migrate from drama to dramatic monologue and tragedy to satire, these generic transformations signalling new efforts to understand old problems.

Whereas the reception of Jonson's play demonstrates the movement of a single text from one genre to another, the following two chapters trace the transformation of a genre, the Anglo-Latin Gunpowder epic, as it gradually evolves from a courtly manuscript genre to a public print one. If James saw in the plot evidence that God protected English Protestant monarchs, he also noted in its timing an opportunity to promote the project that was to have dominated the parliamentary session disrupted by its discovery – the political union of England and Scotland. Although the king wanted his reign to be seen in some ways as a continuation of Elizabeth's, he also wanted to emphasize that he was creating a new Britain.[96] The Gunpowder Plot was thus to become the founding event for both his new dynasty and a new Protestant nation. Those who wrote congratulatory poems to solicit patronage from members of the court after the plot's discovery seem to have recognized this ambition and chosen Anglo-Latin epic as the most appropriate genre in which to represent the plot as the founding event of this new nation.

Nevertheless, they also used the occasion to counsel James on his handling of the Catholic problem. Early epics such as those by Michael Wallace and Francis Herring congratulated the king on his deliverance, but also reminded him of the dangers of allowing Catholics to remain in the country, particularly at court. As some of these poems found their way into English print culture, they helped transform epic from a royalist to a puritan genre in the mid-seventeenth century. Beginning with Herring's 1609 sequel describing the Midlands rebellion, the epics grew more militantly Protestant as publication and translation moved them down the social and economic ladder. Later writers such as Phineas Fletcher combined panegyric praise with apocalyptic warning, representing forcefully Satan's control of the Catholic Church through tropes of monstrosity and demonic councils. Although part of an academic rather than a courtly tradition, Milton's *In Quintum Novembris* also demonstrates diminishing faith in the ability, and perhaps the will, of a godly monarch to preserve the Protestant nation. John Vicars's escalating emphasis upon the abortive revolt and the plotters' characters in his "dilations" of Herring's poem completed the genre's transformation from court panegyric into godly propaganda, raising puritan struggles into an epic subject and creating an audience for the new Christian heroism of patient faith that the mature Milton would celebrate in *Paradise Lost*. The role of gunpowder in Milton's depiction of heavenly warfare demonstrates how godly Protestant writing had transformed the meaning of the Gunpowder Plot and how Milton's response helped to reshape the English epic.

Audiences are the primary subject of the sixth chapter, which documents how annual Gunpowder sermons preached, and sometimes printed, between 1606 and 1688 participated in perpetuating but also transforming memories of the plot. Here we see not the transformation of a single text or a genre, but the creation of a new genre, the anniversary sermon. Both a means for the ruler to display his power and authority to his subjects, and at the same time the minister's opportunity to offer counsel to his governors, sermons participated in the often contentious process of defining the English church in its relations both to the state and to its rivals, Catholicism and puritanism. Although this was the primary genre through which James had chosen to keep alive the official memory of his deliverances, the sermons provided ordinary individuals, even those who could not read, with the skills they needed to understand and participate in religious, political, and ultimately literary discourse by teaching them to negotiate among messages to multiple audiences.

Since the number of surviving sermons does not permit analysis of each one, and generalizing from a body of texts produced over such a long and tumultuous period is dangerous at best, I have selected four sermons for in-depth textual and contextual analysis, focusing particularly on their relationships with their audiences.[97] John Donne, preaching at Paul's Cross in 1622, responded to both James's recent *Directions to Preachers* and Samuel Ward's controversial "Double Deliverance" cartoon by offering a methodology of listening and reading that balances obedience to royal authority with the subject's freedom to interpret. Wolfgang Iser's theory of "blanks" and "negations" may be usefully employed to examine how Donne creates spaces for interpretation through the structure of his sermon, particularly in the later published version. Three printed responses to the 1636 sermons for which Henry Burton lost his ears (those of Archbishop Laud, Peter Heylyn, and Christopher Dow) demonstrate the Laudian administration's uneasiness with the close reading and interpretation that Burton advocates, particularly when performed by the godly. Matthew Newcomen's 1642 sermon to Parliament continues the tradition of counselling governors. Responding to the prospect of a negotiated peace settlement with Charles I that he felt would threaten further ecclesiastical reform, he justifies continuing the war against the king for religious reasons. The preservation of sermon notes taken on this occasion, attributed to Walter Yonge (second son of the diarist), allows us to consider how Newcomen may have adapted his sermon for performance and print audiences. Preaching before the restored Charles II at Whitehall on 5 November 1661, Seth Ward viewed his audience not as competent interpreters, but as potential subversives to be coerced into submission. Nervous about any kind of interpretation, Ward clarifies relations between church and state by articulating the duties of both monarchs and subjects. His sermon was reprinted during the controversy over Henry

Sacheverell's best-selling, and highly inflammatory, Gunpowder sermon of 1709, but the message of passive obedience had lost its effectiveness. Analysis of these four sermons suggests some of the ways in which readers and listeners helped to develop the genre of the anniversary sermon, enabling their own participation in the changing interpretation of the Gunpowder Plot.

In conclusion, I reiterate that the literature that took the Gunpowder Plot as its primary subject did not simply comment on its political occasion. Instead, it reshaped the narrative of the plot that was fundamental to its public memorialization. This constant revision involved not only writers, but also readers, who developed the skills to interpret complex messages in the theatre, in print, and in church, and by responding to them helped to create new genres and transform others. Although I make a case here for the significance of one particular incident – the Gunpowder Plot – I believe the methodologies used in these chapters could be effective in considering the reciprocal relationships between literary and non-literary history in the context of other seventeenth-century events. Not the least of the intriguing possibilities is the effect that the literature of the Gunpowder Plot had on the creation of the Popish Plot, to which I have barely alluded.[98]

2 "like *Sampsons* Foxes": Creating a Jacobean Myth of Deliverance

Early seventeenth-century readers perceived the Gunpowder Plot not as an isolated incident but as the climax in a series of Catholic assaults upon England and her church dating back at least as far as the Northern Rising and the papal bull against Queen Elizabeth.[1] Examining the genesis of this interpretation in the earliest official responses to the plot, I argue that between 1569 and 1605 the English church and state had developed a providential account of English Protestant history through liturgies, sermons, and prose narratives celebrating deliverances from a succession of Catholic threats, and that James I seized the opportunities of the Gowrie Conspiracy and the Gunpowder Plot to expand this English narrative into a British one. Upon his accession to the English throne, one of the king's challenges was to identify his reign as an extension of Elizabeth's while making it clear that he was founding a new Stuart dynasty and a British nation.[2] By inserting the Gowrie Conspiracy into a series of English deliverances, James hoped to make a cultural connection between the two countries through his own person, miraculously preserved in both places.[3] As we shall see in subsequent chapters, however, overcoming resistance to political union was even more difficult than convincing some of his preachers to accept his narrative of the Gowrie incident.

In using the phrase "myth of deliverance" to describe this phenomenon, I rely upon Paul Connerton's distinction between "myth" as verbal act and "ritual" as performance.[4] The *Oxford English Dictionary* defines a myth as a "traditional story, typically involving supernatural beings or forces, which embodies and provides an explanation, aetiology, or justification for something such as the early history of a society, a religious belief or ritual, or a natural phenomenon."[5] Common usage sometimes denigrates myth by associating it with exaggeration or lies; however, here it is not intended to suggest that James and his advisors perpetrated deliberate falsehoods. While the word "myth" is not used in contemporary accounts, the word "deliverance" appears repeatedly and carried much weight for seventeenth-century readers. Blair Worden explains that deliverances were considered "pleasant providences" or "mercies." These "were not random or arbitrary displays of God's sovereignty, but formed a pattern, a 'chain' or 'series', visible to the true believer." Thus, "Providence was the thread of divine purpose which drew together the seemingly disparate events of history."[6] The story of the Gunpowder Plot, retold annually, acquired mythic status as a link in the chain of deliverances from the papal Antichrist that demonstrated God's approval of English Protestantism. As interpreter of the cryptic Monteagle letter, James could claim an instrumental role in this divine work, justifying both his reign and the ongoing marginalization of Catholics.

To remind his subjects continually of the providential status of his reign, James introduced a new focus upon perpetual memorialization that was paradoxically to offer later writers opportunities to critique both his and his son's actions. Even in November 1605, however, not all readers and listeners credited the news of the plot. While dissenting interpretations frequently had to rely upon manuscript or oral transmission, their proliferation required the government to engage with them in a series of texts and oral performances over the following months. The evidence that official texts were developed to target specific counternarratives complicates the prevailing view, expressed by David Cressy, that consensus regarding the nature of the plot did not fragment until the 1630s. Instead, I suggest that such a consensus was illusory from the beginning.[7] Consequently, the Protestant narrative of the Gunpowder Plot was not simply imposed by the state and accepted by a passive populace, but developed through dialogue and debate among competing accounts from the beginning.

2.1 Liturgies: Thanksgiving and Vengeance

On 12 July 1603, two weeks before James I's coronation, the Privy Council instructed Archbishop John Whitgift to devise a thanksgiving service according to his own "Judgment and Wisdom" to celebrate the anniversary of the king's escape from an alleged plot by the Gowrie brothers in Scotland on 5 August 1600. The next day, Whitgift in turn requested assistance from his bishops, but suggested that

> in the meantime, and for the speedier Dispatch of your Letters, I think it fit, that some Order be observed in this Action as was used upon the 17th of *November* in our late Sovereign's Time; with special Charge, that in every particular Church there be a Sermon and Service, with a Declaration of the great Blessing of God for his Majesties Deliverance from that Danger, with hearty Prayer to God for the Continuance of his Goodnes towards him and us; and to the like effect.[8]

As Whitgift's letter indicates, special thanksgiving services in honour of the monarch were not unprecedented. Beginning in the late 1570s, annual liturgies and sermons celebrated the anniversary of Elizabeth's accession, but occasional thanksgivings for her deliverances had begun even earlier.[9] What is striking about Whitgift's direction, however, is the priority the king apparently accorded this activity in the first months of a new reign. Clearly, James had grasped the potential that such occasions offered for moulding his public image as both Elizabeth's rightful successor and the founder of a new dynasty and a British nation.

As Richard Helgerson and Timothy Rosendale have shown, the regular services of the Book of Common Prayer contributed to emergent English nationalism by continuously reinforcing England's distinctive religious character. I would like to suggest, however, that occasional liturgies played a crucial and largely unexamined role in this process by developing a narrative of English history in which God protected the nation against its enemies, particularly Rome and Spain.[10] This providentialist narrative was reflected in literary as well as polemical works well into the next century. While the tradition began with Elizabeth's reign, James eagerly adopted and expanded it, first by introducing the annual memorialization of his deliverances and second by making attendance at such services compulsory.

The practice of ordering special prayers on political occasions began after the Northern Rising and continued with the gradual institution of an annual service of thanksgiving, sometimes accompanied by a sermon, on 17 November, the queen's accession day.[11] The first accession day service was published in 1576 and was followed by a proliferation of occasional liturgies drawn up to offer thanksgiving for Elizabeth's deliverances from assassination plots by William Parry (1585), Anthony Babington and his fellow conspirators (1586), and Doctor Lopez (1594), as well as a special service to celebrate the defeat of the Armada in 1588.[12] Since Elizabeth's accession was understood as the country's liberation from the reign of her Catholic half-sister, all of these occasions presented opportunities for anti-Catholic rhetoric. Although public participation in these liturgies was not required, and the accession day celebration remained controversial, the "Admonition to the Reader" in the 1594 service concludes with the hint of a threat: the "duetie of praying and thankesgiuing there is no doubt, but euery true hearted *English* man and faithfull *Subiect* will both priuately and publickely from the bottome of his heart performe."[13] Nevertheless, it would be a mistake to regard the purpose of these services as simply coercive. In accordance with prevailing beliefs in divine providence, the authorities expected subjects to recognize that maintaining God's favour benefitted them individually as well as collectively.[14]

For rulers, prayer was a double-edged sword. In *The True Law of Free Monarchies*, James identifies prayer as the subject's only legitimate means of resisting an evil or tyrannical ruler. Conversely, by insisting that his subjects routinely pray for him, the monarch could encourage the development, as well as the demonstration, of obedience and loyalty. As a political instrument, liturgy offers the advantages of both inclusiveness and active participation. While some parishes lacked trained ministers who could preach occasional sermons, almost everyone in England participated in the liturgies of the church.[15] Furthermore, in her studies of the English prayer book, Ramie Targoff argues that church authorities justified communal prayer by insisting upon the reliability of external signs in mirroring inward devotion. At the same time, "mainstream Renaissance Protestants frequently imagined performative behavior to have a causal as well as reflective relation to the internal self: according to such accounts, the individual's assumption of external gestures prompted the corresponding internal conditions." Consequently, "Behind the church's emphasis on external conformity lies its commitment to the transformative power of practice."[16] While Targoff is mainly concerned with individual religious devotion, the assumption that speaking words of prayer and praise for the queen will inspire subjects with love for her doubtless underlies the institution of special services on political occasions. Paul Connerton argues further that such shared and repeated speech acts and gestures reinforce communal identity and that such rituals resist change over time.[17] Although Connerton sees participation in liturgy as primarily a performative, bodily action, liturgy also contributes to the creation and dissemination of myth through its use of language. As special liturgies of deliverance developed, a narrative emerged in which first Elizabeth, then James, became the successor to the Old Testament kings, and England merged with Israel.

Like occasional accession day sermons and the *Homily against Wilful Disobedience*, which had been introduced after the failure of the Northern Rebellion in 1569 and was required to be read annually in churches, these services reinforced the connection between treason and false religion, while insisting upon the providential preservation of the queen's person as the means by which her subjects retained access to the gospel. The directions for the use of the 1585 service, to be read in the diocese of Winchester on the occasion of Elizabeth's escape from Parry's plot, ordered that the minister preach a sermon declaring "the authoritie and Maiestie of Princes," and "how streight dutie of obedience is required of all good and Christian subiects, and what a greeuous and heynous thing it is both before God and man traiterouslie to seeke their destruction, and the shedding of their blood."[18] The service was distinctive in requiring the reading of an extract from Parry's confession. When juxtaposed with the full confession as it appears in the official pamphlet detailing the conspiracy, this excerpt seems to have been chosen to emphasize the Jesuits' role and to omit Parry's insistence that he would have preferred to improve the lot of English Catholics by non-violent means.[19] Although ambition was the ultimate source of his fall, the idea of killing the queen only occurred to him after his conversion to Rome, and he did not proceed until both a papal ambassador and a Jesuit had assured him that he could meritoriously commit the deed. The prayer asks that "y cruel spirits of Antichrist that seeke the subuersion of the Gospel, maie by the hand of thy iustice, feele what it is to set to sale for money the innocent bloud of thine annointed Princes, which thou hast prepared and set vp, to be the nurses and protectors of thy truth."[20] Extrapolating from a single example, the service implicates the entire Catholic Church in an attempt to subvert English Protestantism.

Perhaps unsurprisingly, given the political ramifications of Mary Stuart's alleged involvement in the Babington Plot, the 1586 order of service celebrating its failure maintains a more restrained tone, rejoicing in the deliverance of queen, church, and nation from "sundry wicked Conspirators," who remain unidentified.[21] Among the Psalms and lessons from which the preacher may choose, the dominant theme of thanksgiving generally overcomes calls for vengeance.[22] This service provides the germ of the idea of annual memorialization, asking in the preface that "euery one that feareth the Lord among vs, not onely with the *Iewes* in the booke of *Esther* yeerely holds a memoriall with great ioy of so notable deliuerence, but dayly in common assemblies haue this great goodnesse in remembrance," yet there seems to have been no attempt to institute an annual thanksgiving.[23] The same is true of the Armada celebration two years later, for which a brief service was issued consisting of a Psalm and Collect written for the occasion. Thanksgiving was again the dominant theme, vengeance having already been satisfied by the destruction of the Spanish fleet.

Like the 1586 service, that of 1594 addresses a general rather than a specifically clerical audience in its "Admonition to the Reader." This introduction emphasizes the providential protection God accords to kings and kingdoms. The English owe special thanks to God for setting Elizabeth over them, preserving her realm from both internal and external threats, and protecting her person from traitors and conspirators. In contrast to the 1585 service, this one does not even name the individual conspirators, since they are now regarded merely as pawns of Spain and the Catholic Church. All of these treasons "haue they beene continually proiected, caried forwarde, and managed by idolatrous *Priestes* and *Iesuites* his creatures, the very loathsome *Locusts* that crawle out of the bottomlesse pitte."[24] The image of the priests as locusts will be taken up by Phineas Fletcher in *Locustae*, his neo-Latin epic on the Gunpowder Plot, long recognized as an influence on Milton's *Paradise Lost.* The list of conspiracies that follows reinterprets history to demonstrate that priests and Jesuits are aided by kings and magistrates who mask their own ambitions with shows of Catholic devotion. In the Northern Rebellion, the pope sent the priest Morton to stir the earls up to revolt, while Cardinal Allen has boasted that he and other Catholics incited Philip II to send the Armada. Spain and Rome are acting in concert to re-Catholicize England, but only the "wilfully malicious" can fail to see that God protects Protestantism.[25]

In the service itself, three prayers for the queen's preservation follow a series of Psalms proceeding from invocation to assurance. The first prayer implicitly connects Satan and the Catholic Church, asserting that God preserves kings from "the malice of Satan & his wicked ympes," and once again charges Elizabeth with preserving Protestantism, asking: "O Lorde, dissipate and confound all practises, conspiracies, and treasons against her, against this realme of England, and against the trueth of thine holy word here taught and professed."[26] This prayer, however, progresses beyond earlier ones in the pursuit of vengeance, imploring:

> Smite our enemies (good Lorde) vpon the cheeke-bone, breake the teeth of the vngodly, frustrate their counsels, and bring to nought all their deuises. Let them fall into the pit, that they haue prepared for vs: Let a sudden destruction come vpon them vnawares: and the net that they haue laide for others priuily, let it catch themselues, that they may fall into their owne mischiefe.[27]

The second prayer asks God to cause the queen's enemies either to repent or to perish. These services, then, promoted a providential Protestant reading of Elizabeth's deliverances in which God systematically thwarted the devil and his instruments, Spain and the Jesuits, providing that English subjects performed their duties of regular prayer and thanksgiving.

Although these occasional services offered James I precedents for establishing his own services of prayer and thanksgiving, his English memorialization of the Gowrie Conspiracy nevertheless presented several political challenges. Even had its details been more credible than they were, the Gowrie affair had taken place in Scotland and so could easily have been seen as irrelevant by James's new subjects. Nor did the plot fit neatly into the anti-Catholic tradition, for whatever motives may have activated the Gowries, their religious affinities seem to have been presbyterian rather than Catholic. James and Whitgift's solution of modelling the 5 August service on the 17 November one was brilliant, for it papered over the differences between the occasions more effectively than the half-hearted attempts of the preachers, who twisted the evidence to turn Alexander Ruthven into a crypto-Catholic, while insisting that James's Scottish deliverance had preserved him to defend Protestantism in England.

The most salient feature of the service was its emphasis upon continuity. The three kings presented in the Old Testament readings as parallels with Elizabeth had all followed their predecessor David's example in religion, as Elizabeth had continued Henry VIII's reformation. Their stories emphasized that correct worship preserves the monarch, the state, and true religion. Jehoshaphat managed to keep peace in the land because neighbouring kings feared his God; Hezekiah saved himself from death and Israel from the Assyrians through his prayers. Both Hezekiah and Josiah purged their country of idols, and Josiah sent away the priests of Baal, as Elizabeth had ordered priests and Jesuits to leave England. If the authorities wished to identify James as Elizabeth's rightful successor, there could be little better way than by adding him to this sequence of devout monarchs.

Nevertheless, the sugar-coating of persuasion concealed a dose of threat that would be intensified under James. Josiah's story demonstrates God's punishment for disobedience to the laws. Similarly, although the Psalms selected – 21, 85, and 124 – emphasize God's favour to his chosen nation, 85 also sounds a warning against angering God. The second lesson is Romans 13, which reinforces the requirement for obedience to secular authority.[28] The service thus insists that the fates of monarch and nation are interwoven and that divine favour depends upon the people's obedience to a godly monarch. Although retaliation was left to God rather than the state, the service nevertheless reminded subjects of the dangers of disobedience.

By later that year, a new service had been drafted and published. While it incorporated the Psalms from the 17 November liturgy, as well as retaining the Romans 13 reading, the prayers added some features that distinguished James from Elizabeth. The service is notable first for its focus upon the royal family, demonstrating that while James wished to be identified with Elizabeth, he also sought to emphasize the stability of the new monarchy through his provision of heirs. The first prayer for the king reflects the parallel between James and Jacob that was cemented in the official account of the Gowrie Conspiracy, probably written by James himself, which describes his wrestling with Alexander Ruthven.[29] Like the biblical Jacob, James wanted to be regarded as a patriarch, not only of a family, but of a nation. The second prayer for the king is evidently based upon that for Elizabeth in the 1594 service, but whereas the earlier prayer is inclusive, identifying Elizabeth's enemies with those of her people, this one (not surprisingly) highlights the king's personal deliverance. The second of the alternate prayers again savours of vengeance, thanking God that

> in thy iustice diddest thou returne vpon the heads and hearts of those deuilish and disloyall conspirators, the due reuenge of such treasonable attempts, spilling their blood like water vpon the earth, who thought to spill the blood of thine annoynted, and leauing their slaughtered carkesses a worthy spectacle of thy dreadfull iudgements, and their most impious designes.[30]

More cautious than some of the preachers, the liturgy located the conspiracy within a general discourse of obedience rather than attempting to fit it into the mould of Catholic treachery. In the Gowrie service, then, the new Jacobean administration had not only successfully presented James's reign as a continuation of Elizabeth's, but had also held out the promise of future stability that had been so clearly lacking in the queen's later years. By inserting his Scottish deliverance into the earlier English tradition, the new king had also taken a small, symbolic step towards his goal of political union. Finally, unlike the Parry and Lopez thanksgivings, the celebration of this deliverance became an annual event, ensuring that James's role in preserving English Protestantism would not be forgotten.

The final link binding the Scottish monarch to the English tradition was not forged until after the discovery of the Gunpowder Plot on 5 November 1605, when the Gowrie liturgy in turn served as the outline for a new thanksgiving service. Whether or not James and his administrators welcomed this conspiracy is a matter of dispute, but it did create a new liturgical opportunity that they exploited to its full potential. The Gowrie service provided the lessons, gospel, and epistle, contributing to a seamless integration of Scottish and English history through the monarch's person, miraculously preserved in both places, that outlasted his bid for political union. The success of James's efforts to collapse the two reigns in the minds of his subjects may be measured in such literary works as Thomas Dekker's *Whore of Babylon*, in which the playwright alludes to the recent Gunpowder Plot by dramatizing the Spanish Armada.

Although this service also emphasized the king's personal deliverance, references to the royal family once again distinguished James from Elizabeth even as he claimed from her the mantle of embattled Protestant monarch. The selection of Psalms, all of which plead for God to destroy the psalmist's enemies, escalates further the theme of vengeance that had been creeping into the services. Psalms 35 and 68 ask for evildoers to be scattered like dust or smoke, while 69 implores: "Let them bee wiped out of the booke of the liuing: and not be written among the righteous."[31] As in the Elizabethan services, the readings equate preserving the monarch with protecting the church and the gospel. The first prayer of thanksgiving asks God to "infatuate their counsels, and roote out that Babylonish and Anti-christian Sect, which say of Jerusalem, Downe with it, downe with it, euen to the ground." This time, however, God is to receive assistance from the secular authorities, who are urged "with iudgement & iustice to cut off these workers of iniquitie, (whose Religion is Rebellion, whose faith is faction, whose practise is murthering of soules and bodies) and to root them out of the confines and limits of this kingdome."[32] Since the fear of divine wrath might have been insufficient incentive for all subjects to participate in prayers on 5 November, attendance was legislated and the Act of Parliament required to be read each year.

The liturgical tradition into which James inserted himself, then, had already developed through the practice of annual celebrations of Protestant monarchy and occasional thanksgivings for Elizabeth's deliverances from danger. Increasingly these services identified the enemies of the English church as the pope and the Jesuits, and offered more insistent calls for vengeance. Using the Elizabethan liturgies as models for the Gowrie service allowed James to graft thanksgiving for his reign onto the tradition of praising Elizabeth, cultivating her residual popularity while offering a solution to the most vexing problem of her reign, that of a secure succession. By basing the Gunpowder prayers on the Gowrie service, the Jacobean church succeeded in meshing James's two reigns and demonstrating that he had been preserved by God's providence to rule England. Nevertheless, the real innovation James introduced was making his deliverances, both English and Scottish, annual celebrations of Protestantism. Like the *Homilies* and sermons preached on these occasions, the liturgies became part of the fabric of Jacobean life, contributing to a developing narrative in which James's reign looked back to the Old Testament and ahead to the apocalypse.

2.2 Sermons: Obedience and Deliverance

James I's success in establishing annual commemorative sermons in England on the Gowrie and Gunpowder anniversaries has largely been taken for granted. Nevertheless, he was participating in a renegotiation of the sermon's role in the nation's political life that had begun with the Reformation.[33] Although the "Homelie against disobedience and wylfull rebellion," as well as the sermons preached on Elizabeth's accession day, justified preaching obedience to the queen and thanksgiving for her preservation as religious duties, not all subjects considered the church an appropriate forum for such messages. As James's experience in Scotland following the Gowrie Conspiracy and that of the Elizabethan authorities in the aftermath of the Essex Rebellion illustrate, preachers were sometimes uneasy about becoming commentators during political crises. Elizabeth's achievement was to create a providential interpretation of English Protestant history that justified celebrating the monarch from the pulpit, while James's was to secure his own place in that history through annual sermons commemorating his deliverances.

In response to the Northern Rising of 1569, the Elizabethan government assigned Matthew Parker and his chaplains the task of composing the "Homelie against disobedience and wylfull rebellion," which was issued separately in 1570 and added to the *Second Book of Homilies* in 1571. In the introduction to his critical edition of the *Homilies*, Ronald Bond calls this series "one of the most formidable pieces of verbal artillery rushed to guard an old front."[34] The six parts, to be preached on a regular schedule that ensured each would be read annually, progess from a general discussion of universal order to a condemnation of the papacy's threat to civil order. As Daniela Busse points out, the initial use of the "Homelie" enforced obedience first upon the clergy, denying them the opportunity to express sympathy for the rebels in their sermons, even as they preached obedience to the laity.[35] The "Homelie," she observes, addressed the specific context of the rebellion from a religious rather than a political perspective, using biblical texts to demonstrate that even tyrannical rulers must be obeyed and anti-papal rhetoric to juxtapose the ignorance and disobedience fostered by Catholicism with the enlightenment and order of Elizabeth's reign. Whereas the rebels have trampled God's word underfoot, the queen provides her subjects with access to the Word. The assumption in the "Homelie" that the doctrine of resistance was held only by the Catholic Church, although godly Protestants could also have been accused of favouring this doctrine, helped to forge an association between treason and Catholicism that proved remarkably persistent, even when it required manipulating evidence.[36]

The annual celebration of the queen's accession day, begun around this time, provided another occasion for linking the theme of obedience with Elizabeth's deliverance of the nation from Catholicism.[37] Preaching on Titus 3 at Paul's Cross on 17 November 1583, Archbishop Whitgift emphasized the importance of obedience to secular authority, warning against the disobedience of Catholics and Anabaptists. He reminded his listeners and readers that Elizabeth

> hath not onlie deliuered vs from the crueltie and tyranny of the Bishop of Rome, but also opened vnto vs the dore of his Gospell, and as yet keepeth it open, and hath further giuen vnto vs that peace, tranquillitie and aboundance of all thinges, that of all people in the worlde wee are thought to bee the most happie, and as it were an astonishment to our enemies.[38]

Similarly, for Thomas Holland in 1599, Elizabeth's accession was

> A day wherein our Nation received a new light after a fearfull and bloudy Eclipse and al countries subiect to the English Scepter. A day wherein God gaue a rare Phœnixe to rule this land. A day shining graciously to many poore prisoners who long had been wearied in cold and heavy yrons, and had beene bound in the shadow of death, vnto whome shee came as welcome as the sweet shower cometh to the thirsty land.[39]

While obedience is due to any monarch, Elizabeth's subjects should willingly thank God for providing them with a godly sovereign.

Not all subjects, however, approved of celebrating the queen in church, and even in the final years of Elizabeth's reign preachers had to defend the special service. In 1583 Whitgift reproved

> those fantasticall spirits ... which dissalow and mislike this manner of yerelie celebrating this day, (to giue God thankes for the great and wonderfull benefits, which we enioy thorough his goodnes by the ministerie of her Maiestie, whome it pleased him this day fiue and twentie yeares to place in the Throne of this Kingdome, and to praie vnto him for her long life and prosperitie) as though we did it superstitiouslie, or dedicated the day vnto her, as to some Sainct, whereas in deede wee doe but our duetie, and that which is most lawfull for vs to doe.[40]

These remarks were presumably directed primarily towards godly critics who feared that Elizabeth was being worshipped as a saint, and he enlarged them in his letter "To the Christian Reader," added when the sermon was published in 1589.[41] Isaac Colfe, preaching in 1587 before the magistrates of Lydd in Kent, also specifically appealed to Protestant sceptics, insisting that Saint Paul condemned "only the superstitious obseruation of daies and times" and exhorting his congregation "religiously to obserue those dayes wherein the Lord hath done principall thinges either for the benefitte of his Church whether generall or particular amongest vs."[42] In contrast, Catholic critics were the primary audience for Thomas Holland's defence, published with his 1599 sermon, which argues for the celebration as "an office in it selfe sacred, religious, no waies repugnaunt to Gods holy worde" and opposed only by those who favour a return to Catholicism. Holland describes the 17 November office as consisting of

> an exposition of Scripture chosẽ by the Minister that day as such is fitte to perswade the auditory to due obedience to her Maiesty, and to be thankfull to God for her Maiesties happy and flourishing Regiment these 43. yeeres; and to excite them to prayer vnto God long to continue her Grace amongst vs (if it be his blessed will) & to deliver her Highnesse from all malice of her enemies.[43]

John Howson preached another defence in 1602 at St Mary's Oxford, using examples from both the Old Testament and the early Christian church to demonstrate that civil authorities may add festivals to the ecclesiastical calendar.[44] While Howson directs his justification mainly towards Catholics, he also deplores the puritan elevation of the sermon over prayer and criticizes those who "gad" about to hear sermons.

Preaching to their auditors the necessity of both thanksgiving and obedience, these clerics also recognized their own pivotal role in this process. Whitgift tells his audience of his injunction to obedience: "you must be content to heare it, It is our dutie to preache it."[45] Nevertheless, Holland's final line of defence is that the observation

> hath not been imposed vpõ the church of England by any Ecclesiasticall decree, neyther prescribed by any Canon of the Church: but hath bin meere voluntarily continued by the religious and dutifull subiects of this Realme in their thankfulnesse to God, and in their perfit zeale, tendring her Maiesties preservation in desiring the cõtinuance therof to Gods glory, & the good of the church and common wealth of England.[46]

In contrast to the later Gunpowder prayers and sermons, participation by both clergy and laity remained discretionary.

Occasional sermons celebrating the deliverance of queen and country from conspiracy and invasion seem to have developed more slowly than the annual accession day sermons. Ecclesiastical and secular authorities, along with preachers themselves, may not have immediately recognized the political benefits that such preaching occasions could provide. Not so Edwin Sandys, whose undated sermon, simply titled *A Sermon preached at Pauls Cross at what time a Maine Treason was Discovered*, was probably preached in May 1571, during deliberations regarding the punishments of the Ridolfi conspirators, including Mary Queen of Scots. Instead of simply offering thanksgiving for Elizabeth's deliverance, however, this sermon seems to have formed part of a calculated plan to introduce Sandys's argument for the execution of Mary before presenting it in Parliament.[47]

No sermons preached in conjunction with the thanksgiving for Parry's apprehension survive, although the reading of his confession from the pulpit along with the thanksgiving liturgy provides the first evidence of a narrative impulse that would be developed in later sermons. Not until 1586, when John Rainolds celebrated the apprehension of the Babington conspirators from the pulpit at Oxford, do we have evidence of such a sermon. Several features that would become common in later anniversary sermons mark this one, beginning with Rainolds's choice of a text from the Psalms (Psalm 18.47–51) that allowed him to flatter the queen by comparing her to David. Like the accession day preachers, he praised Elizabeth for making the gospel available to her subjects, but he also recognized her prudence in developing the navy to protect the nation. Appealing specifically to his own audience, he also emphasized the queen's concern for education, particularly at Oxford. As later preachers were wont to do, he rehearsed all of the plots from which Elizabeth had previously escaped, but unlike them he provided very few details of the present occasion. This reticence may have reflected caution in the light of Mary Stuart's involvement, or Rainolds may simply have assumed his congregation's familiarity with the details of the conspiracy.

Thanksgiving for the defeat of the Armada posed a difficulty in that it was not until November that the authorities felt confident enough of victory to schedule a celebration. An unidentified cleric preached on the official holiday, 19 November, at Paul's Cross, and John Piers, Bishop of Salisbury, preached on 24 November in the church, to which Elizabeth processed in state from Somerset House. Unfortunately the texts of these sermons have not survived.[48] The queen's accession day, however, provided an earlier opportunity to reflect upon the event. Thomas Cooper, Bishop of Winchester, in another lost sermon, gave thanks at Paul's Cross for the deliverance.[49] Outside of the capital, however, rejoicing may have been more restrained. For an Oxford sermon that day, John Prime chose as his text Psalm 23.4, which offered an appropriate compliment to Elizabeth through a comparison with David. In explicating his text, Prime demonstrates that David was able to overcome natural human fear because God walked with him. Prime then applies the story to Elizabeth, who had no friend except God in her youth. During her reign she has been threatened from the north, the west, and now from the sea, but because God has been with her, most of the Spanish ships perished without being pursued by the English forces. Prime's sermon, however, is not simply a glorification of the queen. Tucked at the end of the explication but carefully separated from the application is a passage in which Prime cautions that the kingdom and the monarch can only be successful together. The ruler is the foundation of the kingdom – if the ruler is not sound then the kingdom will totter for "Like Prince, like people for the most part." He concludes this section by exhorting: "Looke to it ye rulers, but you are not the cheefe rulers, it skilleth not, you are rulers, lesse or more authoritie in rulers, dooth not alter the nature of ruling in your degrees. And water may be pure in the spring, & corrupted in the riuers, if it bee not looked to."[50] Clearly Prime's target is not the queen but the lesser magistrates who enforce her decrees, but his use of the sermon of praise to deliver a political warning points towards the further development of the anniversary sermon in the next reign. If preachers were learning to exploit these occasions, however, the authorities were also beginning to recognize the potential for sermons to participate in emergent political crises rather than simply to memorialize them once the danger was past.

Although most clergy may have been prepared to preach obedience to secular authority and to celebrate the triumph of Protestantism, two incidents, one in Scotland and the other in England, demonstrate that some were uneasy about preaching occasional sermons during political crises. For secular authorities, however, sermons offered an advantage over the *Homilies.* Arnold Hunt argues that sermons are essentially dialogic, preacher and audience sharing in their creation, and were therefore channels of communication rather than a means of imposing uniformity.[51] Thus they could be more effective in situations when the authorities wished subjects to participate actively in constructing an interpretation of an event, such as the aftermaths of the Gowrie Conspiracy and the Essex Rebellion.[52] When James VI commanded his preachers to celebrate his escape from the

Gowries in their churches on 6 August 1600, some offered to thank God for the king's safety, but refused to declare the Ruthvens traitors. Beginning with David Lindsay and Patrick Galloway, James gradually won over the reluctant ministers, and eventually bullied all but Robert Bruce into submission. In James's confrontations with the ministers, Gustavo Secchi Turner suggests that

> What really was at stake … was not what had happened between the Ruthvens and the king's party, but two much larger (and related) issues having to do with the royal prerogative: the right of the monarch to declare people traitors without a public trial, and the privileged position of the king as a special kind of narrator, one whose stories are always true in a religious sense, even if some particulars seem absurd or contradictory.[53]

Also under negotiation was how far the political might intrude on the pulpit.

Clerical obedience was similarly problematic in London following the Essex rising of 8 February 1601.[54] The church attempted to secure the services of a preacher who had previously supported Essex for the sermon at Paul's Cross on the Sunday following the earl's execution, believing that condemnation from a former friend would most effectively communicate the church's repudiation of Essex's treason, but ministers were reluctant to accept directions, and disputes arose between religious and secular authorities.[55] William Barlow finally accepted the commission after Abdias Ashton, one of the other ministers who had attended Essex, refused the task.[56] Nevertheless, Barlow admitted in his introduction to the printed sermon that he had hesitated to preach on an occasion that seemed "matter rather of state then diuinitie."[57] His reluctance was clearly warranted, for he complains that he has been reviled on both secular and religious grounds. He has been accused of profiting from his earlier sermon celebrating Essex's victory at Cadiz, of violating canon law on this occasion by publishing a confession, and of having been imprisoned. Ironically, he rather than Essex has been the victim of unjust rumours. But Barlow concludes shrewdly: "I am not the principall thou aymest at, but according to the prouerbe *Faber cadit cum ferias fulonem*, it is the state thou greeuest at, not my sermon."[58] This was, of course, the problem. Where was the boundary between the state and the sermon?[59]

Barlow's duties as an agent of the crown were to publicize the manner of Essex's death, since the execution had been conducted privately, and to justify the necessity of it; his responsibility as a preacher was to explicate a scriptural text and apply it to the current crisis.[60] The first part of Barlow's sermon on the opening words of Matthew 22.21, "Give vnto Caesar the things of Caesar," focuses on the familiar themes of obedience and sacral kingship, even omitting the second half of this well-known verse from his text to emphasize the pre-eminence of obedience to the earthly monarch.[61] In the first of only two citations of the complete verse, Barlow paraphrases it conventionally as "giue vnto Caesar tribute, whose money it is, giue vnto God your selues, whose people you are," then adds in explanation:

> But first Caesar, and then God, for they two haue interchangeably borrowed names: it pleaseth God to bee called a King in heauen, Psa. 20. and the King is called a God on earth, Psa. 82. therefore hee which denieth his dutie to the visible God, his prince and Soueraign, can not performe his dutie to the God inuisible. Certainely, *a mind inclined to rebellion, was neuer well possessed of religion.*[62]

Although Barlow does not apply these words directly to Essex, his audience likely understood them to imply that the earl had merely used religion as a screen for his ambition, since a truly religious person would never rebel against a lawful monarch.

The opening of the sermon contextualizes the verse within the chapter through images of hunting, describing the series of hostile questions Jesus faces as nets and snares set by various enemies including the Pharisees and Herodians, who thought he could answer the question of whether it was lawful to pay taxes only by committing either treason or blasphemy. Jesus avoids this trap with his astute answer, and Barlow, walking a similar razor's edge, clearly hopes to emulate Christ's example by satisfying both his political masters and his religious conscience. Nevertheless, he must have known that the text was not innocent of associations with Essex. In 1599, John Richardson had found himself under house arrest for an 18 November Paul's Cross sermon on this text that was suspected of comparing the relationship between Essex and the queen to that of Seneca and Nero.[63]

Dividing his text into three parts, Barlow begins by explaining that "Give" refers to the Christian's primary duties of willingly and cheerfully offering alms to the poor and obedience to superiors. "Caesar" is any ruler, whether kind or cruel, legitimate or tyrannical, and exposing him or her to any fear or danger, even without intending murder or deposition, constitutes both irreligion and treason. This definition is broad enough to include Essex's actions, whatever his intentions had been. Edging into application, Barlow condemns Robert Persons for corrupting Essex by dedicating his book on the succession to him.[64] Honour, obedience, fear, subsidies, and prayers are "the things of Caesar," but Barlow pleads lack of time for both preparation and delivery to justify not expanding on each of these duties. Before moving into the occasional part of the sermon, he once again confronts his critics, making himself, like Whitgift, an *exemplum* of the duty of obedience to the authority of the crown.

In the second part of the sermon, Barlow resolves the tensions between his civic and religious duties by creating a Christian narrative of fall and redemption that justifies the earl's execution but allows his followers to hope that his soul has been saved. He anticipates this structure in his preface to this second part when he reminds his auditors that the earl, a man of many talents, had "soared in his highest pitch of fauour" with the queen at the time of the Cadiz victory celebration (B8[v]). "[H]ad he beene contented to haue beene ... a certaine great man, great among the rest; and not affected with Magus, Act. 8. to be ... the onely great man, and none to be great but he," he would have continued soaring. Instead, like Satan and all overreachers, he fell (a verb Barlow repeats frequently in this part of the sermon), and "hath ouerthrowne many of all sortes with himselfe" (C3[r]). While Essex blames his fall on "vanitie and lewd counsell," Barlow insists twice that he suffers from Satan's sin of pride. Two possible parallels are suggested and dismissed – the tragedy of Coriolanus, "a gallant young, but a discontented Romane," and the more ambiguous story of Henry of Lancaster, who revolted against Richard II – for Barlow's story must end in a death redeemed by repentance, not in tragedy or a successful coup (C3[v]).

Barlow had already assured his audience that Essex's "soule, no doubt [is] with the saints in heauen" (C[v]). It remained for him to conduct his auditors to the pinnacle of Essex's pride by describing his defiance after his arrest and then to lead them through the stages of his penitence. Cecil's instructions required the preacher to emphasize the threat to the queen, and he uses Essex's confession to offer his audience a vivid word picture describing Elizabeth at the mercy of armed Catholics, inviting them to "imagine" how frightened she would have been, to "thinke" what it would have been like for her to see her chambers running with blood (D[v]–D2[v]). Although imagining the death of the queen is treason, and despite his own promise to speak only of what he has witnessed, Barlow relies heavily on cultivating the imaginations of his hearers, sweeping them up in the possibility that they could have been harmed or killed as the revolt unfolded. As per his instructions, he must show his auditors not only that Essex deserved death for his disobedience to Caesar, but also that he does not deserve their support, having merely courted the people for his personal ends. Barlow then describes Essex's overnight transformation from defiance to penitence and his good death as a repentant sinner. The proofs of Essex's penitence are his request for humility and his admission of pride, the sin he had previously refused to confess (D7[v]). Essex thus leaves his followers secure in his eternal welfare. In the "Discourse" following the sermon, Barlow carefully renders the scene of execution, allowing his listeners not only to hear Essex's words but even to visualize his appearance and hear his prayers, which reinforce both his guilt and his penitence.[65] While gallows confessions could become sites of contested religious interpretation, excerpting the confession in the sermon allows Barlow to control its meaning.[66] The sermon was not a popular success, but Barlow neatly combined the themes of obedience to secular authority and the monarch's providential deliverance. His narrative of Essex's fall and redemption served a homiletic purpose while his defence of obedience satisfied the authorities.[67]

Only a few years later, Barlow was once again thrust into the spotlight on a political occasion, but this time it was by chance. Doubtless recalling the unpleasantness over the earlier performance, when he published his 10 November 1605 sermon Barlow inserted not his own apology but a preface supposed to have been written by a friend. Those who heard the sermon, the writer says, can best tell how the audience received it, while only the "censorious reader" can judge the printed version.[68] His immediate concern is to insist that Barlow was already scheduled to preach that day, and that circumstances forced him to alter both text and sermon at the last moment. While Barlow had received detailed instructions for the Essex sermon, in this case "*the late receiuing of the* Instructions *which in that short space could not bee many*" meant that he had relied chiefly on the king's speech the previous day and a late conference with Salisbury.[69] Thus, rather than establishing an adversarial relationship with his readers, as he had done before the Essex sermon, either Barlow or his anonymous friend solicits sympathy for his discomfort on this occasion.

While many ministers took the opportunity of publication to insert what the hourglass had required them to omit in oral delivery, Barlow chose not to do so.[70] Thus, he pleads lack of time when he abridges his promised defence of sacral kingship, the subject that had dominated the first part of his Essex sermon. In opening his text, Psalm 18.50 ("*Great Deliuerances giueth he vnto his King, and sheweth mercy to his annointed* Dauid *and to his seede for euer*"), Barlow proposes a much more complex structure than he had employed in the earlier sermon. Rather than crumbling the text, he divides the Psalm into two parts, "intensive" and "extensive": the first refers to the nature of the deliverances (great deliverances); the second refers to how they are distributed or communicated (to David and his seed). The first part subdivides into their double nature (plurality of number and greatness or magnitude) and their double quality (their internal or essential wholesomeness and their external or accidental magnificence or becomingness to God). The second or "extensive" part is divided into the personal (the king's deliverance as an eminent person, a sacred person, and a person approved by God) and the successive (undefined number and unlimited time of the deliverances). Although in the printed version he uses the headings "*The First Part*" and "*The Second Part*," in fact these are the two subtopics of the first part. He does not actually approach the second part until after he has described the plot and its anticipated results, and only then to outline what he planned to say but cannot because he has run out of time. The printed sermon also indicates two breaks where Barlow had read first Fawkes's confession and then "papers" concerning the confession along with his own notes on them.[71] In the first part, he catalogues both the number and magnitude of David's deliverances and the honours he received from God. Barlow concludes this part of the sermon by insisting, as Lancelot Andrewes was to assert in many subsequent Gunpowder sermons, that "All these of *Dauids* were great indeed, but compared to this of our *gracious King*: (the last, I trust, for a worse there cannot be) is but as a *minium* to a *large*, whether we consider therein, eyther the *Plot it selfe*, or the *Con-comitance* with it, or the *Consequences* of it."[72]

Under the heading "*Plot*," Barlow recounts not so much the actual events as those the plotters had intended. Following James's lead, he begins by emphasizing the cruelty of the plotters' plans, but as in the Essex sermon he imagines the results of a successful plot in more immediate and sensational detail than his source. Calling fire and water the cruelest killers, the king noted that whereas Noah's flood had merely purged the world, the fire prophesied to mark the end of time would consume it. Backing away from this apocalyptic vision, however, James later called the plot a "Tragedy" (B3v), enumerating the groups of people who would have been killed while attending the opening of Parliament. Barlow, however, develops the king's hints of an apocalypse by observing that the devil is reputed to have discovered gunpowder and envisioning a "*fierie massacre*" in which individuals would have been torn "parcell-meale" as if by beasts.[73] Whereas James had limited the destruction to king and Parliament, and Barlow's text had referred only to the deliverance of a king, the preacher presented a more frightening vision, in which "(beside the place it selfe at the which he aymed) the H*all of Iudgement*, the *Courtes of Recordes, the Collegiate Church, the Cittie of Westminster*, yea, *White*-H*all* the Kinges house, had been trushed and ouerthrowne" (C3[r]). The impenitent Fawkes is the "*Diuell of the Vault*," an epithet that would shortly be taken up by the author of a popular poem recounting the event (C3[v]).[74] Like Satan, Fawkes wanted to kill souls as well as bodies, but he is worse than Satan, "for this Diuill, with his traine would at once haue pulled downe all the glorious *Starres*, both fixed, and erraticall (those that are fastened to the Court, and those which come and goe as they are called and dismissed) yea euen the Sunne & the Moone themselues, not from heauen to earth, but to the bottomlesse pit, as much as in him lay" (C4[r]). In the following section, as he describes in more detail the consequences of a successful plot, Barlow develops the apocalyptic mode established by his allusion to Revelation 12.4.

Here, the preacher envisions the kind of reverse creation described in John's prophecy by introducing a series of images in which the various lights of the kingdom are extinguished, leaving it in "*Cimmerian* darkness" (D3[r]). While most attempts to change government proceed slowly, this one would have taken place "in the twinkling of an eye," echoing Paul's description of the general resurrection in 1 Cor. 15.52 (D[v]). Benighted, the nation would then have been open to foreign invasion by the Catholic emissaries of the Antichrist or a domestic usurper. Whereas James, speaking to a select group of parliamentarians, had emphasized his personal deliverance, Barlow, speaking to the entire city, demonstrated forcefully that none would have remained unaffected by this event had it taken place.

Taking his cues from James's speech, Barlow highlights the providential nature of the deliverance, the king's personal role in it, and the benefits of having a royal family. James's interpretation of the Monteagle letter, which he reads aloud, is the first evidence of God's providential care. The second is that Fawkes did not leave the cellar after the first search "but when the Priuie watch came in the night, he was the first man that appeared at the dore, as if God himselfe had presented him vnto their handes, and also vpon the rest of the Cõspirators" (E^{r}). Although the king's personal escape represents that of the entire nation, Barlow observes that the royal family and many other people were also delivered. Calling a kingdom with a childless king a "dreadfull case" verges on disrespect to the late queen, but the preacher obviously wants to emphasize the benefits of a stable succession (D2^{v}). He also makes a specific connection between James's English and Scottish deliverances. After almost being killed before birth in Scotland, he was "dismissed from those parts with a dreadfull farewell of a *desperate Treacherie* and entertained among vs with a Conspiracie vnnatural & as dangerous" (D4^{v}).[75] Clearly, James and his family have been preserved to preserve England.

In his speech, James had attempted to stave off panicked reprisals against English Catholics by asserting that "many honest men, seduced with some errors of Popery, may yet remaine good and faithfull Subiects."[76] Barlow's representation of him as a demon in his apocalyptic mode made clear that Fawkes was not such a Catholic. As a human, however, he posed a more difficult problem, since his social status was incompatible with the magnitude of the plot. The perpetrator of this averted catastrophe was not a great or an important man but one described several times by James as a "wretch," and reduced still further by Barlow to "*vermine* of the basest sorte" working underground like a mole.[77] After reading Fawkes's confession, the preacher reiterates, in a dazzling display of accumulatio, his astonishment that

> this *darkenes*, this *blindenes*, this *prophanes*, this *superstition*, this *weakenes*, this *lawles fury*, had with this blowing vp bin blown in & ouer this whole nation, a thing which neither the greatest Potentate of the world, with his strongest inuasion, nor the most dangerous rebel, though most popular & powerfull, coulde haue brought to passe after many repulses, & in many years, namely, to take away at once, *the hope of succession*, the *Oracles* of *wisedome*, the *Chariots of* Israel, the *Beau-peeres* of *Learning*, the *buttresses* of

> *strength*, the *guardians* of *iustice*, the *glory of the Nobilitie*, and in one word, the *Flower* of the whole *Kingdome*. (D2r)

Neither an Essex nor an Armada could have caused the destruction that a man of lowly birth has almost accomplished simply by stockpiling gunpowder and threatening to set a match to it.

In the previous day's speech, James had described the plot as "this great and horrible attempt, whereof the like was neuer either heard or read," and Barlow agrees that there are no adequate classical or biblical parallels, not only for the magnitude and cruelty of the design but also for the status of the perpetrators.[78] As Paul Connerton suggests, naming something categorizes it, and the plot both requires and resists classification.[79]

In these two sermons, then, Barlow seems to have developed a strategy for preaching on political occasions that allows him to fit these events into both religious and secular narrative structures and so both to practice clerical obedience and to defend civil obedience. Although this model for celebrating royal deliverances and enjoining obedience from the pulpit had largely been constructed in the Elizabethan period, the annual memorial sermon was James's creation.[80] The commemorative institution of Gowrie in Scotland might be explained by the king's desire to exact compliance from the presbyterians, but this rationale fails adequately to account for his insistence upon transferring the celebration to England.[81] Gowrie sermons continued to be preached annually at court, at important pulpits such as Paul's Cross, and in parishes with educated clergy for the remainder of James's reign. After the Gunpowder Plot, he introduced regular Tuesday sermons at court in recognition of his deliverances from two conspiracies on the same day of the week, as well as adding 5 November to the public preaching calendar.[82]

Lori Anne Ferrell suggests that the Gunpowder Plot had a "rejuvenating but obliterating effect" on the Gowrie sermons as the English event predominated over the Scottish one the sermons were designed to commemorate.[83] While she sees this as an unintended consequence of the greater appeal exerted by the Gunpowder Plot, it may also reflect James's deliberate linking of these occasions. As Ferrell observes, the post-1605 court sermons on 5 August refer frequently to Gunpowder Plot, sometimes obscuring the distinctions between the two events.[84] Morrissey, however, suggests that court preachers offered Gowrie less attention because there was no need to describe the events of the plot to the king and his immediate circle, while Paul's Cross preachers enjoyed exploiting the inherent drama of the incident for their less informed audiences.[85] Nevertheless, since sermons preached in parish churches offer much shorter applications than those delivered at Paul's Cross, and concentrate on deliverance and thanksgiving rather than describing the conspiracy, Ferrell seems to be correct that preachers were somewhat uncomfortable with the Gowrie narrative. One can, in fact, sense an almost palpable relief on the part of some ministers when they pass from their obligatory references to the Scottish conspiracy to the relatively safer ground of the English one.[86] What I am suggesting, however, is that by drawing parallels between them in his 9 November speech to Parliament, by initiating Tuesday court sermons to commemorate them, and by making both annual preaching occasions, James had deliberately blurred the lines between the two events and had done so to integrate his Scottish deliverance into English history.

Several of the Gowrie sermons illustrate the extent to which the two occasions came to be understood as part of the same sequence of attacks on Protestant England. In his 1615 sermon at St Mary's Oxford, Isaac Singleton links the Gowrie Conspiracy to the later Gunpowder Plot, then reviews Parry's plot against Elizabeth to demonstrate that traitors always have great confidence in their plots, thus equating both of James's deliverances with Elizabeth's. Preaching at Paul's Cross in 1622, Samuel Purchas also emphasizes continuity between Elizabeth and James. Elizabeth was the sun that never set, since James immediately replaced her. The king almost persuaded Gowrie "*to become a Christian*, a Subiect," just as he acted "beyond all reason, and humane capacitie, aboue, yea, againste Arte, to construe those words in the Letter, to bring to light the abstrusest worke of Darknesse, the Masterpiece of Treason, and Monster-prize of Sathanicall Stratagems," the Gunpowder Plot. Here Purchas virtually conflates the two plots.[87] Later in the sermon he recalls James's earlier deliverances as a foetus and a child, and praises once again his ability to decipher the "mysticall *writing*" of the Monteagle letter.[88] August is notable both for James's deliverance from the Gowries and England's from the Spanish invasion, while November is famous for Elizabeth's accession and the foiling of the Gunpowder Plot. The annual calendar of deliverances thus obscures chronological distinctions between the two reigns.[89]

While Purchas seems to have suggested that Gowrie was an atheist, most preachers integrated the Gowrie Conspiracy into this sequence of deliverances by recasting Gowrie as a crypto-Catholic. In an undated sermon preached at St Mary's Oxford, John Prideaux reiterates that Catholics have disrupted the reigns of both Elizabeth and James, and "It is therefore onely *Gods* extraordinary *protection*, that hath hitherto freed him [James] from such apparant and remedilesse dangers. The *Gowries* had dispatched him; *Watson* and his complices had surprised him, the *Powderplot* had blowne vp him and all his, if this mercy of God onely had not preuented the *diuels malice*."[90] In the application of his 1615 sermon, Singleton accuses Gowrie not only of popularity with the people, but also of conferring secretly with Jesuits and taking counsel with the devil.[91] Representing the Gowries as Catholics, however, could also serve as a warning to the king.

Preaching at Paul's Cross in 1607, John Milward urges James to banish priests and Jesuits and enjoins the magistrates to help preserve the king and the state by ridding the country of "these snakes." He concludes by reminding James that God preserved Elizabeth from many treasonous plots only because she maintained true religion. These assaults on the nation have continued since Elizabeth's death, "But aboue all, from that same Salt-*Peter* Treason, or *Peters* salt Treason of Rome." God will not continue to protect England unless James adopts harsh measures against Catholics.[92]

Other preachers observe that the Gowries' failure to kill James has preserved England as a Protestant nation. Singleton concludes that had James not survived to become king of England, Catholics could have conquered the country and deprived the people of the spiritual food of the gospel. Similarly, John Randal ends his 1624 sermon at St Mary's Oxford by reminding his listeners and readers that if the Gowrie Conspiracy had succeeded, not only England, but also Scotland, Ireland, and Germany would have suffered.[93] Daniel Featley opens his 1618 sermon at Croyden by observing that 5 August marks the birth of King Oswald, who first united the crowns of England and Scotland, as well as James's second birth. Despite his initial difficulties with some of the Scottish preachers, then, in England James succeeded in weaving his Scottish and English experiences into Elizabethan history to unify the countries in his person even when political union eluded him.[94]

Lancelot Andrewes's court sermons on the occasion perhaps best demonstrate the yoking of the themes of obedience and deliverance in the thanksgiving sermons. Critics have frequently accused Andrewes of flattering the king excessively on the anniversaries of both the Gowrie Conspiracy and the Gunpowder Plot by endorsing divine right political theory.[95] Nicholas Lossky offers a divergent opinion on this subject, arguing that the events themselves "only serve as a pretext for the preacher to call his congregation to an ever greater awareness of God."[96] Andrewes, according to Lossky, sees these events as symbols of the eternal deliverance available through Christ's resurrection, an idea most clearly expressed in his 5 November 1617 sermon on the *Benedictus*. Thus, Lossky concludes that the understanding of kingship in these sermons is not so much political as religious, containing "perhaps, elements of a theology of man" in which "he who fulfils on earth the real function of king must be the perfect example in order to receive the eternal crown, which he will share with all those who have been entrusted to him and for whom he will have to answer before the supreme Judge."[97] Debora Shuger proposes a synthesis of these views, suggesting that Andrewes is concerned not with political theory but with political theology. For her, the Gowrie and Gunpowder sermons not only "reiterate the basic arguments of absolutist theory, they entwine this with an extraordinary and persistent concern over the location of ‘sacredness’ in history and social structure.” This issue can be traced through these sermons most clearly in the focus on the king’s anointing. Andrewes “thus treats the Gowrie Conspiracy and Gunpowder Plot not as part of the ideological and political struggle between the papacy and the Crown but as part of a cosmic battle between good and evil, with God taking an active role on the English side,” an interpretation that may be traced back to Barlow’s first Gunpowder sermon.[98]

What has perhaps been neglected in these discussions is the context in which Andrewes was working out the boundaries between secular and sacred, politics and theology. As we have seen from the sermons preached on previous occasions, the political sermon was both an injunction to obedience and an act of obedience on the part of the preacher, who provided an example for his listeners. Juxtaposed with those of other preachers on similar occasions, Andrewes’s representations of sacral kingship appear more moderate than they do in isolation. Many other preachers also pointed to the king’s anointing as evidence that he was God’s representative.[99] Although obedience even to a tyrant could be successfully defended on scriptural grounds, representing the monarch as God’s instrument in maintaining English Protestantism helped the preacher to justify the need for obedience, and the king’s deliverances provided irrefutable evidence of God’s providential care for both him and the nation. James’s undeniable achievement was to ensure that on two occasions each year throughout the kingdom, and on every Tuesday at court, his subjects were reminded of their duty to obey a monarch whom God had preserved to continue the work Elizabeth had begun.

2.3 Protestant Narratives: Romance, Tragedy, and Tragicomedy

While sermons and liturgies offered some scope for creating narratives, the most enduring stories of the plot arose from the pamphlet accounts authorized by the state. When read in isolation, these pamphlets seem to reflect the imposition of a uniform interpretation upon the plot’s discovery and the plotters’ trials, but we should remember that they participated in ongoing dialogues with dissenting accounts, frequently transmitted orally or in manuscript. As a result, we can trace an evolutionary process through these pamphlets as emphases shifted in response to rumours, libels, and unofficial texts. The myth of the Gunpowder Plot was thus created not by the state alone but through negotiations between groups within the state and in other nations.

Once again, James and his counsellors sought continuity with the past by modelling their texts upon accounts of earlier events, including the Gowrie Conspiracy. At the same time, as Barlow had recognized, they were faced with an incident that did not readily accommodate itself to existing narrative structures. The complexity of their own investigations also resulted in an unprecedented delay between the discovery of the plot and the trials and executions of the perpetrators, during which time new information became available and primary responsibility was shifted from the lay plotters to the Jesuits.[100] These two factors resulted in a narrative that was generically fractured, creating discontinuities that their opponents could, and did, exploit.

In his study of the "King's Book" containing James I's 9 November 1605 speech to Parliament and the anonymous "Discourse of the Maner of the Discouery of this Late Intended Treason," Mark Nicholls suggests that "as investigations into Essex's revolt informed and guided the subsequent exploration of the Gunpowder Plot, so Bacon's *Declaration* set the pattern in 1605."[101] Nicholls is undoubtedly correct that the official account of the Essex Rebellion informed the Gunpowder Plot narrative, but I believe that both Bacon and the author of the "Discourse" (possibly James I) were working within a tradition that dated back at least to Dr Parry's conspiracy against Elizabeth.[102] Examples of this genre include both numerous English ones and the Scottish one, also known as the "King's Book," that described the Gowrie Conspiracy. While dissimilar in many ways, the Gowrie plot and the Essex revolt shared some significant characteristics, particularly the difficulty of understanding not only the two men's actions, but also their motivations. Equally importantly, both earls were popular with the common people, who were therefore loath to believe them guilty of treason. In both cases, then, there were pressing needs to justify their deaths. When compared with the pamphlets produced on earlier occasions such as the Parry and Lopez conspiracies, what is most striking about these productions is their increasingly sophisticated use of narrative structures associated with literary modes.

The anonymous pamphlet published by the queen's printer describing Parry's treason (*A True and Plaine Declaration of the Horrible Treasons, practised by William Parry the traitor, against the Queenes Maiestie*), like the later Gunpowder pamphlet, presents a collection of documents, including Parry's confession, preceded by a short narrative account. Like Barlow's account of Essex's revolt, it focuses on the sin of pride, which drove Parry, after his unsuccessful attempt to murder Hugh Hare, to reconcile with the Roman church and confer with Jesuits on the Continent before returning to England intent on killing the queen. Providentially his accomplice, Edmund Neville, disclosed the plan. Although initially defiant, Parry ultimately confessed, expressed penitence, and requested mercy. The documentary evidence, however, sometimes fails to support the theme of the main text. Parry's religious and political motives are mixed, and his penitence is marred by his final letter to the Lord Treasurer and the Earl of Leicester in which he attempts to mitigate his guilt by pleading the singularity of his case: "*a naturall subiect solemnely to vowe the death of his naturall Queene (so borne, so knowen, and so taken by all men) for the reliefe of the afflicted Catholiques, and restitution of religion.*" The pamphlet remains, then, more a collection of documents than a unified narrative.[103]

In contrast, the official pamphlet on the Lopez treason written by William Cecil in 1594 is primarily narrative, although it concludes with a selection of confessions and letters.[104] Cecil dedicates his pamphlet to revealing the king of Spain's complicity in all plots against Elizabeth, avowing that his intention is to give alert readers the facts so they can judge the truth of relations between the two sovereigns. The three Portuguese

> who were apprehended and openlie charged, and vppon their owne confessions condemned, & for the same openly at the places of execution, with signes of hartie repentance did aske forgiuenes of Almighty God, and did constantly affirme it to the end, exclaiming against the king of Spaine and his ministers, by whom they had beene set on worke: and in the ende sealed their confessions with their blood to be true.[105]

Cecil accepts the veracity of the gallows confessions, but insists there are many other proofs of Spanish guilt. Thus, he tells a story of Spanish treachery embodied in the current conspirators but extending beyond them. The author's stated purpose of providing an unbiased narrative based upon the conspirators' own words unifies the pamphlet, but the format is legal rather than literary.

In contrast, James VI seems to have shaped his narrative of the Gowrie Conspiracy with a sharper literary consciousness. The urgency for the Scottish king to provide an account of this affair sprang first from the inconvenient fact that he was the only surviving witness to the day's most crucial events.[106] Furthermore, his initial reports had been greeted with considerable scepticism by some presbyterian ministers, who had refused to preach sermons declaring the Gowries traitors.[107] With his access to the nation's pulpits restricted, James looked to print.[108] An anonymous account appeared in Scotland by the end of August, and Valentine Simmes printed an edition in London later that year.[109] Calling *Gowries Conspiracy* "an extremely peculiar textual artifact," Gustavo Secchi Turner describes its style as "a cross between a legal document and a romance."[110] As we have seen, the inclusion of confessions and documentary evidence was typical of the genre. In this case, however, the romance structure provides a narrative framework that emphasizes event over cause. The text begins without preamble, launching immediately into a description of the hunt and Ruthven's conference with the king, reporting details of their conversation that could only have been known to James and the dead man. Throughout the pamphlet the narrator, apparently omniscient as well as anonymous, takes care to represent James's thoughts and actions in the most favourable light possible. He displays no personal desire for the treasure, but only becomes interested when he apprehends that it may be part of a seditious Catholic plot instigated by priests. James's apparent negligence of his personal safety arises from generosity rather than naivety. When Ruthven encourages him to send his companions back, James recognizes danger, "yet his maiestie could neuer suspect any harme to bee intended against his Highnesse by that young Gentleman, with whome his Maiestie had beene so well acquainted, as he had, not long before, beene in suit to be one of the Gentlemen of his Chamber."[111] Even when James became suspicious, he could still "resolue vpon no certaine thing, but rode further on his iourney, betwixt trust and distrust, being ashamed to seem to suspect, in respect of the cleanesse of his Maiesties owne conscience, except hee had found some greater ground."[112] The later part of the narrative contrasts James and his few unarmed men with the earl's three or four score retainers, all well armed, in order to demonstrate that only God could have protected the king. By depicting James as a sort of medieval knight defeating forces of evil, the text avoids having to offer a more plausible motive than long-delayed revenge for the Ruthvens' attempt on his life.[113] The narrative also emphasizes James's sense of being spared by providence for a greater task. While this work is unspecified, anti-Catholic intrusions into the text suggest that James had seen an opportunity to strengthen his claim to the English throne.[114]

In the second part of the pamphlet, consisting of depositions by those "who were either actors, and eye witnesses, or immediate hearers," the author neatly casts the blame for any discrepancies on the guilty by announcing: "wherein, if the Reader shall finde any thing differing from this narration, either in substance or circumstance, he may vnderstand the same to be vttered by the deponer in his own behoofe, for obtaining of his Maiesties princely grace and fauour."[115] The first two deponents, Amos Weimis and William Rinde, both testify to Gowrie's reliance upon charms and his unorthodox philosophy. Turner cites the emphasis placed upon the charms as evidence that the narrative "veers towards the end into one of James's preferred discourses – the language of demonology, damning not only Gowrie but the entire Ruthven family."[116] Curiously, however, most English preachers used this incident primarily to assert that Gowrie, rather than sympathizing with the Presbyterians, was actually a crypto-Catholic. The detail, offered by Rinde, that Gowrie had obtained these charms in Italy was not lost upon at least one English preacher.[117] In Scotland, the text helped to secure the eventual cooperation of the recalcitrant ministers (except Bruce), who were expected to adhere to the narrative as printed in preparing their sermons. Thus, Turner concludes that "After November the little book printed by Charteris in Edinburgh was univocally equal to the matter of Gowrie. In other words, *Gowrie's Conspiracy* was identical to Gowrie's Conspiracy."[118] Having obtained at least outward compliance with the official narrative in Scotland, James turned to an English audience.

The haste with which he relayed an account of the events of 5 August to England suggests that James was concerned from the beginning with international, and particularly English, reception of the news.[119] Unfortunately for the king, Scottish incredulity was mirrored elsewhere. W.F. Arbuckle notes that "Elizabeth did not conceal her scepticism, and the envoy she sent to Scotland to obtain further information admitted in private that he did not himself believe the report he had brought back; while in France the story was greeted with ridicule, especially by those who had known Gowrie there."[120] Nevertheless, James persisted in disseminating his version of the story. A Latin edition of *Gowries Conspiracy* was published in 1601 for an international audience, and translations into European vernacular languages followed, while Simmes issued another English edition of the text in 1603, no doubt capitalizing on James's accession to the English throne.[121] The question we must ask, then, is why James insisted so stubbornly upon a story that was clearly subject to widespread disbelief.[122] One of the answers seems to be that he wanted his deliverance to be understood within the context of providential British history. As the liturgy and sermons discussed above demonstrate, James wanted to show that he had been preserved from his enemies, as Elizabeth had been from hers, in order to perpetuate Protestant rule in Britain. The romance narrative of *Gowrie's Conspiracy* presented James as a questing knight who could drive out the forces of evil and keep his kingdom safe.

Since James had ensured that the story of Gowrie's conspiracy was publicized in England, the authorities there were likely aware of its official narrative by the time they needed to provide a public account of a purported attempt on Elizabeth's life the following year. Francis Bacon's *Declaration of the practises and treasons attempted and committed by Robert late Earle of Essex and his complices*, published anonymously, follows the familiar pattern in which a series of confessions follows a narrative account.[123] In this case, however, a third part inserted between these two, detailing the evidence against Essex and Southampton at their trials, legitimizes the proceedings against the earl. Bacon begins by establishing two purposes for his publication. First, he wishes to refute false accounts circulating in libels, which demonstrate that the "leprosie" of treason is indeed contagious. Second, Bacon suggests that his readers should understand "*the præcedent practises and inducements to the Treasons*," insisting upon the distinction between the evidence required for a public trial and that required to satisfy the public.[124] Whereas in a trial the only evidence required is that an action took place, in narrative actions require contexts. Thus, Bacon admits that the details of Essex's intrigue with Tyrone are irrelevant to the legal case against him but asserts that they are integral to the discovery of truth. If the Gowrie pamphlet narrates a romance, describing actions without causes, Bacon's offers the interpretative structure of tragedy, with its focus upon motivation.

The first act of Bacon's drama takes place in Ireland, although Essex may have been plotting treason even before that time.[125] Like Barlow, Bacon emphasizes the honours the queen heaped upon Essex, which became "nothing els but wings for his ambition" because he aspired "vnto a greatnesse," desiring only power.[126] By representing Ireland as a corrupting influence upon the earl, however, the narrator allows him to remain heroic until then, thereby hoping to satisfy his supporters while justifying his execution. In Ireland, "*Essex* drawing now towards the *Catastrophe*, or last part of that Tragedy, for which he came vpon the Stage in *Ireland*, his Treasons grew to a further ripenesse," and he made a secret bargain with the rebel leader (C^{r}). Blunt and Southampton have attested to dissuading Essex from returning to England with an army, "So as nowe the worlde may see how long since my Lord put off his vizard, and disclosed the secrets of his heart to two of his most confident friends, falling vpon that vnnaturall and detestable treason, whereunto all his former Actions in his gouernement in *Ireland*, (and God knowes howe long before) were but Introductions" (C4$^{r–v}$). Thereupon he planned "the second act of this Tragedy ... which was, that my Lord should present himselfe to her Maiestie as prostrating himselfe at her [Elizabeth's] feete, and desire the remoue of such persons, as he called his enemies, from about her" (E^{v}). The earl's alleged plans for distributing his men about the palace read like a set of stage directions, enabling the reader easily to visualize the action intended, and perhaps to forget that it never actually occurred. The tragedy's third act occurs at Essex House on Sunday, 8 February. This day's events are situated carefully in both space and time, observing the unity of time since the action begins with Essex's assembly of his friends at 8 am and concludes with his surrender at 10 pm. While most of the action takes place at Essex House, the real stage for this act of the drama is London, around which Essex processes in a parody of a royal progress or coronation procession as he attempts to win followers. Speeches and dialogue enliven the account as the Lord Keeper delivers the queen's message, Essex is eventually proclaimed traitor in the streets, and the earl negotiates the conditions of his surrender.

This account characterizes Essex as a tragic hero whose flaw is ambition, a secular manifestation of the pride that Barlow had identified in his sermon as Essex's sin. God "often punisheth ingratitude by ambition, and ambition by treason, and treason by finall ruine" begins the text (A4^{v}). Concentrating upon ambition enables Bacon to avoid proving specific religious or political motives. Instead, Essex and Henry Cuffe "had soone set downe betweene them the ancient principle of Traitors and Conspirators, which was: *To prepare many and to acquaint few*; and after the maner of Mynes, to make ready their powder, and place it, and then giue fire but in the instant" (D3^{v}). The insistence that few knew the details of the plot explains the absence of substantive confessions, a strategy that had also served James well in the Gowrie narrative.[127]

As in the Scottish pamphlet, the providential nature of the events is strongly emphasized. God directed the queen's actions so that "When this man was come ouer, his heart thus fraughted with Treasons, and presented himselfe to her Maiestie: it pleased God, in his singular prouidence ouer her Maiestie, to guide and hem in her proceeding towards him, in a narrow way of safetie betweene two perils," and she resolved to place him under house arrest.[128] Similarly, although the queen's sending for Essex on 7 February may have seemed sudden to men, God "had in his diuine prouidence long agoe cursed this action, with the Curse that the Psalme speaketh of, *That it should be like the vntimely fruit of a woman, brought foorth before it came to perfection*," and so foiled the earl's plans.[129] During the actual revolt, "it pleased God, that her Maiesties directions at Court, though in a case so strange and sudden, were iudiciall and sound."[130] Even after the revolt ended and Essex had been executed, his schemings in Ireland came to light providentially when Blunt confessed to them "most naturally and most voluntarily" after his arraignment (C4^r). Finally, providence turns Essex into "an example of disloyaltie" (F3^v). The providential framework thus propels the story into the genre of *de casibus* tragedy.

Part II describes the trials of Essex and Southampton on 19 February before twenty-five peers, including some who had supported the earl. The pamphlet presents the proceedings as a dialogue in which the judges refute each of the accused's defences, thus offering evidence of a fair trial to potentially sceptical readers. The final section consists of a series of "voluntary Confessions," reported "*word for word*" (K4^r). Although they were taken later, the confessions relating to the Irish background are placed first to show that the plot had its roots there, and Blunt's speech at his execution again emphasizes that the troubles began in Ireland. The second set of confessions, relating to the rebels' intentions on the final Sunday, is clearly designed to show that Essex's first goal was to secure the court.[131] Thus, the later part of the pamphlet, rather than merely presenting supporting documentation, reinforces the narrative shape of the first by insisting upon the plot's Irish genesis even when this interpretation requires manipulating the investigation's chronology.

The tragic mode suits Bacon's secular and legal purposes – like Barlow he needs to acknowledge Essex's greatness to satisfy his supporters and to justify his own earlier friendship, but unlike Barlow he is not required to assert the earl's final redemption. Essex simply mounted to the top of Fortune's wheel before beginning his inevitable decline. Bacon dismisses in a single paragraph Essex's confession of his "great," his "bloudy," his "crying," and his "infectious" sins, which Barlow had lingered over.[132] Bacon will only grudgingly admit that Essex seems to have experienced "a kind of remorse" and quote his assertion that he has "become a new man" since the trial.[133] Whereas Barlow concentrates on Essex's reconciliation with God, Bacon concludes somewhat acidly that he continued to blame his confederates and died without farewells to family or friends.

In some ways, the English and Scottish authorities confronted similar situations in the Essex and Gowrie incidents, and both chose to provide prose justifications for their actions against popular rebels. Whereas James represented himself as the romantic hero of the Gowrie affair, however, the queen was mostly absent from the Essex pamphlet except in its prominent display of the royal arms. In contrast, Ruthven himself remained in the background of the Gowrie narrative, allowing James to take centre stage, while Essex played the tragic hero in his story. Both represented the deliverances of their monarchs as providential and sought to prove the traitors both legally and morally guilty. Essex, whose religious sympathies are difficult to discern, and Gowrie, whose inclinations were apparently presbyterian, both became crypto-Catholics.[134] James's use of the romance genre presented him to readers as a successful hero, whereas by allowing Essex heroic stature the English authorities offered readers the cathartic experience of pitying the fallen favourite while warning against the dangers of incurring the queen's displeasure.

The Gunpowder Plot narratives once again demonstrated God's protection of the monarch, but genre became more problematic. The official Gunpowder Plot publications, *His Maiesties speech in the last session of Parliament … Together with a discourse of the maner of the discouery of this late intended Treason* and *A True and Perfect Relation of the Whole Proceedings against the late most barbarous traitors, Garnet a Iesuite, and his confederats*, both continue earlier traditions and depart significantly from them. Juxtaposed, the two authorized texts provide a curious contrast, for they describe the same plot engineered by two separate sets of plotters. Mark Nicholls argues that the "King's Book" represents a preliminary effort to provide credible information to a frightened and confused populace and to stifle anti-Catholic rumours. Two examples of these sorts of rumours appear in John Chamberlain's letter of 7 November to Dudley Carleton: first that Johnson (Fawkes) is thought to be a priest, and second that a Sir Edward Bainham is being sought and "some five or sixe Jesuites and priests taken in a privie search."[135] The pamphlet presents two texts, the king's 9 November speech to Parliament and an anonymous narrative of the plot containing the confessions of Fawkes and Winter. The origins of the "Discourse" remain mysterious, although contemporaries believed James himself had written it. In his *Answer to certaine scandalous Papers*, Salisbury praises "this Princely and religious worke" in which

> his Maiestie (like to those kings of whome Seneca speaketh, that doe more good by Example then by Lawes) hath increased our obligation, by leauing vnder his owne hand, such a plaine & perfect Record of his own true thankefulnes to Almighty God, for his so great and miraculous graces; as neither the present Time, nor ages to come can euer be so ingrate, as not to retaine the same in perpetual memorie.[136]

Based on its inclusion in James Montagu's collection of the king's writings, Thomas Bayley Howell, in his *Collection of State Trials* (vol. 2, 1809), also assumed James's authorship. When David Jardine revised this work later in the century, however, he speculated that the "Discourse" might be Francis Bacon's work. More recently, Mark Nicholls has concurred that stylistic elements may support Jardine's conclusion, although he recommends caution in attributing authorship.[137] The pamphlet appeared before Barlow's sermon, which had been entered in the Stationer's Register on 11 December, but was not printed until 1606, and seems to have helped Barlow to resolve the dilemma of Fawkes's status in the printed sermon.

In the printer's letter, "To the Reader," Robert Barker claims he was about to print the speech when he received the "Discourse," so he simply put the two together. The author identifies himself only as a member of the court, telling his readers:

> My threefold zeale to those blessings, whereof they would haue so violently made vs all widowes, hath made mee resolue to set downe here the true Narration of that monstrous and vnnaturall intended Tragedy, hauing better occasion by the meanes of my seruice and continuall attendance in Court to know the trueth thereof, then others that peraduenture haue it only by relatiõ at the third or fourth hand.[138]

He thus establishes his own authority, buttressed by that of the government printer, without divulging his identity.[139] As Nicholls notes, however, the "Discourse" also "offers the reader a vivid, exciting account, and both excitement and clarity are enhanced by the deliberate decision to tell the story in the first person."[140] This use of the first person, even in the confessions, recalls the dramatic format of Bacon's account of the Essex Rebellion.

Although the pamphlet appears disjointed structurally, it is unified by the themes of memory, paternity, and providence. The "Discourse" most clearly illustrates God's providence in the fate of the rebels after Fawkes's capture. Burned by their own gunpowder, "they presently (see the wonderfull power of Gods Iustice vpon the guiltie consciences) did all fall downe vpon their knees, praying GOD to pardon them for their bloody enterprize."[141] Furthermore, rather than being accorded any special treatment, they were captured by the ordinary sheriff and placed in the common jail, "Seruing so for a fearefull and publike spectacle of Gods fierce wrath and iust indignation" (M4[r]). Although these experiences do not engender true repentance, Winter admits that he has learned the will of providence and now sees that "such courses are not pleasing to Almighty God" (I[r]). The king's speech, however, highlights not the direct workings of God but his own instrumentality in the divine plan.

As in the Essex pamphlet, in which the queen's sound judgment helped to prevent the revolt, so in this one James claims that his personal qualities effected the deliverance. In his speech to Parliament, he caps the plot's extraordinary characteristics with his own discovery of it, which was miraculous because, although not ordinarily suspicious, he immediately suspected gunpowder. His observation that he considers suspicion the mark of a tyrant actually makes a virtue of his credulity in the Gowrie narrative, although he does not mention this earlier deliverance. James insists that his divinely inspired interpretation of the words of the Monteagle letter, "contrary to the ordinary Grammer construction of them," and as no lawyer or minister would have interpreted them, was the only one that could have saved them (B4^{r}). The author of the "Discourse" also stresses the king's close reading of the letter, demonstrating that only James had the skills to save the country (F3^{v}–G^{r}). England, then, needs not only the office of kingship, but also the abilities of this particular king.

In his speech, however, James focuses not upon the nation's deliverance, but upon his own, making an explicit link between Gowrie and Gunpowder Plot. Both occurred on Tuesdays and on the fifth of a month, "thereby to teach me, That as it was the same deuill that still persecuted mee: So it was one and the same GOD that still mightily deliuered me" (D4^{v}). This observation enables him to conclude by emphasizing again the personal and providential nature of the deliverance. The similarities between the two plots had already been remarked by others, for on 7 November Chamberlain had reported to Carleton that "Curious folkes observe that this deliveraunce hapned to the King the fift of November aunswerable to the fift of August, both Tewsdayes, and this plot to be executed by Johnson as that at Johnstowne."[142] James's speech, however, connects his person and his office through the theme of paternity, which the "Discourse" takes up in its characterization of the plot as an attempted parricide.

The speech continues James's first address to Parliament on 19 March 1603/4, responding to issues raised during that session as well as to the plot. In opening his first Parliament, James had emphasized paternity by alluding to his direct descent from Henry VII and by promising a stable succession through his own sons. Parliamentarians, however, were disturbed by James's assertion, during the session, that Parliament's rights were not immemorial but a gift from the king. Fearful that James wanted to reduce their powers, some members drew up an *Apology of the Commons* expressing their frustrations over parliamentary disunity. While Conrad Russell notes that the document was never passed and did not necessarily represent the views of the entire body, he concludes that "Perhaps the most significant thing about this laborious self-justification is that it was drawn up at all."[143] In his 9 November 1605 speech, James remains committed to limiting parliamentary influence, informing the members that Parliament "is nothing else but the Kings great Councell, which the King doeth assemble either vpon occasion of interpreting, or abrogating old Lawes, or making of new, according as ill maners shall deserue, or for the publike punishment of notorious euill doers, or the praise and reward of the vertuous and well deseruers."[144] In order to locate his views within the context of his earlier discourse on kingship, he returns to images of fatherhood and the human body, proposing that Parliament is the body, but the king the head. Whereas in the first speech he had emphasized his natural fatherhood, here he focuses on his metaphoric paternity in images of the king as father and as head of the body that are familiar from James's earlier writings. In *The Trew Law of Free Monarchies*, he argues that "By the law of nature, the king becomes a natural father to all his lieges at his coronation," using this similitude to demonstrate the evils of rebellion, since it is unnatural for a son to kill his father.[145] A diseased limb may have to be amputated, but a body cannot endure if severed from its head. He represents the king as God's Lieutenant and the head of the civic body represented by Parliament, thus establishing the monarch as the crucial link between God and the people. The "Discourse" echoes James's description of a successful plot as both a "Parricide" and a beheading of the body politic, twice equating such violence with the loss of national memory.[146]

Describing the plot finally as a "Tragedie to the Traytors, but tragicomedie to the King and all his true Subiects," the narrative begins in the comic mode.[147] Whereas the Gowrie pamphlet provides no context for that conspiracy, this one takes place "While this Land and whole Monarchie flourished in a most happie and plentifull PEACE, as well at home as abroad, sustained and conducted by these two maine Pillars of all good Gouernement, PIETIE and IVSTICE, no forreine grudge, nor inward whispering of discontent any way appearing."[148] So secure in the peace of the kingdom was the king that he had gone hunting. Tragedy threatens, but the foiling of the plot and the executions of the conspirators provide an appropriate comic ending. While representing the plot as a tragicomedy accounts not only for its failure but also for the low social status of the plotters, it seems unsatisfactory given the magnitude of the conspiracy, and the writer soon begins to appropriate Barlow's apocalyptic mode.[149] Expanding upon the sermon's list of those who would have been killed, the author describes a national apocalypse, a return to Chaos, that includes the destruction of buildings and records, so that "not onely we, but the memory of vs and ours, should haue beene thus extinguished in an instant."[150] The plot's threat to both past and future makes it unique, and the author of the "Discourse," like Barlow, struggles to determine whether the deliverance represents a comic ending to a potentially tragic incident planned by fallible human beings, or yet another victory in the cosmic battle against the Antichrist that merely delays the apocalypse.

Ultimately, this generic confusion splits the narrative into two parts. Following Winter's confession, the narrator intrudes: "Bvt here let vs leaue *Fawkes* in a lodging fit for such a guest, and taking time to aduise vpon his conscience; and turne our selues to that part of the History, which concernes the fortune of the rest of his partakers in that abominable Treason."[151] The confessions provide a sharp break between the powder plot, in which Fawkes is the devil of destruction, and the subsequent rebellion, in which Digby becomes the gentleman rebel whose human ambition ensures his downfall. Although the pamphlet represents religion as the primary cause of the powder plot, Digby's attempted armed rebellion is reported as merely "pretending the quarrell of Religion."[152] Sir Everard, the highest ranking plotter, is characterized as Nimrod, described in Genesis 10.9 as "a mighty hũter before the Lord" but identified in the margin of the Geneva Bible as "a cruel oppressor & tyrant."[153] Casting Digby in the role of would-be tyrant allows James to appear more effectively as the model of a virtuous king; James hunts with a clear conscience, whereas Digby conceals the true purpose of his gathering by pretending to hunt. Young and handsome as Digby apparently was, his rank was merely that of a gentleman pensioner recently knighted by the new king, and so his fall could not be truly tragic. Burned by their own gunpowder, the rebels opened the gates to the sheriff, whereupon "these resolute and high aspiring Catholikes, who dreamed of no lesse then the destruction of Kings and kingdomes and promised to themselues no lower state then the gouernment of great and ancient Monarchies; were miserably defeated, and quite ouerthrowne in an instant, falling in the pit which they had prepared for others."[154] Their fall becomes merely humiliating – those not killed are "taken and led prisoners by the Sheriffe the ordinarie minister of Iustice, to the Gaole, the ordinarie place, euen of the basest malefactors" and finally gaped at by crowds of women and "fools" who regard them as monsters as they are transported back to London.[155]

This comic ending, however, in no way mitigates the plot's potential for cataclysmic destruction. Thus, the "Discourse" moves uneasily between the poles of comedy and tragedy, tragicomedy and apocalypse. The author finally resolves, inconclusively, that the plot is a "horrible attempt (lacking due epithetes)."[156] As Connerton suggests, naming something categorizes it, and the plot at this point resists classification, for it is both an assassination attempt sparked by misguided religious zeal and a thwarted rebellion fired by excessive ambition, and its agents are simultaneously demonic and human.[157] The story's resistance to generic classification also defamiliarizes it despite the use of the standard pamphlet format. Pointing to the confusion of the later parts of the pamphlet and to variations among surviving copies, Nicholls concludes that "There is yet some scope to discuss whether the apparent candour and rough edges in the 'Discourse' arise from honesty and haste at one extreme, or from sophisticated propaganda techniques at the other."[158] This question of intention may not be as important as Nicholls suggests, however, since the pamphlet bears the marks of this generic confusion, even if the compilers acted unconsciously.

The second official document, *A True and Perfect Relation of the Whole Proceedings against the late most barbarous traitors*, is a detailed account of the trials of the surviving conspirators and the Jesuit superior, indicted as an accomplice.[159] I discuss this pamphlet and its representation of the trials and executions as theatre in the next chapter; here, however, we should note that the pamphlet illustrates again the authorities' difficulties in presenting the plot as a cohesive narrative within an existing literary genre, especially when faced with the additional problem of revising the narrative presented in the earlier "Discourse." In his letter to the reader, Barker admits that, justice having been done, some might deny the need for another book, but insists that

> *it is necessary, and wil be very profitable to publish somewhat concerning the same, Aswell for that there do passe from hand to hand diuerse vncertaine, vntrue,,and incoherent reports, and relations of such Euidence, as was publiquely giuen vpon the said seuerall Arraignments; As also for that it is necessary for men to vnderstand the birth & growth of the said abominable and detestable Conspiracy, and who were the principal Authors and Actors in the same.*[160]

Whether Barker intended the double meaning on "profitable" or not, the authorities were obviously anxious about the circulation of unofficial information in manuscript and oral forms. In addition, they clearly wished to shift responsibility for the plot to the priests. Whereas the "Discourse" had made no mention of clerical involvement, the *True and Perfect Relation*, as its full title indicates, represented the Jesuits as the primary conspirators.

This project, however, required elevating the lay plotters' social status somewhat to make them worthy victims of the ambitious Jesuits. While Barlow had stressed Fawkes's lowly station, Sir Edward Coke takes pains to assert that the plotters are "Gentlemen of good houses, of excellent parts, howsoeuer most perniciously seduced, abused, corrupted, and Iesuited, of very competent fortunes and States," concluding "that the principall offendors are the seducing Iesuites."[161] By representing the Jesuits as agents of corruption he not only attacks Catholicism but also depicts the lay plotters as "gentlemen," if not great men, who succumbed to evil influences through misguided religious zeal. The pamphlet consequently highlights the case of Digby, the only plotter whose social status permitted his fall to be represented in the terms of *de casibus* tragedy. Nevertheless, the status of the other plotters and the failure of their conspiracy keep the story closest to the mixed genre of tragicomedy.

If the trial of the lay plotters sits, somewhat uneasily, within this genre, that of Father Garnett comes closest to a polemical discourse. Garnett was effectively silenced, both literally by being interrupted when he attempted to speak and textually by having his speech reported in the third person, while the Earl of Northampton, in a speech expanded for publication, provided a lengthy history of international Catholicism and its attempts to subvert English Protestantism, representing the Jesuits as the servants of the Antichrist. The juxtaposition of this apocalyptic discourse with the earlier tragicomic one results again in a fractured text.

These prose narratives illustrate the perceived need to persuade readers to accept authoritative interpretations of plots and conspiracies. This perception arose from the very real dangers of dissenting accounts, often circulated in oral or manuscript form as rumours, letters, and libels.[162] Typically, official accounts emphasized both the monarch's providential deliverance and divine judgment upon the traitors. Over time, however, writers seem to have recognized the rhetorical advantages of adapting their narratives to specific literary genres, which acted as communication strategies to facilitate common understanding.[163] The magnitude of the Gunpowder Plot, particularly its plans for both assassination and rebellion, and a late decision to change the locus of blame from the lay plotters to the Jesuits, however, resulted in some confusion. Although the intention of both pamphlets may have been to create an official narrative of the plot, the internal inconsistencies of each as well as their uneasy relationship facilitated the development of the dissenting narratives they had been designed to silence.

2.4 Catholic Narratives: Miracles and Martyrdom

As we have seen above, it was not always easy for the authorities to persuade subjects to accept official interpretations of events. Along with reluctant preachers, governments had to counteract oppositional narratives in oral, manuscript, and even print forms.[164] Despite attempts to regulate the print marketplace, books could still be printed in England on illegal presses, as the Martin Marprelate tracts and some Jesuit pamphlets were, or smuggled into the country from overseas.[165] The trial of the lay Gunpowder plotters clearly illustrates the government's failure to contain unwelcome print.[166] In his speech, Coke describes the legacy of the Jesuit mission as a trail of seditious books, virtually admitting the government's inability to control the circulation of such texts.[167] Even more difficult to eliminate were the rumours and libels that passed relatively freely about the country.[168]

Father John Gerard's narrative of the Gunpowder Plot, apparently circulated in manuscript, offers one Catholic response to the official Gunpowder narratives contained in the "King's Book" and *A True and Perfect Relation*.[169] Gerard, in fact, refers to both official and unofficial sources in his text, which demonstrates the way in which these narratives could be reinterpreted by those who contested them.[170] He introduces his text as a shared creation of author and reader, "desiring only this of the pious reader, that as I will perform my part in truth and fidelity in the whole narration, so he will not be wanting of his part to perform the rules of equity and charity both towards me and the matter I write of."[171] While he states that he was asked to write the narrative for friends abroad, it seems that Gerard also hopes to gain loyal English Catholic readers, and perhaps even some sympathetic Protestant ones. In order to win over a moderate audience, he must exonerate the priests without condoning the plot, a feat he accomplishes by exploiting gaps between the two official publications.

Recognizing that the priests' absence from the "King's Book" allows him to assert their innocence, Gerard accepts the confessions of Fawkes and Winter, taking their silence on the subject of clerical involvement as proof that no priests were plotters. He insists that he has examined all the confessions, including those not printed, and that they concur that no one else participated in the plot. Gerard emphasizes his need to rely on Winter's confession for his description of the early plotting because the conspirators guarded their secret so carefully. Thus, the trope of secrecy used effectively by the authorities in the Gowrie and Essex affairs now aids a Catholic narrator, for the plotters' insistence upon secrecy exonerates the priests. James's 7 November proclamation distinguished the plotters from loyal Catholics, a distinction the king attempted to maintain in his 9 November speech. A second proclamation, however, made the priests the principal plotters, even though none of the lay conspirators had implicated them in their confessions, including those that were published. Even some Protestants were suspicious, "But this was no impediment to the forcible authority of the proclamation, which went out under the King's name."[172] The reason for this abrupt change of policy, according to Gerard, is puritan influence upon the king.

Gerard concludes from James's speech that "the Puritans had laboured and in some sort prevailed with His Majesty to make him believe, that it is holden by the doctrine of Catholics lawful to kill and murder Princes, &c."[173] They have used two books to do this, *The Popish Positions* and *The Late Commotion in Herefordshire.*[174] Gerard instead commends to his readers the example of Garnett's answer to Catesby, which demonstrates that Catholics do not condone the murder of innocents. On the other hand, puritans like George Buchanan and John Knox teach that subjects have the right to resist tyrants,

> And surely His Majesty was not ignorant of the mind and doctrine and manner of proceeding of the Puritans in this point; but out of his wisdom, he thought it best

rather to please them for the time in seeming to believe that they had written of us than to rehearse their own doctrine, whereof he had tasted too much, knowing right well that their patience was not able to bear to be rubbed upon the back, which indeed was much galled in that kind of doctrine about government. So that herein we may think it pleased His Highness to practise that in this his grave and princely speech in the Parliament House, which sometimes before he had used to say in mirth, when he would show the difference between the Papists and Puritans, in matter of patient sufferance.[175]

By suggesting that the king is courting puritan favour, Gerard puts his finger on the weak spot in the Jacobean consensus, introducing a third term into the Catholic/Protestant binary that Northampton had set up in his speech.

Whereas the "Discourse" places the genesis of the plot within a peaceful and contented kingdom, Gerard describes an England divided by confessional strife. Catholics, he claims, face increasing persecution.[176] For them, the continuity between the reigns of Elizabeth and James that the king depicts as a benefit is instead a prolongation of suffering. Gerard begins his narrative by describing the persecution of the faithful from Genesis until James's accession.[177] If international readers query his representation of the English situation, Gerard has the ready answer that "It hath ever been one point of policy in the Government of England, since the beginning of persecution there, to hide the same from the knowledge of the world, and from being judged to be such by other kingdoms round about them, as much as could be possible."[178] Even though "the politics ever with printed books endeavour to prove that all was but the execution of justice against traitors and persons disobedient to the State," Catholics are actually being executed for heresy.[179] Gerard concludes with a short history of the legal persecution of Catholics in England since Elizabeth's accession. James not only confirmed the Elizabethan laws in his first Parliament, but also increased recusancy fines and applied them to women, children, and servants.[180] His new canons require ministers to preach against papal jurisdiction at least four times annually, and James has packed his second Parliament with puritans in order to enact even more stringent anti-Catholic laws.[181] By progressing from Elizabeth's measures to James's, Gerard shows that James has indeed proven himself to be Elizabeth's rightful successor, but more dangerous to Catholics because he has Protestant sons to succeed him.[182] While Gerard is careful not to implicate the king directly, he suggests that James has entered into an alliance with puritans to persecute Catholics.

Gerard adamantly denies a providential interpretation of the event as a deliverance, since this would be to admit that God favours a Protestant England. He demonstrates his scepticism of the circumstances surrounding the Monteagle letter as depicted in the "Discourse," grudgingly admitting:

> Thus far the book of the discovery of this treason discourseth of the manner how the same did come to light. And because the same was set forth by authority, with desire that men all should conceive this to be the manner how it came to light, it may be thought that so it was. Yet there want not many others of great judgment, that think His Majesty and divers of those Councillors also, who had the scanning of the letter, to be well able in shorter time and with fewer doubts to decipher a darker riddle and find out a greater secret than that matter was, after so plain a letter was delivered, importing in so plain terms an intended punishment both by God and man, and so terrible a blow to be given at that very time and yet the actors invisible.[183]

Some think "that this letter was but framed and sent of purpose to give another show of casual discovery both to hide the true means and to make the especial preservation of the King and State to be better discerned to come from God Himself." He enumerates the reasons why some have refused to credit the letter, but concedes that "although many were of opinion that this was not the first means of this discovery, yet none that ever I could hear of, was able to give a certain judgment, which way indeed it was discovered."[184] Gerard's attempt to discredit the letter shows that he recognized how important James's interpretation of it was to a providential reading of the plot and of the king's personal contribution to preventing it. This is not to suggest that he doubts the existence of providence, however, for later in the pamphlet he appropriates it to his own church.

In his account of Garnett's trial, for which he turns to the text of *A True and Perfect Relation*, comparing it with notes taken by those present, he tries to show that the priest is being tried for heresy rather than treason. The indictment at the first trial listed not only the known priests, but also "others," permitting the government to add accusations later. In addition,

> to make the matter good against them, here they were accused in this indictment, where none of them were present to answer for themselves; and were joined with the conspirators who were sure to be convicted and condemned of the fact, that the Jesuits might also seem to stand convicted and proved guilty with them; and this not only as partners, but, as I have said, as principal counsellors and causers of the whole treason.[185]

The point of the first trial, then, was less to convict the lay plotters than to provide a basis for prosecuting the priests. Gerard downplays not only his own alleged role in the plot, but its entire religious foundation, claiming that the plotters' printed confessions offer no evidence that he administered the sacrament to them and heard their confessions. Neither Salisbury nor Northampton accused Gerard, but Coke did, and

> we must pardon Mr. Attorney this overlashing in this his discourse, which seemed rather to be intended against the Jesuits, than to prove the prisoners guilty that were there present before him; for it appeared by his words in divers places, that the chief mark he shot at was, like another Aman, to root out the whole Order of them, not out of England only, but out of the world, if he could.[186]

The trial is thus not about the treasonous behaviour of an individual priest, but another example of prosecution for heresy under the guise of a treason trial.

Finally, Gerard contests the Protestant depiction of the conspirators' deaths. Here he must be careful to show that the lay plotters were good but misguided Catholics, not martyrs, while the innocent priests were martyred.[187] Since the official account provided minimal details of the earlier executions, Gerard turns to an even more stridently Protestant account by T.W., arguing that the conspirators'

> state of mind and manner of carriage may in part be discerned by that printed pamphlet, which was presently set forth, entitled *A true report of the Imprisonment, Arraignment, and Death of the late Traitors*, wherein although all their particular words and actions were of set purpose left out, which might sound to their commendation, and many words of contumely and disgrace heaped upon them and their religion also in the most odious manner that could be devised; yet even that which is there set down of them did confirm very many in opinion that they thought themselves clear from offence to God in the matter, and that they were thereby made the more willing to suffer for the same cause.[188]

Similarly, in response to the Winters' testimony he says: "It is not amiss to see what is said of them both by that pamphlet which was then by some base person published of their arraignment and execution; for that being written in as disgraceful manner of them as could be devised, it is the surer witness of anything that may be well interpreted of their mind."[189] Using the sensational pamphlet allows Gerard to provide a dissenting account without contradicting the official narrative. Whereas Protestant sources refer to the Catholics as defiant before their trial, Gerard describes them as resolute. He takes particular exception to the comment that Digby seemed afraid to die and offers his own more favourable gloss, claiming that Sir Everard impressed many spectators with his courage and faith. His face had the same composed expression after death, even though he had still been alive when butchered. Gerard reports the other executions in less detail but insists that the plotters all died as good Catholics, except Bates, whose participation was motivated by personal loyalty to Catesby rather than religious zeal and who had betrayed the priests. T.W., in contrast, observed that Bates was the only one who seemed penitent.

By relating the various miracles associated with the priests' deaths, particularly Garnett's, Gerard appropriates providence to the Catholic side.[190] In addition to the more famous miracle of Garnett's straw, Gerard recounts two signs attesting to Oldcorne's saintliness: first, the fire into which his bowels were thrown burned for sixteen or seventeen days afterwards (the same number as the years of his ministry); and, second, a crown of distinctively coloured grass grew up in the courtyard at Henlip where the priests were taken. While in previous cases accusations of treason had evidently been manufactured, this time there was clear evidence of a plot, and "Therefore in this case Almighty God did think it more needful in His divine providence to give testimony of His servant's innocency than in former times, when the cause itself was so plain, that it could not be contradicted."[191] God, then, has shown favour to the Catholic cause rather than the Protestant.

Gerard's text demonstrates the possibility of constructing a dissenting narrative from the very fabric of the official accounts.[192] He never contests the main facts of the government's case – that there was a plot and that Garnett learned about it under the seal of confession. It is difficult to determine how well known Gerard's text was in England, but subsequent complaints that some consider the plot as the work of "a few unfortunate gentlemen" suggest that many of the ideas expressed here were readily available.[193] Although Gerard had his own reasons for insisting that not even all Protestants supported the authorized interpretation, he may have had some justification for his assertions. By early 1606, Robert Cecil had been goaded into responding to a series of Catholic libels, but we can be fairly certain that criticism was coming from other quarters as well.[194] In his defence, printed by the king's printer, he complains that he has been "calumniated, with many contumelious Papers and Pasquils, dispersed abroad in diuers parts of the Citie, without any Author, and yet so continually comming vpon" him that he did not know whom to answer. At last, "hauing also heard from Forraine parts, how farre ... [his] Name was there proscribed for a man of blood," he has felt compelled to respond.[195] As evidence of his persecution, he prints one of the libels, in which he is accused of attempting "*to roote out all memory of* Catholicke *Religion, either by sudden banishment, Massacre, imprisonment, or some such vnsupportable vexations, and pressures; and perhaps by decreeing in this next Parliament, some more cruell and horrible Lawes against Catholicks, then already are made*" (B3r). The letter threatens that five Catholics have vowed to kill him and sealed their vows with the sacrament, none of the five knowing the identities of the other four. They claim this is the only avenue open to them, since Salisbury is acting as a match giving fire to the king, making him the instrument of a reverse Gunpowder Plot directed against Catholics (B4v).

Salisbury responds by assuring his readers that not only are Catholics not being prosecuted for heresy, but that the current regime is more moderate than the previous one. The rumour that James intends to enact harsher laws against Catholics has been started to justify Catholic resistance, since Elizabeth shed less blood than Mary, and James has not retaliated, even after the plot. If Catholics believe they are prosecuted as heretics it is not the fault of the English government but of their own ignorant obedience to a church "whereof the faith is lapped vp in such ignorant & implicite obedience; and so much the rather, because it hath fallen out so often, that the scruples of Conscience and seeds of Treason, haue growen vp as close together, as the huske and Corne in one eare" (D3v). Like the writer of the "Discourse," Salisbury recreates England's peaceful state before the plot, with "a iust & gracious King, when euery man reioyced vnder his Vine and vnder his figge Tree" (E3r). The biblical reference (1 Kings 4.25) compares James to Solomon and implies God's particular favour towards England, which promises prosperity to Catholics as well as Protestants, so long as they remain loyal to the crown. His readers' duty is to "make it appeare vnto the world, by the difference of our constant measure of thankefulnesse, that we esteeme not this an ordinary acte of Gods prouidence, nor a thing to be imputed to any fault or fayling in their plots or proiects, but a miraculous effect of the transcendent power, farre beyond the course and compasse of all his ordinary proceedings" (E3v). Salisbury here introduces the importance of memorialization alluded to in the "Discourse" and enforced in the sermons and liturgy. Forgetfulness not only shows disrespect to God, but also encourages enemies of church and nation to believe that England can be attacked with impunity. The duty of memory thus ensures God's care by discouraging both foreign invasion and domestic conspiracy.

2.5 Conclusion

As the foregoing analysis demonstrates, the Elizabethan authorities gradually developed a strategy for informing both English subjects and foreigners of national crises, offering authoritative interpretations through sermons, liturgies, and prose narratives. Before his accession to the English throne, James I had not only practised this strategy in his response to the Gowrie Conspiracy, but had built upon it by instituting an annual commemoration of the event. Having inserted this memorial into the English calendar early in his reign, he used the occasion of the Gunpowder Plot to perpetuate the myth that all the plots against both himself and Elizabeth were, like Samson's foxes, joined at their tails. Through this "myth of deliverance," the new monarch sought not only to portray himself as a worthy successor to Elizabeth and the inheritor of God's providential care, but also to distinguish himself from his predecessor by emphasizing his paternal care for his subjects and his provision of sons to succeed him. More importantly, by linking the English and Scottish conspiracies, he strove to create a cultural connection between the two countries to promote his project of political union.

While the rituals of bonfires and bell-ringing documented by Cressy were important to the creation of this myth, it developed primarily through narrative. Liturgy offered a univocal account of the deliverance intended to be absorbed by the whole nation, but sermons and prose pamphlets participated in a more dialogic working out of the story among individuals and interest groups. From the beginning, preachers and authors sought to accommodate their narratives, with varying degrees of success, to existing literary genres, both anticipating and responding to competing versions. Although memories of the Gunpowder Plot may have been intended to unify the population, it is less certain that they actually accomplished that goal. The next chapter describes how the spectacle of the plotters' trials and executions, intended safely to dispose of the perpetrators, left questions about rhetoric, ambition, and religion to be debated on the London stage.

3 "And no religion binds men to be traitors": The Plot on Stage

3.1 Drama, Politics, and Religion in Early Jacobean London

While the Gunpowder Plot provided sensational matter for both the printed pamphlet and the sermon throughout 1606 and beyond, it seems to have appeared on stage only in disguises that modern scholars have frequently had difficulty penetrating. As Frances E. Dolan observes, "The stage refers to the Gunpowder Plot only through allusion, indirection, and displacement."[1] Although critics have caught glimpses of the plot in a number of plays produced after 1605, evidence of a direct connection is lacking in most cases.[2] Resorting to what Annabel Patterson calls "functional ambiguity," playwrights set their plays in other times or places to avoid or deflect challenges from the authorities.[3] Since the state itself scripted the first dramatic representations in the form of public trials and executions, authors were probably wise to use discretion in offering unauthorized interpretations. Far from providing univocal demonstrations of state power, however, these performances reflected ambivalences that influenced later representations on the commercial stage.

In this chapter, I consider first how the official representations of trials and executions attempted to limit public interpretation of these events and how playwrights Thomas Dekker, John Day, and Ben Jonson responded by questioning and debating those interpretations on the stage in the year following the plot's discovery. Jonson, I argue, reconsidered his original response at the beginning of the next decade in *Catiline, his Conspiracy*, which explores larger issues of institutional corruption involving religion and ambition. Following through on connections made by previous critics, I conclude by tracing this play's influence on the development of the satiric ghost poem at the time of the Popish Plot crisis. As the theatre's capacity to stage dialogue and debate became compromised during the Exclusion Crisis, Jonson's ideas found renewed expression in a new genre, thus demonstrating the potential of Gunpowder texts to stimulate generic blending and transformation long after their original production.

Whereas the authorities did not routinely scrutinize sermons prior to delivery, dramatic performances were always subject to a system of pre-performance authorization that may explain the absence of any surviving play taking the Gunpowder Plot as its primary subject.[4] Nevertheless, William C. Woodson offers tantalizing evidence that such a play may have existed, citing addresses to the reader in Oliver Ormerod's *Picture of a Papist* and William Hubbock's *Great Brittaines Resurrection*.[5] Hubbock defends his decision to write a psalm of thanksgiving, observing that

> Others in great varietie of inuention in verse & prose; in Latine and English, in sermon & otherwise, haue trauelled in this argument laudably and fruitfully: some memorably euen by the voyce of a dolefull Pyramis demolished in *Fraunce*, crauing restitution in noble great *Brittaine*; yea the Theater and English *Roscius* himselfe hath pourtrayed this work of God, and set it aloft, *tanquam in arce Phidiæ*, as it were in the turret of the famous caruer Phidias to the view of all men.[6]

Ormerod, refuting claims that he had authored the *Double PP* pamphlet now attributed to Thomas Dekker, says "I hold both it, and another that was thrown abroad vpon the stage at the late execution of the traitors, together with many other[e] toyes lately printed against the Papists, as fit for the fire as the coniuring bookes in the 19 of the *Acts, verse* 19." Woodson takes Hubbock's mention of Roscius as a possible reference to Richard Burbage that would identify the theatrical company as the King's Men. A marginal note in Ormerod's text, not printed by Woodson, may offer a further clue: "It is a very vnfit thing, that histrionicall iesters and stage players should bee suffred to writ books of such matters and indeed a greate disgrace to our Religion."[7] The reference to "stage players" in conjunction with the possible allusion to Burbage immediately brings Shakespeare to mind, but the absence of any other evidence for a lost play leaves such an identification entirely conjectural. If Ormerod was referring to Shakespeare, he could have been thinking of *Macbeth*'s allusions to the plot discussed below.[8]

While they express distaste for the play, Ormerod's and Hubbock's comments offer little indication of why this play, if it existed, should have disappeared from the records. Ormerod's reference to it as "a greate disgrace to our Religion" seems to be directed at the presumption of the author rather than any irreligious content in the play. In fact, he associates it with "other" anti-Catholic works, which suggests religious orthodoxy and makes the negative reaction to the play more puzzling. Hubbock's more favourable comments place the play above sermons and pamphlets, associating it with the esteemed works of Phidias. Neither author suggests that the authorities had attempted to stop the performances.

Nevertheless, there were reasons why a stage play dramatizing the plot directly might have been dangerous. According to Janette Dillon, "Popery and treason represented the two kinds of subject matter most likely to run into trouble with the authorities: matters of religion and matters of state."[9] In 1559, Elizabeth I had issued a proclamation specifically regulating the performance of plays on these topics. While this document has generally been quoted to prove that religion and politics were banished from the stage, Richard Dutton points to the qualification that these subjects are not "to be wrytten or treated vpon, but by menne of aucthoritie, learning and wisedome, nor to be handled before any audience, but of graue and discrete persons."[10] Like James I's 1622 *Directions to Preachers*, the proclamation attempted to control rather than to prohibit the public discussion of controversial topics. Paul Yachnin contends that such controls led to a subtle form of self-censorship in which dramatists, actors, and audiences were complicit. In his view a combination of repressive censorship, increased commercialization, and a growing sense that poetry was irrelevant to the real world conspired to render drama toothless, and by about 1600 "the authorities do not seem to have counted on the players to support the established political order by instructing the public in the official view on matters of state and religion, and they do not seem to have thought it possible for the players seriously to disrupt the political order."[11] Evidence for the comprehensive censorship to which Yachnin alludes comes from a series of notorious cases in which playwrights and actors were punished for representing potentially seditious ideas.[12] Other scholars, however, believe that focusing on these high-profile cases has skewed our perceptions of the licensing process, which actually sought to balance protecting the interests of the court with allowing performances on a wide range of subjects.[13]

Janet Clare notes that although playwrights wished to avoid trouble, they also felt a commercial imperative to stage topical issues that would engage their audiences. One way of avoiding awkward questions was by encoding meanings into texts in subtle ways that enabled an author to deny any political offence with which he was charged. Concealing meanings, however, restricted the playwright's assurance that any message in his play would be "correctly" decoded by either theatrical or print audiences. As Patterson cautions, "authors who build ambiguity into their works have no control over what happens to them later," so plays could accumulate additional, even contradictory, meanings when performed under different political circumstances.[14] Reminding us that political readings are the creations not of texts alone but of texts within their contexts, Jerzy Limon offers a useful distinction between political texts and political functions, suggesting that "the political function of a literary text, acquired within the particular context in which the communicational process takes place, is independent both of the author's 'intentions' and of the autonomous meaning of the text." Thus, "it may be said that a literary text is capable of functioning as a political piece only in a communicative process during a particular historical period, within a given society and within the social and political context that the given period creates."[15] When the Jacobean authorities took action against plays, it was because they were serving, or could serve, political functions. In two of the most notorious cases of the early seventeenth century, the performance of a play about Richard II on the eve of the Essex Rebellion and the nine performances of Thomas Middleton's *A Game at Chess* shortly after Prince Charles returned unwed from Spain in 1624, critics have debated the political functions of the plays, but clearly the dangers that the authorities associated with the performances related to their perceived abilities to influence actions both within and outside the country.[16] These two cases succinctly demonstrate two major concerns that lay behind the regulation of drama – the threat of domestic rebellion and the fear of jeopardizing delicate international relations. The first performance fuelled suspicions that the theatre could be used to incite insurrection, while the second threatened the fragile peace with Spain once the Spanish ambassador, Diego Sarmiento de Acuña, had lodged a complaint with the king. A play that dealt openly with the Gunpowder Plot could have risked offending if it suggested Spanish complicity, while any portrayal of rebellious Catholics might have offered the wrong kind of example to practitioners of the old religion.

Our own abilities to understand the political functions of these plays are limited not only by gaps in our knowledge of their performative contexts, but also by uncertainties about the status of the texts as we have received them. Clare notes that since plays had to be licensed for both performance and publication, those that have survived passed two tests, but may have been so altered in the process that the original performance text is not recoverable.[17] As Dillon admits: "One of the difficulties of trying to make sense of controversial plays after the event is that the printed text is rarely likely to represent what was performed, and we are not usually in a strong position to second-guess what was cut out and why."[18] At best we have fragmentary accounts of the reception of individual plays on stage and printed texts that may have been subjected to various non-authorial interventions. A modern critic, attempting to reconstruct early responses from such imperfect and incomplete evidence, is then faced with a formidable task that, as Dutton observes, will always "be more an art than a science."[19] Given the importance of time and place of performance to the audience's ability to decode political meanings, we are required to construct the best possible contextualization for these events with the available evidence.

A parallel case that can help us to understand the difficulties of representing recent history on the stage is that of a lost Gowrie play by the King's Servants to which John Chamberlain alluded in a letter to Ralph Winwood on 18 December 1604. Chamberlain admitted he did not know why the play was controversial but confided that it was likely to be disallowed, having displeased "some great counsaillors."[20] Dillon argues that the disappearance of all other traces of the play indicates that it was indeed censored, and while Raymond Burns opines that the play may have offended by exposing marital discord between the royal couple, Gustavo Secchi Turner has suggested that the play may simply have trespassed upon the king's desire to be the only narrator of the Gowrie incident.[21] If Turner is correct, then no playwright may have wanted to risk dramatizing the Gunpowder Plot, of which James was also rumoured to have written the official account.[22] Perhaps an additional source of authorial caution was the trouble Samuel Daniel and the Children of the Queen's Revels had incurred over their alleged commentary on the Essex Rebellion in *Philotas*, likely first performed in the winter of 1604–5.[23]

If no company took up the challenge of unambiguously representing the plot, the number of contemporary plays that refer to it, however obliquely, suggests that audiences were interested in the topic or at least that playwrights expected them to be. Unfortunately, in some of these cases uncertain dating makes difficult the kind of contextualization needed to understand the relationship of a particular play both to the plot and to other contemporary events. While most critical studies have examined individual plays, and a few have attempted to sort them into thematic groupings, in the first part of this chapter I take a chronological approach to three plays that can be dated relatively accurately – John Day's *The Isle of Gulls*, Ben Jonson's *Volpone*, and Thomas Dekker's *The Whore of Babylon* – to investigate the possibility that these plays may have been operating in dialogue.[24] Dutton's work has established the importance of the Gunpowder Plot to *Volpone*, the writing of which can be dated to the time of Henry Garnett's trial in early 1606, and the topicality of Dekker's play, probably written about a year later, is unmistakable despite the Elizabethan camouflage. The case for *The Isle of Gulls* is less certain, but the play makes clear references to the trials and executions of the lay plotters, which had just occurred when it was first performed. I argue that if *The Isle of Gulls* and *Volpone* treat the plot sceptically, satirizing Robert Cecil's use of it to consolidate his power, then Dekker's play may be an attempt to restore faith in the representation of the plot as yet another example of Catholic treason. Dekker's conservative treatment, however, also points up the difficulty of determining what the official interpretation was, since his representation of the plot in the guise of the Armada suggested the Spanish involvement that the government carefully denied.[25] Moreover, although in a somewhat obscure scene he repudiates the methods of playwrights like Day and Jonson who practise satire as a means of curing social and political ills, his own representation of royal counsel may be slyly biased against the Cecils.

Looking back on this controversy five years later, Jonson reconsiders his earlier response in *Catiline, his Conspiracy*, significantly moving from comedy to tragedy, from satire of an individual to a more general indictment of those who serve themselves by serving the state.[26] In this play, Jonson exploits the authorities' failure to establish a definitive narrative by seeing the conspiracy as a reprise not of the Catholic plots against Elizabeth, as Dekker had, but of the Essex Rebellion, in which religion had merely provided a cloak for ambition. I argue that the most remarked aspect of the play, the appearance of Sylla's ghost in the first act, and the least remarked, the role of the women, are fundamentally linked to Catiline's ambition and consequent fears of dissolution. A few readers in the play's early history appear to have appreciated this fact, but later reception has obscured the connection. Although notoriously unpopular at its original appearance, *Catiline* became one of the most successful tragedies of the century, enjoying stage revivals and reprintings in the reigns of both Charles I and Charles II.[27] Moreover, it participated in the contentions of the Restoration by serving as a source of ideas, either directly or indirectly, for a number of other Restoration plays and poems.

The events of early 1606, when the authorities self-consciously staged dramas in which Catholic traitors were tried and executed on the public stage of London, enabled all of these interpretations. While Michel Foucault argues that vicious punishments represented the power of the state before the people, more recent work by Peter Lake and Michael Questier has suggested that, at least in early modern England, such spectacles often sent mixed messages.[28] Consequently, in the courtroom, on the scaffold, and in print, the authorities attempted to control the meaning of these dramatic performances for their audiences. The printed record of the trials and executions of the Gunpowder plotters, however, reveals inconsistencies created by various officials playing to different members of the audience for different reasons. Vacillating between presenting the plot as an example of the sins of pride and ambition and offering it as the product of religious fanaticism inspired by the Jesuits, the authorities created the groundwork for a range of future representations.

3.2 Staging Treason: Trials and Executions

The earliest plot dramas may be regarded as the trials and executions of the plotters themselves. Since the initial publication of Michel Foucault's *Discipline and Punish*, scholars have explored the theatrical qualities of Tudor and Jacobean executions primarily by engaging with his assertions that trial and punishment function as spectacles of state power. According to Foucault, the state inscribes its power upon the bodies of individual subjects in public spectacles as a warning to other potential offenders.[29] In recent years, however, a number of early modern scholars have begun to question, if not to reject entirely, Foucault's insistence upon the state's monopoly on power.[30] In particular, Lake and Questier have argued that executions of Catholic priests revealed to subjects the weaknesses as well as the strengths of the early modern English state and its religious policies. They observe that "every time a catholic priest was executed the issue of where legitimate royal authority ended and tyranny and persecution began was, through speech and gesture, re-opened and thrust onto the public stage."[31] Public executions forced the government to convince its audience that it was punishing Catholics for treason rather than for heresy.

These executions, Lake and Questier argue elsewhere, could also expose differences between religious and secular authorities that should call into question our notions of a monolithic Jacobean "state."[32] We should, perhaps, also be wary of postulating homogeneous audiences for these performances. Aware that trials and executions, like other dramatic spectacles, rely upon the interpretative skills and prejudices of individual spectators – variables even more difficult to control than the events themselves – the authorities attempted to pre-empt "incorrect" interpretations by publishing accounts of trials and executions.[33] The narrative of the Gunpowder plotters' trials and punishments, however, inadvertently reveals subtle discrepancies among judges competing for the favour of specific groups or individuals, inconsistencies that some readers were not slow to perceive and exploit.

As we have seen in chapter 2, Elizabethan and early Jacobean England subscribed to two competing theories regarding the motives of conspirators at least from the time of the Parry Plot. While an account of excessive ambition leading to a fall dominated the official pamphlet in this case, it could not completely eclipse the story of misguided religious zeal that triumphed in Philip Stubbes's more sensational narrative. By 1605, the Bye Plot, in which the secular priest William Watson had conspired to kidnap James at Greenwich on 23 June 1603, could be added to an impressive list of treasons attempted by Catholic sympathizers, while the Main Plot that completed Ralegh's political demise was attributed to ambition and atheism.[34] As in Essex's case, pride and the desire for popular acclaim offered a plausible alternative when there was no clear evidence of religious motivation.[35] Although the authorities immediately recognized the Gunpowder Plot as a Catholic conspiracy, suspicions that a peer had been involved, if only as a potential regent for Princess Elizabeth, quickly emerged, and Henry Percy, ninth Earl of Northumberland, was imprisoned on suspicion of treason. As hopes of tying Northumberland directly to the plot faded, however, the authorities focused their attention increasingly upon the Jesuits.[36] By the time of the trials, the official interpretation of the plot was that the lay plotters, none of whom possessed a rank above "gentleman" and could therefore not have expected any personal advancement, were motivated solely by religious fanaticism. Mark Nicholls has astutely observed, nevertheless, that religious and personal motives were both likely at play.[37]

If the plotters' motives were complex, so were those of their judges. Contemporary libels accused Robert Cecil of attempting both to implicate the Jesuits in order to justify harsher enforcement of the penal laws and of scheming to put Henry Percy out of the way by implicating him in the plot.[38] According to Pauline Croft, Cecil in general supported a moderate position in regard to Catholicism, distinguishing, as the king did, between loyal Catholics and traitors, but "his lenity was rarely perceived outside high political circles, and to many catholics it followed that since Cecil ran the country he must be responsible for their hardships."[39] Although he seems to have been less tolerant of Jesuits, his insistence upon their culpability at the Gunpowder trials may have been exacerbated by concerns that Henry Percy's imprisonment would recall his success in eliminating Essex, a previous rival.[40] As a member of a Catholic family and one who had himself been suspected of participating in a religiously motivated conspiracy, Henry Howard, Earl of Northampton, wanted to demonstrate to King James that he was loyal to the crown and repudiated the pope's deposing authority, but he also may have found reason to assert the evils of ambition in his uneasy relationship with Cecil.[41] Although the two had established a political alliance, their religious differences, Northampton's obsession with lineage and breeding, and competition for favour with a new monarch all led them to play different parts at the Gunpowder trials. Sir Edward Coke was allied closely with Cecil, having been patronized first by his father, Lord Burghley. Coke, too, probably hoped to impress James, and in the event he was appointed chief justice of the Court of Common Pleas in June of 1606, shortly after his performances in these sensational trials.[42]

Even had the authorities been completely united, the circumstances of the plot and the aftermath of its discovery would have hampered their efforts to offer a univocal interpretation. The most dramatic events, the quelling of the rebellion and the capture of the priests, occurred outside London where there were few witnesses, and the most prominent conspirators, Robert Catesby and Thomas Percy, were killed along with Christopher and John Wright in the abortive rebellion, thereby escaping exemplary punishments.[43] To complicate matters, two men arrested in connection with the plot died in suspicious circumstances before they could be tried and executed. Nicholas Owen, the carpenter responsible for designing and constructing many of the ingenious priest holes in recusant houses, died suddenly following an interrogation.[44] The official cause was suicide, but many suspected the unintentional effects of torture. Francis Tresham also died in the Tower, apparently of natural causes, but rumours of poisoning almost immediately began to circulate.[45] In a deathbed letter, Tresham recanted his previous confession and claimed that he had not seen Garnett for sixteen years.[46] In perhaps the most frustrating circumstance of all, the priests' success in evading capture forced the crown to proceed against the lay plotters before Garnett and Oldcorne were located. Having determined to make the Jesuits the principal offenders, the authorities were forced to insist upon the guilt of those absent from the courtroom during the first trial.[47]

As in the drama, the relationship between performance and printed text is difficult to reconstruct, but we have reason to suspect that the printed account of the trials and executions was constructed to satisfy a number of conflicting demands by the prosecutors. The first of these was clearly defensive, for the writer of the preliminary address "To the Reader" justifies the publication as necessary to counter rumours and to ensure that people understand what has taken place. This justification seems to affirm Lake and Questier's suspicions that state authority could be compromised rather than enhanced by the spectacles of trial and punishment if individuals interpreted them incorrectly. Consequently, the government needed not only to provide a series of spectacles, but also to ensure a "true and perfect" interpretation of these events for both local and international audiences. The pamphlet, not published until after Garnett's trial and execution, included an account of the entire legal process, which makes it difficult to know how much editing of the earlier trial occurred after the later one.[48] As the final pamphlet stands, it clearly seeks to establish the Jesuits as the real culprits; however, Northampton's speech blames not the Jesuits' religion but their ambition for secular power.

Two lists, first of the prosecutors and second of the lay accused, that function essentially as "Dramatis Personae" follow the address to the reader. The indictment, however, begins with the names of Father Garnett and Father Tesimond, each followed by a list of aliases.[49] Just as this list suggests a larger group, so also the authorities insisted upon alluding vaguely to other Jesuits, a fact that seems to have particularly rankled with John Gerard, who justifiably suspected his inclusion in this number.[50] As for the lay plotters who are actually on trial, Coke asserts that they are "Gentlemen of good houses, of excellent parts, howsoeuer most perniciously seduced, abused, corrupted, and Iesuited, of very competent fortunes and States," concluding "that the principall offendors are the seducing Iesuits."[51] By representing the Jesuits as agents of corruption he not only attacks Catholicism but also represents the lay plotters as men who had the potential to be good middling subjects.

Figure 1 *Princeps Proditorum.* Broadsheet portrait of the Jesuit Superior, Father Henry Garnet, apparently from a set of six portraits entitled *Princeps Proditorum: The popes Darling: or, a guide to his twelve Apostles* …, before 3 May 1607. (The original prints of the other portraits are not extant; however, they were copied by Thomas Trevilian in his 1616 miscellany; see *The Great Book of Thomas Trevilian: A Facsimile of the Manuscript in the Wormsley Library*, ed. Nicolas Barker, Roxburghe Club, 2000.) © Trustees of the British Museum, Prints and Drawings, 1886, 04101.

The prisoners at the bar having pleaded "not guilty" to the charges against them, Coke and Sir Edward Philips spoke. The compiler of the pamphlet insists that Coke's speech has been recorded as nearly as possible, thereby demonstrating his commitment to a "perfect" record. Coke shows himself particularly conscious of an international audience in a cause "vpon the carriage and euent whereof the eye of all Christendome is at this day bent" (D2^{r}), beginning by justifying the delay in mounting this performance. One of the stated reasons is that the king has timed the event to coincide with Parliament, since this was the institution the plotters had attempted to destroy, but the authorities may also have wanted to ensure a larger audience in London.[52] Aware of his international readers and fearful of compromising the new peace with Spain, he is careful to exonerate "Forreine Princes" (D4^{v}). Coke's speech contains strong elements of homiletic rhetoric, offering a detailed description of the punishments meted out to traitors and their symbolism, presumably both to warn audience members against disobedience and to compliment James on his clemency. The pamphlet demonstrates the trial's performative aspect most clearly when, "for further satisfaction to so great a presence and audience, and their better memorie of the carriage of these Treasons, the voluntarie and free confessions of all the said seuerall Traitors in writing subscribed with their owne proper hands, and acknowledged at the Barre by themselues to be true, were openly and distinctly read" (K3^{r}). The "great ... presence and audience" probably refers not only to the size of the crowd, but also to the attendance of the monarch himself, concealed from the view of the other spectators as he was when he listened to sermons in the Chapel Royal.[53] Since guilty verdicts were a foregone conclusion, the event was primarily a spectacle in which members of the Privy Council, acting as judges, performed before the monarch and most of fashionable London. As in the performance of a play based upon a familiar story, these actors could be assured that the spectators knew the outcome. Their parts were to keep the audience entertained while showing them that justice was being done, but the situation must also have provided an unparalleled opportunity to display their political and rhetorical skills before both their sovereign and their peers.[54]

The plotters were unwilling actors in this drama, and it was the judges' responsibility to provide them with characterization and motivation. Most of the conspirators were assumed to have acted out of religious fanaticism, but the arraignment of Sir Everard Digby tells a different story. According to the list of charges, Digby was arraigned separately because he had committed his crimes in a different county, but since attempts to implicate Henry Percy had failed, he was accorded superior status as the highest ranking of the surviving plotters.[55] While Digby's arraignment and indictment are not recorded, the pamphlet reports his speech, in which he offers as his primary motivation not religion but his friendship with Robert Catesby. In a short speech, Northampton then reinterprets Digby's fall according to the terms of *de casibus* tragedy as that, if not of a great man, at least of a man who had the potential to achieve greatness. Digby, he claims, had been high in Elizabeth's estimation and had every prospect of continuing to enjoy favour from James had he not become embroiled in the plot. Behaving as a gentleman, Digby apologizes for his conduct, asks to be beheaded, and responds graciously when this courtesy is denied. Catesby's servant, Thomas Bates, who also apparently acted out of personal loyalty rather than religious fervour, and who turned King's evidence, is treated leniently but no effort is made, given his station, to turn him into a fallen hero.

The second trial, Father Garnett's, begins in much the same way as the first but is distinguished by its more self-conscious theatricality. In his opening speech, Coke repeats his response to those concerned about the delay and again cautions against blaming foreign powers. He directs more attention in this case, however, to the local than the international audience, apologizing for repeating himself as he does not wish to be "tedious" (O3^{r}) but is aware that many were unable to hear at the former trial. Coke immediately makes explicit a distinction between the lay plotters and the priests that had only been implicit in the first trial. In what he now calls the "Iesuites treason," the laymen were merely actors, while the priests were authors. Furthermore, according to Coke: "The Author or procurer, offendeth more then the actor or executor, as may appeare by Gods owne Iudgement giuen against the first sinne in Paradise, where the Serpent had three punishments inflicted vpõ him, as the originall plotter; the woman two, being as the mediate procurer; and *Adam* but one, as the partie seduced" (P^{v}).[56] Although Coke does not use the word "author" in an explicitly literary sense here, this statement in conjunction with a number of theatrical metaphors suggests a distinction of roles between the two sets of conspirators analogous to that under negotiation in the theatre, where the functions of author and actor were splitting apart, but responsibility for seditious performances could still fall upon either.[57]

Coke reinforced his theatrical analogy when he told his audience: "this is but a latter Act of that heauy and wofull Tragedie, which is commonly called the Powder-treason, wherein some have already plaied their parts, and according to their demerits suffered condigne punishment & paines of death" (O2^{v}). Cecil repeated the metaphor later in the trial when he

> tooke an occasion to declare, that the City of London was so deare to the King, and his Maiesty so desirous to giue it all honour and comfort, as when this opportunitie was put into his hands, whereby there might be made so visible an Anatomie of Popish doctrine, from whence these Treasons have their source and support, hee thought hee could not choose a fitter Stage, then the City of London. (Y^{v}–Y2^{r})

The city has become a stage on which to demonstrate the relationship between Catholic heresy and treason.

While the judges created an essentially univocal narrative in the first trial, Garnett's, according to the published account, became a debate among the priest, Cecil, and Northampton, until Garnett eventually ceased to participate and was replaced by Coke, whose systematic rebuttal of the priest's previous answers created a kind of commentary on the earlier proceedings. With the Jesuit doctrine of equivocation one of the main issues at stake, the authorities sought to show that Garnett's word, like that of a stage villain, could not be trusted and that the audience had to be protected from exposure to his rhetoric. In his first speech, Northampton warns that Garnett can move people to sympathy, and he seems to have had some justification, for on 2 April John Chamberlain wrote to Dudley Carleton that Garnett "caried himself very gravely and temperatly."[58] The judges seem consequently to have deliberately pursued a strategy of interrupting the priest in order to contain his influence. In his *Narrative of the Gunpowder Plot*, Gerard claims that even the king complained of Cecil's constant efforts to silence the priest.[59] While Gerard's narrative is hardly an unbiased source, it is corroborated by the official account when Cecil encourages Garnett to speak at one point with a promise that he will not be interrupted.[60]

Despite this containment of Garnett's speech, made more evident in the printed pamphlet through the use of paraphrase rather than direct quotation, the Lord High Admiral, Charles Howard, told the priest at the conclusion of the trial "that he had done more good this day in that Pulpit which he stood in (for it was made like vnto a Pulpit wherein he stood) then hee had done all the dayes of his life time in any other Pulpit" (Cc4^r). If anyone had preached, however, it was Northampton, who wrapped up the proceedings with a lengthy speech, expanded to almost one hundred pages for publication.[61] The speech provides a historical overview, international in scope, of the Catholic Church's increasing interference in European secular affairs. Discoursing at length on Pope Gregory VII, notorious among Protestants as an example of papal interference in state matters, Northampton demonstrates that ambition to rule over kings led the popes to claim powers of deposition. Similarly, Garnett and his malcontent "disciples" (Dd4^r) have hatched a conspiracy that uses religion for political ends. Garnett, as a parody of Christ, is one who has been sent not to save but to destroy English Protestantism. The "invasion" (Zz3^r) of the priests was merely a forerunner to the Spanish Armada. Thus, in contrast to Coke's appeals to avoid implicating other nations in the Gunpowder Plot, Northampton's history makes a connection that would not have been lost on those displeased at the new peace with Spain.

After this speech, the printer inserted a note to the reader accounting for its length. The text he received, he claims, was "unperfect," so he consulted the earl, who offered him a copy of the actual speech as nearly as he could remember it, as well as an expanded version. Anticipating demand from readers, Barker decided to print the longer version. The note makes the decision seem casual, almost accidental, and the printer's sole responsibility rather than a calculated strategy by the authorities. Linda Levy Peck, however, offers documentary evidence that Northampton compiled the pamphlet carefully, assisted by Robert Cotton and supervised by the king.[62] Northampton's authorship was recognized in international circles, for the Venetian ambassador told the doge in December 1606: "The fact that the author has been and still is reckoned a Catholic is expected to lend the work a greater authority."[63]

As we have them, the proceedings read as a curious hybrid of stage and pulpit performances. Throughout the trials, letters and confessions had functioned both as evidence and as stage properties, as they would in many of the dramas associated with the plot.[64] Coke, Cecil, and Northampton had seized opportunities to make speeches as well as to engage in dialogue. Northampton, eager to demonstrate his loyalty despite possible religious irregularities in his life, and Cecil, anxious to display both his indispensability and his impartiality, played these roles before a mixed audience, royal and common, local and international. While Coke, Cecil, and Northampton all ensured that the official pamphlet memorialized their starring roles, the plotters, lay and religious, had been given few opportunities to speak, and most of their words were reported rather than recorded. In fact, their presence at times seems largely irrelevant.

In the next act, too, the authorities attempted to deflect the spotlight from the traitors even as they suffered what were intended to be exemplary deaths. The city of London once again provided the stage as the conspirators were executed in various locations and their severed heads and quartered bodies prominently displayed both at the place intended for destruction and throughout the city. Here again, however, the authorities sent mixed messages. Just as Northampton had linked the arrival of Garnett and the other priests to the Armada, so the decision to execute the Jesuit superior on the west side of St Paul's, where the thanksgiving for the victory over the Armada had taken place in 1588, seemed to reinforce for the local audience a connection that the government had assiduously denied to an international one. There seems to have been a general effort to play down the executions of the lay plotters, which are described in a single sentence at the end of the first part of the pamphlet. Garnett's execution, however, was reported in more detail, almost certainly to counter rumours circulating about the event.[65]

While the authorities had limited Garnett's speaking opportunities at his trial, the priest took responsibility for devoicing himself at his execution, claiming that he was unable to speak to the entire audience because of a weak voice, and therefore restricting his remarks to a select audience in close proximity to the scaffold.[66]

He maintains that he regrets the plot, but reiterates that he had only a "general" knowledge of it and that his sole offence was withholding this information from the authorities.[67] Interventions by the Recorder of London, whose presence had apparently been engaged by the king, demonstrate the state's concern with maintaining control of the occasion.[68] When Garnett attempts to extenuate himself, the Recorder hastens to remind him of the four points to which he had confessed at his trial. Rather than contesting the rebuke, Garnett apologizes both to the government for his negligence and to Anne Vaux for involving her in a scandal. The author of the pamphlet, however, counters Garnett's display of saintly contrition by representing his rejection of the charitable offices of the deans of St Paul's and Winchester as rudeness. The account also highlights the inability of Catholic doctrine to console or support by observing that Garnett "could not constantly or deuoutly pray" because "feare of death, or hope of Pardon euen then so distracted him." Garnett now plays a coward, deserted by his religion in the hour of his death, although the pamphlet records his Latin prayers, presumably to demonstrate their inefficacy. The final words of the account, that he was "hung till he was dead," may have been intended to counter rumours that sympathizers had pulled his legs to prevent him from being cut down alive.[69] By reporting and interpreting details selectively, and by invoking a state official's words, the authorities sought to prevent Catholics from interpreting the execution as a martyrdom.

Lake and Questier observe that in offering accounts of these occasions the authorities were restricted to interpreting the facts – they could not safely tamper with them for the obvious reason that "These were very public performances and the theatre was usually full. Even the most brazenly biased critic knew he could not get away with telling barefaced lies about what was generally known to have happened."[70] These restrictions, of course, also applied to Catholic accounts, although an international Catholic readership may have been more willing to suspend disbelief. Ending the official narrative with Garnett's death was intended to provide closure, but in Catholic accounts it nevertheless became the starting point for the subversive martyrdom accounts that almost immediately attached themselves to the dead priest.

These accounts reflect the limited success of the official "drama," at least in its printed form. The fullest account of Garnett's "martyrdom" appears in Gerard's *Narrative of the Gunpowder Plot* and includes stories of such signs as the grass in front of the house where Garnett and Oldcorne were captured displaying the pattern of a martyr's crown and Garnett's severed head being encircled with a red garland.[71] Gerard also, presumably to counter the official representation of Garnett as a coward, insisted upon the significance of the execution taking place on a holy day, the Invention of the Holy Cross (since Garnett had protested being executed on the secular holiday of 1 May), and claimed that he had died with his arms folded on his chest in the form of a cross and had not struggled.[72] A sympathetic crowd had prevented him from being cut down alive, and when a spectator pulled his legs, "it was much marvelled how the people durst do this so publicly, seeing the State so generally bent against Father Garnett in this cause." According to Gerard, Garnett's behaviour at both his trial and execution moved even Protestants. There may be some truth to this claim, considering Chamberlain's expression of approval regarding Garnett's deportment at the trial, although he added more cynically that

> likewise he was used with goode respect and goode wordes, whether yt were that the King mislikes that fowle railing and reproaching of prisoners at the barre: or that they hope by fayre meanes to drawe more from him, for that he knowes much, and is thought yf he list he may deserve his live.[73]

While Chamberlain ascribes Garnett's mild demeanour to hopes of clemency, he also suspects the authorities of manipulating these hopes for their own benefit.[74] Gerard's account remains problematic, since we do not know how well it may have been known in England, nor is it an eyewitness narrative, since the priest was busy preparing his escape to the Continent at the time and presumably had to rely on news from other Catholics.

At least one of the martyrdom legends, however, was well known in England, that of "Garnett's straw."[75] According to this legend, a relic hunter collected an ear of corn spattered with Garnett's blood at the site of execution. Within a few days, the drop of blood was said to have formed itself into an image of the Jesuit's head wearing a martyr's crown. Gerard claims Archbishop Bancroft attempted to purchase the straw, presumably to silence the rumours.[76] Nevertheless, it may have appeared in a piece of commercial theatre, namely, that single edgy comic scene of the porter in Shakespeare's *Macbeth*. Garry Wills interprets this obscure scene as a "reverse conjuration" in which the porter welcomes Garnett to hell under three of his aliases (emphasized at his trial), just as Macbeth has three identities in the play. He argues that "The Gunpowder Plot would have been suggested [by the play] in two ways – its menace to the king in Macbeth's regicide, and its failure in the final disposition of traitorous Garnet (safely made the butt of scorn in the Porter scene)."[77] As *Macbeth* was probably performed before James, it would have assured him that traitors are destined to hell.[78] Nevertheless, the very need for such comic containment suggests the inability to enforce a more permanent closure through conviction and execution.

The scene in *Macbeth* reflects how deeply secular politics was engaged in representations of the trial and execution. Northampton, with his lengthy speech appended to the account of Garnett's trial, was not the only individual attempting to use the occasion to demonstrate his loyalty and utility to the crown. Cecil, already a powerful man, was apparently determined to extend his influence further. Both Catholics and Protestants seem to have been uneasy with Cecil's position, as many Elizabethans had been with his father's.[79] The family's relative obscurity before William's rise to power and the ways in which father and son had consolidated offices made Robert suspect, and his physical deformity made him appear even more sinister in a time when a crooked back was thought to reflect moral depravity.[80] His role in discovering the Gunpowder Plot was the subject of enough libels to force the response discussed below. Because the king was away hunting when Lord Monteagle received the famous warning letter, he had delivered it to the Privy Council, whose members made the initial decisions on how to proceed. Cecil's determination to await the king's return seems to have initiated many of the subsequent rumours about his conduct. While few dared to accuse him of actually inventing the plot, some suspected that he had known about it before the letter arrived and had concealed the information to give the plotters more time to incriminate themselves thoroughly and to increase his own opportunities for heroism.[81]

3.3 Debating Interpretations: The Plot as Theatre, 1606–7

Most studies of the theatrical response to the Gunpowder Plot have focused either upon individual plays or upon thematic groupings of plays that minimize the role of chronology (see note 2). Instead, I consider three surviving plays that can be dated with some certainty within the year following the plotters' trials and executions. My working assumption is that these plays responded not only to the event itself but to previous representations of it on the stage. This methodology has not generally been applied to early modern drama, but seems potentially useful to a consideration of reinterpretations of a historical event over time. Its disadvantages, however, must be acknowledged at the outset. Not every play written or performed that year referred, either directly or indirectly, to the Gunpowder Plot, nor do we possess copies of all the plays produced, so that these dramatists may have been responding at least partly to plays that are lost. Some of the plays performed that year, like *Sophonisba*, were conceived earlier, and although topical references may have been added in performance or printing, the plays themselves were not designed to offer commentary on the plot.[82] Furthermore, I make no attempt to untangle the relations among the three dramatists or take more than passing note of the companies that performed the plays.[83] Of the three plays, only Day's *The Isle of Gulls* seems to have incurred official displeasure, and probably not because of its references to the plot.

Despite the dangers of representing matters of religion and state on stage, plays retelling stories of revolt and conspiracy from the historical past were performed regularly.[84] Such plays, however, do seem to have risked censorship, particularly when performed in contexts that made parallels with recent events too transparent. The most recent example at the time was probably Samuel Daniel's *Philotas*, performed once by the Children of the Queen's Revels during the winter of 1604–5.[85] The Privy Council accused Daniel not only of representing the Earl of Essex's downfall, but more provocatively of using the performance to demonstrate his support for the disgraced earl. He probably lost his position of licenser to the company, but the play was printed and he apparently suffered no other punishment.[86] While some earlier scholars accepted Daniel's protestations of innocence, the evidence that he deliberately created a parallel between the classical and the English situations seems fairly conclusive.[87]

The use of such parallels, whether classical or modern, provided one of the best opportunities for making veiled political statements, but Daniel's experience illustrates the inevitable risks. With this example before them, it may not be surprising that Day and Jonson looked to literary models rather than historical sources when they wished to critique Robert Cecil's role in the Gunpowder Plot. Suspicions that Salisbury had used the plot not only to discredit Catholics (especially the Jesuits) and to make himself indispensible to James, but possibly also to eliminate a rival, seem to have motivated these attacks. Moreover, this was not the first time such rumours had swirled around Cecil. Both at the time of Essex's execution and at his own death in 1612, libels accused Cecil of arranging the fall of the Elizabethan favourite to advance his political career.[88] An epigram dated by Alastair Bellany and Andrew McRae after the Gunpowder Plot links the disgraces of Essex and Northumberland, implicating Cecil in both:

> Essex did spend, Northumberland did spare,
> He was free, this close; How shall we live then?
> Of Plotts, these courses both suspected are
> No: they are not suspected, but great men.

Another libel, posted over the Burghley pew in Newark in 1606, accuses Cecil's nephew William, third Lord Burghley, of being a Catholic, a charge that Bellany and McRae suggest "was particularly explosive in the immediate aftermath of the Catholic Gunpowder Plot."[89] At the same time, Catholic libels were apparently circulating so promiscuously that Cecil was forced to respond to them. In *An Answere to Certaine Scandalous Papers*, he printed a sample of the threatening letters he had allegedly received along with his response. The letter accuses Cecil of persecuting recusants since the Gunpowder Plot through "*sudden banishment, Massacre, imprisonment, or some such vnsupportable vexations, and pressures*," with the express purpose of rooting out the old religion entirely.[90] These libels indicate how thoroughly popular opinion, both Catholic and Protestant, was ranged against Cecil at this time, and his compulsion to defend himself attests to the seriousness of the attacks upon him.[91] But Cecil's elaborate defence may have been an act of misdirection, drawing attention from the rumours that he had arranged Northumberland's fall and at the same time attempting to win back Protestant support. If first Day and then Jonson took the opportunity to produce anti-Cecil satires, it is probably because they sensed his vulnerability. Whereas Day's play was censored, however, Jonson disguised his satire sufficiently to avoid detection, or at least prosecution, by the authorities.

The Isle of Gulls was performed for the first time c. 16 February 1606, and the reaction against it seems to have taken place relatively swiftly, since a letter from Sir Edward Hoby to Sir Thomas Edmondes dated 7 March 1606 describes the furore and the action taken against those involved.[92] From the letter, the offence appears to have been connected to the portrayal of Scots in the play. The players, rather than the author, may have been punished because they had used costumes and accents to make the satire more pointed.[93] Either the critique of the court, and of Robert Cecil in the person of Dametas, was unremarked or was deemed beneath notice.[94] Given the wide-ranging nature of Day's satire, critics have hesitated to identify Dametas as a specific individual. E.K. Chambers saw the evil courtier as Somerset, but subsequent scholars have pointed out that he had not yet risen to prominence at court.[95] Raymond Burns, in his edition of the play, warns against attempting to make any individual the model for Dametas, and Gary Paul Lehmann echoes his caution, concluding instead that "Day's play is a searing attack on courtiers, their shallow tastes, artificial manners, sham chivalry, and misapprehensions of duty."[96] More confidently, Pauline Croft asserts that "Dametas can be seen as a composite character, incorporating all the vices found at court, but the topical reference was unmistakable."[97] Dutton posits an even more certain identification of Dametas as Cecil. Echoing De Luna, he insists that the play "patently focuses on Cecil in the person of the hunchbacked Dametas."[98] Nevertheless, he too concludes that the play is a diffused satire offering "something transparent and unambiguous, a caricature of a king's wicked counsellor, unabashedly Machiavellian and self-seeking."[99] Day may have been attempting to ensure "plausible deniability" by taking on multiple targets and by using as his source the text of Sidney's *Arcadia*, yet the play offers evidence of topicality that no alert playgoer could have missed.

The Children of the Queen's Revels, then under Anne of Denmark's patronage, performed the play at Blackfriars. In its short history, this company became notorious for staging topical satire, possibly with its patron's encouragement.[100]

Christopher Love questions the tradition that the Blackfriars company served only a "coterie" of courtiers, concluding after a survey of the evidence that while the theatre catered to an urban elite in an upscale neighbourhood, its audience reached beyond the court.[101] According to Croft, the play was "a London sensation in the winter of 1606," and printing would have made it available to an even wider audience.[102] Failure to license the printing was not, Burns points out, in itself suspicious. Textual evidence that a nervous printer made last-minute changes during compositing, however, the most obvious being the replacement of the titles "King" and "Queen" with "Duke" and "Duchess," leads him to conclude that the play was considered "hot property" and that Day intended to provoke trouble.[103]

The title self-consciously refers back to Nashe and Jonson's *The Isle of Dogs*, giving Day an opportunity simultaneously to flaunt and to deny the play's topicality in the Induction when the Prologue assures the First Gentleman that this title has been assigned: "Not out of any dogged disposition, nor that it figures anie certaine state, or private government" (Ind. 38–9). Although *The Isle of Dogs* is lost, we know that it aroused the ire of the Elizabethan government to the extent that Richard Topcliffe was engaged to go through Nashe's papers.[104] In addition, Day's title reveals that the play concerns itself with the "gulling" of an entire island. The *OED* defines a "gull" as a "credulous person; one easily imposed upon; a dupe, simpleton, fool."[105] The unmistakable implication is that the entire nation has allowed itself to be duped and that the hunchbacked Dametas is responsible. The origins of the plot in Sidney's *Arcadia* only complicate our attempts to interpret the play. Michael Andrews calls the play a "travesty" that ridicules the *Arcadia*, while Gary Lehmann justifies Day's appropriation of Sidney's courtly text for political purposes.[106] These interpretations, however, require an uncomplicated reading of Sidney's romance as courtly entertainment, a reading questioned by numerous critics who find evidence for the author's political engagement beneath the surface. Approaching the *New Arcadia* from the perspective of its varied reception through the seventeenth century, Annabel Patterson argues that Sidney has used his "pretty tales" to create "a medium of expression that may, with luck, break through the political restraints and cultural assumptions" of late Tudor England to offer counsel to the court.[107] In her reading, Sidney's ideals of reformation are inscribed into the text, but with sufficient ambiguity to preserve his own safety. If we read the *Arcadia* this way, then Day's use of it in an almost transparent anti-Cecil satire may be at once less surprising and even more audacious, for it invites a critical rereading of the *Arcadia*.[108] While evoking a courtly culture of romance, Day may be positioning himself as a more reliable counsellor than Cecil. Unlike Sidney, however, Day invited analogical readings by drawing attention to Basilius's evasion of his regal responsibilities and by recasting Sidney's rustic clown, Dametas, as an evil counsellor.

From the beginning, the play gestures towards an even more specific political context by alluding to the trials of the lay Gunpowder plotters that had taken place only a few weeks earlier. In the opening lines of the Induction, the Second Gentleman advises his companions to find seats or "quarter" themselves. The First Gentleman responds: "If some had had the wit to doe so in time, they might ha savde the hangman a labour" (Ind. 5–6). Additional references to hanging and quartering sprinkled throughout make the play topical but not dangerous, while offering a kind of serious counterpoint to the plot's comic action. This action revolves around a conspiracy, though a romantic rather than an overtly political one, involving an attempt to isolate the King (or Duke) from his daughters while they are out hunting. The objects of this plot are Basilius's daughters, but the plan itself bears an uncanny resemblance to the outline of the Gowrie Conspiracy as narrated in the official account.[109] It might also have reminded viewers of the Gunpowder plotters' intention to kidnap Princess Elizabeth.[110]

A stronger connection with the Gunpowder Plot involving Dametas/Cecil occurs in Act 1, Scene 3, when Julio says: "The example lives in this *Dametas*, who notwithstanding the Duke hath raised him to that height that hee lookes equall with himselfe, yet for the base hope of incertaine government, hee offers him to sale, but let his treason live to the last minute" (1.3.140–4). These lines seem inescapably to refer to the rumours that Cecil had permitted the plot to "mature" in order to make his "discovery" more dramatic, a strategy that might have endangered the lives of the royal family. The context makes this comment even more suggestive, for in the previous line Aminter refers to the fable of the cold snake that, once revived, turns its venom upon the one who has saved it. Although all of the surviving examples are later, this cautionary tale occurs frequently in post-plot literature, with English Catholics cast in the role of the snake.[111] Instead, Day suggests that the snake is the king's closest advisor. Earlier in the same act, Dametas claims that he could hang Aminter by a "pattent" (1.3.76), boasting: "Ile tell thee how it runnes, It allowes mee 24 knaves, 6 Knights, 10 fooles, 13 fellons, and 14 traytors by the yeere, take em howe, why, when, and where I please" (1.3.77–9). If we count the lay plotters, those who had been tried at the time the play was written and those who had died in the rebellion or in prison, and the two priests, Garnett and Tesimond, the number comes to fourteen, although only eight had been executed at this point.[112] While this line may not refer to Cecil's involvement in the plot trials, it does highlight his ability to catch and prosecute suspected traitors at his discretion. Day's satire may be broader than Jonson's, but it may be even more openly topical.

Jonson's possible involvement with the Gunpowder Plot, particularly as it affects our understanding of *Volpone*, remains one of the most compelling literary mysteries surrounding the plot.[113] Newly released from his imprisonment following the equally mysterious prosecution for *Eastward Ho*, he dined at William Patrick's on 9 October 1605 with a party that included Francis Tresham, Robert Catesby, Sir Jocelyn Percy (a relative of Thomas Percy), and Thomas Winter. On 7 November, the Privy Council asked for his help in locating a certain priest as part of its investigation. Frances Teague argues that this priest was Father Thomas Wright, who had probably converted Jonson to Catholicism, and that he was likely wanted to help with Fawkes's interrogation.[114] Wright was found after several days, possibly by Jonson, but Fawkes had confessed by then. If Jonson did find Wright, Teague speculates that his "success might explain why Jonson was treated so gently when he was brought up on charges of recusancy on 26 April, 1606."[115] Jonson's presence at the dinner party raises more difficult questions about his political and religious affiliations. Some scholars have argued that Jonson was part of Cecil's extensive "spy network," and De Luna even hypothesizes that Jonson leaked the plot to Cecil.[116] These speculations, however, sit uncomfortably with readings of *Volpone* as an anti-Cecil play. While Jonson's return to the Church of England and his diminishing need for literary patronage may explain his possible criticism of Cecil in *Catiline, his Conspiracy*, scholars have debated whether he would have taken such a risk in 1606, when his recent brushes with the law and his recusancy (or, more likely at this time, church papistry) had left him vulnerable.[117] Both Croft and Dutton acknowledge these issues, but while Croft believes they would have inhibited the playwright from criticizing the politician, Dutton argues that Jonson, although unwilling to risk an outright breach, was prepared to offer covert criticism. Jonson's justifiable concerns for his own well-being may account for the elaborate "functional ambiguity" of the play. Given his recent history, he could not afford to risk official censure.[118]

Jonson's only acknowledged contributions to plot literature were his flattering epigrams to Cecil and Monteagle, but Dutton suggests that the sequence in which these appear in the 1616 folio undercuts the praises of both men. He concludes that "It is difficult to ignore the implication that, even as Jonson salutes these two peers, he is seriously questioning their reputations."[119] While this contextualization is specific to the later folio publication, Dutton argues that *Volpone* offers us a good indication of Jonson's attitude to Cecil in the immediate aftermath of the plot. Unlike Day, whose satire of Cecil must have been virtually transparent, however, Jonson made his disguise almost impenetrable except to his closest associates. The critical history of *Volpone* attests, in fact, to Jonson's success in creating a play that could not be tied directly to the Gunpowder Plot or widely recognized as an anti-Cecil satire. Dutton concludes that although there is no direct evidence that *Volpone* is "about" the plot, the accumulation of circumstantial evidence is compelling. Much of his most recent (and most extensive) argument for the play as a response to the plot comes from his detailed analysis of the prefatory materials to the 1607 quarto.[120] He observes Jonson's concerns with establishing his poetic authority through the commendatory verses, an unusual addition to a printed drama at this time. Donne's contribution raises the question of the relationship between the play and Donne's unpublished *Metempsychosis*, also arguably an anti-Cecil satire.[121] Moreover, the action itself, Dutton argues, depicts the paranoia of post-plot England through the character of Sir Politic Would-be, while making use of the tradition of depicting the wily Cecils as foxes. Along with Teague, Dutton finds that the "scrupulous and verifiable Venetian setting must in large part be aimed at deflecting attention away from the play's urgent concern with matters much closer to home."[122] Specifically, Volpone's subversion of Venetian society "is a richly imaginative metaphor of Cecil's exploitation of English society, undermining the law, alienating fathers and sons, and coming between husbands and wives, in (as it might be seen) the remorseless pursuit of his own wealth and gratification."[123]

To Dutton's comprehensive analysis may be added the subtle but pervasive echoing of Day's play in Jonson's repetition of forms of the word "gull" throughout *Volpone*. These occur at least seven times in the play. In Act 1, Scene 4, Mosca, in response to Corbaccio's "I doe not doubt, to be a father to thee," says slyly: "Nor I, to gull my brother of his blessing" (127–8). In Act 2, Scene 1, the newcomer Peregrine, thrown off balance by his conversation with Sir Pol, asks himself: "Do's he gull me, trow? or is gull'd?" (24). After his performance as a mountebank, Volpone asks Mosca: "But, were they gull'd / With a beliefe, that I was SCOTO?" (2.4.34–5), while following their first court appearance, Mosca exults that he and Volpone have been able "To gull the court" (5.2.16). Corbaccio is correspondingly annoyed that he has been "gul'd" (5.3.65) by the parasite. In disguise, Volpone finally taunts Voltore, "Had you no quirke, / To auoide gullage, sir, by such a creature?" (5.9.11–12). In Jonson's Venice, as on Day's arcadian island, it is not always easy to tell who is gulling and who is being gulled. Everyone in this play is in danger of being deceived while attempting to deceive others, whether in personal life, in political life, or even in the courtroom, but Jonson's choice of words suggests that he is flaunting his subtler and more complex exploration of this problem before the less talented Day.[124]

In contrast to, and I suggest in response to, the satiric treatments of post-plot politics offered by Day and Jonson, Thomas Dekker the following year produced what appears to be a conventional treatment of religious conspiracy promulgated by Rome and Spain and averted by Elizabeth with the assistance of her loyal Privy Council. Dekker consciously rejects the satiric mode, placing his work within the patriotic tradition of Heywood's *If You Know Not Me, You Know Nobody*, which had enjoyed immense success in 1604–5, and basing his interpretation upon "sources sanctioned or even inspired by the government."[125] The play was entered in the

Stationers' Register on 20 April 1607, following production by Prince Henry's players at Henslowe's theatre, the Fortune.[126] Although some earlier scholars believed that the play was actually a revision of an earlier one (*Truth's Supplication to Candlelight*), W.L. Halstead argues convincingly that this cannot be the case. Had the drama been an old one subjected to modernization, the new topical references would have been added to the stage copy, whereas these references appear in the holograph copy from which the text was printed.[127] He concludes: "That the text was printed from Dekker's holograph which he kept in his possession is important because the allusions to the death of Essex, the reign of James, and 'The Isle of Gulls' must have been a part of Dekker's original copy."[128] Halstead consequently dates composition to late 1605 or early 1606. Since Day's play was not acted until mid-February 1606, however, and references to the deaths of traitors would have had more topicality about this time, I suggest narrowing this period to the early months of 1606. If, as I propose below, the play also refers to *Volpone*, then the writing must have been completed after the first performances of Jonson's play, situating its composition during the period when Day and Jonson were satirizing Cecil on stage in ventures that were commercially successful, although in Day's case politically awkward.

Dekker's response to the plot, and to the earlier plays, is a relatively conventional anti-Catholic play that uses allegory and dumb show to display the evils of Rome and Spain as well as the glory of England under Elizabeth. Dekker seems to have attempted to capitalize on Heywood's success and was apparently bitterly disappointed by the play's failure.[129] The play begins with what had been the final scene of *If You Know Not Me* – the tableau of Elizabeth receiving the Bible originally scripted as part of her coronation procession. The familiar story of Catholic plotting against the queen follows, focusing particularly upon the assassination attempts of Parry and Dr Lopez, along with the history of the Jesuit mission culminating in the Armada. In order to arrange his material to best dramatic effect, Dekker takes these incidents out of strict chronological order, a procedure he justifies in the "Lectori" by insisting that he writes "as a Poet, not as an historian."[130]

This licence, however, also allows him to draw the same connection between the commencement of the Jesuit mission and the preparation of the Armada that Northampton had made at Garnett's trial. Although the historical setting precludes any overt reference to the latest Catholic plot, evocative words and phrases would have reminded Dekker's audience of the Gunpowder affair. When the Whore gives the kings their orders to court Elizabeth, the Third King responds: "When mines are to be blown up, men dig low" (1.1.128), and when he decides to stay in England after his suit has been rejected, he suggests that while he works to subvert England from within, the others should operate from outside as, among other things, "devils in vaults" (1.2.276).[131] Susan Krantz observes that both of the above references to the plot are made by the King of Spain while a third is made by the Whore, "thus connecting Spain directly to the most recent episode of Roman Catholic treachery against the English-Protestant world."[132] By insisting upon this connection, Dekker refuses one of the tenets of the official interpretation of the plot and accepts instead Northampton's anti-Spanish version of history, contrasting James's foreign policy unfavourably with Elizabeth's. As Krantz argues, the performance of the play by Prince Henry's Men and the evidence of Dekker's earlier post-plot pamphlet, *The Double PP*, indicate his sympathy with militant Protestantism.[133]

Kathleen E. McLuskie supports Krantz's view that Dekker critiques the current monarch by comparing him with the previous one, observing that "In the context of James's policy of peace in Europe and his failure to support Protestant struggles in the Low Countries, the oppositional political message was unmistakable."[134] Perhaps in order to deflect suspicions arising from such potentially subversive references, Dekker ostentatiously compliments James as the phoenix rising from Elizabeth's ashes. He may also offer an implicit critique of Elizabeth's parsimonious treatment of scholars in the lengthy scene in which the King of Spain recruits Campeius. While John Watkins suggests that Dekker may have made the queen appear weak by portraying her as the victim of continuous plotting, his allusions to the more recent plot would have had a similar effect upon James's reputation.[135] Thus, the conventional content and structure of Dekker's play may have helped him to offer veiled criticism of James, using allegory rather than satire to display both the continuities and discontinuities between the two reigns.[136]

In fact, Dekker explicitly rejects the effectiveness of satire in the theatre and criticizes those, like Day and Jonson, who practise it. In Act 2, Scene 1, Plain Dealing decries to the queen the state of an English theatre that thrives on invective. Having rejected Marian Catholicism to become a good English Protestant, Plain Dealing describes the evils of "ordinaries" and the gallants who frequent them, telling the queen that he "left villains and knaves" in Babylon only to find

> knaves and fools here; for your ordinary is your isle of gulls, your ship of fools, your hospital of incurable madmen. It is the field where your captain and brave man is called to the last reckoning and is overthrown horse and foot; it is the only school to make an honest man a knave, for intelligencers may hear enough there to set twenty a begging of lands; it is the strangest chessboard in the world. (1.2.103–11)[137]

All of this takes place, Plain Dealing says, in "one little cockpit," which is "able to show all the follies of your kingdom, in a few apes of the kingdom" (2.1.117–20). When the queen asks if there are not physicians to cure these ills, Plain Dealing responds that many of the physicians are sicker than the patients. In addition, the queen has

> other fellows that take upon them to be surgeons, and by letting out the corruption of a state – and they let it out, I'll be sworn, for some of them, in places as big as this, and before a thousand people, rip up the bowels of vice in such a beastly manner, that like women at an execution, that can endure to see men quartered alive, the beholders learn more villainy than they knew before. (2.1.128–35)

The topicality of this scene poses challenges of interpretation, but it offers a fascinating glimpse into Dekker's attitude towards contemporary theatrical productions.

The references to gallants, the knight's ward, and the "little cockpit" in conjunction with the phrase "isle of gulls" all point to Day's play, acted in the private theatre of Blackfriars.[138] Dekker seems to be pointing a finger at playwrights like Day and Jonson who claim to satirize the follies of the state in order to change them, but become no better than those they criticize when they savagely "rip up the bowels of vice." Dekker does not deny the existence of "follies" in the state, but he insists that satire is not the best method for curing them. In such plays, in fact, these playwrights recreate the spectacle of the scaffold even as they condemn it. It is tempting to connect the phrase "beastly manner" with Jonson's beast fable, *Volpone*, particularly given the proximity of the reference to "a few apes of the kingdom." Evidence from a variety of sources suggests that Cecil's hunchback and his sexual appetites had led to his popular depiction as an ape.[139] Thus, it is difficult not to see this little scene as a condemnation of Day's, and possibly Jonson's, methods of revealing the weaknesses of the Jacobean court and of Cecil in particular. Yet Dekker's portrait of Elizabeth and her advisors, through a minor historical inaccuracy, may present an equally damaging indictment of the Cecils.

Marianne Gateson Riely has identified the four representatives of the Privy Council in the play as Lord Charles Howard (Fideli); William Cecil, Lord Burghley (Parthenophil); Robert Dudley, Earl of Leicester (Florimell); and Henry Carey, Lord Hunsdon (Elfiron),[140] although she admits that the identification of Burghley as Parthenophil "rests on slender evidence."[141] As she points out, the text itself offers little opportunity to differentiate among the counsellors, although the actors' use of accents and costumes might have accentuated their differences in performance. Riely argues that Dekker has used "delicacy" in characterizing Burghley as Parthenophil, but one might question whether this is actually something more subversive, for Leicester, not Burghley, was Campion's patron before his defection to the Roman church.[142] The play represents the Campion affair and the Armada as the most significant attacks not only on Elizabeth but also on Protestant England. Elizabeth's rejection of Campion's suit, despite Parthenophil's efforts, contrasts with the Third King's courting of him. Contextualized in this way, Elizabeth's refusal to reward her scholars appears a dangerous economy, since it leads to the Catholic mission and hence to the Armada. Dekker's audience would almost certainly have taken the next step of adding the Gunpowder Plot to this list of unintended consequences. The disproportionate emphasis upon Campion's early patronage and recruitment by Spain makes the announcement of his death in the simple phrase "But now hee's tan'e" (4.2.97) so jarring that James H. Conover sees this abrupt dismissal as a flaw in the dramatic structure. Dekker's reticence is almost inevitable, however, since to have dramatized the priest's end might have been to court trouble while the authorities continued to resist Catholic representations of Father Garnett as a martyr. . Leaving Campeus's ultimate fate suspended, however, again suggests a failure to contain the Catholic problem. At the same time, associating Burghley with Campion indicts him in initiating the crises of 1588 and 1605 and may cast aspersions upon his son. Dekker's manipulation of historical facts seems to have been purposeful given his attention to such details elsewhere in the play. Once again, this play dramatizes what are at least ambivalent attitudes to the "regnum Cecilianum."[143]

I have suggested that at least three plays written and performed within the year following the Gunpowder Plot responded not only to the plot but to each other. Day places references to this event within a broad context of anti-court satire that nevertheless focuses on Cecil, who had succeeded in "gulling" an entire island into believing in a plot that he had either designed or manipulated. Jonson, more indirectly, describes a politics of misdirection in which sham plots conceal the real plot to take over the state.[144] Dekker seems to contrast a functioning Elizabethan court able to resist both force and fraud with a Jacobean court unable to contain such threats, but the seeds of these troubles have been sown not only by James's predecessor, but also by Robert Cecil's father. Within the parameters permitted by the authorities, then, the theatre seems to have functioned during the year after the plot as a space for debating and contesting interpretations of the event, its causes and effects. By considering these plays in relation to one another, we may see playwrights operating in dialogue with each other and with their audiences, offering a variety of interpretative possibilities in contrast to the authorities' attempts to impose a univocal narrative.

3.4 Reprising the Plot: Jonson's *Catiline, his Conspiracy*

For reasons that we can only guess, Jonson returned to the subject of the Gunpowder Plot in 1611 with a new play based on Sallust's account of the Catilinarian conspiracy. Although De Luna plausibly attributes Jonson's choice of topic to the assassination of Henri IV in France on 14 May 1610, the publication in 1609 of Francis Herring's continuation of his 1606 epic suggests both a revival of interest in the plot before the French king's death and a shift of focus from the attempt on Parliament to the larger project of taking over the country. Herring's sequel was the first literary work to focus on the abortive Midlands rebellion, about which official accounts had been virtually silent.[145] Jonson's engagement with the plot follows the same trajectory, with *Volpone* dramatizing secret plotting while in *Catiline* conspiracy progresses to armed rebellion. Disturbing news from France may have hastened the first English translation of Herring's original poem in 1610, and Jonson's play probably helped inspire Phineas Fletcher's first surviving version of his *Locustae* in 1611 (itself frequently considered an influence upon *Paradise Lost*).[146] This upsurge of attention to the plot, however, may be explained as much by the increasingly acrimonious international dispute over the Oath of Allegiance as by the French situation, particularly given the emphasis upon Latinate publications such as Donne's *Ignatius His Conclave*. Nevertheless, the translation and consequent popularization of elite texts such as Herring's and Donne's may well reflect the renewed fear of Catholic conspiracy that followed Henri's assassination.[147] This context explains Jonson's decision to revisit the plot without requiring us to resort to the unfounded speculations that De Luna offers regarding Jonson's personal life.[148] While most critics have accepted her conclusion that the play offers a belated response to the plot, almost all remain sceptical of her attempt to read it as a "parallelograph" in which each character must correspond to one of the figures involved in the historical conspiracy.[149]

Although De Luna argues initially that most playgoers would not have recognized the allusions to the plot, much of her argument actually relies on this recognition. Since it was only five years since the event, and memories had been kept alive through annual memorial services, it seems unlikely that any perceptive spectator or reader would have failed to discover the analogy.[150] Parallels between the two events were fairly commonplace and not accessible only to the classically educated. The "Discourse" that accompanied James's speech in the "King's Book" described the plotters as "worse then *Catilines*," and Northampton told Garnett in his trial speech that if Catesby were alive, "he might vaunt, and without exception, that he had surmounted and transcended *Catiline* in the spheare of his owne treacherie."[151] In 1608, Thomas Heywood had published his English translation of Sallust's account of the conspiracy, which attests not only to contemporary interest in the classical story but also to its reading as an analogue for the Gunpowder Plot. De Luna notes that while Heywood's translation "makes no explicit allusion to the Gunpowder Plot, many of his seemingly gauche renderings make it clear that he was, instead, skillfully adjusting his word choices wherever possible in order to suggest a topical application," and that "at one point he has so skewed Sallust's Latin as to unmistakably suggest the Jesuit doctrine of equivocation."[152] We should note, however, that Heywood was working from the French, rather than directly from the Latin, which may explain some of these changes.[153] Nevertheless, Heywood's interest in contemporary applications may also have manifested itself in his choice of prefatory materials. His letter "To the Reader," translated from Jean Bodin's *Methods*, addresses the problems of attempting to write recent history, noting that fear of offending inevitably compromises an author's neutrality. Throughout, the prefatory letter emphasizes such problems as the author's need to separate the roles of historian and orator and the reader's need for discernment. Kings, he declares somewhat pointedly, are not the best judges of their own actions. Cloaking himself in Bodin's words, Heywood offers a critical look at the problems of interpreting contemporary events and may even be subtly questioning James's account of the Gunpowder Plot.

In his view, ambition rather than ethical or religious considerations motivated the Catilinarian conspirators. If De Luna is correct that Heywood was offering an unacknowledged parallel with the Gunpowder Plot, then he would have been aware that the official version of the plot narrative made religious fanaticism rather than ambition its cause. It may, in fact, have been Heywood's translation that spurred writers to turn their attention to the rebellion and to the plotters' personal motives. Herring's continuation of his epic painted a picture of Digby as a classic overreacher, proudly lording it over his fellow conspirators before receiving the devastating news that Fawkes had been captured.[154] By 1611, with Northumberland still languishing in the Tower and the "Regnum Cecilianum" clearly drawing to a close as Cecil's health failed, writers like Herring and Jonson may have gained confidence in representing the plot as the product of misplaced ambition as much as religious zeal. Whereas Herring conventionally attributed ambition only to the plotters, however, Jonson more disturbingly questioned the motives of the authorities.

The analogy of the Catilinarian conspiracy confronted the problem of ambition directly and uncomfortably through its connection with the Essex revolt. Like Catiline, Catesby and some of the other Gunpowder conspirators had been involved in a previous plot against the state, a fact noted initially but not even mentioned in the official account of the trial. This discretion may partly have been an attempt to staunch rumours that Cecil would benefit from Northumberland's fall as he had from Essex's. Had Jonson's play been performed in 1606, then, it might have been regarded as more daring. By 1611, however, Northumberland's imprisonment was less likely to have been connected with the ghostly appearance at the beginning of Jonson's play. De Luna, in fact, dismisses the idea that the ghost would have invoked memories of Essex: "If Jonson in employing the

Ghost of Sylla meant to link the Essex Rebellion and the Powder Plot, causally, he surely cannot have intended the suggestion very seriously unless he believed Essex to have been, like Northampton, a secret Papist, merely posing – when it suited his convenience – as the arch Papist-hater of the realm."[155] In her eagerness to establish exact correspondences, De Luna seems to have misunderstood Jonson's larger point – that the cause of the plot was not religion itself but the use of religion for personal gain. Rather than seeing it as a botched religious coup in the tradition of the Elizabethan Catholic plots, Jonson literally raises the spectre of a political plot in which Cecil was suspected of having played a dishonourable part.

More subversively, Essex frequently appeared as a ghost in commemorative poems, functioning as a silent rebuke to those who had participated in his fall.[156] These poems made the late rebel a hero and "the exemplar of a political cause in danger of losing its heroes, its agents, and of a history that has officially been forgotten."[157] Essex's refusal to stay safely buried represented the same kind of failure of containment that the trials and executions of the Gunpowder plotters had. Weldon Williams, however, points out that Jonson's apparition seems to fall within the tradition of the Senecan rather than the *Mirror for Magistrates* ghost and is particularly indebted to the ghost that introduces *Thyestes*.[158] Seneca's play, available to readers in a 1560 translation by Jasper Heywood, opens with a speech by Tantalus's ghost, raised unwillingly from Hades by Megæra to stir up trouble between his grandsons.[159] Jonson's depiction of the ghost as more a noxious breath than a visible presence echoes Seneca's description of Tantalus. The main distinction, however, seems to be that Sylla shows no reluctance to perform his duty of inciting Catiline to additional crimes. Consequently, he also becomes the negative exemplar of the *Mirror for Magistrates* tradition. Although each ghost makes a single speech before vanishing permanently from the stage, Tantalus remains a presence in the play through Thyestes's son of the same name. Similarly, I believe the ghostly presence in *Catiline* lingers throughout the play both in the women's plot and in Catiline himself, attesting to the difficulty of containing the past to avoid repeating it.

The opening is one of the most arresting aspects of the play, garnering later imitations as well as both favourable and unfavourable commentary. In the late seventeenth century, the ghost's insistence upon addressing Catiline alone in his study rather than the entire city of Rome exasperated Thomas Rymer.[160] Nevertheless, as we shall see later in this chapter, the spectral plotter was reinterpreted in a series of anti-Catholic poems later in the century, including John Oldham's first "Satyre against the Jesuits." Jonathan Goldberg describes it as "one of the most remarkable scenes ever written, the apparition of the past in the form of Sylla's Ghost, breathing life into Catiline's conspiracy."[161] In general, however, critics seem not to have appreciated the implications of the ghostly presence throughout the remainder of the play or its reappearance later in the century.

While Sylla's ghost may be unusually effective, ghosts were commonplace on the Renaissance stage. According to Peter Marshall, between 1560 and 1610 at least "fifty-one ghosts were featured in twenty-six plays."[162] In the tradition of *A Mirror for Magistrates*, literary ghosts frequently served as negative exemplars in the *de casibus* tradition. Michelle O'Callaghan argues that the "ghosts populating the Elizabethan and Jacobean stage, pamphlets and dream-vision poems provided their culture with vehicles for animating memory, providing it with form and purpose." For her, the stage ghosts function as embodiments of history who "return from the past to speak persuasively to the living, and the story they frequently tell, the failure of governance, is intended to be corrective."[163] In fact, the very first poem known to have been written on the plot, Edward Hawes's *Trayterous Percyes and Catesbyes Prosopopoeia*, used the form of "prosopopaiae," the rhetorical device of creating fictional, or ghostly, speakers. The Westminster schoolboy's poem conventionally has the spirits and minds of Catesby and Percy engage in a dialogue – one penitent, the other still defiant in death – in order to support loyal political sentiments and conventional Protestant doctrine.[164] All of these ghosts, then, spoke of the need for both individuals and communities to understand and memorialize the past in order to learn from its mistakes.[165]

If we look closely at the play's opening lines, we find that Sylla's ghost is a curiously immaterial spirit compared with the armour-clad figure of Hamlet's father. The apparition's first words question not whether he can be seen, but whether he can be felt, first as a kind of weight, then as a "Breath," "a dire Vapour," or "a Pestilence" (1.10, 12, 14). Later he even speculates on how he would behave had he "a Body again" (1.22). Given this language, we may wonder whether the audience actually saw this ghost or whether they merely heard an off-stage voice.[166] The ghost's immateriality offers a metaphor for those residual elements of the plot, both ambition and Catholicism, that cannot be contained or controlled.because they are difficult to recognize. During the play, Catiline first fears and then experiences a kind of ghostly dissolution. After losing the consulship, he exclaims: "To what a shaddow, am I melted! / ... Strooke through, like aire, and feele it not. My wounds / Close faster, then they're made" (3.165–8). Similarly, at the beginning of Act 5, Petreius, encouraging his army, pictures for them Catiline in hell, "Walking a wretched, and lesse ghost" (5.64). Catiline, like Sylla, is to become a negative exemplar, a picture of failed governance. But to whom will his ghost appear? The most obvious answer is Caesar. Philip J. Ayres claims that Jonson deliberately dehistoricized Caesar in order to make him simply an emblem of future tyranny. This interpretation is consistent with Paulina Kewes's observation that while other types of literature presented Caesar more favourably and represented his assassination as a regicide, the stage maintained a consistently anti-Caesarian bias.[167] James, meanwhile, identified himself first with Caesar and only later with Augustus, becoming convinced that Caesar had been a tyrant. The ghostly appearance of Sylla and the anticipated transformation of Catiline into a ghost support a reading of Caesar as a future tyrant who will, like Sylla and Catiline, eventually have to be disposed of but can never be completely destroyed.

Other spectral presences haunt the play, particularly the women, who disappear unremarked after the fourth act just as the ghost does in the first. Like the "Would-Be" scenes in *Volpone*, the scenes involving the female conspirators have sometimes been considered expendable, and some critics have avoided discussing the women entirely.[168] Readers' disregard for the female characters may not be entirely surprising, for beginning with the first quarto edition of the play in 1611 the list of "Dramatis Personae" throughout the seventeenth century relegated them to the bottom of the list on the left side of the ledger, equivalent with such minor characters as pages and servants on the right. Similarly, the Gunpowder Plot has for so many years been narrated as an exclusively male event that it is almost impossible to recall that women were involved, if not in the plot itself, then certainly in the events that surrounded it.

More recently, popular historians of the Gunpowder Plot such as Alice Hogge and Antonia Fraser have generated interest in the role of women in the plot, while scholars including Arthur F. Marotti, Marie Rowlands, and Frances E. Dolan have begun the task of recovering the roles of Catholic women in post-Reformation England. Fraser observes how unlikely it is that rumours of the conspiracy would not have spread within the Catholic community, particularly to women and servants, while Hogge reviews more generally the female role in hiding priests.[169] Marotti and Dolan have contended that recusant women were considered dangerous because they resisted or subverted male authority.[170] In many cases, they were responsible for the Catholic upbringing of the next generation, while their husbands might conform outwardly in order to avoid the burden of recusancy fines. One of the factors suspected of motivating Catholics to rise in 1605 was a rumour that recusancy fines were going to be extended to women, forcing more wives to conform and thus making it more difficult to maintain and transmit the old religion.[171]

While Dolan still accepts that it was, to all intents and purposes, a males-only conspiracy, she also asserts that "many" women were imprisoned after the plot was discovered.[172] Not surprisingly, wives of suspected conspirators were detained on 16 November, along with women in the Midlands suspected of harbouring priests and knowing or suspecting the plans for a rebellion

Several female members of a prominent Catholic family were more seriously implicated by having hidden Father Garnett and other priests. Anne Vaux and her widowed sister, Eleanor Brooksby, were both questioned, but Vaux was involved more directly in the conspiracy through her personal devotion to Garnett. Arrested in the immediate aftermath of the plot, she was questioned and released on the bond of Lewis Pickering, but was rearrested for corresponding in orange juice with Garnett and not released again until after his execution.[173] Protestants seem to have enjoyed speculating about possible sexual improprieties between this woman and the priest, and Garnett apologized to her on the scaffold for having implicated her in scandal.[174] According to Mark Nicholls, the sisters continued to shelter priests until Eleanor's death in 1625, and Anne "kept what amounted to a school for the sons of Catholic gentlefolk" in Derbyshire until the mid-1630s, when she disappears from the historical record.[175]

Anne Vaux has left few traces on the historiography of the plot; however, many of the plays associated with the plot feature women in political roles, often involving conspiracy. Lady Macbeth, King Lear's daughters, and Lucretia Borgia all play active roles in the male world of politics. In contrast, Jonson's Celia and Marston's Sophonisba are powerless victims of male conspiracy. In Dekker's *The Whore of Babylon* the virtuous Protestant queen is juxtaposed with her evil double, the Roman church, making women both conspirators and victims.[176]

As several critics have noticed, Jonson gives his women larger and more ambivalent roles in *Catiline* than did his Roman sources. Christopher Gaggero observes that "While Sallust ... makes Fulvia a porous and motiveless vessel used by men to convey information between them, Jonson transforms her into a retentive *agent*, who acquires and trades intelligence and states her reasons for doing so."[177] Fulvia's statement of her motives to Cicero, however, is a lie, for she has revealed the conspiracy from personal jealousy rather than from any concern for the state. What is more interesting perhaps is that both Catiline and Cicero treat women not simply as functionaries but as equals. Catiline in the first act gives Aurelia a role parallel to his own, making her a partner in his conspiracy. In Act 3, when she affirms that she has the women prepared, he tells her: "you have your instructions: Ile trust you with the stuffe you have to work on. You'll forme it?" (3. 544–6). In the act of procreation, men were supposed to provide the form and women the matter.[178] Aurelia, however, shares with Catiline the "power to melt, / And cast in any mould" (1.448–9). In the same way, Cicero later makes Fulvia his colleague in exposing the conspiracy. While Dolan suggests that it is sexual activity that enables women to participate in public life, this seems an oversimplification of what actually happens in the play.[179] At the end of Act 1, the Chorus offers an indictment of Roman women:

> Her women weare
> The spoiles of nations, in an eare,
> Chang'd for the treasure of a shell;
> And, in their loose attires doe swell
> More light then sailes, when all windes play. (1.555–9)

The Chorus then admits, however, that the men are worse than the women and even suggests a possible gender inversion. Fulvia's call for a pearl acquired in exchange for sexual favours to be put in her ear at the beginning of the second act validates the Chorus's observation, for her ability to command such wealth depends upon male desire as much as female immorality.

But the women are not only immoral Roman matrons; they also appear to be English recusants. The opening of Act 2 with Fulvia at her toilet first raises this suspicion. Face painting, particularly when it hides decay, is associated with Catholicism through the image of the Whore of Babylon.[180] Galla reports a rumour that Sempronia "paints, and hides / Her decayes very well" (2.61–2), yet she defends the older woman of the charge, insisting that she uses such natural cosmetics as bread and milk to enhance her complexion. The women also attack Catiline's wife for dressing in so much finery "that her selfe / Appeares the least part of her selfe" (2.74–5), just as Protestants frequently accused the Roman church of cloaking its theological errors under rich furnishings. Aurelia, like the church, is more likely to be hiding moral than physical decay, since Catiline has committed a series of heinous crimes in order to marry her.

That these women represent female Catholicism is suggested in a second way when Curius accuses Fulvia of tricking him by feigning overcautiousness. Pretending to fear a jealous husband, she has "runne often to the dore, / Or to the windowe, frome strange feares that were not" (2.255–6), or she has had her "well taught wayter, here, come running, / And crye her lord, and hide [Curius] without cause, / Crush'd in a chest, or thrust vp in a chimney" (2.262–4), when her husband was actually at his farm or could have been bribed into silence. The act of hiding a man could, of course, be what it appears to be, the concealment of a lover, but in early Jacobean London it was as likely to suggest hiding priests. Curius's mention of bribery heightens the suspicion that Jonson intends the latter as well as the former meaning, since offering a husband money to conceal his wife's infidelity makes no real sense. In this way, Fulvia retains the upper hand in the relationship both by making herself responsible for Curius's safety and by withholding herself from him. Later she punishes his foolishness in divulging his participation in the conspiracy to her with betrayal to Cicero. The Roman women, then, are fundamental to Catiline's plot, just as the women who hid priests were crucial to the success of the Catholic mission.

Aurelia, like many recusant wives, works in concert with her husband, but her role must not be suspected.[181] Catiline tells her that his fellow conspirators "must not see, / How farre you are trusted with these priuacies" (1.188–9). Sempronia too operates independently, writing letters in support of Catiline's bid for the consulship, but she works at night. Just as her beauty may be artificial, so her writing may be an unnatural act of feminine rhetorical skill and political participation. Dolan observes that the play depicts women as underminers from within who cannot be trusted by either side, noting that they are never punished for their roles in the conspiracy, and thus, "Jonson's depiction of female traitors is as uncertain as his own shifting and irrecoverable relationship to Catholicism."[182] Women, and particularly Catholic women, may conceal their personal ambitions under a veneer of religious virtue and ethical action.

The play further suggests their covert roles in keeping the old religion alive by the way in which, like Catiline, they seem to be promised a ghostly afterlife. Act 2 begins with Fulvia complaining of a noxious odour in her rooms that recalls the "dire vapor" (1.12) that characterizes Sylla's ghost, while Sempronia approves Fulvia's tooth powder because of its pleasant scent. In Act 3, when Fulvia confides her secret to Cicero, she tells him that

> The extreme horror of it almost turn'd mee
> To aire, when first I heard it; I was all
> A vapor, when 'twas told me: And I long'd
> To vent it any where. (3.288–91)

Fulvia's assertion that she has become "all / A vapor" after hearing of the plot seems to prefigure her actual disappearance from the play at the end of the next act. Ironically, however, Cicero goes on to suggest that her fame will last not merely while she lives,

> But dead, her very name will be a statue!
> Not wrought for time, but rooted in the minds
> Of all posteritie: when brasse, and marble,
> I, and the *Capitol* it self be dust! (3.352–5)

However, this promised memorialization is as immaterial as the ghost in Act 1, and Cicero conveniently forgets Fulvia once she has supplied him with her information. Jonson's audience, however, might recall that in his speech at Garnett's trial, Northampton, conflating two different Fulvias, allowed her the final revenge of "thrusting needles into the tongue of *Cicero* (after hee was dead)" not for this memory lapse but for "his sharpe inuectiues against / *Anthonie*."[183] Female ambition, like its male counterpart, has a lengthy afterlife.

While it is to ambition rather than religion that Jonson attributes Catiline's plot – and, by extension, the Gunpowder Plot – both sides claim the stamp of providential approval. Directing his first address not to Catiline but to the city of Rome itself, Sylla's ghost seems to delight in cataloguing Catiline's crimes, both past and future, although he claims to speak not for himself but on behalf of "*Fate*," which will have Catiline "pursue / Deedes, after which, no mischiefe can be new" (1.43–4). In the opening of his first speech, Catiline too exults that Rome's fate has been "decree'd" (1.73), but he maintains a pragmatic attitude towards religion, using it to stoke the fires of ambition in Lentulus by hiring "flatt'ring AVGVRES" (1.139) to interpret "a vaine dreame, out of the SYBILL's bookes" (1.135) or to ensure the loyalty of his followers through the theatrical gesture of drinking a sacrament with a slave's blood.[184] As they await this ceremony, the conspirators debate the meaning of a series of providential signs – unnatural darkness, groans that seem to come from the city itself, and finally the fiery light above the Capitol – uncertain whether these portents predict their success or failure. While Catiline insists that Providence, or Fate, is on his side, so does Cato. In Act 3 when the Chorus announces that "The voice of CATO is the voice of *Rome*," Cato responds: "The voice of *Rome* is the consent of heauen" (3.60–1). Cicero too believes that the gods would not "sleepe" (3.389) while the state they founded is endangered. As Cato and Cicero dispute their response to the treason at the end of this act, Cato uses the sudden onset of thunder and lightning to threaten Cicero: "The gods / Grow angrie with your patience" (3.836–7). Doomed to death, Lentulus tells Cicero: "'Twas a cast at dice, / In FORTUNES hand, not long since, that thy selfe / Should'st haue heard these, or other words as fatall" (5.588–90). Petreius, recounting Catiline's final battle, claims that the day grew dark "and *Fate* descended neerer to the earth" (5.635) as the final confrontation approached. Among the evils of ambition, Cicero declares that it "treades vpon religion" (3.251). Ambition is shared by conspirators and statesmen alike, however, and both may claim divine support for actions that are ultimately detrimental to the country. It is, after all, *not* religion that binds men to be traitors, but ambition, the common thread that ties together the Essex revolt and the Gunpowder conspiracy.[185]

Despite his reconciliation with the Church of England, Jonson seems unconvinced by the Protestant providential interpretation of the plot that both religious and secular authorities encouraged. Instead, he develops the possibility, introduced in Northampton's trial speeches, that personal and institutional ambitions were responsible. In his speech at the first trial, Northampton had represented Digby as a rebel felled by his own ambition, while at the second he had attributed Garnett's participation in the plot to the secular ambitions that the Catholic Church had developed after Gregory VII's pontificate. Thus he opened up the possibility of seeing the Catholic priests, as well as the lay conspirators, as men motivated by ambition, either for themselves or for the institution they represent. In the second half of *Catiline*, Jonson considers the problem of institutionalized ambition in the figures of both Cicero and Caesar.

Although she concluded that Cicero must represent Cecil, De Luna complained that "Cicero was a poor choice, in terms of his historical personality, of a figure intended to 'shadow forth' Cecil: Cicero had a boastful manner, while Cecil's was quiet and self-effacing."[186] Once again, she has been misled by her insistence upon one-to-one correspondences into oversimplifying the complexities of Jonson's play. The figure of Cicero seems more likely to be intended as a composite of two of the most powerful figures in the Gunpowder Plot trials – Salisbury, the politically savvy upstart, and Northampton, the learned orator obsessed with his family lineage – who had formed a mutually beneficial political alliance. Jonson was not the only one who disliked Northampton. Even before the Gunpowder Plot he had been criticized in a 1603 libel for his willingness to attend Protestant services since Elizabeth's death in exchange for a place on the Privy Council.[187] In the plot's immediate aftermath, Thomas Dekker had similarly questioned his conversion, depicting him as "*A Papist Couchant*" who "would pull down *stars*, but feares to clime" in his *Double PP* pamphlet.[188] Given Jonson's concerns with the misuse of rhetoric and oratory in the play, it is quite possible that Cicero is intended to represent Northampton as well as Cecil.[189] Moreover, while Salisbury's influence was waning by 1611 as his health failed, Northampton was busily forming a new alliance with the rising star, Robert Carr. The same opportunism that leads Cicero to compromise his moral integrity and ultimately enables the rise of Caesar leads Northampton and Salisbury to form alliances that compromise their religious principles and result in a dangerous consolidation of political influence. Such a conflation of the two politicians makes for greater "plausible deniability" and also focuses squarely upon the negative effects of ambition. In this play, Jonson has extended his satire of individual corruption in *Volpone* to an indictment of institutionalized ambition that can create an alliance even between a crypto-Catholic and an arch-Protestant.

The ending of the play returns us to the problem of containment as the plotters, without trial, are effectively sentenced *in absentia* by the Senate. The crime that Syllanus attributes to the conspirators is the very one with which the Gunpowder plotters were charged. Not only have they attempted to destroy the state from within, but they have even "sought to blot the name of *Rome*, / Out of the world" (5.439–40). Like the English authorities, Caesar determines that no special punishment should be meted out since there can be none "equall to their crimes" (5.459). Consequently, he argues for not executing the traitors. He also, however, recognizes the problems created by the alternative of banishment – forced to leave the country, the rebels will simply flock to Catiline's army. Instead he argues for an enhanced form of exile in which the state would first confiscate the estates of the guilty, then imprison them in free towns where they could have no contact with other Romans. Cato breaks the tie with his vote for death, but Catiline, like Catesby, escapes this ignominious end, dying an unrepentant rebel.

This brief scene reflects the larger problem with which the English authorities were struggling. While individual priests could be captured and executed, there seemed to be an almost endless supply of young English Catholics ready to join the Jesuit mission, thanks in part to the mothers who educated them and the devoted Catholic women who would protect them, operating in the spaces that the recusancy laws had difficulty reaching. Also effectively beyond the law were those who had fled to the Continent to practice their religion. They were, however, still subject to one of the penalties for praemunire – forfeiture of their English property.[190] This procedure enriched the government, but meant that it felt continuously threatened by communities of English Catholics on the other side of the Channel who had not only been forced to leave their homes but were also impoverished by the crown. Caesar's ideal of preventing further rebellion by segregating the exiles is clearly unattainable. Thus, Jonson points out that neither exile nor execution can effectively contain the Catholic problem, particularly as long as administrators are divided by personal ambition.

3.5 From Stage to Page: Ghosts of the Plot, 1611–88

Despite the play's initial failure in the theatre, it too had a ghostly afterlife, one that involved a generic transformation culminating in the creation of a new subgenre in the later seventeenth century. If modern critics have been somewhat slow to appreciate the play's relationship to the plot, seventeenth-century readers seem to have been less wary. G.E. Bentley's list of allusions to *Catiline* demonstrates its popularity later in the century, while De Luna has traced its continued presence in anti-Catholic contexts.[191] Most critically for our purposes, these contexts moved the ghost from drama to poetry and from tragedy to satire.

The play itself was reprinted not only in the folios of 1616 and 1640, but also in the quartos of 1635, 1669, and 1674, where it was tied to new playing contexts. The 1635 quarto reprinted the three original commendatory poems by Francis Beaumont, John Fletcher, and Nathaniel Field that had blamed the original audience for failing to appreciate the play, thus perpetuating the emphasis upon Jonson's unpopular erudition. Dispensing with these commendations, the Restoration editions substituted a prologue and epilogue, "To be Merrily spoke by Mrs. *Nell*, in an *Amazonian* Habit," that seem to have been written to increase the play's popularity.[192] In the prologue, the speaker offers herself as Muse to replace the dead poet. Although she urges men not to slight a female prologue, she directs most of her attention to courting the female members of the audience, with whom she "plots":

> *And ladies sure you'll vote for us entire,*
> *(This Plot doth prompt the Prologue to conspire)*
> *Such inoffensive Combination can*
> *But show, who best deserves true worth in Man.* (Prologue)

Like the prologue, the epilogue seems to neutralize the threat of female plotting by intimating that Jonson must have written for men, since he included none of the lighter elements of song and dance that appeal to women. She claims, alluding to his comedy *Epicoene*, that Jonson only liked one silent woman and so scorned to write for a female audience. Recognizing that women constitute an increasing segment of the theatrical audience, however, she assures them that "For all this, he did us, like Wonders prize; / Not for our Sex, but when he found us wise" (Prologue). The actress's Amazonian attire and her status as one of Charles II's mistresses nevertheless offer a counterpoint to such dismissals of female political influence.[193]

Borrowings and imitations began even before the first stage revival of the play with the 1627 print version of Fletcher's *Apollyonists.* While De Luna has catalogued Fletcher's possible borrowings, she fails to observe the significance of making Garnett rather than Catesby the ambitious plotter, a development that will have consequences for Restoration borrowings. Fletcher's poem, the first version of which was probably written about 1611, provides the first evidence that the problem of ambition had been successfully transferred from the lay to the priestly plotters, likely as a result of Northampton's trial speech. In Thomas Campion's unpublished Gunpowder epic, tentatively dated between 1615 and 1618, another of the priests, Edward Oldcorne [Hall], takes this role. When Garnett addresses the conspirators after Fawkes's capture and interprets the failure of the plot as proof that God did not sanction it, Oldcorne overrules him, insisting that a plan's merit should not be judged by its outcome. It is at this point that the ghost of Ignatius appears before the assembled conspirators to incite them to both war and treachery and to unleash the Furies to assist them.[194] Campion's epic thus moves the demonic council of Fletcher's poem to earth and adds the feature of a ghost who, like Jonson's Sylla, incites others to conspiracy and rebellion. Although the poem was not published or translated into English until the twentieth century, it indicates increasing attention both to the rebellion that was to have followed the destruction of Parliament, and to the representation of the priests as ambitious men inciting their co-religionists to further crimes. As we will see in the next chapter, the attempted rebellion only begins to appear in literature with Francis Herring's 1609 sequel to *Pietas Pontificia.*

While Bentley and De Luna focus upon borrowings in texts by Fletcher, Milton, Crashaw, and other "literary" writers, Susan Wiseman argues "that during the Civil War and Protectorate and at the Restoration, engagement with Jonson's texts was more complex and problematic than the listing of highly literary invocations suggests." She considers, instead, popular allusions to Catiline in the play pamphlets at mid-century and concludes that "insofar as these plays are returning to Jonson's *Catiline* they transform the emotional dynamic of reception, not simply from theatre performance to reading – a large transformation in itself – but from tragedy into topical satire, melding news, politics and dramatic pleasures."[195] In many cases, she cautions, it is difficult to tell whether the allusion is to Jonson's conspirator or to a more appealing Machiavellian figure.[196] We should note, however, that all of these contexts, both popular and literary, were non-performative. Unlike the plays of 1606–7, Jonson's *Catiline* entered into dialogue primarily with non-dramatic texts. While this feature is unsurprising during the Interregnum, while the theatres were closed, Fletcher's and Campion's earlier borrowings demonstrate that this shift to poetry had already occurred.

While Wiseman observes that the play regained its tragic status after the Restoration, non-dramatic borrowings and imitations continued to be mostly satiric, particularly during the religious and political turmoil of the late 1670s and early 1680s, when a series of poems in which ghostly Catholics appeared to new generations of their co-religionists, urging them on to new crimes against the Protestant state, deliberately invoked *Catiline*.[197] Many years ago, Harold Brooks compiled a list of such "fictitious ghost" poems and recommended that a history of this genre be written.[198] Despite increasing interest in literary ghosts, however, there has yet to be a comprehensive study of this phenomenon in the late seventeenth century.[199] Many of these popular poems cluster around various alleged plots late in Charles II's reign. Of them, the best known is the first of John Oldham's "Satyres upon the Jesuits," which explicitly acknowledges, although in rather derogatory terms, its debt to Jonson. Weldon M. Williams notes that the major difference between Sylla's ghost and Garnett's is that the latter addresses a "cabal" rather than a lone man.[200] As I have suggested above, Fletcher's *Apollyonists* and Campion's epic provide intermediate stages in the transformation of Jonson's classical ghost into Oldham's priestly spectre.

The lay plotters, however, could be similarly represented as spectral figures. An anonymous poem that appears to have been inspired by Oldham's has the ghost of Guy Fawkes appear before the poet on the morning of 5 November, a day celebrated by all true Protestants as the anniversary of the defeat of treacherous Catilines.[201] The immediate inspiration for the poem appears to be the Meal Tub Plot, since Fawkes wants to see Elizabeth Cellier made a saint.[202] Once again, the poem illustrates the way in which Catholic ambition could be represented by both priests and lay plotters.

A later addition to this spectral genre is the anonymous "Scylla's Ghost: An Heroick Poem: Being a Satyr against Ambition, and the Last Horrid Phanatick Plot," published in 1684 along with an ode on Charles I's "Murder." What is particularly interesting about this poem is that, although it makes no direct reference to Jonson, it brings together a variety of themes from *Catiline*, particularly the evils of ambition and its relationship to religion. The poet begins by describing the age of Saturn, before ambition broke free from the vault in which it was chained and Jove slew his father. He then narrates a series of classical and biblical events caused by excessive ambition, in which "the more base, and weaker Woman can, / ... out-do the Lordly Creature Man" for Athaliah "fir'd / With hot *Ambition*, and with *rage* inspir'd, / All branches of the Regal-Line cut down."[203] Women, however, have also been the powerless victims of ambition and the wars it caused, in which "Virgins were ravish'd, aged Matrons made / Objects of Lust, and Victims to the Blade." Now, the poet envisions Sylla's ghost "Prompting the *Catilines* of this head-strong Age / To Plots, and Treasons, and Intestine Rage." Sylla's spectre urges his "Pupils" (5) specifically to "*religious Villany*" (4). But religion, as in *Catiline*, is not so much the cause of plotting as a cover for it. Sylla's ghost advises:

> Tell them of dire Portents, and fearful Signs
> (Fit masks to cover all your black Designs)
> Of *Iago-Pilgrims*, *Armies in the Air*,
> And *Traytors*, though you tell not who or where;
> When you your selves the *real Traytors* are. (5)

Any plot may be "Cloath'd with *Religions* fairest out-side" (5) although "*Wealth* and *Interest* at the bottom lyes" (6).[204] The enemy has become not so much a particular faction as faction itself, with Catholics and puritans equally capable of fomenting rebellion for personal gain. The fall of Lentulus, who is identified with the Duke of Monmouth, Charles II's illegitimate Protestant son, compares with that of the angels.[205] The poet compliments Charles II as Caesar and ends with a warning against repeating the horrors of civil war and regicide, apparently unaware of the ambiguities of the comparison.

This anonymous poem traces to its conclusion the relationship between ambition and religion that Northampton's 1606 speech at Garnett's trial had introduced. While Northampton insisted upon narrating the development of secular ambition in the Catholic Church, Jonson and his fellow playwrights recognized that Protestant statesmen were equally capable of using institutional power for their own ends. The civil war and regicide proved that extreme Protestantism could be as dangerous to monarchy as the papal right of deposition. In 1970, Joel Hurstfield argued that the English government kept recollections of the Gunpowder Plot alive in order to justify anti-Catholicism, but more recent scholars have challenged this view, suggesting that the plot was as much an embarrassment as a boon to political authorities.[206] This analysis of plot dramas suggests that the spectacles of trial and execution failed to contain the anxieties surrounding the plot. These included not only fears of Catholic plotting but also apprehensions about a Protestant state that created and represented itself in opposition to Catholicism. As in the development of the Anglo-Latin epic, to which we turn our attention in the next chapter, satire offered the best opportunity of containment, but even this control was ultimately illusory. The spectre of the Gunpowder Plot hung over all of the conspiracies, real and imagined, of the later seventeenth century in ways that have yet to be sufficiently explored. Jonson's dramatic ghost seems to have shifted genres gradually, moving into the Latin epics of Fletcher and Campion, then back into English through the publication of Fletcher's poem in translation. From here, it moved into more popular genres, but retained its connection to classicism.

We could speculate that the generic movement from tragedy to satire reflects increasing disillusionment with political processes in the second half of the century. Similarly, the ghost's migration from the public genre of drama to Latin epic and eventually to satiric poetry may reflect a flight from the public sphere of discussion and debate to the private sphere of individual reading.[207] Jonson's view of ambition, apparently unpopular early in the century, becomes more widespread but also less available to be discussed, reflecting a withdrawal from public life. In contrast, as we will see in the following two chapters, Latin poetry written for a select courtly audience in the plot's immediate aftermath was gradually to acquire a popular audience that would give it an increasingly public role.

4 "In marble records fit to be inrold": Epic Monuments for a Protestant Nation

In the previous chapter, we considered how the public stage queried the "myth of deliverance" that James I sought to create after the plot, drawing attention to how trials and executions failed to contain the threat of Catholic ambition. Whereas playwrights from the beginning appealed to popular audiences by contesting official interpretations, aspiring poets initially reflected these interpretations back to a more select group of individual readers, including their sovereign, choosing epic, the literary form most closely associated with perpetuating myths of origin in Western society, to praise James as the founder of a new Protestant Britain, just as Virgil had glorified Augustus as the father of Rome in the *Aeneid*. Virgil's work was also a singularly appropriate model for these writers because it emphasized three of the themes already present in James's own plot narratives – providence, paternity, and memory.

In this chapter I demonstrate the uneasy construction of a founding myth through the early Latin Gunpowder epics, as poets seeking court patronage balanced flattering the new king with advising him to banish Catholics from his court. Although several Elizabethan writers had memorialized the queen's deliverances in Latin poetry, the Jacobean poets were distinctive first in the explicitly Virgilian overtones of their works, and second in employing the full potential of the genre's epideictic traditions to offer criticism as well as praise. These poems constructed the Jacobean state against a Catholic "other" through tropes of monstrosity and demonic motivation, developing a template that became available later in the century to demonize any religious or political opponent. By the second decade of the reign, as disillusionment with James's religious policies set in, more militantly Protestant poets tempered their praises with increasingly stern warnings against tolerating Catholics. Moreover, by publishing their works rather than circulating them in manuscript, they allowed their critiques to reach a broader audience. Attacking Catholicism through satire, they gradually incorporated elements from popular pamphlets such as the demonic enclave and the journey to hell; and increasingly less optimistic that Catholicism would shortly be eradicated, they allowed their poems to veer away from epic towards open-ended romance narratives. Thus, as the Gunpowder epic moved from manuscript to print and from the world of the court to the broader audience of individual Protestant readers, it focused less on the monarch's deliverance and more on those of individual Christians and the church. In *Literature and Revolution in England 1640–1660*, Nigel Smith observes that the "parliamentarian and puritan appropriation of epic theory and intentions is one of the most exciting literary events of the century, largely because it seems so very daring."[1] Nevertheless, I believe that attending to the histories of this largely neglected group of poems may illuminate the mid-century transformation of English epic from a celebration of imperial heroism modelled on Virgil to a representation of interiorized and individual republican fortitude modelled on Lucan.

4.1 Redefining the Nation: Praise and Blame in the Anglo-Latin Gunpowder Epic

Because James failed to achieve an administrative union of England and Scotland, it is easy to underestimate not only the political but also the cultural importance of this project early in his reign.[2] After 1604, parliamentary resistance to James's attempts at legislating union forced the king to focus upon symbolic representations of unity such as flags and coinage, and those who sought to flatter him recognized the value of couching their appeals in the language of unification.[3] While "orators and clerics," finding "in the Old Testament a divinely sanctioned, auspicious precedent for regal union ... likened James to David, the heroic king who commanded the loyalty of both Israel and Judah," poets revived Geoffrey of Monmouth's legend of Brutus, Aeneas's grandson and mythic founder of Britain, to celebrate not so much the birth of a united kingdom as its re-establishment. The pageants staged for James's entry into London dramatized this myth, and it continued to inform court masques into the 1630s, but it had begun to reassert itself long before James's accession – as early as the 1530s in Scotland.[4]

South of the border, however, references to Britain seldom included the northern kingdom.[5] When Henry VII "cast his accession as the fulfilment of the old prophecies, promising a renewal of ancient empire and ancient unity," he was emphasizing his Welsh descent from Cadwallader, and when his younger son assumed an Arthurian style of kingship upon taking his dead brother's place in the succession, he was also capitalizing on that heritage.[6] Although at mid-century both John Bale (*Scriptorum Illustrium maioris Brytanniæ ... Catalogus*, 1548 and 1557) and John Foxe (*Ecclesiastical History*, 1570) imagined a Britain that comprised the entire island, the alleged plotting and subsequent execution of Mary Queen of Scots in 1587 turned England against her northern neighbour in the last quarter of the century.[7] Consequently, while Spenser's *Fairie Queene* makes use of the Brutus legend, the poem's only Scot is the treacherous Duessa: "Scotland is thus presented exclusively in terms of the Catholic threat to England, one of the chief obstacles that the latter has had to overcome before she can emerge triumphant as (in Milton's phrase) 'this nation chosen before any other.'" Rather than extending Britain to include Scotland, Spenser sought "to provide an English rival to the Trojan heritage claimed by imperial Spain."[8]

As English courtiers were forced to compete for favour with James's imported retainers, hostility towards the Scots increased in the new reign and may even have fuelled the Gunpowder Plot. As Jenny Wormald reminds us, "A Scottish king and his Scottish entourage, as well as his English parliament, were the target of the Gunpowder Plotters."[9] George Blacker Morgan even hypothesizes, without presenting evidence, that the conspirators made no arrangements for governing the country because they anticipated a takeover by those grateful to have the foreigners, in Fawkes's phrase, "blown ... back to Scotland."[10] As we saw in the previous chapter, such anti-Scots sentiments also surfaced in John Day's *The Isle of Gulls*.

In Scotland, however, many Protestants sought union with England as a security measure that could protect them against Continental Catholicism, and Jason C. White, pointing to frequent references to Britain in English poems and polemical treatises written after the Gunpowder Plot, argues that in England, too, some of the godly hoped a truly united kingdom could better defy the papal Antichrist.[11] Alan MacColl also suggests that "the fundamental Protestant principle of a return to an original purity of doctrine and practice found ready analogies and parallels in the old idea of the nation's ancient British origin."[12] Nevertheless, it seems clear that not all writers envisioned the same kind of union. Whereas the Scots imagined the two nations as equal partners in a "Great Britain," the English were willing to offer Scotland only a subordinate place, if any, in their empire.

To complicate matters, antiquarian researches by William Camden and others had confirmed the fictionality of Geoffrey's history of the Britons, contested by Polydore Vergil as early as 1534. As John E. Curran observes, the discovery that the Britons had been a primitive and barbaric people rather than worthy antagonists of the Roman invaders forced Englishmen "to accept truth over self-flattery, and solidified the distinction between history and poetry."[13] In 1607, James dissolved the Society of Antiquaries, a move Derek Hirst attributes to his determination to effect cultural union even when political union eluded him.[14] If this is so, then James took seriously the need to maintain the myth of a British past for political purposes.

For his English subjects, the arrival of Mary Stuart's son, with his retinue of "barbaric" Scots and his imperial aspirations, created conflicts between their desire for patronage and their reluctance to support union with the northern kingdom. Neil Cuddy also suggests that while English assumptions of cultural superiority created some resistance to union, "opposition to the Union served the more politically sophisticated as a means of 'coded' attack on the king's Scottish entourage."[15] Unwilling to risk a direct attack on the powerful Scots of the Bedchamber, politicians like the Earl of Southampton and Edwin Sandys subverted the prospects of political union. Those seeking preferment, however, saw a chance to flatter their new monarch by celebrating in Virgilian epic the foundation of his restored Britain.[16]

Epic not only represented the pinnacle of Renaissance genres, but was also the most political. As David Quint observes: "Virgil's epic is tied to a specific national history, to the idea of world domination, to a monarchical system, even to a particular dynasty."[17] In addition to these attractions, this model offered poets seeking to praise the king in the aftermath of the Gunpowder Plot the opportunity to expand on ideas James had introduced in his own plot narratives – his providential deliverances, his literal and metaphoric fatherhood, and the workings of national memory. One of the most vivid images of the *Aeneid* is the hero fleeing burning Troy carrying his father and leading his young son by the hand. In the "Discourse" printed with his 9 November speech to Parliament, James had called the plot a parricide, describing himself as both the head and father of his country.[18] In addition, accounts of the plot almost invariably presented James literally as a father, reminding subjects that the country could now anticipate a stable succession. For Renaissance readers, the preservation of Aeneas's household gods, carried by Anchises in the flight from Troy, represented the hero's devotion to religion, but his dominant characteristic of *pietas* meant considerably more. M. Owen Lee notes that by Virgil's time the adjective *pius* "had come to mean threefold devotion to family, country, and gods."[19] To be pious is to put duty to these higher goods above one's own concerns, as Aeneas does when he abandons Dido at Carthage.[20] James claimed this kind of piety in his 9 November speech when he told Parliament that had he been killed in the explosion, he would have died in the most appropriate place for a king, while fulfilling his regal responsibilities.[21] Just as Aeneas had ultimately accepted his destiny to found a new Troy, so James has recognized in his history of miraculous deliverances his providential responsibility to restore Britain.

As the *Aeneid* suggests, however, creating a new nation entails looking backward as well as forward. Quint observes that the Trojans must relinquish their legacy of failure not by forgetting it but by rewriting it as success, demonstrating how the Trojans' battles with the Latins reverse their former defeats in the war against the Greeks. The poem thus responds to the question: how does a nation stop reliving its past failures and move on to fulfil its destiny?[22] England's deliverances (and James's) were signs of providential favour, but they also indicated a worrisome inability to overcome decisively the threat of Catholicism. England had faced a destruction equivalent to Troy's – loss of the nation's records, buildings, and monuments that would have effectively erased it from history. James's accession, the new peace with Spain, and the thwarting of the Gunpowder Plot promised a new beginning that could also end the series of Catholic plots that had begun in Elizabeth's reign. Poets thus envisioned their works as monuments to the founding of a Protestant England. But some, in their advice to the king, also recognized the practical difficulties to be overcome, and some came to believe that ultimate victory could only be achieved with the apocalypse. As we shall see, this belief resulted in a turn from epic towards romance narratives that deferred closure in later Gunpowder poetry.

Leicester Bradner observes that Latin poets began to use epic models during the Elizabethan period, particularly in panegyrics to the queen.[23] While the conventions that developed in these poems informed the demonic councils in the Gunpowder epics, they did not evoke the traditions of Virgilian epic as those addressed later to James did. Nevertheless, it is worth noting that although most modern critics refer to these poems as epics or mini-epics, their writers did not identify them as such. Francis Herring called his poem "a brief poetical outline [brevis adumbratio poetica]," while Michael Wallace described his as "A poem of joy [felicissimam carmen]."[24] Neither Phineas Fletcher nor John Milton offered generic clues to their works; however, Dana F. Sutton and Robert Appelbaum have argued that the form of Milton's poem is Alexandrian epyllion, a "mini-epic style [that] was especially serviceable for sixteenth- and seventeenth-century poets who were working on recent history, concerned with post-Reformation political and religious struggle." In Britain, this genre "had even adopted a characteristic story: a story of violence plotted, expressed, and thwarted, with victory redounding to the side of true religion, which begins with a conspiracy against the cause of true religion instigated by Satan."[25] Although the formal aspects of the Elizabethan poetry varied, this imperative to celebrate the establishment of true religion characterizes a wide range of poems including a selection on the Parry Plot – two by William Gager, one attributed to George Peele, and another by an unidentified H.D. – one on the Babington Plot by Gager, and the first book of an epic by William Alabaster describing Queen Mary's imprisonment of Princess Elizabeth. The defeat of the Armada, clearly a fitting subject for epic, inspired Thomas Campion's *Ad Thamesin* and a poem by William Watson. Glancing at some of these poems suggests several ways in which the early Gunpowder poems both emulated these examples and diverged from them.

Like the later Gunpowder Plot, Parry's attempt to assassinate Elizabeth challenged epic writers because Parry's social status prevented his representation as a heroic antagonist. Gager resolved this dilemma by penning three Horatian odes rather than attempting an epic.[26] The first poem ("IN PRODITOREM SERENISSIMAE REGINAE ELISABETHAE CAEDEM MACHINATVRVM ODE 1, 1585"), is directed against Parry, execrating him for plotting against his monarch, while the second, addressed to the queen ("IN SERENISSIMAM REGINAM ELIZABETHAM AB IMMINENTE CAEDIS PERICVLO SERVATAM ODE 2"), offers thanks for her escape. In Poem III, "AD SERENISSIMAM REGINAM ELISABETHAM VT BONVM ANIMVM HABEAT, ET TIMERE TANDEM DESINAT, ODE 3," the writer advises the queen to banish fear and rejoice, "secure both in God's protection and in the support of the Commons and Peerage" (3.13).[27] Although the threat to the queen is unspecified, the context indicates that it too refers to the Parry Plot. The focus of these poems is clearly panegyric and, in accordance with their genre, they are non-narrative. Gager also penned a series of odes on the Babington Plot, comparing it to the Catilinarian conspiracy, a move Sutton finds unsuccessful given the plot's lack of a charismatic leader (3.vii–viii).

Pareus, the poem Tucker Brooke attributes to George Peele, is more relevant to the present discussion, since it shares a number of characteristics with the later Gunpowder epics, particularly the plot's demonic origins, possibly another means of circumventing the problem of Parry's unheroic status. Patronage was clearly the poet's motive, since he concludes by hoping that when Elizabeth and other European rulers destroy Rome he may "Perhaps be famed in future as your bard [felici præcinctus tempora lauro]."[28] Like the post-Gunpowder Plot polemic that White examines, the poem advocates a pan-European war upon Catholicism, but although the opening lines evoke the *Aeneid*'s prefatory inscription, Elizabeth is to conduct this war against the Roman foxes [vulpibus] not as an English Aeneas but as a new Boadicia, yoking three lions to her war chariot and advancing with her Britons [Tuque o magnanimûm virgo sata sanguine regum, / Europæq*ue* decus, quam fata ad tanta reseruant / Munera, trigeminos curru subiunge leones: / Sublimisque incede tuis stipata Britannis, / Et tandem inuictum cœlo caput effer aperto].[29] Sutton argues that *Pareus* offered a model to later poets since "it could readily be adapted to fit a variety of historical situations."[30] In particular, by introducing demonic agency Peele had found a way to write heroic narrative poetry describing threats to the monarch by socially inferior human agents.

While Peele's poem combined realism and allegory, Campion's *Ad Thamesin* is a mythologized treatment of the Armada crisis, in which Dis, god of the underworld, provokes Spain to attack England by arousing his envy with a vision of the country's prosperity. The English victory is achieved by both the river's defensive action and the English sailors' offensive actions, but Campion does not narrate the naval engagement, perhaps again because this would involve the actions of those well below heroic status, or because it would emphasize human over divine agency. The poet ends by praising Elizabeth and praying that she may continue to protect England for many more years. This poem makes a more sustained use of the Galfridian myth, as Oceanus informs Dis: "These are the English, they are Britons from the Trojan race, who cherish peace and worship the spirit and frequent temples."[31] In contrast to the heroic and warlike Britons evoked by Gager, this is a pious and peace-loving race. The poet reiterates their piety when he concludes the story of Spain's defeat with: "So let perish whoever, soon to weep, will set sail against your shores, heirs of Brutus, long friends of the gods, sacred name, Britain."[32] The name is used in this poem to evoke a mythology, not to identify a geo-political entity.

Like these earlier texts, many of the Latin poems produced after the Gunpowder Plot's discovery participated in the culture of patronage, some surviving only in presentation manuscripts, while others, although printed for wider circulation, were dedicated to members of the court. These poems, however, are more narrative and more explicitly Virgilian, seeking to establish monuments to James's new Protestant nation.[33] Michael Wallace asserts in his *In Serenissimi Regis Iacobi* that 5 November "should be inscribed forever upon snow-white stone [niveo signandam in saecla lapillo]," while William Gager makes his poem itself a monument.[34] Gager's non-narrative *Pyramis* exists in a single presentation manuscript (BL MS Royal 12 A LIX) dedicated to James in 1608. The poet begins by addressing the king as "Magnæ Britanniæ regem," despite Parliament's 1604 rejection of James's proposed name change.[35] This gesture appears to be mere lip service, however, since throughout the poem he emphasizes England's deliverance, and at one point he makes a tactless example of "a poor exile in the remote lands of the Picts [ergo ego Pictorum si pauper et exul in oris extremis agerem]" (ll. 263–4) who might be unaware of the plot anniversary.[36] Nevertheless, he includes 5 August, along with 17 November and 25 October (the Battle of Agincourt), as a date for his monument to memorialize (ll. 194–200). Having identified London as "nova Troia" (l. 133) he represents the plot as a reversal of Troy's destruction, as the ruler of these new Trojans delivers his subjects by revealing the men and powder concealed underground.

Despite the royal dedication, however, Gager seems to have a rather unclear sense of his audience, addressing the executed Father Garnett, whose support for the papal power of deposition he deplores, through much of the poem. Gager counters Garnett's claim that he acted piously in observing the seal of confession, contending instead that "no piety permitted him to hold his silence [nulla licuit pietate tacere]" (l. 485). James demonstrates the correct kind of piety, which avoids both the Scylla of Rome and the Charybdis of Geneva. *Pietas* for Gager, then, is the Virgilian blend of devotion to religion and country for which these poets all praise James.[37]

The debt to Virgil in the narrative poems, too, extends beyond verbal echoes to a fundamental conception of the relationship between writer and reader, insisting upon the role of literature in promoting virtuous action. Brian Vickers emphasizes that in the Renaissance "the most significant topic for literature, especially the epic, was the realm of human virtue and vice."[38] For Sidney, heroic poetry was "the best and most accomplished kind" because it could move individuals towards virtuous action more effectively than moral philosophy.[39] Aeneas was a model for monarchs, since he represented all the virtues a king needed. While praising their own king as the modern inheritor of these virtues, the Latin Gunpowder poets also considered it their duty to point out his deficiencies and thus to inspire him to even nobler action.

In offering advice to their monarch, these writers drew upon two models of free speech described by David Colclough – a humanist one outlined in contemporary handbooks of rhetoric and a religious one modelled upon the Old Testament prophets.[40] None of these men held court appointments; they dedicated their poems to the king or members of the royal households in quest of such favours.[41] Advising superiors, however, was a civic duty not only for those with formal conciliar responsibilities, but for all educated men, who hoped both to aid their country and to advance their own careers by demonstrating their potential usefulness as counsellors able to administer correction with discretion. Moreover, believing that a godly nation required a godly ruler, Calvinists claimed a responsibility to chastise magistrates when their actions jeopardized God's continued favour towards England. According to Simon Adams, this Protestant ideal began to change political behaviour fundamentally as early as Edward VI's reign, when "there emerged a novel pressure group of Protestant divines and evangelical laymen more than willing to give kings and magistrates advice."[42] At this early stage in the new reign, when many believed James more accessible and receptive to counsel than his predecessor, the Gunpowder anniversary allowed subjects to solicit personal favour while tendering advice to him on religio-political issues.[43]

The most crucial question the discovery of the gunpowder raised was the effectiveness of the king's policies towards English Catholics. Whereas most Catholics attributed the plot to the severity of the penal laws, and James's failure to rescind them, Protestants generally feared the king was too lenient. Anxieties centred on the presence of Catholics and crypto-Catholics at court, both politicians such as Henry Howard, Earl of Northampton, and members of the royal household, especially the queen. In a 1607 pamphlet entitled *Lucta Iacobi*, the author, who took the precaution of signing himself simply "Univoce-catholicus," flattered James by comparing him with the patriarch Jacob, while identifying the plotters as Esaus. Although he accepted the king's caveat that not all Catholics were disloyal, he advocated banishing them all, declaring: "Away then (Sir) with too much of your olde clemencie: Clemencie, the most dangerous companion that euer your Maiesty caried about with you, howsoeuer a part desiderated in many Princes." However, the biblical analogy enabled the author to broach Queen Anne's Catholicism directly: "We see also in *Iacob* a constant & couragious zeale to reforme both [Court & Country], without exception of persons; yea, he suffered not so much as his own *Rahel* to keepe the stollen gods of her father *Laban*: what lesse can we look for of your Maiesty?" Cleverly, he quotes James's own words in *Basilicon Doron*, admonishing him as the king had advised his son, to "*begin your reformation euen at your elbow*."[44] The author claims to address the king fearlessly, since James, unlike the pope, is a Christian king, not a tyrant. If James then objects to this criticism, he brands himself a tyrant. The writer's careful rhetorical strategies, his anonymity, and the publisher's caution in displaying "*Seene and allowed*" prominently on the title page demonstrate that James was already less amenable to direct criticism; nevertheless, the author's willingness to incur these risks indicates the importance some Protestants attached to creating a godly kingdom by banishing Catholics.

In the plot's immediate aftermath, however, Protestant authors like Michael Wallace warned James more openly against favouring Catholics while praising his deliverance. Wallace, professor of philosophy at the University of Glasgow since 1601, was among the first to dedicate a Latin poem on the plot to James, publishing his *In serenissimi Regis Iacobi* in 1606.[45] He not only congratulates the king on his escape, but also compliments him on unifying the kingdoms in a poem blending fact and fiction into a dramatic narrative. For a Scot, acknowledging James as "a king to whom are subject in a united kingdom Britain, France and Ireland [regi cui unitis coniuncta Britannia sceptris, Francia, Ierna subest]" was perhaps easier than for an Englishman.[46] In the demonic council at which Satan, envying England's peace and piety, proposes the plot, he also admits to authoring the Gowrie Conspiracy and the Bye Plot, linking English and Scottish history through James.[47] Like several of the other epics, this one emphasizes the nation's deliverance through the king, and Wallace heightens the suspense by having the royal family already processing towards Parliament when "the omnipotent father to whose eyes from on high all things mortal are evident, who in his eternity governs the progress of life and of death, ruling the world with perpetual reason, looked out from Heaven upon the secret plot" (385, 387).[48] The depiction of God as father aligns him with James, whose productive fatherhood contrasts with that of the Jesuits, evil parents whose "fatherly advice [Monitus ... paternos]" (379) to Fawkes brings only the threat of destruction and chaos. Providence clearly favours James, for he has survived the Ruthvens' conspiracy, near shipwreck while bringing his bride from Denmark, and the Main Plot, in which Ralegh was implicated, shortly after arriving in England. Even Satan acknowledges the king's *pietas* (ll. 41–2) and fears it is spreading to the whole island.

Nevertheless, Wallace set a precedent for later writers by addressing a stern warning to his king:

> And so that impiety may shudder the more at the crime and mad venture, extirpate from your kingdom the abominable race (410) of the threefold monster which, infected by deadly poisons, rushes into crime and wrongdoing at the impulse of blind fury, despiser of heaven and a universal Erinnys upon earth, which dares to lay its hand upon kings and hallowed crowns with the intention of removing the clear light (415) and enveloping the wretched world in filthy darkness. (391)[49]

Although Satan dresses as a Jesuit to inspire Fawkes to commit treason, Wallace advises the king to banish all Catholics, not just members of the Society. Like many of the early writers, he identifies English exiles on the Continent, men such as Fawkes, as an ongoing source of Catholic intrigue beyond the monarch's control, but reminds the king of his responsibility to act where he does have authority.

Other early poets also complimented the king on both his deliverance from the plot and his unification of the kingdoms, although Englishmen were more reluctant to endorse union, and they too offered discreet advice. Francis Herring, a physician who had first courted royal favour by publishing a congratulatory Latin poem dedicated to "Rex Britonûm" upon James's accession, followed this performance in 1606 with a Latin Gunpowder epic entitled *Pietas Pontificia*, addressed again to his sovereign. Herring, too, dedicated his poem to James as "King of Great Britain, France and Ireland," but his title page also recognized the deliverance of "Her Majesty, Prince Henry and the whole Royal Family and also all the ranks of the kingdom assembled for the supreme meeting of parliament on the fifth of November 1605" (255).[50] After invoking his muse, the poet echoes the first line of the *Aeneid*, but he proposes to sing not of arms and a man but of a monster, Catholicism, later identified as the "monster of Latium [Latio ... monstro]" (267), thus associating it with the enemies of Aeneas's imperial designs rather than more conventionally with Rome. Historians differ in their interpretations of seventeenth-century English attitudes towards Rome. D.R. Woolf claims that "There was a space in the English mind for two Romes, both the corrupt popish Babylon of Foxe's martyrology, a Jezebel to be feared rather than studied, and the great ancient city, whose mighty past and ruinous fall inspired awe," allowing Englishmen to revere and imitate Latin literature while detesting Catholicism.[51] Curran, however, argues that "For many, the Roman Beast was one organism. Classical historiography, the Romans who invaded and occupied Britain, and the Catholics who posed such an immediate threat to England could all be aligned as the enemy of the nation." He proposes instead that reverence for classical learning acknowledged Rome's importance, while the Galfridian tradition insisted "that Rome, the most glorious of nations, had met its match with Britain. The British History positioned Britain directly beside Rome as its eternal foil."[52] In claiming the Virgilian tradition, then, authors faced the challenge of establishing England's founding as analogous, but ultimately superior, to Rome's.

Herring's text, despite complimenting James as "King of Great Britain," illustrates the difficulties of extrapolating an attitude towards union from these poems. That he uses the terms "England" and "Britain" carefully is suggested by his reference to "The Lords of England and counsellors of Britain [Angli satrapae consultoresque Britanni / concilium]" (ll. 169–70) meeting in Parliament. London is the "seat of kings and of British dominion [regum sedis sceptrique Britanni]" (269). Although not elaborated, this distinction reinforces the administrative differences between England and the remainder of the island, offering Scotland subordinate status in an English empire. While it is the British race that annoys Satan and the name of Britain that he attempts to extirpate, it is "all the Christians of England [omnes / Anglo-Christicolas] (ll. 226–7) and England itself [Anglia]" (l. 222) who would have perished.[53] Herring, then, may use the terms "Britain" and "British" to appeal to the king without committing himself to James's vision of union.

Nevertheless, Herring participates in writing the Gunpowder Plot as a founding event by focusing on the themes of providence, paternity, and memory. His account is strongly providentialist, crediting God with the deliverance when he "illuminates the king's mind with amazing shrewdness whereby he can instantly and easily, like a second Oedipus, solve the riddle [of the Monteagle letter], ambiguous in its obscure points of difficulty" (273).[54] After complimenting the entire royal family, Herring singles out Prince Henry for praise in a speech by Fawkes, who argues that if the conspirators simply assassinate James, they will still have to contend with the warlike Henry's inevitable revenge. Although still a child, "This small boy compels us to remember the powerful Henry VIII, who was the first to inflict lethal wounds upon the holy pope" (265).[55] James's son is thus both a reminder of the origins of Protestantism in England and a promise of future glory for a nation that maintains its devotion to the Reformation.

This outcome, however, depends upon the king's willingness to control his Catholic subjects. James's ability to decipher the warning letter has restrained the Catholic monster, but Herring warns that it cannot be vanquished without policy changes. Instead of expressing gratitude when James suspended the penal laws early in his reign, Catholics "began to rear their crests and be puffed up all about with ungovernable pride, to devise new turmoil and noise their loathsome voices abroad among the populace" (261).[56] Herring's strategy for discreetly advising the king is to blame Catholic pride rather than royal clemency, but the result is the same. He then extends his advice to all of his highly placed readers, warning that at least one of the conspirators had walked unimpeded through the court itself.[57] "Lords of the world," he cautions, "you are fostering dreaded Vipers in your bosoms, you who admit papists inside your dwelling" (261).[58] Herring's story of the serpent stinging its rescuer places the blame upon the snake, yet the credulous individual suffers. Alert readers might imagine an allusion to the queen's Catholicism, but Herring diffuses his critique by addressing the entire court.[59]

Publication, however, allowed Herring to address a wider readership than the court, and a few years later he enlarged his audience further. In 1609, he published a Latin sequel describing the brief rebellion in the Midlands after the gunpowder was discovered, and in the following year he seems to have authorized a translation of the original poem (an "old Historie clad in a new English coate") by an A.P., dedicating the translation to Princess Elizabeth and the sequel to John Harington of Exton, who had sheltered the princess during the rebellion and whose son belonged to Prince Henry's household.[60] Such dedications offered readers a shorthand identification of their authors as members of godly Protestant circles.[61] Herring demonstrates his godly leanings most clearly in the first part of the original poem when he credits the rumour that the plotters intended to shift the blame for their crime to the puritans. It is this aspect of the plot, Herring suggests, that makes it truly monstrous, for in the next sentence he comments: "Undoubtedly these are the wiles of the Evil Demon, not of men: to conceal a crime loathsome in its astonishing wickedness, to proclaim the innocent as guilty, punish them with extreme penalties, overthrow entire kingdoms and satiate themselves with the blood of innocents" (269).[62] At this point the conspirators intend only to blame the puritan bishops. In the 1609 sequel, however, Herring alleges a plot to incite wrath against all of the godly by having some conspirators provide Fawkes with a horse belonging to a prominent puritan, then fall upon and murder him as he flees the city after the explosion, disfiguring his corpse to make him unrecognizable. Unable to identify the man and recognizing the horse as the property of a puritan, the common people would have risen against the godly in a civil war.

Herring's decision not to dedicate these new texts to the king registers not only James's decreasing accessibility but possibly also the author's increasing frustration with the king's failure to heed earlier advice. Like others who had hoped James would promote further church reform, Herring may have turned to the militantly Protestant group forming around Prince Henry when he lost faith that James would support a godly agenda.[63] Even in translation, however, the poem did not invite a popular audience, cautioning against Catholics who use "odious speeches vaine" to spread sedition through "th'vnstable commons."[64] Herring's concerns, expressed in printed texts, about the populace's susceptibility to persuasion by factional rhetoric suggest anxiety about the composition of his own audience.

Although sharing Herring's godly Protestantism, Phineas Fletcher was more discreet in the circulation as well as the content of his work, dedicating his manuscript epic to a series of sympathetic court personages through whom he attempted to obtain ecclesiastical preferment. Shortly after graduating from Cambridge, Fletcher dedicated the earliest of three surviving manuscripts of his poem *Pietas Iesuitica* (BL Sloane MS 444, *c.*1611) to James Montagu, then Bishop of Bath and Wells, and identified by Francis Bacon as "one of the three most influential servants in the king's household."[65] Fletcher petitions Montagu on the grounds of his poverty and the bishop's acquaintance with his recently deceased father, telling him: "We are not unaware of the great assistance which you can provide for us; and you can do this not only in accordance with that favour with which the King has always embraced you, but also in accordance with that humanity which you have always embraced, and this most holy gift" (120).[66] He dedicated a roughly contemporary copy (Dobell MS) to Prince Henry, and a later revision (BL Harley MS 3196) to Prince Charles's tutor, Thomas Murray.[67] Fletcher was clearly approaching desperation by this time, for he admits that "a cruel and clearly iron-hearted necessity has driven me to this, namely, that I should take refuge in you, a man known to me only by his face and reputation; whom I have seen only once, and one bound by no obligations to me, and that fearful indeed but not without hope I should implore you for a donation."[68] Fletcher's selection of dedicatees was singularly unlucky: Montagu, although retaining influence at court until his death in 1618, seems to have done nothing for the poet; Henry died in November 1612; and Murray, whose star had been declining for several years, was dismissed for opposing the Spanish Match in 1621, the same year Fletcher finally received his living.[69] More circumspect than Herring, and operating in a new reign in 1627, in his printed text Fletcher commented obliquely on the issue of counsel rather than offering specific advice. Unlike the earlier Gunpowder epics, which focus on celebrating the plot's discovery, his is devoted almost entirely to a secret conclave (discussed below) at which Æquivocus and the Jesuits encourage Lucifer to conspire against Protestant England. Fletcher, however, implicitly contrasts this "horride Court" (1.17) with the legitimate English council the demons seek to destroy, making Parliament rather than the court the heart of a godly nation.[70] Despite concentrating more upon the plot's organization in hell than its frustration upon earth, Fletcher reiterates some of the Virgilian themes of the earlier poems in his Latin text.

Although he employs the terms "England" and "Britain" somewhat interchangeably, avoiding references to union that might have jeopardized his quest for preferment at this late date and calling his dedicatee, Prince Henry, in his dedication of the Dobell manuscript copy "loved by all the English people [Communi Anglorum omnium amori]" (121), in the Latin poem Fletcher alludes to the ancient rivalry between Britain and Rome. He also associates the Jesuits with "Latium," for Fawkes, he claims, is the offspring of a Latin mother and an English father (39).[71] As in Herring's poem, Dis is seeking to redress a past defeat, but now it is not simply the loss of Catholic England but the loss of heaven. In his opening speech, he hopes vainly that God, "forgetful of our sin, will restore us, who have fallen, to the glory to which we were accustomed and will leave to us a heaven and a throne" (5), and to this end he exhorts his followers to "take up again the weapons which you have cast down ... renew the battle-lines and redress the intermission in war" (5).[72] Æquivocus, addressing the denizens of hell, however, also complains: "Alas the hated offspring and destiny of the Britons greater than the destiny of the Latins!" (27).[73] The Roman church's loss of England thus equals the loss of heaven by the rebel angels and threatens a British takeover of Rome itself. A Jesuit inspired by Ignatius consequently proposes a plan "whereby we may be able to break those hard men, and import Latium into the Britons themselves" (35).[74] The pope praises the plan, exulting: "already I see destiny being reversed and Latium flourishing and exhausted Rome growing young once again" (37).[75] There is some ambiguity in identifying the Jesuits with both Rome and Latium, but Fletcher exploits this tension to represent England as consistently successful, both as the heir of Aeneas's victory over the Latins and in the English church's projected ascendancy over the Roman.[76]

Fletcher was not the only aspirant attempting to gain court favour through a Gunpowder poem during the century's second decade. Thomas Campion, most likely between 1615 and 1618, offered to James a manuscript epic, *De Pulverea Coniuratione*, possibly in an effort to rehabilitate a reputation he had tarnished by writing a masque for the Howard/Carr wedding.[77] David Lindley notes that both of the royal dedications indicate the poet's desire to write in panegyric mode, but even in a text so clearly intended to court royal favour Campion does not scruple to remind James of his religious duties.[78] As the plotters dig their mine, Protestantism, "the heavenly Religion" (59), prays at Elizabeth's tomb that God will protect James for preserving true religion as he did Elizabeth for restoring it. Campion delivers his advice both discreetly and authoritatively through Sir Thomas Egerton, who concludes his parliamentary speech on 9 November 1605 by asking: "O mildest of kings, how far will you tolerate such ills? What bound will your ill starred patience set? Now mildness is harmfull, and unpunished the evil will increase, until, too late to remedy, it has finally turned into a disaster"

(79).[79] Ventriloquising his concerns through the mouth of this influential advisor would have been a particularly safe strategy after Egerton's death in 1617, and one that allied Campion with religious moderates rather than radicals.[80] The text, however, remained unpublished and untranslated until the twentieth century, its survival in a single presentation manuscript ensuring it an exclusive readership.[81]

Campion's epic tells the traditional story based upon James's account, but like the earlier sequel to Francis Herring's poem it narrates the Midlands revolt, for which the poet makes the Jesuits chiefly responsible. He contrasts the deliverances of England's monarchs – both Elizabeth and James – with the assassination of Henri IV in France to demonstrate God's fatherly providence towards England. Conversely, the Jesuits are evil fathers who poorly advise their spiritual sons and abandon them to their fate after inciting them to rebellion. Remembering other nations' failures as well as his own's successes, Campion shows how understanding its past is necessary to a nation's future health.

If the Gunpowder epics had ever been successful instruments for obtaining patronage – and we have no evidence that any of these authors benefitted substantially through their efforts – that time had now ended. James's plans for political union were long dead, and his lukewarm support for his Protestant daughter and son-in-law, along with his now public plans to marry his heir to a Catholic princess, declared that he was unlikely to favour the increasingly strident Protestantism and anti-Catholicism of these texts. Furthermore, growing consolidation of patronage in Buckingham's hands limited the effectiveness of royal dedications. With the exception of Milton's *In Quintum Novembris*, written probably as an academic exercise, there would be no more new Gunpowder epics. Instead, English translation and pamphlet culture would reshape the genre by simultaneously broadening its social reach and narrowing its religious appeal.

4.2 Radicalizing the Narrative: The Protestant Epic

Since many of these generic changes resulted from contact between Latin and vernacular texts, we must turn to some of the commemorative poetry written in English immediately after the plot's discovery. While those with court connections represented the plot as an attack upon the king and feared the insidious corruption of court Catholicism, authors outside these circles primarily feared domestic unrest in the plot's immediate aftermath. The authors of two English poems, however, seem to have sought to obtain both favour from members of the court and popularity with puritan print audiences. Richard Williams's "Acclamatio Patriae" survives in a collection of three poems, apparently in his own hand, that he presented to the king (BL MS Arundel 418).[82] The poem is undated but seems to have been written fairly soon after the plot, since Williams claims to have had a copy licensed for the press, "seynge no other had written thereof," but was unable to afford the cost of printing.[83] He also complains that he had given Prince Henry a copy when the royal household was in progress through Nottinghamshire, but had received no word of its reception.[84] Thus, like the Latin poets who printed their works, Williams seems to have hoped both for royal patronage and the benefits of print publication. Since the accompanying two poems are on the Babington Plot and Essex's execution respectively, he may have recognized the king's desire to see his deliverance as a sequel to Elizabeth's. Williams signs himself as the king's "poore Distressed Subiecte," leading to speculation that he may have been a deprived clergyman attempting to regain favour, but nothing more is known of him.

For Williams, the pursuit of favour seems to preclude criticizing the king. Although he makes an oblique reference to Northumberland that indicates his awareness of suspected Catholics at court, he minimizes the role of religion in the plot and offers instead conventional warnings about the dangers of rebellion, focusing upon the plot's potential to have harmed ordinary people and brought about "generall ruyne" (l. 113), particularly a suppression of "godlie lawes" (l. 348). Addressing the plotters directly, he reminds them of their duty to obey even a bad king. All of the traitors, except Fawkes, are motivated by ambition that has been fired by religious zeal. Catholics have been taught to preach treason, and now their pulpit has become the gallows, "A pulpitt where manye haue preached before, / that haue bene traytors agaynst kinge and state" (ll. 442–3).[85] But the guilty include not only those who have been executed, for

> tis thought there bee some of greater states
> that haue bene agents and Dealers therein:
> Tis pittie that ever by suche base mates
> they shoulde bee counselde to suche deadlie synne,
> Or that anye peere shoulde bee sene therein,
> To ecklipse the glorye of Honored fame,
> And bee scandalizde *w*ith touche of the same. (ll. 512–18)

A plot in which commoners have embroiled a peer, presumably Northumberland, inverts the proper social order.[86] Satan was the first traitor, "By polecye turninge darknes to light" (564) and since then, "aspiringe myndes" (607) have never been contented, even when ruled by a king as merciful as James. The poem thus warns would-be traitors to accept their stations and avoid dealings with rebels. Williams ends by rehearsing the qualities for which the king should be praised, particularly his desire to maintain peace abroad and his care for the poor at home.

Like Williams, Robert Pricket, a self-described soldier, saw in the Gunpowder Plot an opportunity to mend strained relations with authority. Pricket had displeased the Privy Council by publishing a panegyric on the second Earl of Essex in 1604, and his release from prison had required Salisbury's intervention. Returning to a loosely connected set of verses he had written several years earlier threatening England with apocalypse should her people continue sinning, Pricket added a thanksgiving for the king's deliverance and a diatribe against Catholics, calling specifically for the removal of the archpriest, George Blackwell, from England. Sprinkling the text liberally with references to a united Britain was doubtless intended to impress Salisbury, to whom he sent a manuscript copy.[87] The 1606 printed version was followed the next year by a poem refuting the various miracles ascribed to the executed priests.[88]

Unrestrained by the need to curry favour, two English authors writing for less educated audiences described an attack on Protestantism by Continental Catholicism. The more literary of the two poems is I.H.'s *Divell of the Vault or the Unmasking of Murder*, which begins with an invocation to Melpomene.[89] As we shall see in the later case of John Vicars, calling the plot a tragedy situates it within an ongoing Protestant struggle in which ultimate victory remains conditional upon religious reform rather than as a unique founding moment. Blaming the Jesuits for having corrupted the Catholic laity, the author reminds his readers of earlier Catholic atrocities, both domestic and foreign, including the Paris massacre, the Marian persecutions, and Henri III's murder, as well as a German plot involving gunpowder.[90] Placing the plot in an international context, I.H. suggests that the Protestant Church, rather than the English state, was the target when "The *Papists* through large *Europe* ranged, / the *Protestants* to sley" (B4^{v}).[91] Yet England does hold a special position in God's sight, for had the plot been successful,

Then *Britons* Angel-garded gates,
    had opened to their hand:
And entrance made for forraigne powers,
    to ruinate the land.[92]

Ambiguously, England is both an insular Eden, protected by God's messengers from foreign invasion, and part of a Protestant Europe. Not content with placing England under foreign domination, the plotters would then have

Brought *Gospellers* and *Protestants*,
    to vndeserued shame:
Diuulging by their forg'd declaimes,
    that they had wrought the same.[93]

The rumour that the plotters would have blamed the puritans for their crime seems to have been fairly widespread in the immediate aftermath of the discovery, but occurs in none of the Latin texts except Francis Herring's, where the plotters intend to implicate only the puritan bishops. I.H. appeals to both king and commoners to stand fast against Rome, thus making both the ruler and ordinary individuals responsible for the kingdom's godliness. In this poem, however, the principal threat remains outside the state and the poet directs no specific advice to the king.

Also published in 1606, John Rhodes's doggerell poem, *A Briefe Summe of the Treason intended against the King*, which offers news to a semi-literate audience, similarly insists upon Jesuit complicity and claims the plotters had prepared a proclamation alleging puritan responsibility.[94] Rhodes, a minister at Enborne, seems to have possessed a ready-made hatred of Jesuits, which may account for his eagerness to vilify them.[95] Like I.H., he emphasizes that the plotters planned on subjecting England to foreign domination. Although acknowledging that the traitors were English, he claims the treason began "beyond Sea" and implicates both Hugh Owen and William Stanley, evoking the familiar suspicion of English exiles on the Continent.[96] The conspirators are both human and demonic, for "Prince of darkenes, and hels blacknes, / was their leader: / *Piercy* Papist, masked *Atheist*," while Fawkes is "Sathans Sonne."[97] Rhodes does briefly narrate the story of the Midlands revolt, in which the traitors, driven by madness and "like Wilde-men," attempt resistance and are burned by their own gunpowder before being killed or captured.[98] Rather than advocating their banishment, he recommends that English Catholics become as loyal as puritans, which can only happen if Protestants recall their deliverances from the Armada, the Gowrie Conspiracy, and the Gunpowder Plot, and teach them to their children. Individuals can also contribute to the country's well-being by praying for the royal family. Both of these poems seem to have been written to offer sensational versions of the story to the poorer classes and to stir up anti-Catholicism by spreading the rumour that the plotters planned to incriminate the puritans. At the same time, they reflect back the conventional messages about the relationship between loyalty and religious conformity that commoners received through the *Homilies* and sermons as well as in other popular media such as ballads.[99] Directed to unlearned, and largely puritan, audiences, they emphasize the individual's role in safeguarding England from the threat not of ambitious nobles who could become tyrants, but of foreigners and English Catholic exiles anxious to reimpose Catholicism by force rather than stealth.[100] Perhaps most significantly, they perceive the plot's primary targets not as the king and state but as the church, specifically its godly wing, and the people.

Herring's sequel to his 1606 epic as well as A.P.'s English translation of the original Latin poem similarly nudge the text away from courtly concerns towards a more popular, and puritan, orientation. This process accelerated in 1617 when John Vicars, a presbyterian usher at Christ's Hospital, published a "very much *dilated*" English translation of both parts of the poem, appealing to a broad audience ranging from those who could translate his Latin marginalia to those requiring annotations to identify events in English history. Vicars offers no rationale for selecting this particular text to translate, but given its multiple editions it was probably the best known of the Gunpowder poems, and it was the only printed Latin poem to narrate the Midlands revolt. Herring's godly credentials may also have recommended it to Vicars, and he enthusiastically expanded upon the rumour of a plot to blame the puritans. His two editions, in 1617 and 1641, both opened the poem to a wider audience and increasingly circumscribed its interpretation by adding paratextual materials as well as by "dilating" the original text. Although Herring survived until 1628, he does not seem to have actively participated in the 1617 publication, thus allowing Vicars to begin the appropriation of the text that he effectively completed in 1641, transforming the poem from court panegyric into godly propaganda.[101]

Vicars (1580–1652) is probably best known for the series of pro-parliamentarian newsbooks he authored during the civil wars, but he was a relatively prolific writer and translator throughout his life, although partisanship coloured seventeenth-century reception of his work.[102] Anthony à Wood claims that Vicars "was esteemed among some, especially the puritannical party (of which number he was a zealous brother) a tolerable Poet, but by the Royalists not, because *he was inspired with ale or viler liquors.*" Most modern readers concur with the royalist view of Vicars's poetic talents, no matter the source of his inspiration. Brought up as an orphan at Christ's Hospital, he returned there after three years at Oxford, spending the remainder of his life at the school, where much of his literary output consisted of translation, including an English Virgil.[103] When translating contemporary Latin poetry, Vicars seems to have followed a pattern of appropriation. Although he identifies himself on the title page of his 1624 translation of George Goodwin's anti-Catholic *Babel's Balm* as "*the* Muses most unworthy *Eccho*" and includes a translation of Goodwin's dedicatory epistle to Robert Naunton, he also inserts his own dedication to William Lord Herbert, a greeting to Catholic readers, an acrostic to the author, a letter "To the Ivdiciovs and Covrteovs Reader," and a commendation by Thomas Salisbury.[104] During the Laudian era Vicars, like William Prynne, conflated formal Protestantism with Catholicism, while by the 1640s he identified both separatists and Catholics as Babylonians.[105] In his later years he engaged in increasingly vitriolic condemnations of the regicides. Thus, the civil wars apparently challenged the faith in individual Protestants that he had asserted in his translations of Herring's poem, leading him to reaffirm the monarch's role in a national, although more reformed, church.

Vicars introduces his 1617 translation with a letter to "All the Loyall-hearted Protestants of England" and a sheaf of commendatory verses that evokes a godly network of writers and readers. Removing the poem entirely from its court context, Vicars expresses little faith in the king to provide godly leadership. Although, he says,

t'is granted that that Letter
Was the first instrument of our blest peace:
Yet certainely little t'had beene the better,
If *God* had not so caus'd that worke to cease
Of vndermining that great Capitoll
By reason of the thicke and stony wall.[106]

Not only does Vicars reduce James's agency in the discovery, but he even deletes Herring's lengthy tribute to the militant Prince Henry.[107] The poem ends not with assurances of Protestant victory, but with Satan vowing to continue undermining England with the help of "choice friends in Court, *Romes* champions bold."[108] Perhaps less explicitly than Fletcher, Vicars situates the court not as the site of godly rule but in opposition to a Protestant God.

While Vicars addressed his criticism of the court to all Protestants, a decade later Fletcher remained ambivalent about popular political participation in the expanded English version of his epic, dedicated to the wife of Francis Bacon's nephew Sir Roger Townsend.[109] Despite having established his career, Fletcher seeks to ingratiate himself with his new monarch using the familiar formula combining praise and advice. His poem concludes by commending Charles for taking up a sword rather than a pen in the Continental religious wars:

Thy royall Sire to Kings this lecture red;
This, this deserv'd his pen, and learned veine:
Here, noble Charles, enter thy chevalrie;
The Eagle scornes at lesser game to flie;
Onely this warre's a match worthy thy Realmes, & Thee. (5.39)

As in the early Jacobean epics, however, flattery anaesthetizes a sting. Fletcher's Æquivocus's Jesuit disciple begins his English conquest by sending priests to gain the confidence of women. Published shortly after Henrietta Maria's arrival with her entourage of Capuchins, the poem revives anxieties about Catholic women at court, implicitly warning Charles against following his father's tolerant policy.[110] If Fletcher portrays English women as credulous, his attitude towards ordinary Protestants remains uncertain. Æquivocus, who can impersonate both courtier and priest, is admired by "the vulgar rout," the "silly Commons" (2.9) in hell who are spellbound by his oratory. Does Fletcher, like Herring, distrust England's lower orders who can be duped by rhetoric, or is Æquivocus's attitude part of his villainy?

While Fletcher may still have hoped to influence Charles, Vicars had clearly determined to seek reform elsewhere by the time he began attempting to publish a new translation of Herring's poem, possibly as early as the late 1620s.[111] In his revised letter "To All Loyall-Hearted English Protestants," Vicars adds a lengthy marginal note excoriating Dr Samuel Baker for refusing to license his "Historie" on the grounds that "we were not so angrie with the Papists now a dayes."[112] He also claims that both Oxford and Cambridge refused to license the poem, making a reference to Thomas Crosfield that dates these efforts after 1627, when Crosfield was elected a fellow.[113] Prynne, however, situates Vicars's initial attempts to publish the poem in the aftermath of the 1637 Star Chamber decree that required writers to obtain new licenses to reprint previously licensed texts.[114] As Gerald MacLean suggests, Vicars uses the story of his struggle to publish the poem as evidence for the country's failure in gratitude to God, which he predicts will lead to disaster if unchecked. MacLean also notes the way the letter is structured, so that

> [a]fter the easy flow of the call to prayer in the opening three stanzas, the verses turn at the emphatic admonition of '*Abundance does us cloy*' to become, themselves, increasingly clogged by parenthetical struggles with syntax in the effort to demonstrate how the history of the poem that follows is itself part of the history of struggle for control of the nation's memory.[115]

According to Vicars, not only have people forgotten the plot, but now, led astray by Catholic and crypto-Catholic propagandists, they deny that it occurred.

Vicars's poem, eventually published in 1641, seeks remedy for the evils of the court not from Parliament, as Fletcher had, but from the common people, asking his "good Reader[s]":

> O English Protestants, why stand you still,
> As if *affraid* to *curbe* Romes cursed will?
> Why seem ye (yet) to hault twixt *two opinions*,
> Pretending *truth*, fostring these Romish *Minions*?[116]

Removing the injunction to rulers and peers not to harbour snakes in their dwellings, he charges his ordinary Protestant readers with responsibility for ridding the country of Catholics. By abridging stanzas in praise of Elizabeth and even depriving James of the epithet "pious," Vicars reduces the role of a godly monarch in the nation's religious life while elevating that of the people.

Whereas the Latin poems praising Elizabeth had lauded her especially for providing the gospel to her subjects, James was praised initially for ensuring dynastic stability that would preserve such access. Writers whose desire for patronage overcame their sometimes ambivalent attitudes towards Anglo-Scottish union used the occasion of the Gunpowder Plot to present James with a founding myth for this new Protestant Britain. Their personal and political aspirations unfulfilled, some exposed their works to readers beyond the court through publication and translation, making their critique of James's court accessible to both larger and more diverse audiences. As the initiatives for which James had been praised, particularly the peace with Spain and the union of the kingdoms, became sources of contention, the hotter sort of Protestants came to dominate the tradition and began looking not to a godly monarch but to their co-religionists for solutions to the nation's religio-political troubles. Reinterpreting the plot as an attack not upon the king but upon the English church became divisive as these writers, and their readers, began to see the king not as providing religious stability but as impeding further ecclesiastical reform.

4.3 Demonizing Catholicism: Monstrosity and the Catholic Other

Authors of both Latin and English poems describe the Catholic threat through a discourse of monstrosity, frequently depicting the plot as a monstrous birth. Although a traditional feature of romance narrative, the monsters here serve the polemical purpose of reinforcing the need to eradicate English Catholicism.[117] Representing the Roman church as an evil mother indicates anxieties about the perpetuation of the Catholic faith in England through wives and mothers who resist conforming but avoid recusancy penalties.[118] Like these women, English priests are monstrous because they fail to reconcile their religious and political identities. Difficult to recognize and contain in daily life, Catholicism could be safely dismissed in literature by labelling its practitioners as monstrous "others." At the same time, however, the seventeenth-century perception of monsters as portents fortelling the apocalypse complicated attempts to dispel the threat of English Catholicism that the Gunpowder Plot represented.

Unlike Wallace and Fletcher, who began their poems with demonic enclaves, Herring chose to locate the origin of the plot in a union between Satan and the Whore of Babylon that produced Guy Fawkes. His feminized representation of the pontiff as the Whore of Babylon belongs to a tradition with a lengthy and complex history. In her study of Catholicism and gender in seventeenth-century print culture, Frances Dolan observes that the phrase "Whore of

Babylon" "yokes together the familiar seduction and corruption of the unruly feminine and the more outlandish threat of the foreign," and suggests that "[b]y persistently associating the Roman church with fallen women, reformers could acknowledge its seductive appeal while simultaneously repudiating it."[119] As both Dolan and Arthur Marotti have noted, recusant women caused persistent uneasiness because they failed to accept the religious authority of the state, and sometimes of their husbands.[120] Fletcher's Gunpowder epic demonstrates how Rome's threat could be feminized. In his English poem, which is more anti-feminist than the Latin version, the seduction of English women by Jesuit priests, spiritually if not physically, and the parallel decline of the Roman church replicate the falls of the angels and the first couple. Æquivocus , addressing the demonic parliament, tells first how he has painted over the decayed Whore to fool the "drunken nations" (2.32) who cannot distinguish the true from the false, and then how priests in England

> with practicke slight
> Crept into houses great: their sugred tongue
> Made easy way into the lapsed brest
> Of weaker sexe, where lust had built her nest,
> There layd they Cuckoe eggs, and hatch't their brood unblest. (2.34)

Just as a union between Eve and Satan produces the deformed Sin, so the priests have worked through women to instigate the Gunpowder Plot.[121] While Fletcher portrays the Whore as a temptress, Herring casts her primarily as an unnatural mother.

Although the former depiction was more common in polemical literature, Craig M. Rustici's study of representations of Pope Joan in this period traces a tendency to conflate the legend of the female pope with that of the Whore of Babylon and thus to make the Whore also a mother. Rustici notes that Protestants employed the Pope Joan legend cautiously during Elizabeth's life, since Catholics might accuse the queen of pretentions to clerical supremacy in the English church. Persistent rumours that Elizabeth had given birth to illegitimate children also sparked attempts to link her to both Pope Joan and the Whore.[122] Thomas Dekker's play *The Whore of Babylon*, in which the Spaniards' ships are described as pregnant with soldiers, and frequent comparisons of the Gunpowder Plot to an unnatural birth demonstrate the evils associated with Catholic maternity.[123] The plot provided particularly rich opportunities for employing the trope of monstrous birth, since the plotters' tunnelling under the earth offered a disturbing image of subversive burrowing into the womb of the mother country.[124] In his 1617 expansion of Herring's poem, Vicars has the plotters actually formulating the details of the treason below ground, a particularly sinister image highlighting England's vulnerability (24).

Dolan notes that

> Protestants associated Catholicism with the stranger ... by associating it, in subtle and inconsistent ways, with monstrosity, contamination, and blackness. When this association was made, it was often via imagery of "unnatural" congress, not between individuals but between abstractions, resulting in monstrous conceptions. Catholic plots were widely described as monstrous births.[125]

I suggest, however, that the monsters are not so much "strangers" as they are misfits, those whose religion is incongruent with their nationality. Fawkes is the most blatant example of this problem – the Catholic son of Protestant parents and an Englishman who has soldiered in a foreign army – but the priests too are men who have lived abroad and embraced an alien religion.[126] In a state that assumes confessional conformity from the beginning of life by recording baptisms rather than births, such deviation must be represented as unnatural.[127] When describing the plot's conception, Fletcher uses the Aristotelian association of the female principle with matter and the male with form. In canto 3 of the English poem, the Jesuits hatch their plots in the frozen north, the "sacred nurseries of the Societie" (3.6), where

> Into the mint fowle hearts, sear'd conscience,
> Lust-wandring eyes, eares fil'd with whispering,
> Feet swift to blood, hands gilt with great expence,
> Millions of tongues made soft for hammering,
> And fit for every stampe, but truths defence:
> .These, (for Romes use, on Spanish anvile) frame
> The pliant matter; treasons hence diflame,
> Lusts, lies, blood, thousand griefes set all the world on flame. (3.7)

As in this stanza, Fletcher frequently juxtaposes images of monstrous birth with ones of coining, suggesting that Catholic rapacity is both sexual and financial. Moving beyond the metaphorical use of this motif, however, he narrates Fawkes's origins as a typical story of a monstrous birth:

> His frighted Mother, when her time shee went,
> Oft dream't she bore a straunge, & monstrous creature,
> A brand of hell sweltring in fire and smoke,
> Who all, and's Mother's selfe would burne and choke:
> So dream't she in her sleep, so found she when she woke. (5.9)

Pamphlets depicting such births frequently blamed maternal imagination for misshapen children.[128] The belief that an image or a dream the mother had seen during intercourse or pregnancy could render her child a monster, given the Protestant uneasiness about images, also implied idolatry, and therefore aroused suspicions of Catholicism. Traditionally, monsters were immediately recognizable by their grotesque physical characteristics and their failure to resemble their parents, particularly their fathers. In his Latin poem, Fletcher also identifies Fawkes, incorrectly, as the product of a racially mixed union between an English father and a Latin mother (39). He thus becomes monstrous not only by hybridity but also by resembling his mother rather than his father. Valeria Finucci notes that such beliefs disturbed the social order because they subverted male authority by offering women a significant role in determining both the appearance and the character of their offspring. Fletcher's publication of this version of the poem in 1627, however, suggests a threat not only to domestic patriarchy, but also to national religion and security. With a Catholic queen consort newly arrived in England, Fletcher reminds his readers that the English succession is controlled by a foreign heretic whose imagination has power to shape the royal heirs.

Julie Crawford suggests that in accounts of monstrous births "the monsters themselves are texts: their bodies are transparent to the crimes they punish, and they render the private beliefs and behaviors of early modern men and women spectacularly legible."[129] Nevertheless, responses to Luther and Melancthon's pamphlet describing the pope-ass and the monk-calf, which had forged the relationship between monstrous birth and Reformation polemic, indicated that each church could interpret physical deformities to support its own cause.[130] In response to this problem, Kathryn Brammall argues, the definition of monstrosity shifted between 1550 and 1570 to include those whose behaviour was repellent, but who had no visible deformity. Thomas Churchyard and Thomas Norton describe the perpetrators of the Northern Rebellion as monsters for their willingness to conspire with foreigners to overthrow their country, and Bacon condemns Essex's decision to treat with Tyrone against the queen's orders as "in a kind monstrous."[131] Like the Jesuits, Fawkes changes identities and names as required, becoming monstrous precisely because his deformity is invisible to the eye. The report that he walked through the court unremarked is calculated to alarm readers, who are forced to acknowledge that villainy can be concealed behind an unremarkable exterior.

Herring's Virgilian opening, "I sing of a monster – terrible, infamous, cruel, arrogant [Monstrum horrendum, infame cano, crudele, superbum]" (257), makes the monster, not the hero, the primary subject of his poem. Fawkes is "a second Proteus readily turning himself into all shapes. Each new district causes him to alter his name in accordance with the locality; his heart remains the same as does his eagerness to cause harm" (259).[132] For Herring, English Catholics are more monstrous than foreign ones: the British exiles at the Austrian court are "monsters of men, who rejoice in fishing in a sea disturbed by a swift storm [monstra hominum, pelago rapido qui turbine moto / piscari gaudent]" (263), and who can teach even a man tutored by Satan and the Whore "how to conceal crime with crime [scelere occultare docent scelus]" (263). These monsters cannot be easily recognized, classified, and deprived of power: only by punning upon the French meaning of Fawkes's name, False, can Herring assert any control over his identity.[133] Thus, representing the priests and plotters as monsters expresses anxieties surrounding Catholics and attempts to reassert the state's ability to identify individuals holding treasonous beliefs by examining their external appearances.[134]

Monstrous births, however, were also regarded as portents, and as such they represented both God's anger with his people and his willingness to delay their destruction.[135] During the Civil War, Vicars published an account of prodigies that he opened with an arresting comparison between God and Tamburlaine.[136] Like the tyrant, God hangs out a white flag urging his people to repent, but if they fail to do so, then he will display his red flag. Although Vicars admits that natural causes may explain the birth of a monstrous child, he insists such events demand religious interpretation.[137] Katharine Park and Lorraine J. Daston note that references to 2 Esdras frequently shaped sixteenth-century attitudes towards monstrous births and that these allusions fostered the beliefs that prodigies occurred in groups and foretold the apocalypse.[138] The depiction of monstrous births in the Gunpowder poems thus fosters an apocalyptic view of history that adds urgency to the writers' pleas for the king to root out Catholicism. The plot becomes not simply a narrative of a past event but an increasingly urgent warning for the future.

The link between Catholicism and the apocalypse arose from the belief that the pope was the Antichrist, which seems to have become common during the Elizabethan period; however, both Bernard Capp and Peter Lake note variations in the deployment of this identification. Capp traces the development of apocalyptic nationalism to the Armada crisis, arguing that the distinction between the true and false churches made by John Bale and popularized in the Geneva Bible and Foxe's *Acts and Monuments* fostered it.[139] Most people consequently accepted Rome's status as a false church, although it was not official church doctrine. Lake, however, distinguishes between the polemical representation of the pope as the Antichrist found in the writings of divines like John Whitgift, and the politicized views of those like William Whitaker, for whom this belief was an "organising principle" requiring a teleological view of history as a struggle between the opposing forces of God and the Antichrist, Protestantism and Catholicism. Throughout the 1620s, as James sought a Catholic match for his son and religious war raged on the Continent, the English church inched towards recognizing Rome as a true but erring church and rejecting the pope's identification as Antichrist, thus relinquishing apocalypticism to the church's most radical elements.[140]

In his English Gunpowder epic, Fletcher depicts the church of Rome as "Clens'd, spous'd to Christ, yet backe to whoordome fel" (1.1), suggesting that Rome cannot regain her status as a true church, for "Fa[l'n]e Heaven's a double hell" (1.1), and his numerous marginal references to the books of Revelation and Daniel highlight his apocalyptic interpretation of the Gunpowder Plot. None of the other epic authors situates the Roman church so carefully or suggests Rome was ever a true church. Milton's depiction of the Roman procession in *In Quintum Novembris*, with the pope carrying his "gods made of bread [Panificosque eos portat]" (17) in what appears to be a parody of Anchises carrying Aeneas's household gods in the flight from Troy, reminds his readers that the Catholic Church rests upon the erroneous doctrine of transubstantiation.

This anti-papal apocalypticism connects with another important change occurring in the Gunpowder poems over time. Capp and Paul Christianson both note that while John Bale had supported the central role of the people in initiating the reformation necessary to thwart the Antichrist, most Elizabethans continued to trust the godly monarch to reform the church.[141] These authors argue that although the Martin Marprelate pamphlets attempted to turn the apocalyptic tradition against the English bishops, not until separatism began to flourish did a significant part of the population cease to place its trust in a godly monarch. The differences between the Latin Gunpowder poems and their later English translations, however, complicate this view. As we have seen above, while the early Latin poems emphasize the king's responsibility for eradicating Catholicism and keeping the nation safe, the English poems offer individuals a greater role in protecting the Protestant nation. As the Latin poems were translated and popularized, they increasingly called upon their ordinary readers to protect English Protestantism, an idea Milton seems to endorse through his favourable portrait of Fama in *In Quintum Novembris*.[142] The Gunpowder epics thus trace the erosion of trust in a godly monarch to prevent the papal Antichrist from subverting the English church.

4.4 Demonic Enclaves: The Marriage of Epic and Satire

Perhaps the clearest sign of the apocalyptic perspective in these poems is the affinity their writers assert between the plotters, the Catholic Church, and the denizens of hell. While the journey to hell and the demonic enclave had lengthy histories in Latin and Continental epic, I want to suggest that in the later Gunpowder poems these fused with a tradition of vernacular prose satire describing

Roman councils and journeys to hell that had grown up in the late sixteenth and early seventeenth centuries. This fusion of the two traditions, I argue, contributed to changes in epic later in the century. Beginning with the 1610 translation of Herring's poem, the Gunpowder epics increasingly opened themselves to satiric impulses that would appear in later works such as *Paradise Lost*, first through their juxtaposition with epigrams, and second by representing demonic councils.[143]

Whereas writers initially used the brief epic primarily to praise the king and secondarily to denigrate the plotters, epigrams generally sought to puncture the plotters' pretensions and less frequently served a panegyric function.[144] Estelle Haan observes that the "established genre of epigram enabled an author to treat of a single idea in terms and tones that were frequently sardonic, ironic, or marked by invective, attack, rhetorical question and exclamation."[145] In contrast to the expansive epic, the epigram was short, written in a plain style without rhetorical figures, and frequently culminated in a witty, pointed conclusion.[146] It could also treat unheroic figures such as the plotters, whose social status made them unsuited to loftier genres. Early Latin epigrams on the plot sometimes appeared as part of miscellaneous collections, as Sir John Stradling's and James Johnson's did, or with other plot-related texts, as Thomas Cooper's did; however, their frequent pairings with epic are of particular interest here.[147]

Herring appears to have initiated this tradition, which Campion followed by appending five epigrams to his manuscript epic. Herring's lengthy epigram first appeared in the 1609 sequel to his original poem along with a miscellany of concluding matter, but was not included with the 1610 translation, leaving Vicars to provide the first English version in 1617. Both Milton and Richard Crashaw wrote brief epigrams on the plot, apparently at the same time as their longer works. Although their epigrams probably arose from the setting of themes in an academic environment, whereas Herring's and Campion's are drawn from the culture of London and the court, their themes are remarkably similar.[148] Mary Thomas Crane suggests that the early sixteenth-century reformers used the model of the Pasquinade to develop the type of epigram that would become, by later that century, "a vehicle for increasingly serious criticism of the Roman Catholic church." Unlike classical epigrams, pasquils usually named their victims, and sought both to embarrass public figures and to "call attention to the vices rampant in the Roman church."[149] This tradition of satirical but morally serious epigrams seems to be the one in which the Gunpowder Plot epigrammatists worked. Lawrence Manley observes that epigrams about urban life reflected an urge to categorize people, and consequently expressed uneasiness about marginal individuals who refused to be confined neatly to a single group.[150] As we have seen above, the Jesuits' ability to disguise themselves and their reliance upon equivocation rendered them a source of anxiety. Along with the discourse of monstrosity, then, satire was a way of expressing the uneasiness created by a group of Englishmen who belonged to a foreign organization that made them outsiders in their own country and necessitated the use of dissimulation. The very length of the epigram appended to Herring's poem suggests a failure to contain the Jesuit threat.[151]

In Vicars's translation, the Jesuits are guilty of the five D's with which Coke had charged them at Garnett's trial: "In *Daunting* subjects; in *Dissimulation*; / To *Depose*, *Dispose*, Kings, Realms, *Devastation*."[152] The poem begins and ends with the conventional complaint that Jesuits have no right to use the name of Jesus when their behaviour contradicts Christ's teachings. Throughout, the author depicts the Jesuits as actors who "play their parts" (98) and "with *religious shows*, shelter *foule-crimes*" (99). Garnett's failure to disclose the plot is bad enough, but praying for its success makes him truly monstrous.[153] Similarly, Herring speculates on whether the civil crime of blowing up a kingdom and destroying a monarch or the religious sin of taking the Eucharist while planning the crime is more reprehensible. Vicars's translation jests that the Jesuits can "Most properly be called the *Kings-evill*" (101), a double-edged pun since the king was supposed to be able to cure scrofula, provided he was willing to do so.[154] Vicars appears to be questioning the king's commitment to curing the Jesuit problem.

While Herring's lengthy epigram comes closer to invective, the shorter, more pointed epigrams appended to the other poems seem to be poised uneasily between the desire to diminish the plotters by ridiculing them and the recognition that Rome poses a serious threat to England. The primary conceit of Milton's four epigrams on the plot is that the recently deceased James has attained heaven by his own piety rather than through the impiety of the plotters, who attempted to send him there before his time by means of the 5 November explosion.[155] Similarly, Herring and Fletcher ironically contrast Rome's false piety with James's true piety in the original titles of their epics, *Pietas Pontificia* and *Pietas Iesuitica*, exploiting the Virgilian tradition identifying piety with heroism. Milton's third epigram, however, takes a more serious turn, admitting how close James came to death when the Latin monster attempted to avenge his jokes about purgatory: "For he did – almost – go to the celestial shores, a cindery ghost, whirled aloft by Tartarean fire [Nam prope Tartareo sublime rotatus ab igni / Ibad ad aethereas, umbra perusta, plagas]" (14). Milton was apparently familiar with James's comment on the existence of purgatory and possibly with Herring's work, which had described Catholicism as the "monster of Latium."[156] Crashaw's rather innocuous epigram plays upon the juxtaposition of "All Saints' Day" with "all sinners day" (the Gunpowder anniversary), but Campion's epigrams share Milton's ambivalence. His first, "Against the Jesuits," rejoices in England's freedom from wolves, first through the extinction of the natural species, second through the Lutheran shepherd's exposure of the hooded wolves stealing from the flock, and finally through Fawkes's capture.[157] The next two jest conventionally with the Jesuits' use of aliases, again concealing uneasiness about the difficulty of identifying, and so containing, the Jesuit threat, while the fourth mocks the plotters for being burned by gunpowder, a monk's invention. The final epigram congratulates Donne on his *Ignatius His Conclave*, alluding indirectly to the ongoing problem of English Catholicism that necessitated the Oath of Allegiance and the ensuing controversy into which Donne had launched his satire. Thus, in the face of the ongoing Jesuit threat, the epigrams seem unable to attain, or at least to maintain, the closure anticipated by their concise form.

This failure of containment may be responsible for the infiltration of satire into the epics themselves in depictions of demonic councils borrowed from both Continental epic and English prose pamphlets. The most immediate sources for these councils are the Latin poems on Elizabeth's deliverances, but these looked back to Continental models, beginning with Marco Girolamo Vida's *Christiad* (first published in 1535), which described in book 1 a meeting in which Satan proposed to his "dire brethren and all their kindred"[158] a plan to capture and mislead one of Jesus's disciples to prevent Christ from accomplishing his mission on earth. Vida's Satan authorizes both force and fraud against the God who has banished them from heaven and now may bar even "these nether realms" to them.[159] The devil operates on what appears to be a conciliar model but manipulates the council in his own favour, just as Milton's Satan does in *Paradise Lost*. Vida's depiction was taken up by Torquato Tasso in canto 4 of his *Jerusalem Liberata*. Tasso's Satan is irked first by his own fall, but even more by the prospect that Christ will cheat death and bring all men to heaven. He also authorizes his minions to use both force and fraud so long as he attains his object.[160]

The biblical tradition also offered an epic model that emphasized man's place in a cosmic struggle between God and Satan. Barbara K. Lewalski observes that in *The Reason of Church Government* Milton identified the Book of Job as the model for a genre of "brief epic," and demonstrates that Job was commonly understood as epic literature from patristic times to the seventeenth century by both Catholics and Protestants. This interpretation of the book focused upon the two heavenly councils "in which Job is singled out to be God's champion in the contest with Satan, and the trials and miseries which Satan inflicts upon Job."[161] As developed by Lewalski, this insight is helpful in understanding the brief Gunpowder epics, which see England's rulers, like Job, caught in a struggle between the divine and the demonic.[162]

In Campion's *Ad Thamesin* and the extant fragment of Alabaster's "Elisæ," Satan initiates the plot action. In the new world of Reformation polemic, however, he has become a Catholic, creating a false church to lure humanity away from the true bride of Christ. In Alabaster's opening book, after Christianity superseded the "gentile myth [gentilis fabula]," "the Destroyer was then distressed at the shameful disgrace, and determining to patch together his fallen empire, he established again in Italy the rubble he had saved from the disfigured ruins" (25), making Italy the new capital of his empire, which continued to spread until first Luther and then Henry VIII began to undermine his conquests.[163] Satan approaches his daughter, the "Babylonian whore [Babylonica pellex]" (39), who uses Bishop Gardiner to sow discord between Mary and Elizabeth, ultimately contriving Elizabeth's imprisonment in the Tower in 1554.

Neo-Latin poetry, however, was not the only literary tradition to conflate Rome with Satan's kingdom. Representations of demonic or Catholic enclaves in two groups of English prose pamphlets beginning in the late sixteenth century – the trip to hell and the Jesuit or papal conference – also contributed to the later transformations of the Gunpowder epics. In the 1590s, the journey to hell became a vehicle for satirical attacks on a variety of urban vices in pamphlets by the so-called university wits, including Thomas Nashe, Barnaby Rich, Thomas Middleton, and the more notorious Robert Greene. Pamphlets written after 1605, however, engage more with religious controversies and particularly with their relationship to political disobedience, often making an example of the Gunpowder Plot. With their roots in Menippean satire, these prose pamphlets utilize dialogic structures that humanize the demonic, giving voices to the forces of evil as well as of good, while their picaresque structures replicate themselves in the increasingly episodic and open-ended form of the later Gunpowder epics.[164]

Although written in English, these pamphlets seem to have been addressed to well-educated readers; the legal references, classical allusions, and Latin marginalia that pepper the texts suggest that the young gentlemen who are both the subjects of the satire and its potential consumers may be those attached to the Inns of Court or the universities. Through the 1590s, these pamphlets remained miscellaneous satirical attacks on various vices rampant among young men, such as overspending and being obsessed with their attire, as well as attacks on specific individuals. Nashe's *Pierce Penilesse his Supplication to the Diuell* (1592) initiated a loosely related series featuring the "Knight of the Post" who carries mail to and from the devil. In this first instalment, Pierce convinces the postman to carry a supplication to Satan. Pierce's complaints rehearse the seven deadly sins, demonstrating how they are currently being pursued by Londoners. In Thomas Middleton's *Blacke Booke* (1604), the Knight returns from hell with news for all the city's villains. Later instances, however, turn the focus from London's sins to proceedings in hell. The second chapter of Dekker's *Lanthorne and Candle-light. or The Bell-mans Second Nights Walke* (1608) describes the devil holding court in a hot and noisy hall. The Knight of the Post arrives during a dispute between an

Englishman and a Dutchman as to who is the worst drinker. When informed that one of his letters accuses the bellman of giving away the devil's secrets in print, Lucifer adjourns the session to hold a council, in which he warns that if the bellman is not stopped, hell will lose its customers and become unbearable. After an animated discussion, the council concludes that a spirit who can change himself into a variety of shapes should go into London to win victims over to the demonic party. Dekker appears to have developed this idea further in his 1612 play, *If it be not good the Diuel is in it: A New Play*, acted at the Red Bull by the Queen's Majesty's Servants. In the play, Pluto, acting upon a complaint from Charon about the lack of both quality and quantity among his new customers, sends three spirits out in the disguises of a courtier, a merchant, and a friar to Naples to subvert the new king, Alphonso. Although the evil spirits enjoy some initial successes, Alphonso ultimately recognizes the deception practised upon him and the devils return in disgrace to hell, where they join Guy Fawkes and François Ravaillac.[165]

This is not Dekker's first reference to the Gunpowder Plot and its perpetrators in such a context. In his 1606 *Newes from Hell; Brought by the Diuells Carrier* the devil tells his messenger to commend "all those that steale subiects hearts from their Soueraignes, say to al those, they shal haue my letters of Mart for their Piracie: factious Gnyziards, that lay traines of seditiõ to blow vp the cõmõ-wealth, I hug thẽ as my children."[166] A more substantial treatment occurs in *The returne of the knight of the poste from Hell* ... (1606), an anonymous contribution to this series, in which the narrator returns to the city after living for some time in the country. Riding into London, he sees guards and soldiers everywhere, and he soon discovers that a terrible plot has just been exposed. Seeking more news, he finds a down-at-heel loiterer who tells him what was plotted. The narrator exclaims that this outrage must have been planned by devils, but his new acquaintance cautions that though they may prove to be devils, they are still men, and he offers the names of Fawkes, Percy, Catesby, the Winters, and the Wrights. The narrator is mystified, since these men are all nobodies who could not have expected advancement, but his new acquaintance chastises him for thinking that discontent cannot be found among the poor and obscure. Questioned, the beggar admits he is an evil spirit in human shape, the knight of the post who carries the devil's mail. In contrast to the later epic treatments, in which the primary responsibility for the plot belongs to supernatural forces, here, as in the earlier epics, the knight of the post places the blame squarely on human agents. Fawkes is a human traitor, not the devil himself.

The visitor, referring to Dekker's pamphlet, then asks how the devil received Piers Penilesse's supplication. The devil's reply identifies pride as the sin that brings men to hell and papistry as another form of pride. Those who

> denie the reading of holy writ, the forme of meditation, the vse and number of sacraments, the function of the elect, the congregation of the belieuing, and heape such infinite authoritie vppon a sinful mans iurisdiction, that casting faith into that ende of the wallet which euer hangs behinde them, they shall rob the great almighty both of his true homage and alleagance and in the ende when their batterie shalbe able not to moue one stone in christianitie, they shall like true souldiours of hels kingdome, practise to make such mines and vndermininges as may blowe vp all truth and religion with vnmerciful gunpowder, adding vnto Cattelins conspiracye and all other treasons how vilde soeuer great showes of charitie in comparison of their inhumanitie.[167]

From this pamphlet we can see that what begins as a satiric genre directed at the ordinary indiscretions of young urban gentlemen becomes inflected with anti-Catholic polemic following the Gunpowder Plot.[168] More importantly, the plot seems to have led to the genre's engagement with more serious problems, particularly political disobedience.

Such a tradition already existed in a body of texts describing papal enclaves. The purpose of this genre from the beginning was clearly to educate readers about the evils of the Roman church. An early example is Bernardino Ochino's *A Tragedy or Dialogue of the unjust and usurped Primacy of the Bishop of Rome*, printed in England in a 1549 translation by John Ponet. The pamphlet consists of a series of dialogues among various parties, beginning with a meeting between Lucifer and Beelzebub in which they agree to subvert the Roman church by giving the Bishop of Rome authority over the other bishops.[169] Among the most interesting of the dialogues are those in which the people attempt to prevent the church's decline into error by querying the pope's declaration of authority over rulers. Although Satan and the pope are too clever for them, the pamphlet suggests that informed Christians know the pope is not entitled to temporal authority.

By 1610, the escalating Oath of Allegiance debate in England, the struggles in Venice, and the assassination of Henri IV in France seem to have created a new demand for texts condemning the papacy's quest for secular power. Already Joachim Beringer, in *The Romane conclave* (1609), had chronicled the relations between various popes and emperors, demonstrating how popes had interfered in human governments throughout history. He justifies his historical methodology by claiming that in learned disputation both sides may appear valid, whereas his technique of using examples defies refutation.[170] Since he follows his survey with a general synopsis of the ways in which the Jesuits have argued against oaths to heretics, this publication seems to have been intended as an intervention in the Oath of Allegiance dispute. George Carleton's *Ivrisdiction Regall, Episcopall, Papall*, published in the following year, followed a similar formula. An English translation of an anonymous French pamphlet, *The Hellish and Horribble Councell, practised and vsed by the Iesuites, (in their priuate Consultations) when they would haue a man to murther a King*, appeared in 1610. The pamplet was dedicated to the French Queen Mother with the stated aim of making her aware of Jesuit doctrine. The author describes a Jesuit council in which the chosen assassin is presented with a knife, shown a picture of Henri III's murderer, Jacques Clément, with the angels in heaven, and promised that a similar reward, rather than purgatory, awaits him if he succeeds in assassinating Henri IV. These texts revealed Rome's errors, particularly its encouragement of civil disobedience and rebellion, to an audience, both Protestant and Catholic, less learned than the audience for disputations.[171] While the epic tradition privileges the heroic perspective, these vernacular pamphlets are inherently dialogic or even multivocal, giving voices to the forces of evil as well as those of good, if only to satirize or refute them.

Although John Donne's *Ignatius His Conclave* was published first in Latin in 1611, it deserves a place in this tradition since it was Donne's English translation that remained popular through the remainder of the century.[172] Previously considered part of the high-culture debate over the Oath of Allegiance, to which Donne had contributed the more intellectual *Pseudo-Martyr*, *Ignatius* has more recently been read as Menippean satire.[173] The first scholar to assert a direct connection to the Gunpowder Plot is Dennis Flynn, who argues that the text satirizes Cecil and his role in the plot and was written for an audience that included Henry Percy, still imprisoned for suspected complicity in the plot. Not only did Northumberland purchase a copy of the Latin text, but Flynn argues that access to the earl's specialized library in the Tower would account for Donne's more obscure references in the satire.[174] In his prefatory "Printer to the Reader," using the transparent fiction of presenting the work of a friend, Donne claims that satire can contribute as much as disputation to the cause of reform. The narrator's travels to hell take him to a secret chamber where a contention has erupted over the seat nearest Lucifer, which will be awarded to history's greatest innovator. Boniface III is likely to win over Mohamet, not only for his own innovations, but also for all those of his successors, particularly the Jesuit order, which has "ever beene fruitfull in bringing forth new sinnes, and new pardons, and idolatries, and King-killings."[175] Ignatius himself, setting out not only to win the competition, but even to usurp Lucifer's own place, rejects Paracelsus's claims by reminding him that the pope controls "the Saltpeter, and all the Elements of Gunpowder, by which he may demolish and overthrow Kings and Kingdomes, and Courts, and seates of Justice." Machiavelli, the next aspirant, determines to address himself directly to Ignatius rather than Lucifer, praising him specifically for his Jesuits' introduction of the art of equivocation, which had figured so prominently in the trial of Father Garnett. Machiavelli flatters Ignatius by observing that the Jesuits have occasionally used others not of their order to effect their purposes, "And therefore as well they, who have so often in vaine attempted it in *England*, as they which have brought their great purposes to effect in *Fraunce*, are indebted only to you for their courage and resolution." Lucifer inclines towards Machiavelli, who has encouraged the laity to sin actively rather than simply through laziness and ignorance, and whom he sees as a potential balance against Ignatius's power, but Ignatius, having deduced Lucifer's plan, grovels before the devil and thunders out

> *With so great noise and horror,*
> *That had that powder taken fire, by which*
> *All the Isle of Britaine had flowne to the Moone,*
> *It had not equalled this noise and horror.*[176]

Flynn notes that "Ignatius's roaring fit of devil worship and his ensuing diatribe against Machiavelli are the turning point of the narration in *Ignatius His Conclave*." Donne "likens the roaring of Ignatius to the importunate outcry and flood of propaganda that helped bring down Northumberland and forever ruled out one of his long-standing political objectives: that the King should grant toleration to English Catholics."[177] Flynn's argument for a direct connection between *Ignatius* and the Gunpowder Plot gains support from the tribute to Donne among the Latin epigrams Campion attached to his plot epic and from Ignatius's presence in later Gunpowder epics by both Campion and Fletcher.[178]

Through the Continental epics, then, we see the development of councils in which Satan and his minions seek to subvert God's plan for the world. The vernacular pamphlet tradition rewrites these councils as anti-Catholic polemic in which Satan collaborates with the Roman hierarchy, while the Elizabethan neo-Latin tradition inherited by the Gunpowder poems offers us the first glimpse of a Catholic, Anglophobic Satan. In the demonic council that begins Wallace's poem, Satan admits to authoring the Gowrie Conspiracy as well as the Bye Plot out of envy for England's peace and piety. In response to his request for advice on formulating a new plot, Abaddon proposes that since force has been ineffective, fraud should be tried.[179] He offers the assistance of Rome, which he has tutored in cruelty and deception. Satan, in agreement, heads to earth, taking the appearance of a Jesuit. In this guise, he befriends Guy Fawkes, convincing him that he would be better to destroy the English Parliament than to waste his life serving a foreign country. Whether he succeeds or fails, he will become a saint. Fawkes finds accomplices in the Netherlands and, after taking the sacrament, they almost complete a tunnel under the Parliament building before discovering the empty cellar and moving their gunpowder into place there. Since the text's panegyric function requires giving James the starring role in the event, Wallace minimizes divine intervention. An inconvenient wall does not providentially prevent the plotters from completing their tunnel, and God merely gives James the opportunity to decipher the Monteagle letter. Although God watches, he allows human agents to carry out his designs, just as Satan operates through the corrupt agency of Fawkes.

Herring's poem similarly focuses upon the plot's human agents, while the most extensive demonic machinery occurs in the later epics of Campion and Fletcher. Campion's Satan is motivated by envy of God generally, and of Jacobean England more specifically, disappointed at seeing "the once doubtful affairs of Britain now settled and peace going olive-crowned through all the realm, sacred worship on the increase, joy resounding in the woods, cities and palaces replete with splendour in varied pomp."[180] In addition to this peace and prosperity, Satan also perceives an unwelcome unity developing among the kingdoms – "that the Irish now of their own accord suppressed their wonted hostility and extended the hand of friendship, that the conspiring arms of the Scots were quiet and that there was no place left for the clank of armour or for secret guile."[181] Satan's agent is Ignatius, whose ghost, appearing to the plotters, helps the priests incite open rebellion once they learn that the powder has been discovered. Ignatius urges them to "Invent a disaster common to all of them: say the thing is being planned secretly, sudden and early violence threatens unless forestalled by earlier force."[182] After he finishes speaking, the earth opens to display Avernus. Ignatius drives the Fears and Furies up to earth to assist the priests, while Lucifer, watching, is not "sorry to yield from equal command, for they both have one heart [suo nec poenitet ipsum / Cedere jam de iure pari, vnum pectus vtrisque est]" (89). As in Donne's satire, Lucifer yields to Ignatius, although here he is resigned to his own loss of authority.

Although Fletcher's epic *Locustae* was not published until 1627, the earliest manuscript copy dates to the same year in which Donne's text was published. It seems unlikely to be coincidental that Fletcher's epic is the first of these poetic accounts to offer both a fully realized and dialogic council in hell and an appearance by Ignatius. Fletcher's epic begins in hell, where Satan tries to rouse his minions to recover their lost empire. Rising to speak after him is Æquivocus, a "swollen-bellied monk" who "once crammed his camp with an idle throng," clearly Loyola himself, who leads a "Jesuit army" of "brethren with shaven faces, whose curved heads were tonsured" (9).[183] Æquivocus offers to "fill the abodes of Styx and its kingdom, which is empty all about, with inhabitants recruited from all sides [Stygiasque domus et inania late / undique collectis supplebo regna colonis]" (15). His plans are grander even than those of the dragon in Revelation – to take away the sun and the stars from the sky. Following a digression on how Rome achieved secular power, Æquivocus takes the problem of English recalcitrance to his Jesuits, and it is a Jesuit "both the greatest in age and powerful in authority [maximus aevo / et sceptris Iesuita potens]" (31) who proposes a solution. First, they will sow discord through women, but "This is the prologue to the tragic scene: we are preparing greater things. It is no ordinary crime that I sow, but one about which no day will be silent, one which no day will believe; I am undertaking a crime great and to be feared by all peoples."[184] The Gunpowder Plot is "the final wickedness [supremum ... scelus]" (35), achieved not directly by Satan, but through the Jesuits. Æquivocus's disciple finds an innovation that Satan cannot, just as Ignatius bests Lucifer in Donne's satire. The poem's structure not only makes the Jesuit mission complicit in the plot, but makes the plot the mission's sole purpose.[185] In his English poem, which is more satirical than the Latin, Fletcher conducts the demonic council in explicitly political terms that parody English government: "A full foule Senate, now they all are set, / The horride Court, big swol'ne with th' hideous Counsel swet" (1.17). Fletcher's demons subvert good by allying "Counsel" with the court rather than with Parliament, where James had located it in his 9 November 1605 speech to that body.

The demonic council proved to be suited to the satiric mode and flexible enough to be used against a variety of opponents, becoming a contested genre in the period of the civil wars as each side attempted to use it against the other. Royalists favoured the prose form for associating the institution of Parliament with hell; however, one of the earliest examples is J.M.'s *Newes from Hell, Rome and the Inns of Court* (1641), which attempts to retain the genre for anti-Catholic polemic. Lucifer praises the pope for sowing discord among English Protestants and provoking the Scots to attack their neighbour, offering that

> In respect of which services, as also for their fidelity to us and our Kingdome, we haue caused our principall Secretary of estate, *Don Antonio Furioso Diabelo*, to make an especiall Inroulement of their names in our Calend amongst those our deare servants the plotters of the *Gun-powder-treason*; and the most renowned the complotters of the former Invasion of England, in the year of grace 1588.[186]

Not only did later royalist writers use this technique to equate parliamentarians with hell's rulers, but one very nearly used J.M.'s own words to do so. The anonymous author of *Hells Triennial Parliament, Summoned five years since, by King Lucifer* (1647) has Lucifer applaud the presbyterians for "sowing the seedes of discord amongst three Kingdomes of my professed enemies, the English, Scotch, and Irish" and declares that as a result he has "caused our principall Secretary of Estate *Dom Antonio Demonibus* to enter your names in our diabolicall Calender, amongst our deare children the complotters of the *Gunpowder Treason*, and of the *Spanish Invasion*."[187] In Francis Wortley's verse *Mercurius Britanicus his Welcome to*

Hell: With the Devills Blessing to Britanicus (1647), written during his imprisonment in the Tower, Lucifer offers to make the parliamentary newsbook his "speciall favourite," promising "And brave *Guy Faux* with famous *Ravilliack* / Shall wait on thee from boord unto thy bed."[188] Similarly, in his *Mercvrivs Infernalis, or Orderlesse Orders* (1644), John Taylor numbers Ravaillac and Fawkes among the devil's counsellors.[189] Thus, associating one's enemies with both Satan and the Gunpowder plotters had become a powerful means of satirizing them.[190]

Beyond these obvious links, however, more subtle echoes of anti-Catholic polemic appear in the anti-parliamentary pamphlets. In Taylor's pamphlet, "*Sultan Sathan*" (1) is irked particularly because "the Kingdomes of Great *Brittain* and *Ireland* have been these many yeares in such a happy condition of Peace, plenty, and all other blessings, to the Envy and admiration of all Nations." Satan's remedy for this situation is remarkably similar to that of Fletcher's Catholic Satan, as he orders "that some of our cunningest Divels should be sent by our Authority into those parts, who should take upon them the shapes and habites of sincere religious persons, and insinuate them selves, first among foolish women, and silly Tradesmen," persuading them to abandon true religion.[191] This Satan sees Britain's subversion as a greater good even than the fall of the angels or the temptation of Adam and Eve. A series of pamphlets satirizing the expanded political roles of women in this period demonstrates that the anti-puritan pamphlets retained the anti-feminist perspectives of the earlier anti-Catholic polemic.[192] Such satire attempts simultaneously to exaggerate and to contain the threats posed by these groups, but it also gives voices to them through its inherently dialogic form. Ironically, then, these texts served to humanize evil even as they insisted upon its Satanic origins. As we will see in the next chapter, their influence upon the Gunpowder epics was to reorient them in the direction of romance.

5 "fit audience find, though few": Militant Protestants and Wandering Ways

This chapter continues to trace the Gunpowder epic as it leaves behind its courtly Latin roots and becomes increasingly identified with a militant and progressively more disillusioned Protestant nationalism. Following James I's death in 1625, the genre ceased to attract patronage-seeking authors, and the last known Latin epic was composed instead as an academic exercise by the young Cambridge student John Milton. *In Quintum Novembris*, with its ambiguous portrait of James I and its suggestion that individual Protestants may protect the nation better than the king, follows a pattern that had emerged with John Vicars's 1617 "dilation" of Herring's poem. However, while Milton's poem ended with the plotters appropriately punished and the promise of yearly celebration, Vicars's poem deferred closure by following the defeated plotters' aimless wanderings during the Midlands revolt. Lack of closure is the most notable of the romance elements Vicars introduces, but he also individuates the plotters, at least temporarily validating their perspectives. These changes subverted the epic genre later in the century when increasing tensions within Protestantism made the simple dichotomies of the early seventeenth century, and Virgilian epic, inadequate for the emerging state. By 1641, English translations and print publication had brought these poems to readers unfamiliar with epic conventions, training individuals to become the "fit audience" that Milton would later seek for his narrative of the fall of humankind.

5.1 Fame and *Fama*: Milton's View of England in 1626

Like the publication of Fletcher's poem the following year, the writing of Milton's *In Quintum Novembris*, probably in 1626, took place in a political and cultural climate far different from the one in which Wallace and Herring had written.[1] Instead of being at peace after decades of war with Spain, England had now plunged into a Continental war after decades of peace. Although he ruled a united kingdom, Charles remained uncrowned as king of Scotland until 1633, and the subsequent failure of his Anglo-Scottish relations stemmed from attempting to impose religious uniformity on the Scots rather than trying to impose political union on the English.[2] More directly, two events in 1623 had redefined the Gunpowder Plot's place in English history: the safe return of Prince Charles from Spain and the collapse of a garret in Blackfriars during a Catholic sermon a few weeks later. Many understood these events, together or separately, as reversals of the Gunpowder Plot as well as demonstrations of God's continuing support for a Protestant England that was once again threatened by too much leniency towards Catholics, both foreign and domestic.

Fears that a Spanish match would bring about a general toleration for Catholics began escalating in 1617–18.[3] In 1622, shortly before issuing *Directions to Preachers* that would reduce opportunities for the clergy to criticize his policies, a topic we will take up again in the next chapter, James added fuel to the fire by formally suspending the penal laws, increasing freedom of worship for Catholics while signalling to Protestants that he was preparing to grant toleration. Anticipating a successful conclusion to the marriage negotiations, particularly once Charles and Buckingham had embarked for Spain in February 1623, Catholics became more visible at court, and some Protestants even converted to the Roman faith.[4] When it appeared that negotiations had stalled, probably fatally, relieved Protestants had only to await the prince's return. They greeted his arrival with unprecedented enthusiasm – Sir Simonds D'Ewes claimed he had never seen so many bonfires in London, and he added tellingly that "Twas prettye to observe the difference betweene the bonefires made by command after his landing in Spaine, being by expresse order from the Privye Councell, and betweene these that weere made upon the matter vountarilye, the first being thinne and poore, these manye and great."[5] While connections with the Gunpowder Plot were not overt, they underlay some of the plot celebrations over the next several years. John Hacket included the prince in the prayer concluding his 1623 Gunpowder sermon at Whitehall, asking God to help both James and Charles to protect the English church and commonwealth.[6] Two years later, George Carleton's *Thankfull Remembrance* (1625) chronicled all of the English Protestant deliverances from the beginning of Elizabeth's reign until the Gunpowder Plot without mentioning the prince's return, but his emphasis upon the complicity of the Catholic Church and the Spanish state pointed directly towards England's most recent deliverance.

The Blackfriars incident was more openly understood at the time in relation to the Gunpowder Plot. On Sunday, 26 October 1623, the floor of a garret in a house adjoining the French ambassador's London residence collapsed under the weight of a large crowd that had gathered to hear a Jesuit preacher.[7] Almost immediately, Protestants noticed that 26 October became 5 November when adjusted for the difference between Roman and English calendars, creating an inevitable link between the two events. This connection was made in pamphlets such as the anonymous *Something Written by Occasion of that fatall and memorable accident in the Blacke-Friers*, but it appeared more graphically in the series of engravings that Alexandra Walsham first identified as a triptych.[8] The first engraving, *A Plot with Powder*, pictures Fawkes's familiar figure stealing towards the Parliament buildings with his lantern; the second, *A Plot without Powder*, depicts the Spanish Match negotiations; and the third, *No Plot No Powder*, illustrates the collapse, the preacher surrounded by masonry and dismembered bodies. The labelling of Fawkes's treachery as "Blacke Deeds" to correspond with "Blacke Friars" in the third engraving and the identification of the first as "November 5th Old Stile" with the third as "November 5th New Stile" emphasized that one action had reversed the other: Catholics had attempted to blow the king and Parliament up towards God; God had caused the Catholics to fall towards the earth and even into hell, which Catholics generally believed was within the earth.[9] The symmetry was inscribed in the first line of the verses below the third engraving: "Vpward had wee gone, downeward goe our foes." Combined with the prince's return from Spain, the incident offered to many what appeared conclusive proof that God favoured English Protestantism.[10] These events extended the life of the Gunpowder Plot in popular memory by demonstrating that it was not simply a past event, nor was it the apex of God's providential care, but that God might continue using it to avenge England's Catholic enemies. Even more importantly, popular rather than courtly texts – rumours, manuscripts, and the pamphlet press – became the primary sites of interpretative activity.

Consequently, these events did not inspire a new series of courtly Gunpowder epics.[11] The new king had been a young child when the plot had been discovered and does not appear to have recalled the anniversary with particular enthusiasm.[12] The annual celebration, however, had become a regular feature of academic as well as civic life, and Richard Crashaw's English poems on the plot were likely written for college performances during his time at Cambridge in the 1630s.[13] A few years earlier, this tradition had also produced the last of the original Latin Gunpowder epics known to have been composed, Milton's *In Quintum Novembris*.[14] We can form some idea of how the anniversary may have been celebrated in the university during Milton's time from an entertainment entitled *Novembris Monstrum*, not printed until after the censorship regulations lapsed in 1641, but "Made long since for the Anniversary Solemnity on the fift day of *November*, In a private Colledge at *Cambridge*."[15] The first part of this pamphlet consists of an eleven-part verse narrative of the plot that the students probably acted out.[16] Although written in English and clearly played for comic effect, it follows the pattern of the epic narratives, beginning with the pope growing so big with the plot, of which the earth is the mother and Fawkes the midwife, that he miscarries, leaving

Figure 2 *A Plot with Powder.* The first panel in a triptych produced after the Blackfriars incident of 1623. The subsequent panels depict the Spanish Match negotiations (*A Plot without Powder*) and the collapse at Blackfriars (*No Plot No Powder*). © Trustees of the British Museum, Prints and Drawings, 1896, 1230.3.

the plot stillborn. The last part reveals the Blackfriars collapse as just retribution upon Catholics. A poem subtitled "The Historicall narration of the Damnable *Pouder-Treason*" follows.[17] Although Sutton finds no evidence that Milton's poem participated in such a celebratory tradition, the poet's concluding emphasis upon the anniversary makes it at least suitable for public presentation, and John K. Hale observes that the poem's "length makes one suppose an occasion, performance and audience."[18]

For many years regarded as an inconsequential piece of juvenilia, *In Quintum Novembris* has begun to occupy an increasingly important place in Milton studies. John M. Steadman calls it a "somewhat bigoted little epic of sectarian nationalism," although he concedes that it displays "in miniature, or indeed in embryo, the techniques ... [Milton] would employ on a more ambitious scale in *Paradise Lost* and *Paradise Regained*."[19] Like Macon Cheek and John Demaray, Steadman sees the poem primarily as a rehearsal for the later epics.[20] David Quint and John K. Hale, however, make larger claims for the significance of the Latin epic to the development of Milton's ideology, Hale arguing "that Milton's political awakening is found in this very poem, and indeed at its ending precisely because of the poem's act of thought." This, he concludes, was "the first time Milton expressed this patriotic, zealot view of history."[21]

Milton's historical consciousness here is noteworthy, for his return to the Galfridian tradition and his celebration of union, appropriate in 1606 panegyric, seem out of date in 1626. Closer analysis, however, reveals that these superficial similarities to the early epics conceal subtle differences in perspective. First, Milton describes the union between England and Scotland as an "inviolable league [inviolabile foedus]."[22] Conrad Russell explains how seventeenth-century persons understood the difference between a "perfect union," in which one nation was subordinated to the other, and an "imperfect union" like that of England and Scotland, in which the countries retained their own institutions and which was seen as more vulnerable to dissolution.[23] Milton's characterization of the union suggests that, like many English Protestants, he favoured a solidarity that would protect the island from Catholic invasion but in which England retained the upper hand. His use of the Galfridian tradition supports such a reading. Referring to the English as the "Troy-born race [Teucrigenas]"(15) whom James has come from the "remote north [arcto]" (15) to lead grants James and the Scots only a subordinate place in the British history that Milton invokes throughout the remainder of the poem. While James has literally come from the north, this region was often the site of hell in medieval lore and is the Jesuits' place of origin in Fletcher's poem.[24] Milton thus describes James as at best an outsider and at worst something more suspicious. Without reading back anti-Stuart sentiments into the poem, I suggest that Milton does not present an unqualified endorsement of the late king.[25]

Despite offering James the epithet *pius* and praising him for establishing peace, Milton seems to recall longingly the days when the Roman church held England's military might in fear and awe. Satan spurs the pope to action by reminding him that the "archer-English [pharetrati ... Britanni]" (18) are mocking him and promising that if he follows the devil's plan he will "rule again over the warlike English [in belligeros iterum dominaberis Anglos]" (18). English naval power rather than God's providence defeated the Spanish Armada. Although he does not condemn the pious James, Milton seems to prefer the policies of "the Amazonian virgin [Thermodoontea nuper regnante puella]" (18) whom he succeeded. While the Catholic authorities want to return England to "the Marian epoch [Saecula sic illic tandem Mariana redibunt]" (18), Milton seems to envision a return to Elizabethan, and even earlier, military glory.[26] If the poem was written in late 1626, then it must have been clear to Milton that this glory had departed. Although Charles and Buckingham had manoeuvred James into military intervention on the Continent in the months before his death, Parliament had offered only lukewarm support. The naval expedition to Cadiz in the autumn of 1625 failed dismally, while Mansfeld's land force, supported by English troops, fared little better.[27] Milton's insistence upon England's former military strength appears to offer an implicit rebuke to the new ruler, and possibly even to the memory of James, who allowed his desire for peace to enfeeble the nation. Unlike Fletcher, Milton does not praise Charles, or even refer to him at all in the poem. The king's unpopular support for Buckingham, culminating most recently in the favourite's appointment to the chancellorship at Cambridge – despite his waffling at the York House conference (which had failed to accept the articles agreed to at the Synod of Dort) and the charges pending against him in Parliament – may have contributed to the poem's nostalgia for an earlier reign.[28]

Milton's attitude to history here is significant in the context of his later *History of Britain* and his chronicle of human history in the final books of *Paradise Lost*.[29] David Loewenstein argues that the *History of Britain* "reveals Milton ... divided between presenting an objective, factual response to history and presenting a more literary and mythopoetic one." He argues that the *History* "begins, like an epic story, with the myth of Brutus and then charts a tragic pattern of failed deliverances in national history, with numerous references made to the troubles of Milton's own age"[30] Graham Parry concurs that Milton "seems determined to recount a protracted history of failure from Roman times onwards, and the chronicle narrative method rather suited his scheme in this regard."[31] *In Quintum Novembris*, written when godly English Protestants were discouraged both by military losses on the Continent and increasing ceremonialism in the church, however, juxtaposes the successes of a mythologized past against the implied failures of a historical present. While Walsham is correct to point out the smug certainties engendered by the Blackfriars collapse, Milton's poem demonstrates how quickly these may have evaporated in the face of dismal news from abroad.

England's decline seems to have begun not with Charles but with James, whose piety is remarkably passive in Milton's poem. Milton assigns the work of discovering and publicizing the plot to Rumour rather than the king, a significant departure from previous Gunpowder epics. In Wallace's imaginative treatment, James and his family are proceeding towards Parliament, unaware of the plot, when Lord Monteagle approaches bearing the letter. Inspired by God, James acts immediately and decisively; he "chose courtiers from the whole company (340) and ordered them to search and examine again and again the building underneath the hall and the underground cellar."[32] Fletcher's Latin poem adheres more closely to historical accounts of the letter's delivery, but also describes how James, "Running over with his clever eye the intricacies and unspeakable ambiguities of wickedness, (while a light scatters the clouds and reveals his mind's illumination), soon ... uncovers all the monstrosities and alone he discloses the crime and dispels the darkness."[33] In Herring's original poem, the "prudent king [Rex prudens]" (273) similarly insists that the Monteagle letter must be taken seriously, instructing his counsellors: "I want to find out who live [*sic*] in the building nearby, if there is any cellar lying beneath the hall. Inform me in the first instance of these facts, having made a careful investigation."[34] But Herring also wants to glorify God more than the king and so has God send an angel to warn James in his sleep as well as to inspire Monteagle to perform his duty. When James receives the letter, he acts more decisively, having already heard "scattered rumours concerning the followers of Rome [rumores quippe recordor / de Romanistis sparsos]" (273). By 1617, however, Vicars had diminished the king's role in the deliverance further, insisting upon the providential placement of the wall through which the plotters were unable to tunnel, and providing five reasons for "the great impossibility / Of hope, of this strange treasons publication / By all the reach of humane policy." He describes rumour spreading the news "through both *Court* and *Country* speedily, / Through *Towne* and *City*, street, and euery place, / Through all the kingdome."[35] Unlike Herring in his original Latin poem, however, Vicars does not personify rumour or associate it with the classical Fama. Most importantly, rumour does not discover the event but merely reports it. Milton is thus the first to assign the plot's discovery to the classical Fama.

While critics have observed the differences between Milton's relatively favourable portrayal of Fama and the unflattering ones of Virgil and Ovid, they have not generally considered contemporary sources or analogues for Milton's treatment.[36] Milton's representation of Rumour contrasts not only with classical ones, but also with Francis Bacon's depiction of fame and rebellion as brother and sister. Martin Dzelzainis, reviewing Bacon's attitudes to Fama, observes that in book 2 of *The Advancement of Learning* (1605) Bacon extrapolated from the *Aeneid* that "rebellion and fame are brother and sister and their mother is the malignity of the people, but they are not co-eval: for feminine fame comes into being only after masculine rebellion has been 'suppressed.'"[37] In his essay "Of Seditions and Troubles," first printed in 1612 but written at least two years earlier, however, Bacon quotes the same lines from the *Aeneid* before commenting that rumours are not merely "the relics of seditions past; but they are no less the preludes of seditions to come."[38] As Dzelzainis concludes, Bacon had apparently come to understand rumour as "a causal factor in its own right rather than a merely post facto phenomenon."[39] In other words, he reflects the suspicion of orally transmitted news that was enshrined in a law allowing seditious words to be prosecuted as treason.[40]

Curiously, and perhaps not coincidentally, in 1626 Jonson equated his news agency in *The Staple of News* with "the house of *fame*" (3.2.115).[41] As Mark Z. Muggli notes, Jonson repeatedly satirized his contemporaries' fascination with the news, and his works explored the relationship between truth and lies, spying and reportage.[42] Interest in foreign news had increased dramatically with the onset of the Thirty Years' War, while the government's efforts to control access to domestic news became rapidly more futile.[43] Although critics have struggled with the complexities of Jonson's satire, he clearly mocks printed news, not only because it ceases to become news once printed, but perhaps also, as Catherine Rockwood suggests, because it advocates English involvement in Europe's religious wars.[44] Joseph Loewenstein suggests that Jonson attacks printed news because it deprivatizes and democratizes information, making it available to popular audiences just as Rumour does.[45] Like Fama's house, the Staple is a place

> Where both the curious, and the negligent;
> The scrupulous, and carelesse; wilde, and stay'd;
> The idle, and laborious; all doe meet,
> To tast the *Cornu copiae* of her rumors,
> Which she, the mother of sport, pleaseth to scatter
> Among the vulgar. (3.2.116–21)

Thus, both printed news and oral rumour are the province of the idle and uneducated.

Rumour's associations with social unrest and even sedition help to explain Milton's defensive assertion that although he may be criticized for his favourable portrayal of Fama, he will "never regret this commemoration of ... [her] at such length in ... [his] song" (20).[46] Rather than merely exploiting classical sources in an academic exercise, Milton seems to be aware of the current debates about news into which Jonson had launched his play. Moreover, there is reason to suspect that Milton had actually seen the play before writing his poem. The poet was notoriously suspended from Cambridge at some point during Lent term (13 January to 31 March) 1625/6, during which time he sent "Elegia Prima" to his friend Charles Diodati, recording among the pleasures of his London exile that of attending the theatre. Timothy J. Burbery argues that Milton attended a performance of *The Staple of News* at Blackfriars during this period, basing his argument upon evidence that the poet's father was almost certainly a trustee of that theatre; that the elegy's description of the building, although vague, could refer to Blackfriars; and, most significantly, that several of the comic characters Milton describes in the elegy may have originated in Jonson's comedy.[47] *In Quintum Novembris*'s reference to Fama adds to the weight of Burbery's evidence to make a strong case for Milton's familiarity with this play. What is perhaps most interesting about this connection is the young poet's willingness to challenge and nuance Jonson's view of Rumour.

Despite recognizing that Fama both lies and withholds truth, Milton nevertheless credits her with the one good deed of exposing the plot, attributing England's safety entirely to her "good offices" (20):

> First, in her usual way, ... [Fama] scatters ambiguous rumors and uncertain whispers through the English cities. Presently, grown clear-voiced, she publishes the plots and the detestable work of treason – not merely the deeds which are abominable to utter, but also the authors of the crime; nor does her garrulity make a secret of the places prepared for the treacherous attempt. (21)[48]

It is only after she has declared the news that "the heavenly Father takes pity on his people from on high and thwarts the outrages which the Papists have dared [Attamen interea populi miserescit ab alto / Aethereus Pater, et crudelibus obstitit ausis / Papicolum]" (21). Milton seems to make prevention of the plot dependent upon public information that enables God to act independently of the king, celebrating the very promiscuity of rumour that Bacon and Jonson deplored.[49]

James's relative passivity in the poem troubles the relationship between the monarch's *pietas* and the providential history established by the earlier epics, in which the king's zeal and wisdom operated in partnership with God's to protect the Protestant nation.[50] Although Quint sees Aeneas as a model for a hero more passive than those of the Homeric epics, within the context of the Gunpowder epic tradition Milton's James strikes the reader as unduly inactive.[51] Moreover, although Milton uses the adjective "pius" to describe James in the poem's first line, at the conclusion he calls the public celebration a kind of piety ("Pious incense and grateful honors are paid to God [At pia thura Deo et grati solvuntur honores]" (21). Like Vicars, Milton seems to be turning away from faith in a godly monarch towards a more populist ideal of the Protestant nation. Similarly, the poem's attitude to memory diverges from the earlier ones. Milton's emphasis upon memorialization may reflect not only a possible performative context, but also the growing concerns with forgetting that prompted authors like Bishop Carleton to publish their chronologies of plots and rebellions. Milton's almost elegaic tribute to England's former glory, however, contrasts with Carleton's optimism. For him, England is not a nation overcoming obstacles with God's assistance, but a people in decline and under attack by both Satan and the pope.

While reasons for the Catholic offensive against Britain vary in these poems, only Milton offers three separate rationales for the plot. In Wallace's poem, Satan is stung to envy and rage by seeing "far and wide cities quiet and kingdoms undisturbed and peoples living their lives in tranquil peace, each person beneath his own vine and the shade of his own tree" (371), a motive that supports the text's panegyric function by alluding to the peace with Spain.[52] In Herring's poem, the Whore of Babylon acts from practical necessity, lamenting the loss of English revenues since the Reformation, for "Through its constant lawsuits the wealthy territory of England more than all others by itself increased the treasury of Rome" (257, 259).[53] Herring thus makes Catholic motives even more venal than Wallace does. In Fletcher's English poem, Satan plots revenge when he sees that England has become a new Eden, where

> every starre sheds his sweet influence,
> And radiant beames: great, little, old, and new
> Their glittering rayes, and frequent confluence
> The milky path to Gods high palace strew:
> Th' unwearied Pastors with steel'd confidence,
> Conquer'd, and conquering fresh their fight renew. (1.28)

Even Virginia is lost to Lucifer, and "What's next but hell?" (1.29).

Milton's Satan, however, sees no evidence for the spread of piety. Instead, he is irked that only England holds him in contempt and rebels against him, making pride his primary motivation. He has the wit, however, to appeal to the pope in the way that will best suit his purposes, castigating him for sleeping "While a savage nation born under the northern sky mocks your throne and your triple crown and while the archer-English insult your rights" (18). Recognizing the pope's vanity and pride, Satan encourages him "to avenge the scattered Spanish Armada" (18).[54] The pope must resort to treachery because England is too strong to attack directly; yet Satan seems to have chosen this moment precisely because he perceives that England has lost its former strength. The devil must persuade the pope, but he can simply order the monstrous twins Murder and Treason to instigate the plot, telling them simply: "A race that is odious to me lives on the western verge of the world amid the surrounding ocean [Finibus occiduis circumfusum incolit aequor / Gens exosa mihi]" (19). The twins merit no complex explanations because they are bound in obedience to the pope, and therefore the devil, as are the kings who follow in his train. Satan attacks Milton's England, then, not because he envies its peace, prosperity, or piety, but because he sees an opportunity to exploit a perceived weakness and avenge insults from a time when England was a worthy opponent. The poet seems to question the benefit of a godly monarch, or at least of the Stuarts as godly monarchs, and to suggest, through his representation of Fama, that the people's role in safeguarding England is more crucial than the king's. Although the poem concludes with Protestant England safe, the final promise of perpetual memorialization cannot overcome the sense of nostalgia pervading its earlier lines. Whether or not Milton had seen Vicars's 1617 expansion of Herring's poem, he too seems to have sensed that celebration might be premature.

5.2 Romantic Subversion: John Vicars Revises the Plot

As monuments to the founding of a Protestant Britain, the early Latin poems on the plot had concluded with the discovery of the gunpowder, sometimes tying up the narrative with the traitors' punishment, but avoiding any reference to the abortive rebellion in the Midlands. When Francis Herring reprinted his original poem with minor corrections in 1609, however, he added a twenty-four-page sequel describing the revolt.[55] In this second part, Herring tells of the plotters' meeting on the pretext of a hunt, their dismay at learning of Fawkes's arrest, and their attempt to rouse the Catholic population before eventually surrendering to the law. The official source for this event was the "Discourse," a narrative that, as we saw above, emphasized the plotters' lack of support, their ignominious arrests by the common sheriff, and their providential burning with gunpowder, doubtless to impress upon readers the futility of open rebellion. Herring seems to have been the first to attempt an aesthetic depiction of these events, and the addition of this narrative fundamentally shifts the balance of the poem, which increasingly tilts away from epic closure towards the open-endedness of romance in John Vicars's later translations and "dilations." Although the plotters themselves are killed or executed, this second part suggests that recusants continue quietly biding their time in the country, a concern that the upsurge in anti-Catholic sentiments unleashed by the acrimonious international Oath of Allegiance debate may have exaggerated. It also demonstrates the difficulties and ambiguities of seeking closure in apocalyptic narrative.

In the early Gunpowder poems, the rejoicing following the plot's discovery and the punishments of the plotters, actual or projected, marked a definitive ending. Although poets warned the king not to trust Catholics in future, the epic structure of their poems left no doubt that the episode was unique and closed, ending a long series of Catholic attacks upon English Protestantism beginning in Elizabeth's reign. Quint succinctly defines epic as the story of history's victors and romance as the story of its losers, arguing that romance narratives "valorize the very contingency and open-endedness that the victors' epic disparages: the defeated hope for a different future to the story that their victors may think they have ended once for all."[56] The boundary between epic and romance, however, has always been indistinct. Virgil's poem progresses from the disconsolate wanderings Aeneas narrates to Dido to the purposeful and heroic conquest of Latium. Beginning with his 1609 sequel, however, Herring's poem reverses this teleological progression, moving from the purposeful actions of the English authorities to the wanderings of the plotters during the failed Midlands revolt, a process that becomes particularly problematic in Vicars's later revisions.

While Herring, or his printer, seems to have considered the original poem's brevity a selling point, Vicars boasts that his 1617 edition is "very much *dilated*," a phrase that would have offered considerable information to Renaissance readers trained in rhetoric. Patricia Parker explains that

> The specifically rhetorical meaning of "dilate" – the amplifying and prolonging of discourse – involves both an expansion and an opening up, the creation of more copious speech through the explication, or unfolding, of a brief, or closed, hermetic "sentence," widening the space between its beginning and ending and generating much out of little, many words (or things) where there had been few.[57]

It was classified as a type of *amplificatio* and was usually accomplished through *divisio* and *partitio*, dividing a sentence into parts and expanding each part. Since it could be used to heighten the importance of a topic, or to add moral weight, it was a staple of sermon rhetoric.[58] Vicars uses this method to add additional descriptive phrases and epithets to Herring's depictions of characters and events, but he makes changes that go well beyond amplification by introducing new material pertinent to the current political situation that also intensifies the poem's godly orientation. The most significant change in the first part of the poem is Vicars's introduction of the Jesuits, who do not appear in the original. Recreating a dialogue between Catesby and Garnett in which the two discuss the problem of killing innocents, he offers a corrective to Garnett's advice, showing that the priest should have argued from scripture rather than analogy, and concluding with a warning against doing evil that good may come of it. This addition not only shifts primary responsibility for the plot onto the Jesuits' shoulders, but also introduces dialogue to instruct his readers in correct reasoning.

Vicars also uses both amplifications and deletions to comment obliquely on current politics, first by adding an account of Fawkes's initial visit to Spain during Elizabeth's reign, at which time Spain had agreed to support the English Catholics.[59] Following James's accession, the Spaniards declined further participation, citing the peace negotiations proceeding between the two countries. Introducing Spain allows Vicars to represent her as an unreliable ally, always intent on her own interests, at a time when James was already known to be negotiating a Spanish marriage for his heir.[60] As we saw in the previous chapter, in this edition Vicars also reduces the king's role in the plot's discovery and eliminates Catesby's lengthy tribute to Prince Henry, indicating increasing scepticism about Stuart rule.[61]

Although he displays little confidence in his readers' abilities to comprehend any kind of figurative language, Vicars introduces a new layer of allegory by identifying Treason, rather than Fawkes, as the son of the pope and the Whore. The original poem had made Fawkes the primary conspirator, a role from which Herring demoted him in the 1609 Latin edition and its 1610 English translation. To justify the introduction of Fawkes before Catesby, Vicars adds a note explaining that, although Catesby is the real author of the plot, Fawkes is introduced first because of his inhumanity. He thus revises the poem's history, explaining on moral grounds what was really the result of incomplete information available at the time of Herring's composition.[62] Allegorizing the monstrous offspring as Treason, who then lodges in Guy Fawkes's breast, requires Vicars to supply additional explanatory notes, but the change supports his interpretation of the plot as merely one episode in an ongoing war between true and false religions. As Guy Fawkes, the offspring of the Whore and the pope can be executed, and closure can be attained; as Treason, this monstrous being will simply move to another host and generate yet more plots. Vicars's deferral of closure nudges the text in the direction of romance, pointing to one of the tensions between apocalyptic history and epic, for while the epic ending is historical, the apocalyptic ending can only be anticipated.

According to Parker,

> The almost cartoon character of the Book of the Apocalypse is a feature of romance dialectical in its tendency. The traditional function of Apocalypse is to portray the enemy as already defeated, in a vision of the end which places us outside the monsters we are still inside – as Job at the end of his trial is shown the externalized forms of behemoth and leviathan – and, by this act of identifying or naming, proleptically overcomes them.[63]

The first part of the poem names the Catholic enemy, despite the difficulties caused by the Jesuits' equivocation and use of aliases, and the defeat of the plotters foreshadows the final victory for God and England. Meanwhile England, like Israel, remains in a state of unfulfilled promise. Lake notes that for those who saw the pope as Antichrist "the assurance of eventual victory (which could only be complete with the Second Coming, the date of which was unknown and unknowable, and which applied only to the universal Church, not to particular, visible Churches) was balanced and held in tension by a lively, indeed perhaps exaggerated, sense of the enormity of the danger."[64] As Parker explains,

> The time between First and Second Coming is itself a respite or "dilation," an interval in which the eschatological Judgment is held over or deferred, a period of uncertain duration when the "end" already accomplished in the Advent is, paradoxically, not yet come, when, though the Promised Land has been conquered, the spiritual Israel still wanders in the wilderness.[65]

At the end of Vicars' poem, Satan vows to continue his offensive against England:

> Indeede, I must confesse, we did expect
> A greater haruest, farre more company:
> But this shall now suffice, and wee'le erect
> Vnto our selues *trophies* of victory
> For this attempt, *Fortune* heereafter may
> Grant vs a time, more mischeefe to display.[66]

This offensive, however, is only part of his larger world plan. Significantly, Satan, not the English poet, is now erecting monuments, although his victory is brief and delusive. While the first part of the narrative demonstrates that Satan cannot win, Vicars makes clear that a battle remains to be fought and that continued vigilance is required to ensure victory. Even a godly monarch is no longer sufficient protection for the church – all Protestants must participate in this work.

According to Helen Cooper, the movement from epic to romance also involves a "shift of emphasis, from the founding of nations to the thoughts and feelings and aspirations of their protagonists."[67] This shift becomes problematic in the expanded Gunpowder epic because in the second part Vicars explores the feelings not of the authorities but of the plotters. As Herring had in his 1609 Latin expansion, Vicars introduces the plotters' perspective immediately by reporting a dialogue between Fawkes and Winter in prison, in which Winter comforts his co-conspirator by reminding him that he and Catesby both leave sons to follow them. Although the plot's failure has left James's succession intact, these men can also console themselves with hopes that their rebellion will not die with them. By allowing the plotters human emotions and aspirations, the second part of the poem opens the door to a viewpoint that complicates authorized versions of the story.

The reorientation towards romance, however, is most evident in the story of the plotters' circuitous wanderings through the countryside as they attempt first to start a rebellion and then simply to evade capture. To some extent, this part of the poem functions as parody, in which Vicars deflates the plotters' pretensions by depriving Digby of the quasi-heroic status accorded to him at his trial. After the hunt, he

> *walkes* and *stalkes* with Princely gate
> Amidst his cursed consorts, traiterous traine,
> Prescribes them statutes, answers, askes in state:
> His brest no triuiall trifles doth retaine,
> His *heart* and *head* negotiate Princely affaires
> He vnto each his place of *honour* shares.[68]

His assumption of kingly airs appears foolish when word of the plot's failure arrives. In contrast to James, who takes control of the situation after reading the Monteagle letter, Digby is so distressed by the news of Fawkes's capture that Thomas Percy must assume leadership of the remaining conspirators. Similarly, describing Catesby and Percy's fall, Vicars begins with what appears to be a conventional epic simile attesting to their heroism, but ends in anticlimax:

> And like two mighty *Oakes*, whose branches high
> May seeme to touch the top of heauen faire;
> But by a rapid whirlewind suddenly
> Are blowne and ouerturn'd, whose branches are
> Laid low vpon the earth, the bowes being meate
> For cattell in the field to brouse and eate.[69]

Vicars portrays the plotters here not so much as monsters but as foolish men badly counselled by the Jesuits. It is Garnett who advises Catesby to proceed with the plot, and Tesimond who incites them to rebel when the original plan fails. The lay plotters are dupes who waste their money and their lives for a church concerned with financial gain rather than the souls of its members.

While Gerald MacLean correctly notes that this part of the poem shows corruption spreading outward from the court to the countryside, the "holy hunt" also disturbingly reverses roles in the religious disputes.[70] Winter, speaking to a Catholic who has joined the hunt, tells him they are actually hunting "*Wolues hereticall*."[71] For a Protestant audience, the idea that Catholics refer to them in the same terms that they refer to Catholics must be disorienting.[72] As Quint reminds us, "the romance narrative bears a subversive relationship to the epic plot line from which it diverges, for it indicates the possibility of other perspectives, however incoherent they may ultimately be, upon the epic victors' single-minded story of history."[73] By developing the plotters' voices in the story, Vicars, regardless of his intentions, validates their perspectives.[74] If, as Quint suggests, romance is the narrative of history's losers, then Vicars's "dilation" reflects a significant decline in confidence, at least among the godly, that in foiling the Gunpowder Plot England had achieved a decisive victory over Catholicism.

5.3 Epic for All: Educating the Protestant Reader

As we have seen above, the Latin epics originally offered compliments, usually seasoned with mild critique, to prospective royal or highly placed patrons. These poems credited the king with saving the country and praised both God and the monarch. In popular English poetry, the plot was more frequently represented as part of an attempt to subvert English, and even European, Protestantism, and thus represented a single battle in an apocalyptic struggle that was won but not yet concluded. Vicars's 1617 translation maintained the patriotic loyalty of Herring's poem, although tinged with increasing scepticism, but he added to it the militant Protestantism of writers such as John Rhodes and I.H. Vicars's translation of Herring's epic brings together the English and Latin traditions, melding them into a militantly Protestant text directed towards godly middle-class readers. Both in his 1617 text and in his paratextual materials, he popularizes the literary conventions of elite culture, while declaring his intention to stimulate his readers' memories so they will not underestimate the Catholic threat.

In his introductory letter to "All the Loyall-hearted Protestants of England," Vicars outlines his purposes: to remind the English that they should thank God for their deliverance, and to move their "*Christian* hearts to *zealous* detestation, / Of *Romes* most impious foule abhomination."[75] Perhaps to support these aims, Vicars introduces three emblems into the text, one serving as the title page for each section of the poem, and the third placed facing the opening lines of the first part.

Margery Corbett and Ronald Lightbown trace the origins of the title page featuring a single picture to German religious disputation during the 1520s, when Lutherans began using such pages as "pictorial propaganda for their religious beliefs," with images "deliberately chosen for doctrinal and controversial significance."[76] Vicars uses woodcut illustrations paired with brief verses in a less obviously controversial way to direct and educate his readers.[77] In his later pamphlet on prodigies, Vicars describes his series of such illustrations as "figures

Figure 3 Emblem from John Vicars's *Mischeefes Mysterie*, his first translation and expansion of Francis Herring's poem *Pietas Pontificia* (London, 1617, A4v). © The British Library, General Reference Collection, G.11266.

or emblems," thus indicating his own understanding of these devices. Alastair Fowler connects the emblem with the mnemonic image, accounting for the simultaneous decline of both in the later seventeenth century.[78] While Vicars's use of the form here supports his goal of stimulating his readers' memories, his appropriation of an elite genre seems to mirror the transformation of a courtly poem to a popular one.[79]

How Vicars perceived his role in creating the text at this point is not easy to determine, since the ideas he articulates are not always either clear or consistent. Flora Ross Amos notes that in this period there was no consensus regarding the need for a translator to acknowledge the original author, and that he or she could freely add to or delete from the original text.[80] Vicars acknowledges Herring's learning and godliness on his title page, but he also presents a series of verse letters commending his own work that fail to acknowledge it as a translation. According to Franklin B. Williams, the practice of prefacing texts with complimentary verses began with serious literature, but trickled down to popular culture after about 1560. In the Stuart period, he suggests, publishers rather than authors usually solicited such letters.[81] Nevertheless, Vicars seems to have participated in a network of writers who regularly exchanged such favours. Both Thomas Salisbury and Nathaniel Chambers contributed verses to other works by Vicars, and his verses appear in works by Joshua Sylvester, also a prolific translator. While not all of the authors of Vicars's commendations can be traced, their names may have been intended to display his relationships to other presbyterians.[82] Thus, both his use of emblems and commendatory verses and his Englishing of a Latin poem point to a project of making high culture traditions accessible to less learned audiences.

Recognizing that his readers might be incapable of understanding literary devices, Vicars both makes accommodations for them and at the same time teaches them, particularly through his marginal notes, to read and understand epic conventions. His change of the main title from *Popish Pietie* to *Mischeefes Mysterie* provides the first indication of how he perceives his audience's abilities. The word "mischief" appears frequently in works about the plot, including the 1610 translation of Herring's text.[83] While the word is now commonly associated with a misdemeanour, the meanings current in the seventeenth century generally implied more serious wrongdoing.[84] More significantly, Vicars's change eliminates the irony of the original title, as though he distrusts his readers' ability to decode the correct meaning.[85] Similarly, the purposes for which Vicars uses marginal notes include pointing out similes and identifying Treason's parents as the devil and the pope, his concern that readers will misconstrue even this simple allegory leading him to mark it twice. Although he uses occasional Latin tags in the margins, he also frequently explains both classical references and events in English history in

English notes that seem directed towards a less knowledgeable audience. Some of these notes also seem to be finding aids for browsers who are not reading the text sequentially, supporting William Slights's observation that margins could serve as rudimentary indices before the modern index became common.[86] The marginal notes also seem to reinforce Vicars's determination to call attention to the plot's historicity and to cultivate his readers' memories. When explaining the plot's unprecedented cruelty, he numbers the points in the margin, apparently to make them more memorable. In a similar vein, he inserts the Monteagle letter into the text. By both summarizing the letter and including the document, he not only offers tangible historical proof of the event, but also gives his readers two opportunities to impress the words upon their memories.

Vicars's 1641edition presented a new translation in which he melded the two parts into a single block of text and added more paratextual material. Resituating the earlier emblematic title pages as illustrations later in the work, Vicars provided a new frontispiece emblem in which Fawkes, now rendered as a demon complete with horns and tail, is caught escaping from the cellar. This time, however, the beam of light falling directly upon the scene from heaven dramatically outshines the feeble light of Knevet's torch.[87] As MacLean notes, the accompanying verse emphasizes the distinction between light and darkness, and explicitly identifies England with Israel. Most of the other new paratextual materials support Vicars's project of demonstrating the truth of his earlier assertion that the plotters had planned to blame the puritans for the destruction. He introduces this theme in his advertisement to the "Covrteovs" reader, promising to provide the testimony of two witnesses. Rather than producing his evidence immediately, however, he defers gratification of the reader's curiosity by interjecting a new dedication to the mayor and governors of Christ's Hospital, followed by a six-page "Table of the Heads of the most materiall passages in this History." As a finding aid, this list is of limited use. Names are indexed inconsistently, some individuals being identified by their titles while others are entered under their last names. Some of the headings appear to have been taken directly from the marginal annotations, including three that point generically to similes. D.R. Woolf notes that indices were becoming more common in historical works during this period, and perhaps this addition was intended to enhance Vicars's efforts to represent his work as creditable history.[88]

Following the table, Vicars returns to his project of demonstrating the existence of a plot to blame the puritans by inserting a supporting letter from a W. Perkins.[89] Perkins's story rests upon information received from Clement Cotton, who claims to have learned it directly from Lewis Pickering. Perkins's story is that Pickering, whose sister was married to Robert Keyes, learned of trouble brewing among the Catholics and gave James a warning about six months before the plot was discovered. Keyes had asked to borrow a horse that Pickering had ridden while hunting with the king, and which therefore would have been familiar to members of the royal household. The horse was to have been waiting for Fawkes in St George's Field on the morning of 5 November, but when he arrived to make his escape he would have been murdered and his corpse disfigured beyond recognition. Pickering, the same morning, was to have been slain in bed and conveyed to the field so that he would appear responsible for the plot. According to Vicars, the result would have been a puritan massacre, followed by civil war.

This story follows the outline of the one Herring had originally proposed, but offers names and details to increase its authenticity. Pickering was a favourite at the early Jacobean court, having been the second Englishman to arrive in Scotland bearing the news of Elizabeth's death in 1603. His promising career was blighted in March 1604/5 when he was accused of authoring a libel that had been pinned to Archbishop Whitgift's hearse. In a landmark libel case, he was found guilty and sentenced to both a fine and imprisonment. Although he was eventually released without paying the fine, he could not regain favour at court.[90] Alastair Bellany suggests that even without this dramatic fall, Pickering's star might have set as James lost sympathy for the puritan agenda. After his release, Pickering disappears from the historical record, even the date of his death being unknown.[91] Given his political troubles, it seems unlikely that he was in a position either to hunt with the king or to offer him advice in the spring of 1605, and, had he done so, it seems unlikely that he would still have been prosecuted on the libel charge.[92] Nevertheless, both Pickering and Keyes were from central England, and a marriage connection seems possible.[93] The evidence that both "Mistress Key wife of Robt: Key" and "Mistress Vaux" were "Discharged vpon Lewis Pickerings bond" in the days after the plot was discovered adds credibility to the possibility of a family relationship, and Pickering's assistance to Keyes's wife is perhaps best explained in this way. [94] Why he stood bond for Anne Vaux remains unclear, but perhaps their mutual ties to Northamptonshire overcame their religious differences.[95] Pickering himself may have originated the rumour that he was to have been killed in the hopes of rehabilitating his reputation at court, but we may never know the truth. Nevertheless, Vicars seems to have assumed that this testimony would impress sceptical readers.

In this second edition, Vicars makes two major revisions to the poem's structure. The first is to change the six-line stanzas of the 1617 edition into couplets. As MacLean notes, Vicars uses the "jingling rhyme of the loose pentameter couplet for conveying the excitement of his message," but it also contributes to the increasing open-endedness of the text.[96] Vicars's couplets generally lack the midline pauses, as well as the balance and parallelism, of more sophisticated writers' couplets, giving them a relentless forward movement. At the same time, since the couplet form is infinitely extendable, it also delays final closure. As a form in which a conversational tone could be achieved, it particularly suited a poem with the substantial dialogical component Vicars had added, likely as a means of popularizing the story.[97] As J. Paul Hunter points out, couplets can also make poems appear more accessible, "as if readers can approach them in a way similar to prose."[98] Thus, Vicars may have been attempting to make his poem more available to those less familiar with more complex stanzaic forms.[99] Although the couplet form makes the poem appear longer, Vicars actually decreases the total number of lines, deleting more material than he adds.[100]

His second major change was to integrate the two parts of the poem into a seamless whole, which undermines the closure of the first part even more than in the previous edition. A scant four lines describes the celebration after the plot's discovery as

> Annoy is turn'd to joy and sweet content,
> Mens *hands* and *hearts and* knees to praises bent:
> Making great *bonfires, feasting*, ringing *bels*,
> Each-one his *neighbour* this Gods goodnesse tells.[101]

Immediately, however, Vicars undercuts this triumphant celebration by turning back to the impenitent Fawkes refusing to concede defeat. He makes few substantial changes in the content of the first part, but increases his emphasis upon details that ground the plot in plausible although unverifiable facts, such as the exact thickness of the wall impeding the plotters' tunnel.[102] Having deleted his invocation to the tragic muse, he seems to have sought to represent the event more as history than as literature.[103] Along with the Monteagle letter, he inserts a copy of the oath supposedly taken by the plotters as further proof of Catholic sacrilege, and to stimulate his readers' memories, he provides additional numbered lists of important points. On several occasions, he addresses his readers directly, first calling the attention of the "good Reader" (11) to the foolishness of the Catholic plotters who believe they will become saints by destroying England, exhorting them, not the king, to banish the Jesuits. Although Vicars continues to support the king, he has shifted responsibility for the nation into the hands of individuals, even Catholics.

Divine providence can no longer be counted on to keep England safe without the continuing political loyalty of individuals. Early in the second part of the poem, Vicars adds to the description of Fawkes's resolution after his capture that "the *King* he did not take / To be his lawfull Soveraign, Gods annoynted" (47), and elsewhere he envisions the horror of a kingdom without a king. In this part Vicars, in accordance with Perkins's letter, provides a more detailed version of the plot to blame the puritans. Despite their attempt to discredit the innocent, however, Vicars increasingly views the lay plotters as men led astray by their leaders, both lay and ecclesiastical. In doing so, he uncovers the dangers of rhetoric used to serve false religion, narrating not only Garnett's false justification for killing innocents but also Tesimond's and Percy's impressive but erroneous appeals to the plotters to continue their rebellion. The idea that individuals may be misled by the very religious advisors who are supposed to care for their souls might have had particular resonance among the godly during the Laudian period. In a marginal note obviously added just prior to publication, Vicars reminds his readers that Satan's vow to continue the war against Protestantism has been "most fully confirmed by Satan and his Agents, our Church & State projectors, in this lately discovered plot, by our blessed Parliament, 1641. Which would have far transcended this of the Pouder-plot had it taken effect" (80), thus crediting Parliament with England's safety.[104] The transformation of the epic, then, mirrors the concerns with bad counsel that emerged in the later Jacobean period and became acute in Charles's reign. At the end of the narrative, Vicars adds two new woodcuts, the first depicting Fawkes's head displayed on the Parliament building and the second illustrating the annual anniversary celebrations, taking place under God's watchful eye.[105] The poem concludes with a lengthy addition that offers first a warning to Catholics and then a reminder to all Englishmen to display gratitude or risk God's wrath.

Vicars, then, gradually transforms this text from a panegyric to a Protestant king to a panegyric to a Protestant God. In his "Letter to all loyall-hearted English Protestants" in the 1641 edition, he reminds his readers "*How powerfully God to our Church did stand*," only adding at the end that king and kingdom were the plot's initial targets.[106] The king's preservation is important only to the extent that he preserves the church. Increasingly, however, puritans have come to represent the persecuted church, and the plot's real targets. The developing emphasis upon the Midlands revolt after 1609 suggests a growing sense that a closed narrative has been reopened. While the Gunpowder plotters may have been punished, Catholics still lurk not only in England's forests, but also in her church and court.

We are faced finally with the irony that a genre originally intended to support the project of a united Protestant state came to participate in the nation's religious and political fragmentation. As the Anglo-Latin Gunpowder epics ceased to be vehicles for obtaining patronage, they lost their panegyric function and sought the support of godly Protestants in printed editions and English translations. Increasing disillusionment with the king's will and ability to eradicate Catholicism led both to attempts to contain false religion through satire and to appeals to godly readers to take up the challenge of maintaining the Protestant nation. Francis Herring's addition of a sequel describing the Midlands rebellion revoked the closure of the earlier epics that had seen the plot as the founding moment for the Protestant nation, nudging this text towards a more open-ended romance narrative that situated England within the broader vision of Christian history and providing the foundation on which John Vicars was able to establish an English epic that both instructed a new class of readers in the genre's conventions and promoted a more militantly Protestant agenda. As conforming Royalists like Abraham Cowley found themselves unable to complete their heroic epics, the godly were inheriting from the Gunpowder tradition a form that offered heroic roles to ordinary Protestants in the ongoing struggle against Satan in his many guises.

5.4 Heaven Turned Upside Down: Satan, Gunpowder, and the Protestant Reader in *Paradise Lost*

One inheritor of this tradition was Milton, whose epic of the fall overturns the closure of his own *In Quintum Novembris*. While the youthful poem ended with joyous annual celebration of a crisis averted, *Paradise Lost* concludes in the knowledge of ultimate triumph through the Son's sacrifice, but in the reality of present uncertainty as Adam and Eve set off to wander through a fallen world infected by a defeated but still powerful Satan. Writing at the end of twenty years of war and chaos, Milton seems, in this poem, to have relinquished both his adolescent militarism and his faith in the collective actions of English Protestants, but not his belief in the individual godly reader's ability to learn from the past. His narrative of Satan's rebellion in heaven, framed as a lesson for the first couple, depicts an "intestine" war that declines from epic heroism to brute savagery when Satan invents, produces, and deploys gunpowder. I argue that Milton gestures back to the Gunpowder Plot in this narrative to recognize it as the first cause of England's own difficult present and uncertain future, just as the rebellion in heaven commences all humanity's woes. He does so not only through Satan's use of gunpowder, but also by focusing his narrative on the original three themes of Gunpowder poetry – providence, paternity, and memory. While Adam and Eve fail to heed Raphael's warning about the dangers of disobedience to the Father, Milton continues to hope his readers will internalize his message.

Milton was not required to include the heavenly war in his epic, and certainly not to accord it the centrality he did, given its limited presence in the biblical narrative and the prevailing assumption that God, with Michael's assistance, had defeated the rebel angels and thrust them from heaven easily, not after a hard-fought, three-day battle. That Milton described the war in detail and also placed it in the centre of the epic, therefore, indicates how vital he considered it to his own designs. Scholars have proposed three credible seventeenth-century analogues for Milton's heavenly war in *Paradise Lost* – the 1605 Gunpowder Plot, the 1641 Irish Rebellion, and the civil wars. The presence of anti-Catholic satire in the text validates the first two, while the argument for the third rests primarily upon the evidence of Milton's disillusionment with the modern warfare he had witnessed. These possibilities, I will argue, are not mutually exclusive; rather, the episode deliberately invokes all three to demonstrate that past errors lead to present trials in both divine and earthly affairs. Moreover, historical events and the literature associated with them do not provide the sole context for this episode. Clearly, Milton relied upon various traditions, and this multiplicity of sources, including the Bible, classical and contemporary epic, vernacular literature, and historical events along with their printed representations compounds the complexities of Raphael's narrative.[107]

As several critics have pointed out, Milton was consistently fascinated with "origins, causes, and beginnings," and Satan's rebellion initiates all the evil that both precedes and follows it in the narrative sequence, just as Milton's contemporaries saw the Gunpowder Plot as the inciting incident for England's seventeenth-century trials.[108] Furthermore, by framing the war in heaven as a lesson for the first couple, Milton makes narrating this battle as vital to his project of educating his Protestant readers in how to avoid Satan's wiles as many still saw the Gunpowder Plot in teaching English Protestants to beware of religious error in its increasingly disparate forms.

Satan's introduction of artillery into heavenly warfare challenges readers who come to the epic steeped in classical representations of heroic combat. As Claude Rawson notes, "Gunpowder was often considered inimical to epic." Not only did technological warfare replace the heroism of single combat with random carnage, consequently blurring distinctions of rank, but it also "reduced the scope of warrior speech-making, a complaint made in respect of both literary texts and real-life military behaviour."[109] In other words, it nudged epic in the direction of mock-heroic, as it does in book 6 of *Paradise Lost*.[110] Milton's decision to have the rebel angels discover and use gunpowder enables him to undercut their pretensions, just as Vicars had done with the defeated plotters in his final version of Herring's poem, as well as to remind his readers of the source of their own troubles. Gunpowder already had popular associations with fraud and the demonic and therefore, for Protestants, with Catholicism. However, Michael Murrin points out that in England "it was the Gunpowder Plot that most deeply impressed the English and linked the new technology to sedition" (132).[111] Consequently, Milton's early readers would likely have had no difficulty in connecting Satan's rebellion with the plot.

Renaissance writers were divided on the question of how gunpowder and artillery first came into use. Polydore Vergil, in his *De Inventoribus rerum* (1499), claimed gunpowder was a German invention, discovered by chance and used first against Genoa by the Venetians in 1380.[112] Among English writers, Camden supported its discovery by a German, while Ralegh believed it had been invented by the Chinese.[113] Camden notes the argument that artillery is so destructive that it must have been invented by the devil, but opts more prosaically for a German inventor, "Berthold Swarte a Monke skillful in Gebers Cookery or Alchimy" (240–1).[114] For Protestants, awarding the discovery to a monk was only one step from blaming it upon the devil. Although the Gunpowder Plot helped to seal the relationship between gunpowder and fraud, Samuel Daniel introduced such a connection in the 1601 addition to his *Civile Wars*. In book 5 he describes artillery as "th'infernall instrument, / New brought from hell, to scourge mortalitie."[115] He associates the discoveries of printing and gunpowder, since printing encourages discordant opinions, which can then be defended by these new weapons.[116] Daniel's poem is particularly relevant as it narrates factionalism and civil discontent. Moreover, Daniel anticipates Gunpowder Plot literature in his description of the quest for gunpowder, describing how

> boldly breaking with rebellious minde
> Into their mothers close-lockt Treasurie
> They [the Yorkists] Mineralls combustible do finde. (5.53)

Perhaps even more suggestively, these arms are used not only in civil strife, but by rebels against the king. In other words, Daniel had already associated the use of gunpowder with sedition and internecine war by 1601. All that remained was to link both with Catholicism, which was to happen only four years later.

Among the writers of brief epics on the Gunpowder Plot, only Francis Herring refers to the popular idea that Satan invented gunpowder as James, wrestling with the meaning of the Monteagle letter, calls it "the invention of the devil [Daemonis invento]" (273). In 1617, Vicars rendered the phrase "that hellish Art" (37), while in 1641 he retreated to the innocuous "*that-art*" (39), possibly foreseeing the use of artillery by his own side in the coming conflicts. Although Herring and Wallace do not identify the origins of gunpowder, they connect its use, and misuse, with both demons and Catholics. In Herring's poem, when the son of Lucifer and the Whore of Babylon comes to England, assuming the name of Fawkes, he proposes to use gunpowder against the king, while Wallace has Abaddon disguise himself as a Jesuit when proposing the plot to Fawkes. Fletcher refers to both the demonic and Catholic origins of gunpowder in his 1627 English poem, as Loyola's son describes how the cellar beneath the House of Lords will be

> Stuf't with those firy sands, and black dry mould,
> Which from blue Phlegetons shores that Frier bold
> Stole with dire hand, and yet hells force and colour hold. (4.34)

Milton, in *In Quintum Novembris*, refers to "Tartarean powder [Tartareoque ... pulvere]" (19), and in his second epigram on the plot, he accuses the "beast in ambush on the Seven Hills" of using "infernal gunpowder" against James, like many contemporary Protestants conflating the beast of Revelation with the Catholic Church. The later part of the epigram narrows his satiric target to monasticism in an image of cowls blown "up to the skies," anticipating the Paradise of Fools in *Paradise Lost* ("In Eandem").[117] Thus, the Gunpowder Plot poetry depicted the Catholic Church making a demonic pact by using gunpowder in its fraudulent attempts to gain secular power.

Stella Revard initially proposed the Gunpowder Plot as background to Satan's revolt in *Paradise Lost*, arguing that, like the plot, it "begins in conspiratorial secret, it is directed against a newly anointed king, and it uses gunpowder to surprise and overwhelm those plotted against."[118] She sees the 5 November sermons as one of Milton's primary sources, emphasizing their depiction's of Guy Fawkes as Satan.[119] Significantly, Revard argues not that the rebellious angels are like the Gunpowder plotters, but that the Gunpowder plotters are like the rebel angels. Satan's use of secrecy, gunpowder, and equivocation in the first rebellion, then, sets the stage for future rebellions, including those that have plagued England since 1605. John N. King has subsequently affirmed the echoes of Gunpowder sermons along with recollections of visual representations of the plot in Satan's rebellion, suggesting that the rebel angels' debasement recalls anti-Catholic satire and polemic connected with the plot.[120] Critics have long recognized Milton's borrowings from and echoes of Fletcher's *Apollyonists*, particularly this poem's influence on his creation of the allegorical Sin and Death.[121] David Quint extended these borrowings to include the consultation in Pandemonium in book 2, where Fletcher's influence is also apparent, while making more sweeping claims for the centrality of the Gunpowder Plot to Milton's epic vision, concluding that "From the beginning to the end of his poetic career, Milton's imagination was haunted by a historical event, the Gunpowder Plot of 1605, and by the literature that described that event, particularly *The Apollynists* [*sic*] of Phineas Fletcher."[122]

Beginning with the evening following the first day's battle, the actions of Satan and his followers closely parallel those of the Gunpowder plotters in their insistence upon secrecy and their subversive burrowing into the floor of heaven. Because this action is initially a rebellion rather than open warfare, subterfuge is necessary; however, Satan's secrecy appears excessive, for it extends even to his closest followers. In his speech at the end of the first day's battle, although making no mention of discovering gunpowder, he slyly alludes to a possibility that

> perhaps more valid Arms,
> Weapons more violent, when next we meet,
> May serve to better us, and worse our foes,
> Or equal what between us made the odds,
> In nature none. (6.438–42)

One might suspect Satan of setting up Nisroch who, after lamenting his first experience of pain, offers that

> He who therefore can invent
> With what more forcible we may offend
> Our yet unwounded Enemies, or arm
> Ourselves with like defense, to me deserves
> No less than for deliverance what we owe. (6.464–8)

Satan responds to this prompt with feigned reluctance, evident in his use of the double negative and the passive voice, that such a device is "not uninvented" (6.470). Satan's depiction as innovator here is consistent with his representation in Gunpowder Plot literature. In the Latin epics, Satan or one of his Catholic emissaries invariably proposes a plot no one else has dared to contemplate, which human agents then carry out. Donne's *Ignatius His conclave* connects Satan even more closely with innovation when he reserves the place closest to him in hell for the greatest innovator in history, thus demonstrating an insatiable thirst for novelty that becomes his downfall. Milton's Satan, too, is ultimately destroyed by his own cleverness, for the Father only stops the war when the loyal angels respond to Satan's artillery by destroying the heavenly landscape. Ironically, Satan's invention, although temporarily effective, is merely a poor copy of the Father's thunderbolt, making him a second-rate innovator.

The rebel angels' subsequent preparations take place "under conscious Night secret" (6.521), although of course this secrecy is ironic since the Father watches but resists intervening. They mine powder from the floor of heaven to manufacture "thir Engines and their Balls / Of missive ruin" (6.518–19), hidden from the eyes of the loyal angels if not from the Father's knowledge. In describing their efforts, Milton echoes much of the imagery employed by earlier poets and preachers to describe the plotters' machinations, including the pervasive images of burrowing into the womb of the mother country and of demonic procreation that we have traced through the Gunpowder poems. In revealing his plans to the other rebels, Satan describes his ingredients as "materials dark and crude," which, "in their dark Nativity," are "pregnant with eternal flame," hidden within the "Entrails of Heaven" (6.478, 482, 483, 517). The feminization of the ground and the images of conception and birth are all familiar from the earlier Latin and English epics as well as from texts such as *Novembris Monstrum*, the Cambridge drama printed in 1641 in which the pope miscarries while pregnant with the plot. Quint notes that, rather surprisingly, "heaven itself is built out of the primordial matter of Chaos – the 'originals of nature' – and this matter has the explosive properties of gunpowder" ("Milton," 261). The traditional association of gunpowder with the demonic generally implies manufacture in hell rather than heaven; however, since the Father creates beauty and goodness from these same materials, it seems that the matter itself is neutral and only becomes harmful when shaped by a rebellious will.[123] Throughout the rebels' production of the gunpowder and deployment of their artillery, Milton reinforces these negative connotations of monstrous birth by simultaneously evoking ideas related to digestive processes and the expulsion of bodily wastes.[124]

Before Satan and his followers fire even a single shot, however, they experience a loss of linguistic purity, falling into misuses of language that begin with punning and lead ultimately to the kinds of equivocations most frequently associated with the Gunpowder plotters, specifically with the Jesuit superior, Father Garnett. Satan, concealing "his devilish Enginry" (6.553), also begins to conceal his meaning in "ambiguous words" (6.568). The loyal angels, unaccustomed to such deception, naively anticipate words rather than weapons and fall "By thousands" (6.594) when the cannons thunder, while Belial triumphantly appropriates his chief's new mode of miscommunication. Equivocation is not mentioned in the original Gunpowder poems, perhaps partly because these poems were written immediately after the plot's discovery, while Fawkes, rather than the priest, was seen as the instigator. Later, however, Father Garnett's trial and the controversy over the Oath of Allegiance gave this aspect of the plot an increasing importance that was reflected in the later poems, particularly Fletcher's, in which Ignatius is given the name "Aequivocus" to signal his linguistic duplicity.[125] Thus, Milton's early readers would almost certainly have connected Satan's changed mode of speech, as well as his secrecy, with the Gunpowder Plot. At the same time, however, duplicitous speech had come to be connected more generally with religious and political strife in the intervening years. Milton himself, in *The Tenure of Kings and Magistrates*, accuses the presbyterians of "paltering with the world," and the animosities of the pamphlet wars demonstrated that each side could use words to its own advantage.[126]

As some critics have persuasively argued, these years provide several other analogues for the war in heaven. The most recent and clearly relevant context is the period of the civil wars, which Christopher Hill and Ronald Bedford both consider essential background, suggesting that specific incidents in the heavenly war may recall occasions in the earthly conflicts.[127] This parallel accounts for both Milton's repudiation of modern warfare based on his personal experience and his characterization of Abdiel, who may represent Milton in his progressively isolated stance in opposition to the Restoration.[128] More recently, several critics have also explored parallels between the heavenly war and the Irish Rebellion of 1641. David Loewenstein first suggested that "the Irish Rebellion and the war which followed, with their associations of royalist conspiracy, secret treachery, and political equivocation, haunted Milton's own imagination from the time of his early revolutionary prose, until the very eve of the Restoration" (301), pointing out that similar secrecy and misuse of language characterize Satan's behaviour in *Paradise Lost.* Expanding upon this suggestion, Catherine Canino observes that the pamphlets from which English readers obtained their news of the revolt frequently characterized the Irish as monsters and demons. In particular, Canino argues that one pamphlet, Thomas Waring's *An Answer to Certain Seditious and Jesuitical Queries*, gave Milton "an immediate model for rebellion as seductive, casuistical, and demonic" in its representation of Edmund Gawre, a Jesuit casuist whose methods and motives in supporting the Irish Rebellion prefigure Satan's in rebelling against God.[129]

The plausibility of all three analogues reflects Hill's admission that "The advantage of Milton's method is that the same narrative can refer to more than one series of historical events."[130] Similarly, Loewenstein cautions: "The relation between the politics of Satan's revolt in *Paradise Lost* and Milton's religious politics in the Revolution and its immediate aftermath ... is neither straightforward nor unidirectional."[131] Rather than arguing for the centrality of a single analogue, I suggest that Milton, like many of his contemporaries, saw all three events as integrally connected. In this world view, as we have seen, the Gunpowder Plot was the seed from which subsequent rebellions and wars grew. In other words, Milton's allusions to the Gunpowder Plot do not equate Satan simply with the Catholic Church or even with the crypto-Catholicism ascribed to Charles I and the royalist party, but show how the failure to learn from a single incident leads England farther into strife. The tradition of Gunpowder poetry we have been examining in these two chapters, then, informs the war in heaven because Milton saw the Gunpowder Plot, like Satan's rebellion, as an event that reverberated through later history.

Popular pamphlet literature continued to connect the Gunpowder Plot with the Irish Rebellion and the civil wars through this period. As we have seen, even before 1641, the plot's original Elizabethan context had been expanded to include the Spanish match negotiations, the Blackfriars collapse, and the growth of

Laudianism. Ethan Shagan's study of how pamphlets describing the Irish situation freely repurposed rhetoric from earlier anti-Catholic discourse demonstrates that this tradition continued into the 1640s.[132] He argues that while conformist pamphlets, including those appearing under the king's auspices, described the rebellion as a sin against order, those written by more militant Protestants looked to the anti-Catholicism promulgated by Foxe and nurtured by accounts of events such as the Armada and the Gunpowder Plot. In puritan pamphlets, however, God and Parliament, instead of God and the King, save the nation. As we have seen, narrative poetry of the Gunpowder Plot had also begun transferring responsibility for the nation's deliverance from king to Parliament.

That news of the Irish Rebellion arrived in London only days before the annual celebration of the Gunpowder Plot's discovery strengthened associations between these events. Perhaps as a result, the rebellion spawned rumours of other plots, many suspiciously similar to the Gunpowder Plot. A 1641 pamphlet, *A Trve Relation of a Damnable Gun-powder Plot* ..., describes two conspiracies reported in November 1641, both connected with the fifth Earl of Worcester, Henry Somerset. The first rests upon the testimony of John Davis, a servant at a Hereford inn who claimed to have accompanied a traveller to "Rugland [Raglan] Castle" in Monmouthshire in Wales.[133] When they arrived, the traveller showed him underground stables with room for about 140 horses, equipment for two thousand men, and a store of gunpowder, matches, and other ammunition, then attempted to recruit him into the plot. In the following year, a brief pamphlet, *A Bloody Plot, Practised by some papists in Darbyshire* (1642), described another conspiracy, in which a Catholic named Needham was alleged to have hidden thirty-four barrels of gunpowder along with iron bars, stones, and other missiles in the vault beneath the village church, intending to light the fuse during Sunday service. The night before, however, after hearing suspicious noises, the sexton gathered some neighbours, who discovered a man with a dark lantern in the cellar along with the gunpowder. The man admitted he had accomplices, and a store of weapons indicated that a rebellion was planned. Like many of the alleged plots in this period, this one implicated the Jesuits specifically. The one interesting detail in this story is the intention to blow up the church, confirming that the threat to the nation is now considered a threat to Protestantism as much as to the ruler.[134]

Perhaps one of the most damaging aspects of the rumours contained in some of these pamphlets was that they recalled the Gunpowder Plot not only in their methods and materials, but also in their participants. As early as 1639, a satirical "squib" accused Sir John Winter, acting as "Secretary and Master of Requests to Queen Henrietta Maria," "whose kindred were some of the chief actors of the Gunpowder Treason" of funnelling money to Catholic causes.[135] Similarly, a 1641 pamphlet entitled *The Iesvites plot discovered Intended against the Parliament and City of*

London very lately accused Sir Thomas Lunsford and George Digby of collecting horses and amunition at the Tower, necessitating the temporary removal of Parliament from Westminster to the Grocers' Hall.[136] The title indicates how fears of Catholics, particularly Jesuits, could whip up popular prejudice against political enemies. Moreover, Digby was cousin to Sir Everard Digby, the highest ranking of the executed Gunpowder plotters, and although a Protestant, he retained the taint of his name. Clearly, the authors of such texts believed allusions to the Gunpowder plotters would give credibility to their allegations. Although warnings of copycat plots died down later in the decade, William Bridge could conclude his 1648 sermon on 5 November with the reminder that God "hath not only delivered us from one *Powder-Treason*, but from many, in these late years."[137]

Connections between the Gunpowder Plot and the Irish Rebellion lingered into the next decade. The anonymous *Papa Patens or the Pope in his Colours*, published in 1652, provides brief accounts of various alleged Catholic conspiracies, situating the Irish Rebellion immediately after the Gunpowder Plot in order to make a strongly marked comparison between them:

> And for the more strongly prosecution of this their most exhorbitant villainy, the Conspirators and Traitors entred into a most accursed Covenant (just as our Popish-Pouder-Traitors did in their damnable designe) and bound themselves by an oath of Confederation and Secrecy, *Reily* a prime Popish-Priest and others (like his father the Devill) compassing the Earth farre and neer to draw into their conspiracy such as had not before bin therwith acquainted, as also to satisfie all scruples (if any arose in any of their minds) about the lawfullnesse of their actions, just as *Garnet* that old *Romish* Jesuiticall Fox did with his Pouder-conspirators, 1605.[138]

That such parallels could still be exploited at this date shows the extent to which the Gunpowder Plot remained a model for treachery.

Nevertheless, its political meanings became increasingly complex during the civil wars as the godly consensus fragmented. As Caroline Hibbard first demonstrated, regardless of any actual ties between Catholics and Laudians, presumption of such connections was widespread in the 1630s. Consequently, the Gunpowder Plot anniversary provided an opportunity for radical preachers such as Henry Burton to insist that Laudianism was simply Catholicism in disguise. Through the early 1640s, militant Protestants persisted in implying continuity between the Catholics who had perpetrated the Gunpowder Plot and the ceremonialists who had caused the wars by misleading the king. In 1642, as we will see in the next chapter, Matthew Newcomen used his sermon before Parliament on 5 November to advocate continuing the war until all traces of Catholicism had been eradicated, implicitly assuming that Royalism and Catholicism were virtually identical. In the

1650s, as the cracks between presbyterians and Independents widened, however, references to the Gunpowder Plot became weapons in increasingly acrimonious rhetorical wars among Protestants. Although Peter Sterry, in his introduction to a 1651 Gunpowder sermon entitled plainly *Englands Deliverance from the Northern Presbytery, Compared with its Deliverance from the Roman Papacy*, admitted grudgingly that the presbytery was better than the papacy, he clearly saw presbyterianism as only one step from prelacy and popery.[139]

Given the persistent connections among these three incidents in popular culture, it may seem less surprising that Milton's depiction of the war in heaven should recall them all and that it should be so difficult to decode Milton's political stance from his narrative of this incident. As Loewenstein suggests, limiting the possible analogues for Satan and his followers to "a duplicitous and impenitent Charles I, divisive Laudian prelates, Cromwell and his supposed political hypocrisy, ambitious Army leaders of the Revolution, a prevaricating Presbyterian clergy, or the Irish Catholic rebels of the 1640s" unnecessarily circumscribes Milton's ability to offer a broader message to his godly readers through his account of heavenly warfare.[140]

Milton gestures to the Gunpowder Plot not only in the details of Satan's revolt, but also, I suggest, in the broader outlines of the episode, which centres, like the early Gunpowder poems, on the three themes of providence, paternity, and memory. The poet who begins by stating his intent to "assert Eternal Providence, / and justify the ways of God to men" (1.24–5) concludes with Adam and Eve setting off "with wand'ring steps" but yet with "Providence thir guide" (12.648, 647), framing the entire narrative with faith in God's care for his people. Throughout the war in heaven, God demonstrates his providential care more intrusively in his vigilance against the rebels. As the Father, with his newly anointed Son, watches and laughs at Satan's plans, a series of allusions from Psalm 2 provides one of the primary biblical contexts for the rebellion.[141] From the moment Satan begins plotting,

> th' eternal eye, whose sight discerns
> Abstrusest thoughts, from forth his holy Mount
> And from within the golden Lamps that burn
> Nightly before him, saw in whom, how spread
> Among the sons of Morn, what multitudes
> Were banded to oppose his high Decree. (5.711–17)

Just as he oversaw the preparations for the Gunpowder Plot, the Father continues to keep his watchful eye upon the rebels. Not only does he see rebellion being fomented, but he also laughs at the plotters. Even while observing Satan's initial meeting with his confederates, the Father smiles as he addresses his Son (5.718). The Son responds with a direct allusion to Psalm 2, validating the Father's satiric perspective: "Mighty Father, thou thy foes / Justly hast in derision, and secure / Laugh'st at their vain designs and tumults vain" (5.735–7). In one of the earliest Gunpowder poems, that of Michael Wallace, "the omnipotent father to whose eyes from on high all things mortal are evident, who in his eternity governs the progress of life and of death, ruling the world with perpetual reason, looked out from Heaven upon the secret plot" (Haan 385, 387).[142] In Francis Herring's epic, the Father's "vigilant eye creeps about everywhere throughout the world, surveying all lands, deep seas and the invisible, secret places concealed in hidden darkness" (269, 271). God then tells the "vast host of angels encircling his throne" (271) of the plot being hatched and sends one angel to warn James in a dream and to remind Monteagle to do his duty to his country by warning the king.[143] While John N. King sees Milton's appropriation of God's eye and God's laughter as "a shift away from the original thrust of Gunpowder Plot satires and sermons as pro-Stuart propaganda" (121), this reorientation had begun to occur in the 1620s.

As we have seen, Vicars's later versions of Herring's poem diminish James's role in the deliverance, while a controversial cartoon "invented" by Samuel Ward in 1621 shows a beam of light from God's eye falling directly upon Fawkes as he steals towards Parliament.[144] Upon the beam of light is printed "Video rideo," followed by the translation "I see and smile." Although the authorities' suspicions of the cartoon arose more from its possible allusions to the Spanish Match negotiations, it also eliminated the king as the instrument of God's providence. I will suggest in the next chapter that Robert Willan's 5 November sermon to the judges in 1622 introduces divine laughter into the Gunpowder sermon tradition partly in an attempt to restore the king's role as God's agent. A few years later, Milton's *In Quintum Novembris* placed Fama in the role of discovering the plot, an honour traditionally assigned to the king. In other words, I suggest that not only are God's eye and God's laughter associated with anti-Catholic polemic, but that after 1622, as Protestants grew suspicious that James was betraying their interests by negotiating a Spanish marriage, they became connected to a more politically subversive reading of history that limited the monarch's role in safeguarding the kingdom, particularly in matters of religion. Milton's allusions to God's eye and God's laughter, then, may not simply reflect the traditions of anti-Catholic satire, but also encode a political, specifically anti-Stuart, message.

Based upon a selection of surviving sermons on texts from Psalm 2, the entire psalm appears to have been far from politically neutral by the 1640s and 1650s. Preachers could apply this text in various ways to the current situation depending upon whether they chose to interpret the psalm historically or prophetically, a situation we will encounter again in the next chapter with John Donne's choice of a text from Lamentations for his 1622 Gunpowder sermon. In 1646, preaching before the Lord Mayor at St Paul's, Edward Terry rested his interpretation upon a historical reading, suggesting that David likely wrote the psalm after his victory over the Philistines. Consequently, taking Psalm 2.3 as his text, he called for obedience to the king and the laws of church and state, identifying "Schismaticks, Hereticks, Pharisees, Papists, Turkes, Infidels, Idolaters of all kinds" as those guided by the spirit of Satan to withhold obedience from their superiors.[145] In his introduction, he admits choosing this text to illustrate the necessity of government in both church and nation. In contrast, an undated assize sermon by Richard Baxter (with an introduction dated 1654) makes plain from its title, "A Sermon of the Absolute Soveraignty of Christ," that obedience is due to the heavenly king rather than an earthly one. Declaring that "The chief scope of the Psalm is, To foretell the extent and pevalency [*sic*] of the Kingdom of Christ, admonishing his enemies to submit to his Government, deriding the vanity of their opposing projects and furie and forewarning them of their ruine if they come not in" (78), Baxter clearly reads the psalm prophetically.[146] William Jenkyn, preaching at St Margaret's Westminster in 1656, took a similar stance, arguing that Christ is the King of Kings and must be worshipped even by the angels (7); therefore, ministers of both church and state must also worship him. "Humility," Jenkyn continues, "is the ornament of angels, and the deformity of Devils" (16), concluding that "As soon as *Angels* ceased to be holy, they began to be Devils, though their other accomplishments of *strength*, *wisdom*, *spirituality*, &c. remained with them" (38). In other words, the psalm seems to have become a focal point for debates about the ultimate source of political authority.[147]

It seems likely, then, that Milton deliberately framed the heavenly rebellion around this psalm to emphasize that Christians are responsible directly to God rather than to God through an earthly king. In linking subsequent historical events such as the Gunpowder Plot with the heavenly rebellion, Milton suggests that these are all ultimately rebellions against God as much as against earthly monarchs, and that God's providence requires no human intermediaries as agents. As the Father orders the Son to end the war, he "on his Son with Rays direct / Shone full" (6.719–20), a reference that recalls the earlier allusions to the eye of God. Patricia Crouch observes that not only does the Father appoint his Son as sole agent in this deliverance, but he also demonstrates the error a subordinate may make in believing himself to be a chosen instrument of God's providence. Michael mistakenly believes the Father has appointed him to drive out Satan, and upon learning that this role belongs to the Son, he is forced to remember his own subordination to Christ. Since many, including an earlier Milton, saw Oliver Cromwell as Michael, this is a lesson about God's ability to work without intermediaries, not only for the archangel but also for the reader.[148]

Milton's allusions to Psalm 2 also seem to underlie one unusual element in his narration of Satan's rebellion, the Son's elevation as the cause of the revolt.[149] Although Milton's Satan, like the plotters, rebels against a newly anointed king, the Son represents for Satan the continuation of an old order against which he is already chafing, just as the accession of James I signalled to Catholics that they could expect no relief from the penal laws, particularly since the new king had sons to succeed him. When Satan speaks first to his recruits, he asks them how they are to accept "Knee-tribute yet unpaid, prostration vile, / Too much to one, but double how endur'd, / To one and to his image now proclaim'd?" (5.782–4). Although Satan has apparently acquiesced in ritual devotion to the Father, it is clear he has not enjoyed it and cannot bear the thought of obedience to both Father and Son. As we have seen, James I interpreted the plot's discovery as a founding event for his new dynasty by focusing upon both his literal and metaphoric fatherhood, a chorus taken up by the early panegyric writers who rejoiced in the promise of a stable succession that had been lacking throughout Elizabeth's reign. In the later epics, authors lost their enthusiasm for the Stuart succession, with Vicars even removing the tribute to the dead Prince Henry from Herring's poem. In 1626, Milton remained silent on the subject of the new king, while the following year, still apparently hoping for royal favour, Fletcher praised Charles only for his willingness to take up a sword rather than a pen in the Continental religious wars. In *Paradise Lost*, Milton creates a dynastic founding event in heaven rather than on earth, enabling God to operate directly through his Son rather than through intermediaries such as Michael, and it is this new development that Satan cannot stomach.

As the Gunpowder epics increasingly asserted, then, God's providence works directly, but it operates through the individual Protestant's capacity and willingness to remember and interpret historical events. Authors like Vicars more and more emphatically insisted their readers remember past deliverances as a means of preventing future dangers. Milton frames the war in heaven explicitly as a warning against disobedience to the first couple, for only by recalling this narrative can Adam and Eve avoid repeating the angels' sin. Concluding his narrative, Raphael exhorts them: "let it profit thee to have heard / By terrible Example the reward / Of disobedience" (6.909–11). At the same time, by telling the story to his readers, Milton reminds them of the horrors of rebellion and war that have ensued in their own day through failures to remember the lessons of the past. Moreover, through his allusions to events such as the Gunpowder Plot, the Irish Rebellion, and the civil wars, he associates the heavenly rebels with those who have disobeyed God and sown the seeds of the current troubles. In future days, Raphael cautions, if Malice should abound,

Someone intent on mischief, or inspir'd
With dev'lish machination might devise
Like instrument to plague the Sons of men
For sin, on war and mutual slaughter bent (6.503–6)

Milton's audience knew that those days had already arrived.

At the same time, the narrative grapples with questions about how to memorialize events without valorizing evil actions. As we have seen above, Vicars's "dilations" of Herring's poem gradually moved towards a potentially problematic memorialization of the plotters' deeds while at the same time he warned his readers that these men deserved no lasting fame. Chronologically rather than narratively, Milton begins to individuate the rebel angels during the war in heaven, giving the first voice to Nisroch, a lower-order angel than those introduced previously in hell, at the moment when Satan introduces gunpowder.[150] Raphael, however, explicitly forbids memorializing the rebels, whose names are "Cancell'd from Heav'n and sacred memory," and who should remain "Nameless in dark oblivion," " doomed to "Eternal silence" (6.379, 380, 385). The loyal angels, Raphael declares, require no memorials, but Milton clearly recognizes the challenges of recording the loyal angels' actions without naming the rebels. Like the Gunpowder poetry, then, Milton's poem is integrally concerned with the importance not only of remembering, but of remembering correctly.

Adam and Eve's failure to remember and learn from the events Raphael describes results in humankind being forced to wander in the wilderness, just as England has been forced to undergo a series of trials, arguably because it has forgotten lessons such as the Gunpowder Plot. To prevent this from being a time of purposeless wandering, however, Milton offers a course in learning through narrative history. We concluded the previous section by looking at how Vicars trained his Protestant readers in the conventions of epic. Milton needed his readers to understand these conventions so that they could recognize his deviations from them, for upon such understanding rested their ability to resist Satan and the wiles of those who would mislead English Protestants into error. In other words, what I have argued here is that Milton saw the beginning of England's problems in the Gunpowder Plot, just as the first problems of humanity sprung from the rebellion in heaven. Milton's allusions to the Gunpowder Plot in this episode reflect his sense of this event as an inciting incident in English history. Even Milton, then, no friend of the Stuarts, had accepted the importance of this episode to England's identity and destiny. It had, indeed, become a founding moment in Stuart history, but hardly as James I had envisioned it.

6 "For God and the King": Preaching on the Plot Anniversary

6.1 Church and Nation: Religion and Politics in the Gunpowder Sermons

When James I initiated the preaching of annual sermons to commemorate the country's, and his own, deliverance from the Gunpowder Plot, he could hardly have anticipated that this tradition would contribute to raising popular discontent in his son's reign, help to justify one grandson's restoration to the English throne, and participate in celebrating another's exile. Although the king's intention was to memorialize a historical event, the sermons also offered preachers a vehicle for commenting on current affairs. Perhaps more importantly, they simultaneously allowed listeners and readers to acquire sophisticated interpretative skills, particularly when preachers' utterances were constrained by generic conventions and political necessity. Unlike the Latin epics, which initially emphasized the role of the Christian monarch in preserving the Protestant state, the sermons from the beginning were based upon the premise that all individuals played a crucial role in the nation's religious and political life. The combination of politically engaged preachers and listeners expanded that role from maintaining the status quo by praying for the king and celebrating his deliverances to participating actively in creating political change over the course of the century. This chapter takes us from one of the earliest crises of interpretation, the Spanish Match negotiations, through the increasing tensions of the Laudian period and the civil wars, to the uneasy restoration of order and obedience after 1660, with a final glance ahead to the early eighteenth century, when it became apparent that the Gunpowder sermon could no longer fufil its original generic function of supporting the authority of church and state.

Political sermons held in tension two separate functions, one controlled by the monarch and the other by the minister. They enabled the ruler to display his power and authority to his subjects, and at the same time they allowed the minister to counsel his sovereign or Parliament. Thus, they participated in the often contentious process of defining the English church in its relations both to the state and to its rivals, Catholicism and puritanism. The four sermons I focus upon in this chapter provide case studies of the ways in which these two functions interacted at some crucial periods during the century. I argue that by learning to negotiate among the messages to multiple audiences that characterized these sermons, listeners, and later readers, developed skills that helped them to engage in a wider range of political and religious discourse.

Although the record of Gunpowder sermons is incomplete, the occasion was the most durable of the political anniversaries, surviving officially until 1859.[1] In 1605, 5 November was added to an English preaching calendar that included the Gowrie anniversary and James's accession day, occasions that David Cressy has argued replaced the saints' days that had punctuated the year before the Reformation with a specifically nationalistic set of occasions.[2] The Gowrie anniversary, always something of an embarrassment to the clergy, was tacitly dropped upon James's death. Less fond of sermons than his father, apparently indifferent to the importance of "representative publicness," and married to a Catholic, Charles I seems to have neglected the Gunpowder memorial and possibly other occasions for political sermons.[3] Godly preachers who saw the occasional political sermon as an opportunity to negotiate the relationship between the church and the monarchy, however, maintained the Gunpowder tradition, exploiting the occasion to increase public awareness of what they considered unacceptable alterations in the Caroline church, while claiming to operate within their traditional role of counselling the monarch. During the Civil War, the anniversary underwent a crucial change from a celebration to one of a series of fast days, but retained its role of justifying hostility to Catholics and crypto-Catholics.[4] In the 1650s, clergy seem to have been uneasy about exactly how the anniversary should be interpreted, and responsibility for the celebration in large measure devolved from the national to the civic level. Surviving the Restoration, however, it was joined by a new set of occasions, most importantly 29 May, the date of the Restoration, and 30 January, the fast day for the regicide, frequently interpreted as a successful Gunpowder Plot perpetrated by Dissenters. The ongoing political importance of the anniversary, perpetuated largely by sermons, is demonstrated by William of Orange's exploitation of its symbolic value in representing his arrival on 5 November 1688 as a new Protestant deliverance.

While some pamphlets, particularly those of Bishop Carleton and Michael Sparke, as well as the original "King's Book," enjoyed wide circulation at various times during this period, sermons provided more regular reminders of the plot.[5] Unlike printed texts that could be accessed at any time, in their original delivery they were tied to a specific time and place, for most individuals the parish church.

Attendance at these annual services was compulsory, at least in law, and Cressy's research demonstrates that laws requiring church attendance on political anniversaries were enforced at least sporadically.[6] Thus, much of individuals' exposure to plot rhetoric was oral, usually received through the experience of liturgy and sermons in parish churches. Other venues, however, were available, particularly to Londoners. Outdoor sermons at Paul's Cross took place until the 1630s and frequently attracted large crowds.[7] Sermons at court, preached regularly during the Jacobean period and reinstated at the Restoration, were accessible to those with court connections. During the Civil War, members of the public could also attend sermons preached to Parliament at St Margaret's Westminster. Although a wide range of individuals, including those unable to read, had access to sermons, we must remember that opportunities to attend commemorative sermons were not ubiquitous. In parishes without trained clergy, subjects would have participated in the liturgy and possibly listened to the "Homelie against disobedience and wylfull rebellion," but would not have received the benefit of an occasion-specific sermon.[8] Increasingly, however, printed copies allowed transmission beyond the original auditories, creating a body of texts not subject to the limitations of their oral performances and engaging in dialogue with each other and with other texts.

This ability to reach a diverse audience had given the political sermon a lengthy history by the seventeenth century. Susan Wabuda suggests that Erasmus's *Ecclesiastes* had first opened the door to political preaching, since he saw the sermon as "an exercise in deliberative oratory, a moralizing force, specifically aimed at the lowliest members of society, the most ordinary of men and women, to teach them the will of God and the wisdom of Scripture."[9] Henry VIII recognized the possibilities of this medium for introducing his subjects to his claim to supremacy in the church and took advantage of Paul's Cross, as the most public pulpit in the country, to justify his new role.[10] In June 1535, Thomas Cromwell ordered the bishops to preach the king's supremacy; at the same time, the Bishop of Lincoln printed copies of his letter to his preachers announcing Cromwell's orders. Wabuda notes that "Few alterations to the political and religious landscape can be more striking than this, that the laity was elevated as watchdogs over the clergy."[11] Every individual, lay and clerical, became responsible for ensuring that every sermon was both politically and doctrinally sound. At the same time, both Mary Morrissey and W.J. Torrance Kirby have observed that the royal use of sermons created a "culture of persuasion," as monarchs recognized that their subjects needed to be convinced, not merely coerced into external conformity.[12] This belief that sermon rhetoric could influence thought and thereby shape action was responsible for the creation of such instruments as the Elizabethan *Homilies*.

Political sermons thus helped to create an English religious identity, particularly in opposition to Catholicism.[13] Preaching itself was on some level an expression of anti-Catholicism, since the elevation of sermon over sacrament in worship was distinctively Protestant. Attacks on Catholics began at the Reformation but became increasingly prevalent in the 1570s, thus establishing repudiation of Catholic doctrine, both theological and political, as a basis of English Protestantism.[14] The institution of Queen Elizabeth's accession day, beginning in the 1570s and celebrated as a deliverance from the reign of her Catholic half-sister, as well as occasional services of thanksgiving for the defeat of the Armada and the discovery of various Catholic plots against the queen beginning in the 1580s, reaffirmed the pulpit's role in promoting the benefits of Protestantism. When James I introduced his annual observance of the Gowrie anniversary into England, he thus grafted it onto an existing tradition of political preaching that required recasting the Gowries as crypto-Catholics.[15] The addition of the Gunpowder Plot anniversary, however, required less political finesse. As I have suggested in chapter 2, James used these occasions to weave together personal and national deliverances through a "vocabulary of celebration."[16] In the occasional sermons, as in the Anglo-Latin epics, however, this rhetoric developed binary oppositions that could later be applied to other religious and political opponents.[17]

The Reformation has frequently been seen as marking a transition from a religion centred upon rituals comprehended largely by the eye to one in which oral instruction was apprehended by the ear; however, Eric Josef Carlson argues that a more significant result of the break with Rome was "the change in the relationship between preacher and audience" required by developments in the theory and practice of preaching.[18] While the thematic sermon characteristic of pre-Tridentine Catholicism consisted of a discourse on a theme derived from a passage of scripture, Protestant preaching emphasized textual explication, refocusing interpretation upon the literal sense of scripture.[19] The standard understanding of English preaching before the Civil War was that "it was an act of biblical interpretation whereby the teachings of the Bible were made relevant (or applied) to the circumstances of the sermon and to the hearers' lives."[20] The preacher's role was not to invent, but to interpret. Most preaching manuals condoned the use of rhetorical techniques, provided they were used for persuasion rather than for mere ornamentation, but their authors encouraged preachers to illustrate the significance of the text to their hearers by interpreting scripture through scripture.[21]

This change in homiletic theory required the auditor to develop a more sophisticated mode of understanding in order to apply scriptural teachings to his or her own life. At the same time, the preacher had to be sensitive to his hearers' abilities to understand and interpret his words. "Decorum" required that he suit his preaching to the educational and social status of his hearers as well as to the time, place, and occasion of the sermon.[22] On anniversaries such as 5 November, the minister's task was to apply the scriptural text to a specific historical and political situation without "wresting" or distorting the meaning.[23]

Two themes predominated in these sermons. The first was the importance of obedience in maintaining the social order. This was an inherently anti-Catholic theme, since the perceived threat of Catholicism was largely based upon the belief that Catholics were permitted to resist a ruler whom the pope had declared a heretic. Under the law, Catholics were punished for treason, not for heresy, and this point was consistently reiterated by preachers as well as by the secular authorities. Some preachers, however, conflated the two, making every Catholic potentially guilty of treason. As both Morrissey and Kirby have pointed out, the very act of preaching such a message acknowledged the need not merely to enforce obedience to the English church and state but to persuade subjects of their duties to uphold these institutions. The second theme was gratitude for God's blessings, usually deliverances from military and political threats. This theme, too, was anti-Catholic because most of the deliverances celebrated in the early part of this period were from Catholic plots. At the same time, reminding listeners of their blessings gave everyone a role in preserving the state, since God's continued favour was regarded as contingent upon gratitude for his earlier assistance. While these were conventions of the occasion, the preacher was also required to suit his discourse to the particular venue and audience. Thus, a sermon before the people from a pulpit such as Paul's Cross required a different preaching style than one before the monarch or the court.

When preaching to the sovereign, the minister was in the position of an authorized counsellor. Peter McCullough has described how the architecture of the royal chapels visually represented the preacher's position as both dependent and spiritual advisor.[24] While the preacher had to look up at the king, the monarch was effectively trapped in the royal closet, where he could be forced to listen to unpalatable truths. Such a position allowed John King to give James I a powerfully worded warning against leniency towards Catholics in his 1608 sermon at Whitehall, and authorized Lancelot Andrewes's critiques of sermon-centred piety at court in his later Gunpowder sermons.[25] Conversely, before the people the preacher was expected to support the king's policies, as John Donne did in his 1622 sermon defending James's *Directions to Preachers*.[26] The medium of print, however, permitted the blurring of boundaries between audiences, a circumstance that caused uneasiness for some clergy. Although James authorized the publication of King's sermon in order to issue a warning to a broader Catholic audience, the same means enabled Henry Burton, later in the century, to feed popular discontent by pointedly dedicating his printed sermons to the king and claiming the privileges of counsel.[27]

Studying the textual remains of these preaching occasions presents several methodological challenges. As Jeanne Shami has pointed out, we still lack any accepted methodology for studying sermons, given their unique status as texts.[28] Historians have sometimes treated them as documentary sources without sufficiently acknowledging their rhetorical character as texts "written to influence events" as well as to document them.[29] Literary scholars, until fairly recently, have focused almost exclusively on a relatively small group of texts by prominent preachers, or have attempted stylistic comparisons of larger groups based on questionable theological or ecclesiological categorizations of their authors.[30] In the case of the Gunpowder sermons, the very volume of texts may have worked against a systematic study and fostered a reliance on a few examples, particularly Andrewes's court sermons, creating an impression of homogeneity that a wider reading dispels.[31] Thus, although the large number of surviving sermons has made them a valuable resource for studying the cultural history of the plot, citations from them have been restricted to a relatively narrow group of texts, and little attempt has been made to understand individual sermons within their specific historical contexts.

This large group of sermons nevertheless represents a relatively low survival rate. Godfrey Davies, many years ago, calculated that on a conservative estimate 360,000 sermons were probably preached in England and Wales between 1603 and 1640, whereas Edith L. Klotz's sampling of *Short Title Catalogue* records suggested that only about 1,600 survive in print.[32] While Davies's calculations could be refined and updated to take in additional sources, including manuscripts as well as sermons included in other publications, he is correct in cautioning that our evidence is woefully incomplete. In addition, W. Fraser Mitchell's assumption that the surviving printed sermons are representative is questionable.[33] Sermons by well-known preachers, those delivered at prominent locations, and those preached at times of political crisis seem to have been the most likely to survive in print. Many more manuscript copies and sermon notes remain effectively buried in local archives and private libraries where they have not been catalogued or made widely available, as well as in major repositories such the British Library.[34] This reminds us particularly of the need for caution when arguing from negative evidence. For example, I have found few printed Gunpowder sermons from the 1660s, but it would be unwise to assume that the preaching occasion lapsed early in Charles II's reign. John Evelyn's diary records attendance at a 1664 sermon by Robert South of which I have found no other trace.[35]

One of the thorniest problems of sermon study, however, is that we have little means of knowing what relationships printed sermons bear to their oral deliveries, or how they were received by their original audiences, either in person or in print. Most preachers spoke from notes and did not write their sermons out in full until a decision had been made to publish.[36] Prefatory materials sometimes indicate that the preacher has expanded the sermon, especially if circumstances forced him to abridge the oral performance. This seems to be particularly true of the sermons preached to the Long Parliament. Both Cornelius Burges in 1641 and Matthew Newcomen in 1642 note that the pressure of business in the House prevented them from delivering their entire sermons. (This was likely true, but it also reminded their readers of Parliament's more immediate task of governing the nation.) Other preachers, however, tell us that care has been taken to reproduce the sermon as originally delivered.

While William Barlow apparently wanted to replicate the experience of the original event for readers of his 1605 sermon, claims of accuracy were more frequently motivated by adverse responses to the preached sermon. Gilbert Burnet admits in the introduction to his 1684 sermon that he cannot guarantee that the words are the exact ones he used, but he insists that he has reproduced the sermon with care, supplementing his own recollections with the memories of his more attentive auditors, in order to vindicate himself of charges that he is disaffected from the government.[37] In contrast, Henry Burton conflated his two 1636 sermons into a "summe," presumably to prevent being charged with uttering specific words.[38] In drawing up the charges against him, Star Chamber circumvented this problem by accusing him in each case of using "the like words in effect & substance."[39] In other cases, however, the decision to merge several sermons into one does not seem to have been politically motivated.[40] While not all preachers offer modern scholars clues to their intentions by including dedications or notes to their readers, some printed sermons bear other marks of their histories, such as imprimaturs and requests to publish from their original hearers – friends, the king, or Parliament. When single sermons were published as pamphlets, their title pages frequently indicate other interpretative contexts, including the original place and date of preaching and scriptural epigraphs.[41] On occasion, auditors made notes in letters or diaries that can also assist us in piecing together the contexts and receptions of early modern sermons as events related to, but distinct from, their surviving traces.

Despite the difficulties in reconstructing the contexts of these sermons, it is vital, as Morrissey has pointed out, to understand early modern sermons both as texts and as events. Political sermons participated in the construction of the "rudimentary public sphere" that Peter Lake and Michael Questier believe began to develop as early as the late sixteenth century during such religious and political controversies as the establishment of the English Jesuit mission and the Elizabethan succession crisis.[42] Sermons were public in two ways. Morrissey, McCullough, and Lori Anne Ferrell have all shown that as public performances sermons reinforced existing social and political hierarchies by presenting the ruler before the people, in person at court and through the preacher at other venues. Thus, they provided a form of "representative publicness" to the monarch, and to Parliament during the civil wars, but they also supplied information and interpretations that could provide the basis for public discussion and debate.

Preachers considered themselves responsible to God as well as to the king, and therefore believed they had the right to chastise a monarch who failed in his spiritual or ecclesiastical duties. Although preaching was subject to various controls, preachers could express dissenting opinions even in the most public pulpits. In fact, Annabel Patterson's thesis that in this period "there was clearly and widely understood a theory of *functional* ambiguity, in which the indeterminacy inveterate to language was fully and knowingly exploited by authors and readers alike (and among those readers, of course, were those who were most interested in control)" seems to apply to oral sermons as well.[43] Preachers appear to have been punished only when they openly crossed the line between critique and sedition. In perhaps the best documented case of sermon-fed controversy in the early seventeenth century, the Spanish Match crisis, both Shami and Thomas Cogswell have demonstrated the importance of sermons in forming public opinion.[44] Their work suggests that James I intervened only when confronted with John Knight's open advocacy of resistance in a sermon at Oxford in April 1622. As Patterson has suggested with reference to print, both sides appear to have known the rules and usually played by them, but this required both ordinary listeners and the authorities to develop sophisticated interpretative skills. Arnold Hunt describes the early modern sermon as an inherently dialogic form, the final product a shared creation between minister and congregation.[45] Particularly in oppositional contexts, the minister relied upon the congregation to make explicit connections that he had not, potentially even those he had specifically denied. McCullough has also observed that court sermons sometimes responded to previous ones, thereby forcing readers to resolve contradictory messages they might have received from the same pulpit on a particular subject.[46] Sermons thus played a crucial role in training individuals to read and interpret in sophisticated ways.

The political sermon straddles, however uneasily, the boundary between the individual's relationship to God and to the community. Eiléan Ni Chuilleanáin suggests that, unlike theatrical audiences, sermon audiences are addressed as individuals.[47] Political sermons, however, exhort listeners both as individuals and as members of a political and religious body. Traditionally, as Morrissey has demonstrated, these sermons were divided into an explication of the text followed by an application to the specific occasion.[48] The preacher's explication of the text frequently implied a comparison between England and Israel, or, less often, between England and the primitive church. The application made this comparison between biblical and modern nations more explicit, but also instructed each member of the congregation on his or her personal obligations within this paradigm. For a sermon preached at Oxford on 5 November 1607, John King chose as his text Psalm 46.7–11.[49] King compared the difficulties from which God saved the Israelites to the English deliverance from the Gunpowder Plot, concluding that the text describes an event very similar to the one commemorated. Although he declared at the outset that his sermon would focus upon applying rather than explicating the text, he established the relationship between God and the children of Israel before demonstrating that God offered the same care to England. In return, God required praise and gratitude. While these were individual duties, they were also responsibilities both of and for the community, since God might punish individual forgetfulness with communal disaster.[50] The "doctrines and uses" style of sermon, more common among puritan divines, similarly required specific tasks of the congregation both individually and collectively. For his sermon entitled "The Church's Deliverances," most likely preached on 5 November 1626, but not published until 1638, Thomas Hooker takes as his text Judges 10.13, "Wherefore I will deliver you no more."[51] He draws from this verse three doctrines: that God does not help those who come to him in their sins, that God delivers his church and his people in times of trouble, and that the state of the church may be such that God will finally refuse any further assistance. In the uses of each doctrine, Hooker moves from the individual's responsibility to repent to the need for collective changes of heart and will to ensure God's continued favour to England.

The frequent identification of England with Israel also highlighted the uneasy boundary between religion and politics that the nature of the English Reformation had created. In her analysis of prophetic sermons preached at Paul's Cross, Morrissey observes that "the 'Israelite paradigm' by which Jacobean preachers made God's dealing with Israel an example to England is *only* that: an example of God's dealing with a nation *as a nation*, a mixed community of saints and sinners. The *typical* signification of Israel is used by preachers only when they speak of the invisible Church, some of whose members are English." The significance of this distinction is that England corresponds to Israel in being a sinful, rather than a chosen nation: "Any nation can be temporarily blessed by God, be it heathen or holy, and any nation can be punished for its sins because no people has a licence to sin with impunity."[52] Nicholas Colt, preaching at Norwich in 1616, distinguishes between the godly, "*they that rightly know the true God, and doe duely worship him in Iesus Christ,*" and the visible church consisting of the religious, the irreligious, and the superstitious.[53]

Increasingly throughout this period, however, the question arose: to what extent were the church and the nation one?[54] On political anniversaries such as 5 November, preachers could emphasize the deliverance of the king, Parliament, the nation as a whole, or the church. While early sermons tended to focus on the king and nation, puritan preachers gradually began highlighting the dangers of the Caroline church by stressing the historical deliverances of the reformed English church. During the civil wars, the church was identified with the godly nation, yet the events of this period demonstrated the impossibility of creating such a nation. After the Restoration, the voices of dissenting preachers were largely silenced, at least in the print record, yet Conformist sermons testify to the strain of attempting to hold together a state and a church that could no longer even pretend to include all of its people.

The intertwining of religion and politics is evident in the relationship between the sermons and their places of preaching. Paul's Cross sermons took place in a location with a unique relationship to the sacred and secular, since this space had been used for both political and religious functions, including the reading of royal proclamations and the Armada celebration, from the beginning of its recorded history.[55] Other sermons were delivered in churches but to congregations organized around political functions – both houses of Parliament, the judges, the Lord Mayor and aldermen of London, and sometimes civil governments in other cities. Many of the surviving sermons from the 1650s were preached to civic authorities, in London and elsewhere, and civic sermons remained important occasions after the Restoration. Their title pages and dedications frequently emphasize the political bases of the gatherings more than the ecclesiastical spaces in which they took place.

Political authorities might pass judgment upon either the oral or the printed sermon in a number of ways, including granting or withholding royal or parliamentary commands to publish. James I called in Donne's 1622 Gunpowder sermon, but thwarted the preacher's apparent hopes of authorized publication.[56] Similarly, although printed orders to publish parliamentary sermons during the Civil War follow a standard formula, not all preachers were invited to print.[57] While preachers may have been disappointed by such slights, they also understood the dangers printing posed. William Strong, in 1654, accepted Parliament's order for publication, but confessed that he would have preferred to remain silent at a time when "some men are made *Transgressors for a word*."[58] Strong's distinction suggests that, at least at times, print was more dangerous than speech. That preachers' fears of legal reprisals were justified at times of political strain is evident from the most notorious cases of Henry Burton in 1636 and Henry Sacheverell in 1709, but Samuel Ward of Ipswich was also questioned for a Gunpowder sermon in the 1630s.[59]

While the people's wrath might be less dangerous than the state's, some clergy feared exposing their sermons to unknown, and potentially critical, print audiences. Some questioned the spiritual efficacy of printed sermons; others were concerned about their own reputations.[60] Although Charles Herle in 1644 called a sermon a kind of miracle, since the crumbs left by the initial auditory could be published for the nourishment of others, James Rigney notes that the proliferation of printed sermons, particularly after 1640, seems to have devalued them.[61] William Cave, in 1680, complained that printed sermons were usually either slandered or tossed aside rather than read for spiritual improvement.[62] At times of heightened political tensions, preachers seem to have been more likely to offer detailed justifications for publication, usually in response to negative rather than favourable reception. Richard Carpenter, in 1656, declares that "*This Sermon had been* nothing but a Voice, *though the* Printers *were the Auditors; had not impudent Slander extorted it from me, and bound it over to the Press.*"[63] Edward Pelling offered the distinction that "*Some discourses may be fit enough for the Pulpit, which may not be so fit for the Press.*"[64] Nevertheless, congregations could also express disapproval of the sermon in performance. In the dedication of his 1679 sermon, Francis Gregory claims that he had originally written the sermon for his village church but was ordered to preach it in London before the Lord Mayor and aldermen at St Mary le Bow. The church, he complains, was large and well filled, making it difficult for his audience to hear him over a din of coughing and other sounds.[65] Were the members of the congregation unusually unhealthy that day, or were they less than engaged by Gregory's performance?

Preachers on this occasion were particularly sensitive to the prospect of Catholic audiences, occasionally addressing them in their sermons, but more frequently acknowledging them as potential, and frequently hostile, readers in paratextual materials. At times when Catholics seemed to be regaining favour, especially at court, preachers seem to have anticipated more criticisms either from them or their supporters. Publishing his series of five virulently anti-Catholic sermons in 1620, Thomas Taylor observed that he expected to arouse the envy and anger of the Catholic population.[66] Thomas Reeve, in a 1629 sermon printed in 1632, addressed "all the adherents of the Romish Church amongst us," exhorting them in a note before the sermon to return to the Church of England and discard their political ambitions.[67] In 1641 Richard Heyrick, publishing three sermons including his 1638 Gunpowder sermon, complained that Catholicism was increasing in Lancashire and Manchester, while conceding that at least papists were easier to identify than Puritans. He preached the sermons, he asserts, "*(with danger enough)*," since they "*breath enmitie to* Rome."[68] Such fears of Catholic audiences returned in the 1670s. John Scott, in 1673, claimed to fear Catholic reprisals, while in 1678 Aaron Baker imagined, perhaps improbably, that he might experience martyrdom for his comments.[69] In 1682, Edward Pelling confessed that his friends had encouraged him to publish to clear himself from charges of being popishly affected because he supported church and king.[70] While these fears may seem excessive in a culture that offered most Catholics little political power, they generally point to fears of highly placed adherents to the Roman church, usually at court. Catholic consorts evoked uneasiness through much of this period, especially in the 1630s and 1680s. Nevertheless, such comments may also have exaggerated the threat of Catholic reprisal for polemical purposes.

Although our glimpses into the reception of these printed sermons are tantalizingly rare and brief, we have evidence from many of the sources noted above – prefatory materials, diaries and letters, and legal proceedings – that sometimes they continued discussion and debate that had begun in the pulpit, broadening the audience for such controversy. In their dedications and prefaces, many preachers attribute the publication of their sermons to the importunities of friends or other auditors, a claim that may frequently be conventional, but that may also reflect either general approval or the desire for the sermon to participate in some larger context. John Chamberlain recorded both the public's approval of Donne's Paul's Cross sermon on James's accession day in 1617, and its lukewarm reception of his September 1622 sermon defending the *Directions to Preachers*.[71] Sermons not only elicited responses, but were themselves frequently both responses to and interventions in existing controversies signalled by other texts. Many of the titles mentioned in the Gunpowder sermons are part of the voluminous Catholic-Protestant controversial literature of this period. Richard Carpenter identified his 1662 sermon as a response to a pamphlet entitled *Reasons why Roman Catholicks should not be persecuted*, while William Lloyd (1680) complained of being maligned for co-authoring a book on suppressing popery.[72] Numerous other discussions and controversies are embedded less overtly both in the texts themselves and in marginal annotations. Lists of Catholic atrocities including the assassinations of Henri III and IV in France, the Paris massacre, the Spanish treatment of the indigenous populations of the Americas, and the various English plots, all sites of contested interpretation, recur frequently in various configurations. Such intertextuality introduced listeners and readers to texts of which they might otherwise have been unaware as well as more generally to methods of interpretation and disputation.

As the event itself receded into history, accounts of the plot became increasingly contentious. Early preachers generally referred their audiences to James I's 9 November speech and its accompanying "Discourse" or to the *True and Perfect Relation*, but as multiple interpretations became available this consensus fragmented. Some sermons perpetuate myths originating in ephemeral sources including ballads, such as the one that the Spanish ships in 1588 carried instruments of torture. Similarly, the tale of Garnett's straw to which Shakespeare had alluded in *Macbeth* reappears occasionally as evidence of Catholic gullibility, and Nicholas Colt refers to Garnett praying twice for the success of the plot.[73] Carleton's narrative became a popular source in the 1620s, while

Puritan preachers occasionally cited Michael Sparke's *Crumms of Comfort.* By the Restoration, Jacques-Auguste de Thou's accounts had become increasingly popular, since citing a Catholic author offered at least the illusion of fairness.[74] Partisanship, however, reasserted itself in the late 1670s and 1680s amid heightened fears of Catholicism. Thomas Wilson (1679) referred his readers to Foulis's *History of Romish Treasons* for further examples of Catholic infamy.[75] Others engaged directly with the opposition. Edward Stillingfleet, in 1673, condemned two Catholic works that described the plot as the work of a few unfortunate gentlemen.[76] In 1684, Gilbert Burnet cited a case analogous to that Garnett was supposed to have proposed in his conversation with Catesby concerning the killing of innocents from Martin Delrio's *Disquisitionum magicarum libri sex.* Occasionally, preachers offered other types of documentation. John Tillotson claimed to have Digby's letters from prison, demonstrating that he had been corrupted by Rome – a use of evidence that apparently impressed John Evelyn.[77] In addition, preachers could set up dialogic relationships with earlier sermons either through direct references or more subtly by selecting the same scriptural texts. While some duplication of texts was inevitable, and probably unintentional, Henry Burton's choice of one that Lancelot Andrewes had used for a conventional sermon in 1614 was not lost upon his hostile readers.[78] Thus, Gunpowder sermons engaged in various ways, and for a variety of rhetorical purposes, with earlier texts. The margins of printed texts allowed for more expansive engagements than the oral sermons were likely to have provided, extending from cryptic references to selective animadversion. By assuming or encouraging familiarity with other texts, these sermons promoted their listeners' and readers' engagement in discussions and debates that required critical listening and reading skills.

The foregoing suggests the impossibility of generalizing from such a large and diverse group of sermons, or attempting adequately to contextualize each within its milieu. Instead, in the following sections, I consider more closely four sermons preached in different venues at various times of political stress. The sermons chosen are not intended to be representative since, as I have suggested, there is no "standard" Gunpowder sermon.[79] Instead, they serve as case studies that can illuminate the various ways in which Gunpowder rhetoric participated in a number of debates and discussions from 1622 to 1688, and even beyond. Moreover, they demonstrate how the genre of the occasional political sermon developed as a result of the Gunpowder Plot from its origin as a means of asserting monarchical authority to an opportunity for subjects to query the actions of those governing both church and state. Preached and published in different circumstances, these sermons all contributed to the construction of audiences capable of reading, and listening, between the lines.

6.2 John Donne (1622): Samuel Ward and Criticizing the King

Donne's 1622 Gunpowder sermon, written for Paul's Cross but delivered in the church because of inclement weather, is situated at a tense moment when James I had curtailed preachers' freedom in response to increasingly vocal challenges from press and pulpit regarding both his attempt to negotiate a Catholic marriage for Prince Charles and his failure to intervene in the Palatinate on behalf of his Protestant daughter and son-in-law.[80] As Shami points out, this sermon deliberately foregrounds issues of interpretation and so offers a number of challenges to modern readers, as it did to Donne's original auditory.[81] Shami's meticulous examination of the circumstances surrounding the sermon nevertheless leaves us to consider how Donne's audiences might have understood and responded to it. Little evidence for actual reception exists in this case; however, we do have two versions prepared for different readers. Many questions remain to be answered about the relationship between the scribal manuscript produced for James I in late 1622 and the text first printed in 1649, but both provide us with hints about how Donne constructed his sermon in order to place the burden of interpretation upon his listeners and readers. Donne seems to have used the occasion to offer a methodology of listening and reading that balances obedience to royal authority with the subject's freedom to interpret, responding not only to James's recent *Directions to Preachers*, but also to one of the challenges that had provoked them, Samuel Ward's *Double Deliverance [Deo Trin-vni Britanniae bis ultori...]*, an engraving linking the Armada, the Gunpowder Plot, and possibly the Spanish Match negotiations. By introducing complex problems of interpretation Donne endorses the individual's right to interpret; however, by highlighting questions of means and responsibilities, he warns against interfering in matters of state beyond one's capacity and position.

Shami and Cogswell have carefully documented the crisis that developed around the role of the pulpit in shaping public opinion during the Spanish marriage controversy. As Millar MacLure phrased it succinctly: "There was trouble in Israel, and for the first time in half a century, the Paul's Cross pulpit got out of hand."[82] Forced to respond to the escalating public discontent that had culminated in John Knight's open advocacy of resistance theory at Oxford on 22 April, James issued *Directions to Preachers* that would inhibit discussions of both his foreign policies and abstruse Calvinist theology from public pulpits and selected Donne to defend them at Paul's Cross on 15 September. Although Donne's support for the king here, as elsewhere in his preaching career, has been read as evidence of "absolutism," Shami and Morrissey have demonstrated that this sermon was characteristic of Donne's casuistical approach.[83] Morrissey points out that Donne typically made the structure of his sermons part of their argument, in this case redividing his text in order inconspicuously to separate the issue of the Spanish Match from the *Directions*. In this way, Donne is able to defend the principle of order, rather than the king's particular instructions, "with all the force of scriptural authority."[84] Shami also notes the division of the sermon into what is effectively two sermons, "on the one hand, a call to active and zealous preaching, within the terms of the *Directions*; on the other, an assertion of monarchical power to restrict controversial preaching."[85] She emphasizes the way in which Donne offered his fellow preachers a model for future sermons that would fulfil their duties to God, their congregations, and their superiors. John Chamberlain, in a letter to Dudley Carleton, indicates that the sermon did not entirely please the public; however, the king was sufficiently satisfied to order it printed and to give Donne his third commission at the Cross, that of preaching on 5 November.[86] As Shami observes, this invitation placed Donne in a difficult situation: "Donne in fact was handed an anti-Catholic occasion and asked to defend the policies of a monarch who seemed to many all too pro-Catholic."[87] In defending James's policies, however, Donne showed his audience that they had the capabilities and the right to interpret the king's actions, as long as they stopped short of giving him advice. If his fellow preachers were a primary audience for the September sermon, then Donne made his audience for this one the entire kingdom, for all would be affected by the *Directions*.[88]

Throughout their seventeenth-century history, one of the recurring themes of the Gunpowder sermons was that of thankfulness for the deliverance itself. Preachers generally approached this theme by choosing a scriptural text that allowed a comparison of England's deliverance from her enemies with one of Israel's. While the Psalms was one of the more popular sources for texts, a range of other books, primarily from the Old Testament, are represented in surviving sermons.[89] Depicting Israel's strivings against its neighbours allowed preachers to make analogies with England's Catholic enemies, local or international. Although the number of surviving sermons preached outside the court from this period is relatively small, they seem to have grown more hostile to Catholics, particularly lay Catholics. Perhaps the most ominous sign in this period, however, is the widening gap between court sermons and those preached in other venues.

With the exception of John King's denunciation of Catholicism at Whitehall in 1608, the publication of which Ferrell argues was politically motivated, the rhetoric of the court sermons was relatively balanced. In fact, Ferrell suggests that the "moderate" discourse of Lancelot Andrewes and other preachers both at court and at Paul's Cross promoted anti-Puritanism as much as anti-Catholicism.[90] Andrewes increasingly used the occasion to attack sermon-centred piety at court, a tactic that allowed him to offer a safer form of criticism than commenting on the king's foreign policies.

In contrast, public sermons became increasingly anti-Catholic. Early sermons blamed the plot upon the Jesuits, and ultimately upon Satan. As the Oath of Allegiance controversy escalated, however, more widespread condemnation of ordinary Catholics seems to have increased. At Paul's Cross, Martin Fotherby had advocated chasing papists out of the English church as early as 1607, and the following year Robert Tynley had preached against toleration.[91] Although Ferrell interprets John Boys's 1613 sermon as more anti-puritan than anti-Catholic, both he and William Goodwyn in the following year emphasized memorialization of Protestant deliverances, while Goodwyn also made a detailed analogy between Rome and Babylon.[92] Unfortunately, a lengthy gap exists in the surviving Paul's Cross Gunpowder sermons between Goodwyn and Donne, but sermons preached in other venues appear to have become more openly anti-Catholic. In 1619, William Jemmat published a set of five vitriolic Gunpowder sermons by Thomas Taylor, the first preached in 1612.[93] These sermons, particularly the later ones, argue against any form of toleration, one of the most controversial topics of the Spanish Match negotiations, as does John Prideaux's sermon at St Mary's Oxford in 1621.

The 1622 *Directions* responded to this blatant anti-Catholicism as well as to Knight's call for resistance by restricting those below the rank of bishop or dean from opening texts not in accordance with the Thirty-Nine Articles or the *Homilies* or preaching on doctrines related to predestination before popular audiences; limiting afternoon sermons to the Catechism, the Creed, the Ten Commandments, and the Lord's Prayer; and restraining all preachers from meddling in affairs of state and attacking either papists or puritans personally.[94] John Wall and Terry Bunce Burgin suggest that one way in which Donne responded to the *Directions* in his Gunpowder sermon was by obtaining a copy of the 1547 *Homilies* and using it for guidance, as James had recommended. He not only echoes the language of the first "Homily" and quotes some of the same scriptures, but he also borrows from the "Homelie against disobedience and wylfull rebellion," which allows him "to undercut the arguments of James' protestant opposition by associating them with the disobedience to royal authority manifested by the Catholic Guy Fawkes and his fellow plotters."[95] This interpretation supports Ferrell's contention that anti-puritanism began to overtake anti-Catholicism in these sermons in the second decade after the plot's discovery.[96] According to Wall and Burgin, Donne also conforms to the *Directions* by shifting his focus from religion to politics, although, as Shami points out, the prayer before the sermon, which is not included in the manuscript version, specifically identifies Catholic doctrine as the plot's source.[97]

The survival of two versions, prepared at different times and for different readers, both enriches and complicates our understanding of this sermon. The king was apparently the intended reader for the first version, a scribal manuscript (BL MS Royal 17.B.XX) corrected by Donne, apparently produced shortly after the sermon's delivery when James requested a copy, and identified by Shami in 1992. Previously, the only known version was that printed first by Donne's son in *Fifty Sermons* (1649), probably based upon a copy Donne revised for possible publication a number of years later.[98] Shami argues that the two texts constitute different versions according to Hans Zaller's definition, since they reflect different intentions.[99] She cautions, however, that we cannot know how carefully Donne corrected the manuscript, and consequently that the "question of authorial intention as it relates to Donne's apparent revisions of his manuscript for publication is crucial to further textual and interpretive decisions." Although many of the alterations in the printed text reflect "the shift from oral to written delivery," many "also show a shift in politics."[100] After examining Donne's three major additions, Shami concludes that the later version is more critical of the king, but the succession of a new monarch in the interval complicates our interpretation of the revisions. In what follows, I wish to consider more closely the structure of the sermon and the rhetorical means by which Donne creates spaces for his readers' critical interpretations in the text, a strategy he seems to have expanded in the later version. This procedure involves shifting our focus slightly from the question of Donne's intentions to his relationships with multiple audiences.

Joan Webber suggests that since Donne's talent lay in communicating his own experience, he focused upon persuasion rather than proof in his prose works, and consequently developed relationships with his audiences.[101] As commentators such as Morrissey and Kirby have argued, the Paul's Cross pulpit had become a site for persuading the people through both the eye and the ear, and in this sermon Donne sought to convince his hearers to accept the king's *Directions* without relinquishing their own interpretative faculties. Whereas Robert Willan in his sermon to the judges on the same day focused solely upon those present, Donne sought to make the entire kingdom his auditory, reminding them in his prayer before the sermon that

> *Now, in these houres, it* [the plot] *is thus commemorated, in the* Kings House, *where the Head and Members praise thee; Thus, in that place, where it should have been perpetrated, where the Reverend* Judges *of the Land doe now praise thee; Thus, in the* Universities, *where the tender youth of this Land, is brought up to praise thee, in a detestation of their Doctrines, that plotted this; Thus it is commemorated in many severall Societies, in many severall* Parishes, *and thus, here, in this* Mother Church, *in this great Congregation of thy Children, where, all, of all sorts, from the Lieutenant of thy Lieutenant, to the meanest sonne of thy sonne, in this Assembly, come with hearts, and lippes, full of thankesgiving.*[102]

Whereas the king's *Directions* divided England into groups, Donne attempts to reunite them through the act of simultaneous worship. Nevertheless, the very effort acknowledges the fragmentation of the political and religious body, not only through separate places of worship, but also through degrees of responsibility, a subject to which Donne will return in the sermon.

Donne's concern with unity is reflected again in his unusual choice of text. Northrop Frye identifies Lamentations 4.20 as an example of the "royal metaphor," in which "the king *is* his people, their existence as a 'body.'" This metaphor "was expressed in terms of unity and integration, as the unity of a social body into which the individual is absorbed." Because the church represented the body of Christ in history, "sacred and secular authority had the same metaphorical construct."[103] Subsequent Gunpowder preachers seem to have understood the verse in similar ways. In 1636, Henry Burton, insisting upon his loyalty, referred to Lamentations 4.20 as proof that subjects should always pray for the king and remain loyal to him.[104] Similarly, Matthew Newcomen in 1642 saw the actions of the king's evil counsellors as taking him into their pits by dividing him from his Protestant subjects.[105] In 1709, Henry Sacheverell, preaching upon the need for obedience, argued that to justify resistance as self-defence would be to authorize any act of rebellion, and then "A Prince indeed, in another Sense, will be the Breath of his Subject's Nostrils to be Blown in, or out, at their Caprice, and Pleasure, and a worse Vassal than even the meanest of his Guards."[106] Thus, despite their different political and religious orientations, all of these preachers seem to have understood this text as an illustration of the monarch's inseparability from his people.

Koos Daley suggests that the situation in the Palatinate, specifically the fall of Heidelberg on 6 September, influenced Donne's choice, arguing that his selection reflects the "literary topos of the grief over a ruined city." Thus, on her view, the sermon becomes "a discreet but pertinent attack on the politically dangerous schemings of James" that "bristles with warnings against Catholicism" as Donne enjoins both king and subjects to be wary of dealings with Spain.[107] While this context is clearly relevant to the sermon, several aspects of Daley's interpretation are problematic. First, Donne does not exploit the theme of the ruined city, although he could easily have done so within the conventions of the Gunpowder sermon. Beginning with Barlow's 1605 sermon, it was not unusual for preachers to describe imaginatively the devastation that would have occurred had the plot been successful.[108] That Donne fails to take this opportunity, focusing upon disunity rather than destruction as the most catastrophic result of a successful plot, suggests this was not a primary motivation in his choice of texts. Second, Daley implies that Donne addresses the king directly, although he was not present at the sermon, a violation of the discretion or decorum ascribed to Donne by other scholars. Morrissey argues that in the three sermons he preached at Paul's Cross in the Jacobean period, Donne uses discretion "in preaching about the subject's duties while avoiding any prescriptions to the king in a sermon *ad populum*," and Shami explains that "discretion is measured by the degree to which the preacher can fit his sermon effectively to his auditory."[109] After examining the ways in which Donne accommodated his preaching style to the Paul's Cross pulpit and the exigencies of the political sermon, Morrissey argues that Donne's highly developed sense of rhetorical decorum prevented him not only from addressing an absent monarch, but also from "wresting" Scripture in order to convey a political message.[110]

Donne seems to have been attracted to the Book of Lamentations over a number of years, preaching two surviving sermons on texts from it and writing a verse translation of the entire book. Scholars have offered a wide range of possible dates and occasions for this translation, ranging from before 1611 until 1621, and from personal affliction (his wife's death in 1617 or his failure to gain ecclesiastical preferment in 1621) to political disillusionment (the situation in the Palatinate).[111] Whatever Donne's personal associations with the book, however, they seem to have been part of a more general attention to it in the late sixteenth and early seventeenth centuries. A glance at the publication dates for commentaries and versifications of this book in the Elizabethan and early Jacobean periods compiled by William B. Hunter suggests substantial interest in Lamentations between 1587 and 1591, while the Spanish threat was particularly acute, and again in 1608–10, when the escalating Oath of Allegiance controversy increased fears of international Catholicism. A number of publications saw at least one reprint, suggesting that they were popular works.[112]

Donne headed his translation "for the most part according to Tremellius," and Ted-Larry Pebworth makes a case for Donne's use of Fetherstone's version of Tremellius. Of particular relevance to this sermon is Pebworth's observation that in the dedicatory epistle "whereas Tremellius placed Lamentations firmly in its historical setting, 'after the death of king Iosias' (The Argvment, 1), Fetherstone saw the book from a millenarian perspective, linking Jeremiah's lament to prophecies of the Second Coming."[113] One of the most notable aspects of Donne's sermon is his insistence on both the historical and prophetic applications of the text, leading him to what Shami identifies as the most challenging aspect of the sermon, the question of whether the text refers to a good or a bad king, a Josiah or a Zedekiah.[114] Similarly, Pebworth's observation that Fetherstone appears to have been Calvinist and violently anti-Catholic raises interesting points and connects it with a text not on Hunter's list, John Hull's *An exposition vpon a part of the Lamentation of Ieremie:Lectvred at Corke in Ireland.* This detailed commentary upon the first five verses of the book was printed in London in 1618 and reprinted in

1620, the later edition revising the subtitle to "First preached and now published by *I. Hull* B. of D. for the benefit of Gods Church" (t.p.). Hull dedicates his text to George Abbot and, after rehearsing the calamities of Jerusalem, adds: "To keepe vs from such calamitie, I haue brought in place this mappe of miserie: bold to present it to your Grace: yet bolde, because by you our Church enioyes prosperity, by deliuering truth, and defending veritie" (A4^{r}). His primary concern is to bring to the archbishop's attention the trials of the Irish church and state. Like Fetherstone, Hull is virulently anti-Catholic, attacking Rome as Babylon. Like Donne, he acknowledges various levels of meaning in the text, although he uses the traditional categories of historical, allegorical, and tropological. Both Hull and Donne seem to have understood Jeremiah particularly as a model for preachers. As Hull puts it, "*Ieremiahs* case is the case of all the Ministery, placed betweene two gulfes, two seas, two rockes, two fires: Gods curse, and the worlds hatred: *Paules* woe if hee preach not, *Ezechiels* Sword if he found not, & *Ieremiah* his end if he speake the truth" (6). This seems an apt description of Donne's situation in November 1622, caught as he seemed to be between the king's orders and his own pastoral duties.

Donne's choice of Lamentations 4.20 on this occasion, however, may also reflect a closer engagement with the public outcry surrounding the Spanish Match. In the previous year, the Ipswich preacher Samuel Ward had printed at Amsterdam an engraving of his "invention" entitled "To God, In Memory of his Double Deliverance From the Invincible Navy and the Unmatchable Powder Treason."[115] The cartoon depicted in the first panel God's playful winds scattering the Spanish Armada, in the second, a Catholic enclave engaged in plotting against England, and in the third, Guy Fawkes caught by the beam of light emanating from God's all-seeing eye as he approaches Parliament to ignite the gunpowder. When the Spanish ambassador, Don Diego Sarmiento de Acuña, Count of Gondomar, complained to James, the engraving was withdrawn from circulation and Ward was arrested and questioned by the Privy Council. Nevertheless, the illustration was evidently popular, even serving as a pattern for several surviving pieces of needlework, and was reprinted as late as 1689.[116]

As Alexandra Walsham has suggested, a reciprocal relationship had developed between the Gunpowder sermons and the engravings that began to be produced to celebrate the plot anniversary, since both were understood as monuments to God's deliverance of England.[117] In a sermon before the Privy Council on the first anniversary of the plot, William Barlow reminded his listeners that God enjoins two kinds of memorials for great deliverances, spoken and unspoken, and that Parliament had provided for both in its legislation of the celebration. William Goodwyn reiterated this need for perpetual memorialization at Paul's Cross in 1614 when he preached on the text Ezekiel 24.2: "Son of man, write thee the name of the day, euen of this same day: the king of Babilon set himselfe against Jerusalem this same day." Both sermons insist on the need to record, both in words and acts, the nation's providential deliverances.

Early visual representations of the plot also functioned as "monuments," interlacing "patriotism, royalism, and providential anti-popery as mutually reinforcing creeds."[118] David Kunzle observes that the Gunpowder Plot is the first of the Catholic conspiracies against the English crown for which pictorial representation survives.[119] The earliest is a 1606 Dutch engraving in which the upper frame depicts the plotters scheming while the lower three frames illustrate their executions. The German and French texts suggest that the engraving was designed primarily for a Continental audience, perhaps both to capitalize on a sensational news story and simultaneously to warn subjects into submission, since they conclude: "This is the reward of traitors, this is what will happen to all others."[120]

The two earliest surviving engravings intended for English audiences, however, are emblematic rather than narrative. *The Papists' Powder Treason*, presumably printed before Prince Henry's death in 1612, and Richard Smith's *Powder Treason* (*c.*1615–23) both feature architectural designs that demonstrate the traditional hierarchy proceeding from God at the top of the illustrations, through the monarch to Parliament, while the demonic plotters crowd the lowest level of the pictures.[121] In her detailed comparison of the two, Christina Carlson notes, among other differences, that the earlier illustration allows human agents, including both good and bad kings, a greater role in human affairs.[122] Nevertheless, as Walsham argues, the monumental framework of each drawing links God's providential deliverances of England to his approval of her institutions – king, church, and Parliament.

The absence of these institutions in Ward's drawing destabilizes the assurance of God's continued preference for England. God does not operate through English institutions, but intervenes directly in national history through his capricious winds and his all-seeing eye. As Northrop Frye has pointed out, however, the eye of God is "always potentially hostile," for God sees and judges all actions, not necessarily in our favour.[123] By drawing attention to God's scornful amusement in the "Video Rideo" caption on the beam of light illuminating Fawkes, Ward calls into question the uncritical assumptions about divine justice favouring England offered by the earlier drawings.

As Carlson suggests, the horizontal, linear focus of the picture, with the Catholic enclave at its centre, "forces the viewer to evaluate this central scene in light of the thematic and political implications of those illustrations that fall to either side of it, performing the work of contextualization and questioning that is the domain of satire, polemic, and propaganda."[124] Interpretation of the degree to which Ward intended a critique of the Spanish Match negotiations rests partly

Figure 4 *The Papists' Powder Treason.* Broadside ballad depicting the foiling of the Gunpowder Plot, 1679 (original produced before 1612). Reproduced with the kind permission of Lambeth Palace Library.

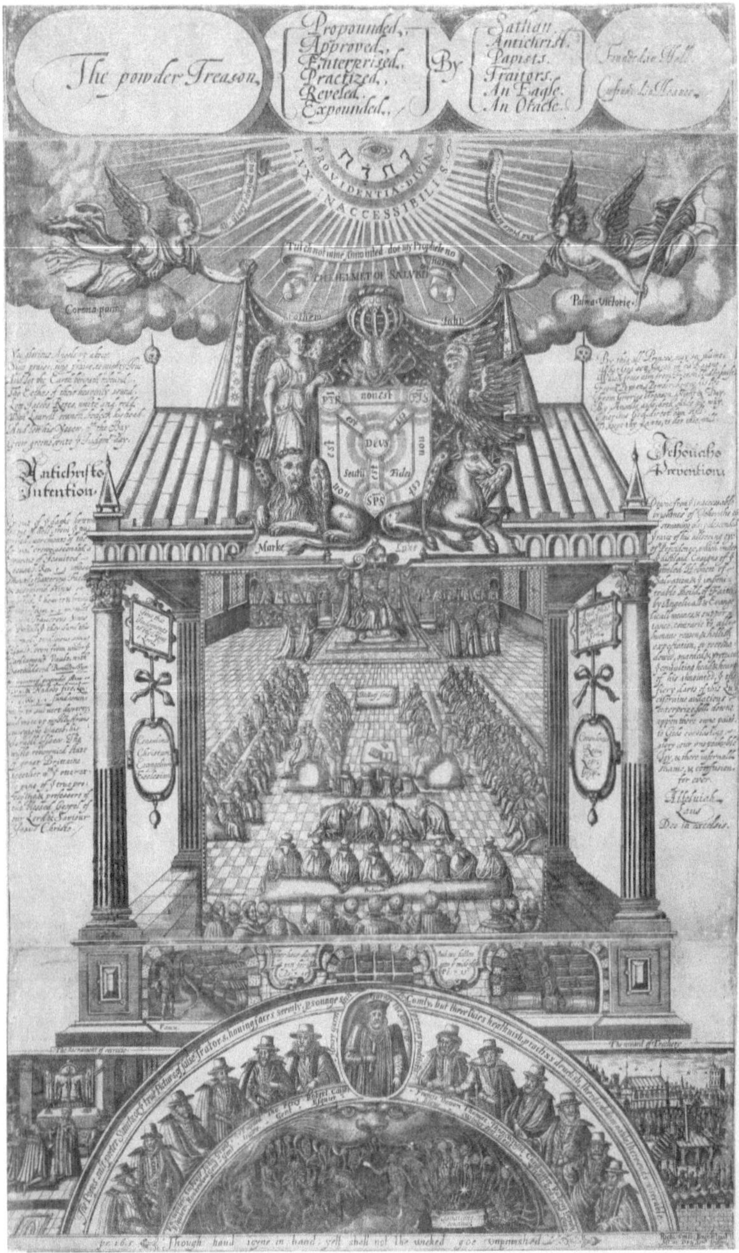

Figure 5 *The Powder Treason … founded in hell, confounded in heaven.* Engraving by Michael Droeshout, apparently from a design by Richard Smith, whose identity remains uncertain, 1620–5? © Trustees of the British Museum, Prints and Drawings, 1852, 1009.248.

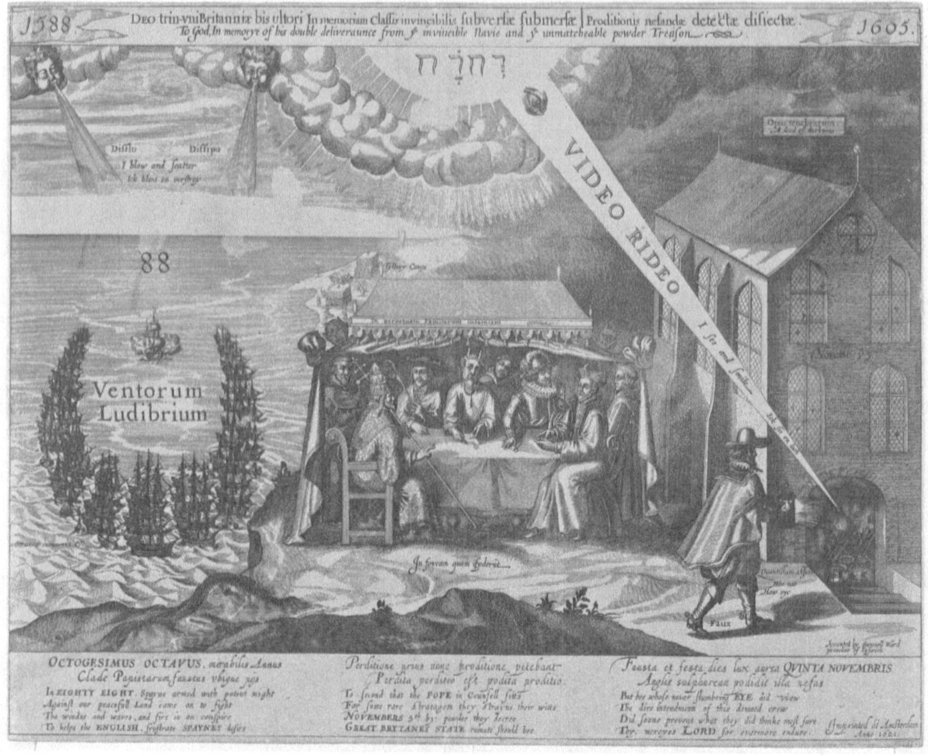

Figure 6 *The Double Deliverance 1588–1605.* Etching "invented" by Samuel Ward of Ipswich and printed at Amsterdam, 1621. © Trustees of the British Museum, Prints and Drawings, 1868, 0808.3353.

on our identification of the figures in the central enclave.[125] Gondomar based his complaint to James I on the alleged misrepresentation of his master, Philip IV, who has been identified by both Frederic George Stephens and Antony Griffiths as the figure in a ruff seated to the viewer's right of the devil.[126] Carlson, however, contends that the devil represents Philip IV and that the figure seated to his right is George Villiers, Duke of Buckingham, making the connection with the Spanish Match much more pointed. Regardless of which figure is seen as Philip IV, it seems clear that contemporaries identified a Spanish presence at the table. Even without such a presence, the flanking of the enclave with the destruction of the Armada and the foiling of the Gunpowder Plot would implicate Spain in the plot, for reading chronologically from left to right the viewer understands the hatching of the plot as an outcome of the failed Armada. A Spanish presence, however, also allows for a thematic reading, in which the enclave can simultaneously represent both the gunpowder plotting and the Spanish Match negotiations.

Ward, of course, denied that he was commenting on James's foreign policies, claiming in his second petition to the king that he had composed the "embleme" (minus the English verses and some additions made by the engravers) five years previously and had sent it to the printer almost a year earlier "without anie other sinister intencion, especiallie of meddling in any of your Majesties secrett affaires."[127] However, Ward was neither the first nor the last to claim the innocence of his intentions when pressed by the Jacobean authorities.

The print itself may have been too costly for many, but Ward's imprisonment doubtless made it a topic of conversation in London.[128] Certainly, it seems to have been on the minds of both Donne and Willan as they composed their 5 November sermons in 1622. Willan preached on Psalm 2.1–4, with the final verse, "He that dwelleth in the heauens shall laugh them to scorne; the Lord shall haue them in derision," allowing the preacher to expand at length in his conclusion on the idea that God laughs or smiles at the designs of wicked men. Since God's ironic laughter does not feature in surviving Gunpowder sermons before 1622, it seems likely that Willan's source was Ward's drawing. Although he cautions that the attribution of laughter to God can only be symbolic, Willan suggests that this derision expresses both how easy it is for God to overthrow the designs of the wicked and how patient he is in restraining his destructive powers. Using a theatrical analogy, the preacher reminds his auditors that "We may not iudge of Gods workes vntill the fift act, the case deplorable and desperate in outward appearance, may with one smile from heauen finde a blessed issue."[129] Willan's sermon, as Shami has pointed out, unquestioningly endorses the king's *Directions*, and therefore reaffirms the conventional providential belief that God will continue to protect England through the institutions of monarchy, religion, and law, directing his scorn only towards her enemies.[130]

Donne's response to the engraving, however, appears considerably more substantial and complex, extending from his unusual choice of text to the structure of the sermon itself. While Morrissey has suggested that Donne deliberately chose a text without the words "king" or "kingdom" in order to avoid tying his discussion of monarchy to a particular scriptural context, it seems more likely that Donne was attracted by the final word in the verse: "The breath of our Nostrills, the Anointed of the Lord was taken in their pitts."[131] Despite the subterranean venue of the Gunpowder Plot, preachers before 1621 seem to have favoured images of nets or fowlers' snares over pits as symbols of treachery. Smith's engraving, however, quotes Psalm 57.2, "They have digged a pit for me," in which Saul's attempt to entrap David redounds upon himself. Under the papal enclave in Ward's drawing are printed the words "In foveam quam foderint" [How they dug themselves into a pit]. Not only does Donne choose a text that offers the image of the pit, but he also draws attention to this word in the later part of the sermon, and even to the Geneva Bible's mistranslation of it as "nets," using this opportunity to distinguish a king merely caught in a net when he "discerns not a flatterer from / a Counsaylor" (1284–5), from one in the more desperate condition of being "taken in their pitts."[132] In Donne's sermon, however, the king remains both historical and potential victim, and retribution upon the plotters is never inevitable.

Donne begins his sermon by drawing his audience's attention to several problems of interpretation regarding the book itself: first, whether it is a distinct book or part of Jeremiah; then, whether it is historical or prophetical, and consequently whether it applies to a good or a bad king. These are questions for which there are no easy answers, nor can they be resolved solely on confessional lines, for Donne points out that while the Council of Trent omitted the book, probably intending it to be subsumed in the Book of Jeremiah, one of their own Jesuits declares it a distinct book. In this dispute, both sides cannot be right – the book must either be independent or part of Jeremiah. Donne then introduces the second, more complex, problem: the book *can* be both historical and prophetical. Having presented these interpretative dilemmas, Donne divides his listeners not by their abilities in understanding, as the *Directions* had, but by their levels of political responsibility – private citizens, preachers, advisors, and the monarch himself. The king is to be supported "by prayer / from them who are private persons, by / Counsayle from them, who haue the / great honor, and the great chardge / to be near them, and by support and / supplie from all of all sorts, from fal= / linge into such dangers" (144–50). Once again, however, division is a means of producing unity, for despite their different tasks, everyone in the kingdom is responsible for preserving the king from falling into "their" pits.

Throughout the first three-quarters of the sermon, however, Donne deliberately refrains from identifying those who dig pits for the king, using only the pronouns "they" and "them." Not until line 1299 of the manuscript version does he confront this question directly. Here he reaches the crux of the second problem of interpretation he had raised at the beginning of the sermon, that of whether the text is to be interpreted historically or prophetically: "If it / were *Josiah*, the persecutor was *Necho* / king of Egipt, for from his army *Josiah* / receyud his deaths wound; It if were / *Zedechiah*, the persecutor the was / *Nebuchadnezzar*, king of *Babilon*" (1299–1304). Throughout the early seventeenth century, Babylon was generally associated with Rome as the false church, whereas Egypt most frequently represented Spain. One, then, defined a religious adversary while the other referred to a political one. Although Donne never mentions Spain in the sermon, and he blames the plot only upon Englishmen (1098), he avoids resolving the question of whether the king has political as well as religious enemies by insisting upon both the historical and the prophetical interpretations. As long as Catholics accept the pope's authority to depose heretical rulers, they will continue to behave in the future as they have in the past. Nevertheless, Donne warns his audience that Protestants who doubt the king's religious fidelity are also digging pits for him. While Ward's cartoon collapses the Armada, the Gunpowder Plot, and potentially the Spanish Match negotiations into a demonstration of the consistent unreliability of both Spain and Rome, Donne refuses this uncomplicated form of anti-popery.[133] Catholic treachery may be both historical and potential, but this knowledge does not exonerate Protestants from their duties to pray for and speak well of the king.

After asserting the status and authority of the book in the first 150 lines, Donne outlines his "handling" of the text, dividing it into three parts: 1) that the cause of lamentation was the decline of the state; 2) that the people did not sever the king from the kingdom but accepted that any king, good or bad, was "the breath of their nostrils"; and, 3) that the past tense of the verb "was falln" (174) ensures that the lamentation presages a deliverance. Morrissey provides a useful outline of these stages as they appear in the marginal notes of the 1622 manuscript, observing that the unusual way in which Donne distinguishes between the division and handling of the text allows the first and final sections of the sermon independence from the text.[134] Donne's mode of working with the text here is particularly significant, since methods or "ways" are one of the sermon's underlying themes.

He describes the sermon at the outset as having both a temporal and a spatial dimension. The temporal trajectory is that of the Lamentations themselves, which fall neatly into the two halves of mourning and rejoicing, just as the sermon falls into two distinct parts. The time of the sermon will thus encompass the entire book, of which the text essentially becomes a microcosm. In an hour, he tells his listeners, his text will grow from mourning to rejoicing; but the sermon is also a "Royall progresse" (186) through the kingdom. The progress was one of the most visible displays of royal power and authority in the early modern period. Nevertheless, it could also invite discussion and critique, as James's 1617 progress to Scotland had done.[135] Beginning at line 186, Donne announces his first step in this progress, highlighted by a marginal note (1. *Regnum*) in both the manuscript and print versions, a history of kingship in which he introduces the issue of means. Between lines 186 and 445, he chronicles the origins of kingship in Israel, focusing on the problem of human meddling with divine design. What the Israelites wanted was not wrong, but their manner of asking for it was, because they failed to understand God's timing. The second step, "Regnum in Rege" according to the marginal note, insists upon the unity of king and kingdom, regardless of whether the king is good or bad. Beginning at line 641, Donne applies this part of the sermon historically to the Catholics who attempted to sever king and kingdom by means of gunpowder, locating the source of Catholic plotting in the doctrine of papal deposition promulgated in the pamphlet literature. As long as Catholics hold these beliefs, they will continue to behave as they have historically, and so the text can also be interpreted prophetically. Donne then broadens the application from Catholics to all individuals who rely on their experience as private individuals to censure kings. Ministers who pray for the king to remain Protestant are misusing prayer; their ends are not wrong but their means are. Donne suggests that individuals rooted in time and space, whether Catholics like the plotters or Protestants like Knight and Ward, are inadequate judges of either God or kings. Thus, Donne begins by refocusing not upon interpretative abilities but upon the hierarchies that determine political participation.

Not until line 798, almost the exact midpoint of the manuscript version, does Donne turn to the first words of the text, which describe the king as "spiritus narium," the breath of our nostrils. In the printed version, Donne clarifies this movement back to the text somewhat by adding "(as it lies in our Text)."[136] In this second part, he turns his attention not only to his text but also to the vertical relationship by which God's will descends through the king and his agents to his people, and it is surely no coincidence that he attributes to the king the two instruments of divine providence Ward represents in his drawing, God's breath and God's eye. Donne refutes the scholastic view that God does not work in secondary causes, insisting: "This is not true; / god doth worke in euery Organ, and in euery / particular action" (903–5), but he immediately qualifies this statement by denying that God causes "the / peruersnes of any action" (906–7). He seems to conflate God and the king as he describes the spirit moving upon the waters to shape an island that is the source of both physical and spiritual sustenance, while the king, "he who is the Spirit of the lord, he who is / the breath of our Nostrills" (816–17), takes special care of the navy. It is the king's "breath and influence of his prouidence / throughout the land" that "makes vsefull ... [God's] blessings vnto vs" (821–3). The king, according to Donne, acts not only as God's eye, but also as God's hands and feet. He is "This ey of god, He by whome god / looks vpon vs, This hand of god, He by / whome god protects vs, This foote of god, / by whome, in his due tyme, ... god shall tread downe his / own and our enemies" (1206–12). Donne thus reinserts the king into the providential hierarchy from which Ward had erased him. What he appears to be creating here is a visual representation of England as God sees it, with a broader vision, both temporally and spatially, than any individual, except the divinely anointed monarch, may have. Through his unusual structure, then, Donne offers two views of England, first as seen by people such as Ward with their limited spatial and temporal perspectives, and second as God sees it from his omniscient viewpoint.

By describing the king as God's lieutenant, however, Donne inverts the problems he discussed in the first half of the sermon.[137] Whereas there he focused on human meddling with God's plans, here the issue is God's, and the king's, use of fallible human instruments. God delegates England's care to the monarch, who is likewise required to employ agents who may, through weakness or malice, corrupt the execution of his plans. Donne raises this possibility almost immediately, but quickly veers away from such a dangerous topic in the first of the abrupt transitions that characterize this part of the sermon. In this second half, Donne repeatedly opens up avenues of thought only to close them off, creating discontinuities that the revisions of the 1649 text intensify. Wolfgang Iser's conception of "blanks" and "negations" helps to interpret some of these shifts. Although Iser has been criticized for failing to define what he means by a "blank," he does provide some guidelines for recognizing one in a text, explaining in *The Act of Reading* that "Wherever there is an abrupt juxtaposition of segments, there must automatically be a blank, breaking the expected order of the text."[138] The blank, however, is not simply a gap to be filled, but something that enables the reader to set up a relationship between two ideas. The referential field set up with the aid of the blank becomes a new theme set against the horizon of the previous one. The more blanks that break up the "*good continuation*" of the text, the more "Second degree images" will be created by the reader. The use of blanks and negations relinquishes more control of the text to the audience and therefore places more interpretative responsibility upon the reader, for "Whatever experience each individual reader may have, he will always be compelled to adopt an attitude, and this will place him into a prearranged position in relation to the text."[139] Since didactic texts generally resist blanks, Donne's rhetorical strategy suggests a desire to offer his readers and listeners the kind of interpretative opportunities that the *Directions* would deny them.

We can trace Donne's method in his scattered references to evil counsellors. In the first passage (823–39), he exonerates the king from responsibility for the evil done by ministers who have executed his orders improperly. He then shifts to a discussion of the need for subjects to speak well of the king, since disrepecting the monarch will lead to disrespecting God. Focusing this time on God rather than the king, he returns obliquely to the problem of secondary causes. God works in all actions, but does not cause evil actions. Similarly, the king must delegate his power to others, and so is excused from responsibility for his ministers' wrongdoing. Then, bringing the focus back to the act of interpretation with an abrupt transition in the words "But here, we carry not this word, *Ruach*, / Spirit, so highe" (840–1), Donne chokes off the line of thought he has initiated, creating what Iser would term a blank. Revoking the analogy he has made between the king and the Holy Spirit, he insists upon a literal interpretation of the word "breath" as speech, reminding his audience of their own duties to speak well of the king. Significantly, he makes this distinction between God and the king immediately after he has warned his audience that God can read our thoughts. The unstated implication is that the king can read only our words. Donne then returns to the problem of works carried out by inferior agents (905–14). In the 1622 manuscript, he excuses kings of responsibility in these situations, placing the blame solely upon the agents who have executed the actions. Rejecting the king's quasi-divine status in favour of an analogy between divine and monarchical government, Donne refocuses upon responsibilities – the king's responsibility to his people and their duties to him.[140] As God's instrument, the king is responsible for his people, but he may be compelled to carry out his duties through imperfect human agents. By insisting upon human accountability at all levels of the hierarchy, Donne refuses a simplistic providentialism.

In the 1649 version, however, Donne opens the gap in the text wider, concluding that kings "communicate power to others, and rest wholly themselves; and then, the *power* is from them, but the *perversenesse* of the action is not. God does work in ill actions, and yet is not guilty, but Princes doe not so much as worke therein, and so may bee excusable; at least, for any cooperation in the evill instrument; but that is another case."[141] In this short section, Donne uses the conjunction "but" three times in order to change directions. God works in all actions, but is not the cause of the evil; kings do not work in all actions, but communicate power to others; kings may not be excusable when they authorize an evil instrument, but that is not the case in this situation. Applying Iser's theory, Donne has not merely created spaces in his text, but by repeatedly juxtaposing interpretations of the king's actions with the need to speak well of him, he has suggested that the two are not incompatible.[142] It is possible, Donne seems to be telling his audience, to remain obedient to the king even when one disagrees with his policies.

Disagreement, however, does not give one the right to criticize the king openly, as Ward and Knight have done. Daley notes that one of Donne's strategies in the sermon is to create his own "ethos," his authority to speak on this subject. The crucial moment in this process is the monstrously long sentence beginning at line 959 and continuing to line 985. Donne starts the sentence by rebuking those who insert caveats into their prayers for the king, then demonstrates through the convolutions of his own syntax that making judgments about the king is not to be done lightly or by those lacking adequate information. The tensions of this sentence seem to be compounded by Donne's desire to establish both his spiritual and his temporal credentials. He begins by identifying himself as a Christian, then as a preacher, placing himself within the earthly church but expressing his hope of future participation in the heavenly church. In contrast, he merely glances over his political experience, offering instead his personal knowledge of the king's "hart" (981) as evidence that James remains committed to a Protestant nation. Nevertheless, Donne does not ultimately presume to speak for the king's constancy of religious beliefs, but only for his consistency of actions as head of the English church. While going so far as to compare James's commitment to the church with Elizabeth's, he also distinguishes their methods, taking us back to his discussion of means in the first part of the sermon. James is dealing differently with the situation in the Palatinate than Elizabeth would have, but "There ways may be diuers, and yet theyr / ends the same" (986–7). Cautiously, however, Donne avoids a preference for either method.

In conclusion, then, Donne's sermon can be seen not only as an attempt to work within James I's *Directions to Preachers*, but also as a response to one of the public challenges to the king's authority that had precipitated them. Samuel Ward's drawing, by eliminating the king and by conflating the origins of the plot with the Spanish Match negotiations, threatened that God would withdraw his earlier favour from England should James conclude a Catholic marriage for his son. Donne, in contrast, reinstates the king as God's agent, his breath and his eye. While the king's actions may appear contrary, God can work through them to preserve his people. Insisting upon English Catholic responsibility for the plot while reminding his auditors of their own responsibilities in the current crisis, Donne problematizes Ward's anti-Catholicism as well as his providentialism. In his later revisions of the sermon, Donne seems to have modified his position to place more responsibility upon flawed human instruments, including the king, but that was in the altered political circumstances of a new reign.

6.3 Henry Burton (1636): The Perils of Interpretation

In the spring of 1637, William Prynne, John Bastwick, and Henry Burton appeared in the Court of Star Chamber charged with seditious attacks on the English bishops.[143] Burton's offences were the preaching of two sermons on 5 November

1636 in his parish, St Matthew Friday Street, London, and their subsequent printing at Amsterdam. Following what David Cressy describes as a "show trial," each of the three authors was fined £5,000, had his ears cropped in the pillory, and was sent into what was to have been permanent solitary exile, deprived of all writing materials.[144] Clegg calls these excessive punishments "anomalous and desperate efforts to contain religious opposition ... a measure not of the success of Caroline press censorship but of its failure."[145] Corporal punishment, however, was not the only avenue open to the authorities in their efforts to counter dangerous writings. A dual strategy involving censorship and printed refutation had been in use at least since the Martin Marprelate controversies of the 1580s, when the government had not only sought out the illegal presses on which the offending tracts were being printed, but had also retaliated with its own texts.[146] While censorship deprived the author of profit and the reader of information, refutation was intended to discredit the author and re-educate the reader.

Burton's 1637 appearance in Star Chamber capped a ten-year history of escalating skirmishes with the bishops. Born near York in 1578, Burton had received his MA from St John's College, Cambridge, and, after a stint as a tutor, become Clerk of the Closet first to Prince Henry (1605–12), then to Prince Charles. Appointed rector of St Matthew Friday Street in 1621, he had lost the living temporarily in 1626, possibly for opposing Laud.[147] As early as 1628, he warned of possible changes to the prayer book, recording in the dedication of his *Tryall of Private Devotions*, a response to John Cosin's *Collection of Private Devotions*, that while visiting a printer he had seen a copy of the prayer book marked up with changes in Cosin's hand.[148] In his own book, Burton conducted a close reading of Cosin's work and concluded that some of the precedents he had cited in his margins did not exist. Although such clashes with authority have led him to be identified as an Independent even at this early date, Clegg insists that Burton "may indeed be among the more radical clergy in the Church of England, but he is conformable, no enemy to ecclesiastical ceremony, and an opponent to Rome. If Wotton, Yates, and Burton are Puritans, as Anthony Milton has classified them, they are so only 'in a second degree.' In the first degree, they regarded themselves loyal ministers of the Church of England."[149] Clegg argues instead that a series of incidents, beginning with his first appearance before the High Commission for dedicating *Babel No Bethel* to Parliament in 1629, gradually radicalized Burton. Through the early 1630s, increasingly in collaboration with Prynne, he repeatedly attacked what he considered Laudian "innovations" in the church. Nevertheless, Clegg argues that Burton, like other critics of his age, was not courting trouble when he dedicated works to Charles or Parliament, but acting under the Renaissance imperative to counsel the governor.[150]

In his 1643 autobiography, he admitted that he chose the Gunpowder anniversary for his inflammatory sermons deliberately to provoke a reaction from the prelates, taking as his text Proverbs 24.21–2: "My sonne, feare thou the Lord, and the King, and meddle not with them that are given to change. For their calamity shall arise suddenly; and who knoweth the ruine of them both?"[151] The sermons question what happens when the subject's duty to the king conflicts with the Christian's duty to God. The text, he argues, does not mean "that wee may not meddle at all, by way of reproofe, detection, conuiction, impeding or impeaching their wicked courses and practises."[152] Since a king being misled in religion should be counselled by his Christian subjects, Burton claims to be informing the king of the bishops' popish innovations, including revisions to the 5 November liturgy. As an experienced controversialist, however, he uses the technique of retortion, juxtaposing contradictory royal pronouncements to cast doubts on the king's trustworthiness. He complains, for example, that he was accused of opposing the king's "Declaration" when he preached the golden chain of salvation in a sermon on Romans 8, even though Charles's declaration on dissolving the 1629 Parliament promised to maintain the Elizabethan Settlement (54–5). Burton presumably knows this was not the "declaration" he was accused of violating, but he wants to demonstrate the king's dangerous inconsistencies of both speech and religious policy. Thus, although Burton insisted on his loyalty to Charles, his readers recognized that he made the king guilty at least of negligence in failing to control his bishops, and possibly of devious and dishonest language.

Burton was not the first Caroline preacher to use the Gunpowder anniversary to critique what he saw as a regression into Catholic error, but he was the most severely punished. The first to incur the government's anger seems to have been Samuel Ward of Ipswich, already suspect because of the 1621 cartoon discussed above, who was questioned for a potentially seditious sermon preached in 1633. Although the sermon does not appear to have survived, it seems that Ward used the occasion to contest Charles's reissuing of the Book of Sports.[153] Like Burton, then, he was protesting changes in ecclesiastical policy that were radicalizing the godly.

Predictably, Burton was charged in the Court of High Commission on 17 November with "uttering 'scandalous and offensive speeches.'"[154] Refusing to appear, he appealed directly to the king. A private commission suspended his preaching license in December and Burton, by his own account, barricaded himself in his house and expanded his two sermons for the press. Pursuivants broke into his house just as he finished and removed him to the Fleet prison.[155] Proceedings against him, along with Prynne and Bastwick, began on 10 March 1637, and the sentence was carried out in the pillory on 30 June, with exile commencing a month later.[156]

Even before the sentence took effect, a strategy for refuting Burton's pamphlet in print had taken shape. Laud's trial speech of 14 June, in which he briefly answered the accusations of all three writers and which contains his only printed defence of Caroline church policies, was published by royal command, the first edition being entered in the Stationers' Register on 1 July. The detailed refutation of Burton's errors promised by Laud was entrusted to Peter Heylyn, whose pamphlet, *A Briefe and Moderate Answer, to the seditious and scandalous challenge of Henry Burton*, had been written several months earlier, bears an imprimatur of 23 June, and was entered in the Stationers' Register, like Laud's speech, on 1 July. A third pamphlet, Christopher Dow's *Innovations unjustly charged upon the present church and state*, does not seem to have had official status but was subject to ecclesiastical control. Dow declares that his text was ready for the press by the end of Easter term, and it bears an imprimatur dated 17 June, three days after the delivery of Laud's speech. When it was half printed, Dow learned of Heylyn's response to Burton's *Apology of an Appeal* and retracted that section of his own work. There was, then, an organized and remarkably prompt series of textual responses by the ecclesiastical establishment.

That only Burton's work generated an official response supports Richard Hughes's contention that the authorities considered him the most troublesome offender.[157] In his final speech to the court, Laud announced: "But when Mr. Burton's book, which is the main one, is answered, ... neither Prynn, nor Bastwick, nor any attendants upon Rabshakeh, shall by me or my care be answered. If this court find not a way to stop these libellers' mouths and pens, for me they shall rail on till they be weary."[158] Refutation, Laud knew, was a strategy to be used cautiously. One of the most common methods of response was selective animadversion, in which the respondent quoted and then refuted selected passages from the original. According to Joad Raymond, "Extensive quotation had manifold effects: it constrained, by rhetorical and typographical means, the ways in which the original work might be read; it also made the original work more widely available, and so undermined it as a commercial enterprise." At the same time, it could have the unwelcome effect of publicizing the original ideas.[159] Laud's words support Clegg's contention that while Calvinists sought discussion and debate, the bishops wanted silence. However, censorship was not the only way to achieve this goal. The ecclesiastical authorities attempted not only to limit *what* readers could read; they also strove to control *how* readers should read. In contrast to the close independent reading advocated by Burton, they attempted to impose modes of interpretation circumscribed by authority.

The clerics who replied to Burton's work, however, were pointedly excluded from the audience he had addressed. Dedicating his text to the king and appealing to him as a judge, Burton literalizes the familiar Renaissance trope of the reader as judge. Anticipating an unfair trial from the bishops on the Star Chamber bench,[160] he sets up an alternative textual court in which his book represents him and he calls his congregation to witness that he preached obedience, not sedition. An anonymous puritan account of the proceedings justifies Burton's concerns, complaining of the court's selective reading from all three authors' works.[161] When asked whether he was guilty, Burton answered: "My Lord, I desire you not onely to peruse my Booke, here and there, but every passage of it." "As for my Answer," he says, "yee blotted out what yee would, and then the rest which made best for your owne ends, you would have to stand."[162] As in his text, Burton made the bishops' reading practices an issue in the court.

In his sermons, Burton represents his godly readers as competent interpreters, whereas the bishops have consistently misread the king's orders, first by compelling all ministers to read from the Book of Sports when the king only wanted it reprinted, and then by incorrectly applying to learned ministers James I's order prohibiting university students from reading Reformed theologians. Now, ordered only to reprint the prayer book, they have also revised the text, thereby acting "contrary to the Kings expresse Proclamation."[163] By making two minor changes in one of the 5 November prayers, Burton argues, they have completely altered its meaning. According to Clegg, Charles and Laud created a culture of censorship by following a process of "transformational literalism," reading "legal precedents so literally that their conservatism effectively produced extraordinary transformation" (101–2). Burton here turns this tactic against them in his own readings of the king's orders and the changes to the liturgy by insisting upon just such a relentlessly literal mode of interpretation. A closer examination of Burton's interpretation of the changes, and the Laudian clerics' responses, suggests that each side had very different attitudes towards reading.

The 1605 prayer asks God to scatter England's enemies, to "infatuate their counsels, and roote out that Babylonish and Antichristian Sect, which say of Jerusalem, 'Downe with it, downe with it, euen to the ground'" (D2^{v}).[164] The revision adds the phrase "of them," reading "root out that Babylonish and Antichristian Sect of them which say of Jerusalem, 'Downe with it, downe with it, euen to the ground'" (D4^{v}). Burton argues that

> whereas the words of the Originall copy doe plainely meane, that all Iesuites, Seminary Priests, and their confederates, are that *Babilonish and Antichristian Sect, which say of Ierusalem*, &c. this latter Booke either restraines it to some few, that are of that mind, or else mentally transferres it to those Puritans, that cry, Down with Babilon, that is, Popery, which these men call Ierusalem, and the true Catholike Religion.[165]

By accusing the bishops of the Jesuit trick of equivocation through mental reservation, Burton has progressed from branding them simply as poor readers to accusing them of wilful misreading, thereby aligning them not only with Catholics, but even with Jesuits.

In the next sentence, the original prayer supplicates God to "cut off these workers of iniquitie, (whose Religion is Rebellion, whose faith is faction, whose practise is murthering of soules and bodies) and to roote them out of the confines and limits of this kingdome" (D2^{v}). Burton insists that the revision, "to cut off these workers of iniquity, who turne Religion into Rebellion, and faith into faction" (D4^{v}), weakens the association between Catholicism and rebellion, "So as by this turning, they plainly imply, that the religion of Papists is the true religion, and no rebellion, and their faith the true faith, and no faction" (131). For proof that Catholicism is a rebellious faction, he refers his readers both to the *Homilies* and to specific chapters in treatises by John White and Richard Crakenthorpe.[166] After quoting several passages from Crakenthorpe, he encourages readers to peruse the text themselves, for "The whole Chapter is worth the reading" (134). His faith in his Protestant audience's reading ability contrasts sharply with his accusations that the bishops have read both incorrectly and maliciously.[167] Nevertheless, he does not advocate uncontrolled reading, conceding that Charles may be wise to restrict reading of the Church Fathers, since "an injudicious Reader, not being well grounded aforehand, comming to read some Fathers and Schoole-men, may in some passages ... bee infected with the poyson of Popish error and Superstition, before hee be aware" (113). His solution, however, is not to deny access to the unwary, but to have students taught by "those uncorrupt Conduit-pipes, the Divines of the Reformed Churches" (113), just as inexperienced seamen are taught by pilots before venturing into dangerous waters on their own. How his adversaries responded to his charges demonstrates their uneasiness with close reading, particularly by the less educated and the godly.

Laud's speech is directed first to Star Chamber and the king, but in its published form to the broader audience of the kingdom. His dedication to the king expresses his distrust of close reading, cautioning that "many things, while they are spoken and pass by the ear but once, give great content; which when they come to the eyes of men, and their often scanning, may lie open to some exceptions." He begs the king to protect both himself and his text from "the undeserving calumny of those men, 'whose mouths are spears and arrows, and their tongues a sharp sword.'"[168] Whereas Burton represents his text as a court, a site for examining conflicting interpretations, his respondents all equate textual disputation with warfare. Laud's extreme reluctance to publish suggests a deep fear of a puritan audience that uses close reading as a pretext for publicly challenging authority.[169]

Dismissing the first change in the prayer as too inconsequential even to merit a response, Laud offers three possible explanations for the second. First, it avoids the "scandal" of calling another faith rebellion. Second, identifying Catholicism as rebellion casts aspersions on all Christians, since all were Catholics before the Reformation. Finally, the state has consistently maintained that it executes Catholics for treason, not for heresy, but "if their religion be rebellion, it is not only false, but impossible, that the same man, in the same act, should suffer for his rebellion, and not for his religion." However, the archbishop concludes cautiously: "Which of these reasons, or whether any other better, were in his Majesty's thoughts when he commanded the alteration of this clause, I know not. But I took it my duty to lay it before you, that the king had not only power, but reason to command it."[170] While willing to offer speculative readings in defence of Charles, Laud disclaims any authority to interpret the king's words or judge his intentions. Elizabeth Skerpan argues that Laud's speech "is a model of forensic oratory" addressed only to Star Chamber:

> With the law on his side, as he sees it, he selects a genre that excludes general readers who do not understand the intricacy of the issues involved. Logical and self-assured, he relies on his own authority and the facts of the case to prove his argument. He makes no effort to unify his audience, assuming that all that truly counts is the Star Chamber, which shares his interpretation of events.[171]

Laud effectively erred in his choice of genre, selecting one that relied upon reason and logic rather than emotion. Skerpan, however, by reading Laud's speech in isolation, fails fully to appreciate the government's strategy in simultaneously publishing Heylyn's and Dow's pamphlets, which *were* intended to engage directly with Burton's original audiences.[172]

According to Anthony Milton, Heylyn's apologetic works "defined government policies in more radical terms, and raised the political and ideological stakes by the extremism which he imputed to the regime's opponents, and the ideological agenda which he glossed onto the government's own policies."[173] In other words, in the absence of clear statements by Laud, Heylyn radicalized the archbishop's program. Here, his assigned tasks are to reassure other clerics that religion is not endangered and to inhibit further discussion by refuting Burton's errors. Like Laud, Heylyn suspects Burton's use of print, complaining in his preface that "*The* Presse, *which was devised at first for the advancement and increase of learning; was by him made a meanes to disperse his* pasquills, *that they might flye abroad with the swifter wing, and poyson mens affections, whom he never saw.*"[174] Burton's words are arrows, directed not only against the king and the bishops, but also against anonymous conforming clergy. Like the Gunpowder plotters, Burton wants to "raise combustions in the state," and seized the opportunity of the plot anniversary, "*that day being by him thought most proper for their execution, whom he had long before condemn'd, and meant to blow up now without helpe of Powder*" (b3^{v}). Heylyn exposes Burton's technique of retortion, accusing him of misreading both scripture and the king, while himself quoting selectively from Burton's pamphlet.

In the body of the pamphlet, Heylyn addresses Burton directly and, through him, other clergy. Although he admits Burton's reading of the first change, he attributes his opponent's perspicacity to a guilty conscience – he too must wish ill against Jerusalem. Burton's fear that the prayer may be invoked against puritans is justified, nevertheless, for Heylyn threatens that "howsoever the *Iesuites*, Priests and their confederates were at first intended: yet if the *Puritans* follow them in their designes of blowing up the Church and State, and bringing all into a lawless and licentious *Anarchie*; the prayer will reach them too, there's no question of it" (152).[175] He thus asserts the government's authority to reinterpret texts for political purposes, regardless of authorial intent, reminding Burton that although recusancy legislation and the Court of High Commission were established to prosecute Catholics, they can also, as Burton is fully aware, be used against the godly.

Burton is also correct that the revision to the second sentence changes its meaning, but since asserting that Catholicism is not necessarily rebellion does not declare it a true religion, he is guilty of a non sequitur. The revision does not extenuate the traitors, for "Before the imputation seemed to rest on the faith it selfe: which being a generall accusation concerned no more the guilty, then it did the innocent. But here it resteth where it ought, upon the persons of the *Traytors*, who are not hereby justified, or their crime extenuated: but they themselves condemned, and the treason aggravated in a higher manner" (154). Burton has offered two proofs that Catholicism is rebellion: priests and Jesuits refuse the Oath of Supremacy and the church promotes disloyalty to kings. Heylyn correctly taxes Burton with confusing the Oath of Supremacy with the Oath of Allegiance and reminds his readers that some priests and lay Catholics have both taken the oath themselves and also urged others to take it. In response to Burton's second proof, Heylyn argues that since John Calvin, David Pareus, and George Buchanan also authorized subjects to rebel against kings, "we may from hence conclude, or else your argument is worth nothing, that out of doubt the *Puritan religion is rebellion*, and *their faith faction*" (156). Burton's error allows Heylyn to suggest that puritans are worse than Catholics, since only a few Catholics were guilty of the Gunpowder Plot, while all puritans may be guilty of sedition. By illustrating the dangers of interpretative warfare, he tries to threaten puritan preachers into silence.

While Heylyn attempts to undermine Burton's clerical support by attacking his text, Christopher Dow seeks to turn Burton's middling readers against him by satirizing his person. Despite complimenting his readers by addressing them as "Ingenuous" (A2r), he does not allow them freedom to interpret.[176] In his first chapter, he observes that although folly should usually be met with silence, some texts require responses in order to educate those who may be misled by popular opinion. Like Laud and Heylyn, he immediately introduces the metaphor of combat. Since both words and weapons function according to the force with which they are employed, we must establish a writer's authority before evaluating his work. Burton, according to Dow, had an uninspiring career at Cambridge followed by a brief stint as a tutor before becoming Clerk of the Closet to Prince Charles, "Which sometime he was wont to execute in his hose and doublet, with a perfuming pot in one hand, and a fire-shovell in another."[177] Dow's observation that during this time Burton "got into Holy orders" (8) implies that there was also something shady about his ordination. Stricken from the list of those to accompany Charles to Spain in 1621 after his baggage was on the ship, Burton became so unpopular in his own parish that when his parishioners learned he was preaching they attended services elsewhere. A harmless bumbler until his dismissal from court shortly after Charles's accession, Burton then became vindictive and extended his animosity from a few bishops to the entire order. While the facts of this sketch are essentially correct, Dow interprets them in the most unflattering manner possible. Had Burton been as unpopular as his adversary claims, the authorities would have had no reason to fear him. Dow's purpose, however, is not to construct an objective biography but to deny Burton's authority to interpret the king's words and actions.[178]

Like Heylyn, Dow identifies Burton with the very Catholics he condemns, but he presents his arguments in a simplified form accessible to a less educated audience. He then dismisses the debate entirely, concluding that since the same authority that originally established the prayers is responsible for revising them, "it is neither for him, nor me, nor any other of inferiour ranke to question them, but with humble reverence to submit to their iudgements, and to thinke them wiser and farre more fit to order those things that belong to their places, than we, whom it neither concernes, nor indeed can know the reasons that move them, either to doe or alter any thing" (136–7). While Dow does not necessarily consider his readers incompetent, he sees interpretation as a form of meddling, unsuitable for those other than authorized counsellors. When practised by the common people, the close independent reading both modelled and advocated by Burton threatens the Laudian church's emphasis on authority and hierarchy.

Burton's case, then, suggests that the Laudian ecclesiastical authorities attempted to impose silence not only through censorship, but also by discouraging textual practices that could foster debate and discussion, particularly among the godly and middling sorts. The Laudian administration, in other words, tried to enforce the kind of hierarchy of interpretation that James's *Directions to Preachers* had also sought to legislate in 1622. While Donne's cautious defence of interpretative freedom had been allowed to pass, however, Burton's attack brought down all the force of the Caroline state upon him. Yet, his use of a sermon, and one preached on one of the nation's most important political anniversaries, as a vehicle for his criticisms suggests that he wanted to bring debate to the very people who had been excluded from the interpretative dilemmas of religious controversy. The reaction to the sermon also indicates clearly the dangers inherent in the anti-Catholic rhetoric developed in Gunpowder sermons, which could be redeployed against other groups, particularly puritans.

6.4 Matthew Newcomen (1642): The Church Besieged

Despite Henry Burton's exploitation of the Gunpowder sermon to create opposition to the Caroline administration in the 1630s, the importance of the occasion declined during the Civil War, perhaps because a series of regular monthly fasts quickly overwhelmed the calendar. The most influential public preaching in London occurred at St Margaret's Westminster, where the House of Commons gathered, and the day of public celebration became a day of fasting. A number of scholars have examined the parliamentary fast sermons, but most either do not distinguish Gunpowder sermons from those of the other fasts or exclude them altogether.[179] Nevertheless, while the relevance of Gunpowder sermons diminished as the 1640s progressed, in the early years of the war both parliamentarians and puritan preachers relied upon them to justify conflict against those perceived to be undermining Protestantism, including the king.

The Commons sermons addressed two distinct auditories, their separateness highlighted by the interior arrangement of St Margaret's. Although Members of Parliament were the primary audience, individual subjects seeking information about the political and military situation frequently joined them. We can explore how this circumstance may have affected these sermons by examining the traces of Matthew Newcomen's 1642 Gunpowder sermon – the printed text published at the request of Parliament and sermon notes attributed to Walter Yonge, son of the diarist. Preaching at a moment of crisis when London had barely escaped assault and Parliament had agreed to pursue a negotiated settlement, Newcomen seized the occasion to reject a possible compromise with those he identified as crypto-Catholics.

In recent decades, historians have contested and revised earlier assessments of the role of religion in the outbreak of the war. Although much remains unresolved, most now accept that religious discontents played a significant part in instigating the conflict. Caroline Hibbard's work usefully reformulated the terms of the discussion around perceptions rather than facts, an approach extended by

Jonathan Scott in his larger study of England's "troubles" in the seventeenth century.[180] Hibbard contends that whether or not Charles and Laud intended to re-Catholicize England is less important than the fact that they were widely believed to be doing so. John Morrill argues that these perceptions in turn created a parliamentary agenda driven more by religious than political issues – moving slowly to address legislative remedies while proceeding swiftly against the men perceived to be Charles's evil counsellors. Morrill warns that "Talk of 'popery' is not a form of 'white noise,' a constant fuzzy background in the rhetoric and argument of the time against which significant changes in secular thought were taking place," but was a crucial feature of the political landscape.[181] Sermons therefore played an important role in politicizing the religious agenda.

Making 5 November a fast day radically altered the Gunpowder tradition. Although sermon attendance had always been mandatory, the day had never been marked by abstinence from food or labour. In contrast to most of the fasts the Long Parliament established, which were new, this one required reorienting an existing calendrical occasion.[182] Like the earlier anniversary sermons, fasts were political acts. Consequently, both Elizabeth and James I had been wary of establishing a fast tradition, and Elizabeth had squelched the first proposal in 1580. In 1614, however, a test communion was proposed as a way for parliamentarians suspected of Catholic sympathies to demonstrate their loyalty to both church and state. The communion, concluding with a sermon, was repeated in 1621 and, according to John F. Wilson, was the genesis of preaching before the House of Commons. In 1624, Edward Cecil proposed a general fast, initiating a second regular preaching occasion, separate from the test communion, that became part of the opening of each session of the Caroline Parliament.[183]

Wilson points out that "This independence of the two religious events served puritan purposes in a significant way. If the fast and the communion were yoked together, only one fast would be appropriate during each session of parliament. Severed from the test ritual, however, there was no theoretical limit to the number of occasions on which Commons could be subjected to preaching."[184] In addition to these authorized fasts, some clergy organized their own fasts to make political statements. Christopher Durston observes: "Throughout the Personal Rule, therefore, the ecclesiastical authorities viewed public fasting with extreme suspicion, identifying it closely with those most implacably opposed to the religious policies being promoted by the king and Laud."[185] As we have seen, the Gunpowder sermons could also provide sites – both physical and textual – for staging opposition and were viewed with similar distrust by the late 1630s. Regular monthly fasts began in early 1642 and continued until 1649, when Parliament outlawed political preaching.[186] Over the course of the war, this proliferation of sermons seems to have diminished their appeal, so that even parliamentarians had to be scolded to attend.[187] Hugh Trevor-Roper suggests that those in the country resented the fasts, which "were always regarded as party propaganda," while Durston argues that the requirement to abstain from both food and work contributed to their unpopularity with the general public.[188] At the same time, Londoners appear to have flocked to the sermons, just as they had earlier to Paul's Cross, to learn the latest news.[189]

The institution of the test communion in 1614 had a second implication for the parliamentary sermons of the 1640s. Refusing to take communion in Westminster Abbey, which continued to use wafers, the Commons moved its service to the smaller St Margaret's. Separating the religious observances of the two houses must only have underlined to observers their political differences during the early 1640s.[190] According to Julia Merritt, an influx of puritan gentry in the 1630s had gradually transformed St Margaret's parish, formerly a bastion of conservatism.[191] Nevertheless, this site flaunted undeniable remnants of its Catholic history as well as its more recent formalist past. At least in the early civil war years, the communion table seems to have required shifting from its altarwise position before parliamentary communions, suggesting that Laudian influence had not been entirely superseded in the parish.[192] In addition, the church was rich in stained glass and statuary.[193] In 1641, a north gallery was built, and it was here that parliamentarians sat during sermons, slightly above and to the right hand of the preacher.[194] Parishioners and the general public sat below facing the preacher but must have been forced to crane their necks to see him, given his distance above them.[195] This development segregated the two groups into separate auditories and privileged the parliamentarians through their proximity to the preacher. While placing the preacher in what appeared to be a subordinate role to Parliament, however, this arrangement also made Parliament effectively a captive audience, much as the king had been in the royal closet during Jacobean court sermons.[196]

Parliamentary authority is replicated in the printed sermons, which are prefaced by the official order to print and by what appears to have been an obligatory dedication to Parliament, frequently expressing patronage relations. Together, the physical site of preaching and the conditions of printing may have contributed, both at the time and for modern scholars, to the perception that the preachers and Parliament spoke as one.

One of the thornier questions about the sermons, then, is the degree to which the preachers represented their own agendas rather than simply acting as the mouthpieces of Parliament. Trevor-Roper's argument that "The real purpose of the monthly fast had been to provide a constant sounding-board of parliamentary policy, a regular means of contact with, and propaganda to, the people" assumes that the clergy acted solely at the prompting of Parliament.[197] More recent scholars have recognized, however, that preachers had theological as well as political motives. David Zaret argues that the "Secular benefits of preaching were always treated as an appendage to its primary purpose, which was to proclaim the gospel."[198] Stephen Baskerville likewise posits a deeper engagement between the two, suggesting that the doctrine of justification by faith gave "to Protestants and especially to Puritanism the claim to be an *ideology*: a system of ideas that creates its own reality, that derives its fulfillment from the very fact that it is believed" and that its ideas became revolutionary simply by being opened to a mass audience. He concludes: "The sermon then was not simply a medium, and the pulpit not simply a platform, for issuing political statements; the promotion of preaching, the very act of delivering a sermon, was itself a political statement."[199] In fact, I suggest that the preachers acted in both their traditional roles of supporting what they saw as divinely ordained authority and providing counsel and critique to their new patrons, the English parliamentarians.

Trevor-Roper asserts that Parliament used the fast sermons "both for strategic and for tactical purposes: both to declare long-term aims and to inaugurate temporary shifts of policy."[200] While he emphasizes the ways in which the sermons prepared people for specific political actions against particular individuals – Laud, Strafford, and eventually the king – the Gunpowder sermons seem to have functioned not only to justify Parliament's actions to the people but also to promote the preachers' own religio-political agendas to Parliament. A primary function of these sermons appears to have been to legitimate the narrative of a popish plot that had developed during the 1630s, thereby justifying hostilities towards a king who appeared inclined towards Rome.[201] In 1641, Parliament was recessed until 20 October due to plague and smallpox. When it resumed, "Commons seized the occasion to authorize the first of an annual series of public thanksgivings for the deliverance from the Gunpowder Treason. November 5 provided an obvious opportunity for the puritan preachers to rehearse the perfidy of papists so dramatically displayed, they believed, in the Irish rebellion."[202] It also provided opportunities to condemn crypto-Catholics closer to home and to glorify Parliament.

Cornelius Burges was the only preacher appointed for the Gunpowder anniversary that year, and even so he notes in his dedication to the printed sermon that the pressure of other business forced him to abridge his delivery, a circumstance that a number of his successors were to echo. From his text, Psalm 76.10, Burges draws the first application that "*the rage of the wicked against God and his people is bottomlesse and endlesse*," but he concludes that this rage only glorifies God and benefits his people, for God will not forsake them.[203] Having described earlier plots, including the Gunpowder Plot, he insists that Catholics continue to scheme even while pleading for toleration, not, as they claim, because they are persecuted, but because their religion compels them to do so. In this, Burges's sermon is completely conventional, but it breaks new ground in making Parliament the site of God's primary deliverance in 1605. The calling and actions of the present Parliament demonstrate the ongoing benefits of the initial deliverance, for this Parliament's work is to continue reforming the church. He rebukes parliamentarians for failing to resolve the religious crisis, but here his main targets are sectarians, not crypto-papists.[204] Thus, while flattering Parliament, Burges also claims the traditional right of chastising his political superiors. The sermon's function as political counsel becomes clearer when it is juxtaposed with one preached by Henry Miller on the same day at his parish church of St Leonard Foster Lane. Miller carefully avoids straying from the historical occasion and conventionally reminds his parishioners to show gratitude to God for their deliverance.[205]

On the same day, preaching at the Cathedral of St Peter at Exon (Exeter) on Judges 5.31, William Sclater, a preacher with royalist connections, pointedly ignored the Irish Rebellion and the question of toleration.[206] Instead, he compared England's situation to that of Israel without a king. The church's puritan enemies are "a crooked and perverse generation" (13) who are reducing the country to anarchy; some of them "are full of all subtilty and all mischief, enemies of all Righteousnes, by their wrangling, and contentions, time-serving disturbance, never ceasing to pervert the ancient, right, and established wayes of the Lord" (13). His allusion to Charles's 18 October letter affirming his intentions to live and die a member of the Church of England counters the popish plot claims Burges advances.

Sclater appropriates for his own cause the authority of tradition, while attributing many of the qualities formerly associated with Catholics, particularly their dangerous tendency to innovate, to the new puritan antagonists. He treads cautiously over the question of whether it is acceptable to hate one's enemies. Although we may think that Christ condemns such action, Sclater insists that Jesus's prohibition in Luke 6.27 comes from tradition rather than scripture and is therefore a guideline rather than a law. When our enemies are also God's, he permits us to curse them – to pray for their physical, but not their spiritual, annihilation. Those who destroy the peace of the state must be eradicated. He concludes this part of the sermon somewhat enigmatically: "Your selves with due Cautions, may make the application: I have spoken unto wise men, who can judge, I doubt not, what I say" (29).[207] Both sides appear to have been troubled by the problem of hating other Protestants, and Sclater turns with some relief to the evils of Rome, particularly of the Jesuits, in the second hour. While this move suits the occasion, it also allows him to distinguish formalists from Catholics. Nevertheless, Sclater's sermon, beginning with his choice of text, renders puritanism the new enemy. Although this sermon, unlike Burges's, was delivered under no special authority, the two preachers seem to have drawn the battle lines in a rhetorical war that Newcomen would escalate in 1642.

Newcomen's was the only parliamentary sermon preached on 5 November 1642, and none appears to have been preached the following year. In 1644, however, both Anthony Burges and Charles Herle preached before the Commons, while William Spurstowe and John Strickland preached to the Lords. On this occasion, the ambiguous success at Newbury and the Scottish capture of Newcastle called forth carefully worded sermons, some optimistic, others more cautious. All fast sermons, including those of 5 November, declined after 1645. According to Wilson, the "fast institution languished, not only because it had outlived its usefulness within parliament and the realm but because its premise – that political men could submit themselves and their interests to divine purposes – was cruelly refuted for all but the most radical and obdurate of believers."[208] Wilson downplays what may have been a more practical obstacle – the fracturing of Parliament on religious matters as separatists began to outnumber presbyterians.[209]

Already a popular preacher before the Civil War, Newcomen continued to play an important role in Parliament during the early 1640s.[210] As a presbyterian, however, his influence waned, perhaps partly because he supported a program that would accommodate both presbyterians and Independents.[211] Like Burges in 1641, Newcomen in 1642 was forced to abridge his Gunpowder sermon due to the pressure of other business in the House. In his dedication to the Commons, he explains that he has nevertheless published the entire sermon in the hope that it will be of use in "establishing Religion, Reforming the Church, rooting out Popery."[212] In fact, the Commons had already offered the sermon such a role, for along with the customary order appointing a parliamentarian (William Massam in this case) to thank Newcomen for his sermon, and directing the preacher to have the sermon printed, appears the request for him "to give a Coppy thereof to the Committee for Religion, that when they shall have liberty to sit, they may consider by it, how to prepare and provide for the extirpation of Popery" (n.p.). Newcomen's sermon, then, is the only Gunpowder sermon known to have been considered as a basis for public policy.

The Committee for Religion had been working since the late 1620s, both pursuing recusants and calling for stringent enforcement of the laws passed after the Gunpowder Plot.[213] Unfortunately, due to the loss of most of the committee records of the Long Parliament, we do not know whether the sermon was ever discussed in this forum. Our two main sources for the work of the committee during the Long Parliament are the records of Sir Edward Dering and Sir Simonds D'Ewes, neither of whose surviving papers covers the period in question.[214] We do know, however, that within a few months some of Newcomen's proposals were being carried out through clerical deprivations and assaults on images in churches, including St Margaret's.[215] Was Newcomen introducing his own program, or was he garnering popular support for plans Parliament had already made?

Newcomen takes as his text Nehemiah 4.11, "And our adversaries said, they shall not know nor see till wee come in the midst among them and slay them and cause the work to cease." The only other surviving Gunpowder sermon on this text was preached by Thomas Reeve in Colby, Norfolk, in 1629 and published in 1632. Although Reeve's sermon is a relatively standard piece of anti-Catholic polemic, it is ominously directed against the upper classes as the chief targets of Catholic proselytizing. Already, he warns, some are willing to work with the Catholic Antichrist, particularly at the Caroline court. During the early years of the Civil War, preachers seem to have considered Nehemiah's struggles to rebuild the walls of Jerusalem an apt parallel for the parliamentarians' task of restoring the English Church. In a commentary published in 1653, but drawing upon an earlier work by Konrad Pellicanus, John Mayer notes that Jerusalem is a figure for the church. The gates in the wall control access to the church, both keeping the faithful in and enemies out. Citing Pellicanus, Meyer notes that "they who doe the like for their native Countrey and Church, labouring to reform things amisse, and to repaire the decays of both are praised, and we are taught always to have them in remembrance, as most worthy instruments."[216] On the 29 June fast in 1642, William Gouge preached from Nehemiah 5.19, offering the Israelite to his audience as the role model of a good patriot. Richard Cust observes that this term had been first invoked as a slogan in the elections of spring 1640 and suggests that in this context patriots were defined as those uncontaminated by contact with the court, Arminianism, popery, or the Caroline administration of the 1630s.[217] Near the end of his sermon, Gouge produces a list of the specific duties of good patriots and parliamentarians: "Heare complaints, receive Petitions, examine Accusations, punish Delinquents, cause restitution of that which is uniustly taken away, and satisfaction for that which is wrongfully done, to be made." Among Nehemiah's patriotic actions, according to Gouge, was his enforcement of a "solemne covenant and oath" to ensure good order among the people. He adds that this is "the rather to be noted for justification and commendation of the course which both Houses of Parliament have taken, about bringing most of this Land into a solemne Covenant."[218] Thus, Gouge endorses Parliament's actions while prescribing an ongoing political agenda.

Between Gouge's sermon in June and Newcomen's in November, the gulf between uneasy peace and open warfare had been crossed, and the story of Nehemiah had acquired a new resonance. On 10 August, Parliament had issued "Directions for the Defence of London," but the urgency to protect the city increased markedly in late October, spurred by Prince Rupert's plan to attack London after the Battle of Edgehill. When he stopped at Oxford to regroup and transform the city into a garrison, the Commons agreed to peace negotiations, and on 3 November the king left Oxford for London. Newcomen's text, then, must have seemed particularly apt. Responding in particular to the prospect of a negotiated peace settlement that he fears would threaten church reform, the preacher justifies continuing the war in the service of religion. As in the oppositional sermons of the 1630s, the Gunpowder anniversary offered a perfect opportunity to preach this message because it provided apparently incontrovertible proof that Catholics plotted against Protestants, and especially against Parliament. It then required only insisting upon the crypto-Catholicism of Charles and Laud to make the Caroline bishops, and by association the king, guilty of a popish plot that would reassert itself in the event of a negotiated settlement.

As with the other Gunpowder sermons, the problem of multiple audiences – performance and print, parliamentarians and people – complicates our understanding of Newcomen's. Juxtaposing two remaining traces of the sermon, the printed pamphlet and notes attributed to Walter Yonge, second son of the parliamentarian and diarist, provides an opportunity to probe Newcomen's interactions with his listeners and readers, since differences between the notes and the printed version suggest that Newcomen may have adapted his message for oral and print audiences. Yonge's notes survive in a small notebook containing records of sermons attended between November 1642 and February 1643/4 (BL Add. MS 18781). On the same day, Yonge also took notes at a sermon by a "Mr. Craynford," probably James Cranford, at an unknown location.[219] We must proceed with caution when considering the evidence of these notes, since our understanding of how early modern listeners took and used notes remains limited.[220] In the first major study of early modern sermon audiences, Arnold Hunt argues that although preachers sometimes resented notetakers, "sermon notes can often be of interest for what they reveal about the sermon as preached, bringing us closer to the preacher's voice than a printed text can do."[221] Since most preachers wrote an outline of the sermon in advance and filled it in during performance, Hunt concludes that

> As a rule, the doctrinal part of the sermon, in which the preacher expounded the sense and meaning of his text and drew out its theological and moral significance, was likely to be written down in the preacher's notes and carried over into any subsequent printed edition, whereas the more practical part of the sermon, in which the preacher drew out "uses" or "applications" suited to a particular occasion, or a particular audience, stood much less chance of being recorded in written or printed form.[222]

In this case, Newcomen tells his readers in the dedication to the printed version that lack of time forced him to abridge both the textual introduction and the application of the sermon now provided for the reader. Yonge's notes, which begin at the bottom of page nineteen of the printed version with Newcomen's transition from the scriptural text to the contemporary application, confirm the abridgement, suggesting that the preacher could have omitted the commentary on his text entirely in the oral delivery.[223] Nevertheless, his claim to have truncated the application due to time constraints may be disingenuous, as he may simply have been more cautious in promoting a radical puritan agenda before the parishioners of St Margaret's than in print.

Based upon Yonge's notes, Newcomen began his sermon that day with a fairly conventional narrative of the plot, but also a more bloodthirsty one than perhaps any preacher since Barlow. The opening was arresting, as Newcomen reminded his listeners that "this day 37: yeares did god make his people to ride in a triumphall chariott of Celebraciõn" (131[v]). He compared the plot to a variety of Old Testament treacheries, claiming in both pulpit and print that it was surpassed in treachery only by the temptation of Adam and Eve. Both Newcomen and Yonge seem to have relished the preacher's catalogue of Satan's works, of which the Gunpowder Plot was to be the grand finale: "the funerall pire of England in Q. maryes dayes, the massacre of Ffrance, the wors of Germany the fresh blood of Ireland, are goodly sights to ... [Satan] & yet this had bin much more delightsome" (130[r]).[224] Having imagined the results of a successful plot in graphic detail, Newcomen attributed its failure to the direct intervention of God, unaided by King James. In the printed version, he makes the same claim that the plot was prevented not by "any *State vigilancy* or *prudence*, but *meerely divine providence*" (28); however, he then refuses to describe the deliverance, claiming that everyone already knows the story. This evasion is probably intended to avoid crediting James with interpreting the Monteagle letter. Perhaps most notably, Newcomen seems to have added to the published version an emphasis upon the role of Parliament. He asserts at the beginning that in 1605 the king had called Parliament "to secure the *Church*, the true Religion and worship of God, with needfull, healthfull Lawes" (20), and he concludes by advising the currrent Parliament that their first action should be to make and enforce more stringent laws against Catholics. These passages do not appear in Yonge's notes.

In the printed sermon, a lengthy textual explication that edges into an application, not to the Gunpowder Plot but to the current crisis, precedes the plot narrative. Newcomen begins by drawing a parallel between Nehemiah's discouragements in rebuilding Jerusalem's walls and England's struggle to reform her church over the previous hundred years, casting Catholics in the roles of Sanballat and Tobias. The doctrine the preacher extracts from his text is that "*The great designe of the enemies of the church, is by craft or cruelty, or both, to hinder any worke that tends to the establishment, or promoting of the churches good*" (3). Beginning with

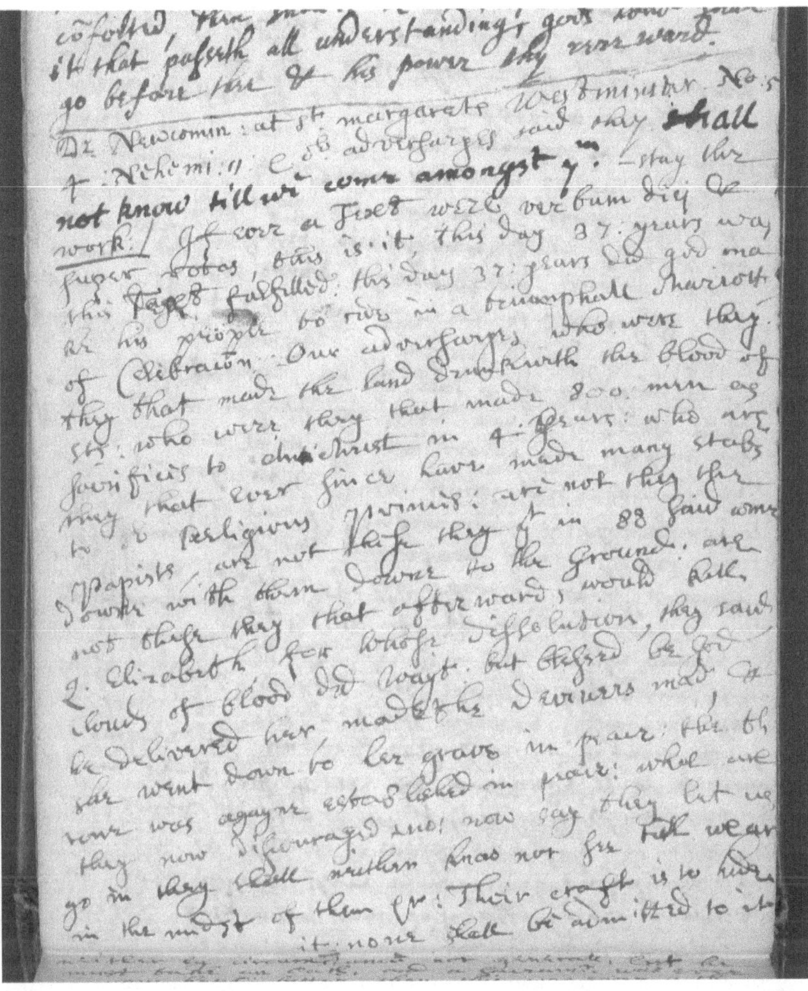

Figure 7 Page from Walter Yonge's notes on Matthew Newcomen's sermon preached to the House of Commons at St. Margaret's Westminster on 5 November 1642. © The British Library Board, Add MS 18,781.

Abel's murder, Satan has instigated all the designs against the church. Frequently, the church's enemies claim to have no plans to alter religion, even when they limit preaching to one sermon per day or allow sports on Sunday. These enemies may also work through promoting intermarriages between believers and non-believers, enacting laws against the church, prosecuting false charges against it, or developing secret conspiracies. Newcomen emphasizes the dangers of "outlandish" women without making specific application to Henrietta Maria, describing the problem of unequal marriage particularly in regard to children corrupted by a Catholic parent. Jesuits are especially practised at creating turmoil, regularly ingratiating themselves with kings and princes. Newcomen thus manages to identify the king's evil counsellors, to whom he returns later in the sermon, with Jesuits, the source of much anxiety during the civil wars.[225] By associating Charles and Laud not only with Catholicism, but even with Jesuitism, he intensifies his attack on those he considers the church's enemies. Although not explicitly, he also suggests that if Parliament negotiates with the king and his crypto-Catholic counsellors, it will become complicit in the plot to destroy England's true church.

Yet, Newcomen also situates himself as a peacemaker by recognizing that "Hatred [*sic*] grounded in differences of Religion, are the most bitter and uncapable of Reconciliation" (15), and that the closer the two groups are in doctrine the stronger the animosity between them. Therefore, the greatest hatred exists between puritans and formalists. God chooses not to restrain this antagonism both to try his people and to increase his own glory. Like Sclater in the previous year, Newcomen seems to have recognized that his listeners might have scruples about Protestants warring against Protestants. But Newcomen's message to his readers is that ending the war would frustrate God's plans for England and so potentially incur his wrath.

After interjecting his plot narrative, Newcomen returns, according to both the printed version and Yonge's notes, to his project of proving that Catholics have conspired continuously since 1605. The Irish Rebellion, he claims, was plotted for seventeen years, while the interruption of Parliaments in England was also part of a Catholic plot, disguised as Arminianism. Although many still insist that the Laudians had no intention of changing England's religion, he insists they followed a template set out in a Jesuit pamphlet for exactly that purpose. This pamphlet claimed to be a translation "*by a Catholicke Spy*" of the eighteenth and nineteenth chapters (Book 2) of a Latin work entitled *Politicorum Libri Decem.*[226] First published in 1630 with the Latin title, it was reprinted in 1641, presumably without authorization since the title page asserts that it was "Printed at the Cat and Fidle for a Dauncing Mouse," as *Look about you. The plot of Contzen, the Moguntine Iesuite, to Cheate a Church of the Religion Established therein, and to serve in Popery by Art, without noise or Tumult.* The text recommends several strategies for restoring Catholicism without unduly alarming a population, much as a musician gradually tightens the strings of an instrument. In other words, it describes a plot that is almost the exact opposite of the Gunpowder Plot.

Rather than being enacted in a moment of terror, this plot reveals itself gradually and almost imperceptibly. A prince may conceal his plans by pretending concerns with his subjects' consciences so that they will applaud him for loving peace rather than suspect him of changing religions. Meanwhile, he may be quietly removing heretics and making laws against the obstinate. Newcomen is careful merely to outline this program and to allow his hearers to make their own analogies with the Caroline administration. Nevertheless, his purpose is to show that Arminianism was only a prelude to restoring Catholicism, a belief that justifies the war against the king. In addition, it shows that the king cannot be trusted – his actions may be concealing his intentions. England harbours at least as many Catholics as at the time of the Gunpowder Plot, according to Newcomen, and their doctrines have not changed. However, the treachery they imagine now exceeds even that of the 1605 plot, for they have laid these plots in the king's heart under the guise of protecting the Protestant faith. And thus, "*The breath of our nostrils, the Anointed of the Lord is taken in their pitts; of whom we said, under his shadow we shall live*" (42 *vere* 50). The king has been captured not by a foreign nation, but by evil counsellors who have divided him from his Protestant subjects.

Newcomen justifies war as the only way to resist popery, but licenses his hearers only to hate Catholicism, not individual Catholics. Yonge's notes end with Newcomen's hope that the king may be divided from his evil counsellors. In the printed version, however, Newcomen expands on the problem of evil counsel. Even a king who converts to Catholicism may be deposed by the pope; therefore, the king will serve himself ill by becoming a papal subject, since neither his crown nor his head will be safe. The bishops, however, will benefit, and therefore must be responsible for the king's actions. Taken together, both this conclusion and the opening scriptural exegesis, neither of which were part of the oral sermon if we trust to Yonge's notes, offer a much more critical view of the king's ecclesiastical advisors and a much more positive view of Parliament and its political advisors.

Newcomen's sermon builds on Gouge's representation of Nehemiah as a patriot, but for him Parliament has become a collective Nehemiah. He claims that James called the 1605 meeting postponed by the plot to enact anti-Catholic legislation to protect the English Church, asking rhetorically: "Wherefore should a Parliament meet, but for that worke?" (20).[227] The question, however, invites agreement to what is clearly a drastic revisioning of Parliament's role in governing the nation.[228] Although only the Commons may have been present, he addresses the members of both houses as "*Princes of the tribes of England*" (33) who "representatively are the whole Nation" (31). Just as Parliament was the primary target of the Gunpowder Plot, so it has been the target of a plot without powder that prevented it from being called for twelve years. Newcomen emphasizes the secrecy with which all of these plots have been carried out in order to demonstrate that the Gunpowder Plot, the Laudian "innovations," and the Irish Rebellion, despite their different modes of operation, are various forms of the same Catholic treachery and warns that the same enemies who tried to divide the king from his counsellors are now trying to divide Parliament from the people. The printed sermon concludes with a list of religious means for eliminating Catholicism – establishing public fasts, eradicating all remaining traces of popery in churches, ridding the church of corrupt ministers, conforming as much as possible with the other Reformed churches (including the Scots), establishing a faithful ministry throughout the country, and suppressing Catholicism in Ireland. Secular means, he says, should be left to the state, thereby claiming for himself a status above politics that is negated for the reader by the authorization to publish.

While we must use caution in reading the differences between the printed sermon and Yonge's notes, they raise some interesting questions about who was being addressed in the parliamentary sermons. Newcomen appears to have been more wary of openly criticizing the king and his counsellors before his audience at St Margaret's and less fulsome in praising Parliament than he was in the printed sermon. This discretion suggests that he wished his general audience to perceive him as a pastor saving his flock from the Roman wolves rather than a political advisor offering counsel. Despite Newcomen's belated attempt to distinguish between religion and politics, however, the printed sermon accepts a direct political function. Clearly he disagreed, for religious reasons, with Parliament's decision to negotiate with the king and sought to sway his parliamentary auditors to his position.

The religious program Newcomen proposed in his printed sermon, but not necessarily on 5 November, included the destruction of the remnants of the Catholic past in churches.[229] Whether such a program had already been planned or whether Newcomen's sermon instigated it, a fresh wave of iconoclasm commenced the following spring. In either case, he may have been reluctant to advocate this project before the very parishioners whose stained glass windows were to be among the casualties. Although he was forced to abridge his sermon that day due to time constraints, the choices he made in both the spoken and the printed sermons may indicate that he recognized several different audiences. The printed sermon, as a document that could be read over, and potentially used as a guide for public policy, included detailed advice to Parliament and a stronger justification for the war, possibly intended both for wavering MPs and for a broader national audience of uncommitted subjects. At St Margaret's, however, Newcomen sensed a greater need to concentrate on his spiritual role, reinterpreting the myth of deliverance created by James I to justify rebellion against his son on the grounds of care for the church. Newcomen's sermon thus represents a development of the political occasion sermon in the preacher's apparent recognition that pulpit and pamphlet could be used to present different messages to different audiences. In other words, these sermons were developing a genre that questioned its own rhetorical purposes and its effects upon audiences.

6.5 Seth Ward (1661): Obedience Restored?

With the Restoration, sermons returned to the court, but the most significant political anniversaries became the 30 January fast marking Charles I's death and the 29 May celebration of Charles II's return, making the Gunpowder anniversary the only pre-war occasion in what was effectively a new political calendar.[230] This change removed 5 November from its earlier contextualization among the records of other Catholic plots and situated it within what was essentially an anti-Puritan calendar, making the failed conspiracy a foreshadowing of the successful one plotted not by Catholics but by the godly.[231] Unlike his father, Charles II seems to have recognized the importance of sermons as a mode of "representative publicness," even if he lacked his grandfather's fondness for the genre. In the first surviving Gunpowder anniversary sermon of the new reign, Seth Ward apparently determined to use the pulpit as his Jacobean predecessors had done, to support the monarch while also offering him counsel. Ward, however, approached his court audience in a new way, seeing them not as competent interpreters, but as potential subversives needing to be coerced into submission. At the same time, he offered Charles II a clear warning about the limitations of his religious authority. Although it was reprinted during the 1710 controversy over Henry Sacheverell's impeachment for another Gunpowder sermon, Ward's message of passive obedience does not seem to have entirely satisfied a new generation.

While relatively few gunpowder sermons from the 1660s survive, the preaching and publication of Ward's Whitehall sermon in 1661 suggest that Charles intended at the beginning of his reign to revive the Gunpowder anniversary as a royal occasion, even if its importance seems to have declined later in the decade.[232] Carolyn Edie notes that sermons made up a significant component in the three official celebrations of the Restoration that took place between late April and the end of June 1660. Her analysis of surviving copies of these sermons indicates that although their tone varied widely, the sermons were guardedly hopeful of a future in which order would return to the nation under a new monarch. In a later study, Edie also observed that Charles carefully selected St George's Day (23 April 1661) as the date for his coronation, reviving an old festival that had languished during the years of puritan rule .[233] The sermon preached by George Morley,

Bishop of Worcester, on this occasion emphasized the restoration of the monarchy itself more than Charles's personal qualities, insisting upon the divine institution of monarchy and its opposition to tyranny. Edie concludes that "There was nothing very remarkable or original in what Morley said, but the point he made was clear. England rejoiced in the restoration of order, propriety, monarchy, and the laws which protected all three."[234] Convocation spent the summer of 1661 writing orders of service for the 29 May and 30 January anniversaries, suggesting that this activity was a priority for the new regime, just as the Gowrie service had been for James I.[235] If Charles hoped to use sermons to reinforce his position as a monarch by divine right, however, his clergy were determined to remind him of the limitations upon his power.

In 1661, Ward preached a message prescribing passive obedience to the monarch, but at the same time he clearly articulated the boundaries of Charles's ecclesiastical authority. He chose his text from the thirteenth chapter of Romans, the standard scriptural source of anti-resistance texts from the Elizabethan period.[236] In fact, he seems to have deliberately harked back to the Elizabethan and Jacobean sermons. In his dedication, he attributes his reluctance both to preach and to publish to anxiety of influence, confiding to the reader his concern "that in a Cause of so great consequence, so clear, so nobly handled by the greatest *Worthies* of the *Church* of *England*, I should not finde any thing to be tolerably spoken, before the greatest, and most revered Judgment under Heaven."[237] Without mentioning names, he seems to be placing himself in a series of royal preachers that includes men like William Barlow, Lancelot Andrewes, and John King, conveniently blotting out the memory of the more recent parliamentary preachers. Despite these attempts to recreate the past, however, Ward clearly addresses issues that had arrived with the Restoration. While Ferrell has suggested that the Gunpowder occasion had always elicited a strain of anti-puritanism, this for the first time completely overshadowed anti-Catholicism. Ward makes an analogy between the Catholic League and the Solemn League and Covenant that clearly identifies the regicide as a successful Gunpowder Plot. In addition, he attacks a notion that would not have occurred to James I or his subjects, that government and religion are opposed. He begins by insisting that the church and the state must operate together. Religion and government cannot be separated, since the bishops are responsible for religion, but their canons must be enforced by civil laws. This state of affairs leaves little opportunity for the monarch to intervene in religious matters, and Ward specifically bars the king from any direct role in the church. Jeffrey R. Collins notes that one of the defining characteristics of the Restoration "was a degree of hostility between the royal court and the English episcopate unprecedented since the Reformation."[238] Unlike Laud, who had allowed Charles I full royal supremacy, the Restoration bishops were unprepared to grant Charles II any prerogatives they considered their own. Ward outlines clearly the king's duties in religious matters – to regulate worship and reform abuses in the church. But, he cautions: "we do not *entitle* him to the *Priest's Office* (the *Spiritual* Function) or the *Execution* of it, in *preaching* the *Word, administring* the *Sacraments, exercising* the power of *Ordination*, or of the *Keyes*, &c" (20). The exclusion of the sovereign from preaching and administering the sacraments had been accepted from the time of the Reformation, so Ward's need publicly to articulate these restrictions seems significant. At the same time, his "etc." offers the threat of expanding the list of exclusions. As Collins points out, this developing insistence upon the separation of royal from episcopal functions resulted in a tendency to view the sacred and secular as parallel but separate spheres of authority.[239] In addition, it opened the episcopacy to charges of popery, which may partly explain the bishops' propensity to draw attention to puritan disobedience as a diversionary tactic.

Relations between the king and the bishops had not yet become so polarized, nor had Ward yet become a bishop, but he was clearly embarking on a career path that allied his interests with those of the episcopate. In August 1660, the king rewarded him for his loyalty during the civil wars with the parish of St Lawrence Jewry, which was in the royal gift. Appointments as precentor, prebendary, and dean of Exeter Cathedral followed the next year, and in the summer of 1662 Ward became Bishop of Exeter, later being translated to the see of Salisbury (1667). Although his biographer, Walter Pope, painted a flattering picture of his conduct during and after the civil wars, some saw him as a consummate politician. According to Pope, he was maligned by Anthony à Wood, who claimed that he had changed his politics and taken the Oath of Engagement "the effect of which was *to be faithful to the Commonwealth of England, as it was then established without a King or House of Lords*" in order to obtain an Oxford professorship in 1649.[240] Anticipating the Restoration in 1660, however, he had arranged to be imprisoned at Cambridge to demonstrate his loyalty to the crown. Once made Dean of Exeter, he had "wound himself in a short time, by his smooth language and behaviour, into the favour of the Gentry of the neighbourhood."[241] While Pope and Wood disagree about Ward's sincerity, neither denies that he had superior rhetorical skills.

According to Pope, Ward's sermons "were strong, methodical and clear, and, when Occasion required, pathetical and eloquent."[242] In this sermon, Ward's choice of text offered little scope for subtlety of interpretation, nor did he exploit any there might have been. Structured in neither of the traditional ways, but as an essay that establishes a thesis in order to refute it, the sermon exemplifies the fear of interpretation that Ward articulates throughout. Treating Romans 13.1–7 as a "theory," he sets out to prove that God never restrains sovereign power. The traditional argument for submission to political authorities, as offered in the

"Homelie against Disobedience and Wylfull Rebellion," was that human government reflected divine government, but Ward seems uncomfortable with arguing from analogy. Instead, he offers Moses, the children in Daniel, the Virgin Mary, and Christ and his apostles as examples of loyalty to civic authority, not devotion to God, and reiterates that God gave none of these individuals, even Christ on the cross, power to resist either just or unjust authority. Although Ward structures his sermon according to the practices of rational discourse, however, he makes no effort to persuade his audience, stating curtly that "The strongest, and most operative *Arguments* upon men ... are Arguments *of Terrour.*"[243] Ward is interested in subdued subjects, not independent, thoughtful ones who will read, or listen, between the lines of his sermon.

While Ward's sermon offers a ringing endorsement of passive obedience, however, it also clearly limits the sovereign's power in religious matters. Later in his reign, when Charles's confrontations with the bishops over these issues had escalated, the king might not have ordered the sermon printed, but at this point he was apparently inclined to overlook Ward's admonition to himself in order to publicize the message of obedience to royal authority.[244] Ward's theme seems to have been echoed in other Gunpowder sermons from the 1660s. John Evelyn noted approvingly that Robert South had preached on obedience to magistrates in 1664, while in 1667 George Morley preached before the king at Whitehall on 1 Corinthians 14.33, defining peace as order and attributing the Gunpowder Plot to the Roman church's elevation of papal over regal authority.[245] He concludes by expanding the causes of confusion in the state to include Protestant dissent and condemning any form of toleration. Preachers like Morley, South, and Ward saw religious uniformity as the key ingredient in maintaining the political order, which enabled them to equate dissenting Protestants with the Gunpowder plotters.

Ward's sermon was reprinted in collected editions of his sermons in 1672 and 1674, then reappeared as a pamphlet during the 1710 exchanges over Henry Sacheverell's immensely controversial sermon the previous November. In the intervening years, Gunpowder sermons had most actively participated in political life during the 1670s and 1680s as fears of a Catholic succession escalated. Charles II's attempt to impose the Declaration of Indulgence initiated a change in relations between church and court that can be gauged from South's 1675 sermon at Westminster Abbey, which insisted upon the king's duty to his subjects along with subjects' duty to the monarch.[246] In particular, South stressed the king's responsibility to care for the church. God preserves kings not because monarchy is divinely ordained, he cautioned, but because it is the best form of government; however, "the greatness or strength of a Monarchy depends chiefly upon the Personal Qualifications of the Prince or Monarch."[247] This is a significant, and ominous, shift from the rationale for obedience presented in the *Homilies* as well as from Morley's coronation sermon, which had downplayed Charles's personal qualities in favour of his place in the divine order. South concludes by reminding subjects to obey the monarch and advising kings to be thankful for their deliverances and not court further mischief. At least eight sermons survive from 5 November 1678, more than for any earlier year, as the discovery of the Popish Plot unleashed the greatest flood of anti-Catholic sermons since the Restoration.[248] Gone are the analogies between Catholic plotters and dissenters, as preachers once again equate religious conformity with political obedience and call upon Protestants to forget their differences in order to establish a united front against Catholicism. Gregory Hascard, after rehearsing the evils of Catholicism, concludes that "being fully perswaded that we are Baptized into this Church of *England*, whose Faith is Primitive, Pure, and Apostolical, her Rules for Manners only leading to Virtue and Goodness, her Discipline wholsome and proper, and her Devotions decent and Manly; let us stick fast unto her, and take *Solomon's* Advice, *My Son, Fear thou the Lord and the King, but meddle not with them that are given to change*."[249] Several other preachers, like John Bedle, referred to the words of the original prayer book service that identified Catholic faith with civil disorder: "If I should say the *Romish* Religion is a Religion whose Faith is Faction, and whose Zeal is Rebellion, 'tis no more than may be proved."[250] By the following year, however, preachers were again attacking both sectarians and Catholics. In an anticipation of post-1688 developments, Francis Gregory conflated the two, asking: "Do we not yet understand, that the *Jesuits* are the men, who, under the notion of *Quakers* and *Anabaptists*, have broken our *Publick Congregations* into *Private Conventicles*?"[251] In an undated sermon published in 1683, William Wray uses a military metaphor to express a similar concern that schisms within the English Church provide opportunities for Catholics: "Alas! our petty *Sects* and *Factions* are our *Weaknesses*, and the Champions of *Rome* are so far from Levelling their Artillery against *them*, that they *connive* at them, they *indulge* them, they make them *more*, in hopes to enter at them, one day, as through *Breaches*."[252] While most preachers still concentrated on attacking Catholicism, there was an increasing emphasis upon the superiority of the English Church as well as the political consequences of any deviation towards sectarian Protestantism.

These issues regarding the relationship between church and state continued to surface intermittently into the eighteenth century. According to Clyve Jones, "The reign of Queen Anne saw the last major flowering of the traditional tory [*sic*] political values and ideals of passive obedience to the monarchy, non-resistance and divine right," and was marked by two significant incidents.[253] First, Tory politicians in 1705 roused the queen's ire by insisting that occasional conformity endangered the church and forcing a lengthy debate in the House of Commons on 6 December 1705. The House eventually voted 61 to 30 that the church was not in danger, and the rhetorical temperature cooled until the actions of Sacheverell and his supporters raised it again in 1710. On 5 November 1709, Sacheverell preached a sermon before the Lord Mayor and aldermen at St Paul's on the text 2 Corinthians 11.26, "In perils among false brethren," in which he identified both Catholics and extreme Protestants, who hatched respectively the Gunpowder Plot and the 1649 regicide, as false brethren.[254] The problem was that after 1688 civil disobedience could not be ascribed solely to puritans and Catholics; those, like Sacheverell, who wanted to warn against the evils of disobedience to the crown had to distinguish the events of the Protestant revolution from those of the regicide. In the ensuing controversy, the doctrine of royal supremacy became a source of the very anarchy Ward deplored, perpetrated this time not by dissenters but by those loyal to the national church.

Although he had arrived in London only a short time earlier, Sacheverell was already making a name for himself as a preacher. Geoffrey Holmes suggests that his success in the pulpit was based more upon the manner of his delivery than the matter of his sermons. He "did not seduce his audiences with words; he bludgeoned them with metaphor and epithet, delivering the blows in such bewildering profusion that the wonder is that all his hearers were not regularly reduced to insensibility" (*Trial* 50).[255] His voice, however, was apparently excellent and his manner entertaining if hardly dignified.[256] London's new Lord Mayor, Samuel Garrard, later claimed he had not witnessed any of Sacheverell's pulpit performances before issuing the invitation for him to preach the annual Gunpowder sermon at St Paul's.[257] Curiously, Sacheverell did not compose a new sermon for the occasion, but revised one he had preached several years previously in a different location. According to an entry in Thomas Hearne's diary, it had first been delivered at St Mary's Oxford on 23 December 1705, immediately following the "Church in Danger" debate in the House of Commons.[258] Holmes, noting that the content of the sermon was the same doctrine Sacheverell had been preaching for years, suggests that repeating this sermon may have appealed to him precisely because it was unconnected with the occasion of the Gunpowder Plot. In attesting to its irrelevance, Holmes observes that "At the start it took Sacheverell under three minutes to dispose of the Gunpowder Plot and the Papists; and even here, by bracketing 5 November with 30 January as days of equal significance in the English calendar, he was able to brand the dissenters as being no less abhorrent than the Guy Fawkes's Day conspirators."[259] While Holmes is disconcerted by this approach, and Sacheverell may have aligned the unsuccessful Catholic plotters of 1605 with the successful puritan regicides of 1649 more emphatically than the Restoration preachers, the idea itself was not new. For Sacheverell, however, the central problem is the analogy made after 1688 between the rebellion against Charles I and the accession of William and Mary. He insists that in 1688 the throne was vacant, and that William III never claimed to be a conqueror; therefore the "protestant revolution" cannot be used to justify resistance. Like earlier defenders of passive obedience, including Ward, Sacheverell argues that justifying resistance as a form of self-defence is dangerous because it can be used to excuse any act of rebellion. Rule by many is worse even than papal tyranny, for each person will interpret the king's actions differently. Under these circumstances, "A Prince indeed, in another Sense, will be the Breath of his Subject's Nostrils to be Blown in, or out, at their Caprice, and Pleasure, and a worse Vassal than even the meanest of his Guards."[260] A unified church is the only way to maintain the state, for neither can continue without the other.

Sacheverell pays little heed to situating his scriptural text, although he does list Paul's vicissitudes, in which the perils of false brethren cap even shipwreck. Once he divides his text, however, he focuses entirely upon the contemporary application. Even more than Ward's, the sermon speaks entirely to the political situation and not at all to the spiritual considerations of its listeners. Nevertheless, like Ward, Sacheverell harked back to the Elizabethan and Jacobean periods, referring to the *Homilies*, quoting from Lancelot Andrewes's 1610 Gowrie sermon, and reactivating the discourse of monstrosity to describe the "false brethren" threatening the church.[261] While Sacheverell's sermon caused an immediate sensation, it might have been quickly forgotten had he not followed it up immediately with publication.

Sacheverell's threat to the authorities was, as Holmes puts it, that "although he preached Obedience, he failed to practise it."[262] He published the sermon claiming the mayor's authorization, although Garrard later denied granting his approval.[263] The printed sermon immediately became a bestseller, selling as many as one hundred thousand copies within weeks. The Whigs initially attempted to attack Sacheverell through the pamphlet press, but soon realized this tactic would not suffice.[264] Legal counsel advised that prosecuting him for sedition would be difficult because "at a number of crucial points he had chosen his words carefully enough, or inserted enough studied ambiguities or contradictions to make it uncertain, to say the least, that he could be convicted of sedition *on words alone*."[265] Nevertheless, the scope of Sacheverell's audacity in comparing 1688 to 1649 forced the government to resort to impeachment proceedings in early 1710. His trial and ultimate conviction led to a series of disturbances in which his supporters attacked a number of dissenting meeting houses before moving on to other targets. Holmes's studies of the riots indicate that participants came from a variety of social classes and that the destruction seems to have been carefully planned in advance and carried out, at least in the beginning, methodically and efficiently. High Church clergy both preached and prayed publicly in support of Sacheverell.[266] Lee Horsley gives some conception of the pamphlet war that accompanied these proceedings and "to which some of the leading journalists of the day contributed with ingenuity and vigor." She points out that Tories "were of two minds, both pleased by their overwhelming popularity and embarrassed by disorderly demonstrations in their cause," demonstrations that effectively quashed any argument that the Church of England could be unproblematically equated with peace and civil order.[267]

At some time in this period of political tension and excitement, Seth Ward's 1661 sermon was reprinted. The title page bears no date, simply "Printed in the Year of Grace," while the following page contains this unsigned and somewhat cryptic note of instruction to the reader: "*If you are minded to see more of the Spirit of Dr.* Sach – –l, *than what appears in his Sermons, you may look in two Books printed some Years ago at* Oxford, *the one was* The Character of a Low-Church-man, *and the other, as I remember*, The Rights of the Church asserted, &c." The first of the two works to which the reader is referred is Sacheverell's 1702 response to an electioneering pamphlet entitled *The Character of a Church-man*, in which he attacks Latitudinarians for misinterpreting scripture for political ends. The second pamphlet also contributed to an existing debate, this one over the status of dissenters. Whoever reprinted Ward's sermon was thus launching it into the Sacheverell controversy, presumably in aid of the High Church party, but was reluctant to have his own name associated in any way with the publication or to endorse Sacheverell personally. For all this, there is a vast difference between the two texts. Ward's asserts in its direct style two messages, one for the king and one for his advisors. Sacheverell's ornate, and frequently impenetrable, style conceals a single message but in such a way that the authorities had difficulty prosecuting him even though his audience could not have failed to grasp his meaning.

6.6 Conclusion

The publicity over Sacheverell's sermon demonstrates that the Gunpowder Plot anniversary could now promote political agendas unimagined in 1605. As Catholic plotting became an occasional rather than a quotidian threat, it became an analogy for crises created by other religious and political issues. Not until the mid-nineteenth century would a Catholic threat resurface as the primary context for Gunpowder sermons.[268] By this time, however, the people rather than the authorities clearly controlled the agenda.

Throughout the seventeenth century, the Gunpowder anniversary had offered preachers opportunities both to counsel the king and to persuade his subjects to practice obedience. In 1622, Donne had defended not only the king's right to political leadership but also the individual's responsibility to interpret both scripture and current events. Although he used his sermon originally to advise subjects to support the king with both their actions and their prayers, his later revisions implicated the king in the actions of evil or corrupted ministers. The threat of evil counsellors was taken up in 1636 by Henry Burton, who claimed to be informing Charles I about the independent actions of his bishops. Matthew Newcomen, in the first year of the Civil War, counselled Parliament against negotiating with Royalists and crypto-Catholics, while in the residual political instability of 1661, Seth Ward advised Charles II to grant the church a measure of independence even as he proclaimed the king's right to the obedience of his subjects.[269] Throughout this process, the Church of England sought to define itself against first Catholicism and then puritanism, and sometimes both. John Spurr remarks that

> What makes the Church of England's continuing search for her identity such an absorbing historical problem is that, as a church, she is particularly dependent upon her "occasion". She has no irreducible doctrinal core, no confession of faith nor petrine rock, upon which to rest, but must go out, armed only with her Bible, liturgy, Articles and traditions, to do battle with each new set of political, social and cultural circumstances.[270]

I would add sermons to this inventory of linguistic ordnance. The Gunpowder anniversary as an occasion proved particularly resilient in adapting to new circumstances and particularly resistant to threats of extinction.

The history of the Gunpowder sermon in many ways traces the life of the occasional political sermon in the seventeenth century, as no other anniversary was continuously celebrated throughout this period. These occasions could, and did, function on multiple levels, but one of their effects was to teach listeners and readers to decode meanings that the preacher was unable or unwilling to express in hostile, or potentially hostile, political climates. Whereas the Elizabethan *Homilies* had offered regular and consistent royalist messages for public consumption, James I's desire to create a Jacobean myth of deliverance in the wake of the Gunpowder Plot offered preachers opportunities to interpret both scripture and political events according to their own lights and to disseminate these interpretations through both the pulpit and the press. Increasingly uncomfortable with the flood of independent thought he had unleashed, James attempted to dam it with his 1622 *Directions to Preachers*; however, the events of the 1630s proved the floodgates could not be closed. Similarly, attempts by Restoration preachers to enforce passive obedience and religious uniformity were doomed to failure despite the warnings offered by the civil wars. Having learned to read critically, parishioners refused any longer to endorse the "fiction in which nation and church were coterminous."[271] They had recognized the political sermon as an instrument of persuasion that acknowledged their crucial role in the nation's religious and political life. At the same time, the critical listening and reading skills they had learned by hearing and reading occasional political sermons offered individuals opportunities to participate in a wider range of political and religious discourse.

Figure 8 Page depicting the Gunpowder Plot in the Sheares Bible, a verse paraphrase of the Bible written and illustrated by Abraham Sheares, 1701–1731. © The British Library Board, Add MS 62708.

So in six hundered and fiue
the fifth day of Nouember
was another Papis PLOT
that we should all Remember
Gainst ye King and Parlimen
which ware in Beeing then
hell and deuills did contriue
with bloodye Papish men
Vnder the Houce of Parlimen
thes Villans Laid Laid a TRAP
with Powder Piles and borning mach
to giue the Peares a clap
So neare this Bloody PEOT was Brought
the mach bornt neare his End
the Powder All Redye to take
but GOD apeard our frend
Manye more sich Cursed Acts
the Papist Acted in
to take our Gospel light away
and bring the man of Sin
The GunPowder Treason
Januarye: 23: 17
Now for six hundred Eighty Seuen
see what was Acted then
Astmkin Prison was a PLACE
for great and famoues men
For a Popish Prince did rule this Land
had gote him selfe great POWER
he seasd our nowbell bushps then
this was a dismall houre

In the "Sheares Bible" (BL Add. MS 62708), an illustrated verse paraphrase of the English Bible created by Abraham Sheares between 1701 and 1731, one eighteenth-century Anglican left us a glimpse of how the Gunpowder sermons he had heard, and possibly read, influenced his interpretation of current events. Sheares interrupts the biblical sequence in the middle of 1 Kings to insert a series of political verses with accompanying illustrations, beginning with the providential defeat and destruction of the Armada, followed by the Gunpowder Plot, emphasizing in his verse how

> neare this Bloudy PLOT was Brought
> the mach bornt neare his End
> the Powder all Redye to take
> but GOD appeard our frend
> Many more sich Corsed Acts
> the papist Acted in
> to take our Gospel light away
> and bring the man of sin. (290^{r})

The accompanying illustration, dated 23 January 1714/15, shows Fawkes approaching Parliament bearing a huge dark lantern. The beam of God's eye falls directly upon the lantern, as if to cancel out the false light with the true. Sheares skips discreetly over the embarrassing episode of the Popish Plot, progressing directly to 1687, when "a Popish Prince did rule this Land" (290^{r}). A double spread over the next two facing pages illustrates Prince William's arrival on the left as James II, his queen carrying a baby labelled "Pretend," and a priest flee to the right (290^{v}-291^{r}). Queen Anne then enjoyed a peaceful reign until 5 November 1710, when Sacheverell "did Remoue ye Powder PLOT / upon that uery day" (291^{r}).[272] Rather than praising God for the deliverance, "of his text he made an Ax / to spleet ye Church in two" (291^{v}). Sheares equates Sacheverell directly with the Gunpowder plotters, calling him Haman's younger brother: "His tongue was like a borning mach / with brimstone soat on fier" (291^{v}). He illustrates this verse with a drawing of the Sacheverell rioters destroying a church and a reproduction of the title page of an anti-Sacheverell pamphlet. The sequence concludes with an illustration of the devil seizing a pope, a monk, a cardinal, and a friar. What is particularly interesting in Sheares's representation of this historical sequence is that clearly, for him, Catholicism and faction within the church remained equivalent enemies of Anglicanism. This fascinating artefact illustrates the extent to which this version of history had achieved a status of truth that allowed it to be included in a Bible. England and Israel had effectively become one.

Conclusion: Echoes and Reverberations

The cultural impact of the Gunpowder Plot has generally been described in terms of the ritual practices, both official and unofficial, that marked the anniversary, with literary texts understood primarily as traces of these commemorative occasions. Studying these artefacts as texts, however, leads us to new insights about the relationship between the political and literary landscapes of seventeenth-century England. The literature of the Gunpowder Plot demonstrates first how the plot participated in a nascent public sphere, then how memories of it were cultivated for religio-political reasons, and finally how competing interest groups struggled to control the narrative of this significant incident in the nation's recent past.

The plot was discovered at a pivotal historical moment when the arrival of a Scottish monarch, the repudiation of Catholicism, and the growth of puritanism were redefining England politically, religiously, and geographically. For all the peacefulness of James Stuart's accession, tensions simmered beneath the surface as Englishmen were forced to compete for precedence at court with foreigners from the north, while Catholics and puritans both sought concessions from the new king. Whether seeking patronage by warning James against Catholic interests at court or fulfilling conciliar responsibilities by documenting the trials and punishments of the plotters, writers expressed anxieties about the dangers of ambition and the limits of religious toleration in the new reign.

At the beginning of this period, the Protestant nation defined itself largely in opposition to Catholicism, but individual religious identities were more fluid than this binary indicates. Attempts to contain religious diversity manifested themselves in satire and invective directed against English Catholics, and especially Jesuits, whose failure to reconcile their political and religious identities made them seem monstrous, or even demonic. The radicalization of puritanism and the growth of ceremonialism ultimately shattered this fragile Protestant consensus. Within this polarized political climate, associating one's enemies with the Gunpowder plotters identified them as both heretics and traitors.

At the same time, the availability of cheap print and the evolving role of sermons in post-Reformation culture were redefining the literary landscape. Both offered the state new opportunities to disseminate information about and interpretations of events, but by the 1620s both were becoming increasingly difficult to control. Even playwrights, subjected to the most direct control, had developed methods of commenting on current events by situating their dramas in other times and places. Not only could competing interpretations be disseminated to most subjects in these ways, but through reading and listening individuals became increasingly sophisticated interpreters, able to negotiate among multiple messages from various media and even within individual texts directed to more than one audience. Moreover, the development of the occasional political sermon recognized that ordinary people, even the illiterate, contributed, through thanksgiving and obedience, to ensuring their nation's peace and spiritual health. Between 1606 and 1641 writers and translators of Anglo-Latin Gunpowder epics increasingly reinforced this role, as their faith in the will and ability of a godly monarch to sustain God's favour declined.

Joel Hurstfield's contention that the Gunpowder Plot is not merely "the story of an explosion which never took place" but has in it "the basic ingredients of the whole human order" is strikingly echoed in David Quint's observation that Milton revisited the event throughout his literary career because in it he "had found the recurring plot of history itself."[1] Seventeenth-century Englishpersons frequently viewed the Gunpowder Plot as a kind of microcosm of English history. But how they understood that history depended upon the narrative they constructed around it. Some saw England attacked repeatedly from outside by international Catholicism, while others saw it undermined from within by those who appeared to be English but subscribed to foreign religions. Whether viewed as the founding moment for a new Protestant Britain or merely a step on the road towards apocalypse, the plot continued to echo in the English historical and literary consciousness well beyond the seventeenth century.

Notes

1. Introduction: Writing the Gunpowder Plot

1 One conspirator, Francis Tresham, died in the Tower awaiting trial, and Nicholas Owen, a carpenter who had constructed priest holes in numerous Catholic homes but was not directly involved in the conspiracy, was probably fatally injured while being tortured for information. One priest, Father Edward Oldcorne, was charged with treason and executed on the basis of his knowledge and approval of the plot although he had not directly participated in it.

2 I discuss some of these accounts, the details of which vary, below. What follows here is a general outline taken mainly from official Protestant sources; I discuss Catholic accounts, particularly the influential one written by John Gerard, in chapter 2. James Sharpe provides a clear and succinct narrative in chapter 2 of *Remember, Remember: A Cultural History of Guy Fawkes Day.*

3 The original plotters included Catesby, Thomas Winter, and John Wright. Fawkes, apparently recruited for his knowledge of mining, and Thomas Percy seem to have entered the conspiracy at the same time, apparently in the spring of 1604. Over the following winter and spring, John Grant, Robert Keyes, Robert Winter, and Christopher Wright were brought in, along with Catesby's servant, Thomas Bates, sworn into the conspiracy after he guessed his master's plans.

4 Plotters admitted late to the conspiracy included Sir Everard Digby, Ambrose Rookwood, and Francis Tresham, all brought in between late September and 5 November. To minimize confusion, throughout this book I date the beginning of the year to 1 January rather than to 25 March.

5 Parker's title is sometimes given as Mounteagle. I have followed the *ODNB*'s preferred spelling of names and titles when two or more forms are in general usage.

6 Father Oswald Tesimond, listed in the indictment, evaded capture and returned to the Continent. Father John Gerard, sought for his alleged role in saying Mass for the

conspirators, also escaped to the Continent, where he recorded his own version of the incident (see chapter 2).

7 For accusations that Cecil had engineered Essex's fall, see Alastair Bellany and Andrew McRae, *Early Stuart Libels* (http://www.earlystuartlibels.net/htdocs/index.html), section D.

8 Joel Hurstfield, "Gunpowder Plot and the Politics of Dissent," 110. Examples of the kinds of historical detection that Hurstfield mocks begin with Henry Hawkes Spink's 1902 *Gunpowder Plot and Lord Mounteagle's Letter.* Spink claims to be an unbiased "historical philosopher" (196), but his Yorkshire background leads him to emphasize the plotters' connections with that county. His thesis that Christopher Wright revealed the plot, aided by Monteagle's servant Thomas Ward and the priest Edward Oldcorne, is, as he admits, based largely on circumstantial evidence and is discredited by Mark Nicholls (*Investigating Gunpowder Plot,* 235). Similarly, in 1931, George Blacker Morgan declared his interest in the plot was "purely secular and historical" (1.6). Identifying William Vavasour, a clerk sometimes employed by Francis Tresham, as the writer of the warning letter, Morgan hypothesizes that the plotters made no plans for governing because they assumed those grateful to them for ridding the country of Scotsmen would take over. The plotters wanted not only to restore Catholicism, but also to introduce social reforms including changes to wardships and death duties. He offers a "modern" perspective by accounting for Catesby's apparently irresistible attractiveness to the other plotters as a possible genetic predisposition to paranoia (1.125). Tresham and Monteagle contrived the letter scheme to raise money, "having previously stipulated that in divulging the Plot to Lord Salisbury, full opportunity of escape should be given to the conspirators" (1.229). Despite numerous inconsistencies in Morgan's narrative, his inclusion of illustrations and facsimiles of historical documents offers the illusion of historical validity. Various government conspiracy theories continue to be espoused, primarily by authors sympathetic to the Catholic cause: Hugh Ross Williamson and Francis Edwards insist that the Jacobean government fabricated the plot; Alan Haynes concludes there was a plot but that Cecil contrived the Monteagle letter in an attempt to frighten the plotters into relinquishing their plans; Antonia Fraser accepts that there was a plot but questions details such as whether there was a tunnel; both Fraser and Alice Hogge cite the sufferings of Catholics as mitigating circumstances in the plotters' actions.

9 Jenny Wormald, "Gunpowder, Treason, and Scots," 145. One explanation for historians' lack of interest is that once the conspirators had been tried and executed the plot left few material traces. Hans Robert Jauss suggests that "historical meaning" consists in "the conceptual difference between beginning and end" ("The Communicative Role of the Fictive" 41). Conversely, Hayden White proposes that the test of whether or not an event merits treatment by historians is whether we can imagine

"at least two different versions of the same set of events" (*The Content of the Form*, 20). The Gunpowder Plot passes this test, since it can be interpreted as either a government plot or a Catholic conspiracy, each account relying upon different evidence.

10 Alison Shell, *Catholicism, Controversy and the English Literary Imagination, 1558–1660*, 142. I would qualify Shell's observation by noting that Catholic interpretations, while seldom printed, are found in many non-print sources including rumours, libels, and manuscript accounts. See chapter 2.

11 David Jardine, *A Narrative of the Gunpowder Plot*, viii, 23. Jacobite risings in Scotland periodically renewed distaste for the Stuart dynasty and the Scots who wanted to revive it, increasing sympathy for the plotters after the mid-eighteenth century. A movement towards religious toleration during this period also saw publications such as the anonymous *Essay towards a new History of the Gun-Powder Treason* (1765) in which the author of the introduction called the pulpit "the most effectual Means *ever yet* devised" (vi) to sow divisions among people and argued that Cecil had participated in a plot to entrap Catholics. The restoration of a Catholic hierarchy in England in the mid-nineteenth century brought renewed confessional polarization, combined uneasily with residual dislike of the Stuarts, and James I in particular (see Sharpe, *Remember, Remember*, 148–66, for popular displays of animosity towards Catholics in this period).

12 Jardine, *A Narrative of the Gunpowder Plot*, 38.

13 Jardine, *A Narrative of the Gunpowder Plot*, 63.

14 Gardiner, *History of England from the Accession of James I to the Outbreak of the Civil War 1603–1642*, 1.269.

15 The "minute" comprised a description of events up to this date, including the first three examinations of Guy Fawkes, written by Levinus Munck and corrected by Salisbury (*CSPD 1603–1610*, 43).

16 Levine, "Intellectual History as History," 194.

17 Mark Nicholls, *Investigating Gunpowder Plot*, 3.

18 Mark Nicholls, "Discovering Gunpowder Plot," 397.

19 Levine notes that Mark Nicholls not only endorsed Gardiner's conclusions, but also duplicated his methodology when responding to the Jesuit Francis Edwards ("Intellectual History as History," 194–5). Recent historians have focused upon the results rather than the causes of the conspiracy. A.W.R.E. Okines challenges the assumption that the plot benefitted James's administration, a presupposition of government conspiracy theories, arguing that the plot jeopardized the new peace, and hence, trade, with Spain and that James therefore downplayed its religio-political aspects, insisting most Catholics were loyal and, more importantly, that it implicated no foreign powers ("Why was there so little government reaction to the gunpowder plot?"). The role of the Oath of Allegiance, introduced in 1606 with the stated purpose of distinguishing loyal Catholics from potential traitors, remains contentious;

see especially Michael Questier, "Loyalty, Religion and State Power in Early Modern England"; Johann Sommerville's rebuttal, "Papalist Political Thought and the Controversy over the Jacobean Oath of Allegiance"; and Questier's reply, "Catholic Loyalism in Early Stuart England." Recent fictional treatments include Martin Stephen's mystery novel *The Desperate Remedy: Henry Gresham and the Gunpowder Plot* and Christie Dickason's romance *The Firemaster's Mistress.* Probably the most interesting appearance in recent literature is Alan Moore and David Lloyd's *V for Vendetta*, a comic book series turned into a graphic novel, then a successful film. Moore and Lloyd's work, begun in the 1980s, imagines a dystopian Britain in which a man wearing a grinning Guy Fawkes mask wreaks revenge upon an authoritarian government that destroyed his life. The creators capitalize on the plotters' apparent failure to arrange for governing the state by representing the work's protagonist, the anarchist V, as a successful, but highly ambiguous, Fawkes.

20 Rebecca Lemon, *Treason by Words*; Paul Wake "Plotting as Subversion." Other important studies include David Cressy's social history of the plot and its memorialization (*Bonfires and Bells: National Memory and the Protestant Calendar in Elizabethan and Stuart England*).

21 Revard, "Milton's Gunpowder Poems and Satan's Conspiracy."

22 De Luna, *Jonson's Romish Plot.*

23 For example, Jonathan Goldberg's *James I and the Politics of Literature.*

24 See Jauss's original statement of his program in "Literary History as a Challenge to Literary Theory." Robert C. Holub provides a useful introduction and critique of these theories in *Reception Theory: A Critical Introduction*, although Robert Hume provides the most incisive critique of Jauss's seven theses in *Reconstructing Contexts*, 20–5.

25 Jauss, "Literary History as a Challenge to Literary Theory," 31.

26 Other introductions to reception studies include Peter Uwe Hohendahl, "Introduction to Reception Aesthetics," and Janusz Slawinski, "Reading and Reader in the Literary Historical Process."

27 Dutton, *Ben Jonson, "Volpone" and the Gunpowder Plot.*

28 Fowler, "The Formation of Genres in the Renaissance and After," 190.

29 Kevin Sharpe and Steven N. Zwicker, eds., "Politics of Discourse: Introduction," 11, 18.

30 Nigel Smith, *Literature and Revolution in England 1640–1660*, 4, 5.

31 Jason C. White, "Militant Protestants," 154–75. In his more popular cultural history of the plot, *Remember, Remember*, James Sharpe uses literary texts in much the same ways as Cressy does.

32 David Quint, *Epic and Empire*, 15.

33 See the collection of essays edited by Peter Lake and Steve Pincus, *The Politics of the Public Sphere*; Lake and Pincus, "Rethinking the Public Sphere in Early Modern England"; Lake and Michael Questier, "Puritans, Papists, and the 'Public Sphere': The Edmund Campion Affair in Context"; Lake with Questier, *The Antichrist's Lewd Hat.*

34 Rebecca Lemon, *Treason by Words*, 19.

35 See *Censorship and Interpretation*, 10–11.

36 Churchyard, *Come bring in Maye with me, my Maye is fresh and greene.*

37 K.J. Kesselring, "'A Cold Pye for the Papistes,'" 433.

38 *The Execution of Iustice in England for Maintenaunce of Publique and Christian Peace*; *Defence of the Honorable Sentence and Execution of the Queene of Scots.*

39 The intended readers of such documents probably included Catholics abroad as well as those at home.

40 On these difficulties, see "To the Reader" in Barlow's *Sermon Preached at Paules Crosse, on the first Sunday in Lent*, A2^{r}-A8^{v}; and, Arnold Hunt, "Tuning the Pulpits."

41 For example, Lemon does not discuss the role of sermons in developing and publicizing ideas about treason. Peter Hinds also virtually excludes sermons from his discussion of the pamphlet literature surrounding the later Popish Plot (*"The Horrid Popish Plot"*). Efforts by sermon scholars to have sermons recognized as a specific kind of discourse rather than misleadingly used as documentary sources have resulted in a body of excellent sermon scholarship that, sadly, is seldom integrated with studies of other genres in this period.

42 Peter Lake and Michael Questier, "Puritans, Papists, and the 'Public Sphere' in Early Modern England," 590, 625.

43 Peter Lake and Steve Pincus, "Rethinking the Public Sphere in Early Modern England," 289–90.

44 This time Barlow was already scheduled to preach at the Cross and his sermon relied heavily upon the king's 9 November speech to parliament: *The Sermon Preached at Paules Crosse, the tenth day of Nouember being the next Sunday after the discouerie of this late horrible treason.* See also: *His Maiesties speech in this last session of Parliament … Together with a discourse of the maner of the discouery of this late intended Treason*; *A True and Perfect Relation of the Whole Proceedings against the late most barbarous traitors, Garnet a Iesuite, and his confederats.*

45 Scott's work also built upon earlier work by Caroline M. Hibbard (*Charles I and the Popish Plot*) and by Robin Clifton ("The Popular Fear of Catholics during the Revolution").

46 Astrid Erll and Ann Rigney, "Literature and the Production of Cultural Memory," 112.

47 Paul Connerton, *How Societies Remember*, 26; Paul Ricoeur, *Memory, History, Forgetting*, 84–5. Hayden White, in contrast, believes narrative to be imposed by writers of history rather than intrinsic to our experiences. In his view, it is possible to write history without narrative, as the French Annales school demonstrated (*The Content of the Form*, ch. 2). In "The Historical Text as Literary Artifact," he argues that historians match their narratives to existing plot structures such as epic or tragedy. David Carr disagrees, asserting "that the events addressed by historiography are already narrative in character" (*Time, Narrative, and History*, 46).

48 Connerton, *How Societies Remember*, 75.

49 Ibid., 56, 57.

50 Cressy, "The Protestant Calendar and the Vocabulary of Celebration in Early Modern England," 31–52.

51 Both Ricoeur and Halbwachs stress that memory is individual: *Memory, History, Forgetting*, part I, ch. 3; *On Collective Memory*, ch. 3.

52 Ricoeur, *Memory, History, Forgetting*, 30.

53 Paul Wake argues that "In emphasising what might have happened, recast as 'what could not have happened' contemporary accounts of the Gunpowder Plot ... effect an appropriation of the subversive plotting of those who sought to destroy James and his government" (306). He connects the use of popular metaphors such as the destruction of Troy in the early plot literature to anxieties about imagining the death of the king, citing the king's speech and the official trial narrative. While some writers did refuse to imagine a successful plot, others were quite willing to speculate. See "Plotting as Subversion," esp. 302–6.

54 William Barlow, *The Sermon Preached at Paules Crosse, the tenth day of Nouember*, C3^{r-v}.

55 The germ of Barlow's description doubtless came from James's speech to Parliament on 9 November, in which he enumerated the individuals and institutions that would have been destroyed and described a death from fire as the cruellest one possible (*His Maiesties speech*, B3^{r}).

56 Howell, *Epistolae Ho-Elianae*, 13–14.

57 As Jason C. White puts it, many authors "let their imaginations run wild" (166); however, since White sees these texts simply as polemic, he does not discuss the function of such vivid descriptions in developing collective memories.

58 Jeremiah Lewis apparently recognized this problem in his sermon on 5 November 1618, reminding his auditors: "Thou art a member of a commonwealth, of a Towne, of a family, what deliuerance comes to that, comes thee" and that therefore all should praise God for their share in the deliverance (*The Doctrine of thankfvlnesse*, 5).

59 Yonge, *Diary of Walter Yonge, esq., justice of the peace, and M.P. for Honiton, written at Colyton and Axminster, co. Devon, from 1604–1628*, 2. Yonge's synopsis may be compared with John Chamberlain's letter to Dudley Carleton on 7 November 1605 (*The Letters of John Chamberlain*, 1.212–15), which, as Mark Nicholls observes, describes the mood of fear and uncertainty in the city as events unfolded ("Discovering Gunpowder Plot").

60 I use the terms "Catholic" and "Protestant" within this study recognizing their slipperiness in seventeenth-century England. Religious identities, as recent studies have suggested, were fluid and complex in this period. (See, for example, Michael C. Questier, *Conversion, Politics, and Religion in England, 1580–1625*.) In dealing with an incident such as the Gunpowder Plot it is all too easy to resort to the binaries fostered by the literature.

61 For an informative case study of these relationships, see Margaret Sena, "William Blundell and the Networks of Catholic Dissent in Post-Reformation England." Jessie Childs's research on the Vaux family is even more relevant here in tracing close relationships among several of the families whose members were implicated either directly or indirectly in the Gunpowder Plot (*God's Traitors*).

62 The most obvious example is John Day's *Isle of Gulls*, suppressed in all likelihood for its anti-Scots sentiments (see chapter 3). For the possibility that the plot itself was fuelled partly by hatred of the Scots, see Wormald, "Gunpowder, Treason, and Scots."

63 The phrase "sites of memory" (*lieux de mémoire*) was coined by Pierre Nora. See "Between Memory and History."

64 Marshall, *Beliefs and the Dead in Reformation England.* For the literary consequences of these shifts, see Stephen Greenblatt, *Hamlet in Purgatory*. On the replacement of Catholic festivals such as saints' days with political anniversaries, see Cressy, *Bonfires and Bells.*

65 Eric MacPhail, "The Plot of History from Antiquity to the Renaissance," 2–3.

66 Aristotle, "Poetics" 9, in *The Complete Works of Aristotle* (1451a37–1451b26, p. 2322); Philip Sidney, *An Apology for Poetry*, 29–39.

67 MacPhail, "The Plot of History from Antiquity to the Renaissance," 1, 9. For a further discussion about the development of definitions of plotting with specific reference to the Gunpowder Plot, see Paul Wake, "Plotting as Subversion."

68 Hayden White, "The Historical Text as Literary Artifact," 278.

69 Jauss, "The Communicative Role of the Fictive," 30–40.

70 Ricoeur argues for this understanding of testimony; *Memory, History, Forgetting*, 21.

71 The choice of incidents often reflected a decision about whether all Catholics were to be blamed or only Jesuits. Authors wishing to concentrate their venom on the Jesuits sometimes removed conspiracies by non-Jesuits from the narrative.

72 White, *The Content of the Form*, 5.

73 Mason's inclusion of the Gowrie plot is significant, since it suggests that James's strategy of linking the Scottish and English attempts on his life had acquired a measure of success. This strategy is discussed in chapter 2.

74 In 1632, the 1606 "Discourse of the maner of the discouery of this late intended treason" that had been published with James I's 9 November 1605 speech to Parliament was typeset into blackletter as part of an anonymous publication, *A Continvation of the histories of forreine martyrs*, that chronicled Protestant martyrdoms in Europe from the 1550s as well as the Armada and the Gunpowder Plot. When it was reprinted in 1641, prefatory materials asserted that this work was intended to encourage godly English Protestants who might be called to martyrdom in the current conflict.

75 John Speed in 1614 also situated the plot's origins in hell, calling it "A stratageme inuented by him that blowes the bellowes of destruction, fashioned in the forge of the bottomlesse pitte, put in practise in a vault of darknesse, and forwarded by him

that is the father of darknesse" (889). Revising Fawkes's recollection of encountering the solid wall "about Christmas" (*His Maiesties speech* H2[v]) to describe the plotters finishing their mine on Christmas Eve, he creates a powerful image of the birth of treachery attempting to overcome that of the Saviour. Like the poets, he shows little interest in human agency. He praises James, but clearly disapproves of his leniency towards Catholics, exemplified in his pardoning the Earl of Tyrone in Ireland. The glory of the discovery is God's rather than the king's, Speed attributing James's interpretation of the Monteagle letter to simple common sense – not having witnessed any signs of open insurrection, the king concluded it must refer to something less obvious such as gunpowder. Later authors cited this account as an unbiased source despite its providentialist themes. In contrast to the overtly religious orientation of chronicles like Mason's, Speed's account situated itself within a political and chorographic narrative that advertised itself as history while flattering James for restoring ancient British glory.

76 A number of publications are specifically directed to children or families: *A Song or Story, for the Lasting Remembrance of Diuers Famous Works, which God hath done in our time* offers a verse narrative of the Gunpowder Plot as well as a song of thanksgiving for the defeat of the Armada, following an introduction that concludes: "*Let this poore song thy little ones direct*" (A4[v]); Samuel Clarke later advertised in the full title of his *Englands Remembrancer* that his narratives of the Armada, the Gunpowder Plot, and the Blackfriars collapse had been "Collected for the information and benefit of each Family," t.p.

77 Anon. *Papa Patens, or The Pope in his Colours*, t.p. This development supports Jonathan Scott's contention that we need to understand seventeenth-century English anti-Catholicism in an international context (*England's Troubles*, 29–31).

78 Anon. *Papa Patens, or The Pope in his Colours*, 4.

79 This text seems to be unique in its subversion of chronology.

80 Anon. *Papa Patens, or The Pope in his Colours*, 5.

81 J.H. *A True and Perfect Relation of that Most Horrid & Hellish Conspiracy of the Gunpowder Treason*, t.p., 11, 7. According to Fawkes's published confession, the plotters were about halfway through the wall by Candlemas (*His maiesties speech*, H2[v]).

82 Suffolk noticed a pile of kindling while conducting an inspection the king had demanded at Westminster on 4 November 1605 after reading the Monteagle letter. James then ordered the more intensive search by Thomas Knyvett that exposed the barrels of gunpowder (Pauline Croft, "Howard, Thomas, first earl of Suffolk (1561–1626)").

83 See chapter 2.

84 *A true narration of that horrible conspiracy against King James and the whole Parliament of England.*

85 Thomas Barlow, *The Gunpowder-Treason with a discourse of the manner of its discovery ... a preface touching that horrid conspiracy, by the Right Reverend Father in God, Thomas, Lord Bishop of Lincoln*, 1, 57.

86 The Monteagle letter was routinely printed in such texts. An oath supposedly taken by the conspirators was also frequently included, but although Thomas Winter had confessed that an oath of secrecy had been taken, there is no documentary evidence for the actual text of the oath (*His maiesties speech*, I3[v]).

87 Jauss, "The Communicative Role of the Fictive," 46.

88 Guibbory, *The Map of Time*, 9. Some scholars have questioned the pairing of the Armada with the Gunpowder Plot when they were very different events. I think this concern stems from confusion about the nature of the relationship being posited. The Armada was an example of Spanish Catholic treachery, but the events were not viewed as parallels in the way that the Gunpowder Plot and the Popish Plot were. John Watkins, misleadingly I think, uses the word "parallels" in his discussion of the relationship between the Armada and Gunpowder Plot (*Representing Elizabeth in Stuart England*, 30).

89 John Williams, *A History of the Gunpowder-Treason, collected from Approved Authors as well Popish as Protestant*, t.p., 76 ff.

90 In his *History of His Own Time*, Burnet explained that he had been required to preach on this occasion, despite his request to be excused. He insists that in his choice of texts he had not considered that the lion and the unicorn were supporters of the king's escutcheon. Although the king, who had already interfered in Burnet's candidacy for a London parish, could find no crime in the sermon itself, the choice of text condemned the preacher, and after being deprived of his clerical responsibilities he felt he had no recourse other than to leave the country, 2.450–2.

91 Ricoeur, *Memory, History, Forgetting*, 497.

92 Astrid Erll and Ann Rigney, "Literature and the Production of Cultural Memory," 112.

93 There are far more casual references to the plot in other texts than could even be mentioned here and many more, no doubt, lie concealed in unidentified manuscript sources.

94 Coke, in his speech at the trial of the lay plotters, referred twice to the story of Samson's foxes, first claiming that priests and Jesuits "are all ioyned in the tailes like *Sampsons* Foxes" (I3[r]), and later adding the plots of Watson, Raleigh, and Clarke to his list of incidents that "all were ioyned in the endes, like *Sampsons* Foxes in the tayles, howsoeur seuered in their heads" (K[v]). The allusion is to Judges 15.4–5, in which Samson sets loose three hundred foxes, tied tail to tail with burning torches, to destroy the Philistines' standing crops. *A True and Perfect Relation of the Whole Proceedings against the late most barbarous traitors, Garnet a Iesuite, and his confederats.*

95 Frances E. Dolan, *Whores of Babylon*; Arthur F. Marotti, *Religious Ideology and Cultural Fantasy*, ch. 2. The popular histories of Antonia Fraser (*The Gunpowder Plot*) and Alice Hogge (*God's Secret Agents*) also draw attention to female roles in maintaining Catholic traditions and hiding priests.

96 Connerton, *How Societies Remember*, 65–6. For James's attempts to represent his reign as a continuation of Elizabeth's, especially after the plot, see John Watkins, *Representing Elizabeth in Stuart England*, 9–35.

97 This reflects Mary Morrissey's reminder that we need to study sermons not only as texts but as events ("Interdisciplinarity and the Study of Early Modern Sermons," 1112).

98 Peter Hinds's excellent analysis of the pamphlet literature related to the Popish Plot does make mention in passing of the way in which this crisis revived memories of the former one, but the subject merits further study (*"The Horrid Popish Plot,"* passim).

2. "like *Sampsons* Foxes": Creating a Jacobean Myth of Deliverance

1 On this point, I differ with Robert Zaller, who argues that the Long Parliament reinterpreted the Gunpowder Plot "not as a singular act of deliverance but as the beginning of a series of trials whose crisis had only just come and whose hero was not the king but Parliament" ("Breaking the Vessels," 765). Before the civil wars, the Gunpowder Plot was not seen as singular, but was contextualized within a series of earlier events, rather than later ones. At Henry Garnett's trial, Sir Edward Coke began his narrative with the growth of recusancy following the bull against Elizabeth, which precipitated the Jesuits' arrival, numerous attempts upon Elizabeth's life, and the Spanish Armada. In *A Thankfull remembrance of Gods mercy* (1625) George Carleton also begins his catalogue of English deliverances with the papal bull. On Elizabethan plots, see Daniela Busse, "Anti-Catholic Polemical Writing on the 'Rising in the North' (1569) and the Catholic Reaction"; James K. Lowers, *Mirrors for Rebels*; and K.J. Kesselring, "'A Cold Pye for the Papistes'"; Maureen King, "'Essex, that could vary himself into all shapes for a time,'" esp. chs. 2 and 3. On the Gowrie Conspiracy, see Gustavo Secchi Turner, "The Matter of Fact."

2 Much has been written about the representation of Elizabeth during the Jacobean period. Two studies that support my own conclusions are D.R. Woolf, "Two Elizabeths? James I and the Late Queen's Famous Memory"; and John Watkins, *Representing Elizabeth in Stuart England*, ch. 1. Woolf argues that James and his advisors deliberately invoked Elizabeth's memory when it was politically expedient. Watkins notes how Stuart panegyrists and preachers linked the Armada and the Gunpowder Plot as royal deliverances but does not suggest that James encouraged such identification or remark the king's insistence upon memorializing Gowrie.

3 The most thorough study of providentialism in England during this period is Alexandra Walsham's *Providence in Early Modern England.* Walsham discusses the providential interpretation of the plot on pages 245–66. Peter Lake and Michael Questier

support Walsham's work but question her depiction of a seamless transition from medieval piety to Protestant providentialism (*The Antichrist's Lewd Hat*, 320–5).

4 I do not claim originality in the use of this phrase ("myth of deliverance"), since others have used similar phrases; however, I may be using it more self-consciously than some writers.

5 *Oxford English Dictionary Online*, "myth," n. 1. I use the word here in its ordinary dictionary sense, rather than in the more specialized sense used by archetypal critics. Richard Hardin's attempt to see in the early Gunpowder poetry the creation of a particular type of myth in which Fawkes becomes the traditional scapegoat falters, I believe, because he attempts to force the story into too narrow a mould ("The Early Poetry of the Gunpowder Plot"). While Frank Kermode muddies Connerton's distinction between myth and ritual, he usefully distinguishes between myth and fiction, suggesting that myth "presupposes total and adequate explanations of things as they are and were," while "Fictions are for finding things out, and they change as the needs of sense-making change" (*The Sense of an Ending*, 39). James set out to create a myth, but the plot has perhaps functioned more as a fiction.

6 Blair Worden, "Providence and Politics in Cromwellian England," 63.

7 David Cressy, *Bonfires and Bells*, 152. My interpretation is supported, although indirectly, by Lori Anne Ferrell's thesis in *Government by Polemic* that many of the Gunpowder anniversary sermons include a strong anti-Puritan element, ch. 3. Her analysis suggests that dissent about the holiday existed even among Protestants. See below for Catholic efforts to widen the cracks in the Jacobean consensus, particularly in John Gerard's account of the plot.

8 John Strype, *The life and acts of the Most Reverend Father in God, John Whitgift, D.D. ...*, 652.

9 The earliest occasional thanksgiving for deliverance from a political conspiracy recorded is that celebrating the frustration of the Northern Rebellion, which was appended to the first part of the "Homily agaynst wilful disobedience" in 1569 but also appears to have been published as a broadside in 1570. Prayers of thanksgiving for deliverance from natural disasters and for the retreat of the plague predate these more political uses of liturgy. For a full list of the occasional prayers of the Elizabethan period, see William Keatinge Clay, *Liturgical Services of the Reign of Queen Elizabeth*, 458–74.

10 C.J. Kitching notes that the first services to provide lists of previous rebellions and to link them explicitly to Catholicism were those of 1594 and 1598 ("'Prayers fit for the time,'" 249).

11 Natalie Mears reminds us that special services of prayer, both petitionary and thanksgiving, had been used during the Catholic period, but notes that only in the Elizabethan period did events with "a clear confessional edge" begin to be marked ("Public Worship and Political Participation in Elizabethan England," 8). She finds

that this period was also distinguished by increasing standardization of the form of worship and growing use of print to ensure that services were distributed to parishes throughout the kingdom.

12 Clay points out that although the first accession day service was printed in 1576, not until 1578 did it bear the official "*Set forth by authoritie.*" Since the earlier edition was nevertheless printed by the Queen's Printer, he argues that this edition should be regarded as having official status (*Liturgical Services of the Reign of Queen Elizabeth*, 463–4). The 1594 service was reissued with revisions in 1598 (Church of England, *An Order for Prayer and Thankesgiuing (necessary to bee vsed in these dangerous times) for the safetie and preseruation of her Maiestie and this Realme*). The revised service added a paragraph documenting Squire's conspiracy in the "Admonition to the Reader." The original Psalms were retained, but minor changes were made to the prayers for the queen (see note 27 below). Kitching also notes the increasing frequency of these political liturgies in the 1580s and 1590s ("'Prayers fit for the time,'" 249).

13 Church of England, *An Order of Prayer and thankes-giuing (necessary to be vsed in these dangerous times) for the safetie and preseruation of her Maiesty and this realme. Set forth by authoritie*, A4[v].

14 Mears argues that earlier studies have overemphasized the propagandistic functions of these services. Instead she suggests they provided subjects with a form of political agency by encouraging them to recognize that they could influence events through their obedience or disobedience to the monarch's directives. Nevertheless, by equating God's will with the monarch's, the prayers simultaneously circumscribed this agency ("Public Worship and Political Participation in Elizabethan England," 16–24). For views of these liturgies as primarily coercive, see C.J. Kitching, "'Prayers fit for the time'"; and J.P.D. Cooper, "'O Lorde save the Kyng.'"

15 For the availability of the Book of Common Prayer, see Judith Maltby, *Prayer Book and People in Elizabethan and Early Stuart England*, esp. 24–30. Although focused on a later period, Maltby's work suggests the book was readily available to individuals as well as churches. Individuals who failed to attend services conducted according to the Prayer Book faced recusancy fines until 1689 except during the Interregnum. The expedient of occasional conformity makes it difficult to determine the extent of recusancy, but John Coffey claims it increased in James's reign due to laxer enforcement of the penal laws, citing statistics for the village of Egton (*Persecution and Toleration in Protestant England, 1558–1689*, 119). Wealthier families could avoid prosecution by having the husband attend church while the wife stayed home, raising the children in the Catholic faith. For the lack of trained preachers in the early Reformation, see Susan Wabuda, *Preaching in the English Reformation. The second parte of a register, being a calendar of manuscripts under that title intended for publication by the Puritans about 1593 and now in Dr. Williams Library, London,* 2:88, no. 42 documents a 1586 survey claiming that only approximately one-fifth of parishes had preaching clergy.

For the difficulties of interpreting this survey, see *Second parte of a register*, 88. Even accounting for puritan biases, the survey paints a dismal picture of the ministry in late Elizabethan England. Ian Green, however, estimates that by 1600 about half of clergy were licensed and that this percentage increased to about seventy-five per cent by 1640 ("Preaching in the Parishes," 139).

16 Ramie Targoff, "The Performance of Prayer," 5.

17 Connerton argues that the use of collective pronouns plays a major role in this process (*How Societies Remember*, 58–9). Targoff observes that while the 1549 prayer book used both "I" and "we," the 1552 text increased the use of the plural. She suggests that the "shift in pronouns that we find in the 1552 text reflects a more pervasive revision: prayers once read by the priest alone are now presented as congregational utterances" (*Common Prayer*, 29). Timothy Rosendale argues that Targoff and Richard Helgerson (*Forms of Nationhood*, ch. 6) overemphasize the coercive potential of liturgy, which by its nature promotes order and uniformity (*Liturgy and Literature in the Making of Protestant England*, 34–69). Arnoult also emphasizes the communal nature of the prayer book service, in which the minister was both leader of and participant with his congregation, observing that "lay participation was higher in the Prayer Book services than in either Catholic or other reformed services" ("'Spiritual and Sacred Publique Actions,'" 34).

18 Church of England, *An Order of praier and thankes-giuing, for the preseruation of the Queenes Maiesties life and salfetie* [sic]*: to be vsed of the preachers and ministers of the dioces of Winchester*, A^{v}.

19 For the official account, see *A True and Plaine Declaration of the Horrible Treasons, practised by William Parry the traitor, against the Queenes Maiestie.* There is also a shorter and much more virulently anti-Catholic account by Philip Stubbes, *The Intended Treason of Doctor Parrie: and his complices, against the Queenes most excellent Maiestie.*

20 Church of England, *An Order of praier and thankes-giuing ... to be vsed of the preachers and ministers of the dioces of Winchester*, A4^{v}. For the identification of the Pope with Antichrist, see Peter Lake, "The Significance of the Elizabethan Identification of the Pope as Antichrist"; Anthony Milton, *Catholic and Reformed*, ch. 2.

21 Church of England, *An Order of Prayer and Thankesgiuing for the preseruation of her Maiestie and the Realme, from the traiterous and bloodie practises of the Pope, and his adherents ...*, A4^{r}.

22 The Psalms provided are numbers 21, 140, 145, and 106, with permission given to add numbers 83, 103, and 124. Acceptable lessons include Exodus 15, Judges 5, and Esther 6–9.

23 Church of England, *An Order of Prayer and Thankesgiuing for the preseruation of her Maiestie and the Realme, from the traiterous and bloodie practises of the Pope, and his adherents ...*, A2^{v}.

24 Church of England, *An Order of Prayer and thankes-giuing (necessary to be vsed in these dangerous times) for the safetie and preseruation of her Maiesty and this realme. Set forth by authoritie*, A4^{r}. The 1594 plots included that of Lopez and his Portuguese conspirators and one by two Englishmen, Edmund York and Richard Williams, recruited by William Stanley and other exiles at Brussels. A Jesuit named Holt was accused of encouraging these men to commit treason and administering the sacrament to them. See William Cecil's *A True Report of Sundry horrible conspiracies*, published anonymously.

25 Church of England, *An Order of Prayer and thankes-giuing (necessary to be vsed in these dangerous times) for the safetie and preseruation of her Maiesty and this realme* ..., A4^{r}.

26 Ibid., C3$^{r–v}$.

27 Ibid., C3^{v}. Curiously, these particularly vengeful lines were removed from this prayer when the service was reissued in 1598, and two more alternate prayers for the queen, with the final one transferring these imprecations to the priests, were added: "But those priests of Baal, the hellish Chapleines of Antechrist, accursed runnagates from their God and Prince, the bellowes and fuell of these flagrant conspiracies, confound them in thy wrath, since thy Grace will not conuert them, and that which thy power cannot worke on them in defeating their enterprises, let thy fury performe in reuenge vpon their persons, the rather, O Lord, because that most blasphemously they abuse thy holy Word for the furtherance of their deuilish complots" (Church of England, *An Order for Prayer and Thankesgiuing (necessary to bee vsed in these dangerous times) for the safetie and preseruation of Her Maiestie and this realme. Set foorth by authoritie anno 1594. And reuewed with some alterations vpon the present occasion*, D4^{r}). In other words, the 1598 service seems to have increasingly vilified the priests rather than the actual conspirators.

28 There are numerous discussions of the importance of Romans 13 in Renaissance injunctions to secular obedience. See the sources cited by Glen Bowman in "Elizabethan Catholics and Romans 13," 531–2 (notes 3–5).

29 Church of England, *A fourme of prayer with thanksgiving to be used by all the Kings Maiesties louing subiects euery yeere, the fift of August*, D2^{v}. At least one anonymous writer exploited this parallel in the wake of the Gunpowder Plot. The author of the pamphlet *Lucta Iacobi* compares James's wrestling with Alexander Ruthven with Jacob's wrestling with God in Genesis. The parallel is rather strained at times, but evidently intended as a compliment to the king followed by a sting in the tail as the author warns James against excessive clemency to Catholics.

30 Church of England, *A fourme of prayer with thanksgiving to be used by all the Kings Maiesties louing subiects euery yeere, the fift of August*, G2^{v}.

31 Church of England, *Prayers and thankesgiuing to bee vsed by all the Kings Maiesties louing subiects: for the happy deliuerance of His Maiestie* ..., B3^{v}.

32 Ibid., D2^{v}.

33 For examples of public preaching on political themes in Tudor England, see Kirby, "The Public Sermon"; MacLure, *The Paul's Cross Sermons, 1534–1642*; Morrissey, *Politics and the Paul's Cross Sermons, 1558–1642.*

34 Ronald Bond, *Certain Sermons or Homilies (1547) and A Homily against Disobedience and Wilful Rebellion (1570)*, 40.

35 Busse, "Anti-Catholic Polemical Writing on the 'Rising in the North' (1569) and the Catholic Reaction," 14.

36 According to John N. Wall and Terry Bunce Burgin, use of the *Homilies* declined in the early seventeenth century and the book was not reprinted between 1595 and 1623, when James's *Directions to Preachers* seems to have created a new demand for it (""This Sermon … upon the Gun-powder day,"" 25).

37 According to David Cressy, the celebration of 17 November began about the time of Pius V's bull against Elizabeth, placing its inception in the same period as that of the "Homily." This concurs with Thomas Holland's dating of the first celebrations to approximately twelve years after the queen's accession. A sermon by John Jewel that J.E. Neale dates to 1567 refers to the queen's accession day at the end of the text (see Morrissey, *Politics and the Paul's Cross Sermons, 1558–1642*, 75n29). By the 1580s accession day sermons seem to have been a regular feature of the preaching calendar. See Cressy, *Bonfires and Bells* (ch. 4) and Roy Strong, *Cult of Elizabeth* (ch. 4). On sermons at Paul's Cross, see Morrissey, *Politics and the Paul's Cross Sermons, 1558–1642*, 134–41.

38 John Whitgift, *A Most Godly and Learned Sermon preached at Pauls Crosse the 17 of Nouember*, B7^{v}.

39 Thomas Holland, *Paneguris D. Elizabethae Dei Gratiâ Angliae, Franciae, & Hiberniae Regina*, K2^{r}.

40 John Whitgift, *A Most Godly and Learned Sermon preached at Pauls Crosse the 17 of Nouember*, B7^{r}.

41 Whitgift's designation of his opponents as "fantasticall spirits" identifies them with the godly. In a July 1573 letter to a subordinate bishop, his predecessor Matthew Parker had used the same phrase to characterize those who opposed ecclesiastical hierarchy (John Strype, *The Life and Acts of Matthew Parker*, 433). Publication provided another preacher, Thomas White, with a way to express possible qualms about political preaching. White preached an admonition on Luke 3.10–14 at Paul's Cross in 1589 without mentioning the occasion, followed by "An Exhortation vnto Thanksgiuing, for the happie Raigne of Queene Elizabeth" (*Sermon preached at Paules Cross the 17. of Nouember An. 1589*). To what extent the two texts were separate in the original delivery is impossible to determine.

42 Isaac Colfe, *A Sermon Preached on the Queenes Day. Beeing the 17. of Nouember. 1587*, C3^{v}.

43 Holland, *Paneguris D. Elizabethae Dei Gratiâ Angliae*, H^{r}, I2^{v}.

44 The most popular of these justifications throughout this period seems to have been the institution of Purim by the secular authorities in the Book of Esther. Isaac Colfe cited both Esther 9 and 1 Maccabees 13 as precedents for celebrating the queen's accession as a deliverance (*A Sermon Preached on the Queenes Day*, C4^{r}). Thomas Cooper published his pamphlet *The Churches deliuerance contayning meditations and short notes vpon the booke of Hester. In Remembrance of the wonderfull deliuerance from the Gunpoulder-treason* in 1609; Lancelot Andrewes preached on Esther 9.31 on 5 November 1618; and George Hakewill contributed another pamphlet, *A Comparison betweene the Dayes of Purim and that of the Powder Plot*, in 1626.

45 Whitgift, *A Most Godly and Learned Sermon*, B4^{v}.

46 Holland, *Paneguris D. Elizabethae Dei Gratiâ Angliae*, N4^{r}.

47 On this sermon, see Kathryn Murphy ("The Date of Edwin Sandy's Paul's Cross Sermon") and Mary Morrissey (*Politics and the Paul's Cross Sermons, 1558–1642*, 75–8).

48 The ballads describing the celebrations, recently discovered by Arthur Marotti and Steven W. May, are frustratingly silent about the sermon's content ("Two Lost Ballads of the Armada Thanksgiving Celebration").

49 Millar MacLure's register of Paul's Cross sermons indicates that Thomas Cooper's 17 November sermon in 1588 offered thanksgiving for the defeat of the Armada (215, citing Strype, *Annals*, III, [2], 27), but the sermon has not survived.

50 John Prime, *The Consolations of David, Briefly Applied to Queene Elizabeth*, B1^{v}, B2^{r}.

51 Arnold Hunt, "Tuning the Pulpits," 107.

52 This is not to say, of course, that such interpretations were not directed or circumscribed by authority, but the very structure of the early modern sermon with its emphasis upon application foregrounded an act of interpretation.

53 Gustavo Secchi Turner, "The Matter of Fact," 90.

54 Arnold Hunt records an interesting connection between the two situations. Robert Bruce, the most stubborn of the Scottish preachers, had discussions with a number of the English clergy in the spring of 1601 regarding their reluctance to conform to the wishes of the authorities. Anthony Wotton and Edward Philips were, like Bruce, unwilling to declare a man a traitor from the pulpit without proof of his guilt. See "Tuning the Pulpits," 98–9.

55 In a different context, Lake and Questier also warn against assuming unanimity among various branches of authority ("Agency, Approriation and Rhetoric under the Gallows," 64–8).

56 For the possibility that the authorities had even tried to bribe Ashton, see Hunt, "Tuning the Pulpits," 113n55.

57 Barlow, *A Sermon Preached at Paules Crosse, on the first Sunday in Lent ...*, A3^{r}.

58 Ibid., A8$^{r–v}$.

59 Morrissey argues that earlier scholars exaggerated government control of Paul's Cross during Elizabeth's reign. Since most preachers spoke from notes,

the authorities could not scrutinize the content of sermons before presentation. In the tense atmosphere following Essex's revolt, however, the authorities were reluctant to take chances. Cecil's instructions to Barlow survive in TNA SP 12/278/126 (calendared *CSPD* 1598–1601, 598–9). Those in Cecil's hand require the preacher to emphasize the discrepancy between Essex's claim that he wished to avoid violence and the likelihood that his plan could have been achieved bloodlessly. Those below in a scribal hand remind Barlow to rehearse Essex's "obstinate speeches to Mr. Dove," his insistence upon his popularity, and his desire to die privately. Lambeth Palace Library's copy of the sermon, apparently the one to be used by the printer (MS 2872, fols 51–8), is emended in three places by Whitgift. At the end of the manuscript (57^{r}–58^{r}) is a set of directions apparently written in response to an earlier draft, possibly by Whitgift (possibly those Cecil refers to in the first sentence of his note). They begin by cautioning that "It shalbee fitt to speake of this matter as by accident, and not purposely for otherwise ye sermon may bee thought to be wholly for this occasyon" (57^{r}). The preacher is to emphasize Essex's insolence to the queen, her generosity and moderation towards him, and his eventual penitence. Morrissey observes that these directions represent a tactical shift from the ones given to the preachers for the Sunday following the attempted rebellion, which enjoined them to represent Essex as a political and religious hypocrite who had long planned his actions (*Politics and the Paul's Cross Sermons, 1558–1642*, 88–91). Barlow may relate his experience of Essex's penitence "wherein nothing can bee better sett downe, then as you have alreadie done it under your owne handes" (58^{r}). The printed sermon reflects yet another post-delivery intervention by Thomas Montford, the other preacher who had attended Essex's execution and objected to some of Barlow's phrases ($E2^{r-v}$).

60 On the rhetorical structure of political sermons at Paul's Cross, see Morrissey, "Rhetoric, Religion, and Politics in the St. Paul's Cross Sermons 1603–1625," 14–26.

61 Curiously, Barlow omitted the second half of the verse from his text. John Mayer, in his 1622 commentary on Matthew, observes that Jesus added the second part of his response lest his disciples think they should give *themselves* to Caesar, while Richard Ward in a later commentary explains that our duties to Caesar and God are complementary, but our primary duty is to God since Caesar is an inferior magistrate. In the first of only two citations of the complete verse, Barlow paraphrases it conventionally as "giue vnto Caesar tribute, whose money it is, giue vnto God your selues, whose people you are," then adds in explanation: "But first Caesar, and then God, for they two haue interchangeably borrowed names: it pleaseth God to bee called a King in heauen, Psa. 20. and the King is called a God on earth, Psa. 82" ($B3^{r}$). Barlow's emphasis makes it clear that the subject serves God by serving the monarch.

62 William Barlow, *A Sermon Preached at Paules Crosse, on the first Sunday in Lent: Martij 1.1600. With a short discourse of the Late Earle of Essex his Confession, and Penitence, before and at the time of his death* (London, 1601), B3r.

63 Arnold Hunt, "Tuning the Pulpits," 86–114.The synopsis of Richardson's sermon appears in PRO, SP 12/276/107, The National Archives, London. See also Richardson's answers to his examiners: Examination on oath of John Richardson, D.D., MS 2004, fol. 9, Lambeth Palace Library, London.

64 Published under the name R. Doleman, *A Conference abovt the next svccession to the crowne of Ingland, divided into two partes*, s.l., 1594.

65 In this way, the sermon could act as a substitute for public access to the execution, enabling readers to view this event not with their own eyes but with the eyes of the state.

66 On the subject of gallows confessions, see Lake and Questier, *Antichrist's Lewd Hat*, ch. 7.

67 For an excellent analysis of this sermon, see Hunt, "Tuning the Pulpits," 100–3; Thomas S. Nowak's "Propaganda and the Pulpit" offers a reading I find unconvincing.

68 Barlow, *The Sermon Preached at Paules Crosse, the tenth day of Nouember ...*, A3[v].

69 Ibid., A3[v]–A4[r]. Lori Anne Ferrell notes "the preface's subtle acknowledgment of the fact that the eminent personages mentioned had exercised control over his sermon by providing him with a goodly portion of the actual prose – a script for speaking to the situation at hand" (*Government by Polemic*, 76).

70 Ferrell also observes Barlow's decision not to improve upon the sermon prior to publication, noting of its introduction that "Ostentatiously excusing its hasty construction, breathless delivery, and precipitate printing, it sets up the expectation of a thrillingly immediate and raggedly emotional performance" (*Government by Polemic*, 75). She argues that these excuses do not justify the disorganization and stylistic flaws of the printed edition. Mark Nicholls observes the same desire for immediacy in the style of the "King's Book" ("Discovering Gunpowder Plot," 404).

71 Fawkes's confession was the only one available at this early date. Mark Nicholls suggests that the "papers" alluded to might be an outline that had been presented to Parliament the previous day (*Investigating Gunpowder Plot*, 26).

72 Barlow, *The Sermon Preached at Paules Crosse, the tenth day of Nouember ...*, C2[v]. Possibly the most extreme example of this hyperbole comes in a 5 November sermon preached by John Rawlinson at St Mary's Oxford in 1610 in which, taking as his text Luke 22.48, the preacher claims that the Gunpowder Plot was a worse treason than Judas's betrayal of Christ. His inspiration may have been the day's gospel reading from Matthew 27 (*The Romish Judas*).

73 Barlow, *The Sermon Preached at Paules Crosse, the tenth day of Nouember*, C3[r]. James had described the apocalypse with a similar emphasis upon the cruelty of Satan and the

Antichrist in his *Fruitefull Meditation, Containing a plaine and easie Exposition, or laying open of the 7. 8. 9. and 10. verses of the 20. chap. of the Reuelation, in forme and maner of a sermon*, first published in Scotland in 1588 and reprinted in London in 1603.

74 Barlow, *The Sermon Preached at Paules Crosse, the tenth day of Nouember*, C3[v].The poem is: I.H. [John Rhodes], *The Divell of the Vault or The Unmasking of Murder* (London, 1606).

75 Barlow's reference in the same sentence to the Gowrie Conspiracy and the Main and Bye plots, which were discovered even before James's coronation, supports my contention below that attacks against James were being inserted into a sequence of Catholic attacks on England that emphasized continuity despite the change in reigns.

76 *His Maiesties Speech in this last session of Parliament … Together with a discourse of the maner of the discouery of this late intended Treason* (London, 1605), C2[v].

77 Barlow, *The Sermon Preached at Paules Crosse, the tenth day of Nouember*, D[r]. The social status of the plotters continued to trouble the authorities. Convinced that a nobleman must be involved in such a horrendous scheme, they imprisoned Henry Percy, Earl of Northumberland, in the tower until 1621. In the absence of solid evidence against the earl, however, the authorities increasingly focused upon the Jesuits as the more important conspirators.

78 *His Maiesties Speach*, B2[r].

79 Connerton, *How Societies Remember*, 27.

80 There was no annual memorial for the defeat of the Armada. The queen's accession day sermons indirectly celebrated Elizabeth's deliverances, but the dates of these events were not memorialized. The only sermon I have found to date that celebrates a specific deliverance was that preached by John Rainolds at Oxford on the discovery of the Babington Plot, discussed above (*A Sermon vpon part of the eighteenth Psalm*).

81 See above for an account of how quickly James initiated an English commemorative service for the Gowrie Conspiracy. Peter McCullough notes that the "Privy Council had rationalized the annual English observance of the Scottish deliverance in terms of England's partaking the fruits of it in the person of their new king" (*Sermons at Court*, 118), quoting a passage from Cardwell's *Documentary Annals* in which the Council declared that as a result of James's succession, "we are now made partakers of the same blessings, and of the benefit thereof preceeding equally with his subjects of the Scottish nation" (2.59). This theme appears in a number of the sermons discussed in chapter 6.

82 McCullough notes that James may have originally intended his deliverance to be celebrated publicly every Tuesday, but the Privy Council only approved an annual celebration. Nevertheless, McCullough demonstrates that court preachers on other Tuesdays alluded to the plot (*Sermons at Court*, 117). Edward Montagu proposed the annual memorial when Parliament convened in January 1606. It is usually assumed that Montagu was motivated by the anti-Catholicism and loyalty to James

that Richard Cust identifies as his most salient characteristics; however, Montagu may have had a more personal motive. He had been relieved of his duties on the commission for the peace earlier in 1605 when the king was incensed by his role in petitioning on behalf of deprived clergy and only reinstated with the assistance of his brother James, dean of the Chapel Royal (although McCullough observes that James may also have been suspected of supporting puritan clergy): Richard Cust, "Montagu, Edward, first Baron Montagu of Boughton (1562/3–1644)"; P.E. McCullough, "Montagu, James (1568–1618)." Montagu may thus have used his 5 November proposal as a way to reingratiate himself with the king.

83 Ferrell, *Government by Polemic*, 88. As Godfrey Davies pointed out long ago, only a small percentage of the sermons preached survive, and those that were printed are probably not a representative sample ("English Political Sermons, 1603–1640"). In addition, we seldom know the relationship between preached and printed sermon, since preachers usually wrote out their sermons in full only in the event of publication (John Sparrow, "John Donne and Contemporary Preachers"). Since the king was frequently hunting at this time of year, he heard sermons in various venues. Surviving examples include seven recorded as preached to the king by Lancelot Andrewes (1606, 1607, 1608, 1610, 1614, 1615, 1616, and 1622) and one prepared for but not preached to the king (1623), and an undated one by John Hacket. (For problems with determining which of Andrewes's sermons were actually preached before the king, see McCullough: *Sermons at Court*, 152–3; "Making Dead Men Speak.") Other printed sermons include four preached at Paul's Cross, *Jacob's Great Day of Trouble* (John Milward, 1607), *The Kings Towre* (Samuel Purchas, 1622), *The Temple* (Thomas Adams, 1624), *A Sermon Preached at Pauls Cross* (Barten Holyday, 1625); three at St Mary's Oxford, one by John Randal (1624) and two undated sermons by Isaac Singleton (*The Downfall of Shebna*); two preached at Croyden by Daniel Featley ("Traitor's Guerdon," 1618, and "The Lord Protector of Princes," 1620, in *Clavis Mystica*); and three preached elsewhere, *The Barren Trees Doome* (Bartholomew Parsons, undated), *The Lot or Portion of the Righteous* (Richard Web, 1615), and *Gowries Conspiracy* (John Prideaux, undated). A sermon preached by James Cleland at Canterbury Cathedral in 1616 survives in manuscript (BL Royal MS 17B.XIX, 2r–14v). We also have a record of a Paul's Cross sermon on 5 August 1605 by Richard Vaughan, Bishop of London; however, the sermon appears not to have survived. The account printed by G.B. Harrison indicates that Vaughan defended the king's commitment to Protestantism (*A Jacobean Journal*, 218–19). As in the case of the Gunpowder sermons, additional sermons likely exist in manuscript and in printed collections.

84 Commentators on Andrewes's sermons invariably conflate the two sets of sermons. See McCullough, *Sermons at Court*, 116–25; Debora Shuger, *Habits of Thought in the English Renaissance*, 141–50; Nicholas Lossky, *Lancelot Andrewes the Preacher (1555–1626)*, 292–325; Maurice F. Reidy, *Bishop Lancelot Andrewes, Jacobean Court Preacher*, ch. 8; Paul

A. Welsby, *Lancelot Andrewes, 1555–1626*, ch. 5. Although references to Gowrie are less common in Gunpowder sermons, they appear with some regularity.

85 Morrissey "Presenting James VI and I to the Public," 118–19.

86 Daniel Featley seems to be an exception. Preaching before a select audience, including Bishop John King, in 1618, he seems to have enjoyed recounting the details of the plot in both of his surviving sermons. Morrissey notes that while no Paul's Cross Gunpowder sermons were printed after 1615, Gowrie sermons for 1622, 1623, and 1624 were rushed into print, suggesting "that the Gowrie Conspiracy had become a more attractive, because less politically sensitive, subject on which to preach" (*Politics and the Paul's Cross Sermons*, 153) as James's interest in closer relations with Catholic Spain made anti-Catholic preaching less acceptable.

87 Samuel Purchas, *The Kings towre and triumphant arch of London*, 63. The source for Purchas's assertion that James virtually converted Gowrie (presumably to Protestantism) is unknown to me and does not appear in the official account or in any of the other sermons I have read. Gowrie is generally represented as a crypto-Catholic rather than an atheist.

88 Purchas, *The Kings towre and triumphant arch of London*, 74.

89 Connerton's observation that revolutions almost invariably involve changes to the calendar is relevant here. While one could not call the transition from the Tudors to the Stuarts a revolution, James's insistence on adding annual events to the calendar at the beginning of his reign suggests an attempt to emphasize change along with continuity (*How Societies Remember*, 6).

90 John Prideaux, "Gowries Conspiracie," in *Eight Sermons*, 12–13.

91 Isaac Singleton, *The downfall of Shebna.*

92 John Milward, *Iacob's Great Day of Trouble and Deliuerance*, G2[r], K3[v]. This is a frequent theme in post-plot literature, which I will discuss in the context of Anglo-Latin epic in chapter 4. It recurs also in Gunpowder sermons, most notably John King's sermon at court on 5 November 1608 (*A Sermon Preached at Whitehall the 5. Day of November. Ann. 1608*). For commentary on this sermon, see Ferrell, *Government by Polemic*, 97–104.

93 Randal claims that the death of James in the Gowrie Conspiracy would have spelled the "ruine of *Ireland*, the confusion of *Scotland*, the diuision of *England*, the suppression of all Protestant Religion in *Germany*" (*A Sermon Preacht at St Maries in Oxford, the 5. Of August: 1624. Concerning the kingdomes peace*, 28).

94 This is not to assert that James exercised direct control over these sermons. Clearly, at times such as the sermons against the Spanish and French matches, preachers acted in defiance of royal policies. I am suggesting instead that these preachers had accepted the Gowrie plot as part of English history.

95 This is the opinion of Reidy, who argues that in his later works Andrewes "taught a fairly consistent theory of divine-right monarchy. Kingship was established by God;

kings rule therefore by divine right; their persons are sacred; they may not be resisted; to them by that same divine right subjects owe allegiance and obedience; over kings God exercises a special protection" (*Bishop Lancelot Andrewes*, 188). Welsby, like Reidy, argues that in his earlier works Andrewes saw monarchy as a postlapsarian necessity rather than the perfect will of God but notes that "by the time he became a bishop he had accepted wholeheartedly the full doctrine of divine right" and that this attitude is expressed in his Gowrie and Gunpowder sermons (*Lancelot Andrewes 1555–1626*, 203); see also McCullough's notes on Andrewes's 1610 Gowrie sermon, his fullest treatment of the king's anointing, in *Lancelot Andrewes: Selected Sermons and Lectures*, 414–33). McCullough focuses on the court context of the sermons, particularly Andrewes's rejection of sermon-centred piety and complaints that the occasions were celebrated with revelry rather than prayer. He also notes that the Gunpowder sermons particularly served as an index of anti-Catholic sentiment at court (*Sermons at Court*, 116–25).

96 Lossky, *Lancelot Andrewes the Preacher (1555–1626)*, 292.

97 Ibid., 325.

98 Shuger, *Habits of Thought in the English Renaissance*, 142, 146. For a more general discussion of absolutist theory in relation to preaching in this period, see Shuger's essay, "Donne's Absolutism."

99 Sacral kingship is the predominent theme of Barlow's sermon defending Essex's execution and recurs, although more briefly, in his 1605 Gunpowder sermon.

100 For comparative purposes, Essex was arrested on the evening of 8 February, tried on 19 February, and executed on 25 February 1606. Guy Fawkes was arrested during the night of 4/5 November 1605, and the lay plotters were tried on 27 January and executed on 30 and 31 January 1606; Father Garnett was captured on 23 January, tried on 28 March, and executed on 3 May 1606. At Garnett's trial, Coke justified the delay on the basis of the king's clemency in insisting upon a fair trial and the court's care in compiling its case (*The True and Perfect Relation*, O4^{r-v}).

101 Mark Nicholls, "Discovering Gunpowder Plot," 400.

102 Dana F. Sutton proposes the Parry pamphlet as the model for the official Gunpowder narrative ("Milton's *In Quintum Novembris, anno aetatis 17* (1626)," 357).

103 *A True and Plaine Declaration of the Horrible Treasons, practised by William Parry the traitor, against the Queenes Maiestie*, 21. The counterpart to this text is the shorter and much more sensational *Intended Treason of Doctor Parrie* by Philip Stubbes. As might be expected, Stubbes's pamphlet is virulently anti-Catholic and uses the example of Parry to argue that all papists are traitors at heart.

104 *A True Report of Sundry horrible conspiracies of late time detected to haue (by barbarous murders) taken away the life of the Queenes most excellent Maiestie*, 6. Burghley and his son Robert specialized in these pamphlets. Burghley helped the Queen draft a defence of her reign after the Northern Rebellion and subsequently wrote *The Execution of*

Iustice in England for Maintenaunce of Publique and Christian Peace defending Edmund Campion's death. Contemporaries acknowledged his son as the author of the anonymous *Defence of the Honorable Sentence and Execution of the Queene of Scots.*

105 The three were Lopez, Stephano de Ferrera de Gama, and Manuel Lews Tinoco.

106 Arbuckle notes that the king was the only surviving witness to his dialogue with Ruthven at the hunt and to the events in the locked room at Gowrie House, both vital to the event's interpretation ("The 'Gowrie Conspiracy,'" 10–11).

107 David Calderwood, clearly unconvinced by the king's narrative, provides a concise account of James's difficulties with the ministers. When, on 6 August, the king's council instructed them to praise God for James's deliverance from a treasonous plot, the preachers agreed only to say that the king had been rescued from a great danger. David Lindsay, who had heard the story directly from James, went with the Council to the Market Cross in Edinburgh where he related the story and the people praised God, celebrating with bonfires, bell ringing, and the discharging of cannons. Upon James's return from Falklands, he went to the Kirk, where Lindsay exhorted him to exercise justice in the matter, and then to the Market Cross, where his chaplain, Patrick Galloway, preached a sermon "to perswade the people, that *Gourie* and his Brother had verily conspired the Kings death, and were slaine in their execution of the enterprise" (444). Since Galloway was known as a "flattering preacher," however, his sermon was not given great credence. The other ministers were charged to appear before the king on 12 August, and when they refused to give in, James deprived them of their preaching responsibilities. Eventually all but Robert Bruce conceded. Calderwood reports that when Bruce went into exile a great light shone on his boat, enabling him to read although it was almost midnight. See *The True History of the Church of Scotland from the beginning of the Reformation unto the end of the Reign of King James VI*, 443–6.

108 It seems likely that James intended some kind of printed account from the beginning. Arbuckle reports that the king wrote an account for his Privy Council on the night of 5 August, noting that "The letter, which reached the Secretary in Edinburgh by nine the next morning, has unfortunately not survived, but its contents were communicated orally by the Secretary to Nicolson, the English envoy, who wrote the same day to Cecil reporting the story" (11). The letter to Cecil, according to Arbuckle, "contained all the essential elements of the version from which James never afterwards departed" (12). Galloway's 11 August sermon introduced details that he claimed he had received directly from the mysterious Andrew Henderson.

109 Turner finds it significant "that more cautious printers had stayed clear of *Gowries Conspiracy*, a curious little book about treason, hidden treasures and sorcery, sponsored by a superstitious king with dangerous pretensions to the Elizabeth's [*sic*] crown" (140).

110 Gustavo Secchi Turner, "The Matter of Fact," 102, 103.

111 *The Earle of Gowries conspiracie against the Kings Maiestie at Saint Ionstoun vpon Tuesday the fift day of August*, B^{r-v}.

112 Ibid., B2^{r}.

113 It is this lack of motive that Arbuckle finds the most serious bar to accepting the printed narrative, since most of the other discrepancies can be accounted for. He concludes that the story was not a complete fabrication, suggesting either that there was a conspiracy to seize, if not to kill, the king, or that Gowrie and Ruthven were killed accidentally in some sort of skirmish and the story was fictionalized to account for their deaths without discrediting James ("Gowrie Conspiracy," 106–10). More recently, Maurice Lee Jr, has argued that the only logical explanation is that Gowrie, with support from the English government, lured the king to Gowrie House with the promise of a message regarding the English succession in hopes of preventing him from interfering in English politics at a critical time by kidnapping him (*The "Inevitable" Union and Other Essays on Early Modern Scotland*, 109–10).

114 Turner also suggests that James saw the narrative as significant in his quest for the English throne ("The Matter of Fact," 136).

115 *The Earle of Gowries conspiracie against the Kings Maiestie at Saint Ionstoun vpon Tuesday the fift day of August*, C3^{r-v}.

116 Gustavo Secchi Turner, "The Matter of Fact," 117.

117 In his 1624 Gowrie sermon at St Mary's Oxford John Randal observes that Gowrie was raised in Italy "where the most King-killing doctrine is taught to be the true meaning of the Gospell" (29). Mentioning Padua is particularly suggestive, since the Jesuits had a college there.

118 Gustavo Secchi Turner, "The Matter of Fact," 154.

119 For a full account of the transmission of the news from Scotland to England, see Arbuckle, "The 'Gowrie Conspiracy,'" 11–18.

120 Arbuckle, "The 'Gowrie Conspiracy,'" 89.

121 Again, this does not seem to have been uncommon. Cecil's pamphlet on the Lopez conspiracy also exists in a French translation (STC 7580).

122 This discussion has focused on representations of the event rather than facts. The most useful reconstruction of the Gowrie incident itself is Arbuckle's "The 'Gowrie Conspiracy.'" See also Turner, "The Matter of Fact," for an extensive discussion of representations of this event.

123 The degree of care taken in the preparation of these accounts is particularly clear in this instance. Bacon's narrative required approval by both the Privy Council and the Queen, with revisions taking place at both stages.

124 Bacon, *A Declaration of the practises & treasons attempted and committed by Robert late Earle of Essex and his complices*, A3^{v}. As Turner suggests, in the case of the Gowrie Conspiracy the pamphlet took the place of the king's deposition at a public trial ("Matter of Fact," 153).

125 The emphasis upon Essex's disobedience in Ireland in this pamphlet contrasts with the instructions given to Barlow earlier by the ecclesiastical establishment, in which he was told: "Howe he [Essex] carried himself in ye county of Ireland no man need dilate for that hath been soo notorious" (LPL, MS 2872, f. 57r; the instructions are unsigned and may be from Whitgift). This difference may lend support to Arnold Hunt's observation that religious and civil authorities were sometimes operating at cross purposes during this crisis ("Tuning the Pulpits," 78–9).

126 Bacon, *A Declaration of the practises & treasons attempted and committed by Robert late Earle of Essex and his complices*, A4v.

127 In his second examination, Rinde stated that Gowrie had expressed the opinion that anyone making great plans should keep them confidential, conveniently accounting for the inability to obtain a confession of complicity from the tutor even under torture.

128 Bacon, *A Declaration of the practises & treasons attempted and committed by Robert late Earle of Essex and his complices*, Dr.

129 Ibid., E3r–v. The comparison of unsuccessful treason to the birth of a stillborn child continues in the Gunpowder literature. In 1616 Lancelot Andrewes preached at court on 5 November on Isaiah 37.3: "The children are come to the birth, and there is not strength to bring forth."

130 Bacon, *A Declaration of the practises & treasons attempted and committed by Robert late Earle of Essex and his complices*, F3v.

131 Although the actual events of the Essex incident are clearer than those of the Gowrie Conspiracy, Essex's intentions are not. Paul E. Hammer concludes that Essex wanted a peaceful discussion with the Queen but was forced into open rebellion by his enemies. See "Shakespeare's *Richard II*, the Play of 7 February 1601, and the Essex Rising," 1–35.

132 Bacon, *A Declaration of the practises and treasons*, I3r.

133 Bacon, *A Declaration of the practices and treasons*, I3r.

134 On Essex's associations with both Catholicism and radical Protestantism, see Paul E. J. Hammer, *The Polarisation of Elizabethan Politics*, passim.

135 John Chamberlain, *The Letters of John Chamberlain*, 1.213. Despite Mark Nicholls's depiction of terror and panic in London, Chamberlain's letter seems curiously calm. His first concern is how the plot will affect Carleton's career given his association with the Percy family, and his tone is that of one imparting sensational news but with no serious concerns for the nation's safety. Having quickly exhausted what he has heard about the plot, Chamberlain concludes the letter with his usual catalogue of births, marriages, deaths, and miscellaneous court gossip. The rumour of Fawkes's clerical profession was also incorporated into Francis Herring's Latin epic, *Pietas Pontificia* (Estelle Haan, "Milton's *In Quintum Novembris* and the Anglo-Latin Gunpowder Epic," 259).

136 Robert Cecil, *An Answere to Certaine Scandalous Papers, scattered abroad vnder colour of a Catholicke Admonition* (London, 1606), A3^{v}–A4^{r}. Although this evidence seems fairly conclusive, it is possible that Salisbury was referring to the speech rather than the "Discourse."

137 Nevertheless, Nicholls suggests that the author of the "Discourse" used Bacon's Essex pamphlet as a model. Dana Sutton proposes the pamphlet on Dr Parry's treason as a model. Sutton is correct that Parry's was the first pamphlet in the genre that Bacon developed. I would suggest, however, that the genre evolved not only through these two pamphlets, but also through James's own narrative of the Gowrie Conspiracy in Scotland. Mark Nicholls, "Discovering Gunpowder Plot," 401–2; Dana Sutton, "Milton's *In Quintum Novembris, anno aetatis 17* (1626): Choices and Intentions," 357; Thomas Bayly Howell, *Cobbett's Complete Collection of State Trials and Proceedings for High Treason and Other Crimes and Misdemeanors from the earliest period to the present time*, v. 2, 195; David Jardine, *Criminal Trials supplying Copious Illustrations of the Important Periods in English History during the Reigns of Queene Elizabeth and James I*, v. 2, 4–5; *A True and Plaine Declaration of the Horrible Treasons, practised by William Parry the traitor, against the Queenes Maiestie*; [James I], *The Earle of Gowries conspiracie against the Kings Maiestie at Saint Ionstoun vpon Tuesday the fift day of August.*

138 *His Maiesties speech in this last session of Parliament*, E4$^{r–v}$.

139 Mark Nicholls notes that David Jardine (*Criminal Trials*, 1847) proposed Bacon as the author. He considers this possible but argues for caution in attributing authorship ("Discovering Gunpowder Plot," 404). John Gerard suspected the king of being the author, and Thomas Bayly Howell, in his *Complete Collection of State Trials* (1809–28), also identifies the "Discourse," which he reprints from James Montagu's collection of James's writings, as the king's (2.195).

140 Mark Nicholls, "Discovering Gunpowder Plot," 404.

141 *His Maiesties speech in this last session of Parliament … Together with a discourse of the maner of the discouery of this late intended Treason*, M3^{r}.

142 Chamberlain, *The Letters of John Chamberlain*, 1.213.

143 Conrad Russell, *The Crisis of Parliament: English History 1509–1660*, 270.

144 *His Maiesties speech in this last session of Parliament …*, D^{v}.

145 James I, *The True Law of Free Monarchies and Basilikon Doron: A Modernized Edition*, 57.

146 *His Maiesties speech in this last session of Parliament …*, C4^{r}.

147 Ibid., M4^{r}.

148 *The Earle of Gowries conspiracie against the Kings Maiestie at Saint Ionstoun vpon Tuesday the fift day of August*, E4^{v}.

149 The social status of the plotters continued to trouble the authorities. Convinced that a nobleman must be involved in such a horrendous scheme, they imprisoned Henry Percy, Earl of Northumberland, in the tower until 1621. Those who made Cecil responsible for the plot often saw Northumberland's incarceration as the plot's sole purpose.

150 *The Earle of Gowries conspiracie against the Kings Maiestie at Saint Ionstoun vpon Tuesday the fift day of August*, E4[r].
151 Ibid., L[r].
152 *His Maiesties speech in this last session of Parliament* . . ., L2[r].
153 *Geneva Bible: A Facsimile of the 1560 Edition.*
154 *His Maiesties speech in this last session of Parliament* . . ., M3[r–v].
155 Ibid., M3[v].
156 Ibid., M4[r].
157 Connerton, *How Societies Remember*, 27.
158 Mark Nicholls, "Discovering Gunpowder Plot," 413.
159 The scale of this publication and the reporting of every detail and speech of the trial is unprecedented in popular print. Joad Raymond points out that pamphlets were generally under ninety-six pages in length, while "Books of more than a hundred pages aspired to a more elevated status" (*Pamphlets and Pamphleteering*, 82). Of this 416-page text, barely one-fifth is accorded to the lay plotters (B–N3), with the remainder (O–Fff3) devoted to Garnett's trial and execution. Although the pamphlet was published anonymously, Northampton compiled the manuscript for the king. He in turn, according to Linda Levy Peck, relied upon Robert Cotton to edit the manuscript. Peck, however, argues that Cotton, in addition to helping with the historical details, "may have influenced the central argument ... that the church had to justify its authority by its history" (112). See *Northampton: Patronage and Policy at the Court of James I*, 111–13.
160 *A True and Perfect Relation of the Whole Proceedings against the late most barbarous traitors, Garnet a Iesuite, and his confederats*, A2[v].
161 Ibid., E4[v], F[r].
162 Dennis Flynn quotes a letter from Dudley Carleton to John Chamberlain dated 13 November 1605 (TNA, SP 14/16/69) that suggests even Protestants closer to the centres of power had doubts about the official version of the plot ("Donne's Travels and Earliest Publications," 516).
163 Alastair Fowler observes that since the 1980s we have come to see genres less as fixed categories used by writers and more as the means of creating shared understandings between authors and audiences, and suggests that we should view them as "fields of association" ("The Formation of Genres in the Renaissance and After," 190).
164 As Lake and Questier have pointed out, we should also be wary of assuming unanimity among the authorities, particularly secular and ecclesiastic ("Agency, Appropriation and Rhetoric under the Gallows," 76). In the case of the Gunpowder Plot, criticism of Robert Cecil doubtless came from enemies at court as well as from Catholics.
165 Some of the Catholic polemical texts illegally printed in England shortly after the plot include *A Iust and Moderate Answer, to a most Iniurious, and Slaunderous pamphlet,*

[Richard Broughton] in 1606, and *The First Part of Protestant proofes, for Catholikes Religion and Recusancy*, by the same author in 1607.

166 A similar issue arises in Dr Parry's 1593 trial, in which Parry is considered to have been corrupted by reading William Allen's treatise on the succession.

167 Coke mentions Tresham's book, *De Officio Principis Christiani* (F4[r–v]), and expounds at more length on Garnett's *Treatise of Equivocation* (I[r]–I2[v]) although he seemed unaware of the book's authorship. At Garnett's trial, Coke produces more examples – the book *Philopater* associated with Cullen's treason and Persons's book on the succession with that of Williams and York.

168 Discourses that focus on power have tended to minimize the importance of such dissenting narratives, but scholars are now attempting to reclaim these texts to gain a fuller perspective on beliefs in this period. In particular, we need to recognize that the government's actions were frequently as much defensive as offensive.

169 John Morris provides the history of this manuscript in his "Life of Father John Gerard," in *The Condition of Catholics under James I. Father Gerard's Narrative of the Gunpowder Plot*, ccl–cclii. While Gerard speaks of himself in the third person throughout the text, his indignation at the accusations against himself strongly indicates that he is the author. Morris suggests that the narrative was written in late 1606, although it is possible that it was begun before Gerard escaped to the Continent in May of that year, since early parts of the text suggest that he is still in England, while he refers later to pamphlets published in the spring of 1606. A number of studies have provided valuable information regarding the importance and extent of manuscript transmission among Catholic recusants. See, for example, Arthur F. Marotti, *Religious Ideology and Cultural Fantasy*, especially ch. 3 on martyrdom accounts; Margaret Sena, "William Blundell and the Networks of Catholic Dissent in Post-Reformation England."

170 There is a second, incomplete, Catholic account apparently written by Father Tesimond. It agrees with Gerard's interpretation for the most part but comes closer to approving the plot itself (*The Gunpowder Plot: The Narrative of Oswald Tesimond alias Greenway*).

171 John Gerard, *The Condition of Catholics under James I* ..., 13.

172 Ibid., 149. In fact, a proclamation for the apprehension of the priests (Gerard, Garnett, and Tesimond) does not appear to have been issued until 15 January 1606 (STC 8387). On 5 November a proclamation went out for the capture of Thomas Percy (STC 8379.5) and on 7 November one listing seven other suspected conspirators as well as Percy (Robert Catesby, Ambrose Rookwood, Thomas Winter, Edward Grant, John Wright, Christopher Wright, and Robert Ashfield) (STC 8382). On 8 November a reward was offered for Percy (STC 8383) and on 18 November a proclamation was issued for Robert Winter and Stephen Littleton (STC 8384). On 19 November a warrant was issued permitting sheriffs in other counties to apprehend the plotters

(STC 8386). Texts of these proclamations are reproduced in *Stuart Royal Proclamations* 1.123–33.

173 John Gerard, *The Condition of Catholics under James I* ..., 119.

174 The books Gerard refers to are Thomas Morton's *Exact discouerie of Romish doctrine in the case of conspiracie and rebellion* (STC 18184), (registered 5 December 1605), and Thomas Hamond's *The late commotion of certaine papists in Herefordshire* (STC 25232), which equated recusancy with civil disorder.

175 John Gerard, *The Condition of Catholics under James I* ..., 123.

176 There is little agreement on whether penalties really were becoming harsher. Although James had offered temporary relief upon his accession, he had reinstated the fines before the Gunpowder Plot, likely because they were a steady source of revenue. On the disagreements about the nature and effects of the 1606 Oath of Allegiance, see the references cited in ch.1, note 19, above.

177 Gerard's choice of this beginning is significant given contemporary debates over the age of the English church. Catholics represented English Protestantism as a new religion, while English theologians insisted that their church was the original Catholic Church purged of accreted errors and that the post-Tridentine Roman church was in fact an innovation. Whereas Protestant chronologies (including Northampton's) begin with the introduction of Protestantism in England, Gerard claims a much lengthier history that neatly ignores the hegemony of the Catholic Church during the Middle Ages.

178 John Gerard, *The Condition of Catholics under James I* ..., 315.

179 Ibid., 316. The question of whether Catholics were executed for their religious beliefs or for their political actions was hotly contested. Lake and Questier suggest that early in the Jesuit mission Campion and Persons deliberately chose to foreground the boundary between religion and politics by choosing recusancy as a "wedge" issue ("Puritans, Papists, and the 'Public Sphere' in Early Modern England").

180 James did increase recusancy fines in 1604, but historians have noticed that enforcement remained lax, so that the amount collected did not actually increase (Okines, "Why was there so little government reaction to Gunpowder Plot?" 283–5). Everard Digby expressed the persistent Catholic fear that fines would be extended to women as justification for his participation in the Gunpowder Plot. Ironically, the plot justified additional efforts to discourage female recusancy. Under 3 and 4 Jac. I cap. 4, married women could be imprisoned for refusing the Oath of Allegiance, while 7 and 8 Jac. I cap. 6 made husbands liable for their wives' recusancy. For a history of recusancy fines, see John Miller, *Popery and Politics in England 1660–1688*, 52–58.

181 The 1604 canons required ministers to affirm the king's supremacy in the English church and to repudiate all foreign authority at least four times per year. They did not specifically mention the pope, but Gerard is correct about the intent of the law (Church of England, *Constitutio[ns] and canons ecclesiasticall treated vpon by the Bishop of*

London, president of the conuocation for the prouince of Canterbury, and the rest of the bishops and clergie of the said prouince, D[v]).

182 Once again Gerard has taken up what James represents as a benefit, a stable succession, and repositioned it as a threat to his own community.

183 John Gerard, *The Condition of Catholics under James I* ..., 100.

184 Ibid., 101, 101–2.

185 Ibid., 194.

186 Ibid., 201. This accusation recurs in the libel that Cecil prints in his *Answere to Certaine Scandalous Papers, scattered abroad vnder the colour of a Catholicke Admonition*, B3[r]. The pamphlet is discussed below.

187 Father Oldcorne's execution was unrelated to the plot except that he had made the unfortunate mistake of sharing Father Garnett's hiding place. Nevertheless, Gerard chose to regard him as a victim of the conspiracy.

188 John Gerard, *The Condition of Catholics under James I* ..., 192. The pamphlet to which Gerard refers was one by an anonymous writer, T.W., who offered a more sensational account of the trial and execution of the lay plotters. Athough he claimed to write as a loyal subject intending to warn other idolators against committing similar crimes, his registration of the pamphlet on 4 February, only a few days after the first executions, suggests that the author was anxious to make a profit by being the first to get the news into print. This pamphlet was published in two variants with slightly different titles (STC 24916 and STC 24916.3). For comparative purposes, it is interesting to look at a similar pamphlet narrating the executions of the Babington plotters by George Whetstone, *The Censure of a loyall subiect.* Whetstone structures his pamphlet as a drama in which a fictitious spectator at the executions relates the event to two friends, whereas T.W. tells his story more simply and soberly. The relationship between the pamphlets describing trials and executions for domestic murders studied by Lake and Questier in *The Antichrist's Lewd Hat* and those relating to political crimes needs to be examined. The Stationers' Register indicates that ballads also appeared rapidly but none have survived (see chapter 4, note 99, below).

189 John Gerard, *The Condition of Catholics under James I* ..., 203.

190 Alexandra Walsham, in *Providence in Early Modern England* (241–3), emphasizes that although Protestants made providentialism a centrepiece in their view of the world, Catholics also frequently relied upon providential explanations of events.

191 John Gerard, *The Condition of Catholics under James I* ..., 301.

192 Catholic references to the plot seldom occur outside of these polemical contexts, for, as Alison Shell reminds us, "viewed from the Catholic perspective, the defeat of the Armada in 1588, or the discovery of the Gunpowder Plot in 1605, cease to be landmarks and become embarrassments: sometimes written about from motives of dissociation, mostly ignored" (*Catholicism, Controversy and the English Literary Imagination, 1558–1660*, 115).

193 In the "Epistle Dedicatory" to his 1610 sermon at St Mary's Oxford, John Rawlinson notes that the Jesuits say that the plot was a rash attempt by a few Catholics rather than a considered plan to return the country to Catholicism (*The Romish Iudas*, A3^{v}–A4^{r}).

194 Chapter 3 describes in more detail the wave of anti-Cecil writings that followed the Gunpowder Plot.

195 Salisbury, *An Answere to Certaine Scandalous Papers*, B^{r}, B^{v}.

3. "And no religion binds men to be traitors": The Plot on Stage

1 Dolan, *Whores of Babylon*, 54.

2 Studies connecting specific plays with the plot include Lemon, *Treason by Words*; Wills, *Witches and Jesuits*; Krantz, "Thomas Dekker's Political Commentary in *The Whore of Babylon*"; Buccola, "Virgin Fairies and Imperial Whores"; Gasper, *The Dragon and the Dove*; Taunton and Hart, "*King Lear*, King James and the Gunpowder Treason of 1605"; Dutton, *Ben Jonson, "Volpone" and the Gunpowder Plot* (as well as several other discussions of *Volpone* and the plot); Teague, "Ben Jonson and London Courtrooms"; and De Luna, *Jonson's Romish Plot.* While individual plays examined in these studies include *Macbeth*, *Volpone*, *The Whore of Babylon*, and *King Lear*, other plays including *Sophonisba*, *The Devil's Charter*, and *The Isle of Gulls* receive passing references. In Renaissance theatre criticism, studies of individual authors have been supplemented in recent years by historical studies of particular companies; however, neither methodology is particularly conducive to studies documenting the response of London's commercial theatre to current events. Section 3 of this chapter performs a comparative analysis of three plays produced in 1606–7 to test this methodology's effectiveness with plays that can be dated relatively accurately. More plays could be included, but thorny issues of dating, particularly around *Macbeth* and *King Lear*, complicate such a project.

3 Annabel Patterson uses this term to describe nine principles by which Renaissance authors could encode political meanings into their works while avoiding overt allusions that the authorities would feel compelled to challenge. See *Censorship and Interpretation*, esp. ch. 2, in which Patterson outlines these principles. Dutton makes the point that Renaissance readers were accustomed to reading analogically and that the licencers expected them to do so. Changes required by the authorities were intended to limit these readings (*Licensing, Censorship and Authorship in Early Modern England*, xi–xii and passim).

4 As we have seen in the previous chapter, there were exceptions during the reigns of Elizabeth and James I, such as Barlow's sermon on Essex's execution. Morrissey also records evidence of a demand for an advance copy of a sermon from an unknown preacher in 1622 that suggests the request was unusual. Laud and Juxon,

however, seem to have required such copies after 1627, judging from several surviving appointment letters from the period 1628 to 1638. See *Politics and the Paul's Cross Sermons, 1558–1642*, 99–100.

5 While the title page of the pamphlet gives the author's surname as "Hubbard," both the *ESTC* and *EEBO* correctly identify the author as William Hubbock.

6 Hubbock, *Great Brittaines Resurrection*, A3[r–v]. The allusion to Pyramis seems to refer to an anonymous pamphlet entitled *An Hvmble Petition offered to the right reuerend, honourable, and worshipfull estates of this present Parliament assembled at Westminster Pallace*, in which a French Protestant refugee begs to be made the chronicler of England's, and James's, recent deliverance. The speaker claims to be the ghost of a monument erected to celebrate the eviction of the Jesuits from France, which had been removed in 1604 when the Jesuits were permitted to return. William Gager's brief epic *Pyramis* is known only in a 1608 presentation manuscript, and so is a less likely candidate.

7 Ormerod, *The Picture of a Papist*, A4[v].

8 Ormerod's pamphlet was entered in the Stationers' Register on 5 December 1605, a mere month after the plot's discovery, but the publication date is 1606. The prefatory material must have been written after the pamphlet was entered, since a month would likely not have been enough time for a play to be written and produced. The dating of *Macbeth* is uncertain, but early 1606 is likely, particularly if we accept that the porter's scene makes allusions to Father Garnett. Such a date would fit with Hubbock's reference to the time of the performance as that when the traitors were being executed. Arnold Hunt interprets Ormerod's marginal note as a reference to Dekker; however, there appears to be no evidence Dekker was ever an actor ("Ormerod, Oliver [*d.* 1626]").

9 Dillon, "Theatre and Controversy, 1603–1642," 367.

10 Elizabeth I, *By the Quene. Forasmuche as the tyme wherein common interludes in the Englishe tongue ar wont vsually to be played ...* (London, 1559). In other words, Dutton argues, the proclamation simply established the conditions under which these subjects could be presented, conditions that reflected the standards of the court rather than the city. When plays passed from the court to the commercial theatre, however, they effectively circumvented these controls ("Jurisdiction of Theater and Censorship," 227).

11 Yachnin, "The Powerless Theater," 73.

12 The subject of dramatic censorship has received increasing attention in the past thirty years from critics including Dutton (particularly *Mastering the Revels* and *Licensing, Censorship and Authorship in Early Modern England*); and Clare ("Transgressing Authority in English Renaissance Drama" and "Historicism and the Question of Censorship"). In "Historicism and the Question of Censorship," Clare criticizes historicists for limiting their interests to a small group of texts and focusing excessively on power relations.

13 Dutton concludes that "As a censor it seems that each of the masters was scrupulous, could on occasion be strict, but on the whole applied relatively broad criteria of what was permissible" ("Jurisdiction of Theater and Censorship," 227).

14 Annabel Patterson, *Censorship and Interpretation*, 18.

15 Limon, *Dangerous Matter*, 14, 19.

16 Much critical ink has been spilled upon the question of why Essex and his friends commissioned this play to be performed and whether it was indeed Shakespeare's *Richard II*. Recently, Paul E.J. Hammer has argued that the play performed on Saturday, 7 February, "had no direct connection with what happened the following day because those events were unforeseen on Saturday afternoon, let alone a day or so earlier when the performance was commissioned" ("Shakespeare's *Richard II*, the Play of 7 February 1601, and the Essex Rising," 18). Whether or not this will end the discussion remains to be seen. Critics of *A Game at Chess* continue to debate who might have had an interest in putting on this play (Charles and Buckingham are the most obvious contenders) and why it was allowed to continue playing for so long before it was suppressed. Studies of particular interest in this context include Richard Dutton, "Thomas Middleton's *A Game at Chess*"; Ian Munro, "Making Publics"; and T.H. Howard-Hill, "Political Interpretations of Middleton's 'A Game at Chess' (1624)."

17 Clare, "Transgressing Authority in English Renaissance Drama," 354.

18 Dillon, "Theatre and Controversy, 1603–1642," 369. We have only a few examples of playtexts showing the hand of the Master of the Revels. Dutton has observed, however, that in these cases it appears material was excised only when it could not be rewritten in a way that would make it acceptable (*Mastering the Revels*, esp. ch. 3).

19 Dutton, *Ben Jonson, "Volpone" and the Gunpowder Plot*, 10.

20 Chamberlain, *The Letters of John Chamberlain*, 1.199.

21 See Dillon, "Theatre and Controversy, 1603–1642," 366–9; Burns, in *John Day's The Isle of Gulls: A Critical Edition*, 25–6; Turner, "The Matter of Fact," 90.

22 Although the "King's Book" was printed anonymously, the assumption of James's authorship is reflected in the book's popular appellation. Royal authorship was virtually admitted by Cecil in his *Answere to Certaine Scandalous Papers.*

23 On the controversy over *Philotas*, see Hugh Gazzard, "'Those Graue Presentments of Antiquitie,'" 423–50; Laurence Michel, ed., *The Tragedy of "Philotas."* Gazzard provides significant new evidence to support Michel's conclusion that the play was intended to comment on the Essex affair. For the earlier argument that Daniel had no such intentions, see G.A. Wilkes, "Daniel's *Philotas* and the Essex Case," 233–42.

24 Thematic treatments include Frances Teague's juxtaposition of *Volpone* and *King Lear* on the basis of their trial scenes, and Garry Wills's observation that *Sophonisba*, *The Devil's Charter*, and *Macbeth* all feature witches in political roles, although Wills concentrates his analysis upon *Macbeth.*

25 Dekker's use of the Armada, a historical incident in which Spanish aggression was sanctioned by war, may have been motivated by the demands of "plausible deniability."

26 Barbara De Luna was the first modern critic to study the play as a commentary on the Gunpowder Plot in *Jonson's Romish Plot.* While her successors have questioned her methodology and her insistence that the play is a "parallelograph," requiring that each character in the play be an exact match for a conspirator, few have doubted her overarching conclusion that the play is connected to the plot.

27 Publication occurred in conjunction with stage revivals in 1635, 1669, and 1674. The play was also printed in the folio editions of Jonson's works.

28 Foucault, *Discipline and Punish*, esp. pt. 1, ch. 2, "The Spectacle of the Scaffold"; Lake and Questier, "Agency, Appropriation and Rhetoric under the Gallows"; Lake with Questier, *The Antichrist's Lewd Hat.* On the political complexities of determining and executing punishments in the early seventeenth century, see also Mark Nicholls, "Treason's Reward."

29 Foucault, *Discipline and Punish*, especially pt. 1, ch. 2, "The Spectacle of the Scaffold."

30 Karen Cunningham notes in *Imaginary Betrayals* that the use of the Foucauldian model in literary studies has tended to emphasize court-centred power while ignoring other bases of power such as the Inns of Court, 23. The church clearly formed another centre of power in this period. For Lake's critique of Foucault, see *The Antichrist's Lewd Hat*, xvii–xviii.

31 Lake with Questier, *The Antichrist's Lewd Hat*, 239.

32 See "Agency, Appropriation and Rhetoric under the Gallows," 83–9.

33 The account of the Gunpowder trials, *A True and Perfect Relation of the Whole Proceedings against the late most barbarous traitors,* followed in the tradition of earlier pamphlets including Bacon's account of the Essex affair (see ch. 2) but was unusual in being published separately from the narrative of the event.

34 Attempts to assassinate Elizabeth included the Ridolfi plot (1570), Throckmorton plot (1584), Parry Plot (1585), Babington Plot (1586), and Lopez plot (1594), while in 1603 James had been threatened by the Main Plot, in which Ralegh had been implicated, and the Bye Plot, for which the priest William Watson had been executed.

35 On Essex, see Bacon's narrative, *A Declaration of the practises & treasons attempted and committed by Robert late Earle of Essex and his complices*, as well as my discussion in chapter 2. On Ralegh, see Karen Cunningham, "'A Spanish Heart in an English Body.'" Cunningham argues that at his trial Ralegh attempted to defend his actions while Coke insisted upon his decline in character from courtier to conspirator.

36 Mark Nicholls provides a detailed examination of the attempt to build a case against Northumberland in *Investigating Gunpowder Plot*, 185–210.

37 See "Strategy and Motivation in the Gunpowder Plot."

38 Cecil was moved to respond to the libels charging him with cruelty to Catholics in his *Answere to Certaine Scandalous Papers*, discussed in the previous chapter. For libels charging him with conspiring against Northumberland, see Bellany and McRae, *Early Stuart Libels* (most notably A16) and below.

39 Croft, "The Religion of Robert Cecil," 784. Croft observes that Cecil distinguished the plotters from loyal Catholics, even in his *Answere to certaine scandalous papers* written in early 1606, and that later in life he favoured increased ceremonialism.

40 For the spate of libels accusing Cecil of eliminating Essex, see Bellany and McRae, *Early Stuart Libels*, esp. A and D.

41 Northampton had been suspected many years earlier in a plot to replace Elizabeth with Mary, Queen of Scots. See Pauline Croft, "Howard, Henry, earl of Northampton (1540–1614)." For a more detailed analysis of Northampton's political career, see Linda Levy Peck, *Northampton: Patronage and Policy at the Court of James I.*

42 See Allen D. Boyer, "Coke, Sir Edward (1552–1634)."

43 Their heads, however, were displayed on the Parliament buildings in London, where they made an impression upon Edward Hawes, the young author of *Trayterous Percyes and Catesbyes Prosopopoeia.*

44 On Owen, see Gerard, *Conditions of Catholics under James I*, 182–90. Alice Hogge, *God's Secret Agents*, 364–6, relying heavily on Catholic accounts, accepts the view that Owen's death resulted from torture.

45 Although Tresham's name remained in the pamphlet account despite his death before the trial, Nicholas Owen's is missing. This may be because he was not accused of participating in the plot but was only being questioned to assist in the search for the priests. Nevertheless, his erasure from the record does suggest the authorities wanted to avoid any reference to his fate. Gerard's insistence upon describing and interpreting Owen's death suggests a determination to ensure he is not forgotten, particularly since his lack of direct involvement made him potentially a martyr.

46 Mark Nicholls, *Investigating Gunpowder Plot*, 70.

47 For a detailed analysis of the plot's investigation, see Mark Nicholls, *Investigating Gunpowder Plot.*

48 As in the case of executions, there were enough witnesses at the trials that the authorities could not easily falsify words or actions; however, choices such as summarizing rather than quoting speech and even print conventions such as layout and typeface could be used to influence interpretation in the printed record.

49 Father Oswald Tesimond worked with Oldcorne for eight years on the English mission. His involvement with the plot consisted of relating to Father Garnett the confession Catesby had made to him regarding his involvement in the plot. The priest managed to elude capture after 5 November and eventually made his way back to the Continent. See Francis Edwards, "Tesimond, Oswald (1563–1636)."

50 See Gerard, *The Condition of Catholics under James I*, 193–4. No doubt the authorities wanted to leave open the possibility that additional Jesuits would be apprehended.

51 *A True and Perfect Relation of the Whole Proceedings against the late most barbarous traitors, Garnet a Iesuite, and his confederats*, E4^{v}, F^{r}.

52 Mark Nicholls suggests that it was talk of having the plotters tried in Parliament, as the king had suggested in his 9 November speech, or of devising special punishments for them that ultimately hastened the trial (*Investigating Gunpowder Plot*, 51–2).

53 Mark Nicholls (*Investigating Gunpowder Plot*, 52–3) cites Hawarde (*Les Reportes*, 257) as proof that "'the Kinge and Queene were bothe there in pryuate,' as were most of the peerage and a majority of 'all the whole parlimente.'" John Chamberlain mentions the king's presence at Garnett's trial and also lists a number of aristocratic ladies who attended (1.220). On the king's closet in the Chapel Royal, see McCullough, *Sermons at Court*, ch. 1.

54 Nicholls notes that Coke "liven[ed] up the proceedings" by telling the "old fable" of the cat and the mice (*Investigating Gunpowder Plot*, 53) but concludes that even so "the trial was apparently rather lacking in spectacle for the crowds of onlookers, many of whom had paid high prices to be present" (52).

55 Having been one of the last to join the conspiracy, Digby's primary roles had been to arrange the hunt as a cover for Catholic activity in the Midlands and to provide much-needed financial support. Henry Percy was tried for contempt in June 1606 and stripped of his offices, fined, and committed to prison until he was released in 1621 as part of an amnesty for James's fifty-fifth birthday. See Mark Nicholls, "Percy, Henry, ninth earl of Northumberland (1564–1632)." Of the other peers suspected of involvement, Lord Montagu was released in late 1606 without standing trial and Lord Stourton in 1608, while Lord Mordaunt died in prison in 1609 (Nicholls, *Investigating Gunpowder Plot*, 74–7).

56 Ironically, of course, the priest could expect the same punishment as the lay plotters.

57 For the changing nature of the theatre and relations between authors and actors at the turn of the seventeenth century, see Richard Helgerson, *Forms of Nationhood*, 200–42. According to Douglas A. Brooks, Jonson seems to have been the first playwright made to answer to the government for a potentially treasonous play (*Sejanus*). See *From Playhouse to Printing House*, 22–3. As we will see below, however, the actors in John Day's *The Isle of Gulls* were the ones prosecuted, possibly because they had gone beyond the bounds of their script.

58 Chamberlain, *The Letters of John Chamberlain*, 1.222.

59 Gerard, *The Condition of Catholics under James I. Father Gerard's Narrative of the Gunpowder Plot*, 264.

60 *A True and Perfect Relation of the Whole Proceedings against the late most barbarous traitors*, CC4^{v}.

61 The original speech seems to have been at least an outline of the expanded version, for Chamberlain, who did not attend the arraignment, reports to Carleton that the "summe" of the proceedings "was that Garnet comming into England in 86 hath had his finger in every treason since that time" (1.220).

62 Peck, *Northampton, Patronage and Policy at the Court of James I*, 111–13.

63 *Cal. S P Venice* 1603–7, 438–9, 7 December 1606. Peck argues that Cotton not only edited Northampton's manuscript, but that he also "supplied the historical framework on which Northampton built his case" (*Northampton*, 112).

64 For example, the letters from the Catilinarian conspirators to the Allobroges that Cicero arranges to have intercepted in *Catiline, his Conspiracy*; Edmund's use of a letter to trick Edgar in *King Lear*, and Macbeth's letter to his wife.

65 The extent of public interest in Garnett is attested by the number of surviving accounts of his trial and execution in manuscript. These include BL Add. MS 21203, ff. 26[r]–40[r]; BL Add. MS 34218, ff. 67[r]–81[r]; BL Add. MS 73085 ff. 185[v]–188[v]. Some of these are handwritten copies of, or extracts from, printed texts.

66 Catholics often attempted to obtain positions close to the scaffold in these cases in order to hear the priest's last words, obtain relics, witness miracles, or simply to pull his legs to ensure he would be dead when cut down and disembowelled. This practice also allowed them to contest statements made in official accounts, as Gerard does in his narrative.

67 The extent of Garnett's foreknowledge and the reasons for his decision not to impart that information to the authorities have provided a perennial source of speculation for subsequent writers and historians. Frequently, these have been polarized by confessional interests. Philip Caraman's biography (*Henry Garnet 1555–1606 and the Gunpowder Plot*) painted a largely flattering portrait of the priest, but Protestant commentators have generally been less forgiving. Mark Nicholls concludes that "While great efforts have subsequently been made to clear the names of the three proclaimed Jesuits, it is difficult to believe that any one of them, with the possible exception of Gerard, was ignorant of the plotters' intentions" (*Investigating Gunpowder Plot*, 51).

68 The Recorder of London at this time was Henry Montagu, appointed in 1603. He was subsequently made King's Serjeant in 1610 and became Chief Justice of King's Bench in 1616. See John Noorthouck's *A New History of London, including Westminster and Southwark*, 893.

69 *A True and Perfect Relation of the Whole Proceedings against the late most barbarous traitors*, Fff2[v], Fff3[v].

70 Lake and Questier, "Agency, Appropriation and Rhetoric under the Gallows," 80.

71 For Gerard's interpretation of the execution and subsequent miracles, see *The Conditions of Catholics under James I*, chs 15 and 16.

72 Dudley Carleton, however, attributed the change of dates to fear of tumult, telling John Chamberlain in a letter of 2 May 1606 that "It was looked yesterday that

Garnett should have come a-maying to the gallows which was set up for him in Paul's churchyard on Wednesday, but upon better advice his execution is put off till tomorrow, for fear of disorder amongst prentices and others in a day of such misrule" (*Dudley Carleton to John Chamberlain 1603–1624: Jacobean Letters*, 80).

73 Chamberlain, *The Letters of John Chamberlain*, 1.225.

74 The lengthy delay between sentencing and execution suggests the authorities still hoped to obtain more information from Garnett. See Mark Nicholls, *Investigating Gunpowder Plot*, 72–3.

75 An account of the straw appears with a narrative of Garnet's arraignment in BL Add. MS 21203, f. 23[r]–24[r], which is clearly the work of a sympathetic author, since it appears among items detailing anti-Catholic legislation and the executions of other priests. A hostile account by Charles Cornwallis (1 May 1607) is recorded in BL MS Stowe 169, f. 27.

76 Gerard, *The Condition of Catholics under James I. Father Gerard's Narrative of the Gunpowder Plot*, 303. That the religious authorities were anxious to disprove the legend of the straw is confirmed by H.L. Rogers, who observes that "The Archbishop of Canterbury wrote to the Lord Chief Justice on 25 November 1606 asking for the apprehension of 'one Barret, who went up and down with a miracle of Garnet's head supposed to be on a straw.' The Archbishop also examined witnesses, including Hugh Griffin the tailor, who was questioned on 27 November and 3 December" (45). See "An English Tailor and Father Garnet's Straw."

77 Wills, *Witches and Jesuits*, 98, 105. See also H.L. Rogers, "An English Tailor and Father Garnet's Straw," 44–9.

78 Rebecca Lemon notes that "The spectacle of Macbeth's severed head at the end of the play ... arguably serves to contain the traumatic events of the Gunpowder Plot" (84), but her analysis suggests that this triumph is undercut by the ways in which the play represents the interdependence of kings and traitors (*Treason by Words*, ch. 4).

79 On the rise of the elder Cecil, see Stephen Alford, *Burghley: William Cecil at the Court of Elizabeth I*. For attitudes to both Cecils, particularly in relation to the rise and fall of Essex, see Paul E.J. Hammer, *The Polarisation of Elizabethan Politics*.

80 A number of the libels current at the time of Cecil's death refer to his physical deformity. See Bellany and McRae, *Early Stuart Libels*, e.g., D4, D5, and D8.

81 Dennis Flynn quotes Dudley Carleton, Northumberland's secretary, who dismissed the whole plot as a "fable" "as soon as the government issued its report" ("Donne's *Ignatius his Conclave* and Other Libels on Robert Cecil," 173 and 182n52). Carleton may have been demonstrating his loyalty to Northumberland as well as his incredulity about the official story.

82 Garry Wills, for example, includes *Sophonisba* with *Macbeth* and *The Devil's Charter* as post-plot plays featuring witches (*Witches and Jesuits*, 152–3 and passim). In their edition of the play, Peter Corbin and Douglas Sedge note that Marston referred to

his writing of this play in the preface to *The Fawne* (1604). While the play may not have been completed until after the Gunpowder Plot, its conception was clearly earlier. See *Three Jacobean Witchcraft Plays*, 4. Nina Taunton and Valerie Hart, in arguing for *King Lear* as a response to the plot note that E.K. Chambers dated the play to 1604/5, but that more recent scholars have argued for 1606/7 ("*King Lear*, King James and the Gunpowder Treason of 1605"). For a summary of the dating controversy over *Macbeth*, see Wills, *Witches and Jesuits*, Appendix 1.

83 For example, we know that Jonson had a strong dislike of Day.

84 Such plays include *The Famous Historie of the Life and Death of Captaine Thomas Stukeley* (printed in 1605 but presumably performed earlier as it was originally licensed in 1600), *The Famous Historie of Sir Thomas Wyat* (1607, but licensed in 1600). Although there are textual difficulties with these plays, it seems the authorities handled both with some caution.

85 The exact date of the performance is unknown. Although it has generally been supposed that it took place at court, Christina Alt suggests that the venue may also have been Blackfriars ("Directed Readings: Paratext in *A Game at Chess* and *The Tragedie of Philotas*," 133–4).

86 Daniel's position as licenser was established in the 1604 patent that created the company (Lucy Munro, *Children of the Queen's Revels*, 19), but Munro cautions that "It is difficult ... to be sure exactly when Daniel ceased to be involved with the company" (20). Alt notes that Daniel published the play in such a way as to dissociate the text from its controversial stage performance (134–9).

87 The most recent discussion of the play's political overtones demonstrates that Daniel actually incorporated material from Essex's trial into his play. See Hugh Gazzard, "'Those Graue Presentments of Antiquitie': Samuel Daniel's *Philotas* and the Earl of Essex," 423–50.

88 A selection of libels circulating about Cecil at the time of his death appears in Bellany and McRae's *Early Stuart Libels* (Section D). Some of these are discussed by Pauline Croft in "The Reputation of Robert Cecil." Richard Dutton also notes those relevant to his discussion of *Volpone* in *Ben Jonson, "Volpone" and the Gunpowder Plot*, 114–15.

89 Bellany and McRae, *Early Stuart Libels*, A16, and B12, note.

90 Salisbury, *An Answere to Certaine Scandalous Papers*, B3^{r}.

91 De Luna suggests that Cecil's use of theatrical language in this pamphlet indicates he was aware of being satirized on the stage (*Jonson's Romish Plot*, 145–6). While this is certainly plausible, Cecil's words are also a reminder of his recent performance on stage at the plot trials.

92 For the dating of the performance, see Lucy Munro, *Children of the Queen's Revels*, 174; BL, MS Stowe 168, f. 363.

93 Hoby's letter states cryptically that "sundry were committed to Bridwell" (BL, MS Stowe 168, f. 363^{r}) and Munro postulates this may have included "some of the

actors, the shareholders and/or managers and the dramatist, but Hoby did not regard the dramatist as having sole responsibility for the performance and the offence it caused" (*Children of the Queen's Revels*, 29).

94 W. David Kay, in relation to Jonson's *Eastward Ho*, writes that "King James had been surprisingly permissive about allowing satire on his person, but in this case his anger was apparently fanned by his Scottish courtiers" (*Ben Jonson: A Literary Life*, 75). The same may have been true of Day's play. Hoby's reference to the portrayal of the "highest to the loweste" indicates audiences recognized that the king and his advisors were being satirized.

95 E.K. Chambers, *The Elizabethan Stage*, 3.286.

96 Lehmann, "A Critical Analysis of the Works of John Day (*c.* 1574–*c.*1640)," 151.

97 Croft, "The Reputation of Robert Cecil," 56.

98 Dutton, *Ben Jonson, "Volpone" and the Gunpowder Plot*, 63. De Luna declares that "With amazing boldness and a degree of viciousness that was really reprehensible, Day makes the identity of his principal victim clear from the very first" (*Jonson's Romish Plot*, 147).

99 Dutton, *Ben Jonson, "Volpone" and the Gunpowder Plot*, 64.

100 Tricomi, *Anticourt Drama in England 1603–1642*, 11–12.

101 See "The Private Theaters in Crisis: Strategies at Blackfriars and Paul's, 1606–1607," 1–83.

102 Croft, "The Reputation of Robert Cecil," 56.

103 Introduction, in *John Day's "The Isle of Gulls": A Critical Edition*, 3, 1–8. Burns represents Daniel as the licenser for the Children of the Queen's Revels at this point; however, Lucy Munro suggests his appointment may already have been terminated (*Children of the Queen's Revels*, 20–1).

104 See Dutton's summary of the *Isle of Dogs* controversy: *Ben Jonson, "Volpone" and the Gunpowder Plot*, 13–14.

105 *Oxford English Dictionary Online*, "gull," n. 3.

106 See Michael Andrews, "*The Isle of Gulls* as Travesty"; Gary Paul Lehmann, "A Critical Analysis of the Works of John Day (*c.* 1574–*c.*1640)," ch. 9. The relationship between Sidney's *Arcadia* and Day's play requires further analysis. The most influential political reading of the *Arcadia* remains Blair Worden's *The Sound of Virtue*. Worden notes that "Because Basilius has broken up his court, Sidney has to work hard to inject the theme of courtly evils into the *Arcadia*. The scope that would have been open to him had he placed the work in a court is indicated by a play of 1606 by John Day, *The Isle of Gulls*, which uses Sidney's plot but sets it in a court intended to parallel that of King James I" (218–19). Tracey Sedinger argues that Basilius's rejection of counsel and retreat from active engagement in his kingdom signal failures that lead directly to rebellion in the *New Arcadia* ("Sidney's *New Arcadia* and the Decay of Protestant Republicanism"). In Day's text, the problem centres on the king's reliance

upon an evil counsellor rather than rejection of counsel. One interesting possibility for further investigation is the relationship between Day's play and Samuel Daniel's production of *The Queenes Arcadia* before James I at Oxford in late August 1605, apparently the only one of the five Oxford dramas James attended between 27 and 30 August that he enjoyed (see J.P. Feil, "Dramatic References from the Scudamore Papers," 114n2; Trevor-Roper, "Five Letters of Sir Thomas Bodley," 134–9). If Day hoped that using a story the king favoured would protect him, he miscalculated.

107 Annabel Patterson, *Censorship and Interpretation*, 43.

108 Despite widespread critical recognition that Sidney's text represents some type of political intervention, the evidence does not indicate that contemporaries read it analogically. As Fred Schurink points out, Heidi Brayman Hackel's study of 151 copies of the text published prior to 1700 does not uncover a single instance of an annotator identifying the fictional characters with political figures (Schurink, "'Like a hand in the margine of a booke,'" 14; Hackel, *Reading Material in Early Modern England*, 158–75).

109 See chapter 2 for a discussion of this pamphlet.

110 In addition, it might be recalled that the delay in interpreting the Monteagle letter was due to the king's absence on a hunting excursion. As numerous scholars have observed, the premise of the *Arcadia* seems to offer veiled criticism of monarchs who pursue their own pleasure rather than attending to the business of governing.

111 See particularly Lodowick Lloyd's *The Tragicomedie of Serpents.*

112 Father Tesimond escaped to the continent and so evaded punishment. Father Oldcorne was not suspected of complicity in the plot but was captured with Garnett and convicted of high treason for being in England. He was tried at the assizes in Worcester and executed there on 7 April 1606.

113 See, for example, Frances Teague, "Jonson and the Gunpowder Plot"; Dennis Flynn, "Donne's 'Amicissimo et Meritissimo Ben. Ionson' and the Daring of *Volpone*," 368–9; James Tulip, "The Intertextualities of Ben Jonson's *Volpone*"; and several studies by Richard Dutton culminating in *Ben Jonson, "Volpone" and the Gunpowder Plot.*

114 For more on Wright, see Theodore A. Stroud, "Ben Jonson and Father Thomas Wright." According to Richard Harp, Wright's identification as the priest responsible for Jonson's conversion has not been challenged. Patrick Martin and John Finnis, however, presented an argument for identifying the priest Jonson sought in 1605 as Father Thomas Strange ("A Gunpowder Priest?" 12–13) that is accepted by Ian Donaldson ("Talking with Ghosts: Ben Jonson and the English Civil War," 17n19). In response to Martin and Finnis, however, Mark Bland argues that the inscription in Jonson's Vulgate, upon which their argument largely rests, dates to 1600 rather than 1605 ("Jonson's Vulgate [Letter]," 15).

115 Teague, "Jonson and the Gunpowder Plot," 251.

116 See *Jonson's Romish Plot*, ch. 4, for De Luna's interpretation of Jonson's involvement with the plot.

117 For a recent overview of scholarship on Jonson's complex religious history, see Richard Harp, "Catholicism."

118 That theatrical audiences or readers could identify the character of Volpone with a number of different individuals is attested by Robert C. Evans's evidence that at least one reader thought the play satirized Thomas Sutton. See *Jonson and the Contexts of his Time*, ch. 3. According to De Luna (*Jonson's Romish Plot*, 146), Jonson disliked Day and referred to him as the "vernaculous Orator" who had satirized Cecil in his preface to *Volpone.*

119 Dutton, *Ben Jonson: To the First Folio*, 146.

120 Dutton's previous discussions of the play as a response to the plot include *Ben Jonson: To the First Folio*, 143–54; and *Licensing, Censorship and Authorship in Early Modern England: Buggeswords*, ch. 6. His most recent review of these arguments is in "Jonson's Metempsychosis Revisited: Patronage and Religious Controversy."

121 On *Metempsychosis* as anti-Cecil satire, see especially M. van Wyk Smith, "John Donne's Metempsychosis." Smith's ideas were extended by Brian M. Blackley, "The Generic Play and Spenserian Parody of John Donne's 'Metempsychosis.'"

122 Dutton, *Ben Jonson, "Volpone" and the Gunpowder Plot*, 107. Teague argues that setting the courtroom scenes in Venice enables Jonson to critique English justice at a time when, following the Gunpowder trials, such scenes set in London would have elicited too many questions. See "Ben Jonson and London Courtrooms."

123 Dutton, *Ben Jonson, "Volpone" and the Gunpowder Plot*, 110.

124 Jonson may also be poking fun at Day, who had not succeeded in gulling the authorities.

125 Riely, in Thomas Dekker, *The Whore of Babylon: A Critical Edition*, 56.

126 The first performance's exact date is unknown.

127 Halstead points out that other aspects of the text such as the identifications of the allegorical figures that appear in the margins were unlikely to have been included in a stage copy. For the now discredited view that the play is a revision of an even earlier one, see Mary Leland Hunt, *Thomas Dekker: A Study*, 36–42. Basing her argument partly upon the inclusion of such "archaic" features as dumb show and morality characters, Hunt claims the topical references are later additions or changes and dates the original play between 1594 and 1596. Despite the lingering perception that dumb show had fallen out of fashion by the beginning of the seventeenth century, it was still being used in 1606 in plays such as *The Devil's Charter* (also an anti-Catholic play performed in the wake of the Gunpowder Plot). B.R. Pearn, in fact, counts sixteen plays between 1601 and 1610 that use this convention. See "Dumb Show in Elizabethan Drama," 386; on the convention more generally, see Dieter Mehl, *The Elizabethan Dumb Show.*

128 Halstead, "Dating and Holograph Evidence in *The Whore of Babylon*," 40. Halstead accepts that the passage in Act 4, Scene 2, refers to Essex's execution, as Frederick Gard Fleay had suggested (*A Chronicle History of the London Stage, 1559–1642*). Riely has postulated that the reference is to Thomas Howard, Duke of Norfolk, in relation to the Ridolfi plot. This would account for the changes of gender as well as for the presence of Florimell (Leicester) in the scene, which would be problematic were the warrant for his stepson's death being signed (*The Whore of Babylon*, 29–32). More recently, Julia Gasper has once again identified the warrant as that for Essex's execution (*The Dragon and the Dove*, ch. 3).

129 In the "Lectori," Dekker compares the spoiling of plays by players to the ruin of good fabric by a poor tailor or of children by inferior nurses.

130 Dekker, *The Whore of Babylon*, 25. Kathleen E. McLuskie suggests that this also may have been a jibe at Jonson for his insistence upon historical correctness in plays like *Sejanus* (*Dekker and Heywood, Professional Dramatists*, 52). Dekker may also have been protecting himself from political repercussions, particularly if he suspected his play could be understood as a critique of the new reign. Julia Gasper argues that critics who evaluate it as a history play are misguided, and that the play is an example of a minor genre, "the *comoedia apocalyptica*," which differs from the history play since it aims to interpret events in terms of Protestant historiography derived from the Book of Revelation and other biblical texts (*The Dragon and the Dove*, 62).

131 Riely notes that the Third King's frequent references to "trains" are also ambiguous, referring generally to plots and more specifically to gunpowder.

132 Krantz, "Thomas Dekker's Political Commentary in *The Whore of Babylon*," 273.

133 Although this pamphlet was published anonymously, scholars generally accept Dekker's authorship. See *The Double PP, A Papist in Armes*.

134 McLuskie, *Dekker and Heywood, Professional Dramatists*, 51. It is useful to remember that to praise Elizabeth was not necessarily to critique James at this early date. See Walsham, "'A Very Deborah?' The Myth of Elizabeth I as a Providential Monarch," 159.

135 See *Representing Elizabeth in Stuart England: Literature, History, Sovereignty*, 5–55.

136 James H. Conover sees the play as "pro-Elizabeth" (*Thomas Dekker: An Analysis of Dramatic Structure*, 134), but does not suggest it is anti-Jacobean; George R. Price reads it as a relatively uncomplicated demonstration of patriotism in the wake of the Gunpowder Plot (*Thomas Dekker*, 69–76); Irving Ribner suggests Dekker "may have been deliberately courting the favour of James I by expressing political doctrine with which the king was closely concerned" (*The English History Play in the Age of Shakespeare*, 285).

137 Jean E. Howard reads Plain Dealing's outburst as evidence of Dekker's intention to show that "while the empress and Titania are supposedly moral opposites, their courts are in many ways indistinguishable in terms of the vices they harbor" (*The Stage and Social Struggle in Early Modern England*, 55). Although she sees the play

making use of antitheatrical rhetoric to juxtapose English Protestant plainness with Spanish Catholic theatricality and deception, she does not read this scene in a specifically theatrical context as I do. It may have been this reference to the stage as chessboard that inspired Middleton almost twenty years later when he set out to intervene in contemporary politics. Critics have noticed that *A Game at Chess* borrows from Dekker's play. See, for example, Price, *Thomas Dekker*, 70.

138 This scene has occasioned some critical attempts to identify the theatre in question. Riely argues, *contra* Chambers, that the "cockpit" more likely refers to the Fortune than to a performance at court. Given the context, however, it seems most likely to me that Dekker is criticizing a play or plays performed at another theatre, and the reference would fit Blackfriars.

139 At least one libel circulating at the time of his death referred to Cecil as an ape. See Bellany and McRae, *Early Stuart Libels*. Closer to the time of the play is Donne's unpublished *Metempsychosis*, which critics like Van Wyk Smith have read as anti-Cecil satire. In Donne's unfinished poem, the "great soul" comes finally to inhabit an ape.

140 Felix Schelling had identified Parthenophil as Leicester and Fideli as Burghley (*Elizabethan Drama, 1558–1642*, 1.289).

141 Riely, in Thomas Dekker, *The Whore of Babylon*, 97.

142 Riely, in Thomas Dekker, *The Whore of Babylon*, 68. This relationship was apparently short-lived, commencing in 1566 when his debating skills impressed Leicester at Oxford and ending before Campion left for Ireland in 1571, having determined to join the Catholic Church (Michael A.R. Graves, "Campion, Edmund [St Edmund Campion] (1540–1581)").

143 Gasper, who argues that the idealization of Elizabeth in the play is also a form of critique, corroborates this argument. She believes the death warrant the queen signs in Act 4, Scene 2, is Essex's rather than Mary Stuart's and that the scene shows that Cecil and the queen were mistaken about Lopez while Essex was right (*The Dragon and the Dove*, ch. 3). At the very least, as Howard suggests, the form of the play as a kind of debate indicates that both sides are politically motivated (*The Stage and Social Struggle in Early Modern England*, 53).

144 Dutton, *Ben Jonson, "Volpone" and the Gunpowder Plot*, 110. In this context, it is worth remembering John Harington's famous epigram "Of Treason" ("Treason doth never prosper, what's the reason? / For if it prosper, none dare call it Treason," *The Letters and Epigrams of Sir John Harington*, 25).

145 Paulina Kewes claims that after 1603 fewer plays dealing with rebellion were written, while tyranny and absolutism became more frequent topics on the stage as the threat of a disputed succession receded and was replaced by anxieties about a monarchy that might become too strong. Despite this, Shakespeare's *Julius Caesar* (1599) remained popular. See "Julius Caesar in Jacobean England."

146 On the relations among these texts, see David Quint, "Milton, Fletcher, and the Gunpowder Plot"; Estelle Haan, "Milton's *In Quintum Novembris* and the Anglo-Latin Gunpowder Epic." In an interesting argument, Robert Wiltenburg also proposes that the characterization of Milton's Satan is indebted to Jonson's Catiline; see "Damnation in a Roman Dress." On anti-Catholic satire in *Paradise Lost*, see John N. King, *Milton and Religious Controversy*.

147 The publication of Donne's satire in Latin in 1611, both in England and on the Continent, was almost immediately followed by the author's English translation (*Conclaue Ignati: siue Eius in nuperis inferni comitiis in thronisatio*; *Ignatius his conclaue: or his inthronisation in a late election in hell*). Although Willem Heijting and Paul R. Sellin have suggested the Continental Latin edition was published before the London one, Ernest W. Sullivan II accepts T.S. Healy's evidence that the Continental printer used the London text in printing his edition ("John Donne's 'Conclave Ignati': The Continental Quarto and Its Printing"; Ernest W. Sullivan, II, "Modern Scholarly Editions of the Prose of John Donne," 69, citing T.S. Healy, ed., *Ignatius His Conclave*).

148 De Luna explains Jonson's renewed interest in the context of the news from France, but she also suggests that he had been deeply stung by criticism of his own role in the plot's discovery. This requires her to engage in the highly dubious conjecture that Jonson had been a spy for Cecil at the time (*Jonson's Romish Plot*, 144–70).

149 Dutton accepts De Luna's main conclusion while criticizing her methodology and refusing her positive interpretation of Cicero (*Jonson, "Volpone" and the Gunpowder Plot*, 135–41); Annabel Patterson agrees that the play's "allusion to the Gunpowder Plot must have been unmistakable" ("'Roman-cast Similitude,'" 387).

150 Scholars no longer uncritically accept Joel Hurstfield's assertion that "the government made the maximum political capital out of the Plot" ("Gunpowder Plot and the Politics of Dissent," 116); however, as I have suggested, it did become the cornerstone of a "Jacobean myth of deliverance" that ensured at least annual memorialization.

151 *His Maiesties speech in this last session of Parliament*, E4^{v}; *A True and Perfect Relation of the Whole Proceedings against the late most barbarous traitors*, Dd3^{v}. Northampton identified all of the traitors as Catilines a second time (Bb^{v}) and Catesby as Catiline again later in his speech (Zz3^{r}). He also made a reference to Fulvia (Aaa3^{r}), to which I shall return below.

152 De Luna, *Jonson's Romish Plot*, 91, 94.

153 David Kathman identifies Heywood's source as Lois Meigret Lyonnais's French version of Sallust ("Heywood, Thomas (*c.*1573–1641)."

154 Herring (28–32) compares Digby to Nimrod, the proud and mighty hunter.

155 De Luna, *Jonson's Romish Plot*, 109. De Luna was also puzzled by the line "And no religion binds men to be traitors," which is crucial to my interpretation of the play. While she finds it incongruous in a play set in pagan Rome, the relationship between

religion and treason was intensely important in Jacobean England, particularly in the wake of Henri IV's assassination in France and the Oath controversy.

156 See O'Callaghan, "Dreaming the Dead," 85–9 and 158–9n21.

157 Ibid., 86.

158 "The Influence of Ben Jonson's *Catiline* upon John Oldham's *Satyrs Upon the Jesuits*," 38–62.

159 That Jonson may have been reading *Thyestes* in the early Jacobean period is suggested by an allusion observed by Brock Cameron MacLeod in the quarto of *Sejanus*. See "An Unacknowledged Debt to Seneca in the Quarto *Sejanus*," 427.

160 Thomas Rymer, *A short view of tragedy it's original, excellency and corruption: with some reflections on Shakespear and other practitioners for the stage / by Mr. Rymer* ..., 160–3.

161 Goldberg, *James I and the Politics of Literature*, 193.

162 Marshall, *Beliefs and the Dead in Reformation England*, 257.

163 O'Callaghan, "Dreaming the Dead," 82.

164 Edward Hawes, *Trayterous Percyes and Catesbyes Prosopopoeia.*

165 Philip Schwyzer connects the ghosts in the later revisions of the *Mirror for Magistrates* to a nationalistic agenda, arguing that only shared nationality connects ancient Britons with Renaissance Englishmen. See *Literature, Nationalism, and Memory in Early Modern England and Wales*, ch. 4.

166 Jonathan Gil Harris's observation that the standard pyrotechnics used for the production of special effects such as the appearance of spirits would have left a stench of gunpowder in the air of the theatre is tantalizing here. Although the text gives us no indication that such effects might have been used in this play, the numerous subsequent references to lingering odours make this an interesting possibility. A smell of gunpowder would also have been likely to take the memories of spectators back to November 1605 (*Untimely Matter in the Time of Shakespeare*, ch. 4).

167 Kewes curiously suggests that Caesar's assassination was widely represented as an analogue for the Gunpowder Plot, but I have found little evidence to support this statement. The Catilinarian conspiracy is a much more popular analogy. See "Julius Caesar in Jacobean England."

168 De Luna makes only passing references to the women (*Jonson's Romish Plot*), while Philip J. Ayres ("The Nature of Jonson's Roman History") makes no mention of the women.

169 See Fraser, *The Gunpowder Plot: Terror and Faith in 1605*, 125–7; Hogge, *God's Secret Agents*, passim; Childs, *God's Traitors*. See also Marie Rowlands, "Recusant Women."Certainly, the authorities almost immediately arrested the wives of the plotters, presumably on the assumption that they could offer information about their husbands' plans. For a detailed account of the interrogations of the Vaux women, see Childs, *God's Traitors*, 329–53.

170 See Marotti, *Religious Ideology and Cultural Fantasy*, ch. 2; Dolan, *Whores of Babylon.*

171 On the legal issues surrounding female recusancy, see Dolan, *Whores of Babylon*, 60–72. During the Elizabethan period, women could be prosecuted for debt (35 Eliz., cap I). Legislation enacted after the discovery of the Gunpowder Plot (3 & 4 Jac. I, cap. 4) specified that married women could be imprisoned until they took the Oath of Allegiance, while later laws (7 & 8 Jac. I, cap. 6) made husbands liable for their wives' recusancy. For a detailed explanation of the penalties for recusancy, see John Miller, *Popery and Politics in England 1660–1688*, 52–8.

172 Dolan, *Whores of Babylon*, 47. BL Add. MS 11,402, f. 108[r] lists nine women arrested on 16 November, mostly wives of conspirators and suspected conspirators, as well as Anne Vaux ("Dorothie Grant, Eliz: Cole, Mary Morgan, Martha Percie, Dorothy Wright, Margaret Wright, Mrs. Rookewood, Mistress Key, and Mistress Vaux").

173 On Lewis Pickering's connections with the plot, see ch. 5.

174 *A True and Perfect Relation*, Fff2[v].

175 Mark Nicholls, "Vaux, Anne (*bap.* 1562, *d.* in or after 1637)." Anne Vaux seems finally to be receiving some much-delayed attention. In *God's Traitors: Terror and Faith in Elizabethan England*, Jessie Childs explores in detail Anne's origins in a stubbornly recusant family, the dangerous game she and her sister Eleanor and sister-in-law Eliza played in sheltering priests, and her devotion to Garnett and his memory.

176 Both Regina Buccola and Jean E. Howard suggest that in this play the two come close to collapsing into each other ("Virgin Fairies and Imperial Whores"; *The Stage and Social Struggle in Early Modern England*, 54). I would suggest that the victim/victor dichotomy also comes close to breaking down by the end of the play.

177 Gaggero, "Civic Humanism and Gender Politics in Jonson's *Catiline*," 412.

178 Chapter 4 offers a discussion of how this idea was expressed in post-plot imagery of monstrous births.

179 Sempronia intervenes in politics through the more masculine means of writing letters of support for her favoured candidate.

180 On the representation of face-painting in early modern England, see Dolan, "'Taking the Pencil out of God's Hand': Art, Nature, and Face-Painting in Early Modern England"; Crystal Downing's rejoinder to Dolan, "Face Painting in Early Modern England"; Jo Eldridge Carney, "'God Hath Given You One Face, and You Make Yourselves Another'"; Annette Drew-Bear, "Face-Painting in Ben Jonson's Plays." It is possibly yet another reflection of the disregard for the women's parts in *Catiline* that Drew-Bear does not mention this scene in her survey of face-painting in Jonson's plays.

181 Dolan points out that many Catholic men attended Church of England services with sufficient regularity to avoid penalty while their wives maintained Catholic practices for children and servants in the home (*Whores of Babylon*, 69–70).

182 Dolan, *Whores of Babylon*, 59.

183 *A True and Perfect Relation of the Whole Proceedings against the late most barbarous traitors*, Aa3[r–v]. De Luna suggests that both Jonson and Northampton incorrectly believed the two Fulvias to be the same person (*Jonson's Romish Plot*, 78 and nn. 15 and 16). Northampton's inclusion of this anecdote indicates some anxiety about the consequences of placing one's rhetorical talents at the service of the state.

184 Catiline, however, does seem to be somewhat convinced by his own rhetoric later in the play, particularly when he insists upon his soldiers reverencing the silver eagle of his standard.

185 De Luna was puzzled by Cicero's assertion that "no religion binds men to be traitors" (3.369), insisting that the conspiracy is never given a religious motivation. Jonson has, however, put his finger here on the problem of interpretation shared by the Catholic and Protestant communities – the reason for which Catholics were put to death. Cicero, as the representative of the state, insists upon the ability to separate religious belief from subversive action, just as James had.

186 DeLuna, *Jonson's Romish Plot*, 198.

187 Bellany and McRae, *Early Stuart Libels*, B2. The popularity of this libel is attested by its survival in multiple copies. Bellany and McRae (*Early Stuart Libels* BS) record five manuscript copies: Bodleian MS Malone 23, p. 1; BL MS Harley 3910, f. 11r; Folger MS V.a 339, ff. 189r; Huntington MS HM 198, 1.164; Rosenbach MS 1083/15 p. 153.

188 Dekker, *The Double PP*, C2[r].

189 De Luna, I think, is correct to see that some of the characteristics of Jonson's Cicero, such as his elaborate spy network and his humble origins, are more applicable to Cecil than to Northampton. Mark Nicholls suggests that the scope of Cecil's network has been exaggerated; however, we are dealing here more in perceptions than facts.

190 Praemunire was "the offense of appealing to or obeying a foreign dignitary (namely, the pope), thus challenging the supremacy of the monarch and thereby committing treason" (Lemon, *Treason by Words*, 192n6). Lemon points out that the 1606 Oath of Allegiance and the pope's response to it left Catholics in the unenviable position of risking excommunication if they took the oath and guilty of treason if they did not. According to John Miller, the penalties for praemunire were seldom enforced (*Popery and Politics in England, 1660–1688*, 57).

191 See G.E. Bentley, *Shakespeare and Jonson: Their Reputations in the Seventeenth Century Compared*; De Luna, *Jonson's Romish Plot*, 328. Dutton (*Jonson, "Volpone" and the Gunpowder Plot*) sees the popularity of both *Volpone* and *Catiline* as evidence that seventeenth-century readers understood both were connected with the Gunpowder Plot, 141–50.

192 For the changing conventions of the prologue in Restoration drama, see *Prologues, Epilogues, Curtain-Raisers, and Afterpieces*; *Of Books and Humankind: Essays and Poems Presented to Bonamy Dobree.*

193 Given the anti-Catholic contexts in which the play was revived, Gwyn's Catholicism must have added to the tension.

194 Thomas Campion, *De Puluerea Coniuratione (On the Gunpowder Plot) Sidney Sussex MS 59*, Book 2.

195 Wiseman, "'The Eccho of Uncertaintie,'" 209, 214.

196 Ian Donaldson observes in conjunction with *Catiline*'s popularity that during the Civil War and Restoration periods Jonson himself was frequently represented as a ghost ("Talking with Ghosts," 13–14).

197 The most extensive borrowing in a dramatic context occurs in Thomas Otway's *Venice Preserv'd*, which, as De Luna has shown, borrows both language and ideas from *Catiline* (*Jonson's Romish Plot*, 349–53). Like Jonson's play, Otway's offers women ambiguous roles in the foiling of a plot that has been seen by modern critics as commentary upon various contemporary events. The play also features the ghostly appearances of Pierre and Jaffeir to Belvidera, although these ghosts participate in the admonitory tradition. On the role of women in the play, see Katharine M. Rogers, "Masculine and Feminine Values in Restoration Drama"; Elizabeth Gruber, "'Betray'd to Shame.'" For the debate about the play's politics, see John Robert Moore, "Contemporary Satire in Otway's *Venice Preserved*"; David Bywaters, "Venice, Its Senate, and Its Plot in Otway's *Venice Preserv'd*"; Phillip Harth, "Political Interpretations of 'Venice Preserv'd'." Without any mention of Jonson or the Gunpowder Plot, Susan J. Owen offers some interesting points for comparing the play with literature produced after the Gunpowder Plot. She notes in particular that one of the play's central issues is the problem of the bad father and that monstrosity is associated with rebellion and republicanism. As in the case of Jonson's *Volpone*, the Venetian setting complicates political readings since there is no monarch (*Restoration Theatre and Crisis*, 229–38).

198 H.F. Brooks, "The Fictitious Ghost: A Poetic Genre."

199 The catalyst of recent interest in early seventeenth-century ghosts seems to have been Stephen Greenblatt's *Hamlet in Purgatory*, but this subject has attracted less interest in Restoration studies.

200 See Weldon M. Williams, "The Influence of Ben Jonson's *Catiline* upon John Oldham's Satyrs Upon the Jesuits"; on this group of satires more generally, see also Williams's "The Genesis of John Oldham's Satyres upon the Jesuits." Harold F. Brooks offers a more exhaustive catalogue of Oldham's borrowings from a variety of sources, proposing in particular that Fletcher's *Locustae* (both the original Latin poem and the English translation) provided much of Oldham's inspiration. Among other sources, he notes Foulis's *History of Romish Treasons* (1671), George Hall's *Triumph of Rome over Despised Protestancy* (1667), Milton's *Paradise Lost*, Donne's "Satire II," plays by Dryden, Otway, and Nathaniel Lee, and Cowley's *Davideis*. My point is not to identify specific borrowings but to observe the anti-Catholic company that Jonson's

play is keeping in this poem, much of it referring specifically to the Gunpowder Plot. See Harold F. Brooks, "Oldham and Phineas Fletcher."

201 Anon., *Faux's Ghost, or, Advise to Papists.* Oldham's poem also appears to be the progenitor of the anonymous *Father Whitebreads Walking Ghost*, which pilfers two passages of three lines, each virtually verbatim from Oldham's poem. Thomas Whitbread became provincial of the English Jesuit province in 1677, was arrested in 1678 on charges of treason, and executed in 1679 (Joy Rowe, "Whitbread, Thomas (*c.*1618–1679)"). The ghostly speaker reminds his audience of Garnet's example, but the poem makes no reference to the Catilinarian conspiracy.

202 On Elizabeth Cellier, see Dolan, *Whores of Babylon*, ch. 4.

203 *Scylla's Ghost an heroick poem*, 3. Athaliah ruled Judah for six years after the death of her husband and promoted the worship of Baal (2 Chronicles 22.10). This allusion thus extends the poem's concerns with the relationship between ambition and religion.

204 Like Jonson's ghost, this one leaves his "*loathsom, sulphurous Breath* behind" (*Scylla's Ghost*, 6).

205 Among the other conspirators, Catiline seems to be identified with Shaftsbury and Cethegus with William Lord Russell, executed as a traitor in 1683, while the "Scotch Augur" is probably Argyll. It is worth noting that, while clearly critical of Monmouth, the writer avoids making him the chief conspirator, perhaps aware that Monmouth and his father might still reconcile.

206 Hurstfield, "Gunpowder Plot and the Politics of Dissent," 116–17. See in particular Okines, "Why was there so little government reaction to the Gunpowder Plot?"

207 George W. Whiting points out that as theatre attendance declined during the Popish Plot crisis due to fears of unrest playwrights were effectively forced to write and stage partisan plays to maintain their livelihoods. Plays critical of the official church and the government risked censorship, resulting in a predominance of Tory plays ("The Condition of the London Theaters, 1679–83"). See also Susan J. Owen, *Restoration Theatre and Crisis.*

4. "In marble records fit to be inrold": Epic Monuments for a Protestant Nation

1 Smith, *Literature and Revolution in England 1640–1660*, 212.

2 Neil Cuddy argues that a courtly rather than a parliamentary perspective allows us to see the project of union "not as a unique, inconsequential and purely legislative failure, but as a central political preoccupation throughout the reign" ("Anglo-Scottish Union and the Court of James I, 1603–1625," 108).

3 Kerrigan, *Archipelagic English*, 13.

4 Ibid., 13.

5 For the complexities of what "Britain" meant to early moderns, see Alan MacColl, "The Meaning of 'Britain' in Medieval and Early Modern England." MacColl argues

that most medieval and early modern historians used the term "Britain" to mean England alone, but that another tradition referred to the whole island as "England" without including Scotland. In the fifteenth century, some Scots began referring to the entire island as "Britannia maior."

6 Scott-Warren, *Early Modern English Literature*, 164.

7 According to MacColl, by the late sixteenth century, the English feared that Scotland was vulnerable to invasion by Catholic Spain, which could use the country as a landing stage to invade England ("The Meaning of 'Britain,'" 268).

8 MacColl, "The Construction of England as a Protestant 'British' Nation in the Sixteenth Century," 604–5.

9 Wormald, "Gunpowder, Treason, and Scots," 161.

10 Fawkes used this phrase in his first examination by the king on 5 November (qtd. in Wormald, 161). Morgan's argument is based largely on conjecture (*The Great English Treason for Religion known as Gunpowder Plot*, 19).

11 Jason C. White, "Militant Protestants: British Identity in the Jacobean Period, 1603–1625," 165–7. On Scottish Protestants' desire for a united island, see also Arthur H. Williamson, "Scotland, Antichrist and the Invention of Great Britain."

12 MacColl, "The Construction of England as a Protestant 'British' Nation in the Sixteenth Century," 583.

13 Curran, "Spenser and the Historical Revolution," 276.

14 "The English Republic and the Meaning of Britain," 471n94. Others, however, attribute James's actions to the debate about whether monarchy or Parliament was the older tradition. See, for example, Pauline Croft, "Sir John Doddridge, King James I, and the Antiquity of Parliament."

15 Cuddy, "Anglo-Scottish Union and the Court of James I, 1603–1625," 113.

16 Despite complaints about James's importation of Scots retainers, the new king was also generous with his English subjects, creating almost half as many knights on the day of his coronation alone as Elizabeth had in her entire reign (Linda Levy Peck, *Court Patronage and Corruption in Early Stuart England*, 32).

17 Quint, *Epic and Empire*, 8.

18 James's Scottish frame of reference may have inspired his use of the paternal analogy. Wormald observes that in Scotland killing the king was "parricide" rather than "treason" ("Gunpowder, Treason and Scots," 164). Both of James's other analogies for his relationship to his country, marriage and the body politic, were potentially problematic. Since England and Scotland remained joined in an "imperfect union" in which each retained its own laws and institutions, the countries were effectively two wives with one husband or two bodies with one head. On James's marriage metaphors, see Anne McLaren, "Monogamy, Polygamy and the True State."

19 Lee, *Fathers and Sons in Virgil's "Aeneid,"* 18.

20 Not all critics agree that *pietas* entails suppression of personal emotions. See, for example, Colin Burrow, who argues that it requires "emotions, such as gratitude and affection" as well as impersonal justice (*Epic Romance*, 40). In contrast, Robin Sowerby argues that "As the chosen instrument of the gods and of the fates that lead inexorably to the foundation of Rome, he [Aeneas] finds that he is required to subdue his personal inclinations at every stage" (*The Classical Legacy in Renaissance Poetry*, 34).

21 James actually began his speech by recognizing piety and justice as the pillars of government.

22 *Epic and Empire*, 63–83.

23 Bradner, *Musae Anglicanae: A History of Anglo-Latin Poetry, 1500–1925.*

24 All references to Herring's and Wallace's 1606 poems are to Estelle Haan's editions. Haan's English translations are cited in the text by page numbers; references to the Latin are cited in the notes by line numbers ("Milton's *In Quintum Novembris* and the Anglo-Latin Gunpowder Epic," 255, 369).

25 Appelbaum, "Milton, the Gunpowder Plot, and the Mythography of Terror," 471. Appelbaum also identifies *Pareus* and James's poem on the Battle of Lepanto as examples of this genre. See also Dana F. Sutton, "John Milton's *In Quintum Novembris* (1626)."

26 These poems appear in a manuscript collection of Gager's poetry (BL Add. MS 22583), described by Dana F. Sutton in his edition of Gager's poetry (3.xviii–xxiii). They were first edited by Tucker Brooke ("William Gager to Queen Elizabeth"). I quote from Sutton's edition.

27 "In quos patrari grande nefas, Deus / Qui sacra fecit corpora, non sinit, / Quêis alta maiestas tributa est / Haud manibus violanda sæuis" (ll. 21–4).

28 Latin and English quoted from Tucker Brooke, "A Latin Poem by George Peele(?)," 48, 67.

29 Quoted from Brooke, "A Latin Poem by George Peele(?)," 67.

30 Sutton, "Milton's *In Quintum Novembris, anno aetatis 17* (1626)," 359.

31 Thomas Campion, *The Works of Thomas Campion*, 367.

32 "Sunt Angli, sunt Troiana de gente Britanni, / Qui pacem, numenque colunt, et templa fatigant"; "Sic pereat, quicunque tuas fleturus in oras / Vela inimica dabit, Brutique nepotibus, et diis / O vetus hospitium, sanctumque Britannia nomen," *The Works of Thomas Campion*, 367, 377.

33 My discussion of the Virgilian overtones of these poems is restricted to a thematic one. For the linguistic echoes of various classical sources in the poems, see the following: Estelle Haan, "Milton's *In Quintum Novembris*"; Estelle Haan, ed., *Phineas Fletcher: Locustae Vel Pietas Iesuitica*; Thomas Campion, *De Puluerea Coniuratione*. Haan's work is particularly useful for comparing the use of specific incidents and motifs in Milton's poem with those of Wallace, Herring, and Fletcher.

34 Quoted from Haan, "Milton's *In Quintum Novembris* and the Anglo-Latin Gunpowder Epic," 389.

35 Gager, *William Gager: The Complete Works*, 134. All subsequent references are to line numbers. Bruce Galloway asserts that in the pamphlet literature of 1604 "there was much more discussion of the name of Great Britain than of any other single proposal for union" (*The Union of England and Scotland 1603–1608*, 35). Parliament rejected the name change, fearing it would affect England's common law, but in October 1604 James used his own authority to change his title to "King of Great Britain." According to Conrad Russell, the English generally ignored this proclamation, seeing it as an attempt to usurp divine authority, but the "question of the change of name to Great Britain had opened up some very big questions about the nature of authority in the English state" ("James VI and I and Rule over Two Kingdoms," 161).

36 Tucker Brooke, in an earlier translation, rendered "Pictorum" as "of Scotland," but Sutton's translation accurately recognizes that the individual is described not as a subject of a kingdom but as a member of a race considered backward and barbaric.

37 Gager praises James in a verse paragraph, ll. 857–70, that Sutton translates thus: "May we venerate our king with the greatest honor, the delight and glory of our kingdom, the pillar of his people, the sublime soul of the British nation and race, the splendor of his people, born of the high blood of gods, an example of supreme good fortune, virtue, and honor. Him should our estate extol with all its might, revered and venerable, as if a god on earth, whom we believe to be more than mortal, who assuredly wields his scepters in a manner next to that of a god, standing on the highest earthly pinnacle, nearest to them. We think there is some divine power in him. It has seemed to his subjects that not even his voice is human, and our piety is genuine, not false flattery or fawning, it is simple faith, not a slavish gesture" (p. 175). While Brooke's earlier translation of l. 859 acknowledged James as the "Parent" of his country, Sutton's translation loses the Virgilian sense of Gager's word "patriaeque" (l. 859).

38 Vickers, "Epideictic and Epic in the Renaissance," 502.

39 Sidney, *An Apology for Poetry*, 119.

40 See *Freedom of Speech in Early Stuart England*, chs 1 and 2 as well as Richard Cust, "The 'Public Man' in Late Tudor and Early Stuart England."

41 On patronage, see Linda Levy Peck, "'For a king not to be bountiful were a fault.'" On the politics of dedicating printed books and manuscripts to royal patrons, see John A. Buchtel, "'To the Most High and Excellent Prince,'" 104–33, esp. 104–6.

42 Simon Adams, "Faction, Clientage and Party," 35.

43 James's accessibility is disputed. Kevin Sharpe claims that James, in contrast to his son, was "accessible, open to influence" ("Faction at the Early Stuart Court," 41); however, Neil Cuddy cautions that the king's accessibility was illusory

("Anglo-Scottish Union and the Court of James I," 111). On the importance of personal access to the monarch, see also the review article by Robert Shephard, "Court Factions in Early Modern England," 723.

44 [Univoce-catholicus], *Lucta Iacobi*, 32, 38, 38.

45 Since we know very little about Wallace, it is difficult to ascertain what his motives may have been. (Estelle Haan summarizes the scanty information about him in *Phineas Fletcher*, xxxixn110.) The royal dedication, however, suggests that he sought patronage of some kind.

46 Quoted from Haan, "Milton's *In Quintum Novembris* and the Anglo-Latin Gunpowder Epic," 371.

47 The Bye Plot was a conspiracy instigated by the secular priest William Watson to capture the king at Greenwich on midsummer eve of 1603 and extract a promise of toleration from him.

48 "At pater omnipotens, cuius mortalia ab alto / cuncta patent oculis, vitae qui tempus ab aevo / ire necisque iubet mundum ratione gubernans / aeterna, insidias prospexit ab aethere caecas," (ll. 306–9). This seems to be the first reference to the Eye of God, which was to become a standard feature of plot iconography in the 1620s, popularized particularly in Samuel Ward's "Double Deliverance" engraving, withdrawn upon the Spanish ambassador's complaint (see chapter 6). Wallace's fictionalization seems to conform to Sidney's dictum that the poet may change the past to make it more instructive. Wallace seems to have wanted to emphasize how close England had come to disaster.

49 "Utque magis scelus et male sanos horreat ausus / impietas, gentem sceptris exscinde nefandam / tricipitis monstri, diris quae infecta venenis / in scelus inque nefas caeco ruit acta furore, / contemptrixque poli et terrae communis Erinnys, / principibus quae inferre manum sacrisque tiaris / audet ut amoto lucis splendore serenae / involvat miserum tenebris squalentibus orbem," (ll. 408–15).

50 "Magnae Britanniae Regem, Augustam, Principem Henricum totamque Familiam Regiam." Quoted from Haan, "Milton's *In Quintum Novembris* and the Anglo-Latin Gunpowder Epic," 254, 255.

51 Woolf, *The Idea of History in Early Stuart England*, 171–2.

52 Curran, *Roman Invasions*, 18, 19.

53 That Herring uses Britain to indicate the entire island is suggested by his description of Fawkes approaching "the Britons who are divorced from the whole world" (259).

54 "principis et miro collustrat acumine mentem, / solvere quo obscuris perplexa aenigmata nodis / extemplo et facile possit velut Oedipus alter" (ll. 313–15).

55 "Parvus hic octavum cogit meminisse potentem / Henricum, sancto letalia vulnera papae / qui inflixit primus" (ll. 162–4). Herring's version of Protestant history here is decidedly Anglocentric, ignoring Luther and Calvin.

56 "indomito passim turgescere fastu / molirique novas turbas et spargere voces / in vulgum invisas" (ll. 91–3).

57 The rumour that Fawkes had been at court seems to have been fairly widespread, appearing in several poems.

58 "Vos, rerum domini, diras nutritis Echidnas / in gremiis vestris, aulae qui admittitis intra / limina papicolas" (ll. 105–7).

59 Herring does not ignore the problem of the English Catholic exiles, "monsters of men, who rejoice in fishing in a sea disturbed by a swift storm" (263), but Fawkes finds his fellow conspirators in England.

60 Herring, *Popish Pietie or the First Part of the Historie of that Horrible and Barbarous Conspiracie*, A3[r]. I base my assumption that Herring authorized the translation on his contribution of the introduction to the poem. This is not the case with the later translations and "dilations" by John Vicars described below. The title was entered in the Stationers' Register on 2 November 1610, suggesting that Herring, or his translator, was alert to commercial opportunities, timing the publication to cash in on the annual celebration. At the same time, Herring warned in his dedication about the danger of forgetting, a common theme in the wake of Henri IV's assassination. Forgetting is considered a sign of ingratitude to God that puts the entire nation at risk.

61 Later, Herring contributed Latin verses to accompany an etching of the younger Harington that was appended to the published version of his funeral sermon (Richard Stock, *The Churches Lamentation for the losse of the Godly*). On Herring's verses, see Pebworth, "'Let Me Here Use that Freedome,'" 29–30.

62 "Sunt hae Cacodaemonis artes, / non hominum indubie: facinus celare stupendo / exosum scelere, innocuos traducere sontes, / plectere suppliciis summis, pervertere regna / integra et insontum sese satiare cruore" (ll. 260–4).

63 For the disappointment of puritan hopes after the 1604 Hampton Court conference, see Frederick Shriver, "Hampton Court Re-visited." Herring's other works mostly concerned prevention and treatment of the plague. His 1603 treatise (reprinted in 1625, 1636, and in 1641, 1665, and 1757 under a variant title) offered advice on combatting the disease, with special application to the poor. Like many of his contemporaries, Herring saw the plague not simply as a disease, but also as a punishment for sin, and he urged his readers to repent before applying other remedies. He describes the infection as "*not a disease, but a Monster, over matching, and quelling, offtimes both Art and Nature*" (1625, A2[v]). See also Joy Shakespeare, "Plague and Punishment." In 1604, he produced a companion text defending his exhortation against poisoned amulets in the first pamphlet. These were obviously popular pamphlets, regularly reprinted in times of severe plague. The 1625 edition of his earlier pamphlet hints at his political views, concluding his dedication to Charles I: "*The Lord of glory & mercy keep your Highnesse, with your most Honorable Councell of*

Parliament from the rage of this man-slaying Hyrda, and all other both open and secret evills and enemyes, and make you wise and skilfull Physitiās to prevent the dangers, & cure the maladyes of Common-wealth and State" (A2v). Herring's warning reflects what appears to have been a growing dissatisfaction with Stuart political and religious policies.

64 Herring, *Popish Pietie or the First Part of the Historie of that Horrible and Barbarous Conspiracie*, St. 20.

65 McCullough, "Montagu, James (1568–1618)."

66 According to Haan, the first two manuscripts are very similar, while the Harleian differs fairly substantially and is closest to the version that was printed in 1627. Haan's edition is based upon a collation of the 1627 printed texts with notes indicating variants in the earlier manuscript texts. I cite the Latin text, as well as prefatory materials, from her edition by line numbers, and her English translations by page numbers. Based upon a reading of Fletcher's *Eclogues*, Lloyd E. Berry has pieced together the story of Fletcher's father, who died in 1611. The older Fletcher was poorly rewarded for his services and died in debt after participating in the Essex Rebellion. Phineas apparently embarked on a clerical career having been disappointed that his academic one had been unrewarded ("Phineas Fletcher's Account of his Father").

67 According to Peck, it was not unusual for clients to apply to several potential patrons until Buckingham began consolidating patronage after 1615 ("'For a king not to be bountiful,'" 44).

68 "Huc tamen dura et plane ferrea necessitas usque impulit ut ad te hominem facie mihi tantum et fama stipemque timidus quidem sed non omnino exspec flagitarem." Fletcher, *Locustae vel Pietas Iesuitica*, 123.

69 Stanwood, "Fletcher, Phineas (1582–1650)."

70 I quote the 1627 English version of the poem from *The Locusts, or Apollyonists*, in *Poetical Works [by] Giles and Phineas Fletcher* (ed. Frederick Boas). References are to canto and stanza numbers.

71 In fact, Fawkes's parents were both English. He was born to Edward Fawkes and Edith Jackson in York in 1570. Although his parents were apparently both Protestant, his father died when Guy was nine years old, and his mother married Denis Bainbridge (also spelled Dionis Baynbrigge) of Scotton, a recusant (Mark Nicholls, "Fawkes, Guy (*bap.* 1570, *d.* 1606)"). On Fawkes's early history, see also Sharpe, *Remember, Remember*, 48–51.

72 "fors solito lapsos, peccati oblitus, honori / restituet caelumque nobis soliumque relinquet" (ll. 41–2); "accendite pugnas, restaurate acies, fractumque reponite Martem" (ll. 54–5). The first of these passages does not appear in the Sloane ms.

73 "Heu sobolem invisam et fatis maiora Latinis / fata Britannorum!" (ll. 412–13).

74 "qua frangere duros possimus Latiumque ipsis inferre Britannis" (ll. 542–3).

75 "Iam versis Latium florescere fatis / aspicio effoetamque iterum iuvenescere Romam" (ll. 590–1).

76 Allusions to classical Rome and Latium are much reduced in the English version, while allegorical details (such as the depiction of Sin frequently seen as a model for Milton) only appear in the English version.

77 His modern editors provide a broad range of possible dates (1613–19), but suggest that the poem was most likely composed between 1615 and 1618 and presented for this purpose (2–5).

78 A verse dedication was pasted over the original prose dedication in the same manner as smaller corrections were made to the manuscript. The original dedication refers to presentation upon the plot anniversary while the verse dedication alludes to springtime. The editors hypothesize that a delay in completing the manuscript or in opportunities to present it may have rendered the original dedication invalid. See the textual introduction to the Lindley edition (1–2).

79 Campion, *De Pulverea Coniuratione*, "Quo, rex, vsque feres mala tot mitissime multa? Infoelix sibi quem statuet patientia finem? / Iam placabilitas nocet, impunitaque crescet / Nequitia in seram tandem nutrita ruinam" (ll. 181–4). English translation by Robin Sowerby.

80 The outline of Egerton's speech recorded in the *Journals of the House of Lords* (v. 2: 1578–1614, p. 357) indicates that he condemned the attempted treason and credited providence with the deliverance. If the chancellor did dare to chide the king on his religious policies, the *Journals* maintained silence on this indiscretion. A more detailed record of the speech is available in the *Journal of Sir Roger Wilbraham* (printed in *The Camden Miscellany*, 10.72–3). The early part of the speech praised the union of the kingdoms, the king's own abilities, and the queen's fruitfulness all as bulwarks against Catholicism before turning to the subject of the plot. Although he encouraged James to punish the traitors harshly as examples to other Catholics, he appears not to have implied any fault in the king's previous policies. Either Campion invented this detail for his own purposes or had access to a copy of the entire speech, no longer extant.

81 Leicester Bradner proposed that "some time between 1595 and 1619 Campion had secretly joined the Roman Church" ("References to Chaucer in Campion's *Poemata*," 323), which accounted for his failure to print *Elegia I*, *Ad Thamesin*, and *De Pulverea Coniuratione* in his collected Latin works. More recent scholars such as Haan have dismissed Bradner's evidence as unconvincing.

82 The description of the manuscript in the British Library's catalogue indicates that it appears to be holographic. I quote by line reference from the copy printed by F.J. Furnivall in *Ballads from Manuscripts*, 2.39–59. The poem is unusual as an English text written in hopes of royal favour.

83 Richard Williams, "Acclamatio Patrie," in *Ballads from Manuscripts*, 2.39. This assertion must result from either exaggeration or ignorance, since the first poem on the plot, Edward Hawes's *Trayterous Percyes and Catesbyes Prosopopoeia*, appeared very early in

1606. If Williams did present the poem to Prince Henry on the 1612 progress (see note 84, below), and the extant copy postdates that presentation, then Williams's verses joined a large and growing body of poetry on the plot. The Stationers' Register provides no evidence that Williams's poem was ever registered.

84 According to Williams, the king was staying with Sir John Byron at his home (Newstead Abbey) in the forest of Mansfield. On a 1612 progress, the king and Prince Henry met 8 August at Belvoir Castle (the king having arrived on 7 August and his son the following day). The king proceeded to Newstead on 14 August and subsequently to Nottingham on 17 August, arriving in Leicester on the following day. While there are no references to Henry's whereabouts between Belvoir and Leicester, it is likely that he accompanied his father. This occasion seems most likely to be the one Williams refers to (Nichols, *The Progresses, Processions, and Magnificent Festivities*, 2.459–68). Since Henry died in November of that year, it is hardly surprising that Williams had received no response to his presentation. The appeal to the prince, however, suggests that Williams may have associated himself with the godly wing of the church.

85 The reference to the gallows as a pulpit suggests that the poem was written after Father Garnett's trial, in the account of which his prisoner's box had been compared to a pulpit.

86 Northumberland had first come under suspicion early in James's reign for advocating toleration. After that he was suspected of connections to the Main and Bye plots.

87 Salisbury had arranged Pricket's freedom some time before 6 September 1604 ("Cecil Papers: September 1604," *Calendar of the Cecil Papers in Hatfield House, Volume 16: 1604* [1933], 299–323). *Time's Anotomie: Containing: the poore mans plaint, Brittons trouble, and her triumph* (1606) and Salisbury MS. 16.302.

88 Robert Pricket, *The Iesuits Miracles.*

89 In his introduction, the author claims that he could have produced a more polished piece of work had he been permitted more time, but that he had only three hours in which to write the poem, although he gives no reason for this limitation. The sprinkling of Latin phrases in the introduction seems intended to represent him as an educated author. He also promises a sequel after the plotters' trial, but this does not seem to have materialized.

90 The German story is also mentioned by Walter Yonge, who describes it more specifically as an attempt to blow up the Princes Electors at Minden in Westphalia in his account of the plot (*Diary of Walter Yonge*, 4). I have been unable to trace such an event.

91 I.H., *The Divell of the Vault*, B4^{v}.

92 Ibid., C4^{v}. While Jason C. White is correct to notice the references to Britons and Britain scattered through these poems, as I have suggested above it is not always

easy to determine to what extent the authors are consciously including Scotland in these terms.

93 I.H., *The Divell of the Vault*, C4[v].

94 In his letter to the reader (unconventionally placed following the text), Rhodes claims that his book is intended "*for the instruction of the ignorant, and the recreation of others, and not otherwise*" (D[v]), affirming Walsham's observation that more educated individuals might read for amusement works apparently intended for less literate audiences (*Providence in Early Modern England*, 37–8). Those unable to read might become familiar with such texts by hearing them read. Although the idea that the puritans were to be blamed for the explosion seems to have been fairly widespread, this seems to be the only appearance of this particular version of the story in print. It is interesting that while most of these stories rely upon the circulation of oral rumours, Rhodes suggests that the Catholic plotters intended to use print to create an anti-puritan backlash.

95 In 1602 he had published *An Answere to a Romish Rime lately printed*, a series of Protestant responses to Catholic criticisms in simple verse. In this pamphlet's opening letter, "To the indifferent Readers, be they Protestants, Papists, or neyther," he speculates that numerous pamphlets similar to the one he is answering may be being sold by women and pedlars around the country, possibly priests and Jesuits in disguise (*An Answere to a Romish Rime lately printed, and entituled*, A2[r]).

96 Rhodes, *A Briefe Summe of the Treason*, A2[v].

97 Ibid., A2[v], A4[v].

98 Ibid., A4[v].

99 That surprisingly few broadside Gunpowder ballads have been discovered probably indicates a low survival rate of a popular genre rather than a failure to produce such items. For example, John J. McAleer found that few of the twenty-seven ballads on the Armada victory registered between 29 June and 27 November 1588 survive ("Ballads on the Spanish Armada," 608). Demonstrating that additional ballads may continue to surface in manuscript collections, Arthur F. Marotti and Steven W. May recently discovered two ballads describing the official celebration of the Armada defeat ("Two Lost Ballads of the Armada Thanksgiving Celebration"). Hyder Rollins's index to ballad entries in the Stationers' Registers identifies four ballads clearly about the Gunpowder Plot (516, 800, 945, and 2411), and another two that may be related (2149 and 2694). All were licensed between 31 January and 5 May 1606, and the titles indicate that most narrate the plotters' arraignments and executions (*An Analytical Index of the Ballad-Entries (1557–1709) in the Registers of the Company of Stationers of London*). In addition to those Rollins lists is one entered 31 January 1606 ("*Londons gladd tydinges*"). Unlike the Armada ballads, however, ones on the plot continued to be produced or reprinted long after the event, including "Gun-powder Plot: or, A Brief Account of that bloudy and Subtle Design laid against the King, his Lords

and Commons in Parliament, and of a Happy deliverance by Divine Power," clearly printed after 1625, since it identifies James as the late king (reproduced in *Broadside Ballads ... Selected and edited by Lucie Skeaping*, 64–5).

100 Although the priests of the Jesuit mission were English, they belonged to a foreign organization and thus could be described as neither English nor foreign. This ambiguous status made them particularly suspect.

101 Anthony à Wood's list of Vicars's publications identifies the 1617 text as a translation of Francis Herring's poem and records Baker's refusal to license the revision (*Athenae Oxonienses*, 2.86). In his list of Vicars's publications, he does not identify the 1641 poem as a translation, or as the text Baker declined to license, merely noting "'Tis a Poem and printed in a large oct[avo]" (2.86).

102 These include *Jehovah-jireh. God in the mount, or Englands parliamentarie-chronicle* (1644) and *Gods arke overtopping the worlds waves, or the third part of the Parliamentary chronicle* (1645).

103 Wood, *Athenae Oxonienses*, 2.85, 2.86.

104 The *STC* lists a variant edition with a cancel dedication to John Egerton, Earl of Bridgewater. Egerton's association with Buckingham at this time may account for Vicars's change of heart.

105 In a broadsheet published in 1649, Vicars makes an explicit comparison between Jesuits and sectarians: *Speculum scripturale schismaticorum or, A Scripture looking-glasse, most exactly characterizing all sorts of schismaticks* (London, 1649), Wing V329.

106 Herring, *Mischeefes Mysterie*, 43.

107 It is possible that Vicars withdrew the tribute to Henry considering it inappropriate after the prince's death in 1612; however, delicacy seems an inadequate motive when five years had already elapsed since the prince's death.

108 Herring, *Mischeefes Mysterie*, 94.

109 The Latin text was dedicated to Sir Roger.

110 Fletcher also in the English poem makes a veiled allusion to the more open practice of Catholicism in the wake of the queen's arrival (2.34).

111 MacLean assumes that Vicars first attempted (unsuccessfully) to publish his poem during the 1620s (*Time's Witness*, 111), but this raises the question of how Fletcher was able to publish his *Apollyonists* in 1627. Although the answer may be that Fletcher published his poem in Cambridge rather than London, Vicars claims he also approached the university presses. In 1626, Charles I prohibited publication of works contrary to the Church of England, but Clegg points out that "The most interesting feature of press controls in 1627 is that the books the government sought to suppress were not the kind of books that had been prohibited by the 1626 proclamation" (*Press Censorship in Caroline England*, 75). Instead, they were politically motivated works addressing the king or Parliament as literature of counsel. John Guy concurs that Charles was not only unreceptive to advice, but

"doubted the value of counsel itself" ("The Rhetoric of Counsel in Early Modern England," 306). Vicars's text may have been considered offensive in this regard; however, Walsham argues convincingly that it was the book's new illustrations that prevented its approval. She traces two of the illustrations, the frontispiece and a depiction of the annual celebrations, to Michael Sparke's *Crumms of Comfort*, and suggests that these "vulgar depictions of 'Heavens All-seeing Eye' thwarting the fatal designs of 'Fauks and his Father-Satan' can hardly have been aesthetically pleasing to the Laudian regime" (*Providence in Early Modern England*, 264). See ch. 6 for discussion of the illustrations.

112 Vicars in Francis Herring, *November the 5. 1605. The Quintessence of Cruelty*, A3[r]. Prynne also identifies the book as a history, suggesting that Vicars's attempts to claim the veracity of his narrative were successful (*Canterburies Doome*, 184).

113 See A.J. Hegarty, "Crosfield, Thomas (1602–1663)." Frederick S. Boas's printed selections from Crosfield's diary, which he claims comprise about three-quarters of the entries, make no mention of Vicars's attempt to publish the poem; however, the entry for 6 May 1636 records "Certaine Articles II. in number urged upon some Ministers, before their admission into Benefices, together w[t]h Mr H. Burtons answer to some passages of B*isho*p Whites booke of the Doct*rine* of the Sabbath sent to me by Mr Vicars Schoole m*aste*r of Chr*is*ts Hospitall London, whose censure of the times is that, MS are nowe the best help Gods people have to vindicate the Truth, printing being now a dayes prohibited to them, especially if their writings have the least tang or tincture of opposition to Arminianisme yea or even to Poperie itselfe–vide l*itte*ras suas." Vicars's disgruntled tone clearly reflects personal experience (*The Diary of Thomas Crosfield, Selected and edited from the ms. in the Queen's College Library by Frederick S. Boas*, 89).

114 On the provisions of the 1637 decree, see Clegg, *Press Censorship in Caroline England*, esp. ch. 5. The new law also required the licensing of paratextual material, thus recognizing the important role such materials played in textual interpretation.

115 MacLean, *Time's Witness*, 114.

116 *November the 5. 1605. The Quintessence of Cruelty*, 53. Not surprisingly, Vicars has returned to the problem of court Catholicism. On concerns about Catholics at court in this period, see Caroline M. Hibbard, *Charles I and the Popish Plot*, and Clifton, "The Popular Fear of Catholics during the English Revolution."

117 As David Loewenstein points out, monstrosity was frequently associated with rebellion (*Representing Revolution in Milton and his Contemporaries*, ch. 6).

118 Frances Dolan notes that although recusant wives could be imprisoned, and even executed if they refused to swear the Oath of Allegiance or harboured priests, their financial dependence saved them from the more common punishments for praemunire to which men were subject (*Whores of Babylon*, 63).

119 Dolan, *Whores of Babylon*, 43, 52. Similarly, Jeffrey Jerome Cohen offers the thesis that monsters evoke in us both fear and desire ("Monster Culture (Seven Theses)," in *Monster Theory*, 16–20).

120 See Marotti, *Religious Ideology and Cultural Fantasy*, ch. 2; Dolan, *Whores of Babylon*, esp. ch. 1.

121 Several critics have noticed the similarity between this incident and Milton's depiction of the origins of Sin and Death. See especially Quint, "Milton, Fletcher, and the Gunpowder Plot," 262–3.

122 Both Rustici (*The Afterlife of Pope Joan*) and Regina Buccola ("Virgin Fairies and Imperial Whores") have noticed that even in a virulently Protestant text like Dekker's *Whore of Babylon*, Titania and the Whore have more in common than the playwright perhaps would have liked to admit. I discuss Dekker's play in chapter 3. For the rumours that Elizabeth had given birth, see Adam Fox, "Rumour, News and Popular Political Opinion in Elizabethan and Early Stuart England," 614–16.

123 The plot was also described frequently as a Trojan horse, again an image of a sinister and unnatural birth.

124 Fletcher describes the earth as the grandmother of the plotters. On the gendering of London as feminine, see Lawrence Manley, "From matron to monster." Manley argues that the city could be seen as orderly and submissive (matron) or unruly (monster) but that its status midway between nature and culture made it consistently feminine.

125 Dolan, *Whores of Babylon*, 39.

126 Richard F. Hardin also observes Fawkes's ambivalent status as an outsider; however, I disagree with Hardin's conclusion that this makes him a scapegoat ("The Early Poetry of the Gunpowder Plot"). The precedence initially accorded to Fawkes resulted from early assumptions that he had instigated the plot. Once the facts were known, Fawkes's prominence declined until the nineteenth century, when he became as much romantic hero as scapegoat. See, for example, Frank Emson's *The Gunpowder Plot: An Historical Melodrama* (1874), in which Fawkes remains loyal to the plotters, of whom Garnett is the chief, despite his belief that the plan is doomed to failure, and who tries to save the heroine, Viviana Radcliffe, from Catesby's machinations.

127 The change to recording births rather than baptisms occurred during the civil wars.

128 See Marie Hélène Huet, *Monstrous Imagination*, 13–30; Valeria Finucci, "Maternal Imagination and Monstrous Birth," esp. pp. 55–61.

129 Crawford, *Marvelous Protestantism*, 3.

130 The first English edition is Philipp Melanchthon, *Of two wonderful popish monsters to wyt, of a popish asse which was found at Rome in the riuer of Tyber, and of a monkish café, calued at Friberge in Misne*, (1579).

131 Bacon, *A Declaration of the practises & treasons attempted and committed by Robert late Earle of Essex and his complices*, C3[v]. See also Thomas Norton, *To the Quenes Maiesties poore*

deceiued subiects of the northe countrey, E3[v]; Thomas Churchyard, *Come bring in Maye with me*, A2[v].

132 "alter / Proteus in formas facile versatilis omnes. / Pro ratione loci regio nova singula nomen / mutat; mens eadem remanet studiumque nocendi" (ll. 65–7).

133 Punning on the names of the plotters was common to many plot texts, including Richard Williams's "Acclamatio Patriae," in which, for example, Catesby became a "wilye catt" (l. 163) and readers "must grante" (l. 225) that Grant deserved to be hanged.

134 Apparently in an effort to make their Catholicism more recognizable, later writers frequently described Fawkes wearing a crucifix and a hair shirt when he was captured and Catesby clutching an icon as he died.

135 Valeria Finucci traces the providential interpretation of monsters back to Augustine's *De Civitate* in "Maternal Imagination and Monstrous Birth." David Williams takes the tradition back farther, to divergent versions of Genesis 6. Williams points out that "Beyond historical detail the symbolic force of the story of the origin of monsters was meant to express the reality that the evil introduced by the first fratricide survived, and that those who practised such evil became monstrous members of his race." Taking into account the human race's failure to improve even after Christ's death and resurrection, "a particular perspective of history was developed in which it was shown that from the beginning two movements in human history could be discerned, the one virtuous and essentially identical to Christianity, the other evil and a constant contradiction to Christianity," a view expressed most clearly by Augustine (*Cain and "Beowulf,"* 36, 38). On the contested interpretation of prodigies during the Laudian period, see William E. Burns, "Signs of the Times," 21–33.

136 *Prodigies and Apparitions, or Englands warning piece.*

137 In their 1981 article on monstrous births, Park and Daston argued that the religious interpretation of such births gradually died out during the seventeenth century and was replaced by a more scientific attitude. In their more recent book, the authors have revised their previous conclusions to recognize that both interpretations existed simultaneously through this period. See "Unnatural Conceptions" and *Wonders and the Order of Nature 1150–1750*, ch. 5. They note that "the fact that a monster could be explained by natural causes did not always disqualify it as a prodigy" (*Wonders*, 192).

138 Katharine Park and Lorraine J. Daston, "Unnatural Conceptions," 25–6.

139 On this development, see also Paul Christianson, *Reformers and Babylon*, 15–44.

140 Lake, "The Significance of the Elizabethan Identification of the Pope as Antichrist," 164. For a detailed discussion of the debates over Rome's status as a true or false church and the pope's identity as the Antichrist in this period, see Anthony Milton, *Catholic and Reformed*, chs 2 and 3.

141 According to Capp, "The role of the godly prince in protecting religious truth was central to Elizabethan thought" (95). Christianson, however, observes that before Elizabeth's accession, some subjects were sceptical about the monarch's role in preserving religion (*Reformers and Babylon* 11, 31).

142 See ch. 5.

143 On anti-Catholic satire in *Paradise Lost*, see John N. King, *Milton and Religious Controversy*.

144 Some epigrams did flatter their subjects. Stradling's Gunpowder epigrams in *Epigrammatum Libri Quattuor* (1607) praise the king and Lord Monteagle. Milton also praised James in one of his epigrams and Campion congratulated Donne on his *Ignatius His Conclave*. For a discussion of Stradling's epigrams, see Haan, *Locustae vel Pietas Iesuitica*, xxiii–xxiv.

145 Haan, in *Locustae vel Pietas Iesuitica*, xxi.

146 On the nature of the epigram in the seventeenth century, see Hoyt Hopewell Hudson, *The Epigram in the English Renaissance*; Daniel Russell, "The Genres of Epigram and Emblem"; Mary Thomas Crane, "*Intret Cato*." On the political uses of epigrams in this period, see James Doelman, "Epigrams and Political Satire in Early Stuart England." Doelman notes that epigrams, unlike satire, might contain both compliment and criticism. A poet could "combine the two halves of the epigram's epideictic project into a single short poem, which might be read as either praise or blame" (39).

147 Johnson published his in *Epigrammatum Libellus* (1615). Thomas Cooper prefaced a Latin treatise on the plot with a series of epigrams (*Nonae Novembris Aeternitati Consecratae*, 1607). See Haan, *Phineas Fletcher*, xxii–xxv.

148 The repetition of the same themes throughout the anti-Jesuit epigrams composed on the Gunpowder Plot may not be surprising when we consider Doelman's observation that political epigrams in particular tended to become common property. He suggests that it "would be best to assume that most political epigrams of the period went through an initial period of mixed transmission, during which they were both written down and posted, and then also remembered and passed along by word of mouth, perhaps once again to be written down" ("Circulation of the Late Elizabethan and Early Stuart Epigram," 63). On the academic epigram tradition, see Hudson, *The Epigram in the English Renaissance*, ch. 4.

149 Crane, "*Intret Cato*," 170, 171.

150 Manley, "Proverbs, Epigrams, and Urbanity in Renaissance London," 266–8.

151 Manley suggests that "As its neat devices begin to soften and expand, the epigram admits to a difference between the order it desires and the alien, mysterious life that order would contain" ("Proverbs, Epigrams, and Urbanity in Renaissance London," 275). Herring may have included the epigram as a compliment to Sir John Harington, to whom he had dedicated the second part of the poem, since Harington's

uncle was a noted epigrammatist. See *Epigrams both pleasant and serious*, 1615. Many of Harington's epigrams in this collection are also lengthier, although still significantly shorter than Herring's poem.

152 Herring, *November the 5. 1605. The Quintessence of Cruelty*, 98. Coke's speech at Garnett's trial accused the Jesuits of "Dissimulation, Deposing of Princes, Disposing of Kingdomes, Daunting and deterring of subiects, and Destruction" (*A True and Perfect Relation*, T2[r]).

153 Curiously, in the epic the plan to shift the blame to the puritans confirms the monstrosity of the plotters' design.

154 D. Harris Willson notes that although James overcame his initial reluctance to perform the touching ceremony, he remained sceptical of the royal power to heal scrofula. See *King James VI and I*, 172–3.

155 On Milton's epigrams, see Stella Revard (*Milton and the Tangles of Neaera's Hair*, 54–6), who reads them as "epitaphs" for the newly deceased James but admits it is "curious" that they are modelled on "satiric epitaphs from the late fifteenth and early sixteenth century that mocked controversial popes" (55). She concedes that since his "questions indirectly warn that the Catholic conspiracy of 1605 could recur in the England of 1626" (56), he may be issuing a warning to the new king.

156 The reference appears to be to James's 1621/2 *Declaration Touching his Proceedings in the late assemblie and conuention of Parliament* in which the king sarcastically told the house "*So as this plenipotencie of yours invests you in all power vpon Earth, lacking nothing but the Popes to haue the keyes also both of Heauen and Purgatory*," 23–4). This context is potentially interesting as James complains in this document of Parliament's lack of gratitude for his peaceful reign and their obstreperousness on the subject of a Catholic marriage for Charles. Haan's analysis of similarities between Milton's poem and Herring's suggests that Milton was familiar with the earlier poem ("Milton's *In Quintum Novembris*, 221–47).

157 While one could assume that Campion is referring to the original expulsion of the Romans from the island, his failure to identify an occasion leaves the reference open to interpretation.

158 Vida, *Christiad*, 1.133; 1.184.

159 This is likely the origin of Fletcher's Satan's apprehension that the spread of Protestant piety to the New World may be followed by its arrival in hell itself.

160 On earlier Christian and classical sources that influenced Vida and Tasso, see Olin H. Moore, "The Infernal Council."

161 Lewalski, *Milton's Brief Epic*, 20. For a detailed examination of the epic characteristics Milton might have seen in the book of Job, see Charles W. Jones, "Milton's 'Brief Epic.'"

162 This model would account for James's passivity in Milton's *In Quintum Novembris*, which most commentators have considered complimentary to the king. It seems to

me, however, that James as king is in a different position than Job, and is responsible to take a more active role in protecting the country. Nevertheless, Hale observes that Satan's flight above the earth at the beginning of *In Quintum Novembris* is modelled on Job.

163 "Deducus hic uero indignum miseratus Apollo / Res lapsas sarcire parat: foedaeque ruinae / Rudera in Hesperiam magnam sublecta reponit" (ll. 60–2). William Alabaster, *Elisæ*, 25.

164 The most comprehensive study of these texts as Menippean satire remains Benjamin Boyce's "News from Hell."

165 As we have seen above, Fawkes is frequently characterized as a shape-shifter or Proteus.

166 Dekker, *Newes from Hell*, F4[r].

167 *The returne of the knight of the poste from Hell*, D4[r].

168 As late as 1614, John Taylor, the water poet, in a pamphlet entitled *The Nipping and Snipping of Abvses* that includes "A Proclamation from Hell in the Deuils name concerning the propagation, and excessive vse of Tobacco," extends his compliment to James with a short poem praising him on his deliverance from the Gunpowder Plot.

169 Unlike later pamphlets, this one works from the assumption that Rome was once a true church and lost that status by becoming obsessed with worldly domination, the main theme of Northampton's speech at the lay plotters' trial.

170 Beringer, *The Romane Conclaue*, A2[r–v].

171 Other examples of this genre include George Carleton's *Vrisdiction Regall, Episcopall, Papall* (London, 1610) and William Fennor's *Pluto his Travailes, or the Diuels Pilgrimage to the Colledge of Iesuites* (London, 1612).

172 Stefania Tutino notes that *Ignatius* was reprinted five times in English between 1611 and 1652, but not in Latin until 1680 ("Notes on Machiavelli and Ignatius Loyola in John Donne's *Ignatius his Conclave* and *Pseudo-Martyr*," 1309).

173 On *Ignatius* as Menippean satire, see Eugene Korkowski, "Donne's *Ignatius* and Menippean Satire," 419–38; Reuben Sanchez, "Menippean Satire and Competing Prose Styles in *Ignatius His Conclave*."

174 Flynn argues for Donne's friendship with Northumberland on the basis of Izaak Walton's identification of Northumberland as the messenger who conveyed news of Donne's marriage to his unsuspecting father-in-law. See "Donne's *Ignatius his Conclave* and Other Libels on Robert Cecil."

175 Donne, *Ignatius His Conclave*, 11.

176 Ibid., 25, 29, 31.

177 Flynn, "Donne's *Ignatius his Conclave* and Other Libels on Robert Cecil," 172, 174.

178 Campion must then be considered an early reader of *Ignatius*, quite likely in Latin. The wit of the Latin epigram is, as Estelle Haan points out, lost in translation. The original reads: *Alludens ad Ignati conclaue / Ioh:Dun Doct:Theol:/ Dun taxat libro Iesuitas*

non tamen vno / Duntaxat, lingua ridet at Ausonia;/ Ausonia in lingua semel est dun sillaba prima / Duntaxat, primas Dun vbi taxat habet. Haan translates this as: *Alluding to Ignatius his Conclave / John Donne, Doctor of Theology / Donne taxes the Jesuits not however in one book / Simply [when he (Donne) taxes] but he mocks them in the Latin language; / In the Latin language 'dun' is the first syllable once / Simply [of duntaxat], when Donne taxes he has more than one first.* Haan interprets the epigram's final line as indicating that Donne has "taxed" or castigated the Jesuits twice, once in *Pseudo-Martyr* (in English) and once in *Ignatius* (in Latin).

179 Abaddon in the Old Testament is equivalent to Sheol, the place of the dead. In the New Testament (Rev. 9.11), however, Abaddon is personified as the angel who rules the land of the dead and directs the locusts who hunt and destroy men. His Greek name is Apollyon, the name used by Fletcher in the title of his 1627 English version of his epic, while Fletcher's Latin title, *Locustae*, refers to his followers (*International Standard Bible Encyclopedia*, 1.2).

180 Campion, *De Pulverea Coniuratione (On the Gunpowder Plot)*, 41. "Res Britonum dubias, oleaque per omnia pacem / Ire coronatam, templis accrescere sacros / Cultus, laetitiam siluis resonare, decusque / Multiplici pompa replere palatia et vrbes" (ll. 36–40).

181 Campion, *De Pulverea Coniuratione (On the Gunpowder Plot)*, 41. "vltro jam ponere suetas / Hesperios jras, [sociasque extendere dextras; / Nunc et Hybernorum requiescere conscia tela, / Nullum adeo superesse locum crepitantibus armis, / Seu tacitae fraudi" (ll. 42–6).

182 Campion, *De Pulverea Coniuratione (On the Gunpowder Plot)*, 89. "Impendere illis communem fingite cladem, / Occulte peragi rem, maturamque minari / Vim subitam, nisi vi contra maturius itur" (ll. 380–2).

183 Fletcher, *Locustae vel Pietas Iesuitica*, 9. "Illi castra olim numero farcibat inerti / crescens in ventrem monachus, simul agmine iuncti / tonsi ore et tonsi lunato vertice fratres. / At nunc felici auspicio Iesuitica princeps / agmina ducebat veteranoque omnia late / depopulans magnas passim infert milite clades" (ll. 110–15).

184 Fletcher, *Locustae vel Pietas Iesuitica*, 34–5. "Hic tragicae prologus scenae – maiora paramus: / non facinus vulgare sero quod nulla tacebit, / credetnulla dies; magnum populisque tremendum / omnibus incepto."

185 Northampton's speech in the published account of Garnett's trial may have been the source of this idea, since by linking Garnett's arrival in England with the Armada, the earl implied that treachery had always been the purpose of the English mission.

186 J.M., *Newes from hell, Rome and the Innes of Court*, 2. Although this pamphlet has been attributed to Milton, the attribution is considered apocryphal.

187 *Hells Triennial Parliament*, 1, 2.

188 Francis Wortley, *Mercurius Britanicus his Welcome to Hell*, 3, 6.

189 John Taylor, *Mercvrivs Infernalis, or Orderlesse Orders*, 2.

190 When the plot was paired with the Armada, it also drew attention to the failure of attempts to subvert God's plans for England. The association of Fawkes with Ravaillac was more ambiguous, since Ravaillac had been successful in assassinating Henri IV.

191 Taylor, *Mercvrivs Infernalis, or Orderlesse Orders*, 1, 2.

192 See, for example, *Now or never: or, A new Parliament of women assembled and met together neer the Popes-Head in Moor-Fields, on the Back-side of Allsuch; adjoyning upon Shoreditch* (London, 1656) and a series of pamphlets by Henry Neville including *The Ladies Parliament* (1647), *An Exact Diurnall of the Parliament of Ladyes* (1647), and *The Ladies, a Second Time Assembled in Parliament* (1647).

5. "fit audience find, though few": Militant Protestants and Wandering Ways

1 Although the poem is undated, the heading "Anno Aetatis 17" points to 1626 as the composition date.

2 On the reasons why Charles's attempts at religious unity failed, see Conrad Russell, "The British Problem and the English Civil War."

3 Cogswell, *The Blessed Revolution*, 16.

4 In August 1622, John Chamberlain reported: "And now to make a compleat geol-deliverie all priests, Jesuites, or other papists imprisoned are set at libertie and are not henceforward to be troubled, for sayeng or (as I heare the words go) prayeng of masse, or refusing the oath of allegeance or supremacie and the like" (*Letters of John Chamberlain* 2.449). On the increasingly open practice of Catholicism in London in 1623, see Cogswell, *The Blessed Revolution*, 37–49.

5 D'Ewes, *The Diary of Sir Simonds D'Ewes (1622–1624)*, 162.

6 Hacket, *A Century of Sermons upon Several Remarkable Subjects Preached by the Right Reverend Father in God, John Hacket*, 751.

7 According to the author of *Something Written*, at least one hundred people were killed, but there is no reliable estimate of the casualties. According to most accounts, the curious Protestants who had formed at least part of the audience sneaked away if they were unharmed.

8 For a comprehensive listing of pamphlets, see Walsham, "'The Fatall Vesper,'" 41n6.

9 Although scholars have observed that doctrines regarding hell were not a major site of contention between Catholics and Protestants after the Reformation, there was some difference of opinion on the geographic location of the place of torment. Because Catholics generally located it within the earth, their hell had a finite space and was therefore subject to concerns about overcrowding. Protestants, in contrast, did not maintain a consistent opinion on the location of hell, a strategy that Marshall suggests "was in large measure intended to disrupt and disparage" the Catholic system with its multiple afterlife destinations" ("The Reformation of Hell?" 295). See

also: Rasmussen, "Hell Disarmed? The Function of Hell in Reformation Spirituality"; Patrides, *Premises and Motifs in Renaissance Thought and Literature*, ch. 11; Marshall, "'The map of God's word.'" Milton dramatizes the distance between heaven and hell in one of his epigrams on the plot, suggesting that while the plotters had attempted to consign James to the infernal regions, he had ascended to heaven instead.

10 While some Protestants gloated, others recognized that delighting in others' misfortunes could seem uncharitable and mitigated their enthusiasm. Sir Simonds D'Ewes is clearly torn between his delight in the working out of providence and his humanity when he records in his diary: "Wee must iudge charitablye of this, yett sure it was the speciall worke of God" (*The Diary of Sir Simonds D'Ewes (1622–1624)*, 168).

11 The sole Latin poem to survive from this occasion seems to have been Alexander Gil's *In Ruinam Camerae Papisticae*, which utilized the story of Samson and may have been a source for Milton's *Samson Agonistes*. Gil's father, Alexander Gil the Elder, taught Milton at St Paul's School, and 1628 Latin letters between Milton and the younger Gil indicate they exchanged their poetry (Donald Lemen Clark, "Milton's Schoolmasters," 122–3).

12 As we will see in chapter 6, public Gunpowder sermons, which may have decreased in frequency during the Caroline period, became a tool of opposition clerics.

13 Crashaw wrote three English poems and an epigram. The longer poems are largely non-narrative and so do not fall within the scope of this discussion. See *The Complete Poetry of Richard Crashaw*, 74, 458–63.

14 While John K. Hale suggests that interest in the Gunpowder Plot was declining in this period ("Milton and the Gunpowder Plot," 355–6), as we have seen, interest had in fact been renewed by the Blackfriars incident; however, it manifested itself more in providential histories such as Carleton's than in epic poetry.

15 *Novembris Monstrum*, t.p.

16 The variety of stanzaic forms suggests that this was either a group effort or a text that evolved over time or both.

17 Although the volume is continuously paginated, this poem has a separate title page and is preceded by a note to the reader.

18 John K. Hale, "Milton and the Gunpowder Plot," 352.

19 Steadman, *Milton and the Paradoxes of Renaissance Heroism*, 188.

20 Critical explorations of the relationship between *In Quintum Novembris* and *Paradise Lost* range from Estelle Haan's identification of the ways in which Milton translated Latin phrases in the earlier poem into English ones in the later work ("The 'Adorning of My Native Tongue,'" 64) to Paul Stevens's observation that "the earlier poem provides a template for the plot of the later one" ("Milton and National Identity," 349).

21 David Quint, *Epic and Empire*, 281; John K. Hale, "Milton and the Gunpowder Plot," 353, 366.

22 Milton, *In Quintum Novembris*, 15. English references to this poem are to Merritt Y. Hughes's translation and both English and Latin references are to page numbers (*Complete Poems and Major Prose*, 15–21).

23 "James VI and I and Rule over Two Kingdoms," 151–63. Cuddy argues that Edwin Sandys proposed to Parliament a "perfect" union that would subordinate Scotland, intending to scupper the entire union debate ("Anglo-Scottish Union and the Court of James I, 1603–1625," 115).

24 The idea that Satan inhabits the north seems to originate in Isaiah 14.13, in which the prophet charges Satan: "You said in your heart, 'I will ascend to heaven; above the stars of God I will set my throne on high; I will sit on the mount of assembly in the far north" (RSV). In *Paradise Lost*, the unfallen Satan takes possession of "The Quarters of the North" (5.689), from which he plots against God.

25 David Loewenstein cautions against reading radicalism back into Milton's early poetry, warning that "a view that transforms the young Milton into a radical, who from the beginning consistently blasts the establishment ... presents the danger of creating a monolithic, schematic account of his early career – one that can too easily flatten out or overlook contradictory and heterogeneous impulses in the writings rather than recognizing the complexity and ambiguity of his attitudes" ("'Fair Offspring Nurs't in Princely Lore'").

26 Thomas Cogswell (*The Blessed Revolution*, 12–14) suggests that James inherited a myth of English military, particularly naval, supremacy that proved dangerous to the king, whose inclinations towards peace were probably influenced by an empty treasury as well as a distaste for religious warfare. See W.B. Patterson, who credits the king with a sincere desire to act as a peacemaker; but see also Arnold Hunt's review in which he suggests Patterson may have been seduced by James's rhetoric (*King James VI and I and the Reunion of Christendom*; "A Jacobean Consensus?" 132–4). N.A.M. Rodger similarly finds that this myth hurt the early Stuarts but also explicitly connects it to a Protestant world view ("Queen Elizabeth and the Myth of Sea-Power in English History," esp. 153–60). Susan Krantz suggests that Dekker's post-plot play *The Whore of Babylon* implicitly critiques James's pacifism by praising Elizabeth's militarism: "Thomas Dekker's Political Commentary in *The Whore of Babylon*," 279.

27 On the situation in Europe, see Peter H. Wilson, *Europe's Tragedy*. Wilson notes that the Cadiz failure "damaged Britain's standing in Europe and reduced Charles I's credibility as an ally" (369); for the troubles of Mansfeld's troops, see p. 365.

28 While one can read the poem as an expression of hope that Charles will revive the nation's glory, Milton's failure to mention Charles suggests this is not the case. On Buckingham's situation during the spring of 1626, see Roger Lockyer, *Buckingham: The Life and Political Career of George Villiers*, ch. 8).

29 Despite the wealth of studies on Milton's attitudes to and representations of history, I am aware of none that include significant discussions of *In Quintum Novembris*.

30 Loewenstein, *Milton and the Drama of History*, 82. He cites "Prolusion III" ("History, when it is handsomely related, can allay and compose the anxious troubles of the mind or anoint it with joy or, again, evoke tears, but gentle and calm tears, tears that bring a strange pleasure with their flow," 605) as evidence that Milton "is remarkably sensitive not only to the effect of rhetoric and embellishment in historical narrative, but to its poetic and emotive power – especially when it is well narrated" (82).

31 Parry, "Milton's *History of Britain* and the Seventeenth-Century Antiquarian Scene," 245.

32 "Continuoque omni comites ex agmine lectos / aulae subiectas aedes infernaque tecta /timando semel atque iterum explorare iubebat" (ll. 339–41, pp. 386–7).

33 "Ille oculo nodos facili scelerumque nefandas / percurrens animo ambages (dum nubila spargit / lux lucis mentemque aperit), mox omnia pandit / monstra aperitque nefas solus tenebrasque resolvit" (ll. 750–3). English translation by Haan, *Locustae vel Pietas Iesuitica*, 47.

34 "Cupio cognoscere quinam / vicinas habitent aedes, num cellula quaevis / aulae subiaceat. Primo me tempore certum / rebus de his facite, accurata indagine facta" (ll. 343–6). English translation by Haan, "Milton's *In Quintum Novembris* and the Anglo-Latin Gunpowder Epic," 273.

35 Herring, *Mischeefes Mysterie: or Treasons Masterpeece, the Powder-plot. Translated and very much dilated by John Vicars*, 42, 43.

36 In general, the focus upon classical elements in the poem has obscured attention to its contemporary contexts. Even John K. Hale, who situates the poem within events at Cambridge, for example, puzzles over Milton's choice to have Satan disguise himself as a Franciscan rather than a Jesuit. This decision makes sense, however, when we consider that in 1625 Henrietta Maria had arrived with an entourage of Capuchins, an order related to the Franciscans.

37 Dzelzainis, "'The Feminine part of every Rebellion,'" 145.

38 See *The Essays or Counsels Civil and Moral*, 142. For the earlier interpretation of Fama, see *The Two Bookes of Francis Bacon*, 2.19.

39 Dzelzainis, "'The Feminine part of every Rebellion,'" 148.

40 See Adam Fox, "Rumour, News and Popular Political Opinion in Elizabethan and Early Stuart England"; also Lemon, *Treason by Words*.

41 In addition to Muggli, see Joad Raymond, *Pamphlets and Pamphleteering in Early Modern Britain*, 138–43.

42 William W.E. Slights explores Jonson's concerns with the boundaries between public and private information in *Ben Jonson and the Art of Secrecy*.

43 See Richard Cust, "News and Politics in Early Seventeenth-Century England"; Cogswell, *The Blessed Revolution*, 27.

44 Rockwood, "'Know thy side,'" 148.

45 Joseph Loewenstein, "Pennyboy's Delight," 341–2.

46 "Sed tamen a nostro meruisti carmine laudes / Fama, bonum quo non aliud veracius ullum, / Novis digna cani, nec te memorasse pigebit / Carmine tam longo" (ll. 194–7). Paul Stevens finds the discovery of the plot through "the confused words of rumour" anti-climactic, another reason why Milton might have felt compelled to defend his choice. Clearly, this was a deliberate decision and needs to be understood as significant to the interpretation of the poem ("Milton and National Identity," 350).

47 For Burbery's full argument, see "John Milton Blackfriars Spectator?"; *Milton the Dramatist*, 1–17.

48 "Et primo Angliacas solito de more per urbes / Ambiguas voces, incertaque murmura spargit, / Ambiguas voces, incertaque murmura spargit, / Mox arguta dolos, et detestabile vulgat / Proditionis opus, nec non facta horrida dictu, / Authoresque addit sceleris, nec garrula caecis / Insidiis loca structa silet" (ll. 211–16). John Demaray sees Milton's depiction of Fama introducing a theatrical element into the poem's epic structure, leading to generic confusion and aesthetic failure ("Gunpowder and the Problem of Theatrical Heroic Form," 11).

49 As Dzelzainis's article on Bacon suggests, writers regarded rumour negatively because they associated it with popular rebellion. David Loewenstein points out that Milton, like Bacon, saw an integral relationship between revolt and the misuse of language (*Representing Revolution in Milton and his Contemporaries*, ch. 6). Scholars have had difficulty pinning down Milton's attitudes to popular political participation partly because his definition of "the people" is not easy to assess. While Annabel Patterson has described Milton as an "Elitist radical" who was suspicious of the uneducated masses, others have noted in texts such as "Areopagitica" a desire for an informed and educated populace capable of political participation ("'Forc'd fingers,'" 22). Hugh Jenkins notes that Milton's definition of the people in *The Second Defense* has been regarded, perhaps justifiably, as elitist, but concludes that ultimately for Milton the English people "are what they can make themselves as well as what they can be made into" ("'Quid nomine populi intelligi velimus'"). Similarly, Sharon Achinstein argues that "Milton never gave up on the people of England" (*Milton and the Revolutionary Reader*, 14).

50 This also seems to be the direction in which Vicars is taking Herring's poem.

51 Quint, *Epic and Empire*, 95–6.

52 "cum late placidas urbes pacataque regna, / tranquilla et populos degentes pace videret, / quemque sua sub vite saeque sub arboris umbra / auspiciis" (ll. 22–5). "Hesperiae disiectam ulciscere classem" (102).

53 "Anglia Romanum fiscum provincia dives / litibus assiduis auxit magis omnibus una" (ll. 36–7).

54 "Dum cathedram, venerande, tuam diademaque triplex / Ridet Hyperboreo gens barbara nata sub axe / Dumque pharetrati spernunt tua iura Britanni" (ll. 94–6).

55 Herring's corrections in the first part are mainly minor revisions to wording. The most substantial changes are the insertion of two new lines at the introduction of Fawkes to explain that while he is introduced first he is not the most important conspirator, and a change of speakers that allows Catesby rather than Fawkes to propose the plot, since the original poem had been written when Fawkes was considered the primary conspirator.
56 Quint, *Epic and Empire*, 9.
57 Parker, "Dilation and Delay," 520.
58 Nigel Smith notes that Vicars's newsbooks were "written in the sermon rhetoric of popular puritanism" (*Literature and Revolution in England 1640–1660*, 340). The standard source for the technique in the Renaissance was Longinus's *On the Sublime*, sections 11 and 12.
59 Albert J. Loomie discusses Fawkes's dealings with Spain in *Guy Fawkes in Spain.*
60 The emblem that precedes the text also includes Spain as one of the figures attempting to subvert England.
61 In addition, Vicars removes tributes to both Elizabeth and Prince Henry from the concluding materials that Herring had introduced into the 1609 edition.
62 Sutton concludes that the change to Catesby as instigator of the plot "was ruinous to the literary effect Herring originally strove to create," since it shifted responsibility for the plot from a supernatural to a human agent, thus rendering the demonic machinery superfluous ("Milton's," 364).
63 Parker, *Inescapable Romance*, 77.
64 Lake, "The Significance of the Elizabethan Identification of the Pope as Antichrist," 169. Although Lake notes that the visible church could not attain victory over the Antichrist, Vicars's version of Protestant nationalism seems to credit the English church with this final victory.
65 Parker, *Inescapable Romance*, 58.
66 Herring, *Mischeefes Mysterie*, 94.
67 Helen Cooper, *The English Romance in Time*, 25.
68 Herring, *Mischeefes Mysterie*, 74.
69 Ibid., 88.
70 MacLean, *Time's Witness*, 105.
71 Herring, *Mischeefes Mysterie*, 73.
72 See, for example, the first of Campion's epigrams.
73 Quint, *Epic and Empire*, 34.
74 It is also possible that Vicars, on some level, identified with the disempowered Catholics because of his own marginal position as a presbyterian.
75 Herring, *Mischeefes Mysterie*, A^{r}. It is worth noting that Vicars does not limit those addressed, as is customary, to readers, but addresses all Protestants, and that he also implicitly connects Protestantism with political loyalty.

76 Corbett and Lightbown, *The Comely Frontispiece*, 3.
77 Daniel Russell notes that the length of the emblem text remained flexible, but that the texts generally became longer as the epigram became a separate genre. See "The Genres of Epigram and Emblem."
78 Fowler, "The Emblem as a Literary Genre," 8–9.
79 On the uses of the Renaissance emblem both in literature and decoration, see Rosemary Freeman, *English Emblem Books*, esp. ch. 4.
80 Amos, *Early Theories of Translation*, 99.
81 Franklin B. Williams Jr, "Commendatory Verses," 7.
82 Nathaniel Chambers mentions in his verse that he does not know Vicars personally. Some of the verses are signed only with initials, making identification difficult.
83 John Speed also used the word "mischiefs" to describe the plot in his *History of Great Britaine* (1614), 889.
84 Contemporary meanings of "mischief" include the following: "Harm or evil considered as attributable to a particular agent or cause. Freq. to do mischief and variants (esp. in early use)" (*OED* II.2.a.); "Originally: a disease or ailment; sickness. Later (chiefly *Med.*): a pathological condition or process. *Obs.*" (*OED* II.3.); "Evildoing, wickedness. *Obs.*" (*OED* III.5). For the full range of contemporary meanings, see the *OED*.
85 This seems to have been an ongoing concern for Vicars. In an address to the readers of his 1644 pamphlet, *Babylons beautie*, he explicitly informs his readers that the title is ironic and that he actually plans to make them loathe Catholicism.
86 Slights, "The Edifying Margins of Renaissance English Books," 697.
87 As Walsham has pointed out, the source of the illustration is Michael Sparke's *Crumms of Comfort* (*Providence in Early Modern England*, 264).
88 See *Reading History in Early Modern England*, 82–4.
89 I have been unable to trace this individual.
90 On the case against Pickering, see Alastair Bellany, "A Poem on the Archbishop's Hearse"; and Philip Hamburger, "The Development of the Law of Seditious Libel and the Control of the Press," esp. pages 690–4. Bellany also summarizes Pickering's career in the *ODNB* ("Pickering, Lewis (*bap.* 1571)."
91 Bellany, "Pickering, Lewis (*bap.* 1571)."
92 It also seems unlikely that the plotting would have been allowed to continue unless the king himself was complicit in a sham plot.
93 Pickering was born into a puritan family in Northamptonshire and attended Emmanuel College, Cambridge (Bellany, "Pickering, Lewis (*bap.* 1571)"). Keyes's father was a Protestant minister at Stavely, Derbyshire, while "his mother was a Catholic relative of Lady Ursula Babthorpe. He was converted by the Jesuits. His wife was governess at Turvey (Bedfordshire) to the children of the Catholic Lord Mordaunt" (Haynes, *The Gunpowder Plot*, 49–50).

94 Privy Council, "Abstract, including large Excerpts of the Privy Council Registers, from 1550 to 1610" (BL Add. MS 11402, f. 108r).

95 Mark Nicholls mentions that Vaux was discharged on Pickering's bond, but does not propose any explanation. See "Vaux, Anne (*bap.* 1562, *d.* in or after 1637)."

96 MacLean, *Time's Witness*, 115.

97 The most extensive study of the couplet remains William Bowman Piper's *The Heroic Couplet.* On the "conversational" tone of the couplet, see J. Paul Hunter, "Couplets and Conversation."

98 J. Paul Hunter, "Couplets and Conversation," 25.

99 Another indication that Vicars was moving the poem down the social scale is the change from quarto format in 1617 to octavo in 1641.

100 The 1617 edition is approximately 3486 lines, while the 1641 is approximately 3034 lines.

101 Herring, *November the 5. 1605. The Quintessence of Cruelty*, 46.

102 Historians remain divided on the question of whether there really was a tunnel. James Sharpe cautiously states that "[t]he plotters apparently planned to dig a tunnel" (*Remember, Remember*, 55), while Antonia Fraser argues that the story of the tunnel was invented to vilify Catholics, and Alan Haynes accepts the existence of the tunnel. Fraser points out the practical difficulties of concealing the excavated earth in support of her argument.

103 Early in the second part, Vicars also eliminates a lengthy digression (pp. 62–7 of the 1617 edition) that includes representing the plot as a tragedy.

104 On the fears of popish plots in this period, see Caroline M. Hibbard, *Charles I and the Popish Plot* and Robin Clifton, "The Popular Fear of Catholics during the English Revolution."

105 The latter is the second illustration that had appeared previously in Sparke's *Crumms of Comfort.*

106 Vicars in *November the 5. 1605. The Quintessence of Cruelty*, A3r.

107 See James Sims, *The Bible in Milton's Epics* on Milton's use of the Bible, particularly his list of biblical references in *Paradise Lost*, 259–73.

108 Loewenstein, *Representing Revolution*, 198.

109 Rawson, "Mock-heroic and English Poetry," 170.

110 Rawson notes that although injuries occur in Milton's epic, no one is killed. He suggests that Milton switched from the heroic to the mock-heroic mode in "mid-poem" because he had become disillusioned with the epic genre ("War and the Epic Mania in England and France," 434).

111 Murrin, *History and Warfare in Renaissance Epic*, 132.

112 J.R. Hale, "Gunpowder and the Renaissance," 391–2.

113 Ralegh, *History of the World*, bk. 5.

114 For a detailed examination and debunking of the "Legend of Black Berthold," see J.R. Partington, *A History of Greek Fire and Gunpowder*, ch. 3. Partington concludes

that guns are mentioned and pictured in English and Italian documents before they appear in German ones.

115 Samuel Daniel, *Civile Wars*, 5.29 (all references cited by book and stanza numbers). According to J.R. Hale, this idea originated with John Mirfield, c.1390 ("Gunpowder and the Renaissance," 394).

116 This material becomes part of Book 6 in the better known edition of 1609 (re-printed 1623).

117 See Merritt Hughes' notes on this epigram in *John Milton: Complete Poems and Major Prose* 14.

118 Revard, *The War in Heaven*, 88.

119 See Revard, "Milton's Gunpowder Poems and Satan's Conspiracy"; *The War in Heaven.*

120 John N. King, *Milton and Religious Controversy*, 115–20.

121 Although critics generally accept its influence upon *Paradise Lost*, Milton probably did not have access to Fletcher's poem before he wrote *In Quintum Novembris.*

122 Quint, "Milton, Fletcher, and the Gunpowder Plot," 261.

123 Nevertheless, the fallen angels are persistently associated with mining. In hell, one of their first actions is to commence mining the resources of their new abode to create Pandemonium.

124 See Lieb, *The Dialectics of Creation*; Lehnhof, "Scatology and the Sacred in Milton's *Paradise Lost*," and "'Intestine War' and 'the smell of Mortal Change.'" It is worth remembering that saltpetre, one ingredient of gunpowder, was frequently produced from excrement leaching into soil.

125 See also Paul Wake, "A Monster Shapeless," on equivocation in the Gunpowder Plot trials.

126 Milton, *The Tenure of Kings and Magistrates*, in *John Milton: Complete Poems and Major Prose*, 751. On misuses of language in Cromwellian propaganda, see Sharon Achinstein, "The Uses of Deception."

127 See Bedford, "Milton's Military Heaven Revisited," esp. 130–9; Hill, *Milton and the English Revolution*, 372–3.

128 John R. Hale, however, points out that opposition to artillery was standard in literature, whereas no one seriously suggested giving it up in military contexts ("Gunpowder and the Renaissance").

129 Canino, "The Discourse of Hell," 21.

130 Hill, *Milton and the English Revolution*, 373.

131 David Loewenstein, *Representing Revolution in Milton and his Contemporaries*, 203.

132 See Shagan, "Constructing Discord."

133 Raglan belonged to the earl, whose wealth provided an important source of funding for Charles I. See Stephen K. Roberts, "Somerset, Edward, second marquess of Worcester (*d.* 1667)."

134 Similar pamphlets include: *A True Relation of a Divelish Designe by the Papists to Blow up the City of Oxford with Gunpowder* (n.d.); *A Discoverie of the Hellish Plot Against Diverse*

Particular of the Nobility of the Kingdome of England. Also the Papists Gunpowder-Plot, brought to Light (1642).

135 *CSPD* Charles I, 1639–40, v. 438, p. 246, item 93.

136 On 22 December 1641 Charles appointed Lunsford Lieutenant of the Tower (apparently on Digby's recommendation), a move many saw as offering the potential for a coup. On 24 December Parliament declared him unfit for office: Basil Morgan, "Lunsford, Sir Thomas (*b. c.*1610, *d.* in or before 1656)."

137 Bridge, *England Saved with a Notwithstanding*, 30.

138 *Papa Patens, or The Pope in his Colours*, 32.

139 Sterry was closely associated with Cromwell. See: Nabil Matar, "Sterry, Peter (1613–1672)."

140 Loewenstein, *Representing Revolution in Milton and his Contemporaries*, 203.

141 See Rovang, "Milton's War in Heaven as Apocalyptic Drama"; Donnelly, *Milton's Scriptural Reasoning*, 105–17. On references to the Eye of God in the poem, see also Waddington, *Looking into Providences*, 102–16.

142 "At pater omnipotens, cuius mortalia ab alto / cuncta patent oculis, vitae qui tempus ab aevo / ire necisque iubet mundum ratione gubernans / aeterna, insidias prospexit ab aethere caecas" (ll. 306–9).

143 "cuius per totum vigilans perreptat ubique / mundum oculus, terras omnes, maria intima lustrans, / abdita et abstrusis penetralia caeca tenebris"; "aligerum immensa thronum cingente corona" (ll. 269–71, 276).

144 This cartoon is discussed in the following chapter.

145 Terry, *[Pseudeleutheria] Or, Lawless Liberty*, 25.

146 Baxter, "A Sermon of the Absolute Sovereignty of Christ," 78.

147 Other sermons preached on texts from this psalm during the period include Temple, *Christ's Government in and over his People* (1642); Hussey, *The Magistrates Charge, for the Peoples Safetie* (1647); Barker, *The Faithful and Wise Servant* (1656).

148 Crouch, "Fighting for Saint Michael." Waddington also notes that Milton distrusted Cromwell's tendency to attribute all of his successes to providence (*Looking into Providence*, 25–34).

149 See Burrow, *Epic Romance*, 256–8.

150 Nisroch is an Assyrian agricultural god mentioned briefly in the Old Testament, where his temple is the site of Sennacherib's murder by his sons (2 Kings 19.36–7, Isaiah 37.38).

6. "For God and the King": Preaching on the Plot Anniversary

1 The liturgies for all of these services remained in the prayer book until 1859. The date of 5 November was celebrated, at least when politically useful (except when the prayer book was prohibited during the civil wars), until that time. Sermons on 30 January and 29 May continued through the eighteenth century, although Howard D.

Weinbrot ("The Thirtieth of January Sermon") notes that later sermons on 30 January paid scant attention to the original occasion.

2 Queen Elizabeth's accession day did not survive as an official preaching occasion, although it continued to be celebrated informally, frequently as a protest against the policies of the reigning monarch. See Roy Strong, *The Cult of Elizabeth* (ch. 4); Cressy *Bonfires and Bells* (esp. ch. 4) and "God's Time, Rome's Time, and the Calendar of the English Protestant Regime."

3 The phrase "representative publicness" comes from Habermas's *Structural Transformation of the Public Sphere* (5), where he uses it to describe how a sovereign power appears before the people without interacting with them. He or she is seen at a distance under carefully controlled circumstances and as an embodiment of the church or state rather than an individual. Morrissey notes that "Charles I failed to follow his father's lead in making public sermons on political anniversaries an important part of his political image making" ("Presenting James VI and I to the Public," 111). Only one Paul's Cross 5 November sermon is known to survive, in manuscript, from Charles's reign (Joseph Nailor, 1631, St Paul's Cathedral Library MS 52.D60.01) and only four of the sermons preached either at Paul's Cross or in the cathedral in honour of the king's accession day are known to survive in print (see Morrissey, *Politics and the Paul's Cross Sermons, 1558-1642*, 154n80).

4 Only two parliamentary sermons are known to survive in print from this period, both by Peter Sterry (*Englands Deliverance from the Northern Presbytery*, 1651, and *The Way of God with his people in these Nations*, 1656). In contrast, sermons preached before the Lord Mayor and aldermen include: William Ames, *The saints security*, 1651; William Strong, *A Voice from Heaven*, 1653; Thomas Horton, *The Pillar and Pattern of Englands Deliverances*, 1654; Ralph Venning, *Mercies memorial*, 1656; and Edward Reynolds, *The Brand pluck't out of the fire*, 1659.

5 Carleton's popular catalogue of deliverances from the Elizabethan accession to the Gunpowder Plot was reprinted many times after its first appearance in 1624. While Carleton was a bishop who dedicated his work to Charles I, Sparke was a printer of puritan sympathies who published what began as a single broadsheet with plates illustrating the deliverances from the Armada, the Gunpowder Plot, and the plague of 1625. The plates were later adapted for John Vicars's 1641 edition of Herring's epic and the pamphlet expanded into an enormously popular collection of prayers that was printed repeatedly through the late 1620s and 1630s. On Carleton and Sparke, see Alexandra Walsham, *Providence in Early Modern England*, 258–65. The "King's Book" remained a standard source for the history of the plot, although Restoration authors wishing to appear neutral based their accounts on those of Jacques-Auguste de Thou and other Catholic authors (see ch. 1).

6 Cressy, "God's Time, Rome's Time, and the Calendar of the English Protestant Regime," 404. Ian Green estimates that about half the clergy were licensed to preach

by 1600 and about three-quarters by 1640 in most areas of the country ("Preaching in the Parishes," 139).

7 Laud may have discouraged popular Gunpowder sermons as part of an effort to downplay the occasion. The destruction of the Paul's Cross pulpit is unrecorded, but probably occurred in 1634 or 1635, and certainly before 1641 (see Morrissey, *Politics and the Paul's Cross Sermons, 1558–1642*, 223). The last Gunpowder sermon known to have been preached at the Cross is Joseph Nailor's in 1631 (St Paul's Cathedral Library, MS. 52.D60.01). Nailor's sermon unequivocally condemns the "Antichristian-Romanists" (17) who perpetrated the plot and warns against a "dangerous & intollerable Toleration" (32). Although Nailor praises Charles for having all his father's virtues along with that of youth, and chastises the puritans for criticizing the king from their pulpits, the anti-Catholicism of the sermon was unlikely to have pleased Charles, and the sermon was apparently never printed.

8 Bryan Crockett reminds us that preachers took a political risk in composing their own sermons rather than using the *Homilies* (*The Play of Paradox: Stage and Sermon in Renaissance England*, 15–17). As will become apparent below, preachers could court trouble by using political occasions to advance their own causes.

9 Wabuda, *Preaching during the English Reformation*, 89.

10 On Paul's Cross and its preaching traditions, see MacLure, *The Paul's Cross Sermons, 1534–1642*; Morrissey, *Politics and the Paul's Cross Sermons, 1558–1642*.

11 Wabuda, *Preaching during the English Reformation*, 95.

12 Kirby takes the phrase "culture of persuasion" from Andrew Pettegree's book, *Reformation and the Culture of Persuasion*. See Kirby, "The Public Sermon," 23n10.

13 Kirby, "The Public Sermon," 5. The question of popular response to the Reformation has been debated for many years. While some have seen the Reformation as imposed from above on a largely unwilling population, others have argued for substantial popular support. For summaries of this debate, see Nicholas Tyacke, *Aspects of English Protestantism c. 1530–1700*, ch. 1; Christopher Haigh, "The Recent Historiography of the English Reformation."

14 According to MacLure, anti-Catholic rhetoric at Paul's Cross became part of official policy beginning in the 1570s. See *The Paul's Cross Sermons, 1534–1642*, 65.

15 See chapter 2.

16 "Vocabulary of celebration" is David Cressy's phrase. See Cressy, "The Protestant Calendar and the Vocabulary of Celebration in Early Modern England."

17 By "occasional political sermon" I mean a sermon preached on a specifically political occasion such as the Gunpowder or Gowrie anniversary. That preachers recognized these sermons as a distinctive type is suggested by Daniel Featley's observation to his congregation on the anniversary of the Gowrie conspiracy in 1618 that "the occasion of our meeting at this present is rather to offer unto God the fruits of

our devotion for his Majesties and our enemies destruction, than to gather fruits of knowledge from Scripture for our instruction" ("Traitor's Guerdon," 60). Clearly, sermons on other occasions frequently contained political commentary.

18 Eric Josef Carlson, "The Boring of the Ear," 250. On these changes, see Gregory Kneidel, "*Ars Prædicandi*: Theories and Practice," esp. p. 10 on the structure of the thematic sermon.

19 According to J.W. Blench, most sixteenth-century Protestants, both English and Continental, insisted upon the literal sense of scripture, although some preachers continued to use typological and even allegorical interpretations (*Preaching in England in the late Fifteenth and Sixteenth Centuries*, ch. 1). For the history of Catholic preaching in this period, see Thomas Worcester, "Catholic Sermons."

20 Morrissey, "Scripture, Style and Persuasion in Seventeenth-Century English Theories of Preaching," 693.

21 The most influential of the preaching manuals in England seem to have been Keckerman and Andreas Hyperius's *De Formandis Concionibus Sacris* (1553). Keckerman was popularized in England through William Perkins's *Art of Prophecying*. On homiletic theory in this period, see Blench, *Preaching in England in the late Fifteenth and Sixteenth Centuries*; Eric Josef Carlson, "The Boring of the Ear"; Davies, *Like Angels from a Cloud*, esp. 10–50; Ford, "Preaching in the Reformed Tradition,"; Lares, *Milton and the Preaching Arts*, ch. 2; Lewalski, *Protestant Poetics and the Seventeenth-Century Religious Lyric*, ch. 7; Mitchell, *English Pulpit Oratory from Andrewes to Tillotson*.

22 On the concepts of "decorum" and "discretion" in preaching, see Shami, "Donne on Discretion"; and Morrissey, "Scripture, Style and Persuasion in Seventeenth-Century Theories of Preaching," 694–6. This recognition that the minister adapts his preaching to the occasion and auditory complicates the older critical practice of classifying preachers into rigid categories such as "plain" or "metaphysical."

23 Application was normally the second part of the sermon. The preacher's first responsibility was the regular homiletic duty of explicating the text's religious meaning.

24 See *Sermons at Court*, ch. 1.

25 On King's sermon, see Ferrell, *Government by Polemic*, 99–106; on Andrewes's sermons, see McCullough, *Sermons at Court*, 116–25.

26 For analysis of Donne's sermon on this occasion, see Shami, *John Donne and Conformity in Crisis*, ch. 4, and "'The Stars in their Orders Fought Against Sisera.'"

27 On the political situation of King's sermon, see Ferrell, *Government by Polemic*, 97–102.

28 "Women and Sermons in Early Modern England: An Immodest Proposal," Unpublished paper, 1. Shami observes that despite calls for interdisciplinarity in sermon studies, we lack methodologies even for their use within disciplines.

29 Morrissey, "Interdisciplinarity and the Study of Early Modern Sermons," 1121.

30 Such studies include Mitchell's *English Pulpit Oratory from Andrewes to Tillotson*, and more recently Davies's *Like Angels from a Cloud: The English Metaphysical Preachers 1588–1645*, which perpetuates Mitchell's distinctions between "plain" and "metaphysical" styles.

31 For example, Revard and Haan both focus upon Andrewes's sermons when discussing the relationship between the Gunpowder sermons and epic literature. The only study of the Gunpowder sermons as a group is Thomas Nowak's dissertation "'Remember, Remember the Fifth of November.'" While some of Nowak's insights are useful, the dissertation is dated by its categorization of preaching styles according to Horton Davies's rhetorical distinctions.

32 Davies, "English Political Sermons, 1603–1640," 1.

33 Mitchell concludes a useful summary of the ways in which printed sermons have come down to us with the surprising statement that "diverse as the sources of the printed texts are, they may be taken on the whole as a fairly true representation of typical sermons of the period" (38), a conclusion unsupported by his own evidence.

34 Sermon notes in particular remain a relatively unexplored source for understanding how individuals responded to sermons as well as the relationship between oral delivery and print. Arnold Hunt offers the first significant study of these issues in *The Art of Hearing*, esp. 94–114 and 139–47.

35 Evelyn says that South "preached at Westminster Abbey an excellent discourse concerning obedience to magistrates, against the pontificians and sectaries" (*The Diary of John Evelyn*, 1.384).

36 Mitchell suggests that early conformists and puritans tended to memorize their sermons, while Restoration preachers preferred to use notes (*English Pulpit Oratory from Andrewes to Tillotson*, 5–38); however, John Sparrow notes that the "approved method of preaching ... in the first half of the century was to speak a sermon with as little dependence on manuscript as possible. Yet a sermon was not given *ex tempore*: the preacher when he entered the pulpit would have it in his head, and he might have copied it out in full. How fully it had been written out, and how minutely he knew what he was going to say, varied no doubt with circumstances and individuals" ("John Donne and Contemporary Preachers," 151).

37 Gilbert Burnet, *A sermon preached at the Chappel of the Rolls on the fifth of November, 1684*.

38 Henry Burton, *For God and the King*. Another edition was printed in London later that year (STC 4141).

39 "Articles objected by his majesties command for causes ecclesiastical against Henry Burton Clerk parson or vicar of St Mathews Friday Street London" (SP16/335), Article 4.

40 For example, Daniel Dyke's sermons before Princess Elizabeth were published in 1616, although evidently delivered before the princess's marriage: Daniel Dyke, *Certaine comfortable sermons vpon the 124. Psalme ...*

41 These are sometimes preserved in sermon collections, particularly those in which the original title pages of previously published sermons are retained. In many cases, however, particularly in later compilations, even the date and occasion of preaching may be missing.

42 See Lake and Questier, "Puritans, Papists, and the 'Public Sphere' in Early Modern England."

43 Patterson, *Censorship and Interpretation*, 18. Patterson articulates nine principles that she believes are important to understanding the ways in which potential censorship influenced printed texts. See *Censorship and Interpretation*, ch. 2. Shami observes that "moderate" preachers "could rely on choice of text, application of biblical example to present circumstances, and analogy to comment discreetly on the spiritual and political condition of England" (*Conformity in Crisis*, 18).

44 See Cogswell *Blessed Revolution*, ch. 1, and "England and the Spanish Match"; Shami *Conformity in Crisis*, ch. 2.

45 See Hunt, "Tuning the Pulpits," 107. Hunt observes the difficulties in convicting ministers of seditious preaching when political messages could be conveyed simply by "stating a general doctrine and leaving it to the audience to supply the obvious application to current events" (107). In these cases, "the 'meaning' of the sermon was not something that could be read off from the written text, but resulted from an act of interpretative collaboration between preacher and audience, specific to the occasion on which it was preached" (107).

46 See *Sermons at Court*, 113–15. McCullough adds that the process might be further complicated when one sermon was published by royal authority and the other was not. On at least one 5 November, Andrewes presented his sermon as a continuation from that of the previous year, apparently expecting his auditors to recall the previous sermon. He begins his 1614 sermon with the words: "We begin, this year, where we left the last" (4.296).

47 Eiléan Ni Chuilleanáin, "Time, Place, and the Congregation in Donne's Sermons," 203–4.

48 On the typical structure of political sermons, see Morrissey, "John Donne as a Conventional Paul's Cross Preacher," 160–1.

49 John King, *A Sermon preached in Oxon: the 5. of November, 1607.*

50 See Walsham, *Providence in Early Modern England*, ch. 3.

51 Thomas Hooker, "The Church's Deliverances." On the date of the sermon, see the editor's introduction, 53–9.

52 Morrissey, "Elect nations and prophetic preaching," 51, 53.

53 Nicholas Colt, *The Seale of the Churches Safety; or a Sermon preached at Norwhich, the fift of Nouember, 1616*, 43.

54 Achsah Guibbory calls the idea that "nation and church were coterminous" a "fiction" created by James and parliament ("Israel and English Protestant Nationalism," 116).

55 On the history of Paul's Cross, see Millar MacLure, *The Paul's Cross Sermons, 1534–1642*, esp. chs 1 and 2; Mary Morrissey, *Politics and the Paul's Cross Sermons, 1558–1642*, esp. ch. 1.

56 Donne wrote to Sir Thomas Roe on 1 December 1622, sending him a copy of his 15 September sermon and regretting that he could not also send a copy of his 5 November sermon, since he had sent his manuscript to the king and it would, in any case, be indiscreet of him to circulate the sermon "whilst it is in that suspence" (SP 14/134/59, qtd by Shami in the introduction to *John Donne's 1622 Gunpowder Plot Sermon: A Parallel-Text Edition*, 12). Shami suggests that "Donne's language in the letter to Roe is deliberately ambiguous" (13), since he understood the dangers of circulating a sermon that had not received royal approval, even though he does not seem to have anticipated any difficulties arising from the sermon.

57 John F. Wilson estimates that between 60 and 65 per cent of the parliamentary fast sermons were published. See *Pulpit in Parliament*, 11.

58 William Strong, *A Voice from Heaven, calling the People of God to a Perfect Separation from Mystical Babylon* …, a^{r}.

59 "Answers of Samuel Ward to 43 articles objected against him by the commissioners for causes ecclesiastical, 19 Dec. 1634," PRO SP 16/278/65, fo. 144r. The sermon has not survived.

60 See Eric Josef Carlson, who observes that John Rogers and John King argued that only the live sermon had saving power; "The Boring of the Ear," 281–2.

61 James Rigney, "'To lye upon a Stationers stall, like a piece of coarse flesh in a Shambles.'"

62 William Cave, *A Sermon preached before the Right Honourable, the Lord Mayor, Alderman and citizens of London, at S. Mary-le-Bow on the fifth of November, 1680*, A3^{v}.

63 Carpenter, *The Iesuit, and the Monk*, A2^{v}.

64 Pelling, *The True Mark of the Beast*, A4^{v}. Pelling was still professing unwillingness to publish in the dedication to his sermon the following year (*A Sermon preached before the Lord Mayor and Court of Aldermen, at St. Mary le Bow, on Nov. 5, 1683*, A2^{r-v}).

65 Gregory, *The religious villain*, A4^{v}. Recent scholarship has provided a clearer picture of how disorderly early modern worship might be. See, for example, Laura Feitzinger Brown, "Brawling in Church"; and John Craig, "Psalms, groans and dogwhippers."

66 "The Authors Apologie," Thomas Taylor, *A Mappe of Rome*, A4^{v}.

67 Reeve, *The Churches hazard*, A2^{r}.

68 Heyrick, "The Third Sermon," in *Three Sermons preached at the Collegiate Church in Manchester*, a3^{r}, a^{r}.

69 In his introduction, Scott observes with some asperity that "perhaps the Protestant Reader, who is unacquainted with the transactions of the last 600 years, may think *I* have been too severe upon the *Roman* Religion," but he takes responsibility for what he has written, most of which has been taken from Catholic authors: *A Sermon preached before the Right Honorable* …, unpaginated. Baker used the analogy of Protestants as sheep to the Roman wolves, but insisted that he hoped to be an example to his flock, even if captured by these predators: *Achitophel befool'd: a sermon preached November 5, 1678 at St. Sepulchres*, A2$^{r–v}$.

70 Edward Pelling, *The True Mark of the Beast*, A4^{r}.

71 Chamberlain, *The Letters of John Chamberlain*, 2.67, 2.451.

72 Carpenter, *Rome in her fruits being a sermon preached on the fifth of November, 1662 near to the standard in Cheapside*, t.p.; Lloyd, *A Sermon Preached before the House of Lords on November 5,1680*, A3^{r}–A4^{v}.

73 Colt, *The Seale of the Churches Safety*, 70.

74 By the 1670s, Thou's account was available in several English versions: *A True narration of that horrible conspiracy against King James and the whole Parliament of England*; *The histories of the gunpowder-treason and the massacre at Paris together with a discourse concerning the original of the Powder-Plot*; *A True History of the Roman Catholicks designs and bloody contrivances for the subversion of the Protestant Religion in England.*

75 Wilson, *A Sermon on the Gunpowder Treason with Reflections on the Late Plot*, 32.

76 Stillingfleet, *A Sermon preached November V 1673 at St. Margretts Westminster*, 42. The two works Stillingfleet cites are: *A Reply to the Answer of the Catholique Apology* by Roger Palmer, earl of Castlemaine, 203; and, *The Advocate of Conscience Liberty*, attributed to Peter Walsh, 218.

77 For Evelyn's account of the sermon, see *The Diary of John Evelyn*, 2.130–1.

78 See Heylyn, *A Briefe and Moderate Answer, to the seditious and scandalous challenge of Henry Burton*, ch. 3.

79 Even in response to the much smaller sample of Gunpowder sermons preached at Paul's Cross, Morrissey concludes that "What is most surprising about the Gunpowder Plot sermons at Paul's Cross is how heterogeneous they are" (*Politics and the Paul's Cross Sermons, 1558–1642*, 150).

80 See Cogswell, *The Blessed Revolution* (ch. 1), and Shami, *Conformity in Crisis.*

81 Shami observes that many of the printed sermons from this period placed a similar emphasis upon interpretation (*Conformity in Crisis*, 53–4).

82 MacLure, *The Paul's Cross Sermons, 1534–1642*, 101.

83 Shami, "'The Stars in their Orders Fought Against Sisera'"; Morrissey, "John Donne as a Conventional Paul's Cross Preacher." For "absolutist" readings of Donne's sermons, see John Carey, *John Donne: Life, Mind and Art* and Debora Shuger, "Absolutist Theology in the Sermons of John Donne." For contrasting views, see David Nicholls, "Divine Analogy: The Theological Politics of John Donne"; Paul Harland,

"Donne's Political Intervention in the Parliament of 1629"; and Jeanne Shami, "Donne's Sermons and the Absolutist Politics of Quotation." See also Shuger's reassessment of this debate in terms of seventeenth-century understandings of the concept of "absolutism" ("Donne's Absolutism," 690–703).

84 Morrissey, "John Donne as a Conventional Paul's Cross Preacher," 170.

85 Shami, *Conformity in Crisis*, 114.

86 Chamberlain, *The Letters of John Chamberlain*, 2.451.

87 Shami, *Conformity in Crisis*, 114, 132.

88 Wabuda points out that preachers at Paul's Cross were expected to serve as models for younger clergy (*Preaching during the English Reformation*, 48).

89 Some preachers, however, did use New Testament texts. Both Lancelot Andrewes (1609) and Arthur Lake (1614) preached from Luke 9.54–6, while Andrewes turned to Luke 1.74–5 in 1617. John Rawlinson compared the plot to the betrayal of Christ in Luke 22.48 (1610) and Nicholas Colt (1616) chose 2 Peter 2.9.

90 See *Government by Polemic*, Ch. 3. On King's sermon see pp. 97–103.

91 Fotherby, *Foure Sermons, lately preached … The third at Paules Crosse*, 85.

92 Ferrell interprets Boys's sermon as the first published instance of combining anti-puritanism with ceremonialism (*Government by Polemic*, 107–9). I believe she has over-estimated the sermon's anti-puritanism somewhat. Boys, I suggest, sees holy days, including political anniversaries, as a means of defeating international Catholicism by restoring the strength of Protestant community. I believe Goodwyn's sermon of the following year, which also focuses on the importance of memorialization in creating a nation, supports this interpretation (William Goodwyn, *A Sermon Preached at Pauls Cross ye 5. of Nouember. 1614. by Doctor Goodwyn. then Vice Chanceller of Oxford*, Doctor Williams's Library, ms.12.10). Although Goodwyn's sermon was not published, it suggests that the theme of memorialization had particular resonance at this time and was not only an obsession of Boys.

93 Although the place of preaching is not specified, the introduction suggests that the sermons were preached at Reading, possibly in the parish of St Laurence, where his brother was preacher. Jemmat was Taylor's assistant in a seminary he held at Reading and subsequently preached his funeral sermon at St Mary Aldermanbury in London. Taylor may have hidden behind Jemmat because he had fallen foul of the authorities at Cambridge for his puritanism and may have been seeking a benefice (J. Sears McGee, "Taylor, Thomas (1576–1632)").

94 For the full text of the *Directions*, see James I, "Directions to preachers, 1622," in *Visitation Articles and Injunctions of the Early Stuart Church*, 211–14.

95 Wall and Burgin, "'This sermon … upon the Gun-powder day,'" 29.

96 See Ferrell's argument that the anti-puritanism of Gunpowder sermons has been under-estimated (*Government by Polemic*, ch. 3). While I largely agree with Ferrell's analysis, I think she fails to distinguish sufficiently between court and public sermons on this occasion.

97 Shami, "Comparison with the first printed version in *Fifty Sermons* (1649)," in Donne, *John Donne's 1622 Gunpowder Plot Sermon*, 28.

98 Potter and Simpson cite Donne's letter of 25 November 1625 to Sir Thomas Roe in which he said he had written out eighty of his sermons and hoped to complete more. Donne seems to have bestowed them on Henry King with his other papers at his death. See Potter and Simpson, *The Sermons of John Donne*, 1.46–7. The manuscript upon which the 1649 text was based is not extant.

99 See Shami's introduction to her parallel-text edition of the sermon, *John Donne's 1622 Gunpowder Plot Sermon: A Parallel-Text Edition.*

100 Shami, "Comparison with the first printed version in *Fifty Sermons* (1649)," in Donne, *John Donne's 1622 Gunpowder Plot Sermon*, 24, 26.

101 Webber, *Contrary Music*, 12–13.

102 Donne, *The Sermons of John Donne*, 4.235–6.

103 Frye, *The Great Code*, 108, 118.

104 Burton, *For God and the King*, 43.

105 Newcomen, *The craft and cruelty of the churches adversaries*, 42, *vere* 50.

106 Sacheverell, *The Perils of false brethren*, 20.

107 Daley, "'And Like a Widdow Thus,'" 61, 58, 65.

108 For example, in his 1612 court sermon on Lamentations 3.22, Andrewes contrasted the averted destruction of London with the actual destruction of Jerusalem in the text ("A Sermon Preached before the King's Majesty at Whitehall, on the fifth of November, A.D. MDCXII" in Lancelot Andrewes, *Ninety-six Sermons by the Right Honourable and Reverend Father in God, Lancelot Andrewes*, 4.261–276).

109 Morrissey, "John Donne as a Conventional Paul's Cross Preacher," 177; Shami, "Donne on Discretion," 61.

110 Morrissey, "John Donne as a Conventional Paul's Cross Preacher."

111 Frontain notes Helen Gardner's suggestion that Donne completed the translation in the summer of 1621 when he was frustrated by his failure to obtain ecclesiastical preferment as well as by the situation in the Palatinate ("'the man which have affliction seene,'" 134). William B. Hunter suggests the versification might have been written upon Anne's death in August 1617, noting that the liturgical readings for the days leading up to her death were from this book ("An Occasion for John Donne's 'The Lamentations of Jeremy,'" 19). One of the crucial issues involved in dating the translation has been which version of the Bible Donne used. Ted-Larry Pebworth suggests that the echoes of the Geneva Bible in Donne's poem may have come through Fetherstone's translation of Tremellius rather than through the Authorized Version, which means Donne's poem could have been written before 1611 ("John Donne's 'Lamentations' and Christopher Fetherstone's 'Lamentations ... in prose and meeter' (1587)," 92). Graham Roebuck also argues that the translation could have been written before 1611 ("Donne's *Lamentations of Jeremy* Reconsidered"). On

Donne's interest in Lamentations more generally, see Reuben Sánchez, *Typology and Iconography in Donne, Herbert, and Milton: Fashioning the Self after Jeremiah*, chs. 4 and 5.

112 John Udall's *A Commentarie upon the Lamentations of Jeremy* was printed in 1593, 1595, 1599, and 1608. Hugh Broughton's *The Lamentations of Jeremy ... with Annotations* was printed at Amsterdam in 1606 and 1608, while Michael Drayton's "Praier of Ieremiah, bewailing the captiuity of the people. In the fift Chap. of his Lamentations" appeared in *The Harmonie of the Church* (1591, C4^{v}–D^{r}) and again in *A Heauenly Harmonie of Spirituall Songes*. A translation by Anne Jenkinson, *Meditations vpon the Lamentations of Ieremy translated out of French into English by A. I.* was printed in London in 1609. See Hunter "An Occasion for John Donne's '*The Lamentations of Jeremy*,'" 18–23.

113 Pebworth, "John Donne's 'Lamentations' and Christopher Fetherstone's *Lamentations ... in prose and meeter* (1587)," 87.

114 Shami, *John Donne and Conformity in Crisis*, 131.

115 By using the term "invented," Ward was probably trying to minimize his responsibility for the cartoon. As Walsham points out, what Ward had done was simply to juxtapose three existing images; however, Christina Carlson argues that this was what made the engraving so politically explosive. See Walsham, *Providence in Early Modern England*, 255–8; Christina Carlson, "Free-Speaking Cartoons," 63–6.

116 The needlework adaptations are discussed by Alexandra Walsham in *Providence in Early Modern England*, 261–2, and by Ann Rosalind Jones and Peter Stallybrass in *Renaissance Clothing and the Materials of Memory*, 162–5. Xanthe Brooke describes the embroideries in *The Lady Lever Art Gallery: Catalogue of Embroideries*, 18–20. Dorothy Selby's stitchery was mentioned prominently in her funerary epitaph, which led, curiously, to her being identified in some strands of tradition as the writer of the "Monteagle letter." For additional sources of information, see Walsham, *Providence in Early Modern England*, 261n140.

117 Walsham, *Providence in Early Modern England*, 250–1.

118 Walsham, *Providence in Early Modern England*, 255.

119 Kunzle, *The Early Comic Strip*, 123.

120 Trans. by Kunzle, *The Early Comic Strip*, 123.

121 Richard Smith's *The Powder Treason*, British Museum, Department of Prints and Drawings. Griffiths and Gerard date the Smith engraving to 1621/23 on the assumption that it participated with Ward's drawing and Thomas Scott's *Vox Populi* as part of the anti-Spanish and anti-Catholic propaganda surrounding the Spanish match negotiations, but nothing is known of Smith or his relation to Droeshout, who engraved the image. Both Walsham and John N. King accept an earlier date, c. 1615 (*Providence in Early Modern England*, 254; *Milton and Religious Controversy*, 47–8).

122 See "Free-Speaking Cartoons," ch. 1. For other discussions of these images, see Antony Griffiths with Robert A. Gerard, *The Print in Stuart Britain 1603–1689*,

144–54; John N. King, *Milton and Religious Controversy*, 115–22; Walsham, *Providence in Early Modern England*, 250–66, and "Impolitic Pictures."

123 Frye, *The Great Code*, 130.

124 Christina Carlson, "Free Speaking Cartoons," 95.

125 Although the verses beneath the enclave clearly identify the occasion as the plotting of the Gunpowder Plot, this attempt to prevent a broader interpretation seems unlikely to have been effective given the emotive power of the visual.

126 Griffiths and Gerard identify the figures as the king of Spain, "the Pope, a cardinal, a Jesuit and two monks" (*The Print in Stuart Britain 1603–1689*, 152).

127 Quoted in John Bruce, "The Caricatures of Samuel Ward of Ipswich," 2.

128 Chamberlain tells Dudley Carleton in a 10 March 1621 letter that "one Ward a speciall preacher of Ipswich is but newly released out of prison (where he lay a good while) for having a picture of the Spanish fleet in 88 with the gun-powder treason, and some other additions of his owne invention and hand (having some delight and skill in limming) which his friends say had lien by him at least seven or eight yeares, and not looked into till now" (*The Letters of John Chamberlain*, 2.351). Interestingly, Chamberlain implies that Ward's offence was not interfering in the marriage negotiations, but drawing attention to the poor performances of both land and naval forces in the Continental war.

129 Willan, *Conspiracie against kings, heavens scorne*, 38.

130 Like the conventional engravings, Willan's sermon seems to be indebted to the official account of the plot, in which the author identified piety and justice as the pillars of good government (*His Maiesties speech*, E4^{v}).

131 Morrissey, "John Donne as a Conventional Paul's Cross Preacher," 173.

132 Except where noted, quotations are from Shami's transcription of the manuscript version of the sermon and line references are to this edition, which probably bears the closest relationship to the preached sermon. I have not reproduced the underlining by which the editor has identified differences from the 1649 print version.

133 For divergent views on anti-Catholicism in Donne's sermons, see Marotti, "Donne's Conflicted Anti-Catholicism"; Shami, "Anti-Catholicism in the Sermons of John Donne."

134 Morrissey, "John Donne as a Conventional Paul's Cross Preacher," 173.

135 Interestingly, Donne's first invitation to preach at the Cross, on James's accession day in 1617, had coincided with this controversy.

136 Donne, *The Sermons of John Donne*, 4.251.

137 Donne's use of the word "lieutenant" suggests that, like Willan, he had reviewed the official plot pamphlet, since James had referred to kings as God's "Lieutenans and Vicegerents on earth" (B^{r}) at the beginning of his 9 November speech to Parliament, and had subsequently reminded the members that the "weales" of king and country could not be separated (*His Maiesties speech in this last session of Parliament*, D3^{v}).

138 Iser, *The Act of Reading*, 195. Although Iser's work is concerned with fictional texts, I believe the idea of "blanks" may also apply to texts such as sermons where authors wished to leave space for readers to interpret without compromising their own safety.

139 Iser, *The Act of Reading*, 188, 186, 217.

140 David Nicholls argues that Donne used the analogy between God and the king both to support and to limit the king's authority ("Divine Analogy: The Theological Politics of John Donne," 576).

141 Donne, *The Sermons of John Donne*, 4.253. If Donne revised the sermon in late 1625, he was likely thinking of Charles's actions rather than James's, which may have caused him to sharpen his criticism of the king for employing evil counsellors. Even at this early stage of Charles's reign, many of his subjects seem to have questioned his ability to govern. See Shami's analysis of the major changes between the manuscript and print versions (*John Donne's 1622 Gunpowder Plot Sermon*, 24–32).

142 Donne's strategy here also seems to reflect Annabel Patterson's ninth principle regarding censorship, that "in a work of oblique sociopolitical import any markedly topical allusions will tend to be widely scattered through the text, so that they appear to be random shots at local irritations, rather than a sustained and coherent attack on a government or a court" (*Censorship and Interpretation*, 63).

143 All three had been charged previously in other matters and Prynne had already had his ears cropped for the publication of *Histrio-Mastix*.

144 Cressy, *Travesties and Transgressions in Tudor and Stuart England*, 219. Burton was imprisoned briefly at Lancaster Castle before being removed to Castle Cornet on Guernsey. In fact, the exile lasted only until 1641, when the Long Parliament returned the three to London and released them.

145 Clegg, *Press Censorship in Caroline England*, 181.

146 On the responses to the Marprelate tracts, see Raymond, *Pamphlets and Pamphleteering in Early Modern Britain*, ch. 2; Joseph Black, "The Rhetoric of Reaction."

147 There is no consensus on when and why Burton first lost his living. Clegg cites Kenneth Gibson's *ODNB* article indicating that the cause was Burton's letter accusing Laud and Neile of Catholic sympathies, but Gibson appears to be referring to the loss of Burton's position as Clerk of the Closet rather than loss of his living (*Press Censorship in Caroline England*, 56, 248–9n63).

148 Burton, *Tryall of Priuate Deuotions*, A^{v}.

149 Clegg, *Press Censorship in Caroline England*, 57.

150 Although I agree that Burton was not a separatist at this point, I find it difficult to share Clegg's faith in the transparency of his own claims. Burton's insistence upon his rights of counsel seems to have been part of his careful self-representation as a martyr.

151 According to his autobiography (*A Narration of the Life of Mr. Henry Burton*), it was not the first time that Burton had taken advantage of the plot anniversary. He admits he had, in an earlier (undated) "Sermon on the 5. of *November* spoken of

sundry fore-running signes of the ruine of a State, which upon that return of the Duke [Buckingham], would not (it seemes) indure the Examination" (6). Unfortunately, the sermon does not survive. After that he claims he began deliberately preaching on controversial topics and neglecting ceremonies, watching "for an occasion to try it out with them, either by dint of Arguments, or force of Law, or by the King and his Counsell, resolving of this, that by this means I should either foile my adversaries (though I had no great hope this way) or at least (which I was sure not to faile of) discover the mystery of iniquity, and the deceit of hypocrisie, which like a white vaile they had cast over all their foule practices, and false pretences" (8).

152 Burton, *For God and the King*, 6.

153 "Answers of Samuel Ward to 43 articles objected against him by the commissioners for causes ecclesiastical, 19 Dec. 1634," TNA, PRO SP 16/278/65, fo. 144r.

154 Clegg, *Press Censorship in Caroline England*, 179. The choice of the anniversary of Queen Elizabeth's accession may have been completely fortuitous, or it may have been intended to help brand Burton as disrespectful to the monarchy. One of the mysteries of the case is exactly what crime the three were charged with. Philip Hamburger suggests it was likely *scandalum magnatum*, although the crown originally wanted to prosecute them for treason ("The Development of the Law of Seditious Libel and the Control of the Press," esp. 678–9). Roger B. Manning argues that the crown increasingly prosecuted those who had spoken against the authorities for sedition because it was difficult to get a treason conviction given the extreme penalties: see "The Origins of the Doctrine of Sedition." For the most complete account of the case and of Burton's earlier troubles with the law, see Clegg, *Press Censorship in Caroline England*, passim.

155 Burton also claims that the book was printed sheet by sheet as he wrote it, both himself and the presses being hounded by pursuivants. According to the *STC*, the first edition was printed at Amsterdam, so Burton was probably overdramatizing the situation in retrospect (*A Narration of the Life of Mr. Henry Burton*, 10). An edition was subsequently printed in London.

156 For a puritan account of the trial and punishment of the three, see the anonymous *A Briefe Relation of Certain Speciall and Most Materiall Passages, and Speeches in the Starre-Chamber, occasioned and delivered Iune the 14th 1637 ...*

157 Despite this fact, Prynne has attracted significantly more attention from modern scholars than has Burton, possibly because of his attack on the theatre in *Histrio-Mastix*. The only full-length studies of Burton are two dissertations: Richard Hughes, "Henry Burton: A Study in Religion and Politics in Seventeenth-Century England" (University of Iowa, 1972); Stephen Rowlstone, "Religion, politics and polemic in seventeenth-century England: The public career of Henry Burton, 1625–1648" (University of Kent, 2005).

158 Laud, "A Speech delivered in the Starr-chamber, on Wednesday, the xiv. Of Iune MDCXXXVIII …," 68.

159 Raymond, *Pamphlets and Pamphleteering in Early Modern Britain*, 211. See ch. 6 of this book on the strategies and dangers of response more generally.

160 See H.E.I. Phillips, "The Last Years of the Court of Star Chamber, 1630–41." Phillips argues that the demise of Star Chamber was largely due to public hatred of the bishops. Ecclesiastical representation in the Court had increased markedly in the Stuart period and by the 1630s the bench included both archbishops and the Bishop of London.

161 See *A Briefe Relation of Certain Speciall and Most Materiall Passages, and Speeches in the Starre-Chamber.*

162 *A Briefe Relation of Certain Speciall and Most Materiall Passages, and Speeches in the Starre-Chamber*, 14.

163 Burton, *For God and the King*, 141.

164 Quotations from the original service are from *Prayers and thankesgiuing to bee vsed by all the Kings Maiesties louing subiects: for the happy deliuerance of His Maiestie* (1606). Quotations from the revision are from *Prayers, and thanksgiuing* (1635).

165 Burton, *For God and the King*, 130–1.

166 Burton refers to a "Treatise of the Popes temporal Monarchy," which is presumably Crakanthorpe's *A treatise of the Fifth General Councel held at Constantinople, anno 553*, and to John White's *Defence of the way to the true church against A.D. his reply.*

167 Burton is not the only one of the Gunpowder preachers in the 1630s to express confidence in the abilities of his Protestant audience. In his 1638 sermon (published in 1641), Richard Heyrick encourages his congregation to "reade the whole eighteenth of the *Revelations* at your leisure, hee that reades it may understand, for the Text you see is plaine enough, it must downe" (88). Esther Gilman Richey, in *The Politics of Revelation in the English Renaissance*, observes that the Caroline court had begun discouraging the reading of Revelation because of its susceptibility to anti-Catholic interpretations (3–7).

168 Laud, "A Speech delivered in the Starr-chamber, on Wednesday, the xiv. Of Iune MDCXXXVIII …," 37.

169 According to the *ESTC*, only twenty-five copies of the first edition of the speech may have been printed, and they seem to have been intended for distribution among the authorities rather than for a general audience. There were at least two additional printings in 1637.

170 Laud, "A Speech delivered in the Starr-chamber, on Wednesday, the xiv. Of Iune MDCXXXVIII …," 54.

171 Skerpan, *The Rhetoric of Politics in the English Revolution 1642–1660*, 44.

172 Skerpan also fails to account for the wide distribution of Laud's speech. Although Laud himself seems to have targeted an elite audience, sending copies to Wentworth

in Ireland and offering copies to the ambassador in Holland, Alastair Bellany also notes that "Shortly after its publication, one newsmonger reported that the book was selling so fast it was hard to get a copy" ("Libels in Action," 111).

173 Anthony Milton, "The Creation of Laudianism," 173.

174 Heylyn, *A Briefe and Moderate Answer, to the seditious and scandalous challenge of Henry Burton…*, b2r.

175 Heylyn is determined to make a direct association between Burton and the Gunpowder plotters. While Lori Anne Ferrell has documented the increasing anti-puritanism of the Gunpowder sermons, it seems that as the puritans began openly accusing conformists of Catholicism, conformists retaliated by sharpening their accusations against puritans, openly making analogies with the Gunpowder plotters (*Government by Polemic*, ch. 3).

176 According to the *OED*, the word at this time could be used to indicate honourable nature, disposition, or birth, or could be used interchangeably with "ingenious." *OED* records the first use of the word with the more dismissive sense of guileless innocence as 1673.

177 Dow, *Innovations unjustly charged upon the present church and state*, 8. The Clerk of the Closet was responsible for the care and repair of the furnishings of the closet in which the king or queen sat during worship in the royal chapels. By this date, however, Bickersteth and Dunning suggest that the practical work of the office was done by subordinates. Clerks of the Closet, including future bishops Richard Neile and William Juxon, not infrequently rose within the ecclesiastical hierarchy (*Clerks of the Closet in the Royal Household*, ix, 1–10). See also McCullough, *Sermons at Court* (110–11) on the significance of this role. Thus, Dow's dismissive remarks either were intended for an audience unfamiliar with court offices, or were spoken in the belief that humour would persuade his audience.

178 Richard Hughes accepts Dow's statement that Burton's congregation did not support him, but Dow hardly seems a reliable or unbiased source ("Henry Burton: The Making of a Puritan Revolutionary," 433–4).

179 Studies of the fast sermons include: Christopher Durston, "'For the Better Humiliation of the People'"; Jacqueline Eales, "Provincial Preaching and Allegiance in the First English Civil War, 1640–6"; Hugh Trevor-Roper, "The Fast Sermons of the Long Parliament"; Barbara Donagan, "Did Ministers Matter?"; Edward Vallance, "Preaching to the Converted: Religious Justifications for the English Civil War"; Christopher Hill, *The English Bible and the Seventeenth-Century Revolution*, ch. 3; Achsah Guibbory, "Israel and English Protestant Nationalism." The most comprehensive study remains John F. Wilson's *Pulpit in Parliament.* On the role of the Puritan clergy and sermons in the war more generally, see Stephen Baskerville, *Not Peace but a Sword: The Political Theology of the English Revolution*; Tai Liu, *Discord in Zion: The Puritan Divines and the Puritan Revolution, 1640–1660*; Michael Walzer, *The Revolution of the Saints: A Study in the Origins of Radical Politics.*

180 Caroline Hibbard, *Charles I and the Popish Plot*; Scott, *England's Troubles*. Hibbard's work built on that of Carol Z. Wiener, who first considered English Protestant perceptions of international Catholicism in the late sixteenth and early seventeenth centuries ("The Beleaguered Isle"). On popular belief in a popish plot, see also Clifton, "The Popular Fear of Catholics during the English Revolution." Scott (*England's Troubles*) reminds us that England must be seen within a European context and that the nervousness of English Protestants may have been justified by the continental resurgence of Catholicism.

181 Morrill, "The Religious Context of the English Civil War," 172.

182 Based upon surviving printed sermons, 17 November does not appear to have been celebrated after 1640, when Stephen Marshall preached. The application of his sermon enjoined his hearers to be thankful for England's access to "a setled, faithfull, preaching Ministery" for the past eighty years (*A Sermon preached before the Honourable House of Commons, now assembled in Parliament, at their publicke fast November 17, 1640*, 48).

183 Isaac Bargrave preached on this occasion (*A Sermon Preached before the Honorable Assembly of Knights, Citizens, and Burgesses of the Lower House of Parliament*).

184 Wilson, *Pulpit in Parliament*, 36.

185 Durston, "'For the Better Humiliation of the People,'" 132.

186 *An Act for Setting Apart a Day of Solemn Fasting and Humiliation; and Repealing the Former Monethly-Fast*, cited in Wilson, *Pulpit in Parliament*, 96n186.

187 In his 12 September 1644 sermon preached before both Houses of Parliament, Newcomen accused the members of angering God by failing to keep their fast days (*A sermon, tending to set forth the right vse of the disasters that befall our armies*).

188 Trevor-Roper, "The Fast Sermons of the Long Parliament," 309; Durston, "'For the Better Humiliation of the People,'" 139–42.

189 On 8 May 1646, Clarendon recorded that "It was an observation in that time, that the first publishing of extraordinary news was from the pulpit; and by the preacher's text, and his manner of discourse upon it, the auditors might judge, and commonly foresaw, what was like to be next done in the Parliament or Council of State" (Clarendon, *History of the Rebellion*, 4.194). A greater sensation was caused in May 1642 when Edmund Waller's plot was first made known at St Margaret's: "At a solemn fast, when they were listening to the sermon, a messenger entered the church, and communicated his errand to Pym, who whispered it to others who were placed near him, and then went with them out of the church, leaving the rest in solicitude and amazement." St Margaret's, then, seems to have taken over the role of Paul's Cross in the transmission of news.

190 From the published sermons, it appears that on occasion the houses did meet together at St Margaret's.

191 Medieval and early modern Westminster has been the subject of several studies. See Merritt, *The Social World of Early Modern Westminster*; Merritt, "The Cradle of

Laudianism?"; and Rosser, *Medieval Westminster 1200–1540*. Studies of St Margaret's include Philip Holland, *St Margaret's Westminster: The Commons' Church within a Royal Peculiar*, Charles Hugh Egerton Smith, *Church and Parish: Studies in Church Problems, illustrated from the Parochial History of St. Margaret's, Westminster*. For additional sources, including ephemeral ones, see the very useful bibliography compiled by Tony Trowles, *A Bibliography of Westminster Abbey between 1570 and 2000*.

192 There are two references to motions to move the communion table before parliamentary communions in *The Journal of Simonds D'Ewes from the beginning of the Long Parliament to the opening of the trial of the Earl of Strafford*, 43, 46. Nevertheless, Merritt has found "no evidence that the parish seized the opportunity of the Laudian reforms to invest more heavily in church ornamentation – there are no references to an enhanced communion table or rails" (*The Social World of Early Modern Westminster*, 348).

193 On the interior of the church, see Merritt, *Social World of Early Modern Westminster*, 15–17; Gervase Rosser, *Medieval Westminster 1200–1540*, 271–5; Albert Edward Bullock, *Westminster Abbey and St. Margaret's Church*.

194 An ordinance of 1644, after the signing of the Solemn Oath and Covenant, required parliamentarians to sit in the gallery in order to accommodate other spectators (Holland, *St Margaret's Westminster*, 54).

195 According to Merritt, the church either replaced or refurbished its pulpit in 1638–39 (*The Social World of Early Modern Westminster*, 348nn192–3).

196 The similarities between this arrangement and the spatial dynamics of court preaching that McCullough has described in *Sermons at Court* (ch. 1) are worth noting.

197 Trevor-Roper, "The Fast Sermons of the Long Parliament," 342.

198 Zaret, *The Heavenly Contract*, 83.

199 Baskerville, *Not Peace but a Sword*, 8, 8–9.

200 Trevor-Roper, "The Fast Sermons of the Long Parliament," 294.

201 On the development of this narrative, see Hibbard, *Charles I and the Popish Plot*.

202 Wilson, *Pulpit in Parliament*, 54.

203 Burges, *Another sermon preached to the Honorable House of Commons now assembled in Parliament, November the fifth, 1641*, 9.

204 Ibid., 160.

205 See Henry Miller, *God the protector of Israel*.

206 The sermon is dedicated to Henry Murray, one of the grooms of the king's bedchamber. William Sclater, *Papisto-Mastix: or Deborah's Prayer against Gods Enemies Judg. 5.31*.

207 Sclater's cautious authorization of his auditors' interpretative faculties suggests that as royalists moved into an oppositional role they were more inclined to permit individual interpretation, but that they remained sceptical about the abilities of the average listener or reader.

208 Wilson, *Pulpit in Parliament*, 97.

209 Wilson's discussion of individual preachers indicates that after 1645 most of the ministers invited to preach were Independents rather than presbyterians, an indication of the Independents' increasing power (*Pulpit in Parliament*, ch. 4).

210 The anonymous author of the preface to Newcomen's funeral sermon, preached by John Fairfax, described Newcomen as "*a* solid, painful, pathetick *and* perswasive *Preacher*" (*The Dead Saint Speaking*, Ar).

211 Tom Webster, "Newcomen, Matthew (*d.* 1669)." The print record attests that Newcomen preached before Parliament on at least two subsequent fast days: *Jerusalems Watch-men, the Lords Remembrancers: A Sermon Preached at the Abbie at Westminster before both Houses of Parliament, and the Assembly of Divines, upon their Solemn Fast, Iuly 7.1643*; *The All-Seeing Vnseen Eye of God. Discovered, in a Sermon Preached before the Honourable House of Commons; at Margarets Westminster, December 30. 1646. being the day of their solemne Monethly Fast.*

212 Newcomen, *The craft and cruelty of the churches adversaries*, A3v.

213 Sheila Lambert, "Committees, Religion, and Parliamentary Encroachment on Royal Authority in Early Stuart England."

214 Simonds D'Ewes, *The Journal of Sir Simonds D'Ewes from the beginning of the Long Parliament to the opening of the trial of the Earl of Stafford* and *The Journal of Sir Simonds D'Ewes; from the first recess of the Long Parliament to the withdrawal of King Charles from London*; Lambert Blackwell Larking, *Proceedings, principally in the county of Kent, in connection with the Parliaments called in 1640 ..., 1627–1644.*

215 The spring of 1643 saw a wave of iconoclasm in which the stained glass east window of St. Margaret's was destroyed and the statue of the saint herself defaced. On 1 April 1643, an act was passed sequestering the estates of "notorious delinquents," both lay and clerical. See John Walker, *An attempt towards recovering an account of the numbers and sufferings of the clergy of the Church of England* ..., 54.

216 Mayer, *A Commentary upon the whole Old Testament* ..., 56.

217 Richard Cust, "'Patriots' and 'popular' spirits," 46.

218 Gouge, *The Saints Support, set out in a sermon preached before the honourable House of Commons assembled in Parliament*, 24, 26.

219 A Jacobus Cranford was appointed vicar in Sherbourne, Oxfordshire, in 1641. It is possible that he preached in London on this particular day (Clergy of the Church of England database, http://theclergydatabase.org.uk).

220 Previous research on the subject of notetaking in the Renaissance generally related to making notes from printed texts rather than sermons. The most useful study in this context is perhaps Ann Blair's "Note Taking as an Art of Transmission." Hunt's study offers a wealth of contemporary sources to help us understand how early modern listeners took notes at sermons; see *The Art of Hearing*, esp. 94–114.

221 Hunt, *The Art of Hearing*, 108.

222 Ibid., 154–5.

223 It is of course possible that Yonge simply did not take notes on this part of the sermon, or that he arrived late. Nevertheless, the notes provide the outline of an effective abridgement, suggesting that the sermon may have been preached in this form.

224 As the writer began from both ends of the notebook towards the centre, the foliation of the sermon notes is in reverse order.

225 Arthur Marotti cites Hugh Aveling's assertion that there were only nine Jesuit priests in England in 1593 and John Bossy's estimate that by 1641 there were almost 400 Jesuits in England, 180 of them missionaries (Arthur F. Marotti, *Religious Ideology and Cultural Fantasy*, 52). While these estimates can only be approximate, it seems clear that there was at least a public perception that the numbers were increasing.

226 The first English edition (1630) is STC 16800; the second (1641) is Wing L3004. Contzen's seems to have become one of the texts routinely used as proof of Catholic plotting in this period. Selections were printed in 1653 in *The Plots of Jesuits* and in 1663 by Richard Baxter in *Fair warning, or XX prophesies concerning the return of popery.*

227 Here Newcomen, without documenting his sources, accepts the veracity of Catholic commentators on the plot, who attempted to justify the conspiracy as a reaction to fears of harsher measures against their religion. Newcomen, however, applauds this intention, seeing the sole purpose of Parliament as the maintenance of Protestantism.

228 Cornelius Burges, in the sermon of the previous year, had claimed that the role of this particular parliament was to continue reforming the church, but Newcomen expands this idea to make church reform the primary purpose of all Parliaments.

229 Guibbory, who explores the ways in which parliamentary preachers used Jewish history, particularly references to rebuilding the temple, in their sermons, observes that despite scholarly interest in iconoclasm, preachers were generally more interested in the work of building rather than destroying. Newcomen's sermon, which she does not discuss, is interesting in this context, since he uses a text alluding to the rebuilding of Jerusalem's walls to call for a program that includes destroying the remnants of Catholicism in churches. See "Israel and English Protestant Nationalism."

230 Edward Boys made the connection between 30 January and 5 November explicit in a Gunpowder sermon apparently preached in Norwich in 1662. Recalling his regicide sermon, he said that had the plot not been discovered, 5 November 1605 "should have been very like" 30 January 1649 ("The Powder-Plot blown up," in *Sixteen Sermons*, 83).

231 On the role of 5 November in this new calendar, see Cressy, *Bonfires and Bells*, ch. 11. Paul Connerton observes that revolutions are frequently marked by the implementation of a new calendar (*How Societies Remember*, ch. 2). While the Restoration was not a revolution, its founders also saw the calendar as a means of justifying political change.

232 In 1667 George Morley preached at Whitehall, although the sermon was not printed until 1683 (*A Sermon Preached before the King at White-Hall, November 5. 1667*). Surviving sermons from other pulpits include Richard Carpenter's 1662 diatribe against Catholicism and toleration, which ended by advising Parliament to conduct a just war against the Roman church and asking God to make Charles an example to his people (*Rome in her fruits being a sermon preached on the fifth of November, 1662 near to the standard in Cheapside*, 32). More restrained is Richard Allestree's 1665 sermon at Oxford, which contrasts the Catholic doctrines that encourage resistance of authority with the Church of England's insistence upon the monarch's right to enforce a national religion ("The Tenth Sermon, preached at Christ-church in Oxford, Novemb. 5. 1665" in *Forty Sermons*). Edward Boys's "The Powder-Plot blown up" is undated but notes that his last sermon preached in the same pulpit was 30 January 1662 (in *Sixteen Sermons*). Matt Jenkinson reminds us of how rare publication even of court sermons was in the Restoration, noting that only about 10 per cent of court preachers had individual sermons printed ("Preaching at the Court of Charles II," 444). Moreover, the Great Fire in 1666 temporarily disrupted the printing trade and destroyed stocks of books and pamphlets that may have included sermons. Consequently, the absence of surviving sermons does not necessarily indicate that they were not preached or printed. Since Nonconformists were ejected from their pulpits in 1662 and denied opportunities to publish their sermons, it is difficult to determine from the print record to what extent dissenters continued to use 5 November as a preaching occasion.

233 See Edie, "Right Rejoicing: Sermons on the Occasion of the Stuart Restoration, 1660," 69, and "The Public Face of Royal Ritual," 313.

234 Edie, "The Public Face of Royal Ritual," 316.

235 Spurr, *The Restoration Church of England, 1646–1689*, 40.

236 See Glen Bowman, "Elizabethan Catholics and Romans 13."

237 Ward, *Against resistance of lawful powers*, A3[v].

238 Collins, "The Restoration Bishops and the Royal Supremacy," 549.

239 Ibid., 566.

240 Wood, *Athenae Oxonienses*, 2.627. Ward was a notable mathematician and astronomer who also had an interest in the development of a universal language, although he gave up these pursuits after the Restoration. For a more balanced summary of Ward's career, see John Henry, "Ward, Seth (1617–1689)."

241 Wood, *Athenae Oxonienses*, 2.628.

242 Pope, *The Life of the Right Reverend Father in God Seth, Lord Bishop of Salisbury*, 24.

243 Seth Ward, *Against resistance of lawful powers*, 8.

244 In 1608 James had apparently acted from similar motives when he ordered John King's virulently anti-Catholic 5 November court sermon published despite King's

blunt warning about the king's dangerous leniency towards papists. See Ferrell, *Government by Polemic*, 99–106.

245 *The Diary of John Evelyn*, 1.384; George Morley, *A Sermon Preached before the King at White-hall, November 5. 1667.*

246 Spurr, *The Restoration Church of England, 1646–1689*, 64–5.

247 South, "The Peculiar Care and Concern of Providence for the Protection and Defense of Kings, set forth in a sermon preached at Westminster-Abbey, Nov.5. 1675," 3.587.

248 The late 1670s also saw the institution of various popular celebrations that included burnings of effigies of the pope and the Whore of Babylon (see Cressy, *Bonfires and Bells*, ch. 11).

249 Hascard, *A Sermon preached upon the fifth of November, 1678*, 20.

250 Bedle, *A Sermon preached in S. Lawrence-Jewry Church on the fifth of November, anno dom. 1678*, 27.

251 Gregory, *The religious villain*, 35.

252 Wray, *Loyalty protesting against popery*, 25.

253 Clyve Jones, "Debates in the House of Lords on 'The Church in Danger,' 1705, and on Dr Sacheverell's Impeachment, 1710," 759.

254 It is perhaps not surprising that both Ward and Sacheverell chose texts from the New Testament. Attempts to map England onto biblical Israel were suspect after the Restoration. Gerard Reedy argues that the major divines had almost completely rejected the use of political typology in their sermons after the first few years of the Restoration (*The Bible and Reason*, 79–84).

255 Holmes, *The Trial of Doctor Sacheverell*, 61–2.

256 For a fuller description of Sacheverell's preaching style and the 5 November 1709 sermon in particular, see Holmes, *The Trial of Doctor Sacheverell*, ch. 3. On reactions to Sacheverell more generally, see Farooq, "The Politicising Influence of Print."

257 Mark Knights refuses to credit Garrard's claims of ignorance, arguing that he "deliberately chose a high-flying firebrand to provoke his overwhelmingly whig colleagues on the aldermanic bench and in the common council. By 1709 Sacheverell was well known for his high church rants against whigs, dissenters and 'fanatics' of all kinds" ("Introduction" 19).

258 See Clyve Jones, "Debates in the House of Lords on 'The Church in Danger,' 1705, and on Dr Sacheverell's Impeachment, 1710."

259 Holmes, *The Trial of Doctor Sacheverell*, 64.

260 Sacheverell, *The Perils of false brethren*, 20.

261 These references did not go unnoticed by contemporaries. In his speech at Sacheverell's impeachment, Gilbert Burnet noted that Sacheverell had quoted eleven times from the *Homilies*, and analyses these references in order to show that only one of them related to rebellion in general, while the others related to rebellion

against wicked princes only. Burnet concludes that between 1558 and 1628 the church's consistent doctrine was that rebellion was justified in self-defence; between 1628 and 1640, the doctrine that the king was God's agent came back into vogue. Consequently the Civil War did constitute a rebellion and was never justified as self-defence. Under these circumstances, it was unsurprising that the doctrine of passive obedience should be urged so strongly after the Restoration. See Gilbert Burnet, *The Bishop of Salisbury his Speech in the House of Lords on the First Article of the Impeachment of Dr. Henry Sacheverell*, 1–12.

262 Holmes, "The Sacheverell Riots," 61.

263 Holmes, *The Trial of Dr. Secheverell*, 91–3.

264 Lee Horsley, "'Vox Populi' in the Political Literature of 1710."

265 Holmes, *The Trial of Doctor Sacheverell*, 81.

266 Holmes, "The Sacheverell Riots."

267 Horsley, "'Vox Populi' in the Political Literature of 1710," 339, 340. On Sacheverell's representation of himself and his cause at the trial, see Brian Cowan, "The Spin Doctor: Sacheverell's Trial Speech and Political Performance in the Divided Society," in *Faction Displayed*, 28–46.

268 This situation was the controversy over the re-establishment of a Catholic hierarchy in England.

269 Jonathan Scott reminds us that the Restoration is best seen as an era of continued instability. See *England's Troubles,* ch. 7.

270 Spurr, *The Restoration Church of England, 1646–1689*, xiii–xiv.

271 Guibbory, "Israel and English Protestant Nationalism," 116.

272 Sheares dates the sermon incorrectly. It was actually preached on 5 November 1709.

Conclusion: Echoes and Reverberations

1 Hurstfield, "Gunpowder Plot and the Politics of Dissent," 100; Quint, *Epic and Empire*, 281.

Works Cited

Manuscript Sources

"Answers of Samuel Ward to 43 articles objected against him by the commissioners for causes ecclesiastical, 19 Dec. 1634." PRO SP 16/278/65. The National Archives, London.

"Articles objected by his majesties command for causes ecclesiastical against Henry Burton Clerk parson or vicar of St. Mathews Friday Street London." PRO SP 16/335. The National Archives, London.

"Collection of State Papers and Correspondence of Sir Thomas Edmondes, Knt.; 1592–1633." MS Stowe 168, fol. 363. British Library, London.

Goodwyn, William. "A Sermon Preached at Pauls Cross ye 5. of Nouember. 1614. by Doctor Goodwyn. then Vice Chanceller of Oxford." Ms.12.10. Doctor Williams's Library, London.

Nailor, Joseph. "Paul's Cross Gunpowder Anniversary Sermon (1631) on Psalm 124.5–7." MS. 52.D60.01. St Paul's Cathedral Library, London.

"Papers mainly concerning Robert Devereux, 2nd earl of Essex." MS 2872, fols. 51–8. Lambeth Palace Library, London.

Privy Council. "Abstract, including large Excerpts of the Privy Council Registers, from 1550 to 1610." Add. MS 11,402. British Library, London.

Sheares, Abraham. "'The Sheares Bible,' versified and illustrated by Abraham Sheares, 1701–1731." Add. MS 62,708. British Library, London.

"Vpon Henry Howard Earle of Northampton 1603." Malone MS 23 1a. Bodleian Library, Oxford.

Yonge, Walter. "Reports of Sermons preached by various ministers in London." Vol. 1. Add. MS 18,781. British Library, London.

Pre-1700 Texts

[A.B.C.D.E.]. *Novembris Monstrum, or Rome brought to bed in England. with The Whores Miscarying.* London, 1641. Wing E3.

Adams, Thomas. *The Temple: A Sermon Preached at Pavls Crosse the fifth of August. 1624.* London, 1624. STC 129.

Allestree, Richard. "The tenth Sermon, preached at Christ-church in Oxford, Novemb. 5. 1665." In *Forty Sermons.* London and Oxford, 1684. Wing A1114.

Ames, William. *The saints security.* London, 1652. Wing A3009.

Bacon, Francis. *A Declaration of the practises & treasons attempted and committed by Robert late Earle of Essex and his complices.* London, 1601. STC 1133.

Baker, Aaron. *Achitophel befool'd: a sermon preached November 5, 1678 at St. Sepulchres.* London, 1678. Wing B478.

Bargrave, Isaac. *A Sermon Preached before King Charles, March 27. 1627.* London, 1627. STC 1414.

– *A Sermon Preached before the Honorable Assembly of Knights, Citizens, and Burgesses of the Lower House of Parliament.* London, 1624. STC 1415.

Barker, Matthew. *The Faithful and Wise Servant. Discovered in a Sermon Preached to the Parliament ... Jan. 9. 1656.* London, 1657. Wing B773.

Barlow, Thomas. *The Gunpowder-Treason with a discourse of the manner of its discovery ... a preface touching that horrid conspiracy, by the Right Reverend Father in God, Thomas, Lord Bishop of Lincoln.* London, 1679. Wing B833.

Barlow, William. *A Sermon Preached at Paules Crosse, on the first Sunday in Lent: Martij 1.1600. With a short discourse of the Late Earle of Essex his Confession, and Penitence, before and at the time of his death.* London, 1601. STC 1454.

– *The Sermon Preached at Paules Crosse, the tenth day of Nouember being the next Sunday after the discouerie of this late horrible treason.* London, 1606. STC 1455.

Baxter, Richard. "A Sermon of the Absolute Sovereignty of Christ; And the Necessity of Mans Subjection, Dependence, and Chiefest Love to him." In *True Christianity; or, Christs absolute Dominion, and Mans Necessary Self-Resignation and Subjection. In two Assize Sermons preached at Worcester*, 77–136. London, 1656. Wing B1437.

Bedle, Joseph. *A Sermon preached in S. Lawrence-Jewry Church on the fifth of November, anno dom. 1678.* London, 1679. Wing B1675.

Beringer, Joachim. *The Romane Conclaue.* London, 1609. STC 24526.

Boys, Edward. "The Powder-Plot Blown Up." In *Sixteen Sermons, preached upon several occasions, by Edward Boys, B. D. Late rector of Mautby in Norfolk,and sometime fellow of Corpus Christi Colledge in Cambridge*, 83–106. London, 1672. Wing B4065.

Boys, John. *An Exposition of the Last Psalme, Delivered in a Sermon Preached at Paules Cross.* London, 1615. STC 3465.4.

Breton, Nicholas. *The Hate of Treason with a touch of the late treason.* London, 1616. STC 3658.

Bridge, William. *England Saved with a Notwithstanding: Represented in a sermon to the Honorable House of Commons, assembled in Parliament, Novemb. 5. 1647. The Day of Thanksgiving for Deliverance from the Powder-Plot.* London, 1648. Wing B4452.

A Briefe Relation of Certain Speciall and Most Materiall Passages, and Speeches in the Starre-Chamber, occasioned and delivered Iune the 14th 1637. At the censure of those three worthy Gentlemen, Dr. Bastwicke, Mr. Burton and Mr. Prynne, as it hath been truly and faithfully gathered from their owne mouthes by one present at the sayd Censure. N.p., 1637. STC 1569.

Broughton, H[ugh]. *The Lamentations of Jeremy ... with Annotations.* [Amsterdam], 1608. STC 2781.

[Broughton, Richard]. *The First Part of Protestants Proofes, for Catholikes Religion and Recusancy.* England [secret Catholic press], 1607. STC 20448.

[Broughton, Richard]. *A Iust and Moderate Answer to a most iniurious and slaunderous pamphlet.* England [secret Catholic press], 1606. STC 18188.

Burges, Cornelius. *Another sermon preached to the Honorable House of Commons now assembled in Parliament, November the fifth, 1641.* London, 1641. Wing B5668.

Burnet, Gilbert. *A Collection of Several Tracts and Dsicourses [sic] written in the years 1678, 1679, 1680, 1681, 1682, 1683, 1684, and 1685.* London, 1685. Wing B5770aA.

Burton, Henry. *For God and the King: The Summe of Two Sermons Preached on the fifth of November last in St. Matthewes Friday-Street.* [Amsterdam], 1636. STC 4142. Rprt at London, 1636, STC 4141.

– *A Narration of the Life of Mr. Henry Burton.* London, 1643. Wing B6169.

– *Tryall of Priuate Deuotions. Or, A Diall for the Houres of Prayer.* London, 1628. STC 4157.

Calderwood, David. *The True History of the Church of Scotland from the beginning of the Reformation unto the end of the Reign of King James VI.* N.p., 1680. Wing C280.

Carleton, George. *Ivrisdiction Regall, Episcopall, Papall Wherein is declared how the Pope hath intruded vpon the iurisdiction of temporal princes.* London, 1610. STC 4637.

– *A Thankfull remembrance of Gods mercy.* London, 1625. STC 4641.

Carpenter, Richard. *The Iesuit, and the Monk: or, The serpent, and the dragon. Being a sermon preached on the fifth of November, 1656.* London, 1656. Wing C622.

– *Rome in her fruits being a sermon preached on the fifth of November, 1662 near to the standard in Cheapside.* London, 1663. Wing C626.

Cave, William. *A Sermon preached before the Right Honourable, the Lord Mayor, Alderman and citizens of London, at S. Mary-le-Bow on the fifth of November, 1680.* London, 1680. Wing C1606.

Cecil, Robert. *An Answere to Certaine Scandalous Papers, scattered abroad vnder colour of a Catholicke Admonition.* London, 1606. STC 4895.

[Cecil, William]. *The Execution of Iustice in England for Maintenaunce of Publique and Christian Peace.* London, 1583. STC 4902.

[Cecil, William]. *A True Report of Sundry horrible conspiracies of late time detected to haue (by barbarous murders) taken away the life of the Queenes most excellent Maiestie.* London, 1594. STC 7603.

Church of England. *A fourme of prayer with thanksgiving to be used by all the Kings Maiesties louing subiects euery yeere, the fift of August.* London, 1603. STC 16489. [1606 STC 16490; 1618 STC 16491].

– *An Order for Prayer and Thankesgiuing (necessary to bee vsed in these dangerous times) for the safetie and preseruation of Her Maiestie and this realme. Set foorth by authoritie anno 1594. And reuewed with some alterations vpon the present occasion.* London, 1598. STC 16529.

– *An Order of Prayer and Thankesgiuing for the preseruation of her Maiestie and the Realme, from the traiterous and bloodie practises of the Pope, and his adherents: to be vsed at times appointed in the Preface.* London, 1586. STC 16517.

– *An Order of praier and thankes-giuing, for the preseruation of the Queenes Maiesties life and salfetie* [sic]*: to be vsed of the preachers and ministers of the dioces of Winchester.* London, 1585. STC 16516.

– *An Order of Prayer and thankes-giuing (necessary to be vsed in these dangerous times) for the safetie and preseruation of her Maiesty and this realme. Set forth by authoritie.* London, 1594. STC 16525.

– *Prayers and thankesgiuing to bee vsed by all the Kings Maiesties louing subiects: for the happy deliuerance of His Maiestie* … London, 1606. STC 16494.

– *Prayers, and thanksgiuing, to be vsed by all the Kings Maiesties louing subiects, for the happy deliuerance of His Maiestie, the Queene, Prince, and states, of the Parliament, from the most traiterous and bloody intended massacre by gun-powder, the fift of Nouember. 1605.* London, 1635. STC 16499.

– *A Psalme and Collect of thankesgiuing, not unmeet for this present time: to be said or sung in churches.* London, 1588. STC 16520.

Churchyard, Thomas. *Come bring in Maye with me, my Maye is fresh and greene: (a Subiectes harte, an humble mind) to serue a mayden Queene. A discourse of Rebellion, Drawne forth for to warne the wanton witte how to kepe their heads on their shoulders.* London, 1570. STC 5224.

Clarke, Samuel. *Englands Remembrancer, a true and full narrative of those two never to be forgotten deliverances, the one from the Spanish invasion in eighty eight, the other from the hellish powder plot, November 5, 1605.* London, 1657. Wing C4510.

Colfe, Isaac. *A Sermon Preached on the Queenes Day. Beeing the 17. of Nouember. 1587. at the towne of Lidd in Kent, by Isaac Colfe, Preacher of the Word of God.* London, [1588]. STC 5552.

Colt, Nicholas. *The Seale of the Churches Safety; or a Sermon preached at Norwhich, the fift of Nouember, 1616.* London, 1617. STC 5585.

A Continvation of the Histories of Forreine Martyrs from the Happy Reigne of the Most Renowned Queen Elizabeth to these times. London, 1632. STC 11228. Rprt. 1641, Wing C5965.

Contzen, Adam. *Looke about you nam stultissimum credo, ad imitandum non optima quaequae proponere. plin. sec. ad vocon: learne from a deuill.* London, 1630. STC 16800. Reprinted as *Looke about you. The plot of Contzen, the Moguntine Iesuite, to Cheate a Church of the Religion Established therein, and to serve in Popery by Art, without noise or Tumult.* n.p., 1641. Wing L3004.

Cooper, Thomas. *Nonae Nouembris aeternitati consecratae in memoriam admirandae illius liberationis principis, et populi Anglicani a proditione sulphurea.* Oxford, 1607. STC 5702.

Crakanthorpe, Richard. *A treatise of the Fift General Councel held at Constantinople, anno 553. under Iustinian the Emperor, in the time of Pope Vigilius.* London, 1634. STC 5984.

Daniel, Samuel. *The Works of Samvel Daniel. Newly augmented.* London, 1601. STC 6236.

A Defence of the Honorable Sentence and Execution of the Queene of Scots. London, 1587. STC 17566.3.

Dekker, Thomas. *The Double PP. A Papist in Armes.* London, 1606. STC 6498.

– *Newes from hell brought by the Diuells carrier.* London, 1606. STC 6514.

A Discoverie of the Hellish Plot Against Diverse Particular of the Nobility of the Kingdome of England. Also the Papists Gunpowder-Plot, brought to Light. London, 1642. Wing D1653.

Dow, Christopher. *Innovations unjustly charged upon the present church and state.* London, 1637. STC 7090.

Drayton, Michael. *In the Harmonie of the Church.* London, 1610. STC 7199.

Dyke, Daniel. *Certaine comfortable sermons vpon the 124. Psalme: tending to stirre vp to thankefulnesse for our deliuerance from the late Gunpowder-treason: preached before the Lady Elizabeth her Grace, at Combe: by Daniel Dike preacher of the Word of God.* London, 1616. STC 7395.

The Earle of Gowries conspiracie against the Kings Maiestie at Saint Ionstoun vpon Tuesday the fift day of August. London, 1603. STC 21467.5.

Elizabeth I. *By the Quene. Forasmuche as the tyme wherein common interludes in the Englishe tongue ar wont vsually to be played ...* London, [1559]. STC 7897.

Featley, Daniel. *Clavis Mystica a key opening divers difficult and mysterious texts of Holy Scripture.* London, 1636. STC 10730.

Fennor, William. *Pluto, his Trauails, or, The Diuels Pilgrimage to the Colledge of Iesuites.* London, 1612. STC 10785.

Fetherstone, Christopher. *The Lamentations of Jeremie, in Prose and Meter, with Apt Notes ... Together with Tremellius his Annotations.* London, 1587. STC 2779.

Fotherby, Martin. *Foure Sermons, lately preached ... The third at Paules Crosse.* London, 1608. STC 11206.

Goodwin, George. *Babels Balm: or the Honey-combe of Romes Religion.* London, 1624. STC 12030.

Gouge, William. *The Saints Support, set out in a sermon preached before the honourable House of Commons assembled in Parliament.* London, 1642. Wing G1397.

Gregory, Francis. *The religious villain: a sermon preached before the Right Honourable Sr. Robert Clayton, Kt., lord mayor of London, and the Court of Aldermen, upon the fifth day of November, 1679.* London, 1679. Wing G1903.

Hacket, John. *A Century of Sermons upon Several Remarkable Subjects Preached by the Right Reverend Father in God, John Hacket.* London, 1675. Wing H169.

Hakewill, George. *A Comparison between the Dayes of Purim and that of the Powder Treason.* Oxford, 1626. STC 12615.

Hamond, Thomas. *The late commotion of certaine papists in Herefordshire.* London, 1605. STC 25232.

Hascard, Gregory. *A Sermon preached upon the fifth of November, 1678*. London, 1679. Wing H1113.

Hawes, Edward. *Trayterous Percyes and Catesbyes Prosopopoeia*. London, 1606. STC 12940.

The Hellish and Horrible Councell, practised and vsed by the Iesuites, (in their priuate Consultations), when they would haue a man to murther a king. London, 1610. STC 5862.

Hells Triennial Parliament, Summoned five years since, by King Lucifer. London, 1647. Wing H1388.

Herle, Charles. *Davids Reserve, and Rescue, in a Sermon preached Before the Honourable, the House of Commons, On the Fifth of November. 1644*. London, 1645. Wing H1554.

Herring, Francis. *Certaine rvles, directions, or advertisments for this time of pestilential contagion: with a caueat to those that weare about their neckes impoisoned amulets as a preseruatiue from the plague*. London, 1625. STC 13240.

– *Mischeefes Mysterie: or Treasons Masterpeece, the Powder-plot. Translated and very much dilated by John Vicars*. London, 1617. STC 13247.

– *A modest defence of the caueat giuen to the wearers of impoisoned amulets, as preseruatiues from the plague*. London, 1604. STC 13248.

– *November the 5. 1605. The Quintessence of Cruelty*. Trans. John Vicars. n.p. 1641. Wing H1602.

– *Pietas Pontificia seu Conjurationis illius prodigiosae, et post natos homines maxime execrandae*. London, 1606. STC 13244.

– *Pietas Pontificia seu Coniurationis sulphureae contrae Iacobum Magnae Britanniae Regem ...* London, 1609. STC 13245.

– *Popish Pietie or the First Part of the Historie of that Horrible and Barbarous Conspiracie, Commonly Called the "Powder-Treason."* Trans. A.P. London, 1610. STC 13246.

Heylyn, Peter. *A Briefe and Moderate Answer, to the seditious and scandalous challenge of Henry Burton* … 1637. STC 13269.

Heyrick, Richard. "The Third Sermon." In *Three Sermons preached at the Collegiate Church in Manchester*, 113–73. London, 1641. Wing H1751.

His Maiesties speech in this last session of Parliament … Together with a discourse of the maner of the discouery of this late intended Treason. London, 1605. STC 14393.

Holland, Thomas. *Paneguris D. Elizabethae Dei Gratiâ Angliae, Franciae, & Hiberniae Regina. A Sermon Preached at Pavls in London the 17. of November, ann. Dom. 1599*… Oxford, 1601. STC 13597.

Holyday, Barten. *A Sermon Preached at Pauls Crosse, August the 5. 1623*. London, 1626. STC 13615.

Horton, Thomas. *The Pillar and Pattern of Englands Deliverances. Presented in a Sermon to the Right Honourable Lord Mayor and Aldermen … in their solemn meeting at Pauls on the Lords Day, Novem. 5, 1654*. London, 1655. Wing H2878.

Howson, John. *A Sermon Preached at St. Maries in Oxford, the 17. Day of Nouember, 1602. In defence of the festivities of the Church of England, and namely that of her Maiesties coronation*. Oxford, 1602. STC 13884.

Hubbock, William. *Great Brittaines Resurrection: or the Parliaments passing bell.* London, 1606. STC 13898.5.

Hull, John. *An Exposition vpon a part of the Lamentations of Ieremie.* London, 1618. STC 13931. Rprt 1620, STC 13932.

Hussey, William. *The Magistrates Charge, for the Peoples Safetie ... May 26, 1647.* London, 1647. Wing H3818.

I.H. *The Divell of the Vault or The Unmasking of Murder.* London, 1606. STC 12568.

J.H. *A True and Perfect Relation of that Most Horrid & Hellish Conspiracy of the Gunpowder Treason.* London, 1662. Wing H82C.

J.M. *News from Hell, Rome and the Inns of Court.* London, 1642. Wing M42B.

James I. *His Maiesties Declaration Touching his Proceedings in the Late Assemblie and Conuention of Parliament.* London, 1621. STC 9241.

– *The Kings Maiesties speech, as it was deliuered by him in the vpper house of the Parliament, to the Lords spirituall and temporall, and to the knights, citizens and burgesses there assembled, on Munday the 19. day of March 1603.* London, 1604. STC 14390.

King, John. *A Sermon preached in Oxon: the 5. of November. 1607.* Oxford, 1607. STC 14985.

– *A Sermon Preached at Whitehall the 5. Day of November. Ann. 1608.* Oxford, 1608. STC 14986.

Lake, Arthur. "A Sermon preached at Saint Maries in Oxford on the fifth of November, 1614." In *Sermons with some religious and divine meditations*, 307–22. London, 1629. STC 15134.

Lewis, Jeremiah. *The Doctrine of thankfvlnesse: or, Israels trivmph, occasioned by the destruction of Pharaoh and his hoste, in the Red-Sea.* London, 1619. STC 15557.

Lloyd, William. *A Sermon Preached before the House of Lords on November 5,1680.* London, 1680. Wing L2712.

Marshall, Stephen. *A Sermon preached before the Honourable House of Commons, now assembled in Parliament, at their publicke fast November 17, 1640.* London, 1641.Wing M776.

Mason, Thomas. *Christs Victorie over Sathans Tyrannie.* London, 1615. STC 17622.

Mayer, John. *A Commentary upon the whole Old Testament ...* Pt. 4. London, 1653. Wing M1424.

Melanchthon, Philipp. *Of two wonderful popish monsters to wyt, of a popish asse which was found at Rome in the riuer of Tyber, and of a monkish café, calued at Friberge in Misne.* London, 1579. STC 17797.

Miller, Henry. *God the protector of Israel: a commemoration sermon, for our gracious deliverance, from that monster of treacheries, the gunpowder treason.* London, 1641. Wing 2060A.

Milward, John. *Iacob's Great Day of Trouble and Deliuerance.* London, 1610. STC 17942.

Morley, George. *A Sermon Preached before the King at Whitehall, November 5. 1667.* London, 1683. Wing M2795.

Morton, Thomas. *An exact discouerie of Romish doctrine in the case of conspiracie and rebellion.* London, 1605. STC 18184.

Neville, Henry. *An Exact Diurnall of the Parliament of Ladyes Ordered by the ladyes in Parliament.* London, 1647. Wing N504.

– *The Ladies, a second time, assembled in Parliament.* London, 1647. Wing N507.

– *The Ladies Parliament.* London, 1647. Wing N508.

Newcomen, Matthew. *The craft and cruelty of the churches adversaries.* London, [1643]. Wing N908A.

– *A sermon, tending to set forth the right vse of the disasters that befall our armies.* London, 1644. Wing N913.

Norton, Thomas. *To the Quenes Maiesties poore deceiued subiects of the northe countrey, drawn into rebellion by the Earles of Northumberland and Westmerland.* London, 1569. STC 18680.

Now or never: or, A new Parliament of women assembled and met together neer the Popes-Head in Moor-Fields, on the Back-side of Allsuch; adjoyning upon Shoreditch. London, 1656. Wing N1434.

Ochino, Bernadino. *A Tragedy or Dialogue of the unjust and usurped Primacy of the Bishop of Rome.* Trans. John Ponet. London, 1549. STC 18770.

Ormerod, Oliver. *The Picture of a Papist: or, A Relation of the damnable heresies, detestable qualities, and diabolicall practises of sundry hereticks in former ages, and of the papists in this age.* London, 1606. STC 18850.

Papa Patens, or The Pope in his Colours. London, 1652. Wing P278.

Parsons, Bartholomew. *The barren trees doome.* London, 1616. STC 19344.

Pelling, Edward. *A Sermon preached before the Lord Mayor and Court of Aldermen at St. Mary le Bow, on Nov. 5. 1683.* London, 1683. Wing P1095.

– *The True Mark of the Beast.* London, 1682. Wing P1106.

Pope, Walter. *The Life of the Right Reverend Father in God Seth, Lord Bishop of Salisbury.* London, 1697. Wing P2911.

Pricket, Robert. *The Iesuits Miracles, or New Popish Wonders ...* London, 1607. STC 20340.

– *Times Anotomie. Containing The Poore Mans Plaint, Brittons Trouble, and Her Triumph ...* London, 1606. STC 20342.

Prideaux, John. *Eight Sermons.* London, 1621. STC 20351.

Prime, John. *The Consolations of David, Briefly Applied to Queene Elizabeth: In a Sermon preached in Oxford the 17. of Nouember.* Oxford, 1588. STC 20368.

Purchas, Samuel. *The Kings towre and triumphant arch of London. A Sermon preached at Pauls Crosse, August. 5. 1622.* London, 1623. STC 20502.

Rainolds, John. *A Sermon vpon part of the eighteenth Psalm preached to the publik assembly of scholers in the Vniuersity of Oxford the last day of August, 1586.* Oxford, 1586. STC 20621.5.

Randal, John. *A Sermon Preacht at St Maries in Oxford, the 5. Of August: 1624. Concerning the kingdomes peace.* Oxford, 1624. STC 20685.

Rawlinson, John. *The Romish Iudas. A sermon preached at Saint Maries in Oxford the fifth of Nouember, 1610.* London, 1611. STC 20775.

Reeve, Thomas. *The Churches hazard.* London, 1632. STC 20832.

The returne of the knight of the poste from hell. London, 1606. STC 20905.

Reynolds, Edward. *The Brand pluck't out of the fire, a sermon preached before the Ld Maior Aldermen & Sherriffs & Companies of London, 5 Novemb last at Pauls.* London, 1659. Wing R1240.

Rhodes, John. *An Answere to a Romish Rime lately printed, and entituled, A proper new ballad wherein are contayned Catholicke questions to the Protestant* … London, 1602. STC 20959.

– *A Briefe Summe of the Treason intended against the king* … London, 1606. STC 20960.

Rymer, Thomas. *A short view of tragedy it's original, excellency and corruption: with some reflections on Shakespear and other practitioners for the stage.* London, 1693. Wing R2429.

Sandys, Edwin. "A Sermon Preached at Pauls Crosse at what time a maine treason was discouered." In *Sermons Made by the Most Reuerende Father in God, Edwin, Archbishop of Yorke, Primate of England and Metropolitane.* London, 1585. STC 21713.

Sclater, William. *Papisto-Mastix: or Deborah's Prayer against Gods Enemies Judg.5.31. Explicated and applyed.* London, 1642. Wing S919.

Scott, John. *A Sermon preached before the Right Honorable* … London, 1673. Wing S2065.

Scylla's Ghost an heroick poem: being a satyr against ambition and the late horid phanatick plot. London, 1684. Wing C300bA.

Seneca. *The Second Tragedy of Seneca entitled Thyestes faithfully Englisshed by Jasper Heywood fellowe of Alsolne College in Oxforde.* London, 1560. STC 22226.

Singleton, Isaac. *The downfall of Shebna together with an application to the bloudie Gowrie of Scotland.* London, 1615. STC 22574.

Something Written by Occasion of that fatall and memorable accident in the Blacke-Friers. London, 1623. STC 3101.

A Song or Story, for the Lasting Remembrance of Diuers Famous Works, which God hath done in our time. With an addition of certaine other Verses (both Latine and English) to the same purpose. London, 1626. STC 22922.

South, Robert. "The Peculiar Care and Concern of Providence for the Protection and Defense of Kings, set forth in a sermon preached at Westminster-Abbey, Nov.5. 1675." In *Twelve Sermons upon Several Occasions*, 3:551–99. London, 1698.

Sparke, Michael. *Crvmms of Comfort, the Valley of Teares, and the Hill of Ioy.* 6th ed. London, 1627. STC 23015.7.

Speed, John. *The History of Great Britaine* … London, 1614. STC 23046.

Spencer, Thomas. *Englands warning-peece or the history of the gun-powder treason.* London, 1658. Wing S4961.

Stephens, Edward. *A discourse concerning the original of the powder-plot together with a relation of the conspiracies against Queen Elizabeth and the persecutions of the Protestants in France to the death of Henry the fourth.* London, 1674. Wing S5426.

Sterry, Peter. *Englands Deliverance from the Northern Presbytery, Compared with its Deliverance from the Roman Papacy: or a Thanksgiving sermon preached on Nov. 5 1651.* London, 1652. Wing S5479.

– *The Way of God with his people in these Nations.* London, 1657. Wing S5487.

Stillingfleet, Edward. *A Sermon preached November V 1673 at St. Margretts Westminster.* London, 1674. Wing S5645.

Stock, Richard. *The Churches Lamentation for the losse of the Godly.* London, 1614. STC 23273.

Stradling, John. *Epigrammatum Libri Qvatvor.* London, 1607. STC 23354.

Strong, William. *A Voice from Heaven, calling the People of God to a Perfect Separation from Mystical Babylon* … London, 1654. Wing S6012.

Stubbes, Phillip. *The Intended Treason of Doctor Parrie: and his complices, against the Queenes most excellent Maiestie.* London, 1585. STC 23396.

T.W. *The Arraignement and Execution of the late Traytors* … London, 1606. STC 24916.

Taylor, John. *Mercvrivs Infernalis, or Orderlesse Orders.* Oxford, 1644. Wing T482.

– *The Nipping and Snipping of Abvses.* London, 1614. STC 23779.

Taylor, Thomas. *A Mappe of Rome.* London, 1620. STC 23838.

Temple, Thomas. *Christ's Government in and over his people Delivered in a Sermon Before the Honourable House of Commons ... Octob. 26. 1642.* London, 1642. Wing T634.

Terry, Edward. *[Pseudeleutheria] Or, Lawlesse Liberty. Set forth in a Sermon Preached before the Right Honourable Lord Major* [*sic*] *of London, &c. in Pauls, Aug.16. 1646.* London, 1646. Wing T781.

Thou, Jacques Auguste de. *A True Narration of that Horrible Conspiracy against King James and the whole Parliament of England.* London, 1674. Wing T1078.

Tillotson, John. *A Sermon preached November 5, 1678 at St Margarets Westminster.* London, 1678. Wing T1231.

A True and Perfect Relation of the Whole Proceedings against the late most barbarous traitors, Garnet a Iesuite, and his confederats. London, 1606. STC 11618.

A True and Plaine Declaration of the Horrible Treasons, practised by William Parry the traitor, against the Queenes Maiestie. London, 1585. STC 19342a.

A True Relation of a Divelish Designe by the Papists to Blow up the City of Oxford with Gunpowder. London, n.d. Wing T2875.

A Trve Relation of a Damnable Gun-Powder Plot, Found out at Rugland-Castle ... London, 1641. Wing T2873.

Tynley, Robert. *Two Learned Sermons. The One, of the mischievous subtiltie, and barbarous crueltie, the other of the false Doctrines* … *of the Romish Synagogue.* London, 1609. STC 24472.

Udall, John. *A Commentarie upon the Lamentations of Jeremy.* London, 1608. STC 24497.

[Univoce-Catholicus]. *Lucta Iacobi: or a bonefire for his maiesties double deliuerie, from the deluge in Perth, the 5. of August, 1600. And the doomesday of Britaine, the 5. of Nouember 1605.* London, 1607. STC 14426.

Venning, Ralph. *Mercies memorial, or, Israels thankful remembrance of God in their high estate for his merciful remembring of them in their low estate.* London, 1657. Wing V205.

Vicars, John. *Babylons beautie.* London, 1644. Wing V293.

Vicars, John. *Gods arke overtopping the worlds waves, or the third part of the Parliamentary chronicle.* London, [1645]. Wing V309.

– *Jehovah-jireh. God in the mount, or Englands parliamentarie-chronicle.* London, 1644. Wing V313.

– *Prodigies and Apparitions, or Englands warning piece.* London, 1643. Wing V323.

– *Speculum scripturale schismaticorum or, A Scripture looking-glasse, most exactly characterizing all sorts of schismaticks.* London, 1649. Wing V329.

Ward, Samuel. *The Papists Powder Treason 1588 … To God, in memorye of his double deliverance from ye invincible navie and ye unmatcheable powder treason, 1605.* London, 1680. Wing W810A.

Ward, Seth. *Against resistance of lawful powers. A Sermon preach'd before the King at White-hall, November 5.1661.* London, 1661. Wing W812. Reprint, [1710].

Web, Richard. *The Lot or portion of the Righteous, A Comfortable Sermon, preached at the Cathedrall Church of Glocester, vpon the fift day of August.* London, 1616. STC 25151.

Whetstone, George. *The Censure of a loyall subiect upon certain noted speech …* London, 1587. STC 25334a.

White, John. *Defence of the Way to the True Church against A. D. his reply.* London, 1614. STC 25390.

Whitgift, John. *A Most Godly and Learned Sermon preached at Pauls Crosse the 17 of Nouember, in the yeare of our Lorde 1583.* London, 1589. STC 25432.

Willan, Robert. *Conspiracie against kings, heavens scorne, A Sermon preached at Westminster-Abbey before the Iudges, vpon the fifth of Novemb. 1622.* London, 1622. STC 25669.

Williams, John. *A History of the Gunpowder-Treason, collected from Approved Authors as well Popish as Protestant.* London, 1678. Wing W2705.

– *A Vindication of the History of the Gunpowder-Treason and of the Proceedings and Matters Relating Thereunto.* London, 1681. Wing W2741.

Wilson, Thomas. *A Sermon on the Gunpowder Treason with Reflections on the Late Plot.* London, 1679. W2936.

Wood, Anthony à. *Athenae Oxonienses an exact history of all the writers and bishops who have had their education in the most ancient and famous University of Oxford …* Vol. 1. London, 1692. Wing W3383A.

Wortley, Francis. *Mercurius Britanicus his welcome to hell.* London, 1647. Wing W3641.

Wray, William. *Loyalty protesting against popery.* London, 1683. Wing W3672.

Secondary Sources and Modern Editions of Pre-1700 Texts

Achinstein, Sharon. *Milton and the Revolutionary Reader.* Princeton, NJ: Princeton University Press, 1994.

– "The Uses of Deception: From Cromwell to Milton." In *The Witness of Times: Manifestations of Ideology in Seventeenth Century England,* edited by Katherine Z. Keller and Gerald J. Schiffhorst, 174–200. Pittsburgh: Duquesne University Press, 1993.

Adams, Simon. "Faction, Clientage and Party: English Politics, 1550–1603." *History Today* 32, no. 12 (1982): 33–9.

Alabaster, William. *Elisæ*. Edited and translated by Michael O'Connell. *Studies in Philology* 76, no. 5 (1979): 15–65.

Alt, Christina. "Directed Readings: Paratext in *A Game at Chess* and *The Tragedie of Philotas*." *Philological Quarterly* 83, no. 2 (2004): 127–44.

Amos, Flora Ross. *Early Theories of Translation*. New York: Octagon, 1973. First published 1920.

Andrewes, Lancelot. *Lancelot Andrewes: Selected Sermons and Lectures*, edited by Peter McCullough. Oxford: Oxford University Press, 2006.

– *The Works of Lancelot Andrewes, sometime Bishop of Winchester*. Vol. 4. Oxford: John Henry Parker, 1854. Reprinted. New York: AMS Press, 1967.

Andrews, Michael. "*The Isle of Gulls* as Travesty." *Yearbook of English Studies* 3 (1973): 78–84.

Appelbaum, Robert. "Milton, the Gunpowder Plot, and the Mythography of Terror." *Modern Langauge Quarterly* 68, no. 4 (2007): 461–91.

Arbuckle, W.F. "The 'Gowrie Conspiracy.'" *The Scottish Historical Review* 36 (1957): 1–24, 91–110.

Aristotle. "Poetics." *The Complete Works of Aristotle*. Vol. 2. Bollingen Series LXXI-2.

Arnoult, Sharon L. "'Spiritual and Sacred Publique Actions': *The Book of Common Prayer* and the Understanding of Worship in the Elizabethan and Jacobean Church of England." In *Religion and the English People 1500–1640: New Voices New Perspectives*, edited by Eric Josef Carlson, 25–47. Kirksville, MO: Thomas Jefferson University Press, 1998.

Ayres, Philip J. "The Nature of Jonson's Roman History." In *Renaissance Historicism: Selections from English Literary Renaissance*, edited by Arthur F. Kinney and Dan S. Collins, 207–22. Amherst: University of Massachusetts Press, 1987.

Baldwin, R.G. "Phineas Fletcher: His Modern Readers and his Renaissance Ideas." *Philological Quarterly* 40, no. 4 (1961): 462–75.

Baskerville, Stephen. *Not Peace but a Sword: The Political Theology of the English Revolution*. London: Routledge, 1993.

Bedford, Ronald. "Milton's Military Heaven Revisited." *AUMLA* 106 (2006): 123–48.

Bellany, Alastair. "Libels in Action: Ritual, Subversion and the English Literary Underground, 1603–42." In *The Politics of the Excluded, c. 1500–1850*, edited by Tim Harris, 99–124. Houndmills: Palgrave, 2001.

– "Pickering, Lewis (*bap.* 1571)." In *Oxford Dictionary of National Biography*, online ed., edited by Lawrence Goldman. Oxford: Oxford University Press, 2004. http://www.oxforddnb.com.libproxy.uregina.ca:2048/view/article/62363. Accessed 13 December 2015.

– "A Poem on the Archbishop's Hearse: Puritanism, Libel, and Sedition after the Hampton Court Conference." *Journal of British Studies* 34 (1995): 137–64.

Bellany, Alastair, and Andrew McRae. *Early Stuart Libels*. http://www.earlystuartlibels.net/htdocs/index.html. Accessed 16 March 2010.

Bentley, G.E. *Shakespeare and Jonson: Their Reputations in the Seventeenth Century Compared.* Chicago: University of Chicago Press, 1945.

Berry, Lloyd E. "Phineas Fletcher's Account of his Father." *Journal of English and Germanic Philology* 60, no. 2 (1961): 258–67.

Bickersteth, John, and Robert W. Dunning. *Clerks of the Closet in the Royal Household: Five Hundred Years of Service to the Crown.* Stroud: Alan Sutton, 1991.

Birch, Thomas. *The Court and Times of James the First.* Edited by Robert Folkestone Williams. 2 vols. London: H. Colburn, 1848.

Black, Joseph. "The Rhetoric of Reaction: The Martin Marprelate Tracts (1588–89), Anti-Martinism, and the Uses of Print in Early Modern England." *Sixteenth Century Journal* 28, no. 3 (1997): 707–25.

Blackley, Brian M. "The Generic Play and Spenserian Parody of John Donne's 'Metempsychosis.'" PhD diss., University of Kentucky, 1994.

Blair, Ann. "Note Taking as an Art of Transmission." *Critical Inquiry* 31, no. 3 (2004): 85–107.

Bland, Mark. "Jonson's Vulgate. [Letter]." *TLS* 9 December 2005, 15.

Blench, J.W. *Preaching in England in the Late Fifteenth and Sixteenth Centuries: A Study of English Sermons 1450–c.1600.* Oxford: Basil Blackwell, 1964.

Bond, Ronald, ed. *Certain Sermons or Homilies (1547) and A Homily against Disobedience and Wilful Rebellion (1570).* Toronto: University of Toronto Press, 1987.

Bowman, Glen. "Elizabethan Catholics and Romans 13: A Chapter in the History of Political Polemic." *Journal of Church and State* 47, no. 3 (2005): 531–44.

Boyce, Benjamin. "News from Hell: Satiric Communications with the Nether World in English Writing of the Seventeenth and Eighteenth Centuries." *PMLA* 58, no. 2 (1943): 402–37.

Boyer, Allen D. "Coke, Sir Edward (1552–1634)." In *Oxford Dictionary of National Biography.* Ed. H.C.G. Matthew and Brian Harrison. Oxford: Oxford University Press, 2004. Online ed. Ed. Lawrence Goldman. Jan. 2009. http://www.oxforddnb.com.libproxy.uregina.ca:2048/view/article/5826. Accessed 5 April 2010.

Bradner, Leicester. *Musae Anglicanae: A History of Anglo-Latin Poetry 1500–1925.* New York: MLA, 1940. Reprinted. New York: Kraus Reprint Co., 1966.

– "References to Chaucer in Campion's *Poemata.*" *Review of English Studies* 12, no. 47 (1936): 322–3.

Brammall, Kathryn M. "Monstrous Metamorphosis: Nature, Morality, and the Rhetoric of Monstrosity in Tudor England." *Sixteenth Century Journal* 27 (1996): 3–21.

Bromiley, Geoffrey W., ed. *International Standard Biblical Encyclopedia.* Rev. ed. Grand Rapids: W.B. Eerdmans, 1979. v. 1.

Brooke, Tucker. "A Latin Poem by George Peele (?)." *Huntington Library Quarterly* 3 (1939): 47–68.

Brooke, Tucker. "William Gager to Queen Elizabeth." *Studies in Philology* 29, no. 2 (1932): 160–75.

Brooke, Xanthe. *The Lady Lever Art Gallery: Catalogue of Embroideries.* Stroud: A. Sutton in association with the Trustees of the National Museums and Galleries on Merseyside, 1992.

Brooks, Douglas A. *From Playhouse to Printing House: Drama and Authorship in Early Modern England.* Cambridge: Cambridge University Press, 2000.

Brooks, H.F. "Oldham and Phineas Fletcher: An Unrecognized Source for Satyrs upon the Jesuits." *Review of English Studies* 22, no. 88 (1971): 410–22 and 23, no. 89 (1972): 19–34.

– "The Fictitious Ghost: A Poetic Genre." *Notes and Queries* 29 (1982): 51–5.

Brown, Laura Feitzinger. "Brawling in Church: Noise and the Rhetoric of Lay Behavior in Early Modern England." *Sixteenth Century Journal* 34, no. 4 (2003): 955–72.

Bruce, John. "The Caricatures of Samuel Ward of Ipswich." *Notes and Queries*, 4th ser., 1 (1868): 1–2.

Buccola, Regina. "Virgin Fairies and Imperial Whores: The Unstable Ground of Religious Iconography in Thomas Dekker's *The Whore of Babylon.*" In *Marian Moments in Early Modern British Drama*, edited by Regina Buccola and Lisa Hopkins, 141–60. Aldershot, Hampshire: Ashgate, 2007.

Bullock, Albert Edward. *Westminster Abbey and St. Margaret's Church.* London: J. Tiranti and Co., 1920.

Burbery, Timothy. "John Milton Blackfriars Spectator? 'Elegia Prima' and Ben Jonson's *The Staple of News.*" *Ben Jonson Journal* 10 (2003): 57–76.

– *Milton the Dramatist.* Pittsburgh: Duquesne University Press, 2007.

Burnet, Gilbert. *History of His Own Time.* Edited by Martin Joseph Routh. 6 vols. Hildesheim: Georg Olms Verlagsbuchhandlung, 1969.

– *The Bishop of Salisbury his Speech in the House of Lords on the First Article of the Impeachment of Dr. Henry Sacheverell.* London, 1710.

Burns, William E. "Signs of the Times: Thomas Jackson and the Controversy over Prodigies in the Reign of Charles I." *Seventeenth Century* 11 (1996): 21–33.

Burrow, Colin. *Epic Romance: Homer to Milton.* Oxford: Clarendon, 1993.

Busse, Daniela. "Anti-Catholic Polemical Writing on the 'Rising in the North' (1569) and the Catholic Reaction." *Recusant History* 27, no. 1 (2004): 11–30.

Bywaters, David. "Venice, Its Senate, and Its Plot in Otway's *Venice Preserv'd.*" *Modern Philology* 80, no. 3 (1983): 256–63.

Campion, Thomas. *De Pulverea Coniuratione (On the Gunpowder Plot) Sidney Sussex MS 59.* Edited by David Lindley with translation and additional notes by Robin Sowerby. Leeds Texts and Monographs, New Series 10. Leeds: Leeds Studies in English, 1987.

Campion, Thomas. "Ad Thamesin." In *The Works of Thomas Campion: Complete Songs, Masques, and Treatises with a Selection of the Latin Verse*, edited by Walter R. Davis, 362–77. Garden City, NY: Doubleday, 1967.

Canino, Catherine. "The Discourse of Hell: Paradise Lost and the Irish Rebellion." *Milton Quarterly* 32, no. 1 (1998): 15–23.

Capp, Bernard. "The political dimension of apocalyptic thought." In *The Apocalypse in English Renaissance Thought and Literature: Patterns, Antecedents and Repercussions*, edited by C.A. Patrides and Joseph Wittreich, 93–124. Ithaca: Cornell University Press, 1984.

Caraman, Philip. *Henry Garnet, 1555–1606, and the Gunpowder Plot.* New York: Farrar, Straus, 1964.

Carey, John. *John Donne: Life, Mind and Art.* London: Faber and Faber, 1981.

Carlson, Christina M. "Free Speaking Cartoons: The Rise of Political Prints and Drama in Seventeenth-Century England." PhD diss., University of Chicago, 2008.

Carlson, Eric Josef. "The Boring of the Ear: Shaping the Pastoral Vision of Preaching in England, 1540–1640." In *Preachers and People in the Reformations and Early Modern Period*, edited by Larissa Taylor, 249–96. Leiden: Brill, 2001.

Carr, David. *Time, Narrative, and History.* Bloomington: Indiana University Press, 1986.

Chamberlain, John. *The Letters of John Chamberlain.* Edited by N.E. McClure. 2 vols. Philadelphia: American Philosophical Society, 1939.

Chambers, E.K. *The Elizabethan Stage.* 2nd ed. Vol. 3. Oxford: Clarendon, 1951.

Cheek, Macon. "Milton's 'In Quintum Novembris': An Epic Foreshadowing." *Studies in Philology* 54 (1957): 172–84.

Childs, Jessie. *God's Traitors: Terror and Faith in Elizabethan England.* London: Vintage Books, 2014.

Christianson, Paul. *Reformers and Babylon: English Apocalyptic Visions from the Reformation to the Eve of the Civil War.* Toronto: University of Toronto Press, 1978.

Clare, Janet. "Historicism and the Question of Censorship in the Renaissance." *English Literary Renaissance* 27 (1997): 155–76.

– "Transgressing Authority in English Renaissance Drama." *Textus* 19, no. 2 (2006): 352–69.

Clarendon, Edward. *The History of the Rebellion and Civil Wars in England begun in the year 1641.* Vol. 4. Oxford: Clarendon, 1958.

Clark, Donald Lemen. "Milton's Schoolmasters: Alexander Gil and His Son." *Huntington Library Quarterly* 9, no. 2 (1946): 121–47.

Clay, William Keatinge. *Liturgical Services of the Reign of Queen Elizabeth.* Cambridge: Cambridge University Press for the Parker Society, 1847.

Clegg, Cyndia Susan. *Press Censorship in Caroline England.* Cambridge: Cambridge University Press, 2008.

Clifton, Robin. "The Popular Fear of Catholics during the English Revolution." In *Rebellion, Popular Protest and the Social Order in Early Modern England*, edited by Paul Slack, 129–61. Cambridge: Cambridge University Press, 1984.

Coffey, John. *Persecution and Toleration in Protestant England, 1558–1689.* Harlow: Pearson, 2000.

Cogswell, Thomas. *The Blessed Revolution: English Politics and the Coming of War, 1621–1624.* Cambridge: Cambridge University Press, 1989.

– "England and the Spanish Match." In *Conflict in Early Stuart England: Studies in Religion and Politics 1603–1642*, edited by Richard Cust and Ann Hughes, 107–33. London: Longman, 1989.

Cohen, Jeffrey Jerome. "Monster Culture (Seven Theses)." In *Monster Theory: Reading Culture*, edited by Jeffrey Jerome Cohen, 3–25. Minneapolis: University of Minnesota Press, 1996.

Colclough, David. *Freedom of Speech in Early Stuart England.* Cambridge: Cambridge University Press, 2005.

Collins, Jeffrey R. "The Restoration Bishops and the Royal Supremacy." *Church History* 68, no. 3 (1999): 549–80.

Connerton, Paul. *How Societies Remember.* Cambridge: Cambridge University Press, 1989.

Conover, James H. *Thomas Dekker: An Analysis of Dramatic Structure.* The Hague: Mouton, 1969.

Cooper, Helen. *The English Romance in Time: Transforming Motifs from Geoffrey of Monmouth to the Death of Shakespeare.* Oxford: Oxford University Press, 2004.

Cooper, J.P.D. "'O Lorde save the Kyng': Tudor Royal Propaganda and the Power of Prayer." In *Authority and Consent in Tudor England*, edited by G.W. Bernard and S.J. Gunn, 179–96. Aldershot: Ashgate, 2003.

Corbett, Margery, and Ronald Lightbown. *The Comely Frontispiece: The Emblematic Title-Page in England 1550–1660.* London: Routledge and Kegan Paul, 1979.

Cowan, Brian. "The Spin Doctor: Sacheverell's Trial Speech and Political Performance in the Divided Society." In *Faction Displayed, Reconsidering the Impeachment of Dr Henry Sacheverell*, edited by Mark Knights, 28–46. Malden, MA: Wiley-Blackwell for the Parliamentary History Yearbook Trust, 2012.

Cowley, Abraham. *The Civil War.* Edited by Allan Pritchard. Toronto: University of Toronto Press, 1973.

Craig, John. "Psalms, Groans and Dogwhippers: The Soundscape of Worship in the English Parish Church, 1547–1642." In *Sacred Space in Early Modern Europe*, edited by Will Coster and Andrew Spicer, 104–23. Cambridge: Cambridge University Press, 2005.

Crane, Mary Thomas. "*Intret Cato*: Authority and the Epigram in Sixteenth-Century England." In *Renaissance Genres: Essays on Theory, History, and Interpretation*, edited by Barbara Kiefer Lewalski, 158–86. Cambridge, MA: Harvard University Press, 1986.

Crashaw, Richard. *The Complete Poetry of Richard Crashaw.* Edited by George Walton Williams. Garden City, NY: Anchor, 1970.

Crawford, Julie. *Marvelous Protestantism:Monstrous Births in Post-Reformation England.* Baltimore: Johns Hopkins University Press, 2005.

Craze, Jack M. "Balls of Missive Ruin: Milton and the Gunpowder Revolution." *Cambridge Quarterly* 26 (1997): 325–43.

Cressy, David. *Bonfires and Bells: National Memory and the Protestant Calendar in Elizabethan and Stuart England.* London: Weidenfeld and Nicolson, 1989.

– "God's Time, Rome's Time, and the Calendar of the English Protestant Regime." *Viator* 34 (2003): 392–406.

– "The Protestant Calendar and the Vocabulary of Celebration in Early Modern England." *Journal of British Studies* 29, no. 1 (1990): 31–52.

– *Travesties and Transgressions in Tudor and Stuart England.* Oxford: Oxford University Press, 2000.

Crockett, Bryan. *The Play of Paradox: Stage and Sermon in Renaissance England.* Philadelphia: University of Pennsylvania Press, 1995.

Croft, Pauline. "Howard, Henry, earl of Northampton (1540–1614)." *Oxford Dictionary of National Biography.* Ed. H.C.G. Matthew and Brian Harrison. Oxford: Oxford UP, 2004. Online edition. http://www.oxforddnb.com.libproxy.uregina.ca:2048/view/article/13906. Edited by Lawrence Goldman. January 2008. Accessed 5 April 2010.

– "Howard, Thomas, first earl of Suffolk (1561–1626)." *Oxford Dictionary of National Biography.* Edited by Lawrence Goldman. Oxford: Oxford UP. Online edition. http://www.oxforddnb.com.libproxy.uregina.ca:2048/view/article/13942. Accessed 10 November 2010.

– "The Religion of Robert Cecil." *Historical Journal* 34, no. 4 (1991): 773–96.

– "The Reputation of Robert Cecil: Libels, Political Opinion and Popular Awareness in the Early Seventeenth Century." *Transactions of the Royal Historical Society*, 6th ser., 1 (1991): 43–69.

– "Sir John Doddridge, King James I, and the Antiquity of Parliament." *Parliament, Estates and Representation* 12, no. 2 (1992): 95–107.

Crosfield, Thomas. *The Diary of Thomas Crosfield M. A., B.D. Fellow of Queen's College, Oxford.* Selected and edited by Frederick S. Boas. London: Oxford University Press, 1935.

Crouch, Patricia. "Fighting for Saint Michael: The Typology of Defeat in Milton's Celestial and Sublunary Civil Wars." *Milton Studies* 53 (2012): 149–79.

Cuddy, Neil. "Anglo-Scottish Union and the Court of James I, 1603–1625." *Transactions of the Royal Historical Society* 39 (1989): 107–24.

Cunningham, Karen. *Imaginary Betrayals: Subjectivity and the Discourses of Treason in Early Modern England.* Philadelphia: University of Pennsylvania Press, 2002.

– "'A Spanish Heart in an English Body': The Ralegh Treason Trial and the Poetics of Proof." *Journal of Medieval and Renaissance Studies* 22, no. 3 (1992): 327–51.

Curran, John E. *Roman Invasions: The British History, Protestant Anti-Romanism, and the Historical Imagination in England, 1530–1660.* Cranbury, NJ: University of Delaware Press, 2002.

– "Spenser and the Historical Revolution: Briton Moniments and the Problem of Roman Britain." *CLIO* 25, no. 3 (1996): 273–92.

Cust, Richard. "News and Politics in Early Seventeenth-Century England." In *Reformation to Revolution: Politics and Religion in Early Modern England*, edited by Margo Todd, 232–51. London: Routledge, 1995.

– "'Patriots' and 'popular' Spirits: Narratives of Conflict in Early Stuart Politics." In *The English Revolution c. 1590–1720: Politics, Religion and Communities*, edited by Nicholas Tyacke, 43–61. Manchester: Manchester University Press, 2007.

– "The 'Public Man' in Late Tudor and Early Stuart England." In *Politics of the Public Sphere in Early Modern England*, edited by Peter Lake and Steven Pincus, 116–43. Manchester: Manchester University Press, 2007.

Daley, Koos. "'And Like a Widdow Thus': Donne, Huygens, and the Fall of Heidelberg." *John Donne Journal* 10 (1991): 57–69.

Daniel, Samuel. *The Tragedy of Philotas.* Edited by Laurence Michel. Hamden: Archon, 1970.

Daston, Lorraine, and Katharine Park. *Wonders and the Order of Nature 1150–1750.* New York: Zone Books, 2001.

Davies, Godfrey. "English Political Sermons, 1603–1640." *Huntington Library Quarterly* 1 (1939): 1–22.

Davies, Horton. *Like Angels from a Cloud: The English Metaphysical Preachers 1588–1645.* San Marino, CA: Huntington Library, 1986.

Day, John. *John Day's "The Isle of Gulls": A Critical Edition.* Edited by Raymond S. Burns. New York: Garland, 1980.

Dekker, Thomas. *The Whore of Babylon: A Critical Edition.* Edited by Marianne Gateson Riely. New York: Garland, 1980.

De Luna, B.N. *Jonson's Romish Plot: A Study of "Catiline" and Its Historical Context.* Oxford: Clarendon Press, 1967.

Demaray, John G. "Gunpowder and the Problem of Theatrical Heroic Form: *In Quintum Novembris.*" *Milton Studies* 19 (1984): 3–19.

D'Ewes, Simonds. *The Diary of Sir Simonds D'Ewes (1622–1624).* Edited by Elisabeth Bourcier. Paris: Didier, 1974.

– *The Journal of Simonds D'Ewes from the beginning of the Long Parliament to the opening of the trial of the Earl of Strafford.* Edited by Wallace Notestein. New Haven, CT: Yale University Press, 1923.

Dillon, Janette. "Theatre and Controversy, 1603–1642." In *The Cambridge History of British Theatre.* Edited by Jane Milling and Peter Thomson. Cambridge: Cambridge University Press, 2004. 1:364–82.

Doelman, James. "Circulation of the Late Elizabethan and Early Stuart Epigram." *Renaissance and Reformation* 29 (2005): 59–73.

Dolan, Frances E. *Whores of Babylon: Catholicism, Gender, and Seventeenth-Century Print Culture.* Notre Dame, IN: Notre Dame University Press, 1999.

Donagan, Barbara. "Did Ministers Matter? War and Religion in England, 1642–1649." *Journal of British Studies* 33, no. 2 (1994): 119–56.

Donaldson, Ian. "Talking with Ghosts: Ben Jonson and the English Civil War." *Ben Jonson Journal* 17, no. 1 (2010): 1–18.

Donne, John. *Ignatius His Conclave: An Edition of the Latin and English Texts with Introduction and Commentary by T.S. Healy, S.J.* Edited by T.S. Healy. Oxford: Clarendon, 1969.

– *John Donne's 1622 Gunpowder Plot Sermon: A Parallel-Text Edition transcribed and edited and with critical commentary by Jeanne Shami.* Pittsburgh: Duquesne University Press, 1996.

– *The Sermons of John Donne.* Edited by George R. Potter and Evelyn M. Simpson. 10 vols. Berkeley: University of California Press, 1984.

Donnelly, Phillip J. *Milton's Scriptural Reasoning: Narrative and Protestant Toleration.* Cambridge: Cambridge University Press, 2009.

Durston, Christopher. "'For the Better Humiliation of the People': Public Days of Fasting and Thanksgiving during the English Revolution." *Seventeenth Century* 7, no. 2 (1992): 129–49.

Dutton, Richard. *Ben Jonson: To the First Folio.* Cambridge: Cambridge University Press, 1983.

– *Ben Jonson, "Volpone" and the Gunpowder Plot.* Cambridge: Cambridge University Press, 2008.

– "Jonson's Metempsychosis Revisited: Patronage and Religious Controversy." In *Ben Jonson and the Politics of Genre*, edited by A. D. Cousins and Alison V. Scott, 134–61. Cambridge: Cambridge University Press, 2009.

– "Jurisdiction of Theater and Censorship." In *A Companion to Renaissance Drama*, edited by Arthur F. Kinney, 223–36. Oxford: Blackwell, 2002.

– *Licensing, Censorship, and Authorship in Early Modern England: Buggeswords.* New York: Palgrave, 2000.

– *Mastering the Revels: The Regulation and Censorship of English Renaissance Drama.* Basingstoke: Macmillan, 1991.

– "Thomas Middleton's *A Game at Chess*: A Case Study." In *The Cambridge History of British Theater, v. 1: Origins to 1660*, edited by Jane Milling and Peter Thomson, 424–38. Cambridge: Cambridge University Press, 2004.

Dzelzainis, Martin. "'The Feminine part of every Rebellion': Francis Bacon on Sedition and Libel, and the Beginning of Ideology." *Huntington Library Quarterly* 69, no. 1 (2006): 139–52.

Eales, Jacqueline. "Provincial Preaching and Allegiance in the First English Civil War, 1640–6." In *Politics, Religion and Popularity in Early Stuart Britain: Essays in Honour of Conrad Russell*, edited by Thomas Cogswell, Richard Cust, and Peter Lake, 185–207. Cambridge: Cambridge University Press, 2002.

Edie, Carolyn A. "The Public Face of Royal Ritual: Sermons, Medals, and Civic Ceremony in Later Stuart Coronations." *Huntington Library Quarterly* 53, no. 4 (1990): 311–36.

– "Right Rejoicing: Sermons on the Occasion of the Stuart Restoration, 1660." *Bulletin of the John Rylands Library* 62, no. 1 (1979): 61–86.

Edwards, Francis. *The Enigma of Gunpowder Plot, 1605: The Third Solution.* Dublin: Four Courts, 2008.

– *"The Gunpowder Plot": A Lecture delivered on 10th November, 1972.* Ilford: Royal Stuart Society, 1972.

Emson, Frank. *The Gunpowder Plot: An Historical Melodrama.* London, 1874.

Ennis, Daniel J., and Judith Bailey Slagle, eds. *Prologues, Epilogues, Curtain-Raisers and Afterpieces: The Rest of the Eighteenth-Century London Stage.* Newark: University of Delaware Press, 2007.

Erll, Astrid, and Ann Rigney. "Literature and the Production of Cultural Memory." *European Journal of English Studies* 10, no. 2 (2006): 111–15.

An Essay towards a New History of the Gun-powder Treason. London, 1765.

Evans, Robert C. *Jonson and the Contexts of His Time.* Lewisburg, PA: Bucknell University Press, 1994.

Evelyn, John. *The Diary of John Evelyn.* Edited by William Bray. 2 vols. London: Dent, 1966.

Farooq, Jennifer. "The Politicising Influence of Print: The Responses of Hearers and Listeners to the Sermons of Gilbert Burnet and Henry Sacheverell." In *Readers, Audiences and Coteries in Early Modern England*, edited by Geoff Baker and Ann McGruer, 28–46. Newcastle: Cambridge Scholars Press, 2006.

Feil, J.P. "Dramatic References from the Scudamore Papers." *Shakespeare Survey* 11 (1958): 107–16.

Ferrell, Lori Anne. *Government by Polemic: James I, the King's Preachers, and the Rhetorics of Conformity, 1603–1625.* Stanford, CA: Stanford University Press, 1998.

The Fifth of November; or, The Gunpowder Plot. An Historical Play, supposed to be written by William Shakspeare. London, 1830.

The Fifth of November Plot. London, [1840?].

Finucci, Valeria. "Maternal Imagination and Monstrous Birth: Tasso's *Gerusalemme liberata.*" In *Generation and Degeneration: Tropes of Reproduction in Literature and History from Antiquity through Early Modern Europe*, edited by Valeria Finucci and Kevin Brownlee, 41–77. Durham, NC: Duke University Press, 2001.

Fleay, Frederick Gard. *A Chronicle History of the London Stage, 1559–1642.* New York: B. Franklin, 1964.

Fletcher, Phineas. *Phineas Fletcher: Locustae vel Pietas Iesuitica.* Edited and translated by Estelle Haan. Supplementa Humanistica Lovaniensia IX. Louvain: Leuven University Press, 1996.

– *The Locusts, or Apollyonists.* In *Poetical Works [by] Giles and Phineas Fletcher*, edited by Frederick S. Boas, 1.128–86. Cambridge: Cambridge University Press, 1908; Grosse Pointe, MI: Scholarly Press, 1968.

Flynn, Dennis. "Donne's 'Amicissimo et Meritissimo Ben. Ionson' and the Daring of *Volpone.*" *Literary Imagination: The Review of the Association of Literary Scholars and Critics*, 6 (2004): 368–69.

– "Donne's *Ignatius his Conclave* and Other Libels on Robert Cecil." *John Donne Journal*, 6, no. 2 (1987): 163–83.

– "Donne's Travels and Earliest Publications." In *The Oxford Handbook of John Donne*, edited by Jeanne Shami, Dennis Flynn, and M. Thomas Hester, 506–22. Oxford: Oxford University Press, 2011.

Ford, James Thomas. "Preaching in the Reformed Tradition." In *Preachers and People in the Reformations and Early Modern Period*, edited by Larissa Taylor, 65–88. Leiden: Brill, 2001.

Forsyth, Neil. "Rebellion in *Paradise Lost*: Impossible Original." *Milton Quarterly* 30, no. 4 (1996): 151–62.

Foucault, Michel. *Discipline and Punish: The Birth of the Prison*. Translated by Alan Sheridan. New York: Vintage, 1979.

Fowler, Alastair. "The Emblem as a Literary Genre." In *Deviceful Settings: The English Renaissance Emblem and Its Contexts*, edited by Michael Bath and Daniel Russell, 1–32. New York: AMS, 1999.

– "The Formation of Genres in the Renaissance and After." *New Literary History* 34, no. 2 (2003): 185–200.

Fox, Adam. "Rumour, News and Popular Political Opinion in Elizabethan and Early Stuart England." *Historical Journal* 40, no. 3 (1997): 597–620.

Fraser, Antonia. *The Gunpowder Plot: Terror and Faith in 1605*. London: Weidenfeld and Nicholson, 1996.

Freeman, Rosemary. *English Emblem Books*. New York: Octagon, 1966.

Frontain, Raymond-Jean. "'the man which have affliction seene': Donne, Jeremiah, and the Fashioning of Lamentation." In *Centered on the Word: Literature, Scripture, and the Tudor-Stuart Middle Way*, edited by Daniel W. Doerksen and Christopher Hodgkins, 127–47. Newark: University of Delaware Press, 2004.

Frye, Northrop. *The Great Code: The Bible and Literature*, edited by Alvin A. Lee. Toronto: University of Toronto Press, 2006.

Furnivall, F.J., and W.R. Morfill, eds. *Ballads from Manuscripts*. Vol. 2. Hertford: Ballad Society, 1873.

Gager, William. *William Gager: The Complete Works*. Vol. 4, Juvenilia, "Pyramis," Collected Prose. Edited by Dana F. Sutton. New York: Garland, 1994.

Gaggero, Christopher. "Civic Humanism and Gender Politics in Jonson's *Catiline*." *SEL* 45, no. 2 (2005): 401–24.

Galloway, Bruce. *The Union of England and Scotland 1603–1608*. Edinburgh: John Donald, 1986.

Gardiner, Samuel R. *History of England from the Accession of James I to the Outbreak of the Civil War 1603–1642*. Vol. 1: 1603–1607. London: Longmans, Green, and Co., 1883.

– *What Gunpowder Plot Was*. London: Longmans, Green, and Co., 1897.

Gasper, Julia. *The Dragon and the Dove: The Plays of Thomas Dekker*. Oxford: Clarendon, 1990.

Gazzard, Hugh. "'Those Graue Presentments of Antiquitie': Samuel Daniel's *Philotas* and the Earl of Essex." *Review of English Studies* 51, no. 203 (2000): 423–50.

Geneva Bible: A Facsimile of the 1560 Edition. Intro. Lloyd E. Berry. Peabody, MA: Hendrickson Bibles, 2007.

Gerard, John. *The Condition of Catholics under James I. Father Gerard's Narrative of the Gunpowder Plot*. Edited by John Morris. London: Longmans, Green, and Co, 1871.

Gerard, John. *What Was the Gunpowder Plot? The Traditional Story tested by Original Evidence.* 2nd ed. London, 1897.

Goldberg, Jonathan. *James I and the Politics of Literature: Jonson, Shakespeare, Donne, and Their Contemporaries.* Baltimore: Johns Hopkins University Press, 1983.

Goodman, Godfrey. *The Court of King James the First; by Dr. Godfrey Goodman, Bishop of Gloucester.* Edited by John S. Brewer. 2 vols. London, 1839.

Green, Ian. "Preaching in the Parishes." In *The Oxford Handbook of the Early Modern Sermon*, edited by Peter McCullough, Hugh Adlington, and Emma Rhatigan, 137–54. Oxford: Oxford University Press, 2011.

Greenblatt, Stephen. *Hamlet in Purgatory.* Princeton, NJ: Princeton University Press, 2001.

Griffiths, Antony and Robert A. Gerard. *The Print in Stuart Britain, 1603–1689.* London: British Museum Press, 1998.

Gruber, Elizabeth. "'Betray'd to Shame': *Venice Preserved* and the Paradox of She-Tragedy." *Connotations* 16, no. 1–3 (2006–7): 158–71.

Guibbory, Achsah. "Israel and English Protestant Nationalism: 'Fast Sermons' during the English Revolution." In *Early Modern Nationalism and Milton's England*, edited by David Loewenstein and Paul Stevens, 115–38. Toronto: University of Toronto Press, 2008.

– *The Map of Time: Seventeenth-Century English Literature and Ideas of Pattern in History.* Urbana: University of Illinois Press, 1986.

Guy, John. "The Rhetoric of Counsel in Early Modern England." In *Tudor Political Culture*, edited by Dale Hoak, 292–310. Cambridge: Cambridge University Press, 1995.

Haan, Estelle. "The 'Adorning of My Native Tongue': Latin Poetry and Linguistic Metamorphosis." In *The Oxford Handbook of Milton*, edited by Nicholas McDowell and Nigel Smith, 51–65. Oxford: Oxford University Press, 2009.

– "Milton's *In Quintum Novembris* and the Anglo-Latin Gunpowder Epic." *Humanistica Lovaniensia* 41 (1992): 221–95; 42 (1993): 368–93.

Habermas, Jürgen. *The Structural Transformation of the Public Sphere.* Translated by Thomas Burger with Frederick Lawrence. Cambridge, MA: MIT, 1989.

Haigh, Christopher. "The Recent Historiography of the English Reformation." In *Reformation to Revolution: Politics and Religion in Early Modern England*, edited by Margo Todd, 13–32. London: Routledge, 1995.

Halbwachs, Maurice. *On Collective Memory.* Edited by Lewis A. Coser. Chicago: University of Chicago Press, 1992.

Hale, John K. "Milton and the Gunpowder Plot: *In Quintum Novembris* Reconsidered." *Humanistica Loveniensia* 50 (2001): 351–66.

Hale, J.R. "Gunpowder and the Renaissance: An Essay in the History of Ideas." In *Renaissance War Studies*, 389–420. London: Hambledon Press, 1983.

Halstead, W.L. "Dating and Holograph Evidence in *The Whore of Babylon.*" *Notes and Queries* 180 (1941): 38–40.

Hamburger, Philip. "The Development of the Law of Seditious Libel and the Control of the Press." *Stanford Law Review* 37, no. 5 (1985): 661–762.

Hammer, Paul E. "Shakespeare's *Richard II*, the Play of 7 February 1601, and the Essex Rising." *Shakespeare Quarterly* 59, no. 1 (2008): 1–35.

Hardin, Richard F. "The Early Poetry of the Gunpowder Plot: Myth in the Making." *English Literary Renaissance* 22 (1992): 62–79.

Harington, John. *Letters and Epigrams of Sir John Harington, together with The Prayse of Private Life*. Edited by N.E. McClure. Philadelphia: University of Pennsylvania Press, 1930.

Harland, Paul. "Donne's Political Intervention in the Parliament of 1629." *John Donne Journal* 11 (1992): 21–37.

Harp, Richard. "Catholicism." *Ben Jonson Journal* 14, no. 1 (2007): 112–16.

Harris, Jonathan Gil. *Untimely Matter in the Time of Shakespeare*. Philadelphia: University of Pennsylvania Press, 2009.

Harris, Tim. *Restoration: Charles II and his Kingdoms, 1660–1685*. London: Allen Lane, 2005.

Harth, Phillip. "Political Interpretations of *Venice Preserv'd*." *Modern Philology* 85, no. 4 (1988): 345–62.

Haynes, Alan. *The Gunpowder Plot: Faith in Rebellion*. London: Grange, 1994.

Hegarty, A.J. "Crosfield, Thomas (1602–1663)." *Oxford Dictionary of National Biography*. Edited by H.C.G. Matthew and Brian Harrison. Oxford: Oxford UP, 2004. Online edition. http://www.oxforddnb.com.libproxy.uregina.ca:2048/view/article/65929. Edited by Lawrence Goldman. January 2008. Accessed 18 November 2010.

Heijting, Willem, and Paul R. Sellin. "John Donne's 'Conclave Ignati': The Continental Quarto and Its Printing." *Huntington Library Quarterly* 62, no. 3/4 (1999): 401–21.

Helgerson, Richard. *Forms of Nationhood: The Elizabethan Writing of England*. Chicago: University of Chicago Press, 1992.

Henry, John. "Ward, Seth (1617–1689)." *Oxford Dictionary of National Biography*. Edited by H.C.G. Matthew and Brian Harrison. Oxford: Oxford University Press, 2004. Online edition. http://www.oxforddnb.com.libproxy.uregina.ca:2048/view/article/28706. Edited by Lawrence Goldman. May 2006. Accessed 7 October 2010.

Hibbard, Caroline M. *Charles I and the Popish Plot*. Chapel Hill: University of North Carolina Press, 1983.

Hill, Christopher. *Antichrist in Seventeenth-Century England*. London: Oxford University Press, 1971.

– *The English Bible and the Seventeenth-Century Revolution*. London: Penguin, 1993.

– *Milton and the English Revolution*. London: Faber and Faber, 1977.

Hinds, Peter. *"The Horrid Popish Plot": Roger L'Estrange and the Circulation of Political Discourse in Late Seventeenth-Century London*. Oxford: Oxford University Press for The British Academy, 2010.

Hirst, Derek. "The English Republic and the Meaning of Britain." *Journal of Modern History* 66, no. 3 (1994): 451–86.

Hogge, Alice. *God's Secret Agents: Queen Elizabeth's Forbidden Priests and the Hatching of the Gunpowder Plot.* New York: HarperCollins, 2005.

Holland, Philip. *St Margaret's Westminster: The Commons' Church within a Royal Peculiar.* Nuffield Henly on Thames: Aidan Ellis Publishing, 1993.

Holmes, Geoffrey. "The Sacheverell Riots: The Crowd and the Church in Early Eighteenth-Century London." *Past & Present* 72 (1976): 55–85.

– *The Trial of Doctor Sacheverell.* London: Eyre Methuen, 1973.

Holub, Robert C. *Reception Theory: A Critical Introduction.* London: Methuen, 1984.

Hooker, Thomas. "The Church's Deliverances." In *Thomas Hooker: Writings in England and Holland, 1626–1633*, edited by George H. Williams et al., 53–88. Cambridge, MA: Harvard University Press, 1975.

Horsley, Lee. "'Vox Populi' in the Political Literature of 1710." *Huntington Library Quarterly* 38, no. 4 (1975): 335–53.

Howard, Jean E. *The Stage and Social Struggle in Early Modern England.* London: Routledge, 1994.

Howard-Hill, T.H. "Political Interpretations of Middleton's 'A Game at Chess' (1624)." *Yearbook of English Studies* 21 (1991): 274–85.

Howell, James. *Epistolæ Ho-Elianæ: The Familiar Letters of James Howell.* Edited by Joseph Jacobs. London: David Nutt in the Strand, 1890.

Howell, Thomas Bayly. *A Complete collection of state trials and proceedings for high treason and other crimes and misdemeanors.* London: Longmans, 1809–28. 1.160–358.

Hsia, R. Po-chia. "A Time for Monsters: Monstrous Births, Propaganda, and the German Reformation." In *Monstrous Bodies / Political Monstrosities in Early Modern Europe*, edited by Laura Lunger Knoppers and Joan B. Landes, 67–92. Ithaca, NY: Cornell University Press, 2004.

Hudson, Hoyt Hopewell. *The Epigram in the English Renaissance.* Princeton, NJ: Princeton University Press, 1947.

Huet, Marie Hélène. *Monstrous Imagination.* Cambridge, MA: Harvard University Press, 1993.

Hughes, Richard T. "Henry Burton: A Study in Religion and Politics in Seventeenth-Century England." PhD diss., University of Iowa, 1972.

– "Henry Burton: The Making of a Puritan Revolutionary." *Journal of Church and State* 16 (1974): 421–34.

Hume, Robert D. *Reconstructing Contexts: The Aims and Principles of Archaeo-Historicism.* Oxford: Oxford University Press, 1999.

Hunt, Arnold. *The Art of Hearing: English Preachers and their Audiences, 1590–1640.* Cambridge: Cambridge University Press, 2010.

– "A Jacobean Consensus?: The Religious Policy of James VI and I." *Seventeenth Century* 17, no. 1 (2002): 132–4.

– "Ormerod, Oliver (*d.* 1626)." In *Oxford Dictionary of National Biography*, edited by H.C.G. Matthew and Brian Harrison. Oxford: OUP, 2004. Online edition. http://www

.oxforddnb.com.libproxy.uregina.ca:2048/view/article/20838. Edited by Lawrence Goldman, January 2008. Accessed 5 March 2014.

– "Tuning the Pulpits: The Religious Context of the Essex Revolt." In *The English Sermon Revised: Religion, Literature and History 1600–1750*, edited by Lori Anne Ferrell and Peter McCullough, 86–114. Manchester: Manchester University Press, 2000.

Hunt, Mary Leland. *Thomas Dekker: A Study*. New York: Russell and Russell, 1964.

Hunter, J. Paul. "Couplets and Conversation." In *The Cambridge Companion to Eighteenth-Century Poetry*, edited by John Sitter, 11–35. Cambridge: Cambridge University Press, 2001.

Hunter, William B. "An Occasion for John Donne's 'The *Lamentations* of Jeremy.'" *ANQ* 12, no. 3 (1999): 18–23.

Hurstfield, Joel. "Gunpowder Plot and the Politics of Dissent." In *Early Stuart Studies: Essays in Honor of David Harris Willson*, edited by Howard S. Reinmuth Jr, 95–121. Minneapolis: University of Minnesota Press, 1970.

Ihalainen, Pasi. "The Political Sermon in an Age of Party Strife, 1700–1720: Contributions to the Conflict." In *The Oxford Handbook of the Early Modern Sermon*, edited by Peter McCullough, Hugh Adlington, and Emma Rhatigan, 495–513. Oxford: Oxford University Press, 2011.

Iser, Wolfgang. *The Act of Reading: A Theory of Aesthetic Response*. Baltimore: Johns Hopkins University Press, 1978.

James I. "Directions to preachers, 1622." In *Visitation Articles and Injunctions of the Early Stuart Church*, edited by Kenneth Fincham, 211–14. Woodbridge: Boydell, 1994.

– *The True Law of Free Monarchies and Basilikon Doron: A Modernized Edition*. Edited by Daniel Fischlin and Mark Fortier. Toronto: Centre for Reformation and Renaissance Studies, 1996.

Jardine, David. *A Narrative of the Gunpowder Plot*. London: John Murray, 1857.

Jauss, Hans Robert. "The Communicative Role of the Fictive." In *Question and Answer: Forms of Dialogic Understanding*, translated by Michael Hays, 3–50. Minneapolis: University of Minnesota Press, 1989.

– "Literary History as a Challenge to Literary Theory." In *Toward an Aesthetic of Reception*, translated by Timothy Bahti, 3–45. Theory and History of Literature, 2. Minneapolis: University of Minnesota Press, 1982.

Jenkins, Hugh. "'Quid nomine populi intelligi velimus': Defining the 'People' in *The Second Defense*." *Milton Studies* 46 (2007): 191–209.

Jenkinson, Matt. "Preaching at the Court of Charles II: Court Sermons and the Restoration Chapel Royal." In *The Oxford Handbook of the Early Modern Sermon*, edited by Peter McCullough, Hugh Adlington, and Emma Rhatigan, 442–59. Oxford: Oxford University Press, 2011.

Jones, Ann Rosalind, and Peter Stallybrass. *Renaissance Clothing and the Materials of Memory*. Cambridge: Cambridge University Press, 2000.

Jones, Charles W. "Milton's 'Brief Epic.'" *Studies in Philology* 4 (1947): 209–27.

Jones, Clyve. "Debates in the House of Lords on 'The Church in Danger,' 1705, and on Dr Sacheverell's Impeachment, 1710." *Historical Journal* 19, no. 3 (1976): 759–77.

Jones, P.P. *An Account of the Gunpowder Plot.* n.p., n.d.

Journals of the House of Lords. V. 2: 1578–1614. University of London and The History of Parliament Trust, 2012. http://india.british-history.ac.uk/image-pageScan.aspx?pubid=117&sp=1&pg=357.

Kay, W. David. *Ben Jonson: A Literary Life.* Houndmills: Macmillan, 1995.

Kermode, Frank. *The Sense of an Ending: Studies in the Theory of Fiction with a New Epilogue.* Oxford: Oxford University Press, 2000.

Kerrigan, John. *Archipelagic English: Literature, History, and Politics, 1603–1707.* Oxford: Oxford University Press, 2008.

Kesselring, K.J. "'A Cold Pye for the Papistes': Constructing and Containing the Northern Rising of 1569." *Journal of British Studies* 43, no. 4 (2004): 417–43.

Kewes, Paulina. "Julius Caesar in Jacobean England." *Seventeenth Century* 17 (2002): 155–86.

King, John N. *Milton and Religious Controversy: Satire and Polemic in 'Paradise Lost.'* Cambridge: Cambridge University Press, 2000.

King, Maureen Claire. "'Essex, that could vary himself into all shapes for a time': The Second Earl of Essex in Jacobean England." PhD diss., University of Alberta, 2000.

Kirby, W.J. Torrance. "The Public Sermon: Paul's Cross and the Culture of Persuasion in England, 1534-1570." *Renaissance and Reformation* 31, no. 1 (2008): 3–29.

Kitching, C.J. "'Prayers fit for the time': Fasting and Prayer in Response to National Crises in the Reign of Elizabeth I." In *Monks, Hermits and the Ascetic Tradition*, edited by W.J. Sheils, 241–50. Oxford: Oxford University Press, 1985.

Kneidel, Greg. "*Ars Prædicandi*: Theories and Practice." In *The Oxford Handbook of the Early Modern Sermon*, edited by Peter McCullough, Hugh Adlington, and Emma Rhatigan, 3–20. Oxford: Oxford University Press, 2011.

Knights, Mark. "Introduction." In *Faction Displayed: Reconsidering the Impeachment of Dr. Henry Sacheverell*, edited by Mark Knights, 1–15. Malden, MA: Wiley-Blackwell for the Parliamentary History Yearbook Trust, 2012.

Krantz, Susan E. "Thomas Dekker's Political Commentary in *The Whore of Babylon.*" *SEL: Studies in English Literature, 1500–1900* 35 (Spring 1995): 271–91.

Kunzle, David. *The Early Comic Strip: Narrative Strips and Picture Stories in the European Broadsheet from c. 1450 to 1825.* Berkeley: University of California Press, 1973.

Lake, Peter. "The Significance of the Elizabethan Identification of the Pope as Antichrist." *Journal of Ecclesiastical History* 31 (1980): 161–78.

Lake, Peter, with Michael Questier. *The Antichrist's Lewd Hat: Protestants, Papists and Players in Post-Reformation England.* New Haven, CT: Yale University Press, 2002.

Lake, Peter, and Michael Questier. "Agency, Appropriation and Rhetoric under the Gallows: Puritans, Romanists and the State in Early Modern England." *Past and Present* 153 (1996): 64–107.

– "Puritans, Papists, and the 'Public Sphere' in Early Modern England: The Edmund Campion Affair in Context." *Journal of Modern History* 72, no. 3 (2000): 587–627.

Lake, Peter, and Steve Pincus. "Rethinking the Public Sphere in Early Modern England." *Journal of British Studies* 45, no. 2 (2006): 270–92.

– eds. *The Politics of the Public Sphere in Early Modern England*. Manchester: Manchester University Press, 2007.

Lambert, Sheila. "Committees, Religion, and Parliamentary Encroachment on Royal Authority in Early Stuart England." *English Historical Review* 105, no. 414 (1990): 60–95.

Lares, Jameela. *Milton and the Preaching Arts*. Pittsburgh: Duquesne University Press, 2001.

Larkin, James F., and Paul L. Hughes. *Stuart Royal Proclamations: Volume I: Royal Proclamations of King James I 1603–1625*. Oxford: Clarendon, 1973.

Larking, Lambert Blackwell. *Proceedings, principally in the county of Kent, in connection with the Parliaments called in 1640, and especially with the Committee of religion appointed in that year ... from the collections of Sir Edward Dering, bart., 1627–1644*. [Westminster]: Camden, 1862.

Laud, William. "A Speech delivered in the Starr-chamber, on Wednesday, the xiv. Of Iune MDCXXXVIII ..." In *The Works of the Most Reverend Father in God, William Laud, D.D. sometime Lord Archbishop of Canterbury*, 6.37–70. Oxford: John Henry Parker, 1862.

Lee, M. Owen. *Fathers and Sons in Virgil's "Aeneid": Tum Genitor Natum*. Albany: State University of New York Press, 1979.

Lee, Maurice, Jr. *The "Inevitable" Union and Other Essays on Early Modern Scotland*. East Linton, UK: Tuckwell, 2003.

Lehmann, Gary Paul. "A Critical Analysis of the Works of John Day (*c.* 1574–*c.*1640)." PhD diss., Duke University, 1980.

Lehnhof, Kent R. "'Intestine War' and 'the smell of Mortal Change': Troping the Digestive Tract in *Paradise Lost*." *The Sacred and Profane in English Renaissance Literature*, edited by Mary A. Papazian, 278–300. Newark: University of Delaware Press, 2008.

– "Scatology and the Sacred in Milton's *Paradise Lost*." *English Literary Renaissance* 37, no. 3 (2007): 429–49.

Lemon, Rebecca. *Treason by Words: Literature, Law, and Rebellion in Shakespeare's England*. Ithaca, NY: Cornell University Press, 2006.

Levine, Joseph. "Intellectual History as History." *Journal of the History of Ideas* 66, no. 2 (2005): 189–200.

Lewalski, Barbara Kiefer. *Milton's Brief Epic: The Genre, Meaning, and Art of "Paradise Regained."* Providence, RI: Brown University Press, 1966.

– *Protestant Poetics and the Seventeenth-Century Religious Lyric*. Princeton, NJ: Princeton University Press, 1979.

Lieb, Michael. *The Dialectics of Creation: Patterns of Birth and Regeneration in "Paradise Lost."* Amherst: University of Massachusetts Press, 1970.

Limon, Jerzy. *Dangerous Matter: English Drama and Politics in 1623/24.* Cambridge: Cambridge University Press, 1986.

Liu, Tai. *Discord in Zion: The Puritan Divines and the Puritan Revolution, 1640–1660.* The Hauge: Nijhoff, 1973.

Lockyer, Roger. *Buckingham: The Life and Political Career of George Villiers, First Duke of Buckingham, 1592–1628.* London: Longman, 1981.

Loewenstein, David. "'Fair Offspring Nurs't in Princely Lore': On the Question of Milton's Early Radicalism." *Milton Studies* 28 (1992): 37–48.

– *Milton and the Drama of History: Historical Vision, Iconoclasm, and the Literary Imagination.* Cambridge: Cambridge University Press, 1990.

– *Representing Revolution in Milton and his Contemporaries: Religion, Politics, and Polemics in Radical Puritanism.* Cambridge: Cambridge University Press, 2001.

Loewenstein, Joseph. "Pennyboy's Delight: Ben Jonson, News, and the Conditions of Intellectual Property." *Daphnis* 37, no. 1–2 (2008): 333–50.

Longinus. *Longinus on the Sublime.* Translated by A.O. Prickard. Oxford: Clarendon, 1906. Reprinted with corrections, 1961.

Longueville, Thomas de. *The Life of a Conspirator: Being a biography of Sir Everard Digby.* London: K. Paul, Trench, Trübner and Co., 1895.

Loomie, Albert J. *Guy Fawkes in Spain: the 'Spanish Treason' in Spanish Documents.* London: University of London, Institute of Historical Research, 1971.

Lossky, Nicholas. *Lancelot Andrewes the Preacher (1555–1626).* Oxford: Clarendon, 1991.

Love, Christopher. "The Private Theaters in Crisis: Strategies at Blackfriars and Paul's, 1606–1607." PhD diss., University of Maryland, 2006.

Lowers, James K. *Mirrors for Rebels:A Study of Polemical Literature Relating to the Northern Rebellion, 1569.* Berkeley: University of California Press, 1953.

MacColl, Allan. "The Construction of England as a Protestant 'British' Nation in the Sixteenth Century." *Renaissance Studies* 18, no. 4 (2004): 582–608.

– "The Meaning of 'Britain' in Medieval and Early Modern England." *Journal of British Studies* 45 (2006): 248–69.

MacLean, Gerald M. *Time's Witness: Historical Representation in English Poetry, 1603–1660.* Madison: University of Wisconsin Press, 1990.

MacLeod, Brock Cameron. "An Unacknowledged Debt to Seneca in the Quarto *Sejanus.*" *Notes and Queries* 50, no. 4 (2003): 427.

MacLure, Millar. *The Paul's Cross Sermons, 1534–1642.* Toronto: University of Toronto Press, 1958.

MacPhail, Eric. "The Plot of History from Antiquity to the Renaissance." *Journal of the History of Ideas* 62, no. 1 (2001): 1–16.

Maltby, Judith. *Prayer Book and People in Elizabethan and Early Stuart England.* Cambridge: Cambridge University Press, 1998.

Manley, Lawrence. "From Matron to Monster: Tudor-Stuart London and the Languages of Urban Description." In *The Historical Renaissance: New Essays on Tudor and Stuart Literature and Culture*, edited by Heather Dubrow and Richard Strier, 347–74. Chicago: University of Chicago Press, 1988.

– "Proverbs, Epigrams, and Urbanity in Renaissance London." *English Literary Renaissance* 15, no. 3 (1985): 247–76.

Manning, Roger B. "The Origins of the Doctrine of Sedition." *Albion* 12, no. 2 (1980): 99–121.

Marotti, Arthur F. "Donne's Conflicted Anti-Catholicism." *Journal of English and Germanic Philology* 101, no. 3 (2002): 358–79.

– *Religious Ideology and Cultural Fantasy: Catholic and Anti-Catholic Discourses in Early Modern England.* Notre Dame, IN: University of Notre Dame Press, 2005.

Marotti, Arthur F., and Steven W. May. "Two Lost Ballads of the Armada Thanksgiving Celebration [with texts and illustration]." *English Literary Renaissance* 41, no. 4 (2011): 31–63.

Marshall, Peter. *Beliefs and the Dead in Reformation England.* Oxford: Oxford University Press, 2002.

– "'The map of God's word': Geographies of the Afterlife in Tudor and Early Stuart England." In *The Place of the Dead: Death and Remembrance in Late Medieval and Early Modern Europe*, edited by B. Gordon and P. Marshall, 110–30. Cambridge: Cambridge University Press, 2000.

– "The Reformation of Hell? Protestant and Catholic Infernalisms in England, c. 1560–1640." *Journal of Ecclesiastical History* 61, no. 2 (2010): 279–98.

Marston, John. "Sophonisba." In *Three Jacobean Witchcraft Plays*, edited by Peter Corbin and Douglas Sedge, 33–84. Manchester: Manchester University Press, 1986.

Martin, Patrick, and John Finnis. "A Gunpowder Priest? Benedicam Dominum – Ben Johson's Strange 1605 Inscription." *TLS* 4 (November 2005): 12–13.

Matar, Nabil. "Sterry, Peter (1613–1672)." In *Oxford Dictionary of National Biography*, edited by H. C. G. Matthew and Brian Harrison. Oxford: OUP, 2004. Online ed. Edited by Lawrence Goldman. October 2005. http://www.oxforddnb.com.libproxy.uregina.ca:2048/view/article/26416. Accessed 13 December 2015.

McAleer, John J. "Ballads on the Spanish Armada." *Texas Studies in Language and Literature* 4 (1962): 606–12.

McCullough, Peter E. "Montagu, James (1568–1618)." *Oxford Dictionary of National Biography*. Ed. H.C.G. Matthew and Brian Harrison. Oxford: Oxford UP, 2004. Online ed. Ed. Lawrence Goldman. http://www.oxforddnb.com.libproxy.uregina.ca:2048/view/article/19021. January 2008. Accessed 15 November 2010.

McCullough, Peter E. *Sermons at Court: Politics and Religion in Elizabethan and Jacobean Preaching*. Cambridge: Cambridge University Press, 1998.

McGee, J. Sears. "Taylor, Thomas (1576–1632)." *Oxford Dictionary of National Biography*. Ed. H.C.G. Matthew and Brian Harrison. Oxford: Oxford UP, 2004. Online ed. Ed.

Lawrence Goldman. http://www.oxforddnb.com.libproxy.uregina.ca:2048/view/article/27083. January 2008. Accessed 17 July 2012.

McLaren, Anne. "Monogamy, Polygamy and the True State: James I's Rhetoric of Empire." *History of Political Thought* 25, no. 3 (2004): 446–80.

McLuskie, Kathleen E. *Dekker and Heywood, Professional Dramatists.* Houndmills, Hampshire: Macmillan, 1994.

Mears, Natalie. "Public Worship and Political Participation in Elizabethan England." *Journal of British Studies* 51, no. 1 (2012): 4–25.

Merritt, J.F. "The Cradle of Laudianism? Westminster Abbey, 1558–1630." *Journal of Ecclesiastical History* 52, no. 4 (2001): 623–46.

– *The Social World of Early Modern Westminster.* Manchester: Manchester University Press, 2005.

Mehl, Dieter. *The Elizabethan Dumb Show: The History of a Dramatic Convention.* Cambridge, MA: Harvard University Press, 1966.

Milton, Anthony. *Catholic and Reformed: The Roman and Protestant Churches in English Protestant Thought, 1600–1640.* Cambridge: Cambridge University Press, 1995.

– "The Creation of Laudianism: A New Approach." In *Politics, Religion and Popularity in Early Stuart Britain: Essays in Honour of Conrad Russell,* edited by Thomas Cogswell, Richard Cust, and Peter Lake, 162–84. Cambridge: Cambridge University Press, 2002.

– *Laudian and Royalist Polemic in Seventeenth-Century England: The Career and Writings of Peter Heylyn.* Manchester: Manchester University Press, 2007.

Milton, John. *John Milton: Complete Poems and Major Prose.* Edited by Merritt Y. Hughes. New York: Odyssey, 1957.

– "John Milton's *In Quintum Novembris* (1626): A Hypertext Critical Edition." Edited by Dana F. Sutton. Philological Museum, University of California, Irvine. Rev. 2006. www.philological.bham.ac.uk/milton/.

Mitchell, W. Fraser. *English Pulpit Oratory from Andrewes to Tillotson: A Study of Its Literary Aspects.* New York: Russell and Russell, 1962.

Moore, Olin H. "The Infernal Council." *Modern Philology* 16, no. 4 (1918): 169–93.

Morgan, Basil. "Lunsford, Sir Thomas (*b. c.*1610, *d.* in or before 1656)." In *Oxford Dictionary of National Biography.* Online ed. Edited by Lawrence Goldman. http://www.oxforddnb.com.libproxy.uregina.ca:2048/view/article/17197. Oxford: OUP, 2004.

Morgan, George Blacker. *The Great English Treason for Religion known as Gunpowder Plot and the (Faked) Miraculous Manner of its Public Discovery with its Hitherto Unknown Greater Betrayal, in the Year 1605.* 2 vols. Oxford: Oxford University Press [privately printed], 1931.

Morrill, John. "The Religious Context of the English Civil War." In *The English Civil War,* edited by Richard Cust and Ann Hughes, 159–81. London: Arnold, 1997.

Morrissey, Mary. "Elect Nations and Prophetic Preaching: *types* and *examples* in the Paul's Cross Jeremiad." In *The English Sermon Revised: Religion, Literature and History 1600–1750,* edited by Lori Anne Ferrell and Peter McCullough, 43–58. Manchester: Manchester University Press, 2000.

– "Interdisciplinarity and the Study of Early Modern Sermons." *The Historical Journal* 42, no. 4 (1999): 1111–23.

– "John Donne as a Conventional Paul's Cross Preacher." *John Donne's Professional Lives*, edited by David Colclough, 159–78. Cambridge: D.S. Brewer, 2003.

– *Politics and the Paul's Cross Sermons, 1558–1642*. Oxford: Oxford University Press, 2011.

– "Presenting James VI and I to the Public: Preaching on Political Anniversaries at Paul's Cross." In *James VI and I: Ideas, Authority, and Government*, edited by Ralph Houlbrooke, 107–21. Aldershot: Ashgate, 2006.

– "Rhetoric, Religion, and Politics in the St. Paul's Cross Sermons 1603–1625." PhD diss., Cambridge University, 1998.

– "Scripture, Style and Persuasion in Seventeenth-Century English Theories of Preaching." *Journal of Ecclesiastical History* 53, no. 4 (2002): 686–706.

Muggli, Mark Z. "Ben Jonson and the Business of News." *Studies in English Literature* 32, no. 2 (1992): 323–40.

Munro, Ian. "Making Publics: Secrecy and Publication in *A Game at Chess*." *Medieval and Renaissance Drama in England* 14 (2001): 207–26.

Munro, Lucy. *Children of the Queen's Revels: A Jacobean Theatre Repertory*. Cambridge: Cambridge University Press, 2005.

Murrin, Michael. *History and Warfare in Renaissance Epic*. Chicago: University of Chicago Press, 1994.

Murphy, Kathryn. "The Date of Edwin Sandy's Paul's Cross Sermon, '… at which time a maine treason was discouered.'" *Notes and Queries* 53, no. 4 (2006): 430–2.

Myers, Nick. "Hercule Gaulois, Great Britain's Solomon – Myths of Persuasion, Styles of Authority." In *The Stuart Courts*, edited by Eveline Cruickshanks, 29–42. Thrupp, Stroud, Gloucestershire: Sutton, 2000.

Neale, J. E. *Elizabeth I and Her Parliaments, 1559–1601*. 2 Vols. London: Jonathan Cape, 1953–7.

Ni Chuilleanáin, Eiléan. "Time, Place, and the Congregation in Donne's Sermons." In *Literature and Learning in Medieval and Renaissance England: Essays Presented to Fitzroy Pyle*, edited by John Scattergood, 197–216. Dublin: Irish Academic Press, 1984.

Nichols, John. *The Progresses, Processions, and Magnificent Festivities, of King James the First, His Royal Consort, Family, and Court* ... Vol. 2. London: J.B. Nichols, 1828.

Nicholls, David. "Divine Analogy: The Theological Politics of John Donne." *Political Studies* 32 (1984): 570–80.

Nicholls, Mark. "Discovering Gunpowder Plot: The King's Book and the Dissemination of News." *Recusant History* 28, no. 3 (2007): 397–415.

– "Fawkes, Guy (*bap.* 1570, *d.* 1606)." *Oxford Dictionary of National Biography*. Ed. H.C.G. Matthew and Brian Harrison. Oxford: OUP, 2004. Online ed. Ed. Lawrence Goldman.

May 2009. http://www.oxforddnb.com.libproxy.uregina.ca:2048/view/article/9230. Accessed 15 November 2010.

– *Investigating Gunpowder Plot.* Manchester: Manchester University Press, 1991.

– "Percy, Henry, ninth earl of Northumberland (1564–1632)." *Oxford Dictionary of National Biography.* Oxford University Press, Sept. 2004. Online ed. January 2008. http://www.oxforddnb.com.libproxy.uregina.ca:2048/view/article/21939. Accessed 5 April 2010.

– "Strategy and Motivation in the Gunpowder Plot." *Historical Journal* 50, no. 4 (2007): 787–807.

– "Treason's Reward: The Punishment of Conspirators in the Bye Plot of 1603." *Historical Journal* 38, no. 4 (1995): 821–42.

– "Vaux, Anne (*bap.* 1562, *d.* in or after 1637)." *Oxford Dictionary of National Biography.* Ed. H.C.G. Matthew and Brian Harrison. Oxford: OUP, 2004. Online ed. Ed. Lawrence Goldman. January 2008. http://www.oxforddnb.com.libproxy.uregina.ca:2048/view/article/28159. Accessed 22 Nov. 2010.

Nora, Pierre. "Between Memory and History: 'Les Lieux de Mémoire.'" *Representations* 26 (1989): 7–25.

Noorthouck, John. *A New History of London, including Westminster and Southwark.* London, 1773.

Nowak, Thomas S. "Propaganda and the Pulpit: Robert Cecil, William Barlow and the Essex and Gunpowder Plots." In *The Witness of Times: Manifestations of Ideology in Seventeenth Century England,* edited by Katherine Z. Keller and Gerald Schiffhorst, 34–52. Pittsburgh: Duquesne University Press, 1993.

– "'Remember, Remember the Fifth of November': Anglocentrism and Anti-Catholicism in the English Gunpowder Sermons, 1605–1651." PhD diss., State University of New York at Stony Brook, 1992.

O'Callaghan, Michelle. "Dreaming the Dead: Ghosts and History in the Early Seventeenth Century." In *Reading the Early Modern Dream: The Terrors of the Night,* edited by Katharine Hodgkin, Michelle O'Callaghan, and S.J. Wiseman, 81–95. New York: Routledge, 2008.

Okines, A.W.R.E. "Why was there so little government reaction to the gunpowder plot?" *Journal of Ecclesiastical History* 55, no. 2 (2004): 275–92.

Park, Katharine, and Lorraine J. Daston. "Unnatural Conceptions: The Study of Monsters in Sixteenth- and Seventeenth-Century France and England." *Past and Present* 92 (1981): 20–54.

– *Wonders and the Order of Nature 1150–1750.* New York: Zone, 2001.

Parker, Patricia. "Dilation and Delay: Renaissance Matrices." *Poetics Today* 5, no. 3 (1984): 519–35.

– *Inescapable Romance: Studies in the Poetics of a Mode.* Princeton, NJ: Princeton University Press, 1979.

The parliamentary or constitutional history of England; being a faithful account of all the most remarkable transactions in Parliament, from the earliest times. Collected from the journals of both Houses, the records, ... By several hands .... London, 1751–61. *Eighteenth Century Collections Online.*http://find.galegroup.com.libproxy.uregina.ca:2048/ecco/infomark.do?&source=gale&docLevel=FASCIMILE&prodId=ECCO&userGroupName=ureginalib&tabID=T001&docId=CW3326048375&type=multipage&contentSet=ECCOArticles&version=1.0. Gale. University of Regina. Accessed 13 December 2015. 6.126.

Parry, Graham. "Milton's *History of Britain* and the Seventeenth-Century Antiquarian Scene." *Prose Studies* 19, no. 3 (1996): 238–46.

Partington, J.R. *A History of Greek Fire and Gunpowder.* Cambridge: Heffer, 1960.

Patrides, C.A. *Premises and Motifs in Renaissance Thought and Literature.* Princeton, NJ: Princeton University Press, 1982.

Patterson, Annabel. *Censorship and Interpretation: The Conditions of Writing and Reading in Early Modern England.* Madison: University of Wisconsin Press, 1984.

– "'Roman-cast Similitude': Ben Jonson and the English Use of Roman History." In *Rome in the Renaissance: The City and the Myth*, edited by P.A. Ramsey, 381–94. Binghamton, NY: Medieval and Renaissance Texts and Studies, 1982.

Patterson, W.B. *King James VI and I and the Reunion of Christendom.* Cambridge: Cambridge University Press, 1997.

Pearn, B.R. "Dumb Show in Elizabethan Drama." *Review of English Studies* 11, no. 44 (1935): 385–405.

Pebworth, Ted-Larry. "John Donne's 'Lamentations' and Christopher Fetherstone's *Lamentations ... in prose and meeter* (1587)." In *Wrestling with God: Literature & Theology in the English Renaissance: Essays to Honour Paul Grant Stanwood*, edited by Mary Ellen Henley and W. Speed Hill, 85–98. Mary E. Henley, 2000.

– "'Let Me Here Use that Freedome': Subversive Representation in John Donne's 'Obsequies to the Lord Harington.'" *Journal of English and Germanic Philology* 91, no. 1 (1992): 17–42.

Peck, Linda Levy. *Court Patronage and Corruption in Early Stuart England.* Boston: Unwin Hyman, 1990.

Peck, Linda Levy. "'For a king not to be bountiful were a fault': Perspectives on Court Patronage in Early Stuart England." *Journal of British Studies* 25, no. 1 (1986): 31–61.

– *Northampton, Patronage and Policy at the Court of James I.* London: Allen and Unwin, 1982.

Phillips, H.E.I. "The Last Years of the Court of Star Chamber, 1630–41." *Transactions of the Royal Historical Society*, 4th ser., 21 (1939): 103–31.

Piper, William Bowman. *The Heroic Couplet.* Cleveland: Case Western Reserve University Press, 1969.

Pitcher, John. "Samuel Daniel and the Authorities." *Medieval and Renaissance Drama in England* 10 (1998): 113–48.

Price, George R. *Thomas Dekker.* New York: Twayne, 1969.

Questier, Michael. "Catholic Loyalism in Early Stuart England." *English Historical Review* 123 (2008): 1132–65.

– *Conversion, Politics and Religion in England, 1580–1625*. Cambridge: Cambridge University Press, 1996.

– "Loyalty, Religion and State Power in Early Modern England: English Romanism and the Jacobean Oath of Allegiance." *Historical Journal* 40, no. 2 (1997): 311–29.

Quint, David. *Epic and Empire: Politics and Generic Form from Virgil to Milton*. Princeton, NJ: Princeton University Press, 1993.

– "Milton, Fletcher, and the Gunpowder Plot." *Journal of the Warburg and Courtauld Institutes* 54 (1991): 261–8.

Rasmussen, Tarald. "Hell Disarmed? The Function of Hell in Reformation Spirituality." *Numen* 56 (2009): 366–84.

Rawson, Claude. "Mock-heroic English Poetry." In *The Cambridge Companion to the Epic*, edited by Catherine Bates, 167–92. Cambridge: Cambridge University Press, 2010.

– "War and the Epic Mania in England and France: Milton, Boileau, Prior and English Mock-Heroic." *Review of English Studies* 64, no. 265 (2013): 433–53.

Raymond, Joad. *Pamphlets and Pamphleteering in Early Modern Britain*. Cambridge: Cambridge University Press, 2003.

Reedy, Gerard. *The Bible and Reason: Anglicans and Scripture in Late Seventeenth-Century England*. Philadelphia: University of Pennsylvania Press, 1985.

Reidy, Maurice F. *Bishop Lancelot Andrewes, Jacobean Court Preacher: A Study in Early Seventeenth-Century Religious Thought*. Chicago: Loyola University Press, 1955.

Revard, Stella P. *Milton and the Tangles of Neaera's Hair: The Making of the 1645 "Poems."* Columbia: University of Missouri Press, 1997.

– "Milton's Gunpowder Poems and Satan's Conspiracy." *Milton Studies 4*. Edited by James D. Simmonds, 63–77. Pittsburgh: University of Pittsburgh Press, 1972.

– *The War in Heaven: "Paradise Lost" and the Tradition of Satan's Rebellion*. Ithaca, NY: Cornell University Press, 1980.

Ribner, Irving. *The English History Play in the Age of Shakespeare*. New York: Barnes & Noble, 1965.

Richey, Esther Gilman. *The Politics of Revelation in the English Renaissance*. Columbia: University of Missouri Press, 1998.

Ricoeur, Paul. *Memory, History, Forgetting*. Translated by Kathleen Blamey and David Pellauer. Chicago: University of Chicago Press, 2004.

Rigney, James. "'To lye upon a Stationers stall, like a piece of coarse flesh in a Shambles': The Sermon, Print and the English Civil War." In *The English Sermon Revised: Religion, Literature and History 1600–1750*, edited by Lori Anne Ferrell and Peter McCullough, 188–207. Manchester: Manchester University Press, 2000.

Roberts, Stephen K. "Somerset, Edward, second marquess of Worcester (*d.* 1667). In *Oxford Dictionary of National Biography*. Edited by H.C.G. Matthew and Brian Harrison.

Oxford: OUP, 2004. Online ed., edited by Lawrence Goldman, May 2006. http://www.oxforddnb.com.libproxy.uregina.ca:2048/view/article/26006. Accessed 13 December 2015.

Rockwood, Catherine. "'Know thy side': Propaganda and Parody in Jonson's *Staple of News*." *English Literary History* 75, no. 1 (2008): 135–49.

Rodger, N.A.M. "Queen Elizabeth and the Myth of Sea-Power in English History." *Transactions of the Royal Historical Society* 14 (2004): 153–74.

Roebuck, Graham. "Donne's *Lamentations of Jeremy* Reconsidered." *John Donne Journal* 10, no. 1–2 (1991): 37–44.

Rogers, Katharine M. "Masculine and Feminine Values in Restoration Drama: The Distinctive Power of *Venice Preserved*." *Texas Studies in Literature and Language* 27, no. 4 (1985): 390–404.

Rollins, Hyder E. *An Analytical Index of the Ballad-Entries (1557–1709) in the Registers of the Company of Stationers of London*. Hatboro, PA: Tradition, 1967.

Rosendale, Timothy. *Liturgy and Literature in the Making of Protestant England*. Cambridge: Cambridge University Press, 2007.

Rosser, Gervase. *Medieval Westminster 1200–1540*. Oxford: Clarendon Press, 1989.

Rovang, Paul. "Milton's War in Heaven as Apocalyptic Drama: 'Thy Foes Justly Hast in Derision.'" *Milton Quarterly* 28, no. 2 (1994): 28–35.

Rowlands, Marie. "Recusant Women." In *Women in English Society 1500–1800*, edited by Mary Prior, 149–80. New York: Routledge, 1985.

Rowlstone, Stephen. "Religion, Politics and Polemic in Seventeenth-Century England: The Public Career of Henry Burton, 1625–1648." PhD diss., University of Kent, 2005.

Russell, Conrad. "The British Problem and the English Civil War." In *The English Civil War*, edited by Richard Cust and Ann Hughes, 111–33. London: Arnold, 1997.

– *The Crisis of Parliament: English History 1509–1660*. Oxford: Oxford University Press, 1971.

– "James VI and I and Rule over Two Kingdoms: An English View." *Historical Research* 76, no. 192 (2003): 151–63.

Russell, Daniel. "The Genres of Epigram and Emblem." In *The Renaissance*, Vol. 3, *The Cambridge History of Literary Criticism: The Renaissance*, edited by Glyn P. Norton, 278–83. Cambridge: Cambridge University Press, 1999.

Rustici, Craig M. *The Afterlife of Pope Joan: Deploying the Popess Legend in Early Modern England*. Ann Arbor: University of Michigan Press, 2006.

Sacheverell, Henry. *The Perils of false brethren set forth in a Sermon preach'd before the Right Honourable the Lord-Mayor, Aldermen, and Citizens of London, at the Cathedral-Church of St. Paul, on the 5th of November, 1709*. London: Printed for Henry Clements, at the Half-Moon in St Paul's Church Yard, 1709.

Sánchez, Reuben. *Typology and Iconography in Donne, Herbert, and Milton: Fashioning the Self after Jeremiah*. New York: Palgrave Macmillan, 2014.

Schelling, Felix. *Elizabethan Drama, 1558–1642.* Vol. 1. New York: Russell, 1959.

Schurink, Fred. "'Like a Hand in the Margine of a Booke': William Blount's Marginalia and the Politics of Sidney's *Arcadia 1.*" *Review of English Studies* 59, no. 238 (2008): 1–24.

Schwyzer, Philip. *Literature, Nationalism, and Memory in Early Modern England and Wales.* Cambridge: Cambridge University Press, 2004.

Scott, Jonathan. *England's Troubles: Seventeenth-Century English Political Instability in European Context.* Cambridge: Cambridge University Press, 2000.

Scott-Warren, Jason. *Early Modern English Literature.* Cambridge: Polity, 2005.

Sedinger, Tracey. "Sidney's *New Arcadia* and the Decay of Protestant Republicanism." *SEL* 47, no. 1 (2007): 57–77.

Sena, Margaret. "William Blundell and the Networks of Catholic Dissent in Post-Reformation England." In *Community in Early Modern England: Networks, Place, Rhetoric,* edited by Alexandra Shepard and Phil Withington, 54–75. Manchester: Manchester University Press, 2000.

Shagan, Ethan Howard. "Constructing Discord: Ideology, Propaganda, and the English Responses to the Irish Rebellion of 1641." *Journal of British Studies* 36, no. 1 (1997): 4–34.

Shakespeare, Joy. "Plague and Punishment." In *Protestantism and the National Church in Sixteenth Century England,* edited by Peter Lake and Maria Dowling, 103–23. London: Croom Helm, 1987.

Shami, Jeanne. "Anti-Catholicism in the Sermons of John Donne." In *The English Sermon Revised: Religion, Literature and History,* edited by Lori Anne Ferrell and Peter McCullough, 136–66. Manchester: Manchester University Press, 2000.

– "Donne on Discretion." *ELH* 47, no. 1 (1980): 48–66.

– "Donne's Sermons and the Absolutist Politics of Quotation." In *John Donne's Religious Imagination: Essays in Honor of John T. Shawcross,* edited by Raymond-Jean Frontain and Frances M. Malpezzi, 380–412. Conway, AR: UCA Press, 1995.

– *John Donne and Conformity in Crisis in the Late Jacobean Pulpit.* Cambridge: D.S. Brewer, 2003.

– "'The Stars in their Orders Fought Against Sisera.'" *John Donne Journal* 14 (1995): 1–58.

– "Women and Sermons: An Immodest Proposal." Unpublished paper.

Sharpe, James. *Remember, Remember: A Cultural History of Guy Fawkes Day.* Cambridge, MA: Harvard University Press, 2005.

Sharpe, Kevin. "Faction at the Early Stuart Court." *History Today* 33, no. 10 (1983): 39–46.

Sharpe, Kevin, and Steven N. Zwicker, eds. "Politics of Discourse: Introduction." In *Politics of Discourse: The Literature and History of Seventeenth-Century England,* 1–20. Berkeley: University of California Press, 1987.

Shell, Alison. *Catholicism, Controversy and the English Literary Imagination, 1558–1660.* Cambridge: Cambridge University Press, 1999.

Shephard, Robert. "Court Factions in Early Modern England." *Journal of Modern History* 64, no. 4 (1992): 721–45.

Shriver, Frederick. "Hampton Court Re-visited: James I and the Puritans." *Journal of Ecclesiastical History* 33, no. 1 (1982): 48–71.

Shuger, Debora. "Absolutist Thelogy in the Sermons of John Donne." In *The English Sermon Revised: Religion, Literature and History 1600–1750*, edited by Lori Anne Ferrell and Peter McCullough, 115–35. Manchester: Manchester University Press, 2000.

– "Donne's Absolutism." In *The Oxford Handbook of John Donne*, edited by Jeanne Shami, Dennis Flynn, and M. Thomas Hester, 690–703. Oxford: Oxford University Press, 2011.

– *Habits of Thought in the English Renaissance: Religion, Politics, and the Dominant Culture.* Berkeley: University of California Press, 1990.

Sidney, Philip. *An Apology for Poetry or The Defence of Poesy.* Edited by Geoffrey Shepherd. London: Nelson, 1965.

Sidney, Philip. *A History of the Gunpowder Plot: The Conspiracy and Its Agents.* 2nd rev. ed. London: The Religious Tract Society, 1905.

Sims, James. *The Bible in Milton's Epics.* Gainesville: University of Florida Press, 1962.

Skeaping, Lucy, ed. "Gunpowder Plot." In *Broadside Ballads: Songs from the streets, taverns, theatres and countryside of 17th-century England*, 64–5. Harlow, England: Faber Music, 2005.

Skerpan, Elizabeth. *The Rhetoric of Politics in the English Revolution 1642–1660.* Columbia: University of Missouri Press, 1992.

Slights, William W.E. "The Edifying Margins of Renaissance English Books." *Renaissance Quarterly* 42, no. 4 (1989): 682–716.

Smith, Charles Hugh Egerton. *Church and Parish: Studies in Church Problems, illustrated from the Parochial History of St. Margaret's Westminster.* London: SPCK, 1955.

Smith, M. van Wyk. "John Donne's *Metempsychosis.*" *Review of English Studies* 24, no. 93 (1973): 17–25, 141–52.

Smith, Nigel. *Literature and Revolution in England 1640–1660.* New Haven, CT: Yale University Press, 1994.

Smith, Victor, and Peter Kelsey. "The Lines of Communication: The Civil War Defences of London." In *London and the Civil War*, edited by Stephen Porter, 117–48. Houndmills: Macmillan, 1996.

Sommerville, Johann. "Papalist Political Thought and the Controversy over the Jacobean Oath of Allegiance." In *Catholics and the 'Protestant Nation': Religious Politics and Identity in Early Modern England*, edited by Ethan Shagan, 162–84. Manchester: Manchester University Press, 2005.

Sowerby, Robin. *The Classical Legacy in Renaissance Poetry.* London: Longman, 1994.

Sparrow, John. "John Donne and Contemporary Preachers: Their Preparation of Sermons for Delivery and for Publication." *Essays and Studies by Members of the English Association* 16 (1930): 145–78.

Spink, Henry Hawkes. *The Gunpowder Plot and Lord Mounteagle's Letter: being a proof, with moral certitude, of the authorship of the document: together with some account of the whole thirteen gunpowder conspirators, including Guy Fawkes.* London, 1902.

Spurr, John. *The Restoration Church of England, 1646–1689.* New Haven, CT: Yale University Press, 1991.

Stanwood, P.G. "Fletcher, Phineas (1582–1650)." *Oxford Dictionary of National Biography.* Ed. H.C.G. Matthew and Brian Harrison. Oxford: Oxford UP, 2004. Online ed. Ed. Lawrence Goldman. May 2008. http://www.oxforddnb.com.libproxy.uregina.ca:2048/view/article/9738. Accessed 25 November, 2010.

Steadman, John M. *Milton and the Paradoxes of Renaissance Heroism.* Baton Rouge: Louisiana State University Press, 1987.

Stevens, Paul. "Milton and National Identity." In *The Oxford Handbook of Milton*, edited by Nicholas McDowell and Nigel Smith, 342–63. Oxford: Oxford University Press, 2009.

Strong, Roy. *The Cult of Elizabeth: Elizabethan Portraiture and Pageantry.* N.p.: Thames and Hudson, 1977.

Stroud, Theodore A. "Ben Jonson and Father Thomas Wright." *English Literary History* 14, no. 4 (1947): 274–82.

Strype, John. *The Life and Acts of Matthew Parker, the First Archbishop of Canterbury in the Reign of Queen Elizabeth.* London, 1711.

– *The life and acts of the Most Reverend Father in God, John Whitgift, D.D. the third and last Lord Archbishop of Canterbury, in the reign of Queen Elizabeth; ... In four books. Together with a large appendix of the said papers, ... By John Strype, ...* London, 1718. *Eighteenth Century Collections Online.* http://find.galegroup.com.libproxy.uregina.ca:2048/ecco/infomark.do?&source=gale&docLevel=FASCIMILE&prodId=ECCO&userGroupName=ureginalib&tabID=T001&docId=CW3321701226&type=multipage&contentSet=ECCOArticles&version=1.0. Gale Group.

Sturgeon, Elizabeth. "Ghostly Speech: Writing History and Reading Literature in the Renaissance." PhD diss., Northwestern University, 2004.

Sullivan, Ernest W., II. "Modern Scholarly Editions of the Prose of John Donne." In *The Oxford Handbook of John Donne*, edited by Jeanne Shami, Dennis Flynn, and M. Thomas Hester, 65–80. Oxford: Oxford University Press, 2011.

Sutton, Dana F. "Milton's *In Quintum Novembris, anno aetatis 17* (1626): Choices and Intentions." In *Qui Miscvit vtile Dvlcu: Festschrift Essays for Paul Lachlan MacKendrick*, edited by Gareth Schmeling and Jon D. Mikalson, 349–75. Waconda: Bolchazy-Carducci, 1998.

Targoff, Ramie. *Common Prayer: The Language of Public Devotion in Early Modern England.* Chicago: University of Chicago Press, 2001.

– "The Performance of Prayer: Sincerity and Theatricality in Early Modern England." *Representations* 60 (1997): 49–69.

Tasso, Torquato. *Jerusalem Delivered (Gerusalemme liberata).* Edited and translated by Anthony M. Esolen. Baltimore: Johns Hopkins University Press, 2000.

Taunton, Nina, and Valerie Hart. "*King Lear*, King James and the Gunpowder Treason of 1605." *Renaissance Studies* 17, no. 4 (2003): 695–715.

Teague, Frances. "Ben Jonson and London Courtrooms." In *Solon and Thespis: Law and Theater in the English Renaissance*, edited by Dennis Kezar, 64–77. Notre Dame: University of Notre Dame Press, 2007.

– "Jonson and the Gunpowder Plot." *Ben Jonson Journal* 5 (1998): 249–52.

Tesimond, Oswald. *The Gunpowder Plot: The Narrative of Oswald Tesimond alias Greenway*. Edited by Francis Edwards. London: Folio Society, 1973.

Trevor-Roper, Hugh. "The Fast Sermons of the Long Parliament." In *Religion, the Reformation, and Social Change and Other Essays by H.R. Trevor-Roper*, 294–344. London: Macmillan, 1967.

– "Five Letters of Thomas Bodley." *Bodleian Library Record* 2, no. 24 (1946): 134–9.

Tricomi, Albert H. *Anticourt Drama in England 1603–1642*. Charlottesville: University Press of Virginia, 1989.

Trowles, Tony. *A Bibliography of Westminster Abbey between 1570 and 2000*. Woodbridge: Boydell Press, 2005.

Tulip, James. "The Contexts of *Volpone*." In *Imperfect Apprehensions: Essays in English Literature in Honour of G.A. Wilkes*, edited by Geoffrey Little, 74–87. Sydney: Challis Press, English Department, University of Sydney, 1996.

– "The Intertextualities of Ben Jonson's *Volpone*." *Sydney Studies in English* 20 (1994): 20–35.

Turner, Gustavo Secchi. "The Matter of Fact: 'The Tragedy of Gowrie' (1604) and Its Contexts." PhD diss., Harvard University, 2006.

Tyacke, Nicholas. *Aspects of English Protestantism c. 1530–1700*. Manchester: Manchester University Press, 2001.

Vallance, Edward. "Preaching to the Converted: Religious Justifications for the English Civil War." *Huntington Library Quarterly* 65, no. 3/4 (2002): 395–419.

Vernon, E.C. "Jenkyn, William (*bap.* 1613, *d.* 1685)." *Oxford Dictionary of National Biography*. Ed. H.C.G. Matthew and Brian Harrison. Oxford: Oxford UP, 2004. Online ed. Ed. Lawrence Goldman. January 2008. http://www.oxforddnb.com.libproxy.uregina.ca:2048/view/article/14743. Accessed 10 April 2009.

Vickers, Brian. "Epideictic and Epic in the Renaissance." *New Literary History* 14, no. 3 (1983): 497–537.

Vida, Marco Girolamo. *Christiad*. Translated James Gardner. Cambridge, MA: Harvard University Press, 2009.

Wabuda, Susan. *Preaching during the English Reformation*. Cambridge: Cambridge University Press, 2002.

Waddington, Raymond B. *Looking into Providences: Designs and Trials in "Paradise Lost."* Toronto: University of Toronto Press, 2012.

Wake, Paul. "'A Monster Shapeless': Equivocation and the Treasonous Imagination." *Textual Practice* 25, no. 5 (2011): 941–60.

– "Plotting as Subversion: Narrative and the Gunpowder Plot." *Journal of Narrative Theory* 38, no. 3 (2008): 295–316.

Wall, John N., Jr. "Godly and Fruitful Lessons: The English Bible, Erasmus' Paraphrases, and the Book of Homilies." In *The Godly Kingdom of Tudor England: Great Books of the English Reformation*, edited by John E. Booty, 47–135. Wilton, CO: Morehouse-Barlow Co., 1981.

Wall, John N., Jr, and Terry Bunce Burgin. "'This sermon … upon the Gun-powder day': The Book of Homilies of 1547 and Donne's Sermon in Commemoration of Guy Fawkes' Day, 1622." *South Atlantic Review* 49, no. 2 (1984): 19–30.

Walker, John. *An attempt towards recovering an account of the numbers and sufferings of the clergy of the Church of England, ... who were sequester'd, harrass'd, &c. in the late times of the Grand Rebellion: occasion'd by the ninth chapter (now the second volume) of Dr. Calamy's Abridgment of the Life of Mr. Baxter. Together with an examination of that chapter. By John Walker, ...* Vol. 1. London, 1714. *Eighteenth Century Collections Online.* Gale. http://find.galegroup.com.libproxy.uregina.ca:2048/ecco/infomark.do?&source=gale&docLevel=FASCIMILE&prodId=ECCO&userGroupName=ureginalib&tabID=T001&docId=CW3319683918&type=multipage&contentSet=ECCOArticles&version=1.0. University of Regina. 13 December 2009.

Walsham, Alexandra. "'The Fatall Vesper': Providentialism and Anti-Popery in Late Jacobean London." *Past and Present* 144, no. 1 (1994): 36–87.

– "Impolitic Pictures: Providence, History, and the Iconography of Protestant Nationhood in Early Stuart England." *Studies in Church History* 33 (1997): 307–28.

– *Providence in Early Modern England.* Oxford: Oxford University Press, 1999.

– "'A Very Deborah?' The Myth of Elizabeth I as a Providential Monarch." *The Myth of Elizabeth*, edited by Susan Doran and Thomas S. Freeman, 143–68. Houndmills: Palgrave Macmillan, 2003.

Walzer, Michael. *The Revolution of the Saints: A Study in the Origins of Radical Politics.* Cambridge, MA: Harvard University Press, 1965.

Watkins, John. *Representing Elizabeth in Stuart England: Literature, History, Sovereignty.* Cambridge: Cambridge University Press, 2002.

Watt, Tessa. *Cheap Print and Popular Piety 1550–1640.* Cambridge: Cambridge University Press, 1991.

Webber, Joan. *Contrary Music: The Prose Style of John Donne.* Madison: University of Wisconsin Press, 1963.

Webster, Tom. "Newcomen, Matthew (*d.* 1669)." *Oxford Dictionary of National Biography.* Ed. H.C.G. Matthew and Brian Harrison. Oxford: Oxford UP, 2004. Online ed. Ed. Lawrence Goldman. http://www.oxforddnb.com.libproxy.uregina.ca:2048/view/article/19995. October 2006. Accessed 26 September 2009.

Weinbrot, Howard D. "The Thirtieth of January Sermon: Swift, Johnson, Sterne, and the Evolution of Culture." *Eighteenth-Century Life* 34, no. 1 (2010): 29–55.

Welsby, Paul A. *Lancelot Andrewes 1555–1626.* London: SPCK, 1964.

White, Hayden. *The Content of the Form: Narrative Discourse and Historical Representation.* Baltimore: Johns Hopkins University Press, 1987.

– "The Historical Text as Literary Artifact." *CLIO* 3 (1974): 277–303.

White, Jason C. "Militant Protestants: British Identity in the Jacobean Period, 1603–1625." *History* 94, no. 314 (2009): 154–75.

Wilkes, G.A. "Daniel's *Philotas* and the Essex Case: A Reconsideration." *Modern Language Quarterly* 23 (1962): 253–42.

Williams, Franklin B., Jr. "Commendatory Verses: The Rise of the Art of Puffing." *Studies in Bibliography* 19 (1966): 2–15.

Williams, Richard. "Acclamatio Patrie." In *Ballads from Manuscripts*, edited by F.J. Furnivall, 2.39–59. New York: AMS Press, 1968.

Williams, Weldon. "The Influence of Ben Jonson's *Catiline* upon John Oldham's Satyrs upon the Jesuits." *ELH* 11, no. 1 (1944): 38–62.

Williamson, Arthur H. "Scotland, Antichrist and the Invention of Great Britain." In *New Perspectives on the Politics and Culture of Early Modern Scotland*, edited by John Dwyer, Roger A. Mason, and Alexander Murdoch, 34–59. Edinburgh: John Donald, n.d.

Williamson, Hugh Ross. *The Gunpowder Plot.* Long Prairie, MN: The Neumann Press, 1996.

Wills, Garry. *Witches and Jesuits: Shakespeare's 'Macbeth.'* New York: Oxford University Press, 1995.

Willson, D. Harris. *King James VI and I.* London: Jonathan Cape, 1956.

Wilson, Elkin Calhoun. *Prince Henry and English Literature.* Ithaca, NY: Cornell University Press, 1946.

Wilson, John F. *Pulpit in Parliament: Puritanism during the English Civil Wars 1640–1648.* Princeton, NJ: Princeton University Press, 1969.

Wilson, Peter H. *Europe's Tragedy: A History of the Thirty Years War.* London: Allen Lane, 2009.

Wiltenburg, Robert. "Damnation in a Roman Dress: *Cataline*, Cataline, and *Paradise Lost.*" *Milton Studies* 25 (1989): 89–108.

Wiseman, Susan. "'The Eccho of Uncertaintie': Jonson, Classical Drama and the English Civil War." In *Refashioning Ben Jonson: Gender, Politics and the Jonsonian Canon*, edited by Julie Sanders et al., 208–29. Houndmills: Macmillan, 1998.

Woolf, D.R. *The Idea of History in Early Stuart England: Erudition, Ideology, and 'The Light of Truth" from the Accession of James I to the Civil War.* Cheektowaga, NY: University of Toronto Press, 1990.

– *Reading History in Early Modern England.* Cambridge: Cambridge University Press, 2000.

– "Two Elizabeths? James I and the Late Queen's Famous Memory." *Candian Journal of History* 20 (1985): 167–91.

Worcester, Thomas. "Catholic Sermons." In *Preachers and People in the Reformations and Early Modern Period*, edited by Larissa Taylor, 3–33. Leiden: Brill, 2001.

Worden, Blair. "Providence and Politics in Cromwellian England." *Past and Present* 109 (1985): 55–99.

– *The Sound of Virtue: Philip Sidney's "Arcadia" and Elizabethan Politics.* New Haven, CT: Yale University Press, 1996.

Wormald, Jenny. "Gunpowder, Treason, and Scots." *Journal of British Studies* 24 (1985): 141–68.

Yachnin, Paul. "The Powerless Theater." *English Literary Renaissance* 21, no. 1 (1991): 49–74.

Yonge, Walter. *Diary of Walter Yonge, esq., justice of the peace, and M.P. for Honiton, written at Colyton and Axminster, co. Devon, from 1604–1628.* Edited by George Roberts. London: Camden Society, 1848.

Zaller, Robert. "Breaking the Vessels: The Desacralization of Monarchy in Early Modern England." *Sixteenth Century Journal* 29, no. 3 (1998): 757–78.

Zaret, David. *The Heavenly Contract: Ideology and Organization in Pre-Revolutionary Puritanism.* Chicago: University of Chicago Press, 1985.

Index